The Collected Works of Lodowick Muggleton: Letters and Epistles

Edited by Mike Pettit

Visit us online at www.muggletonianpress.com **and view our entire range of Muggletonian Literature**

A Muggletonian Press Book

Copyright © Mike Pettit 2010

All rights reserved. No portion of this publication may be reproduced, stored in a retrieval system, or transmitted in any form or by any means, electronic, mechanical, photocopy, recording or otherwise, without prior written permission of the copyright owner. While many of the original texts which form the basis of this publication are to be found in the public domain the texts found herein have been typographically modernised and reformatted at great expense. Please respect the resulting copyright that such work has created.

ISBN 978-1-907466-09-0

Cover Image: G. V. Caffeel engraving attached to the 1699 first edition of "Acts of the Witnesses of the Spirit"

Published by:
Muggletonian Press
129 Hebdon Road
London SW17 7NL
England

I would like to make it clear that in editing and publishing this volume I am not seeking to advocate any element of *Muggletonian* theology. I fully subscribe to historic orthodox Christianity as expressed in the Reformed Confessions of Faith and would plead with all the readers of this work to consider the claims of the triune God.

From the Heidelberg Catechism

Question 26. What believest thou when thou sayest, "I believe in God the Father, Almighty, Maker of heaven and earth"?

Answer: That the eternal Father of our Lord Jesus Christ (who of nothing made heaven and earth, with all that is in them; who likewise upholds and governs the same by his eternal counsel and providence) is for the sake of Christ his Son, my God and my Father; on whom I rely so entirely, that I have no doubt, but he will provide me with all things necessary for soul and body and further, that he will make whatever evils he sends upon me, in this valley of tears turn out to my advantage; for he is able to do it, being Almighty God, and willing, being a faithful Father.

Question 27. What dost thou mean by the providence of God?

Answer: The almighty and everywhere present power of God; whereby, as it were by his hand, he upholds and governs heaven, earth, and all creatures; so that herbs and grass, rain and drought, fruitful and barren years, meat and drink, health and sickness, riches and poverty, yea, and all things come, not by chance, but be his fatherly hand.

Question 28. What advantage is it to us to know that God has created, and by his providence does still uphold all things?

Answer: That we may be patient in adversity; thankful in prosperity; and that in all things, which may hereafter befall us, we place our firm trust in our faithful God and Father, that nothing shall separate us from his love; since all creatures are so in his hand, that without his will they cannot so much as move.

Mike Pettit

CONTENTS

	Page
Introduction	7
Dictionary of National Biography	9
A Volume of Spiritual Epistles	11
A Stream from the Tree of Life	323
Supplement to the book of Letters	393

INTRODUCTION

Lodowick Muggleton had a surprising aversion to writing books, he records in the "epistle to the reader" that formed the introduction to his 1665 work "A True Interpretation of all the Chief Texts, and Mysterious Sayings and Visions Opened, of the Whole Book of the Revelation of Saint John" that:

> "I had thoughts when I writ the Interpretation of the eleventh of the Revelation, to have written no more books, thinking in myself that there were sufficient mysteries written to have satisfied the spirit of any man, as well as myself, who came to understand the mysteries of the true God, and the right devil, as I myself did."

Further works followed as he:

> "thought it was better to break covenant with myself, than to bury those heavenly mysteries, and divine secrets with myself."

Persecution came, with Muggleton suffering fines and imprisonmnet in 1677 on trumped up charges relating to his 1663 work "The Neck of the Quakers Broken". Muggleton never published again, but maintained a steady stream of correspondance that was zealously collected by his disciples, notably Alexander Delamaine. The entry from volume 14 of the "**Dictionary of National Biography**" (1888) in repect of Alexander Delamaine, written by the great Muggletonian historian Alexander Gordon, is reproduced in this volume.

These letters (written by both Muggleton and his co-prophet Reeve) were finally published in the 1755 work "**A Volume of Spiritual Epistles**", which is reproduced in full in this volume.

Further letters were published in the 1778 collection of "**A Stream from the Tree of Life**" that is also reproduced in full in this volume, as is outlined in the title page they:

> "were not included in the Volume of SPIRITUAL EPISTLES because of the great expence"

A final book entitled "**Supplement to the Book of Letters**" was published in 1832 (and is reproduced in full in this volume) with the publishers stating that:

"WITH the authority of the Church we have made diligent search through the Manuscript Records of the Church, and have found the following Letters, not in print in the "Book of Letters." The following Letters may be considered the conclusion of all the Writings of the Prophets REEVE and MUGGLETON, both of spiritual matter and temporal advice, as far as the Church is in possession of."

These collections of letters are mainly the work of Muggleton, with no attempt being made to remove any letters by John Reeve, in order that the integrity and breadth of the works are maintained.

THE DICTIONARY OF NATIONAL BIOGRAPHY

DELAMAINE, ALEXANDER (1654-1683), Muggletonian, was probably originally a baptist; his brother Edward was, in 1668, a baptist preacher at Marlborough, Wiltshire. In 1654 he was a quaker, as appears from his letter of 27 June in that year. He first appears as a Muggletonian in 1671, and it is probable that he attached himself to the following of Lodowicke Muggleton [q. v.] about the time when Muggleton obtained complete control over his sect by putting down 'the rebellion against the nine assertions,' which began in 1670. At this period Delamaine was a London tobacconist, carrying on business 'at the sign of the three tobacco pipes' on Bread Street Hill. He became a very staunch disciple of Muggleton, collecting money and receiving letters for him during his troubles with the authorities. After the release of Muggleton from Newgate on 19 July 1677, Delamaine composed a 'song,' dealing with the circumstances of his trial before Chief-justice Rainsford in the previous January. This was first printed in 'Divine Songs of the Muggletonians,' 1829, 12mo, p. 267. In 1682 he finished transcribing into a folio volume the letters of Muggleton (with a few by John Reeve [q. v.]), addressed to various persons, from 1653 onward. On 19 April 1682 he began a second volume of additional letters 'that would not goe into my grate Book. Both these manuscript volumes are preserved among the Muggletonian archives. Their contents have been edited in 'A Volume of Spiritual Epistles,' &c., 1755, 4to; 2nd edit. 1820, 4to.

Delamaine died between 25 June 1683 and 26 Dec. 1687. His second wife, who survived him, was Anne Lowe, first married to William Hall. By his first wife he had a son, Alexander, and several daughters, of whom the last survivor was Sarah, married to Robert Delamaine. All were zealous Muggletonians.

[Letters of Early Friends, 1841, p. 5; Supplement to the Book of Letters (Muggletonian), 1831; works cited above.]

A. G.

Verse Fidei Gloria est Corona Vitas.

A

VOLUME

OF

SPIRITUAL EPISTLES:

BEING THE

Copies of several Letters

WRITTEN BY

The two last PROPHETS and MESSENGERS of GOD,

JOHN REEVE AND LODOWICKE MUGGLETON;

CONTAINING

Variety of Spiritual Revelations, and deep Mysteries, manifesting to the Elect Seed the Prerogative Power of a true Prophet; who, by Virtue of their Commissions, did truly give Blessings of Life Everlasting to those that believed their Declarations; and to all despising Reprobates the Curse or Sentence of Eternal Damnation.

COLLECTED BY THE GREAT PAINS OF

ALEXANDER DELAMAINE, THE ELDER,

A true Believer of God's last Commission of the Spirit,

INTENDED

At first only for his own spiritual Solace; but finding they increased to so great a Volume, he leaves it to his Posterity, that Ages to come may rejoice in the comfortable View of so blessed and heavenly a Treasure.

TRANSCRIBED FROM

ALEXANDER DELAMAINE's ORIGINAL COPY

BY TOBIAH TERRY,
A true Believer of the like precious Faith in the true God the Man Christ Jesus, which most holy Faith the reprobate World despises.

FRINTED, BY SUBSCRIPTION, IN THE YEAR 1755:

RE-PRINTED, BY SUBSCRIPTION, IN THE YEAR 1820,

BY W. SMITH, KING STREET, LONG ACRE.

PREFACE.

IN this paper book is contained several writings and letters to several particular persons; some to the believers of this commission of the Spirit, and others to unbelievers that were moderate, and some to those that were despisers, as will be seen in those that read them.

These writings and letters were written by John Reeve and Lodowicke Muggleton, the two last Witnesses and true Prophets that God will ever send, to the end of the world.

These writings and letters were gathered from many parts of England, and copied out of the original letters sent by John Reeve and myself, by a true believer, and one of the blessed of the Lord to eternity, namely, Alexander Delamaine the elder. He hath taken a great deal of pains to gather these letters from all parts, and to copy them out in this book, and to send the originals to the parties again. These writings and letters are distinct from all that have been printed, and never was public to the world, although we have printed and published many books to the world, wherein life and death hath been set before all people.

And some few hath chosen life rather than death, and hath believed our report concerning those two great mysteries, how God became flesh, and how the devil became flesh.

Upon these two dependeth salvation and damnation of men and women; which multitudes of people, who hath seen these books, and heard of them, their eyes being blinded, and their hearts hardened, hath gone that broad way of despising the mystery of God, and the mystery of the right devil, and so hath gone the broad way into eternal destruction, and hath chosen death rather than life.

And though there is enough printed to make the man of God perfect, as to life and salvation, to eternity; yet, after my decease, whoever shall come to hear these letters read in this book, if they have any true light, of faith in them, will see how the blessing of heaven did run in the days of a prophet, and how happy were those persons that were under it; and shall wish they had lived in those days, and shall rejoice they are counted worthy to hear these letters that never were printed.

LODOWICKE MUGGLETON.

AN ACROSTIC.

P eruse with Joy, my Friends, the sacred Lines

R eeve and Muggleton wrote by Power divine,

I nspir'd by Christ the God whom we adore,

N o more our God will send till Time's no more.

T his writing long in Manuscript did lie,[1]

E v'n now made publick to the faithful eye,

D ominion, Power, and Praise to God on high.

B y Friends [2] these Letters together were collected,

Y ea then transcribed, and now in Print perfected.

S uch was the soul's desire of a dear friend that sleeps[3],

U nto us hath made known these sacred sheets;

B ut Praise to God 'tis done by some expence,

S uch Truths to see, how great the recompence!

C ombine in Love ye Sons of Faith, and sing,

R eturn all Praise to Christ your God and King.

I t was for us his precious Blood was spill'd,

P our'd forth his Soul, yea the Almighty kill'd:

T hen at the Time decreed my God arose,

I n Triumph over death and all his Foes;

O n high ascends eternally to reign,

N ow we are longing till he comes again.

---

[1] In the hands of Mr. Cook, Distiller, at Vauxhall, Surrey.
[2] Alexander Delamaine and Tobiah Terry.
[3] Thomas Tompkinson, in his preface to the Acts.

LIST OF SUBSCRIBERS, 1820.

Mr. and Mrs. George Browne*
Mr. Thomas Browne*

Mr. William Gates

Mr. John Drummond

Mr. and Mrs. James Frost
Mr. and Mrs; James Frost, jun.
Mr. and Mrs. Joseph Frost
Mr. and Mrs. Isaac Frost
Mr. and Mrs. Joseph Flemming
Mrs. Sarah Fever

Mrs. Sarah Gandar
Mr. and Mrs. Joseph Gandar
Mr. Edward Gandar
Mr. and Mrs. Timothy Gandar
Mr. Elhanan Gascoyne
Mr. and Mrs. Joseph Glaskin
Mr. and Mrs. William Graham†

Mr. and Mrs. Thomas Hewett
Mrs. Hannah Hunt*
Mr. and Mrs. George Hunt *
Miss Hannah Hunt*
Mr. Samuel Hunt*
Miss Theodocia Hunt *
Mr. John Hunt*

Mr. Benjamin Hall*

Miss Theodocia Hogg *
Mr. John Hogg, jun.*
Mr. Robert Hogg *
Mrs. Amy Hall
Mr. Stephen Hodgkinson*

Mr. and Mrs. William Lepper †

Mr. James May ‡

Mr. and Mrs. Thos. Pickersgill, sen.

Mr. and Mrs. George Robinson

Mr. Richard Smith
Mr. James Pearce Smith
Mrs. Susannah Spooner
Miss Ann Slates *

Mr. Richard Tyley

Mr. and Mrs. Vincent, sen.
Mr. and Mrs. William Vincent, jun.

Mr. James Windsor
Mr. Robert Wallis
Mr. James Wood
Mrs. Esther Wilthew
Mr. and Mrs. John White.*

---

* Derbyshire. † Maidstone. ‡ Deal

An Epistle to Recorder Steel 25
A Letter presented unto Alderman Fouke, Lord Mayor of London, from the two Witnesses and Prisoners of Jesus Christ, in Newgate, as an eternal Witness unto him; with a Declaration unto the Recorder Steel, and the Lord Chief Justice Rowles, with the whole Bench and Jury; and in general, unto, all Civil Magistrates and Juries in the World: John Reeve, and Lodowicke Muggleton, the two last spiritual Witnesses, and true Prophets, and only Ministers of the everlasting Gospel, by Commission from the Holy Spirit of the true God, the Lord Jesus Christ, God and Many in one Person, blessed to all Eternity. 26
The Prophet Reeve's Epistle to his Friend, discovering the dark Light of the Quakers; written in the Year 1654, September 20 27
An Epistle of John Reeve to Christopher Hill 30
An Epistle of John Reeve to Christopher Hill, dated London, July 17, 1757. 31
The Prophet Muggleton's Blessing to Mrs. Elizabeth Dickinson of Cambridge, dated August 28, 1658. 31
An Epistle from the Prophet Muggleton to Christopher Hill, dated January 2, 1660. This concerning Claxton to be given with Care to his loving Friend, Christopher Hill, at Maidstone in Kent. 32
An Epistle of the Prophet Lodowicke Muggleton's to Christopher Hill, &c. 35
An Epistle of the Prophet Lodowicke Muggleton to Christopher Hill, Feb. 25, 1660. 37
A Copy of a Letter written by the prophet Lodowicke Muggleton, to pull down the high Exaltation of Lawrence Claxton. Dated from London, December, 25, 1660. 38
A Copy of a Letter, written by the Prophet Lodowicke Muggleton, to his loving Friend Christopher Hill, at Maidstone, in Kent, Jan. 2, 1661. 40
A Copy of a Letter written by the Prophet Lodowicke Muggleton to Mrs. Dorothy Carter, near Chesterfield, bearing date February 13, 1660. 41
A Copy of a Letter written by the Prophet Lodowicke Muggleton, to Mrs. Dorothy Carter of Chesterfield, Feb. 16, 1661 43
An Epistle of the Prophet Lodowicke Muggleton's to Mrs. Ellen Sudbury. Feb. 17, 1661. 44
A Copy of a Letter written by the Prophet Lodowicke Muggleton, to the Believers in Cambridgeshire, bearing Date from London, Aug. 9, 1661. 46
A Copy of a Letter wrote by the Prophet Lodowicke Muggleton, to Mrs. Ellen Sudbury, bearing date November 28, 1661. 48
A Copy of a Letter written by the Prophet Lodowicke Muggleton, to Mrs. Ellen Sudbury. April 7, 1662. 49
A Copy of a Letter wrote by the Prophet Lodowicke Muggleton, to Mrs. Dorothy Carter, of Chesterfield, bearing date April 12, 1662. 50

A Copy of a Letter wrote by the Prophet Lodowicke Muggleton, to Mrs. Bladdwell, a Believer, bearing date May 30, 1662. 51

The Prophet Lodowicke Muggleton's Blessing to Mrs Sarah Short. Transcribed from a Copy drawn from the Original. Given to her by him, June 2, 1662. 52

A Copy of a Letter written by the Prophet Lodowicke Muggleton, to Mrs. Dorothy Carter, of Chesterfield, bearing date July 14, 1662, from London. 53

A Copy of a Letter written by the Prophet Lodowicke Muggleton, to Mrs. Ellen Sudbury, July 19, 1662. 56

A Copy of the Prophet Lodowicke Muggleton's Blessing, given by him to Mrs. Ellen Sudbury, Aug. 11, 1662. 58

A Copy of a Letter written by the Prophet Lodowicke Muggleton, to Mrs. Dorothy Carter. Dated September 12, 1662. 59

A Copy of a Letter written by the Prophet Lodowicke Muggleton, to Mr. John Leavens, bearing date October 6, 1662. 60

A Copy of a Letter from the Prophet Lodowicke Muggleton, to Mr, Richard Sudbury, dated Nov. 3, 1662. 62

A Letter from the Prophet Lodowicke Muggleton, to Mrs. Dorothy Carter, of Chesterfield, dated November 7, 1662. 63

A Copy of a Letter from the Prophet Lodowicke Muggleton, to Christopher Hill, November 16, 1662. 63

A Copy of a Letter written by the Prophet Lodowicke Muggleton, to Mrs. Dorothy Carter of Chesterfield, dated from London, Nov. 28, 1662. 64

A Letter written by the Prophet Lodowicke Muggleton, to one Susannah Frith, a Quaker, bearing Date the 28th of Nov. 1662, from London. 65

A Copy of a Letter wrote by the Prophet Lodowicke Muggleton, to Mr. Richard Sudbury, bearing date the 8th of December, 1662. 66

A Copy of a Letter written by the Prophet Lodowicke Muggleton, to Mrs. Elizabeth Carter, of Chesterfield, from London, dated the 11th of December, 1662. 69

A Copy of a Letter written by the Prophet Lodowicke Muggleton, to Mrs. Ellen Sudbury, from London, bearing date December 15, 1662. 70

A Copy of a Letter wrote by the Prophet Lodowicke Muggleton, to Sir Thomas Twisden, dated from Rootam in Kent, January 6, 1663, as followeth. 72

A Copy of a Letter written by the Prophet Lodowicke Muggleton, to Mrs. Elizabeth Carter, dated April 3, 1663 74

A Copy of a Letter written by the Prophet Lodowicke Muggleton, to Mrs. Dorothy Carter, of Chesterfield, bearing date April 3, 1663. 75

A Copy of a Letter written by the Prophet Lodowicke Muggleton, to Mrs. Dorothy Carter, bearing date from London, May 8, 1663. 77

A Letter of the Prophet Lodowicke Muggleton's to Mr. Richard Sudbury, May 19, 1663. 78

A Copy of a Letter written by the Prophet Lodowicke Muggleton, to Mrs. Ellen Sudbury, bearing date from London, May the 19th. 1663. 79

A Copy of a Letter written by the Prophet Lodowicke Muggleton, bearing date from London, June 19, 1663. 81

A Copy of a Letter written by the Prophet Lodowicke Muggleton, to Mrs. Dorothy Carter in Chesterfield, bearing date from London, July the 18th, 1663. 83

A Copy of a Letter written by the Prophet Lodowicke Muggleton, to Thomas Highfeild, Gardener in Nottingham, bearing Date from Chesterfield, July 31, 1663. 84

A Copy of a Letter written by the prophet Lodowicke Muggleton, to Goodwife Wylds, William Young, and Thomas Martyn of Kent, dated from London, August 27, 1663. 86

A Copy of a Letter written by the Prophet Lodowicke Muggleton, to Christopher Hill Sept. 23, 1663. 89

A Copy of a Letter written by the Prophet Lodowicke Muggleton, to Mrs. Dorothy Carter, of Chesterfield, bearing date November 14, 1663. 91

A Copy of a Letter written by the Prophet Lodowicke Muggleton, to Mrs. Dorothy Carter, bearing date the 27th of November, 1663, as followeth. 92

A Copy of a Letter written by the Prophet Lodowicke Muggleton, London, December 13, 1663. 93

A Copy of a Letter written by the Prophet Lodowicke Muggleton, to one Rice Jones, at his House in Nottingham, without any Date or Place it came from, as follows; 95

A Copy of a Letter written by the Prophet Lodowicke Muggleton, to Mrs. Elizabeth Carter, of Chesterfield, dated April 19, 1664. 97

A Copy of a Letter sent by the Prophet Lodowicke Muggleton, to one Robert Beake, of Coventry, in Answer to one that he wrote to Captain Wildy, July 11, 1664. 98

A Copy of a letter written by the Prophet Lodowicke Muggleton, to Mr. Thomas Tompkinson, of Sladehouse, in Staffordshire, bearing Date from London, December 9, 1664. 107

The prophet Lodowicke Muggleton's Letter to William Cleve, near Cambridge, 1665. 110

A Copy of a Letter wrote by the Prophet Lodowicke Muggleton, to Mrs. Ellen Sudbury, London, Feb. 10, 1665. 111

A Copy of a Letter written by the Prophet Lodowicke Muggleton, to Mrs. Dorothy Carter, of Chesterfield, bearing date Feb. 7, 1665. 112

A Copy of a Letter written by the Prophet Lodowicke Muggleton to Charles Cleve, a Believer of the Commission of the Spirit, living then near unto Cambridge. 114

A Copy of a Letter written by the Prophet Lodowicke Muggleton, to Mr. Thomas Tompkinson, of Sladehouse, in Staffordshire, bearing Date from London, March 17, 1665. 115

A Copy of a Letter written by the Prophet Lodowicke Muggleton, to Mr. Joseph Whitworth, at Abbots-Bromely, in Staffordshire, bearing Date May 19, 1665.. 116

A Copy of a Letter written by the Prophet Lodowicke Muggleton, to one John Hyde, living in Jewen, a bookseller, bearing date October 27, 1665. 121

A Copy of a Letter written by the Prophet Lodowicke Muggleton, to Mr. Martyn, Minister of Orwell, in Cambridgeshire, dated from London, January 16, 1666. 124

A Copy of a Letter written by the Prophet Lodowicke Muggleton, to Mr. William Fershall, High Constable of Orwell, in Cambridgeshire, bearing date from London, January the 19th, 1666........................ 126

A Copy of a Letter written by the Prophet Lodowicke Muggleton, to Mr. James Brocke, bearing date from London, March 30, 1666, directed to Mile-End, near Stepney. 128

A Copy of a Letter written by the Prophet Lodowicke Muggleton, to one Mr. Fletcher, of London, June 25, 1666................................. 130

A Copy of a Letter written by the prophet Lodowicke Muggleton, to Mr. Harrison, called Minister of Blithfeild, in Staffordshire, dated from London, October 6, 1666. 134

The prophet Lodowicke Muggleton's Blessing to Mrs. Anne Lowe, now the wife of Alexander Delamaine, senior. Given to her July 5, 1667. 136

A Copy of a Letter written by the Prophet Lodowicke Muggleton, to Mrs. Ellen Sudbury, November 4, 1667.. 137

A Copy of a Letter written by the Prophet Lodowicke Muggleton, to Elizabeth Hooton, Quaker, January 26, 1668. 138

The Copy of a Letter written by the, Prophet Lodowicke Muggleton, to Mrs, Parker, May 25, 1668. 141

The Copy of a Letter written by the Prophet Lodowicke Muggleton, to Mrs. Ellen Sudbury, May 25, 1668. 142

The Copy of a Letter written by the Prophet Lodowicke Muggleton, to Thomas Tompkinson, May 26, 1668. 143

A Copy of a Letter written by the Prophet Lodowicke Muggleton to Mrs. Dorothy Carter; being a relation of some Passages in a Discourse with George Whitehead, and Josias Cole, two Speakers of the Quakers in the Year 1668; as also some relation of that cursed Devil Thomas Loe, Speaker of the Quakers, and how the Ejects of God's Vengeance did seize upon him, immediately after the Return of an Answer to his cursed blasphemous Letter sent to me, and in less than three Weeks after was dead and buried. 144

A Copy of a Letter wrote by the Prophet Lodowicke Muggleton, to Mr. William Hall, in the Year 1668, concerning his Marriage................. 148

A Copy of a Letter wrote by the Prophet Lodowicke Muggleton, to Mr. Edward Delamain, a Baptist Preacher, living in Marlborough, bearing date the 16th of June, 1668, ... 150

A Copy of a Letter wrote by the Prophet Lodowicke Muggleton, to Mrs. Mary Parker, August 13, 1668. 160

A Copy of a Letter written by the Prophet Lodowicke Muggleton, to Mr. Thomas Tompkinson, bearing date from London, September 21, 1665. 161

A Copy of a Letter sent by the Prophet Lodowicke Muggleton, to Mr. Thomas Tompkinson, of Sladehouse, in Staffordshire, bearing date from London, December 14, 1668. 162

A Copy of a Letter written by the Prophet Lodowicke Muggleton, containing the Blessing of Eternal Life, sent unto Lydia Brooks, of Sheasby, in Leicestershire, (this was John Saddington's sister) bearing date from London, October 24, in the year 1668. 163

A Copy of a Letter written by the Prophet Lodowicke Muggleton, to Mr. Thomas Tompkinson, of Sladehouse, in Staffordshire, bearing Date from London, January 31, 1669. 164

A Copy of a Letter sent by the Prophet Lodowicke Muggleton to Mr. Goodwyn, of Chesterfield, bearing date February 4, 1669. 165

A Copy of a Letter wrote by the Prophet Lodowicke Muggleton to John Lad. 166

A Letter from the Prophet Lodowicke Muggleton, June 14, 1669. 166

A Letter from the Prophet Lodowicke Muggleton to Mrs. Ellen Sudbury, June 14, 1669 167

A Copy of a Letter written by the Prophet Lodowicke Muggleton to Mr. Thomas Tompkinson, of Sladehouse, in Staffordshire, bearing date from London, June 19, 1669. 168

A Letter from the Prophet Lodowicke Muggleton, to Mrs. Ellen Sudbury, August 30, 1669. 170

A Letter from the Prophet Lodowicke Muggleton, to Mrs. Mary Parker, August 30, 1669. 171

Letter from the Prophet Lodowicke Muggleton, to Mr. Thomas Tompkinson, Sept. 6, 1669 172

A Letter of the Prophet Lodowicke Muggleton to Christopher Hill, September 9, 1669. 173

A Copy of a Letter written by the Prophet Lodowicke Muggleton, to Mr. Thomas Tompkinson, of Sladehouse, in Staffordshire, bearing date from London, October 4, 1669 174

A Copy of a Letter written by the Prophet Lodowicke Muggleton, to Mr. Thomas Tompkinson, dated from London, December 4, 1669.. 175

A Copy of a Letter written by the Prophet Lodowicke Muggleton to Mr. Thomas Tompkinson, bearing date from London, March 20, 1670. Directed to Sladehouse, in Staffordshire. 176

A Copy of a Letter written by the Prophet Lodowicke Muggleton to Mr. Thomas Tompkinson, of Sladehouse, in Staffordshire, bearing date from London, April 25, 1670. 177

A Copy of a Letter written by the prophet Lodowicke Muggleton to Mr. Thomas Tompkinson, of Slade-house, bearing date from London, December 7, 1670. 178

A Copy of a Letter written by the Prophet Lodowicke Muggleton to Mrs. Ellen Sudbury, of Nottingham, bearing date January 13, 1671. 180

A Copy of a Letter wrote by the Prophet Lodowicke Muggleton to Mrs. Elizabeth Atkinson, bearing date London, February 12, 1671. 182

A Copy of a Letter sent by the Prophet Lodowicke Muggleton to Mrs. Dorothy Carter, of Chesterfield, March 23, 1671 184

A Copy of a Letter written by the Prophet Lodowicke Muggleton to Mrs. Ellen Sudbury, bearing date April 7, 1671, directed to Nottingham. 186

A Copy of a Letter written by the Prophet Lodowicke Muggleton to Mr. Charles Cleve, Mr. Thomas Parke, Mr. Francis Hampson, all of Cambridge, bearing date April 24, 1671. 187

A Copy of a Letter written by the Prophet Lodowicke Muggleton to Mr. Alexander Delamaine, senior, bearing date from Southampton, June 8, 1671. 190

A Copy of a Letter written by the Prophet Lodowicke Muggleton to Mr. George Gamble, a Merchant in Cork, in Ireland: the first to him after he came to set his seal to the true faith. Bearing date from London, March 6, 1672. 190

A Copy of a Letter sent by the Prophet Lodowicke Muggleton to Mr. Jeremiah Moss, Physician, living in Cork, in Ireland, being the first after his believing the Commission of Truth, bearing date from London, March 6, 1672. 193

A Copy of a Letter wrote by the Prophet Lodowicke Muggleton to Mrs. Preston, of Little Towerhill, Mrs. Henn's Mother, and to her Father likewise, dated in London, May 14, 1672. 195

A Copy of a better sent by the Prophet Lodowicke Muggleton to Mrs Elizabeth Marsden, of Chesterfield, May 20, 1672, ... 198

A Copy of a Letter written by the Prophet Lodowicke Muggleton to Mrs. Dorothy Carter, of Chesterfield, dated August 30, 1672, as followeth. 199

A Copy of a Letter written by the Prophet Lodowicke Muggleton, to one William King a Quaker, who came from New England, dated from London, October 3, 1672. 202

A Copy of a Letter written by the Prophet Lodowicke Muggleton to Mr. Thomas Tompkinson, bearing date from London, October 16, 1672. 204

A Copy of a Letter written by the Prophet Lodowicke Muggleton to Mr. Thomas Tompkinson, of Sladehouse, in Staffordshire, bearing date from London, January 19, 1673. 205

A Copy of a Letter wrote by the Prophet Lodowicke Muggleton to William Penn, Quaker, bearing date from London, January 23, 1673. 207

A Copy of a Letter sent by the Prophet Lodowicke Muggleton to Mr. George Gamble, in Ireland, Feb. 14, 1673. 207

A Copy of a Letter written by the Prophet Lodowicke Muggleton to Mr. Thomas Tompkinson, bearing date from London, February 16, 1675. 209

A Copy of a Letter written by the Prophet Lodowicke Muggleton to Mr. Alexander Delamaine, senior, May 16, 1673. 210

A Copy of a Letter wrote by the Prophet Lodowicke Muggleton to John Harriot, bearing date from London, July 16, 1673. 211

A Copy of a Letter sent by the Prophet Lodowicke Muggleton, to Cork, in Ireland, being the sentence of damnation upon twentysix Quakers there. 213

A Copy of a Letter sent by the Prophet Lodowicke Muggleton to Mr. Joseph Moss, a Physician, in Cork, in Ireland, August 11, 1673. 223

A Copy of a Letter written by the Prophet Lodowicke Muggleton to Mr. Thomas Tompkinson, of Sladehouse, bearing date from London, August 11, 1673. 224

A Copy of a Letter written by the Prophet Lodowicke Muggleton to Mrs. Dorothy Carter, bearing date January 16, 1674. 225

A Copy of a Letter written by the Prophet Lodowicke Muggleton, to Mrs. Frances Man, containing her blessing, dated January 23, 1674. 226

A Copy of a Letter written by the Prophet Lodowicke Muggleton to Elizabeth Dickinson, Jun, being her Blessing, bearing date March 6, 1674. 227

Postscript of a Letter to Mrs. Futerell. 228

A Copy of a Letter wrote by the Prophet Lodowicke Muggleton to Mrs. Hampson of Cambridge. 229

A Copy of a Letter written by the Prophet Lodowicke Muggleton to Isabella Malum, Quaker, dated from London, October 1, 1674, directed to her at Nottingham. 230

A Copy of a Letter wrote by the Prophet Lodowicke Muggleton to John Gratton, of Derbyshire, bearing date October 8, 1674. 236

A Copy of a Letter written by the prophet Lodowicke Muggleton to Mr. Thomas Tompkinson, of Sladehouse, in Staffordshire, dated from London, July 1, 1675. 237

A Copy of a Letter wrote by the Prophet Lodowicke Muggleton to Mr. Henry Henn, bearing date from London, August 20, 1675. 238

A Copy of a Letter written by the Prophet Lodowicke, Muggleton to Mrs. Susanna Moss, of Dublin, in Ireland, bearing date September 5, 1675. 239

This is the Copy of the Answer of the Prophet Lodowicke Muggleton's, unto a Letter which our brother Lad had sent him. 243

A Copy of a Letter written by the Prophet Lodowicke Muggleton to Mr. James Whitehead, of Braintree, bearing date from London, December 31, 1679. 245

A Copy of a Letter written by the Prophet Lodowicke Muggleton to Mr. George Gamble, in Cork in Ireland, bearing date the 12th of January, 1678. 248

A Copy of a Letter written by the Prophet Lodowicke Muggleton to Major John Dennison, of Dublin, in Ireland, bearing date February 24, 1678. 251

A Copy of a Letter written by the Prophet Lodowicke Muggleton to Michael Pett, in Kent, bearing date the 25th of February, 1678. 253

A Copy of a Letter written by the Prophet Lodowicke Muggleton to Mr. Thomas Nosworthy, in Antigua, bearing date the 3d of March, 1678. 256

The Prophet Lodowicke Muggleton's Blessing to Alexander Delamaine, junior, bearing date November 18, 1678. 257

A Copy of Mrs. Elizabeth Roe's Blessing:, written by the Prophet Mr. Lodowicke Muggleton, bearing date December 5, 1678. 257

A Copy of a Letter written by the Prophet Lodowicke Muggleton to his Kinsman, Mr. Roger Muggleton, of Wilbarston, in Northamptonshire, bearing date December 14, 1678. 258

A Copy of a Letter written by the Prophet Lodowicke Muggleton to Mr. Thomas Tompkinson, bearing date July 29, 1679; directed to Sladehouse, in Staffordshire. 259

A Copy of a Letter written by the Prophet Lodowicke Muggleton to Mr. Thomas Tompkinson, bearing date from London, July 24, 1680. 261

Lodowicke Muggleton's Letter to Robert Peirce, concerning the Holy Ghost. 264

A Copy of a Letter written by the Prophet Lodowicke Muggleton to Mr. Edward Burton, in Derbyshire, bearing date the 12th of January, 1681. 268

The Copy of the Prophet Lodowicke Muggleton's Blesssing, sent to Mrs. Sarah West, of a place called Uver, in Cambridgeshire, dated February 22, 1681. 270

A Copy of a Letter written by the Prophet Lodowicke Muggleton, bearing date August 22, 1681, to Charles Yeeles, Thomas Millerd, and John White, in or near Cork in Ireland. 271

A Copy of a Letter written by the Prophet Lodowicke Muggleton to Mr. James Whitehead, of Braintree, in Essex, bearing date from London, August 30, 1681. 273

A Copy of a Letter wrote by the Prophet Lodowicke Muggleton to William Wood, of Braintree, in Essex, dated September 26, 1681... 274

A Copy of a Letter written by the Prophet Lodowicke Muggleton to Mrs. Mary Scott, of Bristol, bearing date October 12, 1681. 275

A Copy of a Letter wrote by the Prophet Lodowicke Muggleton to Mrs. Dorothy Carter, of Chesterfield, in Derbyshire, bearing date from London, February 1, 1682. 276

A Copy of a Letter written by the Prophet Lodowicke Muggleton to Mrs. Elizabeth Flaggerter, of Cork in Ireland, bearing date from London, June 22, 1682. 278

A Copy of a Letter wrote by the Prophet Lodowicke Muggleton to Mr. William Sedley, a Weaver and Dyer, a Believer of the Commission of the Spirit, living in Southampton, bearing date from London, the 12th day of January, 1683. 280

A Copy of a Letter wrote by the Prophet Lodowicke Muggleton to Mr. Capp, upon his death-bed, dated from London, the 15th of March, 1683. 282

A Copy of a Letter wrote by the Prophet Lodowicke Muggleton unto Mrs. Rebecca Hall, of Arnesby, bearing date from London, May 1, 1683. 283

A Copy of a Letter wrote by the Prophet Lodowicke Muggleton to Mrs. Elizabeth Flaggerter, of Cork, in Ireland, bearing date from London, June 25, 1683. 284

Copy of a Letter wrote by the Prophet Lodowicke Muggleton to Alexander Delamaine, senior, dated in London, June 25, 1683. 285

A Copy of a Letter written by the Prophet Lodowicke Muggleton to Mrs. Mary Scott, of Bristol, bearing date from London, July 19, 1683. 286

A Copy of a Letter wrote by the Prophet Lodowicke Muggleton to Mrs. Eleanor Sudbury, in Nottingham, bearing date from London, August 6, 1683. 288

A Copy of a Letter written by the Prophet Lodowicke Muggleton to Mrs. Ann Jackson, living in York, bearing date from London, August 29, 1683. 290

The Copy of Mrs. Anne Tompkinson's Blessing, given her by the Prophet Lodowicke Muggleton, dated in London, July 10, 1684. 292

A Copy of a Letter wrote by the Prophet Lodowicke Muggleton to Mrs. Ellen Sudbury, of Nottingham, bearing date from London, July 19, 1684. 293

A Copy of a Letter wrote by the prophet Lodowicke Muggleton to Mr. James Whitehead, of Braintree in Essex, bearing date from London, August 12, 1684. 294

A Copy of a Letter wrote by the Prophet Lodowicke Muggleton to Mrs. Elizabeth Wheately, of Andover, bearing date from London, dated September 24, 1684. 296

A Copy of a Letter wrote by the Prophet Lodowicke Muggleton to Mrs. Rebecca Hall, of Arnesly, in Leicestershire, bearing date from London, October 18, 1684. 298

A Copy of a Letter wrote by the Prophet Lodowicke Muggleton to Mrs. Ann Jackson, of York, bearing date from London, October 18, 1684. 302

A Copy of a Letter wrote by the Prophet Lodowicke Muggleton to Mrs. Rebecca Hall, of Arnesby, in Leicestershire, bearing date from London, January 20, 1684-5. 303

A Copy of a Letter wrote by the Prophet Lodowicke Muggleton to Mrs. Mary Gamble, of Cork in Ireland, bearing date from London, March 6, 1684-5. 307

A Copy of a Letter written by the Prophet Lodowicke Muggleton, to Mrs. Priscilla Whitehead, containing her Blessing, bearing date from London, September 24, 1685. 309

A Copy of a blessing wrote by the Prophet Muggleton, to Mrs. Mary Whitehead, of Braintree, bearing date 310

A Copy of another Letter wrote by the Prophet Lodowicke Muggleton to Mrs. Anne Delamaine, Widow of Mr. Alexander Delamaine, Senior, bearing Date from London, February 3, 1687. 311

A Copy of a Blessing wrote by the Prophet Lodowicke Muggleton to Mr. John Mellford, of Braintree, bearing date from London, April 12, 1687. 312

A Copy of a Blessing wrote by the Prophet Lodowicke Muggleton to Thomas Ladd, of Braintree, bearing date from London, July 15, 1687. 314

A Copy of a Blessing wrote by the Prophet Lodowicke Muggleton to Mr. James Whitehead, of Braintree, bearing date from London, August 27, 1687. 317

A Copy of a Letter wrote by the Prophet Lodowicke Muggleton to Mary Gamble, dated August 29, 1687 318

A Copy of a Blessing wrote by the Prophet Lodowicke Muggleton to Mrs. Mary Whitehead, the Wife of Mr. James Whitehead, of Braintree, bearing date from London, November 17, 1687. 320

A Copy of a Letter written by the Prophet Lodowicke Muggleton to Mrs. Sarah Delamaine, Daughter to Mr. Alexander Delamaine, Senior, Wife of Robert Delamaine, bearing date December 14, 1691. 321

AN

EPISTLE

To

THE RECORDER STEEL,

OCTOBER 28, 1653.

SIR,

YOU may remember at the Sessions in the Old Bailey, on October 14, and 15, we had a trial before your honour; and, sir, you may remember we gave your honour notice before our trials that you had no commission from God to be the judges of matters of faith concerning God; for you must understand that all spiritual power wholly resides in God's person, or in the person of God, until his pleasure is to communicate it unto his creatures; whose pleasure it was to make choice of us two only to be the judges of blasphemy against the Holy Spirit, because no man clearly knew the Lord until we were commissionated by voice of words from heaven, to declare what the true God is; yet notwithstanding, your honour, with the jury, gave sentence against us as blasphemers, because we declared Jesus Christ to be the only God, and everlasting Father; and that there was no other God in heaven or in earth but the man Jesus only.

Sir, we must tell you, that we cannot break the civil law, but we are made examples in fulfilling of it to the whole world: wherefore whosoever tries us by the law of the land, it is allowed as if he tried his God by the civil law as the Jews did, because we cannot break your law, but fulfil it as aforesaid. Let your honour judge whether the sentence of eternal death upon our accusers be not just; for we did them no wrong in word or in deed.

They came to our houses, and spake evil things they knew not, as most men do; and we, in obedience to the commission of God, returned their blasphemy upon their own heads, which provoked them with a warrant to bring us before the lord mayor; who, joining with our blasphemous persecutors, he came under the sentence of eternal death with them.

Is it not a marvellous thing, that you that are magistrates should want the spirit of discerning to judge between the law of the Scriptures, and the law of the land? Do you not understand that the civil law instructs no man in the knowledge of God; therefore you that are invested with authority from men to judge all manner of accounts concerning the breach of the civil law, you ought not to take upon you to judge prophets, who cannot desire to break your law: for, by the power of Him that sent us, we cannot wrong any man in his person or estate, although they would kill us; yet amongst you there is sentence given against us to remain six months in prison, for declaring the Man Jesus to be the only God and everlasting Father; which you think is blasphemy. Wherefore once more from the Lord Jesus, we forewarn you, before it be too late, forthwith to declare unto us, the Lord's messengers, that you disown the verdict to be blasphemy that the jury brought in against us; which if you disobey, then in obedience unto the commission of the Lord Jesus, with those gentlemen of the jury that are guilty of that unjust sentence, from the presence of the Lord Jesus Christ, elect men and angels, we pronounce you cursed and damned, soul and body, to all eternity.

JOHN REEVE, and
LODOWICKE MUGGLETON,

The Two last Witnesses and Prophets, and only Ministers of the everlasting Gospel, by Commission of the Holy Spirit of the Lord Jesus Christ, God alone, blessed to all Eternity.

A Letter presented unto Alderman Fouke, Lord Mayor of London, from the two Witnesses and Prisoners of Jesus Christ, in Newgate, as an eternal Witness unto him; with a Declaration unto the Recorder Steel, and the Lord Chief Justice Rowles, with the whole Bench and Jury; and in general, unto, all Civil Magistrates and Juries in the World: John Reeve, and Lodowicke Muggleton, the two last spiritual Witnesses, and true Prophets, and only Ministers of the everlasting Gospel, by Commission from the Holy Spirit of the true God, the Lord Jesus Christ, God and Many in one Person, blessed to all Eternity.

BY virtue of our commission, received by voice of words, from the glorious mouth of the only true God upon the throne of Glory, the Lord Jesus Christ, we shall make manifest unto men, what the foundation is of the power of the civil magistrate, and that he ought not to meddle with spiritual things, which God hath reserved himself, not allowing any man to touch them upon pain of eternal death, but those only by him anointed for that purpose: first, we declare that the Scriptures were given by inspiration of the Holy Spirit; therefore, except the magistrates were inspired with the same spirit as those that speak the Scriptures, they ought not to judge any man by them, but ought rather to yield obedience themselves unto holy Writ, or they must perish to eternity. Again, we declare from the Holy Spirit, that since God became flesh, no civil magistrate hath any authority from above to be the judge of any man's faith, because it is a spiritual invisible gift from God, that gives a man assurance of everlasting life; but the magistrate's authority is to judge the civil laws of the land, which is grounded only upon reason; but the things of eternity are from God, who is from eternity to eternity, therefore faith is the evidence of things hoped for, and reason is judge of things that are visible: as for you that are skilful in the law of reason, as soon as you hear an action to be a breach of the law, you understand presently what punishment belongs to the fact; therefore the Apostle saith, *The magistrate is the minister of God for good to them that do well, and a terror to the evil doer*. Again, we declare from the Lord, that no magistrate, by his power from the law of reason, ought to usurp the law of faith into his authority, because the law of reason is utterly ignorant of the law of faith, the one being carnal, and the other being spiritual; therefore, what magistrate soever takes upon him to be the judge of us, who are the messengers of faith in the true God, they are enemies to the Lord Jesus Christ, and shall surely perish to eternity. Again, from the Lord Jesus we forewarn you that are magistrates, before it is too late, that you tread not in the lord mayor's steps, presumptuously to take upon you to judge this commission of the two-edged sword of God put into our mouths, which, if you are left so to do, it will cut you in sunder from the presence of our God to all eternity; for our God is a consuming fire, who did pronounce us cursed to eternity, had we not obeyed his voice; therefore we perfectly know whoever is left, great or small, to speak evil of this commission, which God hath put unto us, by calling it blasphemy, delusion, a devil, or lie; in so doing, they have sinned against the Holy Ghost, and must perish, soul and body, from the presence of our God, elect men and angels, to all eternity; for God hath chosen us two only, and hath put the two-edged sword of the Spirit into our mouths, as beforesaid, that whom we are made to pronounce blessed, are blessed to eternity, and whom we are made to pronounce cursed, are cursed to eternity; and this power no mortal can take out of our hands, neither will our God any more give such power unto men whilst the world endures. Therefore, you that are judges of this earth, be wise and learned, and meddle with those things which you know in this world only, and call not your God to account at your bar; for whoever arraigneth a prophet at his judgment-seat, it is all one as arraigning his God, for a prophet cometh in the name and power of his God; therefore he that despiseth the prophet, despiseth him that sent him. Again, we declare from the Lord Jesus, if any magistrate pretends to be a preacher of the Gospel, he having no commission from our God so to do; if he preach any more after we forbid him, then we have Full power to pronounce the sentence of eternal death upon him, and it is so unrevocable. Again, we declare from the Lord Jesus, that the cause why so many magistrates and ministers must suffer the vengeance of eternal death, is, because with one consent they fight against the true messengers of God, with the temporal law invested upon them by men. Again, woe would have been unto us, if we had come in our own name; but we know that God sent us, as sure as he sent Moses, the prophets, and the apostles; and that great authority, as to be judges of blasphemy against the Holy Ghost, we only are invested withal: Wherefore, you magistrates that are not yet under this sentence of eternal death from the Lord Jesus, our counsel is, if you desire blessedness in the life to come, that you would not meddle to be the judges of spiritual things, knowing you have no commission from the Lord. Remember the counsel of Caiaphas, the high priest, if it be possible, and prevent the lord mayor's eternal curse.

The Prophet Reeve's Epistle to his Friend, discovering the dark Light of the Quakers; written in the Year 1654, September 20.

Loving Friend,

CALLING to mind the letter thou readest to me, which was sent thee out of the country, I am moved to present these lines to the view of thy ponderous spirit; for as words of truth, flowing from a real foundation, drew forth humility and love to God and man, from that soul that hath received an hearing ear, so likewise thou mayest know the glittering words proceeding from man's carnal wisdom, is that which hath occasioned many men to be exalted above measure, and to imagine himself so essentially united to the Divine Glory, that at length that man hath been so bewitched through the adorations of men and women in deep darkness, with high conceits of his own spiritual wisdom, that he hath been willing to deny his creaturely condition, and to embrace the holy titles and honour of an infinite Creator. Yea, and to say in his heartland tongue also, that there is no spiritual God or personal glory in the least, but what is in man only, notwithstanding, as sure as the Lord Jesus liveth, both he and all that is in him must turn into silent death and dust for a moment; yea, and would so remain unto all eternity, if there were not a distinct personal Majesty living without man, to raise him again to everlasting sensible glory or shame, according to the royal pleasure of that God, that neither will nor can give his glory to another.

My dear Friend,

Be not deceived with men's crafty words, who have no true spiritual distinction in them; for if any mortal man have dwelling in him the eternal Spirit, all the motions, thoughts, words and actions of that man must needs be as pure, holy and powerful as God himself, because thou knowest they proceed from a pure, holy, and glorious spirit. But, of the contrary, if thou perceivest a measure of light only abiding in thee, which thou in mercy hast received from an everlasting Jesus without thee, then thou often seest darkness in thee as well as light; for light entered not into sinners to make them spiritual gods one over another, but shined into them to discover their natural enmity, continually warring against a God of eternal love towards them; and not only so, but to prevent also their former darkness from tyrannizing in them for ever, yea, and to consolate their elect brethren by their spiritual experiences.

Wherefore, from a divine gift which I have freely received from an unerring Spirit, I say unto thee, that those men which labour to persuade their hearers, that if they diligently harken to the light that is in them, they may attain to such a power, as to be dead in this body from all kind of inward darkness, sin, or evil, have uttered the falsest doctrine that ever was declared to men. Moreover, if the light of life eternal be thy guide, thou must needs know then, it was neither the justifying light of Christ within man, no, nor the spirit of Christ without man that moved those men to speak or write to the people; but it was their own lying imagination which hurried them about to beget proselytes to themselves in the man Christ Jesus's stead, who alone *is God over all, blessed for ever and ever*. Amen.

He that is born of God sinneth not; that is, he is not left to his own heart, to commit the unpardonable sin of unbelief in the true God, in despising the spirit of Christ Jesus, to be the only Lord God of his salvation. *He that believeth shall be saved, but he that believeth not is condemned already*; not because he hath not believed in a God, or Christ that is within him, but because he hath not believed in a personal God or Christ that is without him, whose Divine Majesty is crowned with such immortal, blight, burning glory, that if he did not veil his fiery nature within his own blessed body, the glory of it is so transcendency infinite, that he in a moment would consume all created beings to powder. He that committed that sin of calling God a liar, which is the sin of not believing in our Lord Jesus Christ as aforesaid, or he that maketh glorious pretences of unfeigned love to Christ and his tender-hearted people, and yet secretly lieth under the power of carnal filthiness; such a man is not only of his father the devil, (cursed Cain) but he also is a very devil himself. *He that saith he hath no sin in him, is a liar, and the truth is not in him*; that is, he that saith Christ is so powerfully risen in him, that all motions, thought and desire of sin against God or man, is perfectly done away, that man is an horrible liar, and a deadly enemy to all humble and broken hearted saints; for their natural rebellious warring against the light within them, and the Lord of Glory without them. Oh! my precious friend, for whom my soul spiritually travelleth, till thou art firmly established with glorious things which are eternal, not with empty notions proceeding from an imaginary God or Christ within men, only which with Syrenian songs is very pleasing to the carnal ear, which may delude some undiscerning spirits for a season, nor with pharisaical looks, sighs and groans, to be seen of men, which is nothing else but the effects of men's crafty words and gestures proceeding from man's fleshly wisdom, which is abominable in the sight of our God, who is the Lord Jesus Christ in the eternal heavens above the stars.

My beloved Friend,

Give me leave a little to reason with thee, about things of the greatest concernment: what excellent truths above other men hast thou heard from the chief speakers of the Quakers? didst thou ever hear them speak to the purpose? or speak at all of any God or Christ, but what is in man only? or didst thou ever hear them speak of a bodily glory and misery to come sensibly to be enjoyed by the saints in the highest heavens, and to be endured by the serpents in this world at the day of eternal accounts? or dost thou see the image or likeness of the true Jesus in that ministry? the true and living Jesus rejected not the company of publicans and dinners, even when his light appeared not in them; but on the contrary, do they not rashly condemn those men that soberly oppose them, and shun the company of those that are not of their opinion, as serpents; much like unto those hypocrites of old, who said, Stand farther off, for we are more holy than you. Moreover, in all their speakings and writings to the people, do they not make a grand idol of the word Light, and occasion men to worship it as their only God; as if mere words were to be adored without a person, or worshipped within the bodies of sinful man as a God: or as if those that enjoy true light in them, have such a measure of God in them, that they stand in no need of any God without them in the least.

My dear Friend,

Thou knowest men of unstable spirits, child-like or rather fool-like, are easily taken with every wind of doctrine; but if thou hast a spirit of true discerning in thee, thou wilt be made thoroughly then to try the spirits and doctrines of men, whether they be of God or no, before thou embrace them having been in the fire of the devil already, I hope thou hast gained experience. Wherefore, for thy clearer sight concerning of the fallacy of all speakers, which say the Lord Jehovah, or Jesus, sent them, I shall give some discovering characters; he that saith the everlasting spiritual God or Father became not a perfect man of unspotted flesh, blood, and bone, was never moved by the spirit of God or Christ, to preach or speak to the people; or he that saith, that spirit which is dwelling in the glorious body of Christ Jesus, is not the alone everlasting Father, God and Man in one distinct person glorified, is none of Christ's messenger; or he that saith God is not in the form of a man, but is an infinite spirit essentially abiding in all creatures, that man is a liar, and the truth is not in him; or he that saith Christ's godhead died not in the flesh, and did not quicken and raise his manhood to life again, and in that body of flesh and bone, did not ascend into a kingdom of glory in another world, the deep things of God is utterly hid from that man; or he that saith all mankind proceeded from the loins of the first man Adam, is ignorant of the two Scripture seeds (namely) the seed of the woman, and the seed of the serpent, therefore he is none of Christ's sending; or he that saith mens souls do not die with their bodies, and sleep together in the dust of the earth, till the Lord Jesus, by the mighty power of his word speaking only, do raise them unto life again at the last day, that man is in deep darkness, not knowing the Scriptures, or the power of God; or he that says mens bodies only perish (and not the souls) will be saved at the last, that man is a liar, and the truth is not in him.

Dear Friend,

Thus far was I moved to write unto thee, as an eternal witness between us, when the secrets of all hearts shall be opened. If thou seest good, thou mayst present this epistle to the view of those men called Quakers; not that I can expect a good issue from any of them, unless God hath endowed them with hearing ears, unjudging, meek and patient spirits.

Thine in all eternal excellencies,

JOHN REEVE.

September 20, 1654.

An Epistle of John Reeve to Christopher Hill

IN the eternal true Jesus, my soul salutes you all: I have received your love-tokens, which is a vessel of cyder and a sixpence: my joy in the Lord is encreased by your communion with each other, I trust to the praise of his glory, his light and love shall abound in you more and more, for the strengthening you in the inward man, and confounding all gainsayers in your outward conversations: neither I nor my wife are in perfect health; especially my wife, who is very ill, and has been so about six weeks: so hoping of your welfare to his infinite grace, I commend you, and remain your friend and brother in Christ Jesus. Our elder brother.

JOHN REEVE,

P. S. Brother Christopher, if my mother comes up, pray tell her she need not trouble herself about any more goods at present, but a bolster and a little more covering for the bed; and as for that you sent for, you shall have it next week, God willing.

An Epistle of John Reeve to Christopher Hill, dated London, July 17, 1757[1].

Loving Friend in pure truth,

I RECEIVED the six shillings and the hat, and the eighteen-pence you sent me as a token. I am not a little joyed for our brother Martyn's likelihood of recovery, with your wife's safe delivery. But my chiefest rejoycing for you all is, your reality to the things you have received from our ever-loving Father, which is the living Jesus in a bodily form; this is a riddle to your elect brethren, even through the whole world, unless it be to a few. Oh! blessed are you that you are of that number, unto whom it is in some measure unfolded; for by this means you are delivered from all carnal bonds of outward forms, and are sate down in peace through inward enjoyments, which none can take from you.

Brother, I shall be careful in what your mother-in-law requireth. Thus not naming any more, but my tender love to all you that enjoys this truth, I commit you to the most High, and remain eternally yours in all righteousness,

JOHN REEVE.

P. S. My wife's kind love to you all.

The Prophet Muggleton's Blessing to Mrs. Elizabeth Dickinson of Cambridge, dated August 28, 1658.

Dear Friend, in the eternal Truth Elizabeth Dickinson; my Love remembered unto you and your Husband, as being in the same Faith also.

I AM very well persuaded of your eternal happiness, and I would willingly say unto you, as our Lord did in another case to the woman that was troubled with a bloody issue, who said within herself, that if she could but touch his garment, she should be made whole; and according to her faith it was unto her, for she felt in herself that she was healing of her plague, and not only so, but she had assurance of everlasting life, which was far beyond the health of her body. Which faith of hers did draw virtue out of our Lord, which made him to say, that virtue was gone out of him; and he looked round about to see her that had done this thing, *and he said unto her, daughter, thy faith has made thee whole, go in peace, and be whole of thy plague*; as if our Lord should say it was her own faith that did fetch virtue out of him, and it was her own faith that did heal herself; as if he had no hand in the thing, he was but the object of her faith; it was her faith that did draw that from the object; and so it is with you, John Reeve and myself, the chosen Witnesses of the Spirit, we having the commission and burden of the Lord upon us. We are made the object of your faith, and as your faith is strong in this commission of the Spirit, so shall the virtue flow

---

[1] Both the 1755 and 1820 editions give the year as 1757, the correct year probably being 1657.

from it to your eternal rest and peace, so that you shall be perfectly whole as to the relation to the fears of eternal death, as that woman was in her body of the bloody issue; and your faith being in me, as the object in relation to the commission of the Spirit, it is your faith will make you whole; for my faith is in you concerning your eternal happiness. Let yours be in me, and you shall fare no worse than I do; for you shall have the end of your faith, even the salvation of your soul, as well as I; and that you may be sure, I do declare you one of the blessed of the Lord to all eternity. But as for those fears that do arise in you from the weakness of your nature, or from a distemper in nature, I cannot promise you deliverance from it, but it is very probable that the assurance of eternal life will mitigate and weaken the other. I thought good to write these few lines unto you for farther confirmation of your eternal happiness after death.

No more at present, but rest your faithful friend and true prophet of the Lord,

LODOWICKE MUGGLETON.

An Epistle from the Prophet Muggleton to Christopher Hill, dated January 2, 1660. This concerning Claxton to be given with Care to his loving Friend, Christopher Hill, at Maidstone in Kent.

Loving Brother, Christopher Hill, in the Spirit of this Commission, and to all the rest of the Believers of this Commission at Maidstone in Kent, I send greeting.

I WOULD have you to seriously mind and consider these lines as follows.

There hath of late days happened a great deal of difference between some of the believers of this commission here in London, and Lawrence Claxton; whereby the believers have complained to me, that Lawrence Claxton hath carried himself so proud and lord-like over others that have been of a lower comprehension than himself; likewise he hath been so full of filthy covetous avarice, which hath not had so much as the very colour or show of natural righteousness in it. So I, taking these things into consideration, did send my daughter to tell him, that if he did exercise his spiritual pride any more, that I would take away his commission from him; which he at the first did seem very scornful at, as if he could stand by virtue of John Reeve's words without me, as did afterwards appear; but yet concerning my daughter's words concerning my authority, he did seem hypocritically to submit, and to acknowledge himself to be but a servant unto me, and unto the believers of this commission. But it hath appeared since to be otherwise, and that there was a cursed pride that lay in his heart; and for that purpose he hath written a book, called *The lost Sheep found*; where in the latter part of that book, he hath proudly exalted himself in John Reeve's place; for he hath quite excluded me out of the commission; so that there is none now but John Reeve and he that hath the spiritual commission; therefore you shall find in that book, and more especially in the epistle of that book: whereas he doth call it very often our commission; so there is no true confidence, as he says, but in our commission: his meaning is John Reeve and himself, for he hath quite excluded me, and hath gotten himself into John Reeve's chair and place; therefore I would have you seriously to mind and peruse that part of the book which doth treat upon the commission. For I suppose you have the books sent unto you, as well as others have; there you shall find a great deal of spiritual pride assuming to himself those high titles which never did belong to him, neither did John Reeve, nor I, ever give to him; which books of his, with other words and passages that hath happened of late, hath made an everlasting difference between us two in this world; therefore I would have you, and all the believers of this commission, to understand, that I have utterly disowned that part of the book, that doth treat of the commission; and for that purpose I did send my daughter to burn some of them before his face.

Likewise I have utterly disowned Lawrence Claxton, for ever being a messenger or bishop, or servant any more unto this commission. Neither shall I own any thing that he shall say or do in reference to this commission. Therefore I do exhort you, and all the rest of the believers, not to stumble or stagger in your faith concerning Claxton, as if your happiness of eternal life did depend upon believing of him to be a messenger or a bishop; for though he should be cut off to eternity, yet is the foundation of God sure and true; that is the commission of God, as it was given to John Reeve and Lodowicke Muggleton, by voice of words from God but as for Claxton, he had his commission from man; therefore man can take it away again; for he hath stood all this while but by my assistance, and at my will and pleasure. Therefore as long as he kept himself in obedience as a servant unto this commission, he had my authority and assistance on his side also.

I did bear with many infirmities of his nature, but this spiritual pride of his hath been much like unto the lost angel, which thought himself as fit to rule and govern as his Maker was; nay, more fit, and therefore he would have been in God's room and place, that he might have governed the holy angels. So likewise this Lawrence Claxton, not thinking it enough to be saved by this commission, or to be a bare messenger or servant to it, but hath, angel-like, aspired so high as to get into John Reeve's chair or place, and so he is now become the chief commissioner, which is far above a servant or messenger; therefore he doth very often in that book call it our commission, as if John Reeve and he were the only commissioners, and that I, which God gave to be John Reeve's mouth, is quite thrust out, so that I am made but a fellow-labourer with him in this commission.

But Lawrence Claxton shall know that there is yet a prophet in Israel that hath power over him. For as John Reeve was like unto Elijah, so am I as Elisha, and that his place was but as Gehazi, and could stand no longer than my will and pleasure was, because the burden of the Lord lyeth wholly upon me, which is the commission of the Lord.

Therefore my counsel and advice to you all of this faith is, that you would stand stedfast in your faith unto the doctrine of the true God, which hath been delivered unto you by John Reeve and myself, and that we two are the last Prophets and Witnesses unto the true God the Man Christ Jesus.

Again, my counsel and advice unto you, and the rest of the believers there about you is, that you would allow Lawrence Claxton no more maintenance weekly as you have done formerly; but let him betake himself to some employment in the world, as well as the rest of the believers do; for I do not see it fit that he and the serpent his wife should be maintained in idleness and pride; for there is no more use for him in this commission; therefore to what purpose should you allow him any maintenance, which is made lower than yourselves in this commission. For I have utterly disowned him upon any such an account, as to be a messenger or bishop, or servant anymore unto this commission. For I shall not own whatsoever he shall write or speak concerning this commission any more; for it will be well if he have so much faith in this commission as will save his own soul. Therefore I should rather advise you to preserve some part of that which you did allow Claxton weekly towards the reprinting of that book of ours which hath the dark print, and towards the printing of the 11th of the *Revelations*, for I shall make as much haste of it as I can; because, I suppose, that this will be the last that ever will be set forth by this spiritual commission: for I cannot conceive that there can, or need be any more spoken concerning this spiritual commission, than hath been related in all our writings, and will now be in this of the 11th of the *Revelations*.

I speak this, because there is very few left of the dark print; for there hath been more enquiring after them of late than formerly, because that book hath the most highest and heavenly mysteries contained in it, but that the print is so bad, that it doth make every one almost weary of reading it.

Therefore my judgment is, that it would be better work, and more glory to God, and honour to this commission, to give something weekly, for or towards the printing of that book again; and let Claxton shift in the world as others have done before him; for you are not bound now I have disowned him, not to look no more upon him than you are to look upon the weakest believers of this commission; no, nor so much neither.

Therefore let not your thoughts be troubled concerning Claxton; for most part of you did believe the commission before Claxton came, and will do after he is gone; therefore as he came to this commission by man, therefore by man is his commission taken from him again; and so your burden, which he hath laid upon you, may be taken off you.

I would desire you to read this letter to all the believers of this commission there about you, though some of them are unknown to me, with my love to yourself and mother Wylde, and Martyn the thatcher, and Martyn the tanner, and his wife, and his daughter, and all the rest that have a love to this commission. I desire you to let me hear from you as soon as you can conveniently.

Written by

LODOWICKE MUGGLETON,

The last true Prophet and Witness unto the true God, the Man Christ Jesus.

P. S. You may send to me in Great Trinity-lane, next door to the sign of the Black-Boy and Hand,

London, Jan. 2, 1660.

An Epistle of the Prophet Lodowicke Muggleton's to Christopher Hill, &c.

To his Loving Friend, Christopher Hill, and to all the rest that love this Commission, or that are in the Faith of it.

February 5, 1660.

I RECEIVED your letter, being dated Jan. 20, but I having other occasions of late than ordinary, so that I could not send you an answer; because, since I have disowned Lawrence Claxton, there hath been more resorting unto me than formerly; for there hath been some strangers that seemeth to have great affection to the doctrine of this commission, and some of them have some things of this world considerably, which hath promised me to be some assistance unto me in the re-printing of the dark printed book again; which hath encouraged me to go on with it; therefore I have almost prepared it for the press; which, if the printer have but a care to do it according to the directions which is given him, it will be a most excellent piece of work; for there is the most deepest mysteries contained in it as ever was penned by man these thirteen hundred years, or ever will be again; therefore there is much looking after them now a late, but there is never a one to be had but that which I must print the others by. I hope it will be ordered so, that it will be very delight some to read, so that people may the more clearly understand those deep mysteries contained in it; but as for that which I am about, will not be ready for the press yet a while, though I have almost gone through the heads of the chapters. Yet I must write it again before it is fit for the press, which will take a great deal of time, which I cannot spare as yet, because this dark print will take up some time in the correcting of it fit for the press, and the looking to it when the printer is a doing it, that it may not be spoiled as it was before. I do intend to put it into the press in a fortnight or three weeks at the farthest; therefore I desire you, that have faith in it, if you can, to raise forty or fifty shillings towards it in three weeks or a month; but if you cannot do so much, let it be what you can only let me hear before, and then I shall order things otherwise here in London, &c. I do find in your letter as if your hearts were troubled because of your meetings being put down, and the oaths to be imposed upon you. But as for your meetings being put down, what need you care? Cannot you live by your own faith for a time, without meeting together on those days called Sundays? Cannot you see and talk with one another as you see occasion on the week or working-days, for what you suffer upon any such account, when as this commission layeth no such bond upon you, but rather to the contrary; for as long as the powers of the nation doth forbid you to go to any meetings, do you obey them, and keep all at home; but if the powers of the nation doth command you to go to church to their public worship, then I say you are to suffer what penalty the powers of the nation will lay upon you, rather than to worship in the house of Baal. For this worship of the Spirit, which is now, hath no visible forms of worship at all belonging to it, neither is there any necessity for any public meetings at all. So that as for your meetings being put down, there is no cause of trouble or sorrow at all, but rather a cause of joy. But the oaths which will be imposed upon you, may cause matter of trouble upon your spirits, because I cannot say that any believer of this commission can, with safety and peace to his own conscience, take any of them"; both because if you take an oath of allegiance, which doth seem to be the most easiest oath, yet there you are bound, if needs be, to fight for the present power, or else you must break your oath; so that there is great inconveniency in taking that oath to a tender conscience.

And as for the oath of supremacy, it cannot be understood by those that have faith in the true God, that the king is the supreme head of the church of God, or that he is their defender of: their faith; for the powers of the nation if they did know of it, they would rather, instead of defending and upholding it, overthrow and destroy it; but those that are of the same faith of the church of England, the king is the supreme head of that church, and the defender of their faith. Therefore those people that are of the faith of the church of England, Scotland, and Ireland, what need they to scruple the taking of the oath of supremacy, seeing they are of the same church as the powers of the nation is of, as aforesaid. But this oath was especially intended and made for the Papists in Queen Elizabeth's time and days, but now it is laid as a snare upon all the free-born people of England, that they might find out all those whose consciences are tender, which dare not swear at all, as there are many here in London that will not swear at all; but I confess that you that live in the country are to be pitied more upon that account than we that are here in the city; because here a man may go in a crowd and never be missed; but in the country there is no place for a man to hide his head, but they will find him out. So that my advice to you is, that you would take no oaths at all, not that hath relation to fighting or unto public worship: for how can you fight for to defend the king, when as you are not to defend yourselves, but rather to suffer what the present powers doth lay upon you; only this, I would advise you to pay according to your abilities, what taxes soever the powers of the nation doth lay upon you, whether it be by way of tithes or any other taxes whatsoever, so that Caesar may have the things that are Caesar's, and God the things that are God's; therefore I shall give you an example of some of the Quakers here in London concerning this thing.

There was in the time of the late troubles, concerning those fifty monarchy-men, search made into every house, which was suspected for arms, whereby they took many of the Baptists and of the Quakers upon suspicion; upon which the Quakers were carried before a justice, which justice proposed the oath unto them: one of the Quakers answered, saying,

"We cannot swear to defend the king, for we cannot defend ourselves, much less to fight to defend another; but this, said he, we are willing to do, to pay what taxes the king shall lay upon us to the utmost of our abilities; and if the king will take those goods we have, he shall freely have them, for to swear for him we cannot do it." The justice being so convinced at their sincerity in that thing, sent them away without taking any oath at all, and bid them go home to their own houses in peace; but on the next Sunday following, these same men would needs go to their meeting again, notwithstanding the proclamation of the king was against all private meetings, yet their zeal was so great, or else wilful, that they could not live by that light within them; but must needs meet together, contrary to the kings proclamation and so the same men were taken at their private meeting, and carried to Newgate, and there they remain to this day; so that now their sufferings is rather for evil-doing, than for welldoing: seeing they are not required to meet together on the Sabbath-day, neither by God nor man. No more at present concerning these things aforesaid, but exhorting you to hold stedfast in the faith of this commission unto the death, that you may receive that crown of eternal glory which is set before you, which is the knowledge of the true God, and the right devil, which hath not been so clearly manifested since the world began, as it hath been in this spiritual and last witnesses of the Spirit.

No more at present, but I rest your brother in the true faith of the true God,

LODOWICKE MUGGLETON.

P. S. We are all well in London, and there is none of the faith here that I know of that have had the oaths propounded to them as yet, I suppose because the number is few. Your Brother Andrew is well, but as for your brother Ralph, I have not seen him ever since he came from you out of the country. I pray let me hear from you as soon as you can conveniently concerning that business in the beginning of the letter.

London, February 5, 1660. Give this with care.

An Epistle of the Prophet Lodowicke Muggleton to Christopher Hill, Feb. 25, 1660.

Brother Christopher, and all the rest of the Faith in Kent,

I RESERVED your letter, and am glad to hear that you are so well satisfied in your minds concerning the oaths, and the other things therein contained. But as for the money I made mention, that cannot be raised, only twenty shillings yon say will be raised, with their names that doth give it. I am very well satisfied with that, for I am very loath to be so much burthensome unto those of the faith in the country, therefore I shall press the more upon some here in London, because it will arise to a great deal of money more for the printing than I thought it would; but I suppose I shall raise friends that will enable me, and I suppose about twelve days hence the printer will begin to put it into the press, therefore you may send the twenty shillings according as you have expressed in your letter.

Also I understand by your letters, that Lawrence Claxton hath sent you a letter, wherein he doth declare, that he is the same in Revelation as he ever was, and thinks by pen it cannot be declared what the difference was; but when he shall see your faces, he shall make appear what the differences is: he did send a letter into Cambridgeshire, which was much to the same purpose as yours was, only there was some expressions in it, which expressions are such like as these. Those unheard transactions concerning him, which he could not express, but when he did see their faces he would open the difference more clearer unto them.

Therefore I would have you observe and consider that his pen and his tongue together, could set forth his spiritual pride and lordliness, with some other practices which hath made this great difference, but his pen is not able, nor his tongue neither, to be humble in his mind, and to see his spiritual pride and filthy covetous avarice, for if he could, his pen might as easily declare what the ground and cause of all this difference is as well and better, than when he shall see your faces; but he doth think by his goodly words and presence, as being the same in Revelation as ever he was, to overpower your spirits, that you might think that the difference between him and I, but that it might easily be reconciled. Likewise your desire is, that I would send you word whether you may relieve him as a believer or no; My answer is this, that you may not relieve him, neither as a messenger nor as a believer of this commission, because he is an excommunicated person of the commissioner himself, and is separated from having any union with me in spiritual matters. Therefore you that are believers in or of this commission, ought not to have any society with him in spiritual matters: let his pretence of revelation be ever so much, you are not to mind him nor regard it, for it is nothing worth unto you, for what the commissioner doth not own, you are not to have any regard unto it.

Therefore let not his pretences of being the same in revelation, nor his goodly words be any way a means to trouble your spirits about it; for he is cast out of heaven, even as the angel was from the presence of God and the holy angel into this earth; so even is Claxton cast out of heaven; that is, from having any communion with the prophet or commissioner of the Spirit, or with those believers of the Spirit, so that as the angels was cast out, not only from the presence of God, but also from the presence of the holy angels; so likewise he is not only cast out from the presence of the prophet, but from the presence of the believers also, and as the angel was cast into the earth, so likewise is he cast into the world, and let the world relieve him, for that is large enough, and as for his revelation, if he hath so much in himself as will bear up his own soul into eternal happiness it is well, but nobody else will be ever a whit the better for it; for I would not have you so ignorant as to think, that after a man is excommunicated or cast out of this commission, though his understanding be greater, and his language more glorious than in any one of the same faith, yet he that hath the least knowledge in a commission is to be minded and respected of all those of the same faith.

But on the contrary, if a man have never such great parts, if he be disowned or cast out by the commissioner, the believers are bound to disown him out of their society, and not to relieve him as a believer of this commission; only this I shall give the liberty to do, that if he comes amongst you, you may eat or drink with him, or give him lodging as you would unto a stranger, but not to mind any of his sayings with reference to his being a believer, or to what I have done concerning him: I say in these things you are not to mind him nor regard what he shall say or do of that nature.

No more at present, but expecting to hear from you as soon as you can, I rest your Brother, in the true faith of Jesus, the only true God,

LODOWICKE MUGGLETON.

London, February 25, 1660.

A Copy of a Letter written by the prophet Lodowicke Muggleton, to pull down the high Exaltation of Lawrence Claxton. Dated from London, December, 25, 1660.

Lawrence Claxton,

I HAVING seriously considered your many foul, proud and covetous actions since you came to the belief of this commission, but more especially of late, since you have been allowed some means from the believers of this commission, which have made you so lord-like, that you are grown so spiritually proud, so that now you are gotten, in your own conceit, to be the chief man in this spiritual commission; so that your pride hath grown by degrees so high until you have gotten to sit in John Reeve's chair and place, so that you are got up as high as you can; therefore it is high time for you to fall.

Therefore, seeing that occasion and offences will come, that the secrets of the heart may be made manifest, therefore I do see a great providence in that business of mason's wife, for that hath been an occasion to bring forth those differences which have been among the believers of this commission « likewise it hath been a means to insearch the bottom of your heart; for ever since the beginning of this difference, after that you did understand that your commission was like to be taken away from you, you have strove with all your might, both with saint and devil, for to uphold your authority without me; therefore you have made use of your beloved Frances and Ananias, and, Saphira-like, you have consulted with that venomous serpent your wife, and have made her your council in all spiritual matters, and that I did perceive by the serpent your wife, in that she did show Mr. Hatter and Mr. Hudson, that place of Scripture concerning Moses and Miriam, which I know she could not do of herself, except she had heard your judgment of it, which conceit of yours on that place could do you little good, only this your judgment on that Scripture, with your continual consultation with the devil your wife, hath enraged your wife so far as to vaunt herself against the believers of this commission, and against me; for which I do pronounce your wife cursed and damned to eternity, though she hath been damned by John Reeve already, therefore I have set to my seal, that John Reeve's damnation shall be true upon her.

As for yourself, because you have strove to maintain your authority without me, and for that purpose you have written this book, wherein you have quite excluded me, and have made the commission only John Reeve's and yours, for your writings do shew forth the very pride of your heart; therefore I do declare against that book, and against you, that I do renounce and disown you upon any such account, as to be a messenger, bishop, or a servant, any more to this commission; neither shall you write any more, or speak any more in the behalf of this commission, for I shall utterly disown whatever you do or say of that nature; neither shall the believers of this commission allow you any maintenance, neither in Cambridgeshire nor Kent, upon any such account, as looking upon you to be a messenger; for you shall become as one of the least of believers of the commission, and you shall become a reproach to saint and devil, which shame and reproach shall strike as a loathsome leprosy unto you during your life; for your shall never come to any honour of this commission any more, for you have had your last that ever you shall have in this world, because you shall know that you have kicked your heel against your master, and that there is a prophet yet in Israel, and hath power over you; notwithstanding you have made yourself equal with John Reeve, you shall know that John Reeve was as Elijah, and that I am in the place of Elisha, and that you are in the place of Gehazi. This is my resolution.

Written by Lodowicke Muggleton, the last true Prophet and Witness unto the true God, the Man Christ Jesus in glory.

December 25, 1660.

LODOWICKE MUGGLETON.

A Copy of a Letter, written by the Prophet Lodowicke Muggleton, to his loving Friend Christopher Hill, at Maidstone, in Kent, Jan. 2, 1661.

Give this with Care.

Loving Friend, Christopher Hill,

MY love remembered unto you and to all the rest of the believers of the commission of the Spirit there with you.

These are to let you understand, that I received your letter, dated November the 29th, 1661, with your kind token; and the eighteen shillings in money; and it came very seasonable, because I have been at more expence of late than ordinary; for my daughter Sarah hath been sick of the yellow jaundice ever since, and doth remain so still, which was the cause I did return no answer all this while; because her death hath been much feared by some in London, and there is no certainty yet that she will escape, though she is not so extreme sick as she was.

Also, there hath been another trouble upon me to add unto the other, which is this; I being a long liver in the parish, it fell to my lot to be chosen scavenger, and I must either hold or fine; and if I should have held I might have lost nothing, but I should have been entangled with oaths; therefore I rather chose to pay down the fine, which was twenty shillings, before the parish would choose another in my room.

Now I shall write a few lines concerning some particular things in your letter.

The first thing is concerning some that do profess an acknowledgment of this commission, but do not live the life of it; because they go to publick meetings, which indeed cannot stand with true faith in a commission. For, look what laws a commission doth set up are to be observed by the believers of it; and the laws of this commission of the Spirit are spiritual, and do worship God in spirit and truth, without any visible forms of worship, as the worshippers of Baal have; for though there was an outward, visible form of worship set up by Moses and the Apostles, and they were to be observed in their times and places, because they had commissions from God so to do; and the believers in their commissions were happy in yielding obedience unto them: but when public worship is set up by men, without a commission from God, it becomes a will-worship and idolatry, a thing which is an abomination unto the Lord. Therefore, whosoever shall make a show, or a profession of faith in this commission of the Spirit, and yet go to worship with the idolaters of the nation, I shall not look upon any such person to have any true faith in the true God, nor in this commission of the Spirit; neither can they have any true peace, nor the assurance of everlasting life; for he that will not deny himself and take up his cross for truth's sake is not worthy of it: and I am sure, there is as little suffering by the believers of this commission for their faith sake, as ever there was of the other two commissions.

Again, this commission of the Spirit doth lay as little, and less bonds upon the believers of it than any of the other two above mentioned did; for this commission requires nothing but faith in the heart, which works by love, without any outward ordinances of visible worship, which is a great burthen to bear to those that are under them.

It would ask a whole sheet of paper to clear this thing; but I suppose, that they which are truly enlightened in the power of the three several commissions, may understand and be satisfied in what I have said in this letter, and in those books of ours that you have amongst you, concerning the worship that doth belong unto the three several commissions, they all of them differing one from the other, neither is the one bound to observe the other; but every commission, and the worship belonging to it, is to be observed by the believers of it, in its time and place, when it is in being, and not when it is out of date.

The other thing, which is of concernment in your letter, is, that you have a monthly contribution, and your desire is to have my judgment in it, which is very pleasing unto me, and I do like it very well, it being a good work, and I am glad that you are so free amongst yourselves; because it was always against my nature and spirit to lay any engagement and burthen upon the believers of this commission, neither shall I: but in regard you are free to lay it on yourselves, it being sure a good work, I do freely give you my consent unto it; therefore do as your own freedom gives you leave and prosper. So resteth your friend in the true faith.

LODOWICKE MUGGLETON.

London, Jan. 2, 1661.

My kind love remembered unto yourself and all the true believers in those parts in general, as if it were in particular to every person.

A Copy of a Letter written by the Prophet Lodowicke Muggleton to Mrs. Dorothy Carter, near Chesterfield, bearing date February 13, 1660.

Loving Friend,

THOUGH unknown to me in the natural or visible sight of the body, yet by that invisible discerning which I have of your spirit by those few words which you have made mention of in your letter, wherein I find that the spirit of truth hath blown upon your heart, in that it hath made you willing for to seek and to enquire after the knowledge of these two witnesses. Therefore I shall give you a word or two to inform you who these two witnesses are, and in some measure how their testimony is received: therefore I would have you to mind and observe these lines as followeth.

That as there are three that bear record in Heaven, *The father, the word and the spirit; and these three are one, that is, these three are one distinct person in the form of a man; so likewise there is three that doth bear witness on earth, namely, the spirit, water and blood, and these three do agree in one.* Now observe, those three upon earth, are these three commissions which should be acted forth upon the stage of this world. Which three commissions are these.

First. The commission of Moses and the prophets.

Secondly. The commission of Christ and the apostles.

Thirdly. The commission of the Holy Spirit, which commission of the Spirit is now extant in the world at this day, and hath been here in England these nine years, and the sound of it hath gone through many parts of Christendom, as in this part of England, Scotland, Ireland, New England, Virginia, Barbadoes, and many other places, I will not here mention; but the doctrine of the commission of the Spirit hath been very little received in the world; but the most that hath received it, is here in London, and in Cambridgeshire, and in Kent.

In these three places there is a few that is very well grounded in the belief of this spiritual commission; but one cause why there is so few that doth receive it, is because there is no visible forms of worship belonging to this spiritual commission, but doth altogether consist of the knowledge of the true God and the right devil, with the place and nature of Heaven and Hell, with the forms and nature of angels and the mortality of the soul.

And upon these six principles in the knowledge of them, dependeth all the eternal happiness of man.

Therefore because it will be too tedious to write all these things, I have sent you a book; these books that were written by these two witnesses; they are bound up together, and, they will inform you who those two witnesses are, with their names, and the voice of God that spake to them, and their messages, with their doctrine, which they should set forth with many deep mysteries which is hard to be understood.

Likewise I have sent you some books of his which he hath written in behalf of this commission; and as for the names of those two prophets, you will find them in the books, and the place where they live; only one of them, since the book of the Mortality of the Soul was written, is dead; namely, John Reeve, but Lodowicke Muggleton is yet living in Great Trinity-lane, over against one Mills's, a Brown Baker.

There is in that book, which is bound, all that was written by the two witnesses and prophets themselves; and there is laid down in those writings the true grounds of all divinity, which doth consist in the knowledge of the true God, and the right devil, with the knowledge of the two seeds, is those two keys that doth open the gates both of Heaven and hell; and there is none now in this world, that hath the keys given unto them, but these two prophets and witnesses of the Spirit only.

Written by

LODOWICKE MUGGLETON,

The last true Witness and Prophet unto the Man Christ Jesus, glorified.

It was your lot to employ a man for to buy those books which hath been damned by the prophets daughter, some eight or nine months since, for opposing of those books; and the revelation of his commission; therefore the man, remembering these books, and the sentence, will neither undertake to carry them, nor to lay down the money for them; because he hath a prejudice both against the books and the persons that wrote them. Therefore I shall desire Mrs Griffith for to take some course that these books may be conveyed to you, and let her give orders how they may be sent, and how the money may be conveyed to her again; for then I shall desire Mrs. Griffith to set her name to the direction of this letter.

LODOWICKE MUGGLETON

A Copy of a Letter written by the Prophet Lodowicke Muggleton, to Mrs. Dorothy Carter of Chesterfield, Feb. 16, 1661.

Friend Dorothy Carter,

I RECEIVED your letter, bearing date February 3, 1661, wherein I perceive you have received some books, and a letter from me, whereby you have received some refreshment of heart, and so understand in some measure those great and high mysteries contained in them; and having one daughter which is partaker with you in the faith of this commission of the Spirit, which I am very glad to hear of, desiring that your faith and hers may grow to perfection here, and to eternal glory hereafter! and I have so much the more hopes of it because there is so few of you, because truth hath but few of its side, nor never had, because the world is given unto reason, the devil's hands, he being the elder brother: but faith the younger brother, his kingdom, is an everlasting kingdom; but a strait and narrow gate or way that leadeth to life eternal; for there is but one truth, the way, and the life; and there is no finding this way without a guide; and there can be no true guide except he knoweth the way himself; and none can know the way to life eternal, but he that hath a commission from God: he knowing the deep mysteries of the true God, and the right devil, doth shew them to the seed of faith, by declaring by word and pen, that strait and narrow way that leadeth unto life, which very few do find, because there is but few ambassadors and shepherds chosen of God; that is, one prophet at a time, one Jesus, one

Peter that had the keys of heaven and hell; and now in this commission of the Spirit but two chosen witnesses of the Spirit, and one of them is not; so that I am as Elijah said in another case, *I am left alone, neither will there be any more sent of God after me while the world endures.* And as for these persecuting times, they are nothing in comparison of what hath been suffered by. the believers of the other two commissions; nay people hath and doth suffer great things for a lie, even to whipping, imprisonment, banishment, and death itself, for a lie: but the believers of this commission are loath to part with a little money, but will rather worship Baal than to pay such a tax as the powers of the nation doth lay upon them, for such a neglect of going to the public meetings; for I cannot advise any one that hath true light in them, to darken that, by going to worship a false God; for no man can serve two masters, neither can a man worship God and Baal: for if God be to be worshipped in spirit and truth, then let not the same man worship the devil with falsities and a lie; for whosoever doth so, will darken their own light; and so lose the peace of their own minds, and the assurance of their eternal happiness, for to save themselves a little in this world. And as for the book of the *interpretation of the eleventh of the Revelations*, I have finished it, and prepared it ready for the press, supposing it will be the last that will be set forth by this commission of the Spirit, and finding such great difficulties to get it printed, the times being changed, and the great charge that must be laid out upon it, I was minded to lay it aside for a time, to see if there should be any alteration in church government. But there is some here in London, and elsewhere in the countries, which have a great desire to have it out now, but it will cost so much money that, it will hardly be raised; for the printing of the Divine Looking Glass did cast me much behind hand, and this will cost more, because the times are so troublesome concerning printing, that I have much ado to persuade the printer to do it at all, being not licensed: yet he printing the Divine Looking Glass, and the Mortality of the Soul, and other books, in relation to this commission of the Spirit, he is willing to undertake to do it, but not without extraordinary gain, more than he had for the Divine Looking Glass.

Therefore, I would desire you or any other of your acquaintance, that have any affections unto truth, if they have any freedom in themselves, to contribute something towards the printing of it, what they are made free to do: I should not lay a burthen upon any if I had it of myself.

The printer will have ten pounds when he hath finished it, and ten pounds he will have down, besides other charges upon it: he doth intend to set about a matter of twelve day hence, and doth intend to finish it by Easter. I would be glad to hear from you before that time, if you can with conveniency; also, I do intend to see you sometime this summer, shall give you notice when I do intend to come: but I would willingly have this book out first.

No more at present, but my love remembered unto yourself, your daughter, and Edward Frewterill.

Your Friend, in the true Faith of Jesus, the only Wise God,

LODOWICKE MUGGLETON.

My daughter remembers her love to you, and to Edward Frewterill, being glad to hear of your love to truth.

An Epistle of the Prophet Lodowicke Muggleton's to Mrs. Ellen Sudbury. Feb. 17, 1661.

Friend in the true faith, Ellen Sudbury,

I RECEIVED your letter, but no date unto it; but for the substance of it doth favour of true light, which doth arise from the seed of faith in you, in receiving the declaration of this commission of the Spirit, which is as light set upon a hill, or in a candlestick, to give light unto all in the house, and not to be put under a bushel.

For every commissionated man is the candle of the Lord, which gives light unto the whole house; which house is the seed of faith, as it was said by Moses, *That he was faithful in all his house*: that is, he was faithful in all his commission, which was of the law, he being the candle of the law, to enlighten the seed of reason in the outward letter of the law. And this commission of the Spirit is the candle of the Lord to enlighten the seed of faith in the spiritual understanding of the Scriptures, which doth consist but upon six principles: As to know the true God, his form and nature, the right devil, his form and nature, the place and nature of heaven, and the place and nature of hell, the persons and nature of angels, and the mortality of the soul.

Upon the knowledge of these six principles dependeth the eternal happiness of man; neither can any man come to the knowledge of them but by this commission of the Spirit, which is the candle of the Lord, to light the seed of faith, the way to eternal blessedness. And though I have named six principles, yet whosoever doth but understand two, namely, the true God, and the right devil; upon these two dependeth the other four, with many deep mysteries, which will flow from the knowledge of these principles aforesaid.

And as for your emptiness and weakness, in respect of what you have formerly had, I am very glad of it; there is the more room for truth, to fill your heart up with faith and experience in the heavenly mysteries, which is declared by the witnesses of the Spirit; for many thousands are so full of their own righteousness, and of talk upon the letter of the Scriptures, that there is no room for truth to enter into their hearts. These now, in this commission, are in the same condition as those were in Christ's time, which had eyes, but did not see, and had ears, but did not hear, and had hearts but did not understand. And the cause was, and is still, men and women being so full of their own righteousness, which is of the Jaw, that there is no room in their hearts for truth, which is the righteousness of faith, to have any entrance into them.

But the thing, which is of the greatest weight in your letter is, concerning the sin against the Holy Ghost; which hath lain heavy upon you, you fearing you had committed it by questioning the truth of the Scriptures, and Christ to be the true God.

I would have you to take notice of this, that none can commit the sin against the Holy Ghost, but that man or woman that hath despised prophecy. Now you cannot despise prophecy except you do oppose, vilify, and speak evil of that man that is sent of God, that hath the spirit of prophesy; for this I would have you to know, that there can be no sinning against the Holy Ghost, but in the time of a commission; for if a man be sent of God, he is sent by the Holy Ghost, and whosoever doth despise that man, that is sent of God, he despiseth him that sent him, and so he cometh to commit that unpardonable sin, which will never be forgiven him in this world, nor in the world to come: and this was committed in the days of Christ, and in the apostles commission, as you may know by these words of Christ to the Jews, when, as they said, *he cast out devils by Belzebub the prince of devils.* Here they called the holy Spirit of Jesus a devil, and this was that sin against the Holy Ghost. And so you may see in Acts, the apostles and Stephen amusing the rulers of the Jews, saying, *you always resist the Holy Ghost as your fathers did*; and this resisting of the Holy Ghost was that unpardonable sin. And there have been more men and women that have sinned against the Holy Ghost within these ten years, than there hath those thirteen hundred and fifty years; for I know of near upon a thousand that have sinned that sin, for which they have been damned to eternity; for which we have given them the sentence of condemnation for no other sin, but for the sin against the Holy Ghost, in that they have despised the spirit of prophecy, because they had it not themselves; for it is the nature of reason to despise prophesy, being convicted of its own wisdom or legal righteousness of the law. For this I do by infallible rule of faith in the Scriptures know, and by my own experience these ten years, that there hath been more religious persons, who had an outside righteousness, hath committed the sin against the Holy Ghost, for which they have been damned to eternity. I may safely say, almost forty to one that hath had no righteousness in them at all; for no man or woman can commit the sin against the Holy Ghost, but in the time of a commission, nor then except he doth despise that prophet, messenger or minister, which is sent of God for his doctrine, and in so doing he hath committed that unpardonable sin, which very few religious persons, that hath talked with me, or seen our writings, that hath escaped it.

Loving Friend,

I have now finished, I suppose, my last book of the interpretation of the eleventh of the Revelations, and have prepared it ready for the press: and there is many here in London, and elsewhere in the country, that have a great desire to have it out, but it will cost such a deal of money the printing, that it will be much ado to be raised; for the printing of the Divine Looking-Glass did cast me much behind hand, and this will cost more, because the times are so troublesome concerning printing, that I have much ado to get it printed at all. But the printer knowing of me, I printing so much, concerning this commission, knowing that they are dispersed unto private persons, and not sold public in the stationer's shops, he is willing to undertake it with some more gain than formerly.

Therefore, if there be any of your acquaintance that hath any affection unto truth, if they have any freedom in themselves, to contribute something towards the printing of it; what they are made free I shall not lay any burthen upon them no where: if I can get money enough to pay the printer one half down, he will set about it a matter of ten days hence, and the other half must be paid when he hath done, which is supposed will be about Easter.

I shall desire to hear from you before that time, if you can: I do intend after this is out to see you this summer.

I have had a letter since I had yours, from your aunt Carter, and am glad to hear of her faith and confidence in the truth, and of the affection that is in her daughter unto truth. I do intend to send her an answer unto it.

No more at present, but rest your friend in the true faith of Jesus, the only God blessed for ever,

LODOWICKE MUGGLETON.

London, Feb. 17, 1661.

A Copy of a Letter written by the Prophet Lodowicke Muggleton, to the Believers in Cambridgeshire, bearing Date from London, Aug. 9, 1661.

Brother Dickinson, and to all the rest of the Believers in Cambridgeshire,

MY love remembered unto you and your wife, and unto all the rest of our friends there with you.

My writing unto you this time is to certify you, that my daughter is come well home, and I am informed by her, that you and other of the believers doth expect that I should come into those parts this Bartholomew-tide, because I did send a letter a great while ago somewhat to that purpose, because then I did expect that my daughter would have come up to London long before that time; but since she did not, my mind is altered as to that thing; because I do not see it necessary, nor convenient to come this year, because my daughter having been there so long with you, hath set such a fire about the country, that will not be quenched in a fortnight or three weeks time, therefore not convenient that I should come suddenly after her.

Therefore my desire is, that you may be stedfast in your faith, and that will rectify and uphold you in the midst of all opinions, and be not fearful and unbelieving, that is, afraid of every reed that is shaken with the wind: for, consider your sufferings for your faith in these times cannot extend unto death, as it hath in other commissions.

And yet you see how the believers in other commissions have suffered the spoiling of their goods, and the passing through death itself, rather than shrink in their faith. And you see the martyrs, which had no foundation, but an infinite spirit; yet, if they should have flinched from their faith, they would never have been able to have gone through those fiery trials as they did; which faith of theirs did carry them through death itself with great joy; for none can tell what the power of faith is until it be tried.

Now there is none of your trials that are the believers of this commission of the Spirit, that can reach so far as death, nor surely to any punishment on your bodies, only some charges, or perhaps imprisonment, which is not worth the naming, and who would sell faith and a good conscience, and the assurance of eternal life, for a mess of pottage! which many a one at this day hath so done, and will do.

I perceive by my daughter, that your thoughts are as if I should not have such affection to you as I had before, because our brother Burton is come away from you. I would have been glad if it had been so appointed, that he might have stayed with you yet; nevertheless my love and desire shall be nevertheless unto you, and shall come and see you as when he was there; for if he should have stayed there I should not have come this year, because of those things aforesaid, and the hinderance of that book that is now in hand. Therefore I shall desire, in the bonds of peace, that ye love one another, and bear with one another's weakness, so that the weakness be not absolute sin or wickedness; for you are but few, and have many enemies, therefore walk as children of the light, that you may know the end of your faith, which is a crown of eternal life; that you may receive the end of your faith, which God the righteous Judge, shall give unto all those whose faith doth hold out to the end in the belief of the true God, which hath been declared by this commission of the Spirit.

My love remembered unto Charles Cleve, Thomas Parke, and goodman Dovie, and the widow Adams, and her daughter Anne, and goodman Warrboys and Singleton, and his wife, and all the rest of the faith. And when your conveniency will serve, certify them concerning my not coming to see them this time.

No more at present, but rest your friend in the eternal truth, the last commissioner of the Spirit,

LODOWICKE MUGGLETON.

August 9, 1661.

A Copy of a Letter wrote by the Prophet Lodowicke Muggleton, to Mrs. Ellen Sudbury, bearing date November 28, 1661.

Friend,

I HAVE received your letter, though unknown to you in the body; yet I perceive by your letter, that light hath shined into your heart, by the declarations of this commission of the Spirit, which I desire may increase and grow in you, so that you may become wiser than your teachers, or that society which you have been formerly acquainted with, notwithstanding it is counted weakness and ignorance in you: yet, if your faith doth grow in the knowledge of the doctrine of this commission of the Spirit, your weakness will be stronger than their strength, and your ignorance will prove wiser than their wisdom; because their wisdom, which counts your wisdom ignorance, is the wisdom of reason, which is the devil, and your wisdom is the wisdom of faith, which is the wisdom of God; because it leads you to the knowledge of the true God and the right devil, with the knowledge of the place and nature of heaven, and the place and nature of hell, with the persons and nature of angels, and the mortality of the soul.

Upon the knowledge of these six principles dependeth the eternal happiness of man, in which Jacob Bemon was utterly ignorant; yet he doth talk of a God, and a devil, and of angels; but knows nothing of the person and nature of them. Yet his philosophical light was above all men that doth profess religion, until this commission of the Spirit came forth, which hath brought Jacob Bemon's light, and many other high lights, down very low within these ten years, as you may read in our writings, if you have them all, and if you have them not all, send to me, and I will help you to them, and they will inform you further than I can by word or pen.

The books that were written by us, the witnesses of the Spirit, are these:

First, *A Transcendant Spiritual Treatise*.

Secondly, *An Epistle to the Ministers*.

Thirdly, *A Letter to the Lord Mayor of London*.

Fourthly, *A Remonstrance*.

Fifthly, *A Divine Looking-Glass*.

Sixthly, *The Mortality of the Soul*

These were all written by us the ministers of the Spirit.

There is one more, which I shall set forth, which I suppose will be the last that will be set forth by me. It is *The Interpretation of the Eleventh Chapter of the Revelation*, which is much desired by many.

You speak as if I had some thoughts to come down, and that somebody did speak something to that purpose: but I do not know why they should say so; for I do not remember that I did say any such thing, neither had I any ground to say so, because I do not know any one in those parts that hath any such affections to me, or to the doctrine held forth by me, except it be one Dorothy Carter, and one Edward Frewterill, at Chesterfield, else I know none by name in those parts that hath any affections to these things. Now this Edward Frewterill was a great Bemonist before he had heard of our books; yet, nevertheless, I am encouraged by your letter to come and see you, but it will be next summer first, and then I am to go into Cambridgeshire, and that is a quite contrary way from you; yet I am unacquainted in those parts, yet I have been at Harborough, in Northamptonshire, and at Ashby de la Zouch, in Leicestershire; there have been some of my name, which did live at Nottingham, they were of kin to me; but kindred hath been of little value to me from a child. If you be acquainted with Dorothy Carter, and Edward Frewterill, let me know it, and whether you had the books by their means or no.

No more at present, but rest your friend in the faith of the true God the Man Christ Jesus in glory,

LODOWICKE MUGGLETON.

You may direct your letter to me as you did before, in Great Trinity-lane, over against the Lion and the Lamb.

A Copy of a Letter written by the Prophet Lodowicke Muggleton, to Mrs. Ellen Sudbury. April 7, 1662.

I RECEIVED your letter elated March 28, with the inclosed to Mr. Hatter, which he coming to my house at that same time the letter came, I gave unto him, at which he was very glad to see, and he reading of mine, was the more refreshed in his mind to hear of your love, faith, and stedfastness in this commission of the Spirit. Also I shewed it to my daughter, and to others of the faith, which doth much rejoice at your faith and satisfaction you have in the understanding of the truth, in that you are made partaker With us in the like precious faith, which doth consist in the right understanding of the true God and the right devil; the rise of the two seeds, and the distinction of the three commissions, which no more in the world doth know at this day, but the believers of this commission of the Spirit only; because they have no true spiritual foundation as a rock, but their foundation is upon the sand, even all the teachers in the world, and the Quaker's principle or foundation is the worst of all; though it seemeth to be the best of all in righteousness of life; yet the worst of all in point of doctrine: and that they will find in the end, though they may flourish for a time; for no Quaker, nor any other that hath heard of this commission of the Spirit, and of the doctrine declared by it, and doth not understand it, and believe it, they cannot be saved, let their holiness of life be never so much; for God hath not regard unto the righteousness of life, except it doth proceed from faith in the true God; which no Quaker, nor any other man hath, but those that have faith in this commission of the Spirit. Therefore it is that they do all fight against the true God, and against the commission of the Spirit; but I am refreshed at your experience and growth in grace and knowledge of the true God; and in that you have eyes, and can see, as Christ said unto his disciples, *Blessed are your eyes, for they see; for many hath eyes, but they see not.* Also I am glad to see that your understanding is enlightened to see the true interpretation of Scripture, which is given by this commission of the Spirit; and this book of *The Eleventh of the Revelation* is very little else but interpretation of many places of Scripture, besides the chapter itself, which will enlighten the understanding in the knowledge of the Scriptures more than all that hath been written before; therefore I have sent you three of them; because if there should be any others besides yourself, that should have any affection to them besides yourself, let them have them; but I shall leave that to your discretion, do what you will with them.

I received a letter from Edward Frewterill, and your aunt Carter, with the money, bearing date March the 19th, 1661; but I have not sent them any answer as yet, nor no books; but I do intend to send this week, if the carrier be in town.

And as for my coming down into the country, I do much rejoice at yours and your aunt Curtis's affection in desiring of me to come, which I do intend to do, but I think it will be about James-tide, for I must go into Cambridgeshire about Midsummer, and after I have been there, I do intend to see you. So being in haste, I rest your friend in the true faith,

LODOWICKE MUGGLETON.

Mr. Hatter remembers his love unto you. My daughter remembers her love, with others of the faith, unto you.

London, April 7th, 1662.

A Copy of a Letter wrote by the Prophet Lodowicke Muggleton, to Mrs. Dorothy Carter, of Chesterfield, bearing date April 12, 1662.

Loving Friend in the true Faith, Dorothy Carter,

I RECEIVED the thirty-five shillings of Holland's man. Also I received the inclosed letter as it was directed.

I am glad to hear of your faith in this commission, and of your affections and forwardness in things of this nature, and of your daughter's faith in the true God. I shall not write to you, but of those things that are expected by you, that is, of my coming down to see you.

I do intend to come about James-tide, for I must go about Midsummer into Cambridgeshire; that journey is but short, I can return again in twelve or fourteen days time.

In the mean time you may read over this book, which I believe will give you more light in the Scriptures, than all that ever you have read; I have sent you six of them. Let Mr. Frewterill have one; as for the rest, dispose of them as you please. If there be any need for any more of them, send to me, and I will send them. I have sent three to your cousin Sudbury on Monday last, by the Nottingham carrier; he goeth forth on Monday.

No more at present, but my love remembered to you and your daughter, having an intent to see you at the time appointed. I rest your friend in the faith, as it is in Jesus,

LODOWICKE MUGGLETON.

Mr. Hatter and my daughter remember their loves unto you, and your daughter, and Mr. Frewterill.

A Copy of a Letter wrote by the Prophet Lodowicke Muggleton, to Mrs. Bladdwell, a Believer, bearing date May 30, 1662.

Friend Mrs. Bladdwell,

I UNDERSTAND by Mrs. Chitwood and my daughter, that you are desirous to be declared one of the blessed ones' of the Lord by me, which I do believe that you are of that seed which is appointed unto eternal happiness, therefore you have been preserved even to the last hour, which is the eleventh hour of the day; for the twelfth hour is the hour of eternity, when, as no man can work, neither will there be any need of the work of faith any more, because eternity enters in at the twelfth hour.

I say you have been preserved as Nicodemus was, to be born again by the words of Christ, when he was old; so now for you to be born again by this commission of the Spirit, when you are old, it is a thing which I have not known, no, not since this commission hath been upon me, that one so old as you are should believe truth, when it is declared, even at the last hour. It cannot be expected by me, neither of God himself, that you should grow to any maturity in the knowledge of the true God, and the right devil, with many other heavenly mysteries, as if you were but in the sixth or ninth hour of your age; but it is well for you that ever you was born, that you were of that seed that was capable to believe in this commission of the Spirit, when as you did hear of it, which is a great Providence unto you, being caught in the net of eternal happiness, which is the commission of the Spirit, before you departed this life.

But however, whether your understanding or knowledge do increase or no, so as to discourse to the convincing of others that are enemies to truth, yet let your faith be strong in what you have received by reading in those books, which have been written by the witnesses of the Spirit, and in vindication of this commission, and you shall fare no worse than I myself shall do. In which faith you so living, and so dying, (I not questioning you in the least) I do declare your soul and body happy and blessed to eternity.

By,

LODOWICKE MUGGLETON,

One of the last two Witnesses and Prophets of the Commission of the Spirit unto the High and Mighty God, the Man Christ Jesus, in Glory.

May 30, 1662.

The Prophet Lodowicke Muggleton's Blessing to Mrs Sarah Short. Transcribed from a Copy drawn from the Original. Given to her by him, June 2, 1662.

Dear Friend, in the eternal Truth, Mrs. Short,

I UNDERSTOOD by a word or two that Mrs. Chitwood spake, that you were not well satisfied in those words that I spake unto you concerning your eternal happiness, as if I did not look upon you to be of the seed of faith, or one of the blessed of the Lord, because I bade you not be troubled in your mind concerning that, for you should fare no worse than myself did, and what could I say more; for if I had not looked upon you as one of the seed of faith, I should never have said so unto you; for I never did say so unto any, but unto those which I do really believe to be of the seed of faith, especially unto those that do ask it out of singleness of heart, as I do believe you did; but this I would have you to consider, that a prophet cannot give faith and revelation unto any, whereby they may find those refreshments and joy of heart. It must arise from your own seed of faith, neither can it arise so in you as it doth in others, neither can it be expected of you, because you are not, neither have you been exercised with the trouble of this world as others are. And then again the weakness of your nature is such, that you cannot exercise your mind about the business and lawful affairs of this world, which would be a great refreshment unto nature, as it were the assurance of eternal life, is which nature hath denied unto you; but it is well for you that ever you were born, that you were of that blessed seed, that will be happy in the end. I should be glad that your faith might grow as strong as that woman's did, which was troubled with the bloody issue, that if she could but touch our Lord's garment she should be whole; and according to her faith it was unto her, and not only so, but she had the assurance of eternal life beside; for virtue went out of our Lord not only to cure the bloody issue, but the peace and satisfaction of her mind concerning a life to come. Therefore it is said he looked round about to see her that had done this thing, and he said, *Daughter thy faith hath made thee whole; go in peace.*

Here you may see, it was not our Lord that did give her faith, but it was her own faith which made her whole, both natural and spiritual; neither can any prophet give faith to any, neither doth God himself give faith to any, it must arise from its own seed. You may say then, why doth the Scripture say, that faith is the gift of God? To which I answer, for these two reasons; because the seed of faith is of his own Divine nature, and that breath of life, which God breathed into Adam, was that breath or seed of faith; and whoever is partaker of the seed of Adam, they are of the seed of faith; so in time it doth arise out of that seed into art, so that the creature come to the peace of assurance of eternal life. And in this sense it may be said, that faith is the gift of God, because God gave the seed in the original unto Adam, and not in particular unto every person, as hath been a long time vainly imagined through the ignorate of man not knowing the two seeds.

Secondly, it may be said, that faith is the gift of God, in that he hath chosen prophets and ambassadors to preach faith. Therefore, saith Paul, *Faith cometh by hearing the Word of God preached, and how can he preach except he be sent.*

The meaning is this, that the act of faith cometh by hearing the Word of God preached by me, or more, that is sent of God, but the seed and roots of faith was in them that did believe before, and not immediately given of God, as I said before.

But in regard God did send messengers to preach faith, and so that seed is awakened, and cometh to act itself forth in power, so as to justify themselves towards God, and towards man; for being justified by faith, we have peace with God.

And in this regard, it may be said, that faith is a gift of God, in that he hath sent men to declare truth, and so them that believe them may be said to receive faith from God; for he that receiveth a prophet, in the name of a prophet, receiveth him that sent him; and whoever receiveth a prophet, in the name of a prophet, shall receive a prophet's reward, which reward is eternal life; for prophets have little, else to give. And if it be well considered it is enough, and as the woman's faith did draw virtue from our Lord, so there will virtue go from the commission of the Spirit as to your eternal happiness. Let your faith wholly depend upon it, and you shall fare no worse than myself doth: you shall have the end of your faith, even the salvation of your souk

And that you may be sure I do declare you one of the blessed of the Lord to eternity. I thought good to write these few lines unto you, for your further confirmation of your eternal happiness after death.

Your faithful Friend,
and true Prophet,

LODOWICKE MUGGLETON.

June 2, 1662.

A Copy of a Letter written by the Prophet Lodowicke Muggleton, to Mrs. Dorothy Carter, of Chesterfield, bearing date July 14, 1662, from London.

Loving Friend, in the eternal Truth, Dorothy Carter,

MY love remembered unto you and to our friend Mr. Frewterill.

I understand by your letter, that you received the six books, and how you disposed of some of them, and of a maid that liveth with you, that is brought to believe this commission, which I am very glad to hear that one so young should be called by this declaration of truth, even as my daughter was, even at the sixth hour of the day, that is, in their infancy; for there is but the sixth hour, ninth, and eleventh hour; for the twelfth hour is the hour of eternity.

The sixth is youth or childhood, the ninth is middle age, the eleventh hour is old age, which is the last hour, then cometh the twelfth hour, which is the hour of eternity.

I do know but of two that are called at the eleventh hour, not these ten years, but at the sixth many, but most of all at the ninth hour of the day, that is, middle age.

Also you desired a book all bound together, for that maid's brother, which Mr. Hatter did send in my absence. I hope you did receive it; I am glad to hear of your faith and refreshment, that you find in this commission of the Spirit, in the understanding of those things declared by this commission. I make no question but that you shall increase in faith, light and life, to the opposing of all those blind and dark lights, the Quakers, that have no God but what is within them, and that light within them will be found in the end to be but darkness; and then how great will that darkness be! For their God and their light within themselves will perish to eternity; for though they seem to be the best of all the seven churches in righteousness of life, and do suffer more by the powers of the nation than any other, yet they are the worst of all the seven churches in point of doctrine; for they are absolutely the spirit of antichrist, which denieth both the Father and the Son; for though the other churches do deny the Father to be a person in the form of a man, yet they will acknowledge that Christ, the Son of God, is now in heaven, in that body that suffered death; but these Quakers do deny, that the same body of flesh is now living, therefore the spirit of antichrist, which denieth both the Father and the Son to be a person; for those Quakers are but the very influence of John Robin's witchcraft spirit, he being the antichrist in this last age, which did shew such signs and wonders as is written of by John Reeve, and many more strange things than what was written, which was acted in my house by some of his prophets, which I am an eye-witness of before I had any knowledge of God, or knew what did belong to a commission, neither will any of his prophets or disciples own any such thing now, though they know that this witchcraft power was taken from him, and so from them, by that sentence of eternal death, which John Reeve had pronounced upon him.

Therefore it matters not whether the Quakers do believe any thing concerning him or no.

Are the Quakers so simple to think, that any of John Robin's disciples will tell him the truth how they were bewitched by him? No, nor no other man, neither could we ourselves, if we had not had a knowledge above him, and a commission too, Ave could neither have brought down his power, nor have known how, and by what means, he did procure it, with divers other actions, which his disciples did act, which I shall relate, if need be, when I see you.

The thing of concern in your letter is concerning these words of Christ: *Swear not by heaven, for that is God's throne, nor by the earth, for that is his footstool*; and so in another place, bade them *swear not at all*.

I know your desire is to know in what sense it may be said, *Swear not at all*.

You may remember it was said by Christ, *Let your conversation he yea, yea, and nay, nay, for what cometh more is evil*.

These words of Christ were not to his disciples, but to those Jews that were under the law of Moses.

Therefore it is that Christ doth expound the law, shewing what was said of old, and then giving in his judgment, which is thus: It was said of old, thou shalt not forswear thy self, but shalt perform the vow that thou hast made, and so forth, but I say, swear not at all, neither by heaven, and the like.

Which words (*Swear not at all*) was only to beat men off from swearing to unrighteous things, and from swearing vainly in their common discourse, as it is usual amongst men in these our days, as they did swear by heaven in those days, and by the earth, and by the city, and by a man's head, and those things did they in their common discourse. Therefore it was that Christ said, *Let your yea be yea, and your nay, nay, be all,* for need you use swearing in your common talk or dealings, for swearing in this kind is evil; for do not they do so now-a-days? Will not men swear by their faith, which true faith is the nature of God, which they know not? They will swear by God, and yet know him not; they will swear by God's blood, and yet they do not believe that he had any blood; and so God damn them, and yet they are loth to be damned, with many other oaths, which are frivolous, in their common discourse, which becomes evil and sin to them that practise it, and a guilt upon the consciences of those that use it.

I would not have you think, that these words of Christ did take you off from all swearing at all, not as the Quakers do blindly imagine, that will not be a witness in any business; let it be of bonds concerning money, or other cases, in which they know that the innocent will suffer and lose their right, for want of their witnessing to it; and they must do it in that form and order, that the law of the land hath ordained, else a man's word is worth nothing, though it be never so true; and the unrighteous hath gotten the better for want of an oath, and the innocent hath lost his right, through the blindness and ignorance of those that strain the letter of the Scriptures beyond the intent of them, neither can the judge help the innocent in such a case.

But as for those oaths, that are imposed upon the Quakers and other people now of late, it is utterly unlawful for any one that hath any light or tenderness of conscience in him to take; for he that takes it receives the mark of the beast, either in the forehead, or in the hand, he shall not be suffered to buy or sell else. He that receiveth the mark in the forehead is he that doth take the oath willingly; and he that receiveth the mark in the hand is he that doth take the oath against his will, only for fear of imprisonment, or the suffering of loss in their estate; neither shall they be suffered to buy or sell except they receive the mark in their hand. And this is the state of this land at this day.

It will be well for those few of this faith that are preserved from that pollution upon the mind.

It will be too tedious to speak what might be said concerning oaths, therefore I shall let it alone until I see you, and then I shall inform you further in it, which will not belong after the receipt of this letter; for I do intend to set out of London on the 28th day of July, being Monday: I do intend to come to Nottingham first. I cannot give our friend Mr. Frewterill any certain knowledge where or when he should meet with us; for I know not as yet whether Mr. Hudson will have two horses or no; he hath one for himself, for he is going into Lancashire to some friends there; so that we know not whether we shall go any further than the carrier or no.

So with my love remembered unto yourself, and Mr. Frewterill, and all the rest of the faith with you, I rest

Your Friend in the eternal truth,

LODOWICKE MUGGLETON,

There is a letter inclosed of Mr. Frewterill's, which should have been sent to you when I was in Cambridgeshire. He remembers his love to you, and is glad to hear of your faith in the truth.

A Copy of a Letter written by the Prophet Lodowicke Muggleton, to Mrs. Ellen Sudbury, July 19, 1662.

Friend in the Faith of the true God, Ellen Sudbury,

I RECEIVED your letter, dated May 26, with a letter inclosed from our friend in the same faith, Dorothy Carter; but I could not send you an answer until now. I had but one day to stay in town, after that I received yours; but I gave order to our friend Mr. Hatter to write unto you, and to send the book which your aunt Carter wrote for, which I hope did come to your hands accordingly, though I have heard nothing of it. Also I do much rejoice to hear of your growth in the faith, and in your understanding, being enlightened so as to see the foundations of all saving truths, by the belief of this commission of the Spirit, which is not a little refreshment unto me; though the present peace, and eternal salvation, will redown unto yourself; or though I was left alone, even as the prophet Elijah was, and as the prophet Esaiah, who saith, *Who hath believed our report? Or to whom is the arm of the Lord revealed?* Yet should I not think nevertheless of the commission, neither is there any saving truth, but in a commission: and as you say well, though you have been a professor, or seeker after the truth, yet you never found the like effect wrought in you, as you have done since you were acquainted with us, the witnesses of the Spirit; which I perceive by your letter, you are given to understand the form and nature of the true God, the form and nature of the right devil: and that it was the Godhead that suffered death upon the cross: and that the believing of this is to eat his flesh, and drink his blood; and this will quench the thirst of sin; for it was for sin that he shed his blood, therefore it is said in Scripture, *In that he died, he died unto sin*; that is, to satisfy sin, which could not be satisfied but by the blood of God, neither would there have been any eternal damnation unto the seed of reason, which is the seed of the serpent, but by his quickening again into life; so that by his passing through death to life again, he hath purchased eternal life for the seed of faith, and eternal death to the seed of reason.

These sayings will be counted hard sayings by most men and women in the world; but blessed are they that understand them and believe them, which I perceive you do; for what greater faith can there be in any, than to understand the form and nature of the true God, the form and nature of the right devil, and to believe the Godhead life to die, as it is held forth in this commission of the Spirit.

I may say by you, as our Lord said in another case; where he saith, *That he had not found such faith, no not in Israel*: so may I say that I have not found such strong faith, not in one, that never saw none of us, nor spake with us: I may say, I have not found such faith, no not in England; and be sure that such a faith can never fail, because it is built upon a rock, even upon the commission of the Spirit, as Peter's was in his time: and when Peter had made a confession of his faith unto our Lord, he said, *Upon this rock will I build my church*; that is, on this faith, which thou art, of Peter, so that the gates of hell shall not prevail against it. So it is with every commissionated prophet, his faith and commission is the rock for all the seed of faith, which is the church to build upon, neither shall the gates of hell prevail against the faith that is built upon this commission of the Spirit, no more than it did in Peter's commission, which was the commission of the blood; but it shall be a rook in this last age. And I am glad for your own sake that you do understand so well the distinction of the three commissions; for I do find that those that do lay the greatest weight upon the commission, do grow most eminent in faith and understanding.

Yet I very seldom press the commission upon any except it be to some wise in reason, that would run away with the doctrine of this commission, thinking to be saved by that, without the commission of the Spirit; as if the doctrine that we declare, may be truth and saving, but we ourselves false messengers, and so in danger to be lost.

These things do I meet withal sometimes, having to do with all sorts, and all dispositions of men, within these ten years: and I do find now of late, that this commission of the Spirit hath put all men, of what opinion in religion soever, unto such a loss, that they know not which way to turn to find rest; all of them being ignorant of the true God, and the right devil; and as for a commission of the Spirit, they stop their ears against it, even against that which should show them the way to their eternal rest and peace, which I am sure cannot be but by this commission of the Spirit; for men and women cannot lay too much stress upon the commission: for if we, the witnesses of the Spirit, be true and happy, (as I know we are,) then all those that believe it shall be happy also: then of necessity, all other opinions that do hear of it, and do not believe in it, must be unhappy, and perish to eternity. But if we be false, (as I have said to many that have been damned by me) then shall they, and all the world be saved, and we only, and those that believe our report, shall be damned to eternity.

Thus it must go; you, and all the seed of faith must venture your eternal happiness upon the commission of the Spirit declared by us, the chosen witnesses of God; and we being happy, you that believe, shall be happy also; and so all other opinions whatsoever besides, which hear of it, and do not believe it, will be unhappy, and perish to eternity.

This is that strait and narrow way that leads to life, and few there be that find it; not as man doth vainly imagine, that men may go to heaven in every opinion; no, there is but one truth, one way, one eternal life; neither is this true way to be found but in the faith of this commission of the Spirit; and blessed are they that have faith in it.

I did think to have come to see you a week before I now shall, through some occasion that Mr. Hudson hath; but I do intend to set out of London on the 28th day of July, but whether I shall come any sooner than the carrier doth, I cannot yet tell; but I suppose you are the first that I shall come unto, because I think your aunt Carter liveth twenty miles further than you.

My daughter and Mr. Hatter remember their loves unto you, rejoicing to hear of your growth of faith, and your understanding you have expressed in your letter concerning the true God and right devil.

This, with my love remembered unto you, I rest your friend in the eternal truth,

LODOWICKE MUGGLETON.

London, July 14, 1662.

A Copy of the Prophet Lodowicke Muggleton's Blessing, given by him to Mrs. Ellen Sudbury, Aug. 11, 1662.

Dear Friend in the true faith of Jesus, Ellen Sudbury,

I CALLING to mind some passages in your letters sent to me at London, which gave great testimony unto me of your faith in the true God, and in this commission of the Spirit, which I find since I have seen you, not only in the head but in the heart also, which my heart is much rejoiced to see that strength, and growth of faith, which you have in these things aforesaid; seeing you are alone, and compassed about with devils, baiting at you as a deceived person, and now I know it will be so much the more because I have been with you; for that William Watson hath been here at your aunt Carter's with another scolding fit me, and not only so, incensing some others here in Chesterfield against me, which maketh people offended at me, yet never saw me; so that if I should stay long here, I should make the world mad.

Also it is upon my heart to be sensible how your faith will be tried, seeing you are alone; but I know according to your trials, your faith shall grow in strength,. And I considering that now some of those of the Bemonist's principles being damned, it will run through the whole body of them; so that I know you will be the more exclaimed at as a deceived person: but I know your faith shall not fail, but increase in more experience and knowledge of the truth of these things, which are held forth in this commission of the Spirit.

Therefore, for your further assurance of your eternal happiness against all gainsayers whatsover, I do declare you one of the blessed of the Lord both soul and body to eternity.

I thought good to write these few lines unto you, because I fear I shall have no time to have any talk with you; for it is not good for me to stay here any longer, because people's minds are, and do begin to be incensed much against me. Therefore it is my intent to see Mr. Hudson on his journey this Monday, and I do think to be on Tuesday night at your house, or on Wednesday at the farthest, and so to London. I shall call and see you before I go.

I cannot tell whether it will be convenient to lie at your house or no, I cannot tell whether there be freedom of both sides, but I shall call and see you however.

No more at present, but rest your friend in the true faith, and alone prophet and witness unto the High and Mighty God, the Man Christ Jesus in glory,

LODOWICKE MUGGLETON.

Chesterfield, Aug. 11, 1662.

A Copy of a Letter written by the Prophet Lodowicke Muggleton, to Mrs. Dorothy Carter. Dated September 12, 1662.

Dear Friend in the true Faith, Dorothy Carter,

I RECEIVED your letter, also I received the linen of Holland's man, according as you specified in your letter, and am glad to hear of your, and the rest of the faith with you, of your refreshments and further enlightening, which you and they received by my society that small time I was with you, which I am glad to hear, and do desire your further increase and growth in the knowledge of the doctrine of this commission of the Spirit, and the power of a commission to declare blessing and cursing to eternity, which faith, depending and resting upon it, will give you easily to see the happiness of the one, and the misery of the other; and you cannot lay too much stress upon the commission, for the more weight you lay upon it, the more comfort and assurance of your eternal happiness you will receive; neither can you expect to be free from reproach, envy and malice from that seed that is condemned by this commission of the Spirit; and though they may seem to rejoice, and make light of it for a season, yet their damnation I am sure doth neither slumber nor sleep, neither will the eternal happiness of the true believers of this commission of the Spirit slumber nor sleep, but will increase from life to life; that is, the faith of it shall pass through the life of assurance into life eternal, the unbelief of reason shall pass through the first death of fear and unbelief, into the second death of eternal damnation, where the worm will never die, nor the fire never go out.

These things are hard sayings unto the seed of reason, but plain and easy where faith is deeply grounded upon a rock, which rock is the true God, and the right devil, which knowledge hath been declared, with many other heavenly wisdom and mysteries, of this commission of the Spirit, which faith in it will abide the greatest blasts that reason the devil can blow, though it be even to death itself; therefore it is said by our Lord, *Fear not him that can kill the body, and hath no more to do, but fear him that can cast both body and soul into hell fire*; as if he should say, that the death of this life is but as the killing of this body, because it is not above a quarter of an hour's work; but the second death will be forever; therefore it is that he must be feared, that can and will cast both body and soul into hell-fire; that is, God doth kill the devil reason with the second death, and reason the devil did kill God, and the seed of faith with the first death, which is called but a killing of the body, and hath no more to do, because reason the devil his wrath can extend no further, but the wrath of God extends to eternity.

And as for those slavish fears which you had when I was there with you, I do suppose too, I do think that some of them were occasioned by that old maid that lived with you; but this you may be sure, that it was not for want of will that they did it not, but for want of power, for I find opposition in all places, both in city and country.

But all opinions being under the hatches of persecutions themselves, therefore it is that they can do nothing to me; for all sects and opinions in religion are against me, and I against them all.

I was in good hopes that you had seen our friend Ellen Sudbury before now, but you have shewed me the cause; but I hope when you are well, and your occasions will permit, that you will see her. I have not received any letter from her since I came from her, only one from her husband, the day after I received yours, which was on Saturday, being the sixth of September. I did send him an answer on the eighth of September. It may fall out so that I may see you and her there; but if not, I shall, be glad to see you here, in London, if your health and occasions will permit, towards the next spring. In the mean time let me hear from you how you all do, as oft as you can. I got very well to Barnet that Saturday night, and am very well at this time, but I have not heard from Mr. Hudson not as yet.

No more at present, but my love remembered unto yourself and your daughter Elizabeth Carter, and Elizabeth Smith, and to Mr. Frewterill and his wife.

So resteth your friend in the true faith,

LODOWICKE MUGGLETON.

My daughter Sarah remembers her love unto yourself and Mr. Frewterill, and all the rest of the faith with you, but she is very ill at this time.

Mr. Hatter desires to be remembered to you.

A Copy of a Letter written by the Prophet Lodowicke Muggleton, to Mr. John Leavens, bearing date October 6, 1662.

This is Mr. Hatter's Brother.

I HAVING been informed that you are a man that have travelled through several principles of religion, even from the Baptist to the Quaker; indeed it is the last, and seemeth to me to be the purest religion or principle of all the seven churches, and so it is in respect of practice, but the worst of all the seven in matter of true doctrine.

And though you are come to the purest life in respect of righteousness towards men, which may give some peace, because every action hath its reward in it, whether it be good or evil; but as for the true righteousness of faith, you have not as yet tasted of it, because you have no true foundation as a rock to set your faith upon; for the Quakers principles is but a sandy foundation for a man's eternal happiness, as well as the others, because there is no true spiritual principle declared nor believed by none of the ministry of the seven churches, because there is, none of the ministry of the Quakers, nor none others that hath ft commission from the true God; therefore they cannot declare and make known what the form and nature of the true God was before he became flesh, nor now that he is become flesh, nor the form and nature of the right devil, before he became flesh, nor what he is now, though no man can see any other devil or devils, but man and woman, that is cloathed with flesh and bone; neither doth any of the ministry know the place and nature of heaven, nor the place and nature of hell, with the persons and natures of angels, nor the mortality of the soul. Those six principles, or grounds of faith, is all that is necessary unto salvation, in which all the teachers of the world are ignorant of, but this commission of the Spirit only.

And as the Quakers ministry is the seventh and last angel that will sound, till time be no more, therefore it seemeth to carry the purest show in righteousness of life, but the most cursed of all in point of doctrine; and the spirit of it in the absolute spirit of Antichrist, which doth deny both the Father and the Son; for though they do confess a Christ within them, yet they deny the very person or body of Christ without them. This I know by experience, for which, at a dispute in East-Cheap, there was five of them damned to eternity, whereof George Fox the younger, and John Harwood, were two of them; and as for Fox the elder, he and Francis Hewgill, and James Burroughes, were all of them damned devils eight years ago; and not only those, but many more of the Quakers, and many other opinions whatsoever; and as the Quakers are the last angel will sound, so is the third and last commission of the Spirit come forth upon the earth, which is to finish the mystery of God, and to encounter and oppose all spiritual counterfeits, whether it be in Quakers, or any others whatsoever, because there is none that hath a commission from God but us two; neither can any man truly interpret Scripture but us two only, neither hath any man the knowledge of those things aforesaid, because we two are to finish the deep and secret mysteries of God's becoming flesh, which Moses, the prophets and apostles so much hinted at, up and down in the Scriptures, so that there cannot be the assurance of eternal happiness but in the belief of a commission.

Therefore, think you what you will of yourself, and of the Quakers principles, it is not all the sanctification of life which you or they can do that will procure your peace with God, except you, that are not under the sentence of this commission, do come to own the doctrine of the true God, and the right devil, which is held forth by this commission of the Spirit, and then your sanctification of life will add to your comfort here, and to your glory hereafter.

I write not this unto you as expecting you to be a disciple of this commission, but because you shall understand that there was a true prophet in these latter days, as well as there was in former times, which you do so much honour, because they are all dead, and that now the deepest mysteries of the true God, the right devil, with many other heavenly secrets which lay hid from the foundation of the earth, but now revealed both by word and power by this commission of the Spirit, or spiritual commission, which you, and many thousands more, cannot be ignorant of, and say that you did never hear of it; but if there be not that in your seed, that should lay hold of life when it is set before you, then the seed is appointed unto cursings; for this commission doth set life and death before men, as truly as Moses did set life and death before the people of Israel.

These lines I have written unto you, that you might, if it be possible, understand truth, that is now alive in the world, and not to depend upon the dead letter of the Scriptures, nor upon the lying imaginations of the Quakers, which bids you hearken to the light within you, but denies the person of the true God without them.,

So resteth the last true witness and prophet unto the true God, the man Christ Jesus in glory,

LODOWICKE MUGGLETON.

A Copy of a Letter from the Prophet Lodowicke Muggleton, to Mr, Richard Sudbury, dated Nov. 3, 1662.

Friend Richard Sudbury,

I RECEIVED your letter, bearing date October the 7th, with the two inclosed letters, and am glad to hear that you are so far enlightened as to understand any of these things; for these things which the commission of the Spirit hath declared are not common, or easy to be understood, but must be comprehended by the single eye of faith, and not by the right eye of reason; for if your right eye offend, pull it out: this right eye is the reason of man, the left eye is the faith of man, and these two eyes do see, and the sight doth arise from these two seeds; so that if your eye be single, your whole body will be full of light; but if you look upon spiritual things with both eyes, is double, and not clear sighted, for reason can see the things of this world better than the things of eternity: and the eye of faith doth see the things of God better than it can the things of this world; therefore it is called a single eye; and the more faith you have in this commission of the Spirit, the more clear you will see in what condition the whole world is in, and how it lieth in darkness, being totally ignorant of the knowledge of the true God, and of the right devil; and being ignorant of these two, they miss of all other heavenly mysteries which flow as a fountain from those two heads; for what knowledge can go beyond the knowledge of the true God and right devil? Have not many men, philosophers and others, lost their wits, nay, their lives, to find out God, and yet could not do it; for if they could have found out God, they would easily have found out the right devil; but because they sought to find out God by the right eye of reason, and not by the single eye of faith, therefore they lost their wits in seeking after God.

I received the Quaker's letter you spoke of, from Dorothy Carter, and I have prepared an answer unto it; I do intend to send it to Chesterfield, for she doth desire me to let her have the reading of it to a Quaker there also: I would have her, or Mr. Frewterill, to take a copy of it, before it comes to you to Nottingham; for it must be delivered to one Highfield, at Nottingham; and when it comes from Chesterfield to you, if you will be at that trouble to take a copy of it, you may; but you must make as much haste of it as you can, for it will be some labour, for it is something large, it is almost four sheets of paper. It will be your best course to let your wife, or somebody, read it as you write it, or else it will be too tedious. I do intend to send it to Dorothy Carter on Friday next. I did think to have written a few lines to your wife, in answer to her letter, for her further confirmation; for I am very joyful to hear of her increase in faith, and assurance of eternal life; for I know that letter was her heart, though not her hand; therefore I shall only remember my love to her at this time, expecting to hear from you and her so soon as you can, after you have received and delivered this Quaker's letter.

No more at present, but my love to yourself and all friends with you, which are few.

Your friend,

LODOWICKE MUGGLETON.

I have never heard from Mr. Hudson since Mr. Frewterill and I parted from him there in the country.

A Letter from the Prophet Lodowicke Muggleton, to Mrs. Dorothy Carter, of Chesterfield, dated November 7, 1662.

Dear friend in the eternal truth, Dorothy Carter,

MY love remembered unto you and your daughter Elizabeth, and Elizabeth Smith.

I am glad to hear that you are all well, and of your stedfastness in the faith of the true God, and this commission of the Spirit. I received the Quaker's railing paper you sent me, and I have given answer to it; and, according to your desire, I have sent it you, and if you please you may let that Quaker woman which you spake of see it, but if you had sent me her name, and the bitter words she spake against this commission of the Spirit, I would have sent her the sentence as well as the other; for I cannot endure that any quaking devil should escape being damned, when as they despise the spirit of truth. I would desire you to let Mr. Frewterill, if his leisure will serve, to take a copy of this letter of mine, for it will be some labour, it being something large; it is almost four sheets of paper; he must do it as soon as possible he can, because you must send it to Richard Sudbury's before it be delivered to Thomas Highfield; and perhaps Mr. Sudbury will take a copy of it before it be delivered to the place aforementioned; therefore it will require what haste you can.

I gave Mr. Sudbury information that I should send it to you first, and that you should send it to him, because it is to be delivered to that town; for Mr. Sudbury, in his letter, doth desire if I send any answer, to send it to him, and he will convey it to you; but I suppose it will be more convenient to send it to you first, seeing it must come back again to Nottingham.

No more at present, but my love to yourself, Mr. Frewterill and his wife.

So resteth your loving friend in the true faith,

LODOWICKE MUGGLETON.

I would willingly hear from you as soon as you can after you have delivered this letter to that Quaker.

A Copy of a Letter from the Prophet Lodowicke Muggleton, to Christopher Hill, November 16, 1662.

Loving friend in the true faith, Christopher Hill,

I RECEIVED our friend Nicholas Miles his letter, with the basket of pippins he sent, your mother also hath them you sent to her, and I have sent the two baskets by Nathaniel the hoyman again; you, or our friend Miles, must look for them at Milton, for I have directed them for you at Maidstone; but I perceive since, that the hoyman doth not come there, but at Milton you may have them; and as for the cyder our friend speaketh of, John White, my daughter's friend, will see this week what may be done in it, and next week I think he will send you word what may be done, yea or nay.

Also! understand by your letter, that our friend John Martin is fallen asleep, and that he hath remembered me, and the poor saints there with you, which was more than I did expect, yet he hath given a great testimony that his faith was grounded upon the truth of this commission of the Spirit, which fruit and effect of his faith would yield him peace, and in the end eternal life, which I do not question but he shall have it in that day when the prophets and apostles and saints shall receive theirs, *For he that receives a prophet in the name of a prophet, and a saint in the name of a saint, he shall not lose his reward*; therefore I would have his wife, son, and daughter not to be troubled, but rather be comforted in this, that his and their names are written in the book of life, and so it will be well with them on the other side of death, for this first death we must all pass through, but blessed and happy are all those that shall escape the second death.

I did intend to have seen them, and all the rest of friends in the faith, before I heard of this letter, this Christ-tide, and my resolution doth hold so still, for I must get out of the way two or three days before Thomas's day, because the parish hath pricked me down to bear office this Christmas, or else fine. The last year I did fine for scavenger, which cost me twenty shillings, and now they have chosen me questman, which fine will cost three or four pounds, and next year it will cost as much more to be constable; therefore I must get out of the way a fortnight or three weeks, until the business is over; so I shall either come and visit you, or else go to Cambridge.

No more at present, but my love remembered unto yourself, and to goodman Miles and his wife, the widow, her son and daughter, and all the rest of our friends in the faith there with you, not forgetting your mother Wills.

I rest your friend in the true faith,

LODOWICKE MUGGLETON.

London, November 17, 1662.

My daughter Sarah desireth to be remembered unto you all; she is very well after her journey.

A Copy of a Letter written by the Prophet Lodowicke Muggleton, to Mrs. Dorothy Carter of Chesterfield, dated from London, Nov. 28, 1662.

Dear friend in the eternal truth, Dorothy Carter,

I RECEIVED your letters, wherein you have given me a relation of things concerning that letter I wrote to Samuel Hooton, and W. S. with some other passages of Susanna Frith, which I am very well satisfied in, and have sent her that which doth belong unto her; for none but the seed of the serpent would have spoken such words as she did: but as for those few lines of your own concerning yourself, concerning the blessing, I did always look upon you to be one of the elect seed, and your having faith in the commission, I know it will bear you up in the day of death; but yet I am glad you are so sensible for to see the benefit of the blessing of a prophet, and that you can discern the power and operation, the curse hath upon the seed of reason, even to blast and wither that comfort and peace they had before: so on the contrary, the blessing will make their peace and joy to flourish, and encrease to their further eternal happiness. And I know this could not have been desired by you had you not been of the seed of faith; therefore, in obedience to my commission, I do pronounce you justified, blessed, and happy, both in soul and body, to eternity. And let not your thoughts be troubled any further, but depend wholly upon it; for you shall fare no worse than I myself doth. And so you may live in assurance here, and when you shall pass through this first death, you shall enter into life eternal, where you shall see your God face to face; also you shall know him according to your faith, him you did believe in, which you never saw, in that you did believe in the commission of the Spirit, which you have seen.

If you have any occasion to write to me again, you must do it within this fortnight; for I am going into Kent: I go a week or ten days before Christ-tide. The occasion of my going is because the parish hath chosen me to bear offices, either I must hold or fine; the last year I did fine for one office, and now they put me upon another, because I have lived long in the parish; therefore, to prevent them, I will go into Kent for a matter of three weeks, 'till the business is over.

So with my love to yourself, your daughter, and Elizabeth Smith, Mr, Frewterill, and his wife, I rest at this present,

Your friend in the true faith,

LODOWICKE MUGGLETON.

I would have you to deliver the inclosed as directed.

A Letter written by the Prophet Lodowicke Muggleton, to one Susannah Frith, a Quaker, bearing Date the 28th of Nov. 1662, from London.

Susannah Frith,

I UNDERSTAND, that being a Quaker, you were at the writing of that letter sent unto me from Samuel Hooton, and W. S. Also I understand, that you cannot see any fruits from the believers of this commission doth bring forth, but these that were filthy are filthy still; for you see some disorderly walking in some. Also you think, that others do fashion themselves too much according to the world; and if any do walk disorderly, or live an intemperate life, it is not my desire they should do so; for I did always love a temperate life from my childhood, much more now since I came to understand truth.

Also I know that those that do live an intemperate life, by overcharging their natures, in what kind soever, they lose their peace, which they would find if it were otherwise: yet nevertheless, this is not a sin unto death, though I do not encourage any one to live an intemperate life.

Yet you may remember, that it was the practice of Christ himself, to keep company with publicans and sinners; therefore the scribes and pharisees, which were so righteous men, speak evil of Christ, saying, he was a wine bibber, and a friend of publicans and sinners; neither did Christ pronounce woes to any as he did to those that were so righteous in their own conceit; it was those that sinned against the Holy Ghost, that unpardonable sin, that will never be forgiven in this world, nor in the world to come. And, you, by the light of Christ within you, leading you to a more preciseness of life than others, you have taken upon you to judge and speak evil of the commission of the Spirit, even as those Jews did by the righteousness of the law in them, they spake evil and blasphemed against Christ, and that Holy Spirit by which he cast out devils, by calling him a deceiver, a blasphemer, and a devil, and this was that sin against the Holy Ghost: so have you sinned that sin unto death, which is not to be pardoned; for you have not only been with others that have written and spoken evil of this commission of the Spirit, in giving countenance and credit to the evil report of others, but you have blasphemed against the Holy Spirit that sent me; by calling the commission of the Spirit a deceit, lies, and a false Spirit; which hath clearly discovered unto me what seed and nature you are of you being one of the seed of the serpent, you have sinned against the Holy Ghost. Therefore, in obedience to my commission, I do pronounce Susannah Frith cursed, and damned, soul and body, from the presence of God elect, men, and angels, to eternity.

Perhaps you will say as you did by Samuel Hooton, and W. S. that you will not matter it; but if you can make as light of it as I do that give judgment upon you, it will be well for you; for I am well satisfied in giving judgment against any person that doth sin against the Holy Ghost, more than any one thing whatsoever. Neither am I willing that any Quaker devil, nor any other should escape, that speaks evil of things they do not know; for I am no more troubled at their condemnation than the judges of the land are, when they give judgment according to the law, for a man to be put to death. And if that man, so condemned, can make as light of it as the judge doth, let him if he can. So will it be with you, and many hundreds more, (flatter yourselves, and make as light of it as you will) I know it is so decreed by the Creator; neither will your light of Christ within you prevent it, because you have despised the commission of the Spirit without you.

By

LODOWICKE MUGGLETON,

One of the Two last Witnesses and Prophets, unto the High and Mighty God, the Man Christ Jesus in Glory.

A Copy of a Letter wrote by the Prophet Lodowicke Muggleton, to Mr. Richard Sudbury, bearing date the 8th of December, 1662.

Mr. Sudbury,

I RECEIVED your letter, bearing date September the first, in which I perceive, that your wife and you did expect to have heard before now how I got through my journey. Also I did expect to have heard from you, or Dorothy Carter, before I did send unto you; which letter I did receive from her the day before I received yours, and she speaketh much to the same purpose as you do, expecting to hear whether I came well to London or no. And as for that, to certify you, I did come well to Barnet that Saturday night, and am well now both in body and mind, but always meeting with opposition both in city and country; for let them be of what sort or opinion soever, though they be under the hatches of persecution themselves, yet will they be against me; so that it may be said by me as it was said in another case by Esau, that his hand should be against every one, and every one's hand against him.

So it is with me, every opinion in the world is against me, and I against every opinion in the world. And the commission of God, which is truth, being given unto us two, shall encounter with all opinions and sorts in the world.

And whereas you say you understand more clear, the Baptist's commission counterfeited, I am glad that you understand any thing that is truth. I could wish that you might understand things of a. more high concernment, that are written in those books; as concerning the true God, his form and nature, the right devil, his form and nature, the persons and nature of angels, the rise of the two seeds, and the mortality of the soul, and the power of a commission; with many other heavenly secrets, never revealed to man before, which are plainly declared in those writings, if understood. And though you do say, the Baptist commission is counterfeit, yet I perceive you are not clear in the mortality of the soul; therefore your desire is, that I would give you the interpretation of those verses, Mat. xxvii. 51, 52, 53 verses. It is a more easy thing to read than to write, and more easy to ask questions, than it is to answer: nevertheless, I shall give you some answer to those things, though there is arguments enough in that book to prove the mortality of the soul and that the soul doth sleep in the dust until the resurrection, to any man that hath but the least measure of true light in him: but because men read scriptures, that do seem to speak to the contrary, and they being not alive to give the interpretation and leaning of their own words, which is the cause that people read their words, and not understanding them, they go away unsatisfied, and loth they are to believe, that God should send any messenger or interpreter of the Scriptures; but would fain find out the meaning by the reading of the dead letter, which they never can do; no more than the eunuch could do without Philip's expounding of it unto him. Neither can any man understand the Scriptures, except there be one or more sent of God to give the interpretation of them. And as for the veil of the temple rending from the bottom to the top, and the stones cleaving asunder, I have spoken of it in the interpretation of the eleventh of the Revelations; yet, for your further satisfaction, I shall open it more particularly.

The veil of the temple, which was rent, it was an outside building, that was not so beautified as the temple; so that no man could see the glory or beauty of it but by piercing through the veil: and this temple was that which Solomon built, which was so highly esteemed by the Jews; and this veil, which was rent, did belong unto it; and those stones that clave asunder did belong to this veil or temple.

These things were done in the natural only to shew the power of Christ's death; for this temple was hot far from the place where Christ was put to death, neither doth the Scripture speak of what stones they were that clave asunder, nor where.

Therefore it must be believed, that it was those stones that did belong to the veil or temple; because they did signify in the spiritual these two things.

First, the veil being rent from the bottom to the top, did signify the worship of the law of Moses, which was a veil upon the people of the Jews face; so that they could not see that spiritual and heavenly glory, which was in the believing that this Jesus was the Son of God, or the Saviour of the world.

Therefore the worship of the law of Moses, which was a veil before the peoples face, was now, by the death of Christ rent in twain from the bottom to the top; so that the reason of man could never sew it or join it together again unto this day, though it hath been much endeavoured by the seed of reason. Therefore it is said, that Moses put a veil upon his face, it did so shine, that the people of Israel could not look upon it, it was so bright and glorious; which veil of Moses was only to signify the worship of the law, which was to be rent from the bottom to the top by the death of Christ; that is, to be torn in pieces, not fit to be used any more by the believers in Jesus.

And this did the natural veil of Solomon's temple rending from the bottom to the top signify.

And as for the stones cleaving asunder, it did signify in the spiritual the breaking of the stony hearts of the Jews asunder, and the Gentiles too, by causing some of their stony hearts to break in pieces, by faith and love, in believing that this was the son of God.

Others again, their stony hearts were broken asunder with wrath and envy, because the worship of the law was now rent in twain; so that they could not have life by the righteousness of the law, which made their hearts of stone with envy even ready to burst, as you may read in the Acts, concerning their malice towards Stephen. And for the earthquake there spoken of, you may read in the book of the interpretation, there I have opened it something large; so that there needeth no more to be said of that.

But the thing that you aim at, as I perceive, is concerning those dead bodies, which slept in the earth, and arose and appeared unto many.

First, You must understand the power of Christ's death; and secondly, the power of his resurrection.

You find at his death the veil of the temple did rend, and the stones did cleave, and the earth did quake.

These things were done at his death, by the power of that; but the graves opening, and the dead bodies arising, was after his resurrection; which thing was to prove the power of his rising from the dead: therefore he raised the bodies of many saints which slept, which arose, and appeared unto many.

Now you must understand, that it was the bodies of the saints that arose, and came out of the graves, and appeared, and not the bodies of the reprobate, that hated and persecuted him.

Also it is to be understood, that those saints that arose out of the graves were but newly fallen asleep or dead, not that they were corrupted or turned to dust, as those are that have been dead a long time; then could they not have risen with the same bodies as was laid in the graves, but they were raised in the same nature as Lazarus was, that had been four days dead: neither were their bodies spiritualized as the body of Christ was; that is, they did not rise spiritual bodies; but the same natural bodies that slept or died, did rise again, and appeared in the temple.

You do not read, that they did ever speak or eat afterwards as Lazarus and Christ did; for Lazarus did live some years afterwards in that natural body which was born, and then died again, and is now asleep in the dust of the earth.

But Christ's body rising a spiritual body, it is alive, and behold it is alive for evermore.

But you may say, what became of those bodies of the saints which arose.

To which I answer, their bodies lay down in the same graves again, and there shall remain until the resurrection: only this was done to shew the power of Christ's resurrection, both in raising up of himself from death to life, and of his power in raising the saints out of their graves.

Which thing was but as a little fast, or but as a sign of his great power, which he hath gained to himself, by his death and resurrection, even power to raise the seed of faith to that eternal happiness, and. to raise the seed of reason to that endless misery, which both seeds shall find at the general day of resurrection; when it shall be said, Come ye blessed, to the seed of faith, and, Go ye cursed, to the seed of reason.

And if you consider these things, they make more for the mortality of the soul than against it.

For it doth not say, that spirits rose out of the graves, but bodies, neither did spirits come into them.

But the power of Christ's resurrection had an influence on their bodies; which did cause their bodies to arise to shew his power as aforesaid.

More might be said on this thing; but where true faith is, may easily be understood the truth of it.

So, with my love to you as a civil man, and to your wife as a true believer, I rest,

LODOWICKE MUGGLETON.

September 8, 1662.

A Copy of a Letter written by the Prophet Lodowicke Muggleton, to Mrs. Elizabeth Carter, of Chesterfield, from London, dated the 11th of December, 1662.

Dear Friend, Elizabeth Carter,

I RECEIVED your letter, and am glad to hear of the benefit that you have received in the belief of this commission, and of your further joy you have received by my being with you. All that I can say in it is, that I am glad to hear that the seed of faith in such tender age should spring up as a fountain of living water unto eternal life; and the more strong your faith is grounded upon this commission of the Spirit, the more firm will you stand. It will be as a rock, which no storms nor winds whatsoever shall be able to make it fall; for every commission from God is a rock, and whosoever doth build upon it will stand sure, when as the sandy foundation, though it seem ever so strong, when the storm of death and the wind of eternal judgment doth come, then it will fall, because it was built upon the sand; for this personal God is the Head Corner-stone, and that Stone which is laid in Sion; and blessed are those that build upon it, which none can do but those that have a faith in a commission.

Therefore all that seeming shew of righteousness in the Quakers and others, it will avail them nothing, because it was built upon the sand, that is, upon an infinite incomprehensible spirit, without a body, which is but a sandy foundation; they will find so in the end, though they make slight of a God that is cloathed with flesh and bone, yet this flesh and bone is the stone which the builders refused, which is become the Head of the Corner. Also it is that stumbling stone and rock of offence, which every man doth stumble at, but those that do believe in this commission of the Spirit; and you having expressed a great measure of faith in this commission of the Spirit, all that I shall say this time in this thing is, that you may grow in further understanding, faith, and knowledge of these things until you come to the possession of that eternal happiness, which your faith in this commission of the Spirit will lead you unto.

Dear Friend,

I have sent you the copy of Mr. Hatter's letter to John Leavins; I would desire you to take a copy of it, and send it me again, because my letter is joined with it. I shall be in London about a month hence; I do intend to take my journey on Tuesday next; so, with my love to your mother and Elizabeth Smith, Mr. Frewterill and his wife, I rest

Your Friend in the eternal Truth,

LODOWICKE MUGGLETON.

A Copy of a Letter written by the Prophet Lodowicke Muggleton, to Mrs. Ellen Sudbury, from London, bearing date December 15, 1662.

Dear Friend in the true Faith, Ellen Sudbury,

I RECEIVED your letter with the inclosed, and I have read it over, and I find very little in it more than there was in the other; nay, the other was the chief master-piece, only towards the latter end of this doth give me better satisfaction than the other did, because in the latter end of this letter doth plainly shew what their God is which they believe in, which is no other but what the Heathen philosophers did declare, and something of Jacob Bemon's philosophy; neither did it arise from their own revelation or experience, nor from the seed of reason within them, but merely by reading other folks works: for I could, if it were of necessity, shew you a book that doth speak the very same words, and doth give the very same definition of God as they do; for every Heathen philosopher will say, that God is love, and life, and wisdom, and glory, with many other excellencies in himself, and yet not to be defined or distinct, neither is he to be known by his creature.

To what purpose then did God send prophets and apostles into the world, to tell people of such a God as cannot be defined, nor made known unto man; when as those that speak the Scriptures, their declarations were only to bring men to the knowledge of God; therefore it is said in Scripture, it is life eternal to know the only true God, and Jesus Christ, whom thou hast sent.

It is but turning the words thus: it is life eternal to know, that this Jesus Christ, which is sent into the world, is the only true God; for it is better, and a more safe way for a man to believe, that a mere mortal man is a God, than to believe God to be an infinite Spirit without a body: for can there be love, life, wisdom, and glory acted forth, and yet have no person or body to act in? Can a man love his wife if she have never a body? Yet by these, people must love God, and yet he hath no person at all, neither can he be defined nor known, which is contrary to the apostle John's faith; for, saith he, if thou doest not love thy brother, whom thou doest see, how canst thou love God, whom thou didst never see. And because we never saw God with this natural eye, will it follow therefore, that we must believe that he is no formal personal all; when as the Scripture doth call upon men to love the Lord their God, with all their hearts, and with all their strength, which is impossible for men to do, if God had no person at all; nay, and not only a person, but the very person and form of a man, else a man could never love God; for men doth love God because he is like God, for every thing doth love its like; therefore it is that God loves man, because man's person and form is the image and likeness of God, therefore God loves man.

Indeed I need not write these things to inform you, for you have given great testimonies of your faith, light, and knowledge in a personal God, which this commission of the Spirit doth declare, which faith of yours shall bear you up above all philosophy knowledge whatsoever.

But I write these things that you may see the more clearly the vanity and emptiness, and how unsatisfied that faith is to the mind whose God hath no form nor person at all, which I know your own experience can witness, you having been acquainted with the Bemonist's principles. You know what satisfaction you found in it, and what you find now in the faith of this commission; for the faith of this commission will uncover all the cloathing of every opinion, though never so seeming righteous, whereby their nakedness will be seen.

Dear Friend,

I would desire you to send this letter inclosed as it is directed.

I would have sent by the Chesterfield carrier on Friday last, but he was gone a little before I came; therefore I thought good to put you to the trouble to send it to her, because I am going into Kent this Wednesday: and about a month hence I do intend to be at home again, therefore for the present I shall rest, with my love to you and your husband,

LODOWICKE MUGGLETON.

My daughter Sarah and Mr. Hatter desireth to remember their loves to you and your husband.

A Copy of a Letter wrote by the Prophet Lodowicke Muggleton, to Sir Thomas Twisden, dated from Rootam in Kent, January 6, 1663, as followeth.

Sir,

I UNDERSTAND that you are a judge of the civil law of the land, and that you are so by commission from the king: I suppose that you are the man which I have heard much of in London, commended for honour and renown in the wisdom and knowledge in the civil laws of England, else I suppose you would not have been chosen for that great place; which authority of yours I do own, and have always been obedient to the civil laws of the land, both to you and all other judges, neither did I ever break any of the king's laws, neither in the old king's time, nor now in this king's time; for I never did bear arms against his father, nor for no power then in being, neither have I had any meetings at my house, nor have been at any no where else, not since his majesty's restoration, nor many years before; so that it seems very strange, that I, being a free-born man of England, and a freeman of the city of London, and one that hath fined for many offices of the parish where I live, I say it is somewhat strange that I should not have so much liberty as to come into the country to see my wife's mother, with other relations, but I must be hunted after as if I had committed some treason or felonies; which things I am more innocent of, I think, than any man in the world is at this day. And yet, through the ignorance and darkness of men and women, which know neither the law of God nor the law of the land, they have reported strange things unto you, which have caused you to have a bad opinion of as pure a truth as ever was spoken by prophet or apostle, and to look upon me to be a deceiver: but I would have your honour to be careful what judgment you give of spiritual things before you know the cause why, lest you sin against the Holy Ghost, a sin which will never be forgiven, neither in this world, nor in the world to come; for though you are knowing above most men in the law of the land, and can give judgment accordingly, even as the demerit shall deserve, yet God hath not made you the judge of spiritual and eternal matters, neither are you to judge of blasphemy against God: God himself is the only judge in those matters, and those whom he hath chosen, anointed, and sealed for that purpose, viz. his prophets and apostles, and those whom he hath sent now in this last age of the world.

But I suppose you know and do read in the Scriptures, that the prophets and apostles of old were counted by the generality of people in their time to be blasphemers and deceivers, and were persecuted thereupon; nay, the Lord Jesus himself was put to death upon that account, as may be read in the Scriptures.

And this I say, those which persecuted men upon the account of blasphemy (they having broke no civil law of the land) I say they would have been the same to the prophets and apostles of old, and to Christ himself, if they had been living in their time.

Also I understand you have a desire to see one of my books. Now I do not conceive that you desire to see it in love only, but that you might see what you could pick out of it, that you might have wherewithal against me, that you might persecute me the more.

Yet nevertheless, I am not afraid of your seeing my writings, nor ashamed of the doctrine contained therein; nay, I am not afraid if the king's majesty himself should see it; for my writings are more for the honour of the king, than any dishonour.

Therefore, if you please to send a messenger or carrier to London, where I live, and send money, they shall have it, for they cost a great deal of money the printing, neither will I lend any; for I find by experience, that when books be lent they are worse liked than when they are paid for: but if I had thought that you had desired to see it in love, you should have had not only one, but three or six presented unto you to peruse.

But I think most magistrates and people have forgot the Scripture language, which saith, forget not to entertain strangers; for some in entertaining strangers have entertained angels: as righteous Lot and faithful Abraham, Isaac, and Jacob, and divers others, that have received prophets in the name of a prophet, and so have received a prophet's reward, which reward is no less than the blessing of eternal life; which I suppose all men would willingly have: but instead of receiving a prophet in the name of a prophet, the people receive him as a blasphemer, a liar, and deceiver, and persecute him, and so instead of a prophet's blessing they receive a curse of eternal damnation.

This I know to be true, by great experience, these twelve years; for I have found more malice in the country where I have been a stranger and a pilgrim (as most prophets were) nay they will neither receive me themselves, nor suffer others that would; yet I meddle with no man, neither do I invite any one to come where I am, but would rather they would forbear coming near me; for most people come to me only to try me, to catch words out of me, as the Scribes and Pharisees did to the Lord Jesus Christ, that they might have something to accuse me of to the rulers.

But I hope you being a ruler of the people (for every judge is a ruler) will not be an accuser and persecutor yourself; but if you be I shall be made able by the power of faith to bear it.

And what I have written, and the sentences I have and do pronounce, I shall willingly (if the laws of England will do it) seal it with my blood.

But it would be better and more commendable to do as Nicodemus (a ruler in Israel) did, which came to Christ by night to ask him questions.

Surely Nicodemus did not come to entrap and catch Christ in his words, whereby to have something against him to persecute him, but asked questions in love, desiring to be resolved; which was a good character, that this ruler came to Christ in love, and that he was an elect vessel.

It would be good for all rulers if they could follow his example in spiritual matters; for indeed rulers are to be learned and wise, to declare the matters of this world (as David doth say in the Psalms) for God hath chosen few rulers to be prophets to declare his mind. And that is the very cause so many rulers did persecute the prophets and apostles; you may read, that the rulers of Israel did persecute the prophets, and the rulers of Israel did persecute the apostles.

Likewise I have had my share of persecution by the rulers of England, for these twelve years; but what they and all persecuting rulers have got by it will do them but little good, for they procured no less than the sentence and seal of eternal damnation to themselves; neither will they be delivered from it; for no persecutor of a prophet, as he is a prophet, can be saved, that prophet not being guilty of the breach of the civil law of the land.

Therefore it is good for judges and rulers of the land to mind the place they are set in, and to judge of those things they know, viz. the laws of the land: and let them do righteous judgment according to the known law of the land, and they shall do well, and not to meddle with that which God hath reserved to himself, and will give power and judgment in spiritual matters to whom he please.

Therefore I should desire you to persist no further in persecuting of men for spiritual matters, lest you persecute the truth instead of a lie, and call that blasphemy which God doth own to be revealed by his Holy Spirit, and so come within the compass of blasphemy against the Holy Ghost, a sin that never will be forgiven in this world, nor in the world to come.

Neither would I have you to think scorn to be advised by one so low, and you so high; for my power is as great in spiritual matters as yours is in things of nature.

And as your commission is to be judge from the king, which I do own, so is my commission in spiritual things from the King of Heaven.

And as your commission will bear you out in all things you do according to the law of the land; so will my commission from God bear me out in what I do upon a spiritual account.

I have been more large than I did intend, but things of this nature cannot be expressed in few words, as other things may be; but I shall say no more at present, but rest,

LODOWICKE MUGGLETON.

And if you would be any further informed of me, and my writings, you may have, for twenty-pence, a book, at my mother Martyn's, called, *The Quaker's Neck broken*, that will inform you further both of me and my writings.

From Rootam in Kent,

January 6, 1663.

A Copy of a Letter written by the Prophet Lodowicke Muggleton, to Mrs. Elizabeth Carter, dated April 3, 1663

My dear Friend, Elizabeth Carter,

I READ over your letter, and though the lines of your letter are but few, yet I find they are very pithy, and full of substance; which I am much rejoiced to see, and so much the more, in that one so young should grow so far in perfection of faith, as to know that the words or writings of faith should speak peace to the soul of a believer, and, to cast yourself upon this rock, and if you perish, to perish there; which you have done well, for you cannot but grow in peace and satisfaction that casts itself upon a true prophet, it is as if they did cast themselves upon God himself, for a true prophet is in God's stead, and they that receive him so, shall receive a prophet's reward, which is no less than eternal life.

For this I would a little inform you further, that there is no man nor woman, but they must have some prophet or minister or other, to pitch their faith upon, else they cannot be quiet in their minds, except they be Atheists.

And seeing there is a necessity that there must be a sandy foundation and a rock, or a false and a true; and this sandy foundation is so large, that almost all the world doth build upon it; and the rock is so little, that there can but few build upon it; it hath but one Chief Corner-stone, even God himself; but the world builds all upon the sand that have never a cornerstone at all to bear up their building, when the storm of death comes.

Therefore you may see what a multitude of messengers, ministers, and ambassadors there is in this world, of all sects and opinions, and every one of the messengers have store of people which do build upon them, which may be evident to a discerning eye that they all build upon the sand; and that there should be but one" true prophet in the world at this day, and that such young ones as you, and Elizabeth Smith, should build upon this commission of the Spirit, which is a sure rock of salvation.

There are other young ones in other places, which I find to be father more confident, and do grow more in the faith of this commission than some that are of older years. The cause why it is so, is, because they were catcht in faith's net before any other form of religion had laid hold on them.

I write these few lines to you for the further confirmation and growth of your faith; so that you may receive the more full assurance here in this life, which is an hundred fold; and in the life to come, life everlasting.

No more at present, but my love to yourself. I rest your friend in the eternal truth,

LODOWICKE MUGGLETON.

April 3, 1663.

A Copy of a Letter written by the Prophet Lodowicke Muggleton, to Mrs. Dorothy Carter, of Chesterfield, bearing date April 3, 1663.

Dear and loving Friend in the true Faith, Dorothy Carter,

I RECEIVED your letter with your daughter's inclosed, and am glad to hear you are well in health, and more especially in your faith and confidence of this commission of the Spirit; and I do find every where, both in city and country, that those that do lay the greatest weight upon this commission do find the greatest peace and satisfaction in their minds, and are the more able to encounter with opposition where they meet with it; for it is a hard matter for any of this faith to escape being opposed, because this commission and the faith of it fight against all the world.

For this being the faith of God's elect, it fights against all sects and opinions in religion in the world, and all opinions have a faith in that opinion they are of; but it is but the faith of devils, whatsoever they pretend. Why? Because there is none knows the true God, in his form and nature; and how is it possible that any man should have true faith, and yet not know the true God.

Therefore that faith which is built upon a false God must needs be no other but the faith of devils: therefore how few is there in the world at this day that can say as Paul did, I have fought a good fight, *I have finished my course, I have kept the faith, and henceforth there is laid up forme a crown of righteousness, which God the righteous Judge shall give?* Can any one fight the fight of faith, and yet not know the true God? And that is the very cause so many die unsatisfied in death; because they know not the true God, yet they despise that man that should declare him unto them; but they would have God to do it himself, and yet their God, in their imagination is so big, so infinite and incomprehensible, that he cannot be known nor comprehended by his creature. And yet they would have this unknown God to save them.

Therefore you that are enlightened in your understanding, who can by faith comprehend what the true God is, in his form and nature, you may see how the whole world lyeth in wickedness, ignorance, and darkness; neither can the world fight a good fight of faith; no, none can truly do so but those that have believed our report.

You speak in your letter of a man that came out of the North; it will be well for him if it be given him truly to understand these things; but I have heard nothing of him as yet.

This letter of yours came when I was in Cambridgeshire; I have been little at home since Christ-tide; and the very morning that I went into Cambridgeshire, I received four letters from Mr. Hudson, two of them from Quakers there in Lancashire, which Mr, Hudson would have me send the sentence to those two Quakers and to a Presbyterian minister, which I have had no leisure to send till now: the same day as I deliver yours to the carrier, I shall send his. He is well, and remembers his love to all our friends of the faith. I have remembered yours and Ellen Sudbury's love to him.

Also I have received since I came home a Quaker's letter, and a copy of Edward Bourne's letter, of Mrs. Griffith, which I cannot have leisure to answer at present; but I do intend to send an answer the next return of the carrier. My daughter is pretty well recovered of her sickness; she received your kindness which you sent, of Mr. Griffith, and desireth to remember her kind love to you and your daughter. I think her husband doth intend to write to you himself; therefore, I shall say no more, only my love remembered to yourself, Elizabeth Smith, and the rest, Mr. Frewterill and his wife, with my love to Ellen Sudbury when you can.

So resteth your Friend in the eternal Faith,

LODOWICKE MUGGLETON.

London, April 3, 1663.

Mrs. Griffith remembers her kind love unto you.

A Copy of a Letter written by the Prophet Lodowicke Muggleton, to Mrs. Dorothy Carter, bearing date from London, May 8, 1663.

My dear Friend in the eternal Truth, Dorothy Carter,

I HAVE had a great desire to have sent to you before now, but I have been much hindered by other occasions, but it is not for want of love that I did not write to you before now; yet I am much straitened for time as ever I was, but I having finished an answer to Richard Farnesworth's letter, and taken a copy of it, have sent it to you, with Edward Bernard's letter; so that if you think good to take a copy of this Richard Farnesworth's letter, you may, before you deliver it; it will be some labour, but it will be necessary, though it may be hereafter it may be put in print.

For there are some friends here in London, that are very desirous to have this letter of Richard Farnesworth's with my answer; and that letter of Samuel Hooton's and W. S. which they sent to me first, and my answer of the four sheets to them, printed; which, perhaps, I may trouble you for some small matter towards the printing of them: but the captain that is,, the most desirous to have them printed, hath a son that did own this commission, and he is dead beyond the seas, in a place called Antego, which is a great grief to his father, both in respect as he was in the faith of this commission, and in respect of his temporal estate, for he had a great charge with him of his father's.

So that I do not know how things will fall out as to that, but when such a thing is resolved upon, I shall give you notice of it.

So, being in haste I shall only remember my love to yourself, and to your daughter, and Betty Smith, and all the rest of our friends of the faith therewith, if there be any; not forgetting my dear friend in the true faith, Ellen Sudbury. I long to hear how she and her husband doth.

So resteth your Friend in the true Faith,

LODOWICKE MUGGLETON.

May 8, 1663.

I should be glad to hear from you as soon as you can. My daughter Sarah and her Husband remember their kind loves unto you, and so doth Mr. Hatter, with many other friends unknown to you, yet remember their love to you.

A Letter of the Prophet Lodowicke Muggleton's to Mr. Richard Sudbury, May 19, 1663.

Loving Friend, Richard Sudbury,

I RECEIVED your letter, bearing date the first of May, 1662.

I am glad to hear that you are in health, and more especially that you do understand something more than you did when I was with you, of the form and nature of God, and the form and nature of the right devil; and the difference betwixt the seed of reason, and the seed of faith, and the nature of a commission.

The knowledge of these things when they are sunk deep into the heart and do not remain only in the head; I say they will make you wiser than your fathers, and will yield you more peace and satisfaction to your mind, than all the religions and opinions in the world besides can do; because the knowledge of these things, it gives a peace which the world cannot give; nor no righteousness which is acted or wrought by the seed of reason, let it be ever so pure, it is but the righteousness of the law; and by the deeds of the law shall no flesh be justified, but by the righteousness of faith are we justified in the sight of God, and hath peace in God; and this justification and peace, it doth arise from the seed of faith which is God's own nature, and this is that which is called in Scripture the divine nature of God; where it is said, speaking to believers, We are partakers of his divine nature: now if God hath a divine nature, of necessity he must have a person, for there can be no nature of God, angels, man, nor any other creature nor thing, but it must have a person or substance; now a spiritual substance hath a nature as well as that which is natural.

So that God having a divine nature, he must needs have a spiritual, heavenly, and divine substance; and according to the faith of the Scriptures, this substance of God is no other but the form of a man, and this God-Man is no other but *Christ Jesus, which is the Alpha Omega, the beginning and the end, the first and the last, he that was dead and is alive, and behold he is alive for evermore.* Neither can there be any true peace to any upon the earth, but in the believing it was God that poured out his soul unto death, and rose again, and is now living in that same body; and the faith in this gives true peace to the mind here, and the assurance of eternal life hereafter, which can never be known but in and by a commission, this being the last, and of the highest nature; which I am glad that you do confess a belief in, which is more than I did think you would have done when I was with you, for you being wrapped up and entangled with Jacob Bemon's principles and disciples with a little smatch of the Quakers, that there would have been no room for truth to take place in you; but I see now it is otherwise, for now you would wish to see me; but when I was with you I could discern no such thing, neither can I tell as yet whether ever I shall see you again, except you do come to London about some business. I shall be glad to see you, but if ever I have any occasion to come within twenty or thirty miles of you, I shall come and see you.

I understand by your letter that you are got into the bishop's court, that is a thing that is common every where in the countries, but as for us at London, we are very quiet as to that; so people will forbear meeting, and pay tithes and taxes, they may live quiet enough here; but I have been in Cambridgeshire and spent the most part of this winter, and they are cited into the bishop's court for not going to church, and some for not baptizing their children, as you are, but there is none of this faith that doth go, except one or two that are weak and fearful, and loth to part with a little money to preserve a good conscience free from idolatry; but some of our friends have been cited in very oft, and would not appear, but at last the apparitors did arrest them with a writ to appear at the Quarter-Sessions, and there they were made to pay ten shillings a piece, so that they could do them no further harm for six month's time; others again, if they did appear at the first summons, they paid seventeen shillings, and were discharged; for it is only a money business.

Therefore my advice to you is to give the apparitor his fee; if you do give him something more than what is stated by their laws, perhaps he will put out your name, if not, appear at the court, and pay the charges of it; for there is no oaths, nor any thing else imposed upon you, but only pay the charges of the court and be gone; but if you let it run till you be suspended, that will be taken off for eight shillings, for it is; only to get money: now there is some baptists, and others, that will not pay any money at all, so that they do proceed to excommunication: now what the event of their excommunication is I cannot hear, but I do advise all our friends rather to part with a little money, for that is it that all courts do look for; and so preserve their temporal well-being, and their conscience, free from idolatry; for money is Caesar's, *Therefore give Caesar the things that are Cesar's, and God the things that are his*; for all tribute and taxes which is laid upon the people, by the power of the nation, whether it be the spiritual courts so called, or the civil courts, it is all Caesar's tax, and so ought to be paid by all those that love peace of conscience better than money.

Therefore my advice is that you would do as before said, for I know a little money will let you free in this matter.

No more at present, but my love to yourself. I rest.

LODOWICKE MUGGLETON.

May 19, 1663.

A Copy of a Letter written by the Prophet Lodowicke Muggleton, to Mrs. Ellen Sudbury, bearing date from London, May the 19th. 1663.

Dear Friend, in the true Faith, Ellen Sudbury.

I AM glad to hear a few lines from you, and though you have not been well in body, yet I perceive you have grown more strong in the faith of this commission, and in the assurance of eternal life, which is the chiefest and greatest thing that can be attained in this life; which faith of yours shall carry you up here in this life, and not only so, but *according to your faith it shall be unto you, for you shall see your God face to face, in that kingdom of eternal glory*. And this faith which you have in this commission of the Spirit, *is that earnest of the Spirit which is the evidence of things not seen, and the substance of things hoped for*. There is no knowing of God, nor any things above the stars, but by faith, therefore *without faith it is impossible to please God*, neither can a man please himself without faith, *for great and wonderful things have been done by the power of faith*; and yet the peace of mind, and the assurance of eternal life, is greater than all. For the time was, when as I would have given the whole world if it had been in my power; nay, I would willingly have laid down my life to have procured favour with God, or to know my eternal happiness, but could not; but now eternal life is freely given me, made known to me, I am not so willing to lay down my life as I was before; for before, I thought to procure peace with God by suffering, which could not be; but now, by faith, I have obtained the assurance of eternal life without laying down my life.

So that what I suffer now it is from life, and not to gain life, which, all men which have not this faith do suffer to gain life, and not from any true life of faith; neither can they say the life that they live is by the faith of the true God, as we can, for if God hath never a person, (as they say) there can be no true faith at all: therefore be not you discouraged because of the fewness that believe or receive this commission of the Spirit; for if there should be none but yourself in those parts, yet your faith and blessedness, which hath been declared upon you, shall bear you up, and confirm you the more, both of the truth of the Scriptures, and of the doctrine that is held forth by this commission of the Spirit, for the Scriptures are full of sure examples; here and there one, *that did receive a prophet in the name of a prophet*. And as for William Watson's tempting of you to speak evil of me, I know that is the nature of the devil so to do. And as for his going up and down with Richard Farnesworth's letter, saying that he durst, and himself speak evil of me, that belongs only to the devil so to do, especially those that are damned by me; for it is not Richard Farnesworth's letter, nor all the men in the world, and letters, that can or shall take off his damnation again. But if William Watson do but read, or hear my answer read to Richard Farnesworth's letter, he will have small cause to boast of that letter.

I hope our friend Dorothy Carter hath taken a copy of it before now, expecting that she will send it to you, though I did not desire her so to do when I sent it, yet I hope you have it before you receive this,

Therefore let the devil Watson, and all they that are under the sentence of this commission, rage and do what they can, they shall never take away that assurance of eternal life from you, neither shall they deliver themselves from that damnation which I have pronounced upon them.

No more at present, but my love to yourself.

I rest your friend in the eternal Truth,

LODOWICKE MUGGLETON.

A Copy of a Letter written by the Prophet Lodowicke Muggleton, bearing date from London, June 19, 1663.

Dear and loving Friend in the eternal Truth, Dorothy Carter,

I RECEIVED your letter bearing date May 18th, 1663, and am glad to hear of your health, and more especially of your faith and confidence in this commission of the Spirit, for that will make your life both comfortable here, and happy hereafter.

I had given you an answer before now, but that I was to go into Kent at that time when I received yours, and was there a matter of eight or ten days; but now being at home again, I shall give you an answer to those things of most concernment in your letter

The first thing is, I am glad your daughter hath so good an opinion of Richard Sudbury, as to give testimony of his faith in this commission of the Spirit.

Indeed I do find by his writing, that he is very much enlightened in the knowledge of many things which this commission doth declare, to what he did when I was there: also I do see by his letters that there is love to truth, which was not in him then.

Indeed I did little expect that ever he would have received the doctrine of the true God, and the right devil, not in the love of it. But this I will say, he will know, to h:s everlasting peace, the difference between Jacob Bemon's doctrine and the doctrine of this commission of the Spirit, which he, nor no other can do, but by faith in this commission of the Spirit.

I hope he and his wife are well, and those friends that were to be at your house this Witsuntide.

The second thing is, that you and Mr. Frewterill are cited into the bishop's court, for which you would have my advice.

I shall give you the same advice as I do all other believers in the countries, for they are cited into the bishop's court every where in the countries; some of the believers do pay their monies, and so they proceed no further; yet they lye liable to be cited again every month, but I do not hear they are so extreme as to do it, for it is but to get a crown or an angel a year of you, that is all they look after; and if a man be able, he had better do it and pay it, for his quietness sake, than to stand it out. Others again that are poor, are excommunicated quite, and so they remain, and that is as far as they can go.

I do not understand that the bishop's courts have any such power not as yet to strain upon any man's goods for the charges of the court, according to the old law formerly they had, but except the Parliament do revive and ratify that law a-new, they dare not put it in execution: else excommunication can go no further than thus, that is to say, you shall be cast out of the church, so that you shall not be partakers of the ordinances of God, not as to receive the sacraments; and if you die, you shall not be buried in the church-yard, nor have Christian burial, as they call it; and if you have any debts owing to you, you shall not have the benefit of the law to get your own.

These, and such-like, are the effects of excommunication:, therefore, in my judgment, it is better to give them their fees now while it is but little, so you can keep the mind free from oaths and worship; it is better let them have some of your money, for that is the world'. God, for money will buy off excommunication, condemnation, and worship; and all that the bishop's courts can do, or they aim at, is but money, for if you be damned afterward they care not, so they can but get your money; therefore you need not much trouble yourself about that, for a little money will deliver you out of that trouble.

We are very quiet here at London as to that, but only taxes go on more and more; but, as for worship, it is not here, so we do not meet nor neglect paying of tythes, we worship who or what we will; the cause, I believe, is of the sectary party, four for one, if not more, so that it is impossible for them to bring the people to an uniformity of worship; and for watching of schools, the bishop's licence will hold good, for there is a friend of mine of this faith, which did keep a school before the king came in, but when the bishop's courts were settled they would not let him keep school without a licence, and that was a hard matter to get without swearing, or going to church: he went to the secretary of the bishop's court, being of his acquaintance, and told him, if he would help him to a licence he would give him content; the secretary told him he could not well do it, except he would show himself at church, or swear. My friend said he could not swear nor go to church, and if he could not do it without those two things, he must lay it down So, at the last, the officer did promise to get him one: and so he did, without swearing or going to church; it cost my friend but six shillings and eight pence, and so he left his conscience free from offence. And because you may see that this, school-master is one of this faith, I have gent you a letter of his, which he sent to me lately, but I would have you send it me again as soon as you can; he liveth near Cambridge, but it Was at the bishop's court at Cambridge that he had his licence.

And as for that Evans at Nottingham, I do not know the man, neither was he of our society, for I know all that have been of our society, and have slunk away, there is none of them that dare speak evil of that which they did formerly own, neither was there ever any families ruined by following us, but many families have been upheld and preserved by us. How is it possible that any families should be ruined by us, when we never lay any burthens upon any; for my part, all the while that John Reeve was living, I never had two-pence of all the believers in England, except it was of one gentleman, but have spent many a pound for the commission-sake; for I do believe I was above forty pounds the worse in my estate for this commission, for I did not live of the Gospel, as the apostles did, without working; I have been more true in that particular than ever any apostle was, or ever any Quaker was, for there cannot be so many speakers of the Quakers but they must be maintained by their disciples, which I never was, neither was John Reeve, for John Reeve's wife and his daughter did get most part of his living, for if he had got no more than what was given him, it was but little, for he never laid no burthen upon any; if they were moved to give him sometimes 1$s.$ 1$s.$ 6$d.$ or 2$s.$ 6$d.$ so it was, he never compelled any, but they did it freely of themselves, which could not ruin any family; neither was he ever drunk in his life, to my knowledge, for he was too innocent and sober-natured a mail to be drunk: but I conceive this Evans is mistaken in the man, I believe it was John Reeve's brother, for he, indeed, towards his latter end, was grown a drunkard and sot, and, perhaps, this Evans was of his society, which was upon the rant, and the ranters indeed did ruin many families. There have been divers others that have laid aspersions upon John Reeve, because of his brother's foolish practice; but, as for himself, he was, in that point, as a child that weaned is; but no body can help people's believing of lies, no more than we can help believing of truth.

Therefore let the Quakers believe what they will of John Reeve, that will not deliver them from the sentence which he and I have passed upon them; and as for this Evans, but that I think he is mistaken in the man, I would have sent the sentence to him for his lies.

And as for my coming down to see you, I cannot possibly promise you at present, but I do think our friend Mr. Hatter must go into Yorkshire about a month hence at the farthest, and he doth intend to be one night at Mr. Sudbury's, for that is in his way, so that he cannot come to you, but I suppose he will send you word when he will be there, so that, if you can, you may meet with him there, and, if I can possibly, I will come along with him, for I have a desire to see you all over again; and the more, because Mr. Sudbury hath given such testimonies of his faith in the true God, and his desire to see me.

No more at present, but my love to yourself, your Daughter, and Elizabeth Smith, and all the rest of our friends in the Faith.

Your Friend in the eternal truth,

LODOWICKE MUGGLETON.

A Copy of a Letter written by the Prophet Lodowicke Muggleton, to Mrs. Dorothy Carter in Chesterfield, bearing date from London, July the 18th, 1663.

Dear Friend,

I THOUGHT good to give you notice, though I am uncertain myself, but, I think, Mr. Hatter will be at Mr. Richard Sudbury's on Wednesday night, being the 23d of July, and if he does come, as I suppose he will, for he must come then or not at all, for he cannot stay above a day longer if he comes at all; and if he comes out on Monday or Tuesday, I did intend to come along with him, but if he doth not come at all, I will come myself the next week after; but, if you can, be at Ellen Sudbury's on Wednesday next, that you may see Mr. Hatter, for he goes no nearer you than Nottingham; and if you do lose your labour in seeing him, you may take comfort in seeing your cousin Sudbury, for I cannot give the certainty of it, yet I thought good to send by the post this Saturday night, else I could not convey any notice of it to you, for he must come at a day's warning, so that no letter could be conveyed unto you, neither can he stay at Ellen Sudbury's but one night; and as for my staying with you longer than I did before, that I cannot do, but I do intend to stay with you about so long time as I did before.

So being in haste, I shall take leave, with my love remembered unto yourself, and unto your daughter, and Elizabeth Smith, and all other friends. I rest

Your friend in the eternal truth,

LODOWICKE MUGGLETON.

A Copy of a Letter written by the Prophet Lodowicke Muggleton, to Thomas Highfeild, Gardener in Nottingham, bearing Date from Chesterfield, July 31, 1663.

Thomas Highfeild,

I UNDERSTAND that you are a Quaker, and that the Quakers do sometimes meet at your house, so that you cannot be ignorant of those letters of Samuel Hooton, and W. S. which they sent to me, and of my answer to them, as also that letter of Richard Furnesworth's, and my answer to him.

In which letters of mine you may see, if you have but the single eye of faith, why I do oppose that sort of people more than any other sect of religion, because, as I have expressed in those letters, the Quakers are the greatest fighters against God's being a person of himself (of any) they being led and guided by the spirit of antichrist in this last age, which is transformed into the likeness of an angel of light, for that they have got their God all within them; so that they deny God to have a person or body of his own without them so that they are that spirit of antichrist that doth deny the Father and the Son, that is, they deny Jesus Christ to have become in the flesh; I mean they deny Jesus Christ to have flesh and bone of his own, which is the same flesh and bone that he suffered death in; I say that same flesh and bone is now living in heaven above the stars, and not as the Quakers do vainly imagine him to be, all diffused into spirits, and so lie is gotten into them; and this is that which they call the light of Christ in them, and so they say that Christ is in them from that Scripture, where it is said, *Know ye not that Christ is in you, except you be reprobates*; never considering that saying in Scripture, *Let Christ dwell in your hearts by faith.* Now that which dwells in a man's heart by faith, it doth not dwell in a man's heart in its person and essence, for if one man had the person and essence of God in him, then I say God can be in one particular person, as he was in the body of Christ; therefore it is said in Scripture, *That the fulness of the godhead dwelt bodily in him*, that is, the essence, substance, spirit and being of God was compassed all within that body of Christ, which was flesh, blood and bone in the state of mortality and so the godhead life was made capable to suffer the pains of death; therefore it is said concerning Christ's death, that he was offered up through the eternal Spirit, so that the eternal Spirit quickening into life again, it raised that flesh and bone again, and in the raising again it was made spiritual, and so became capable to ascend above the stars, where he now is in that same body which he suffered death in; so that Christ cannot be in every man's body, not in his spiritual person and essence, but he may dwell in all men's hearts by faith, though he be not in the, world at all; if men have but so much faith as to believe that flesh of Christ to be the flesh of God, and, that blood of his to be the blood of God; this is to eat his flesh, and drink his blood, and so they shall never die, that is, that eternal death; so that it is not the light of Christ within a man that will deliver from eternal death, but faith in the person of Christ without a man. This I know to be truth, I being, one of the two last chosen witnesses of the Spirit, to; declare what the form and nature of the true God is, the form and nature of the right devil; the place and nature of hell; and the right heaven; the person and nature of angels; the mortality of the soul; with many other heavenly, mysteries which do arise from the knowledge of these six heads,. which hath been declared in our writings, which I do suppose you cannot be ignorant of, and you being of that, form, and others of the Quakers; therefore, by virtue of my commission, I am moved to write these lines; unto you, I knowing that the Quakers are led and guided by the spirit of Antichrist, which is nothing else but the devil transformed into an angel of light; but that light within them being darkness, it is the greatest darkness of all the seven churches. And though you in that way do seem to be the most pure in shew and righteousness of life, yet your righteousness of life is but legal, which is nothing else but the righteousness of the law, which no flesh shall be justified by; for that which you call the light of Christ within you, is nothing else but the light of the moral law which is written in your seed and nature, which is reason, which doth cause your thoughts to accuse and excuse, which is no other but what the heathens had before the law was given to Moses; but as for the righteousness of faith, you Quakers are totally ignorant of, and so not being justified by faith, you cannot have peace with God.

Therefore do not you think that the righteousness of life can save you, for it is but the righteousness of the law; and though you ought not to leave this righteousness of the law undone, because it is good amongst men, but nothing but faith in the true God, and that righteousness that flows from it, can justify the mind, and give true peace as to eternal happiness, which is impossible you Quakers should have, seeing you deny the object of faith, which is the body and flesh and bone of God.

I write not these lines unto you as expecting you to decline your principle, for you are too deeply riveted in that lie to come to truth; yet because you shall be left without excuse, I have written these lines unto you, that you may know there is a true prophet now in England, which hath declared truth unto you, or set life and death before you; but it is the nature of your principle to chuse death rather than life; therefore, by virtue, power and authority of my commission, I do charge and command you (as I have done many of the preachers of the other six churches) that you would leave off speaking or preaching of that lying doctrine which the Quakers teach, which is to mind the light within them, but deny the body and person of Christ without them; neither have you any commission to do as you do, for the light within a man was never a sufficient commission: to make a man a minister, messenger, or ambassador of Christ.

Therefore, if you shall exercise the office of a public preacher, or gather the people to meet at your house upon a religious account (for you do but deceive yourselves, and other ignorant and silly people;) therefore, if you shall do any of these things aforesaid, after the receipt of this letter, then, for this your disobedience unto this commission of the Holy Spirit, I do pronounce you cursed and damned, both in soul and body, from the presence of God, elect men and angels, to eternity.

Written by

LODOWICKE MUGGLETON,

One of the two last Witnesses and Prophets unto the High and Mighty God, the Man Christ Jesus, in Glory.

A Copy of a Letter written by the prophet Lodowicke Muggleton, to Goodwife Wylds, William Young, and Thomas Martyn of Kent, dated from London, August 27, 1663.

I UNDERSTANDING that you three are fallen in your minds from that true faith, and spiritual worship, which doth belong to this spiritual commission, and so have given up yourselves to worship as the priests of the nation do; for I understand that you three do all go to church, to save yourselves from suffering a little damage in your outward estates, which you will find contrary to your expectations. I thought that you had been very well satisfied about that the last time I was with you; but your faith was not tried as it is now.

Yet you, Goody Wylds, had no intent to go to the public worship; then, however, you did pretend unto me it was but for the trial of other believers; but now it doth appear otherwise; and Thomas Martyn could say unto you, that you should lose your peace, and be damned to the grave's mouth, and yet he himself should do the same thing, there being at that time no trial put upon him. Oh! how strong is mens' faith where there is no trial of it; but that faith which doth endure the fiery trial to the end shall receive the crown of life.

But I perceive that you, because you were blessed by John Reeve, think you shall not be damned, though you do bow your knee to Baal, or worship Baal; but I would not have you so ignorant as to think, that you can shew yourselves at church, to save your estates, and yet not to worship a false God. Is not all the worship of the nation set up by man? and if man command you to worship, or else to pay your money, if you do obey to save your money, do you not worship as the nation doth? and if the worship of the nation be true, then the worship of God in spirit and truth (which this commission of the Spirit holds forth) must be false. For, deceive not yourselves, you cannot serve God in spirit and truth, and give your bodies to the worship of the nation; for where the heart is, there is the body also; and where the body is, there is the heart; and it can be no otherwise: therefore do not blind your eyes as to think that you may shew yourselves at church to save yourselves from sufferings, and yet own this commission of the Spirit, you are mightily mistaken if you think to do so. But I have learned experience by this your fall, you Goody Wylds and Thomas Martyn, which were the strongest in faith, revelation, and experience in this commission of the Spirit in all that country, and yet the least able to suffer any thing for it, notwithstanding this commission of the Spirit hath freed you from abundance of bondages and entanglements which other sects do undergo; a yoak which our fathers, the apostles and saints, did undergo in their times. These things this commission of the Spirit hath freed the believers of it from. that bondage, which all other sects are under to this day: and yet now there is a little trial, how few is there that will hold out to the end. And if your faith cannot abide the trial of losing a little money or imprisonment, what would you do if it were death itself, as all other commissions have suffered death for their worshipping of God contrary to the worship of the nation; neither doth this commission lay such a strict law upon the believers of it, as Christ did upon his; for except a man would forsake father and mother, wife and children, house and land, for his sake, they were not worthy of him. But you will not forsake the tempation of your husband, nor the other two the brawling of their wives, for the faith's sake; but you have done muck like unto Ahab; you have sold yourself to work spiritual witchcraft, through the temptation of your husband, and their wicked wives.

For this I say to you, that temptations will come, but happy are they that are not overcome by temptations; for our Lord was tempted of the devil, but not overcame. And so hath all prophets, apostles, and saints, been tempted by the devil without, as well as by the devil reason within. But those as have overcome the temptations of the devil without, and the devil within, they shall come forth as gold tried in the fire. But I perceive you three have been overcome by the temptation of the devil without and within both. You, by the devil your husband without you, and the other two by the serpents their wives without them, with some other by-ends, which your reason the devil did lay hold on, which have overcome the seed of faith in you, and hath carried it captive into prison, and hath made shipwreck and spoil of your faith; neither do I think that you will ever be delivered into that liberty and assurance of eternal life as you had before; for you have quenched the spirit of truth and revelation, which did run as a river of living water in you: it will run but little in you now, hardly to bear you up into the assurance of eternal life; for you know not what you have done in forsaking the worship of the living God, and joined to the worship of the nation. For if their worship be true, then this worship we have professed is false.

Again, did not this commission of the spirit deliver you, Goody Wylds, from all our sins, which were more and greater than ordinarily is committed by other people; and not only so, but your faith in it, and Thomas Martyn's, it made you strong in faith, revelation, and experience, above all in that country. It was a crown of glory upon your heads; but you have pulled it off your head, and trampled it under your feet, by bowing your knee unto Baal, for you were much like unto Sampson for strength.

For your faith and revelation in this commission of the Spirit did break all the cords of the Philistine's asunder; that is, all the arguments and reasonings, which other sects brought from the Scriptures to bind you withal; but now you are become like Sampson, when his, hair was cut he was like another man, and so had his eyes pulled out.

So it is with you, you are become now like other men, for your eye of faith is pulled out, and your eye of reason will be pulled out shortly also; so that you will be as weak in the true faith as other men, or any other experience: for the devil hath caught you fast enough now, he hath got you to bow down to his worship. Let it be out of hypocrisy, or out of sincerity of heart, the devil matters not for that, you have yielded obedience unto him, and you will have much ado to get out of the snares of the devil to your lives end, think of it what you will; for it is a dangerous thing to find that grace might abound, because you think you shall not be damned to eternity for it, therefore you will do despite to the spirit of grace, so that you may be set down, like prophane Esau, who sold his birthright for a mess of pottage.

What have you done less than he, who have valued the fears of the loss of some of the goods of this world more than a good conscience, and faith towards God, which gives the assurance of eternal life, which I am certain you will lose the sense of? Neither will your mess of pottage be any bigger for what you have done, but rather the less; for it must be as Christ said in another case, *he that is willing to lose his life shall save it*; so, on the contrary, you that are willing to save your mess of pottage, you shall lose it. For I say, it is hard for the devil to get a mess of pottage in this world as it is for the saint, let them bow down e'er so much; for you will see, in a short time, what profit it will be unto you in this world. Neither will you eat your mess of pottage with that peace of mind as you had before; for this art of yours, it will be as gall and wormwood in your pottage; it will be worse than playing at cards, and being drunk, or all the sins that you committed in the days of your ignorance. For God was always more angry at Israel's worshipping a false God, than any other sin whatsoever; because other sins were infirmities of nature, which nature cannot avoid, it being naturally prone unto it. But this bowing down to worship that which you know to be false, neither do you do it because you own it to be truth, but only through slavish fear, of suffering some, loss in this, world; which thing is worse seven times than if you had owned it to be the true worship of God, as other people do.

Therefore do not deceive yourselves, and count it your liberty, as if you had more liberty in point of worship, by this commission of the Spirit, than the rest of the believers have; for some of the believers of this commission have suffered more in their outward estates than ever you would have done, yet they have thought themselves happy in that they kept their hearts pure and undefiled from that spiritual whoredom to worship a false God, or bow to the false worship, contrary to the faith they have in this commission of the Spirit: for if all the believers of this commission of the Spirit should do as you have done, it would be but a vain thing for them to dispute or plead for the doctrine of the true God, and the right devil, with many other heavenly mysteries, which no other forms of worship do know. And as you have been instruments to publish and make known this doctrine, which thing was a crown of honour upon your heads, but now you have done the greatest dishonour to this commission of the Spirit that could be done; so that your glory will be your shame. For it will be but a vain thing for you to profess any faith in this commission of the Spirit any more; for I shall never own you as I did before; neither can I have that love and affection for truth's sake, as I had before; neither do I care for ever seeing you any more. Yet I shall bear the shame of it, and though you should all of you fall, so that I should be left alone, as Elijah was, yet my faith shall bear me up.

And if you find the same peace as you did when you lived in the obedience of faith of this commission of the Spirit, then hath God revealed no truth unto me.

I shall say no more, but leave you to the worship of the nation, and as fallen from the true faith in the true God.

LODOWICKE MUGGLETON,

One of the two last Prophets unto the true God

London, August 29, 1663.

A Copy of a Letter written by the Prophet Lodowicke Muggleton, to Christopher Hill Sept. 23, 1663.

Loving Friend, Christopher Hill,

I RECEIVED yours, with the letter inclosed, wherein I perceive that your family is afflicted with the small-pox. If I should say I am sorry for it, it would not ease you e'er the more; for these things are natural to all, and falls all alike to all. So that time puts an end to all diseases, and to life itself. So that death and life is always at strife one with the other, and so it will be as long as the world doth endure. But when time shall be swallowed up into eternity, then shall there be no more death to the seed of faith, nor no more life to the seed of reason; for death shall swallow up the seed of reason's life and heaven into that eternal death. So on the contrary, the seed of faith's life shall swallow up that death and hell into eternal life. For great is the power of faith and the power of reason. The one goes into the power of death and drunkenness, and the other into the power of life and light eternal.

It is well, and I am glad that you are so stedfast in your faith, notwithstanding the last proclamation. I wish you may hold out to the end, and not do as others have done, to put your hand to the plough, and look back; that is, to worship God in spirit and truth, according to the faith of this commission of the Spirit, and them to turn back to the worship of the nation, either to gain or save a suit of apparel, which is but a mess of pottage. And as for you, mother Wyld, if that were her excuse, as you have written, for her going to church to try their spirits, and finding the priest to be a devil, and therefore she would not hear him any more; it is but a poor excuse, not so good as Adam's fig-leaves were to cover his nakedness.

Now I cannot tell whose spirits she went to try, whether the saint's spirits, or the devil's spirits; but let it be which she will, she went the wrong way to try spirits: For if he went to try the devil's spirits, it was that which they did desire; so that the devil tried her spirit to make her fall down and worship him, even as he did unto Christ; so that Christ did not try the devil, but the devil tried him.; And if Christ had yielded to the devil's temptation, as she hath done, what would have become of us all, his own faith and power, and the faith of the elect? There would have been havock and shipwreck made of it, and the devil would have been more than a conqueror, as he hath been in those three. And if she; did it to try the spirits of the weak saints, that was as much as to tempt the spirit of truth. For when the; apostle bad the believers in his time try the spirits, whether they were of God, or no, it was not that they should turn back, again to the worship of the law, for to encourage the devils, that their worship is right, and to weaken the faith of the saints. This is not the right way of trying of spirits: they had better have set their own faith to have been tried by the devil's, like gold in the fire. I am sure it would have yielded them more peace here, and more glory hereafter, and good a livelihood in this world as they will now have.

And as for her knowing the priest to be a devil, she knew that many years before she came to own this commission. She need not to have gone to church to have known that; for she knew all the priests of the nation, and of all sorts, were false, and not sent of God. And as for her peace and satisfaction, I shall let that alone: Yet this I am sure of, if faith hath not its perfect work in the soul, there cannot be that perfect peace. Neither did I slight her faithfulness to this commission, but did honour her upon that account more than all in that country; which the fall of her hath done more mischief to the commission of the Spirit, than all the rest besides: for if she and they had not been declared blessed by John Reeve, I should not have mattered it so much; for I always had a great respect to those which John Reeve did bless, in case I did approve of them. And it was well that Claxton was not declared blessed, either by John Reeve, or myself; if he had, I should not have excommunicated him for ever, as he now is. But I see what a confusion there will be with the believers of this commission when I am dead: For almost all those that disadhere unto John Reeve, are some dead, and many of the rest fallen away from that stedfastness of faith; but blessed and happy are they who hold out to the end. She might have said to bear it with patience, had she given no cause: For I do never use to write so sharply without a cause; for I was always naturally inclined to moderation, patience, and long-suffering with such weaknesses in the saints, which I know John Reeve would never have done nor borne.

But in points of worship, God himself, and all prophets and apostles, were angry at; for that is as the apple of God's eye: and all the controversy in the whole world, persecution, killing and slaying, all about worship, from Gain and Abel, in the beginning of the world, even to this day, and to the end of the world, and so forth.

Mr. Burton would have Goodman Miles to come up and take some order about his cyder; for he hath let his house to another, and that man doth want the room; so that he will not let it stand there. He takes possession of it next Tuesday, therefore let him come as suddenly as possibly he can.

So resteth your friend in the true faith,

LODOWICKE MUGGLETON.

A Copy of a Letter written by the Prophet Lodowick Muggleton, to Mrs. Dorothy Carter, of Chesterfield, bearing date November 14, 1663.

Dear and loving Friend in the true faith, Dorothy Carter,

I DID understand by your last letter, bearing date October 1, 1663, that the next week but one after that, I should hear from William Newcome; but I have not heard from him not yet; but I believe some occasion or other is the cause that doth hinder it.

Also I perceive by your letter that you would willingly have those letters of mine to the Quakers put in print, which in my last letter to you I was willing to have let them alone for a time; for I had not read over his printed pamphlet when I sent you that letter; but since I have read it over, and have shewed it to some other friends in the faith, and they are very desirous that I would write an answer to that printed pamphlet of Richard Farnsworth's, and put it in print with the other letters of the Quakers, with my answers unto them.

It would be the greatest discovery of the deceit of the Quaker's doctrine of any thing that hath been yet written; so I know it well. I had thoughts when the Interpretation of the Eleventh Chapter of the Revelations was printed, not to have printed no more; but seeing truth cannot be so public and made known to the world without printing, because every one cannot read writing; besides, it is too tedious to write much; so, for the desires of others, and that truth may be made more known in the world, and that the Quakers may not tyrannize in their way, as if they had printed such a thing as could not be answered; in consideration of these things I have written an answer to this printed pamphlet, and I have spoken with the printer about it, and we are almost agreed concerning it. I do intend to have that letter of mine to Edward Bourne printed; for that was the first which did anger them. Also I will have Samuel Hooton and William Smith, their first letter to me, and my answer to them, and Richard Farnsworth's first letter to me, and my answer to it, and my answer to this printed pamphlet; all these I do intend to put in print: therefore, what you shall be willing and free, and our friend Mr. Sudbury, and if there be any other there that is able, what they are free, they may contribute towards the printing of them, and I will send you some of them down as soon as they are printed, which I suppose will be about a fortnight or three weeks hence; for the printer doth say, if he doth not do them in that time he will not do them at all.

So in haste I rest at this time, only my dear love to yourself, and to your daughter, and Betty Smith, and all the rest of our friends in the faith.

Your friend in the true faith,

LODOWICKE MUGGLETON.

London, November 14, 1663.

My wife desires to be remembered to you all, though unknown.

Let me hear from you as soon as you can.

A Copy of a Letter written by the Prophet Lodowicke Muggleton, to Mrs. Dorothy Carter, bearing date the 27th of November, 1663, as followeth.

Dear and loving friend in the ink faith of Jesus, Dorothy Carter,

I RECEIVED your letter and the twenty shillings of William Holland's man. I am very glad to hear that you are all well; and also do understand by your letter what the mayor of Chesterfield hath done, and that I must make my personal appearance at Derby assizes, which I do intend to do, that the bail may not suffer. I know nothing to the contrary as yet, for I have asked counsel about it, and they tell me because I did put in bail in the open court, I cannot remove it; so that I must be forced to see you again; but do not you be troubled about it; for if I had ten thousand damned devils before me, I should not be afraid; neither can they do any great matters against me, not according as the laws of England stand at this time; so that the envy of the devils cannot go beyond their own law, only it will be some charge and trouble to come so far; but as to what they can do by their law, I do not much value what they can do, for I shall justify most part of their charge which they have against me; and the more I suffer for it, the more hotter will the fire of hell burn in those that are my enemies.

And as for Mr. Pender and others being bound over to come in against me by the mayor, I say it is more than the mayor can do, except the mayor do take the business upon himself to prosecute and persecute me, which doth not concern him; for he did what was his place to do, and that was to commit me to prison, that was as much as concerned him in his place; neither was he bounds nor no other man, to witness my words against me, not upon any penalty, if I had been tried then, much less now; but if the mayor and others their malice be so great towards me, they thinking to make great matters of my words, which they urged out of me, which I shall justify in the open court to their eternal shame, let their malice be what it can be to me, I shall be made able to bear it. And if they can bear their eternal torment as well, it will be well for them; but if there be any way that I can prevent my coming there and free my bail, I will; if not, I will come, but you shall know further before that time. I had thoughts to have written a few lines to Mr. Pender, to have shewed him that it was more than the mayor could do, to bind him or any other to witness against me, there being no penalty or punishment can be inflicted upon them in case they do not; but if the mayor and priest have bound themselves through their malice to prosecute the business, all that they can do, is to supoena you in for a witness; and if you do not go, what penalty can be inflicted upon you for it? None at all; but some through ignorance and fear, and others through malice and envy, both mixed together, will do what mischief they can to me; but I shall be able to bear it all; so that I shall not persuade Mr. Pender, nor no other, against what their ignorance and fear will lead them unto; but I being in haste at this time, shall say no more in that business.

Dear Friend,

I have here sent you Charles Cleve's letter unto Richard Farnsworth; I would desire you to convey it to him some way or other. I would have you read it over before. I do think it will be too tedious to take a copy of it; yet I have done it here, because of others seeing of it to lend it about. I think the book of the Quaker's Letters and mine will be out the next week, and the next week after I shall send you some of them; for I must go into Kent a week before Christmas, because the parish doth intend to choose me constable this year, so I shall prevent them if I can. I go to my wife's mother, but after the twelve days are over I do intend to come again.

Our friend Mr. Hatter is very well, and doth give us good hopes of a good success of his business; but when he doth intend to come to London he maketh no mention in his letter. He waits as he saith for his wife to be delivered of child-birth, and if she do well it will be much better for him.

Our friend Mr. Hudson doth intend to come to London about Candlemas day, and he says he will come by Chesterfield, to see you, and through Nottingham, to see Ellen Sudbury.

And as for that priest, whose heart is set on the fire of hell, that fain would have me hanged or burned, the same measure shall be meted unto him which he would have done unto me, and that I shall let him know; but at present I have no time to write the sentence unto him, nor to those other two you mention in your letter; but if I can when I send the books, I will.

So I shall say no more, but rest

Your loving friend in the true faith,

LODOWICKE MUGGLETON.

London, November 27, 1663.

My love remembered to your daughter and Betty Smith, and all the rest of our friends in the faith.

My wife desires to be remembered unto you all.

A Copy of a Letter written by the Prophet Lodowicke Muggleton, London, December 13, 1663.

Loving Friend, Mr. Sudbury,

I RECEIVED your letter, with your wife's inclosed, and I am glad to hear you are all well, and of your faith in this commission of the Spirit. I wish you may grow more and more in it, until you be as strong in your faith, as Sampson was in his body, even to destroy a thousand Philistines, with the jaw bone of an ass: so the power of faith in the true God will destroy a thousand of the seed of the serpent, with the word of their mouth, and so it doth every where, where men and women are thoroughly grounded in it; it hath great effect upon the seed of the serpent, all well as my faith hath.

This I know by experience, by several believers of this commission of the Spirit.

I also received five shillings of the carrier.

Also I find in your letter, that William Watson would willingly have me come to Derby, to be tried; and I perceive, rather than I should not come, he would bear my charges. I do see by this how free the devil is4o me, because he doth think there is some evil intended against me, therefore he would willingly be at the charge, that it might be put in execution; for this I know, that if there was any good intended towards me there, then he would be as forward to give money for me to stay away: but, however, if I could not bear my own charges nor if I had no friends in this world to do it, yet I would take no mercy of him, nor any other that is under the sentence of this commission; I never did it to my knowledge, never since I came forth upon this account, when as I had fewer friends than I have now; for I have refused both work and money, many times, of those that have been damned by me, which they would have thought themselves the more happy if I would have, accepted of it, but I would not; but I see what the serpents seed doth aim at, and it is very like that he may have his desire in that thing, and yet keep his money too; for I know nothing to the contrary yet, but do intend to come and, see you before I go to Derby assizes. I know they can do nothing to me when I do come there, not according as the laws of England stand at this time; except ignorance of the law, and envy together, doth that which is contrary to the law; but if it do, I shall bear it: but I shall inform you further of this before that time.

You say in your letter that there is one there that hath a mind to all my books, and if you mean all our books bound together, then I cannot help him to them, for there is none of the commission books left, not one, if I would give five shillings for that alone, that being the ground and beginning of all; but as for the Interpretation, I have sent you one, the price is two shillings. Also I have sent ten of those newly printed, and the price is twelve-pence a piece, they being very chargeable the printing, and much ado to get them at any rate; neither would I have you to lend them to Quakers or others, but if they will buy them, let them have them, and if they do not like them, when they have read them, let them burn them, or do what they will with them; for I have found by experience, a great deal of inconvenience in lending books, for when people see them for nothing, they like them the worse, but when they have paid for it, they will take more notice what they read; neither will those books of the Quakers be long before they be all gone, for most people do desire to see what these things mean, they having a good opinion of the Quakers, and the price being small, there is few will grudge to give a shilling for it; it contains ten sheets of paper, but if that man aforesaid hath a desire of all our works, I do think that William Newcomb, of Derby, bookseller, can help you to one, for he had three of me, and I hear he hath not sold them yet. If you send to Dorothy Carter you may know further of it, for he is there every Saturday.

In your wife's letter I understand that Mr. Tomkinson doth desire an answer to his letter.

But there being such a many particulars, to answer which, if they were answered fully, it would make a great volume; and if it should be answered ever so short, it would be very large, neither have I any time to do it, neither do I know when I shall: and for me to take such a deal of pains to please the unsatisfied fancy of one particular man, it would be but a vain thing; for there is enough written, if understood and believed, to satisfy the mind of any man or woman in the world; for if those things were answered upon his desire, in a month's time there would be as many more places of Scripture, as needful to answer, as those he hath propounded; so that there is no end of answering questions, neither will the reason of man ever be satisfied; for if there be nota growth in faith, upon these two foundations, viz. the true God and the right devil, there can be no true peace. But it is much upon my mind of late, for the good of the seed of faith in general, that if I do but live a few years longer, and have my liberty to interpret the chief principal heads of the whole Book of the Revelations of St, John, for the eleventh chapter being opened already, it will the more easily open all that rich cabinet, where the seed of faith may see the glorious treasure of heaven; but my haste is great at present, therefore I shall say no more in this thing, but if you please you may send me William Smith's letter, and your answer, when you send to me again.

And as for Mr. Hatter he is very well, and his business is like to do pretty well; I have sent to him this day some of those books which I know will be welcome to him, because he doth not know that they were printed. Our friend Mr. Hudson, I think, will be with you about Candlemas.

So in haste I rest, having much business to do, and being alone, for my wife is at her mother's, and my two daughters are from me; the one is married, the other is in Cambridgeshire, and the latter end of this week I do go into Kent; I do intend to be at home again at the twelve holidays end. So with my love to yourself, and to your loving wife, with my love to your maid, though I never had any discourse with her, neither do I well know her if I should see her again; yet this I say, I do look upon that maid to be one of the seed of faith, and that it will grow in her.

Your Friend in the true Faith,

LODOWICKE MUGGLETON.

London, December 13, 1663.

A Copy of a Letter written by the Prophet Lodowicke Muggleton, to one Rice Jones, at his House in Nottingham, without any Date or Place it came from, as follows;

Rice Jones,

ABOUT a twelve-month since it was I saw you, and then I had some little discourse with you: in which discourse I did understand what principle of religion you are of, which principle of God is founded upon Jacob Bemond's writings, which is to believe that God is an infinite Spirit without a body; also Jacob Bemond's angels which he speaketh so much of have no bodies, neither doth he describe the form and nature of them, neither could he tell what the right devil is, nor the true heaven, nor the right hell, nor the mortality of the soul, no, not any of these things did he truly know; neither are his writings any more divine or heavenly than the Heathen philosophers; for they are no other but philosophy, which proceedeth from the wisdom or seed of reason, and not from the seed and nature of faith, which the Scriptures were spoken and written by; neither can any man know these six heads before mentioned, without an infallible Spirit so to do; neither can any man interpret Scripture truly, and be ignorant of those Six principles aforesaid; that is, to know what the form and nature of the true God was before he became flesh, and what he is now;

Secondly, What the form and nature of the right devil was before he became flesh, and what he is now.

Thirdly, Where the place, or heaven of glory is.

Fourthly, Where the place of hell and shame is.

Fifthly, What the persons and natures of angels are.

And, sixthly, To understand the mortality of the soul.

Upon these six heads standeth all those heavenly secrets and mysteries spoken of in the Scriptures, they being hinted at by the prophets and apostles, but were hot so clearly made known unto the soul of man, as they are now by this commission of the Spirit, there being never a true interpreter of the Scriptures in the world at this day, but us two, the witnesses of the Spirit; for God hath given the Scriptures into our hands, so that none ought to officiate the office of a minister or messenger of Christ, but such as are approved of by me.

These things being so, I thought good to write these lines unto you, and by virtue and authority of my commission to forewarn you, and forbid you to exercise the office of a speaker among that society of the Bemonists or Quakers, nor any other sects; for there is very little difference betwixt the Bemonists and the Quakers, only the Quakers are a little more precise in their outward lives, but for your doctrine and theirs it is all one; for your God and theirs is all the same; so that you being ignorant of the true God and the right devil, and so of all other heavenly and saving truths which do arise from these two heads; neither have you any commission to exercise the office of a speaker in spiritual things; for this I would have you to know, that it is not the wisdom of reason upon the letter of the Scriptures, neither revelation, which you call the spirit within you, nor, as the Quakers say, the light of Christ within them. I say, none of these things are sufficient to authorize you to be a preacher or speaker unto the people.

Therefore, by virtue of the authority of my commission, I shall do by you as I have done by many public speakers of the nation (that because they had neither the knowledge of those things before expressed, nor commission from God) to lay down their preaching, and upon the pain of their eternal damnation; so likewise I do say unto you, being a private speaker amongst the Bemonists and Quakers, that if you shall exercise yourself in the way of a public speaker in the society of those people called Bemonists and Quakers, (for you having not the knowledge of the true God nor the right devil, nor a commission from God, you do but deceive yourselves and others).

Therefore, if you shall not lay down that practice which you formerly used, but deny this commission of the Spirit, but practice the same still, after the receipt of this letter, then I do pronounce you, Rice Jones, cursed and damned, both in soul and body, from the presence of God, elect men and angels, to eternity.

Written by

LODOWICKE MUGGLETON,

One of the last Two Witnesses and Prophets, unto the High and Mighty God the Man Christ Jesus in Glory.

A Copy of a Letter written by the Prophet Lodowicke Muggleton, to Mrs. Elizabeth Carter, of Chesterfield, dated April 19, 1664.

Dear Friend in the eternal truth Elizabeth Carter,

I RECEIVED your letter bearing date April 12, 1664, in which I understand your mother is gone into Yorkshire, and that she hath not been well, which I am sorry to hear; but yet I hope she will do Well again, and that we shall see yourself e're it be long, which my wife and others of the faith will be glad to see you; and as for my getting well out of Cambridgeshire, as for that I found no opposition at all there at that time, for I did stay but two or three days in a place, and some places but one night, so that there could be no great notice taken of me, there being a great many of the faith of this commission of the Spirit, yet many of them are excommunicated; but what will become of it know not as yet; but none of our friends are in prison, as there are for meetings, so that they not meeting is a great preservation to the believers and me also. And as for your mother's dream causing a fear to arise in her of my being in prison, dreams do not always prove true; yet sometimes they do; for when I was put in prison there in Chesterfield, your mother had such a like dream a little before it, which did prove accordingly; but now there is no such thing, not as yet; for I am very well, and do not know of any danger in that kind, not at present, though I have many enemies here at London and elsewhere, and some more fiery and bloody-minded here in London, that would destroy me if they could any ways, were it not that they fear to be hanged more than to be damned to eternity; because they look upon damnation at a distance, but hanging is near at hand; but they will find the other to be suddenly enough; and I am much threatened by one bloody-minded man, that if I should pass the sentence upon his wife, that he will do great matters unto me; and he will shew the book to the king, and he will do I know not what, nor himself neither.

So I hearing what wicked words his wife did speak against this commission of the Spirit, it happened before her mother had told me what the words all were, that the maid came where I was, and so I did send the sentence by the maid to her mistress by word of mouth; the mistress sends her man immediately in great wrath, desiring me to send his mistress the sentence under hand and seal, only that she might shew it to her husband, he being a solicitor in the law, thinking that his malice might be the more vented against me; but for that I matter not, so that I damned his man also, and bid him tell his master that he was a damned devil also, and bid him do his worst; yet nevertheless I would give his master and mistress both their damnation in writing, and let them see what they can do in it; but I would not do it at present. But what the event will be when I have sent them the sentence in writing, time will make appear. Therefore I shall say no more at present, but my love and my wife's remembered unto your mother, and Betty Smith, and all the rest of Our friends in the faith.

I shall rest and remain your friend in the true faith,

LODOWICKE MUGGLETON.

London, April 19, 1664.

I have written to you as soon as I can; for I came to London but on Saturday night; therefore I do expect to hear from you as soon as you can, and how your mother doth.

A Copy of a Letter sent by the Prophet Lodowicke Muggleton, to one Robert Beake, of Coventry, in Answer to one that he wrote to Captain Wildy, July 11, 1664.

Mr. Robert Beake,

I SAW a letter of yours, bearing date July 8th, 1664, which you sent to Captain Wildy; and in your letter to him, I understand the Captain, out of love and affection, did lend you some books and paper writings to peruse, he hoping that your understanding would have been enlightened, to have seen the truth of those things, which are written in those books and papers; or at least, that you would have; been so moderate as not to speak evil of things you do not know: which I perceive he gave you a hint of it, but it hath proved altogether to the contrary. For God hath hid the mysteries of the kingdom of heaven from the wise and prudent men of the world; for though they have eyes, yet they see not; and ears, yet they hear not; and hearts, but understand not: and you being one of these wise and prudent men the Scripture speaketh of, the mysteries of eternal life are hid from your eyes, because you are of the seed of the serpent; for this I would have you to know (though it be now too late) for your good, that whoever doth speak evil of these books and papers which the Captain did lend you, are the seed of the serpent, and hath sinned against the Holy Ghost; a sin that will never be forgiven in this world, nor in the world to come; and that you shall find to your eternal pain and shame. Think of yourself what you will, for you have showed yourself the seed of the serpent, a son of the devil, in speaking evil of the Revelation of the Spirit; which hath been declared by us the Witnesses of the Spirit; which hath been in those books and papers, which such devils as you are, are not worthy to look into; but you, from your Pharisaical righteousness, and wisdom of reason, from the letter of the Scriptures, have proudly took upon you to judge prophets that have a commission from God, and to condemn their righteousness by the letter of the Scripture; and because you shall see that you deserve to be damned, I shall relate most of your wicked speeches against those books and papers in your letter.

First. You say, you found expressions therein so uncouth, that made your soul to shrink again.

Answer. As to that I say, truth will make the spirit of reason to shrink, which is the devil; for had you had true light in your understanding, instead of shrinking, you would have rejoiced and have been glad, because the doctrine of salvation was come to your house. For every true prophet hath salvation attending on him, and blessed are they that receive him upon that account, and cursed will they be that despise him on that account.

Secondly. You say, that the authentiques thereof, you thought was to be tried by some known standard rule and balance, and the word of truth being most sovereign, you applied the matter and phrase of the papers. As to this, I suppose your meaning is, that the Scripture is the word of truth, and the standard rule, by which would try the phrase of those papers; so that you would lay those papers in one scale, and the Scriptures in the other, and you found, as I perceive, the papers too light in the balance with the Scripture. This, I suppose, is your meaning.

Answer. I do acknowledge that the Scriptures are the word of God, and a standing rule; and that which will balance truth and error. But then I must tell you, that somebody must put truth and error into the balance, who hath the same spirit of inspiration, as those had that wrote the Scriptures, (that is,) their doctrine must be as authentic as their's was, else they cannot give true judgment between truth and error, which none can do but those that have a commission from the eternal God, as those had that spake the Scriptures. Therefore, for you to weigh the phrase in those papers, in the balance of the Scriptures, or to judge of any thing contained in them, by the letter of the Scriptures, you do but procure your own damnation by it. For God never chose you, that you should know truth from error, nor to give any interpretation, for God hath chosen John Reeve and myself, and hath given the Scriptures into our hands, and hath given us more knowledge to interpret them, than all the men in the world at this day.

And yet you that have no commission nor revelation, will undertake by your reason and education, to judge whether things be agreeable to the Scripture or no; when as you do not know any one principle of religion, no more than the ignorantest man that is doth know the points of law or state affairs.

Thirdly. You say you found so much inequality in them, that if you did admit the one, you must of necessity reject the other. You, through ignorance of the spiritual meaning of the Scriptures, do judge so; but if you had understood the doctrine contained in those books, you would have found the Scriptures and them to agree, so that you would have admitted of them both. But I see it is hid from your eyes.

Fourthly. You say you know no medium in the case; either the drift or design of those papers is envious, and grossly abusive of the Spirit and way of righteousness, or the word of life and salvation is spurious and false.

Answer. Here you have shewed yourself a subtil serpent. What drift or design could we have in writing those papers, when as there was nothing but persecution and sufferings did and doth fall upon it, and wasting our estates, and losing all our natural relations; for men that go upon that account as prophets, and have such a dreadful message to declare unto the world as we have, shall find but few friends in the world to receive it, therefore our drift and design as to the world, or to obtain riches, would have been to little purpose.—And as for our errors, as you call them, grossly abusive of the Spirit, and of the way of life and salvation, here you have belied the Holy Spirit that sent us forth; for the wisdom that God hath given us, hath preached the righteousness of faith, in that we have declared the true God and right devil, with many other heavenly mysteries and secrets which are written in those books, which the Scripture did hint at but darkly, but now by us the witnesses of the Spirit made clear to the seed of faith; so that instead of grossly abusing the Spirit of life and salvation, God hath chosen us to declare the true righteousness of faith and light, and life of salvation, and also the light of the Scriptures, which no man doth truly know but those that have received it from the commission of the Spirit, which God hath given us to declare; but such reprobates as you did say as much by the Lord himself when he was upon earth, as you do by me; but as they had their reward for their blasphemy against him, so shall you.

Fifthly. You call those papers and books false, and no way the foundation of your faith and manners, and do say that God hath given you a more sure word of prophecy, and say that you should highly tempt him to listen to any insinament, or pretended discovery of his will, besides what therein are contained.

Answer. As to this, I would have you to know that those papers and books are the foundation of true faith, but as for manners, that I shall leave to the wisdom of reason, for reason the devil liveth upon manners, for the seed of the serpent hath no faith but the faith of devils, as you have; yet such subtil serpents as you are will presume to say that God hath given you a more sure word of prophecy, when as that saying was never spoken to you, being the seed of the serpent, but it was given to the apostles, and: to the believers of their doctrine, and it is given unto us the witnesses of the Spirit, and to the seed of faith, who are given to believe the doctrine and declaration of the true God, and so they understand the Scriptures, and know them, because they have believed our report. Also, you say you should highly tempt God if you should listen to any insinuations or pretended discoveries of his will besides what is therein contained.

As to that I say, you have highly tempted God, in that you did not listen unto us the prophets and witnesses, and messengers of God, who only can interpret the Scriptures, and discover the will of God which is contained in the Scriptures, though you call us insinuators, and our discoveries but pretended, but all prophets were served so by the seed of the serpent; therefore it is no new thing for us, the witnesses of the Spirit, to be called so by that generation of wise and prudent men, that think they know more than the prophets and apostles do; nay, they think that they know more than God himself, and yet the most blindest in spiritual matters in the true knowledge of the Scriptures of any, but in the matters of the world so subtil and cunning that none can go beyond them, but as dark as pitch in any true knowledge concerning eternal life.

Sixthly. You advise the captain to poise, therefore, in the balance of a sincere judgment, the expressions contained in those books, and if he find not a direct repugnancy therein to the unerring rule of righteous.

Answer. To this I say, God gave you no sincere judgment in the Scriptures, nor in those books, neither do you know the unerring rule of righteousness, so that you are very unfit to poise in the balance the Scriptures of truth, and those books; for if you had known the Scriptures of truth, you would have known those books to be truth also, and no direct repugnancy against one another, but a sweet agreement; for the Scriptures of truth are a sealed book, and those books of ours are the breaking open of the seal, that the seed of faith may see the truth and treasure written within the Scriptures; but the serpent-seed thinks himself so wise, as if he could tell or know God from the devil, truth from error, and truth to be error, and error to be truth. This was always the practice of the seed of the serpent; it was the practice of the Jews to the prophets of old, and those serpents to Christ, and afterwards to his apostles, and the seed of the serpent, such as you are, doth practice the same, thing now to us the witnesses of the Spirit; yet I would have you to know that it doth not lie in the captain's power, nor yours neither, to poise in the balance the Scripture and those books, neither of you being chosen for such a great work; for who shall judge of prophets revelation and doctrine? None will presume to do it but the seed of the serpent. Experience hath shewed me the truth of this,—for many hundreds of your seed have said as much to me as you have said, whereby they have been put in the balance of eternal damnation, and the seed of faith being but few, have been put in the balance of eternal life; for this commission hath weighed you all in the balance, and you the seed of the serpent have been found too light in the balance; for God hath chosen every true prophet to weigh in the balance, so that it doth not belong to you, nor no man upon the earth at this day, to be the judge of us the witnesses of the Spirit, but God only; for we only know the unerring rule of righteousness, and can poise in the balance of the Scripture the seed of the woman, and the seed of the serpent; and as you have done by our books, so have I done by you, I have put you in the balance among the reprobate seed, and you are found too light, notwithstanding you think your wisdom and knowledge in the Scripture to be true light; but it being the wisdom of reason the devil, and not the light and wisdom of faith, which is of God, it will be found the greatest folly and darkness of all, because it led you forth to despise and speak evil of as pure a truth as ever was spoken by prophet or apostle.

Seventhly, You would have it demonstrated to your understanding what we say to be of the Spirit, and in cases of this nature you must be dealt withal as a rational creature, and not as a brute.

Answer. I would ask you this question, whether Moses, and prophets; Christ and apostles, did direct their speech or writings to rational creatures, or to brutes? Surely the prophets' messages, and the apostles epistles were spoken to rational men and Women, and not to brute beasts. And have you been dealt withal as a brute, and not as a rational man? Are those books and papers which you have perused so uncouth, as if they were more fit to be read to brutes than to rational creatures? Do not those books and papers speak as good sense as any other writings whatsoever? And do not those books and papers interpret the Scriptures more than any writings whatsoever?

If you were not stone-blind in spiritual matters, you would have seen it, so have you not been dealt withal as a rational man, as well as others have been; nay, the more clearer the seed of the serpent have life and salvation propounded to them, or set before them, the more he despiseth it; for I must tell, you were not worthy to look into those books, for they coat you nothing but your labour to read them, which if you have not liked them, you might have returned them back again; but truth was always counted by the serpent not worth the reading, but the seed of faith thought nothing too dear for truth, but was willing, as Christ said, to forsake all for the truth's sake; but the wise and subtil serpents will not part with a penny for truth, though they know books cannot be printed for nothing. But however it is well, for every one must act acccording to the seed, the seed they are of, either towards eternal life, or eternal damnation. Also I do wonder how you, that are of the seed of the serpent, would have us to demonstrate to your understanding that which we say we had from the Spirit.

To this I say, it is as much demonstrated to you as to any others, and yet others believe it, and have the assurance of eternal life by it, and you, and such as you are, through your unbelief, eternal damnation by it; for we the witnesses of the Spirit are made a sweet savour unto God both in them that are saved, in those that are damned; and what demonstration would you have more than the declaration of the true God in his form and nature, with the interpretation of many mystical things in the Scriptures, which all the wise and learned men in the world cannot unfold; but I know by experience, that the serpent's seed doth look more at some visible miracle, and yet they read in the Scriptures that the greatest prophet that was born of woman did no miracles; so are we dealt with by the serpents in this last age, though our doctrine and declaration be more spiritual and heavenly than those that went before us, we being the witnesses of the Spirit; yet because we do no outward miracles, we are counted by the reprobate seed to be false prophets, deceivers and liars, so that we cannot demonstrate to the devil understanding by any visible sign that we are sent by the Spirit of God, but time will make it manifest to your eternal pain and shame.

Eighthly. You say, if you must receive that for truth, or this or that man that saith he hath a revelation, you must necessarily then let your faith languish after every man's revelation; and here you say am I a poor soul bewildered.

Answer. To this I say, there is no knowing of any revelation to be true, but by believing of it. Did any know Moses revelation to be true in that time, but those that believed him? Did any of those Pharisees and Sadducees, that came to John's baptism, believe that John was a messenger of Christ? Did any of the Scribes and Pharisees and hypocrites believe that Christ was the Son of God? Yet they heard that John the Baptist had revelation to declare that Christ was the Son of God, notwithstanding he spake nothing else but revelation; yet these had heard of him before, but saw no sign by either of them both, but others that believed their revelation, not expecting a sign, they did see signs also.

So that believing the declaration of men that are living is the only way to establish the soul, for there is no true rest to the soul but in pinning their faith upon that man's sleeve that hath a commission from God, and his revelation must needs be true, and happy are those that venture their souls upon it; but the seed" of the serpent thinks himself so wise, that he will allow of no revelation in himself, neither will he hearken to him that hath a revelation, for fear his soul should be bewildered; for the devil not knowing what revelation is, he will be so wise and cunning that he will neither be received with God nor with man; and this is your condition, you will not hearken to this or that man's revelation, though it be never so true, lest your soul should be bewildered.

But instead of your soul being bewildered, I am sure your soul is bewitched with ignorance and darkness in the Scriptures; you think you see, but are stark blind, and have ears, but are deaf as an adder: but it was always so with the seed of the serpent, for they always thought themselves so wise, that they could tell whether prophets or apostles revelations were true or no, but they were always mistaken, for they ever despised and persecuted them for it, even as you do by me and my revelation.

Ninthly. Here you say, Oh! Sir, your soul grieves within you that those poor souls, meaning us that wrote those books, should be involved in such strange delusions; certainly, you say, a greater judgment cannot be from the Lord here.

Answer. Here you do by us as the devils did by Christ, they pitied and shaked their heads at him when he went to suffer, as if they did grieve that he should suffer, but they thought within themselves that he suffered for his fault; that is, they thought he was a blasphemer, a deceiver, a liar, and took too high things upon him, and so was under a great judgment of God. Do not you do the same things by us the witnesses of the Spirit?

You say your soul grieves within you that we poor people, as you call us, should be involved in such strong delusions. I marvel how you, being the seed of reason, came to know what a strong delusion is, when you never was in the truth, for you never did know truth in your life; for I must tell you, it is not the reading of the Scriptures will give you to know truth, except there be a true interpreter ordained of God, which I am sure you never heard none; but true prophets and true interpreters of the Scriptures were always counted by the seed of the serpent to be strong delusions.

Therefore it is no new thing for us to be called so by you, who are a subtil serpent; and as for a greater judgment from the Lord, there cannot be here.

To this I say so to; and further I say, that if we, that wrote those books and papers, be strongly deluded, or if we be deluders, then I say, let the judgment of God be upon us here and hereafter; but if we be true messengers and chosen witnesses of God, as we know we are, then I say it had been good for you, and such as you are, that you had never been born; and a greater judgment cannot be from the Lord than there is upon your understanding, for God hath given you up to slumbering eyes, that you might despise the light of heaven, so that you might stumble and fall into the pit of eternal damnation.

Tenthly. You say, it were worth the enquiry by what method and wiles the devil doth thus infatuate poor creatures.

Answer. Here you shew yourself a devil, in that you do not know what the devil is, nor the method and wiles by which he doth infatuate or deceive poor creatures; for this I must tell you, that the devil is always mistaken in himself, for he always looks upon the devil to be some ugly thing or spirit without him, when as indeed your own soul is the devil, and that you shall find one day; and the imagination of your own heart hath infatuated your poor soul, which hath made your wits to go in this method, as to despise and blaspheme against the doctrine of the true God, by us the witnesses of the Spirit.

Eleventhly. You say, let me suggest my thoughts to you herein: is it not likely, say you, that the first entrance into this snare, was the perpetration of some conscience-wasting sin which followed the sinner, that no rest could be obtained, till it cast off the word and other ordinances.

Answer. Your suggested thoughts in this particular, is no other but the suggestions of the devil, for your thought therein doth proceed from your lying imagination; for we the witnesses of the Spirit never committed any sin, whereby the peace of our conscience could be any ways wasted for this I must tell you, that God never chose any to be prophets to declare his mind, but such as had escaped the pollutions of the flesh; and if we had not been kept innocent, God would never have chosen us to be his messengers; and this is the greatest comfort we have in this world, that we can justly say we never did this or that evil in the days of our ignorance, much less since we were chosen of God; and this is the very cause, that I have and do tread upon the heads of the serpents, by virtue of my innocency, and the commission of God. I am made as a wall of brass against many hundred of devils, and have cast them down with the two-edged sword of the Spirit that is put into my mouth; so that they have and shall fall into the bottomless pit of eternal damnation, into which place you must go; and as for our attaining no rest until we had cast off the word and other ordinances.

Answer. To this I say, no man doth own the word (if you mean the Scriptures) more than we do, for no man in the world doth truly know the word but us, and those books will testify the same; neither do we cast off any ordinances, neither of God, nor of man; for we know what ordinances God hath set up now in these last days, and we follow and practice them, and have rest and peace in it; but you have none, because you are a traditional follower of the ordinances of the apostles; and instead of entering into this snare, as you call it, it will prove a snare to you, and it will be just like Peter's net, which catched many fishes, and the good he picked out, and the bad he cast away: so it is with the commission of the Spirit, it is as a net or a snare that is set or laid to catch the seed of faith, and so they are brought home unto God, and happy are they that are caught. So likewise the seed of the serpent, they are caught in this snare, and they are cast away, even like the bad fishes, that is, they are cast into the pit of utter darkness, where there is weeping and gnashing of teeth for evermore; and this snare are you fallen into by your despising those books and papers. It would have been better for you but not much, if you had never seen them at all, you would have been damned before, but you would not have known for what; but now you will know for what you are damned to eternity for, and in this regard it had been better you had never seen the writings at all.

Twelfthly. You say, let the first broachers of these wild notions, as you call them, deal ingenuously with God and the world, and he will confess, if I be not mistaken, that there is some wide gash in his conscience, which he labours to dress up with these super-celestial, if not diabolical notions.

Answer. To this I answer, I do acknowledge that we, the witnesses of the Spirit, were the first broachers of these wild notions, as you call them; and I do ingenuously confess, that there is no wider gash in my conscience than there was before, nor so much; for my conscience is as truly justified in declaring these wild notions, as you call them, as ever Moses, the prophets and apostles were in broaching their doctrine. You would have called their doctrine wild notions if you had lived in that time, as you do mine, for they did meet with the same serpents in their time as I do now; neither do I dress up my conscience with those super-celestial, if not diabolical notions, as you call them; it would be well for you if they were diabolical notions, but you will find them to be as true as truth itself, they being broached by the Spirit of truth, therefore you are much mistaken indeed, for the devil is always mistaken in the things of eternity, and never certain in Spiritual knowledge; for, as I said before, he always calls God a devil, and the devil God; truth he calls wild notions, and the imaginations of reason, from the letter of the Scriptures, you call the ordinances of God. And this I am sure, all the notions that shall arise from the imaginations of reason, and study of the letter of the Scriptures, shall never dress up the gash in your conscience which you have made, by speaking evil of things you know not; for you have such a gash cut in your soul by the two-edged sword of the Spirit that is put into my mouth, that there will be no balm in Gilead to be had to cure you, so that it will not be whole to eternity; and I shall deal ingenuously with you, that are of the world, that I am justified of God, and in my own conscience too.

Thirteenth. You say it is the captain's duty and yours to stand in the old way, and to repair to the law, and to the testimonies; therein, say you, we have eternal life, because they testify Christ Jesus.

Answer. As for the true old way, I think the captain nor you did know; for how could you possibly know the true old way without a true preacher? And as for your repairing to the law, and to the testimony, that you cannot do, because you know hot what they are, only you have got those words out of the Scriptures, but know nothing truly what is meant by the law and testimony; for whosoever did repair to the law and testimony, they were to be tried by some commissionated man that was appointed, thereunto; so that God hath given the law and testimony into our hands, who are the witnesses of the Spirit, and you are to be tried by us, both the captain and you also. And I do find by the law and the testimonies, that you deserve to be damned to eternity; for you must not think, that because you read the Scriptures, and find such words there; I say, you must not think that you can try prophets by the law and testimonies, when as you were never chosen of God for such a work; neither do you know what the law and testimony is; though they do testify of Jesus, yet will not you find eternal life by them, because you have judged and despised those whom God hath chosen, anointed, and sealed, to be the interpreters of the law and testimony; therefore, your repairing to the law and to the testimony now, will signify but little benefit to you; so that now you are in the old way of your father Cain.

Fourteenth. You say, and his promise, he that doth his will, shall know of his doctrine, whether it be of God or man.

Answer. That is as true a saying of yours, that he that doth God's will, shall know his doctrine; but you never did know his will, therefore you know not his doctrine, whether it be of God or man; neither are those promises in Scripture made to the seed of the serpent, such as you are; but the promises in the Scriptures were made to the seed of faith, who are made to believe God's messengers; and so they come to know God and his doctrine; for the doctrine of man cannot declare what the true God is in his form and nature, and those books do, which you so much despise; but there can be expected no better from that seed you are of.

Fifteenth. Also you say, what shall we think of those precious souls, who have spent themselves for us in the Lord; you name Hooker, Cotton, Heldersham, Marshall, Burroughs, and Simpson.

These you say taught us, and brought us another doctrine than is contained in your papers.

Answer. You may think what you will of then, I know them to be false ministers, and their doctrine to be false also, because they had no commission from God to be ministers of the gospel; for he that preaches without a commission from God, cannot preach true doctrine; and as for some of those precious souls, as you call them, I know them to be damned devils; that Cotton, I Suppose, was of New England, and that Holland Simpson, I suppose you mean, was of those precious souls that spent themselves for you; it was but the devil that spent himself for the devil, for; that Cotton I know to be damned to eternity; there is none of the others will escape you speak of, before they were sent, though we the witnesses of the Spirit did not pass the sentence of eternal damnation upon them all; yet they taking upon them to preach the gospel without a commission from God, though much good may be done by it; yet it will be said unto them by the Lord Jesus, Depart from me ye workers of iniquity, I know ye not; for Christ will know none but those he hath sent; and as for that Cotton, I am as certain that man will be damned to eternity as Cain and Judas; if they escape, then he shall; and as for the other of your gracious souls, as you call them, must to damnation also, for preaching without a commission from God, because we, the witnesses of the Spirit, did not pass the sentence of damnation upon them, as we did upon Cotton; so they have not the seal of it as he had, yet they were all false, and taught a false doctrine: for this I must tell you, that no man can teach or preach true doctrine, but he that is sent of God; and those gracious souls, as you call them, did bring, as you say, another doctrine than what is contained in those books and papers; for how can a man preach true doctrine, who knows not the true God, nor the right devil; for these men you speak of, their doctrine which they brought in, was their own lying imagination, which they did imagine out of the letter of the Scriptures, merely from the strength of reason even as a tradesman doth his trade; and as tradesmen deceive others that are not skilful in that art, so did these men become deceivers by their doctrine, and you and the captain, with many hundreds more, were deceived by them, for all the hearers of them, so long as they followed them, were, and are as blind as beetles in any spiritual and heavenly matters; neither hath God forbid them to be deceivers, nor you from being deceived by them; for the blind hath led the blind, and you will both fall into the ditch of eternal destruction; and as we and our doctrine shall enter into our master's joy, because we did not go before we were sent, but have been faithful to declare the truth, as it is in Jesus, the only wise God, blessed for ever.

I have spoken of most of the chief things contained in your letter, concerning your wicked speeches against as pure truth as ever was spoken by prophet or apostle, for you would, have said as much by them, if you had been living in their times, as you do by us the prophets of the Spirit; but I perceive you think to deal with prophets as you do with priests of the nation; you can speak evil, and find fault with them and their doctrine when they please not your humour; and when they speak anything from the letter of the Scriptures that pleaseth you, you are good friends again; so that the shepherd and his doctrine must be judged by his sheep. This hath been the custom of formal christians ever since the ten persecutions; but you must not think to do so by prophets that have a commission from God; for he is no true minister of the gospel that hath no power to pronounce those blessed that receive his doctrine, and those cursed to eternity that despise it; therefore this doctrine and commission of ours will seem strange to the seed of the serpent, for little did you think, when you met with those books and papers, that you met with men that have authority from God; neither do we speak or write as the Scribes, viz. as the priests and speakers of the nation; therefore, became you shall know that there is a true prophet in England, to give judgment upon despising spirits, in that you have blasphemed against the Holy Spirit that sent us; for whosoever receiveth him that is sent, receiveth him that sent him, even God; so, on the contrary, he that despiseth a prophet, despiseth him that sent him, even the Spirit of the Lord Jesus; which thing you have done, and that in a high nature, in calling the doctrine, contained in those books and papers, erroneous, strong delusions, and the wiles of the devil, wild notions, diabolical notions, with many more wicked speeches, as I have before mentioned.

Therefore in obedience unto my commission, for these your wicked and hard speeches against the doctrine of truth declared by us, the witnesses of the Spirit, I do pronounce you cursed and damned, both in soul and body, from the presence of God, elect men and angels, to eternity.

Deliver yourself from it if you can.

Written by

LODOWICKE MUGGLETON.

July 11, 1664.

A Copy of a letter written by the Prophet Lodowicke Muggleton, to Mr. Thomas Tompkinson, of Sladehouse, in Staffordshire, bearing Date from London, December 9, 1664.

Loving Friend Thomas Tompkinson,

I RECEIVED your letter, bearing date October 2d, 1664, with the token. Also I have perused your letter, but had not time to give you an answer before now to it; neither have I time as yet, but because I am to go into Cambridgeshire before Christmas, I shall give you some lines for your satisfaction before I go, which are as follow:

I have taken notice of some passages in your letter, which I shall give some answer unto.

The first thing is, whether Christ did know himself to be the only God when he was in a state of mortality, or no? You say you cannot tell; yet the seventh chapter of our commission-book doth say he did: but Mr. Claxton, in his Wonder of Wonders, saith he did not know himself to be the only God.

As to this I say, it is not much material, whether Christ himself did know himself to be God the Father, or not, when he was in a state of morality; but the comfort and benefit that will redown to us; it is for us to believe and know, that Jesus Christ was in the state of mortality, and is the only God and everlasting Father. So that the happiness that will be unto us, it is to know and believe that he is the only God, and everlasting Father; but whether he knew himself to be so at that time, it is not much material. Yet it is my faith, that he did not know; but my happiness is, that I know him to be so: and as for the apostles knowing him to be the only God, it is not much matter neither; but that happiness that is in the faith in this commission of the Spirit, is to know more of the true God than they did.

You likewise say, for the most part you pitch upon this commission of the Spirit, and do begin to close in faith with those six principles which are treated on by me; and further you say, you have had such smugglings and strivings in your mind about your former worship, and until you could, in some measure resolve to close with me, there was nothing but trouble and vexation in your soul.

Furthermore you say you have gone to the church by fits; but now you are resolved to leave it off, though you look for nothing else but great sufferings.

As to this I say, it is well that you do for the most part pitch your faith upon these six principles; and it would be better for you if you did venture your whole soul upon them.

And as for the strugglings in your mind, about worship, there could be no other thing expected; for no man can serve two masters. For if the worship of God in Spirit and truth be the true worship, that will yield peace to the mind, as is held forth by this commission of the Spirit, then, of necessity, the worship of the nation must needs be false, and so produce nothing but trouble. For if the worship of the nation would give peace to the mind, and the assurance of eternal life, then should I have found it when my zeal was in it, and many more that can experience it as well as myself, who have believed in this commission of the Spirit.

Further you say, that, come what will come, you will venture your salvation upon this commission of the Spirit; and that you do feel those strugglings which you formerly had, to cease.

Also you say, be this truth, or no, that we have declared, you cannot help it; but must now, from that seed within you, venture upon it, in pitching your faith upon this commission of the Spirit.

And further you say, if it prove a rock, then you shall be happy, and your soul will stand for ever; and if I be a true prophet, then shall you be safe, and all those that have believed it.

To this I say, it is well for you that there is such a resolution wrought in you, as to venture your soul upon this commission of the Spirit, come what will come. For this I say to you, that nothing venture, nothing have: for if there be no salvation in this, there was never none in any; so that eternal life is but a thing ventured. For if God doth speak to a man, we that do not hear him speak, yet do believe that man speaketh truth, who saith God spake to him, we must venture our salvation on his words, else no peace will arise out of the heart. This hath been God's practice of old to prophets and apostles; and happy have they been that did believe them, and ventured their salvation upon their bare words.

And so it is now by John Reeve and myself, we being the last two chosen witnesses of God; and whoever doth venture their salvation upon this commission of the Spirit, shall not miss of eternal life, no more than those did that depended upon Jesus Christ himself; so that true faith in the thing will make your strugglings cease, as with relation to eternal salvation; neither can you, nor any other, help their believing in it, but happy are those that are so caught, and that venture their souls upon it, it will prove a rock indeed, and safe will those be who truly build upon the commission of the Spirit, in that they believe us to be true prophets. We are as true as truth can make us; and it is by faith that I myself do stand, and it is by faith that you, and all the rest of the believers do stand. For there is, nor can be, no surer standing, as to things of eternity, but by faith: so that you that believe shall fare as well as I myself; and if any would be more sure than I myself, they must seek it where they can find it, which I am sure is no where to be found, but in believing in them that God hath sent:

You say the light of life, which floweth from the interpretation of Scripture, you of late have tasted of, in that you have believed us to be true prophets,; and that is a true commission which hath proved to a refreshing of heart unto you, and so becomes water of life unto your soul, and makes you to see the truth of our doctrine.

Also you say, tho' your faith be but weak, and your knowledge but small, yet doth it put forth its hand towards this commission of the Spirit, and is willing to make itself known unto me, that so it may receive refreshments from me, as it hath already received some golden oil, which doth so chear and glad your heart, that you would not part with it for all the world; for you do perceive now that you do receive it in the love of it. So this I say, that the true interpretation of Scriptures is light and life unto the soul of man. For the Scriptures, when they were spoken by men who were inspired by the Holy Ghost, their words were spirit and life; and the true interpretation of them is as water of life unto those that understand them.

For the same Spirit of inspiration that spake them, did put life into them, so that no man can truly interpret them but such as have the same spirit of revelation as those that spake them. So that true interpretation of Scripture will be as water of life, as the speaking of them was spirit and life: for in the Scriptures is the assurance of eternal life to be found, and no where else; only this, they must have a true interpreter, which none can but those whom God hath chosen for that purpose. So that it will be happy for all those that truly understand the interpretation of Scriptures, which I perceive you do; Which have yielded you some refreshings of heart unto you, and your weak faith may grow to be strong, and your small knowledge may come to be great; and then will your refreshings of heart overflow, and continually spring as a river of living waters. For the seed of faith is a well that is never dry when it is built upon a rock; for when a commission doth smite the rock, by giving the true interpretation of Scripture, there will come water of life out of it; especially when it is received in the love of it. As you say you do; it will be as golden oil to glad your heart, and water of life to quench the thirst of sin, which is of more value than can be expressed. For there is no balm but in Gilead, even a personal God-Man, Christ Jesus, which none could, or can, declare, but us the witnesses of the Spirit. And happy will it be for all those that venture their souls upon the declarations and doctrine of us, the witnesses of the Spirit.

You further say, before you did receive it in the head, but now say you it goes down into the heart; and so your soul begins to cleave to the doctrine as to eternal life, and to cleave to me as the only prophet to shew the way to this life eternal.

And in the latter part of your letter you say you should be glad if you might receive one letter from me, but especially to hear that your condition is a condition of safety, which would be more joy to me than all the world's riches; because you believe me to be a true prophet, and so are able to judge and discern between faith and reason.

As to this I shall say but little; only this, I am glad even for your own sake, that truth did not only remain in your head, but is gone down into the heart; which I make no question but it will take deep root there, which will bring forth the fruits of the Spirit, even the fruits of faith, which is love to God, peace of mind, obedience to his worship in spirit and truth, and unto the assurance of eternal life, which is no where to be found now, but in the doctrine of the true God and the right devil, which is held forth and declared by us, the chosen witnesses of the Spirit: unto which you have given sufficient testimony of your faith in it, and that you do cleave to the doctrine and to me, as the only true prophet to shew you the way to eternal life.

And as for your condition being a condition of safety: to that I say your condition is a safe condition; and whoever buildeth upon this rock, even this commission of the Spirit, shall never fail. And for your further satisfaction, that your joy may encrease, and be established to enable you to suffer in the day of trial when it doth come,

I do pronounce you one of the blessed of the Lord, both in soul and body to eternity, which is of more peace than the tongue of man can express.

Written by me,

LODOWICKE MUGGLETON,

The Prophet of the Most High God, the Man Christ Jesus in Glory.

December 9, 1664.

And as far the book I am about, it will more wonderfully open the Godhead of Christ, than all that hath been said before by us, with many other mysterious things opened in the book of the revelation, which were not made known to us before, even almost all the chief heads in the book of the revelation, except those that I have treated on already; but I suppose it will be towards Easter before I can accomplish it, and when it is ready, you and your brother shall hear of it. And in the mean time my love to your brother.

LODOWICKE MUGGLETON.

The prophet Lodowicke Muggleton's Letter to William Cleve, near Cambridge, 1665.

WILLIAM CLEVE, I received your letter by your brother, dated March the 3d, 1665, which lines I am very sorry to hear or read; though I have heard much more than you relate, but I never did love to hear of other folks sins, but always love to hear of their righteousness; but messengers of God are always troubled with other people's sins more than with their own, neither have the sins of others been a small disgrace and disparagement to me, because they own me upon a spiritual account, so that I even could wish I had never been a messenger of God; yet I knowing it was the portion of my Lord himself, and others of his messengers, to bear the shame and reproach of the sins of others, I am made the better able to do the same; for the shame and reproach of other's sins doth reflect upon me and all in my condition, yet the punishment of sin will be to them that act it. And whereas you say you was drunk with wine and beer, and upon that you committed adultery, to that I say, if it had been but an act of drunkenness, or a bare act of adultery, though they are both wicked acts, yet they would have been more tolerable of forgiveness than this act of yours was; for you acted with one that was neither maid, widow nor wife, but a common whore; and not only so, but a defiled whore, defiled with the pox, for she is now in the hospital for cure, and you having to do with her, you have received of the same diseases with her; for Doctor Powell doth affirm you have it, but not quite cured. Also he doth upbraid Mr. Fort, me, and all the believers that own me; saying this is their faith, they can get the pox and then come to me to be cured; he speaking this to Mr. Newsome and you, so that we are all ashamed to own such believers; that so this commission is mightily ashamed by those things lying heavy on us all. But I have no occasion to aggravate your sins, but would rather have smothered it, neither should I have discovered it to any, though the cry of it hath been sounded in my ears by others; yet I stopped even my ears against it, as one not willing to hear, and the reason why, because you own truth; but had not the power of truth in you, which power I could not, nor cannot give if it be not planted in your nature. I cannot help that, and as for my speaking peace to your troubled soul, I would to God I could do so, and be justified in my own conscience; but I cannot speak peace to sins of that nature, though your sin is not that unpardonable sin which can never be forgiven in the world to come. But your sin is more hard to be forgiven in this world, than the other; for the sins you have acted it carries the curse immediately along with it all the days of a man's life; but the other aforesaid may do well enough in this life; but the curse will follow hereafter. So that this is all that I can say unto you, that for my part I shall neither justify you nor condemn you; neither will God condemn you himself for it; but if you can by your faith, repentance and newness of life, encounter with your sin, and recover the peace of your conscience, and the health of your body, I shall be very glad you may; for sin is a strong enemy.

So I must leave your faith and the guilt of your sin to strive together, and which getteth the victory, will be Lord; and sol rest in sorrow for you,

LODOWICKE MUGGLETON.

A Copy of a Letter wrote by the Prophet Lodowicke Muggleton, to Mrs. Ellen Sudbury, London, Feb, 10, 1665.

Dear Friend in the eternal Truth, Ellen Sudbury,

I RECEIVED your letter, but when it was written I know not, being not dated; but however, I am glad to see your own hand-writing, and more glad to hear of your health, and of your husband's health also. Likewise, it is no small comfort to me, to hear that you are so sensible of the benefit you have received by believing in the true God, and that peace and satisfaction you do find in the death of God: and as you say none can take it from you; indeed none can take it from you; for your faith being built upon that rock, all the powers of hell cannot prevail against it, not so much as to raise a doubt, or a question within you, as concerning your eternal happiness. This experience doth teach me the truth of it, and so I believe it doth you, with divers others also. And this true faith in you, it will be as a well springing up to eternal life, which will cause your peace and joy to fill up, and overflow, and run over; which thing is hid, the knowledge of it, from all people in the world; but only those that build their faith upon a true commission. And this I may speak further for your comfort, that this is the best time for the seed of faith to live in, as hath been since the creation of the world, notwithstanding the many troubles that are in the world at this day, and more troubles are yet like to ensue. But happy are those which have a peace which the world cannot give. For as many prophets and righteous men did desire to see that day as the apostles did, when Christ was upon earth, so I say many of the holy and elect seed, that have died these fourteen hundred years, have desired to see that day which we see, but could not; for what happiness can be greater unto man, than to know his eternal happiness in this life? which thing cannot be made known but by a commission from God: so that now is the best time, in relation to truth, that ever shall be to the world's end.

So, being in haste, I shall take leave, having little or no temporal news, only this, the sickness is very little now in London; but it is supposed this summer will produce much trouble otherways, both by sea and land; but time will shew the effects what they will be.

So I shall say no more, only my love, with my wife's love, remembered to yourself, and to your husband; supposing you have received John White's letter before now; I rest and remain,

Your friend in the true faith,

LODOWICKE MUGGLETON.

London, February 10, 1665.

A Copy of a Letter written by the Prophet Lodowicke Muggleton, to Mrs. Dorothy Carter, of Chesterfield, bearing date Feb. 7, 1665.

Dear Friend, Dorothy Carter,

I RECEIVED your letter about two weeks ago concerning a young man, called John Matten; indeed I have been so busy about a troublesome business for a friend ever since, so that I could not spare time to give you an answer, neither is it yet quite ended, but I suppose that this week it will; yet because I would not have you stay too long, I shall give you an answer as short as I can.

First, I perceive this young man's heart was not right, when he said to Thomas Marsden, that the devil had his mysteries, as well as God had his mysteries, The thing was true enough, but I perceive the words proceeded from a naughty heart, or seed; that is to say, those words were spoken in way of vilifying, or slighting the mystery of God. But to let that pass: I perceive he was smitten a little upon it, but did recover his peace again. But after this, I perceive, he being in league with a maid, who was contrary minded, yet, for fear of losing her love, and her friends, and his own friends love, and fears of persecution together, the temptation of these things did cause him to go to church, even against the light of his own conscience, and so withdrew his affections from you, which formerly he had.

Now I say these are sad omens, or signs; for truth is a straight and narrow way, yet the seed of faith may easily go through this narrow gate; that is, keep the heart entire to the doctrine and worship of this commission of the Spirit.

Thirdly, I perceive he is afraid he is not of the elect seed, and that if he were sure of his eternal happiness, he would not matter the maid, nor any of the sufferings of this world, and such like.

Indeed I cannot blame the man for making such a sure bargain with God, that if God would give him eternal life in one hand, and the losses of the world, and the things he doth affect, in the other hand, I confess then, if he should refuse eternal life, and embrace the other, he would be counted a very fool; but it was always God's practice to propound unto men and women, that if they would forsake, father and mother, brother and sister, nay, wife and children, for his sake, then they should receive eternal life.

So that man must forsake all those things that offend the conscience for it, and trust unto God whether he will give us eternal life or no, and not that he should give us the assurance of eternal life first. But who is it but they would forsake this world, so they might have a better bargain first? But man must give God the heart first, and trust to God for the reward, and no doubt but God will give men a better thing, for he is faithful and true.

And as for his marrying one of this faith, let that fall how it will, you need not matter that, if the seed within him doth not lead him to it, let him alone in that matter; and as for the trouble of his mind, and his fear of the loss of heaven, I cannot see how it can be otherwise; for when a man shall seem to receive truth, and rejoice in it for a season, and afterwards fall away for fear of some loss of friends, and persecution; and not only so, but worship contrary to the light of his conscience: I say, these things will cause trouble of heart enough, and his condition bad enough.

And as for my administering to him: to this I say, that I cannot tell how to administer comfort unto him, not for the present in this thing, so likewise I shall administer no discomfort; but in regard he hath not sinned the unpardonable sin, though his sin was very nigh it; therefore I shall leave it to the seed within him to work it out; so that I shall neither help him in it, nor disable him to encounter with it; but if he be of the true seed, he will overcome it in time, and be settled in the truth and peace of his mind.

This is the consideration I have of your letter, and of, his condition, and accordingly you may demean yourself in your judgment and carriage to him, as you shall see how the seed doth work in him, either for peace or trouble; neither do you provoke him to write to me, but let things proceed from himself what he is moved unto.

Dear Friend,

I received your daughter's letter, dated February 10, with the letter inclosed to Mrs. Ward, and accordingly I delivered it unto her, and I received of her twenty shillings according to your desire. I shall pay the thirty shillings in Gracechurch-street as soon as I can meet with the party. Also I marvel you speak never a word whether your mother received Elizabeth Slater's book, with a letter by the carrier of Chesterfield. It was sent about a month ago.

I confess I received this letter from you, concerning John Gratton, about that time you should have received the book, so I did expect to have heard of the receiving of it in the next, but I heard not a word of it; but I hope it doth not miscarry, though mentioning of it be forgotten.

So not to trouble you any further, only my love to yourself, and all other friends with you. We are all pretty well here at London at present.

So I rest and remain your friend in the true faith,

LODOWICKE MUGGLETON.

London, February 17, 1665.

We shall be glad to see your daughter according to the time you speak of.

A Copy of a Letter written by the Prophet Lodowicke Muggleton to Charles Cleve, a Believer of the Commission of the Spirit, living then near unto Cambridge.

Loving Friend Charles Cleve,

I HAVE perused your lines concerning your brother, and as for the writing or speaking himself, I matter it not, but like it the better that you write it, so I know the better that you are not ignorant how things are with him, though I knew more of the business before than he hath related to you, or that you do yet know, as you will perceive in these lines to him.

And because you may not think it strange that I will nor cannot speak peace to him, as I have done to others, you may know, that I never knew any sin like unto this, since I knew truth, but Mr. Nusom's only. But when I considered that Nusom got his mischief before he came to own truth, besides, it was hid from my eyes that he had the pox, but it went under the name of canker; for had I known what it had been, and by what means he got it, I would not have spoken peace unto him, let his repentance be ever so true or great; but my word being past, I could not call it back again when I did know of it; for sins of this nature are not common, for those sins always carry the curse with them: so that I cannot speak peace to such sort of sinners if I know it: for these two men owning of me hath brought more disgrace to me and this commission, than all the sins of all the believers in England besides; and not only to me, but to all others of the same faith: so that I am very sorry for you also, in that your affections are related to him by the bond of nature as well as of profession, and the more in that no balm can cure that sore but the blood of God. And his faith must arise out of its own seed, and be very strong, else that wound sin hath made will not be cured. So that I shall neither judge him to be of the right seed, nor of the reprobate seed, but should be glad he might recover the peace of his mind by faith, soberness, and chastity; for if he can do that, it will do well, for no such gross sinners will go unpunished in this life. And whereas you say he is resolved to persevere in the belief of this commission though he perish.

To that I say, there is no danger of perishing in the belief of truth, but a preservation and blessing in it; so that for my part, I had rather no man should believe it but myself alone, if they should perish by it; for sinners cannot say they lose by truth, no not in this life, but it is sin that doth cause men to perish in this life and that which is to come; for such believers, are a great disgrace and reproach to truth, and; better it had been for such they had never owned truth, and form also, then should not truth have been dispagraged as now it is. But these things must be borne by prophets and saints; for this I must tell you, that the doctor saith, that your brother's body was more foul with that cursed distemper procured by that unclean woman, far more than Mr. Nusom's was, which grew so long upon him.

I thought good to give you a hint of these things, because I perceive he hath made you acquainted with part of his sin; for had not the curse followed the sin, he would never have confessed it to you, nor to none alive; sq that you may do as you please. Let him hear this letter to you, or not, which you think convenient. So I shall say no more at present, but rest

Your friend in the true faith,

LODOWICKE MUGGLETON.

London, March 15, 1665.

A Copy of a Letter written by the Prophet Lodowicke Muggleton, to Mr. Thomas Tompkinson, of Sladehouse, in Staffordshire, bearing Date from London, March 17, 1665.

Dear Friend in the true Faith, Thomas Tompkinson,

I RECEIVED your letter by a friend, William Hall, which came lately from Mrs. Carter (it was dated Feb. 11, 1665,) and I am glad to hear of your joy and confidence in the truth, and that your wife is so stedfast in the faith of this commission of the Spirit. She will lose nothing by it, neither in this life, nor in the life to come, if she hold out to the end; neither need you much to wonder how much faith should hold all the reprobates in the resurrection to eternity. For I say unto you, this earth is big enough to hold them all, if they were ten thousand times ten thousand more than there is, or will be, at the end of the world. For consider, half the world will be saved, count children of the elect seed, and the reprobate seed; for all children will be saved dying in their childhood; though of the reprobate seed, they shall be raised to the same glory the angels are in, from whence their father, the lost angel, fell.

And as for your being chosen church warden the next year, my advice unto you is, that if they choose you, either fine, or else hire a man in your room, and he will take a churchwarden's oath; for it is unlawful for any believers to take that oath, or to serve that place here in London. Any man whose conscience is tender, or not tender, may either fine or hire, which he please; for there is very few places of this nature in England, but money will buy them out; but if men will go against the light of their own conscience to save their money (as I have known some do) I cannot help that; but it is better to part with silver, than to part with peace of conscience,

I perceive you have received John White's letter; so I shall say nothing unto that, nor concerning the thing you speak of in your letter, but I shewed him your letter, and I suppose his letter to you doth specify something concerning the thing you speak of. But what contract is between you two I know not, but a little glimpse of it, so I shall leave it to you two to treat about it.

This is all at present, only my love to yourself and your wife, and that we are all well at present. I rest and remain,

Your friend in the true faith,

LODOWICKE MUGGLETON.

London, March 17, 1665.

A Copy of a Letter written by the Prophet Lodowicke Muggleton, to Mr. Joseph Whitworth, at Abbots-Bromely, in Staffordshire, bearing Date May 19, 1665.

Joseph Whitworth,

I RECEIVED a letter from you, bearing date April 16, 1665.

In your letter I find something of the seed of faith to arise in you concerning this commission of the Spirit, though there is not that full satisfaction, not as yet, in the thing declared by us, the witnesses of the Spirit, as there is in others, who have more experience of the doctrine of the true God and the right devil, with many other heavenly secrets declared by us, than you have heard of yet.

Nevertheless, your faith in time may arise to that perfect assurance and full satisfaction in your mind as it hath in many others at this day.

Further, I must tell you, that there hath not been a mail upon the earth that hath had the assurance of eternal life abiding in him, not this 1350 years, 'till this commission of the Spirit came forth into the world.

Yet this I say, many were saved through election in that time, but had no assurance of it in themselves; for this is the great benefit people have by a commission, they do by faith attain to the assurance of their particular election, and so consequently to the assurance of their eternal salvation. And it is to be attained to no other way, but by faith in him whom

God doth send; for the true ambassadors of God can declare what the true God is in his form and nature, and what the right devil is in his form and nature, the place and nature of heaven, the place and nature of hell, the persons and natures of angels, and the mortality of the soul.

On these six principles, the knowledge of them, dependeth all the eternal happiness of mankind.

These six principles, and many more heavenly secrets, which were never made known before by prophet or apostle, are declared and published by us, the witnesses of the Spirit, in those writings set forth by us.

And as you say, if you had read them all, most of your queries, if not all, would have been answered.

But I perceive you have had but a little of them, and how the case is with you,

I shall take so much pains as to give answer to your queries, though there is greater things in print, and that which will satisfy the heart of man if understood.

But to satisfy your desire, I shall answer as followeth:

First query is, Whether God. hath elected some men and women to eternal happiness, and reprobated others unto endless misery, or not?

Answer. As to this I say, That God hath elected some men and women to eternal happiness, and reprobated others to endless misery.

This was the faith of Moses, the prophets, and apostles; also it is the faith of us, the witnesses of the Spirit: for God said unto Moses, *I will have mercy on whom I will have mercy, and whom I will I harden.*

This was spoken in relation to Pharaoh, and to rebellious Israel, and with relation to Jacob and Esau.

Therefore it is that the apostle Paul doth instance Jacob and Esau, to those Jews in his time that did question God's election.

All the apostles preached of election, but more especially the apostle Paul doth use many arguments for it, as may be read in the epistle to the Romans; so that he was mighty strong in his faith for election and reprobation; for who shall lay any thing to the charge of God's elect?

So that you must mind, that if there be a number of people elected of God, there must of necessity the other number of people be reprobated of God; for if all were elected, what need there be any talk of reprobation, or eternal damnation?

And if any shall say it was a temporal reprobation, as many have done,

To that I say, the election and reprobation the Scripture speaketh of, it was altogether in relation to a. spiritual and eternal happiness; for if God loved Jacob and his seed, and hated Esau and his seed, he was reprobated.

So that there is two seeds, namely, the seed of Adam, and the seed of the serpent; Esau being the seed of the serpent, therefore reprobated; Jacob being the seed of the woman, that is, the seed of Adam, therefore elected.

So that there being two seeds, there must needs be election and reprobation, for both cannot be saved. This was the faith of the prophets and apostles, and is the faith of us the witnesses of the Spirit.

Second query. And as for those who are so elected, whether by generation according to birth, who are the sons of Adam to eternal felicity, and those which are the sons of Cain to endless misery or not?

Answer. To this I say, That the election of God it lieth in the seed; that is, the seed of faith, who are the sons of Adam, are all elected; for all the seed of Adam, which do become persons, so as to be born, they are all elected. Only this is to be minded, that election comes by generation; not that God doth elect persons after they are born, but in the seed: so that when the seed of faith doth get the pre-eminency in the conception, and so a man or woman comes to be born, they may be said to be of the elect seed. But no person can know his particular person elected, but by faith in the true God; which true God cannot be known but by a prophet, as Moses, the prophets, and apostles, and us the witnesses of the Spirit, who were chosen witnesses of God.

So that election comes by generation, but no man or woman can know they are of the elect seed but by believing in those messengers whom God doth send; and their doctrine and declaration being true, the believers of them do come to the certain assurance of their election, both in the seed and of their persons, So likewise it is on the contrary with the reprobate; that is, when the seed of reason gets the upper hand in the conception, and so a man or woman comes to be born, they may be said to be reprobated persons, they being reprobated in the seed, for reason is the seed of the serpent; so that the whole person is so to be reprobated, being the serpent's seed, though he knows it not. But he that doth know his own election, shall as certainly know another to be a reprobate; for he that doth not know certainly another to be a reprobate, I say he doth not know certainly his own election. I speak not this of children, but of those capable of men and womens estates.

Third question. How a man may know whether he be of the elect seed or not?

Answer. To this I say, as before, that it is known in believing the true messengers of God. So a man comes to know his own election, and another's reprobation; and in knowing a man's own election, he hath certain assurance of his own eternal happiness, and certain assurance of the reprobate's eternal misery.

Fourth question. Whether after the belief of this commission, there will be any divine light, as a testimony evidencing in the believer's spirit a perfect assurance of his election, or not?

Answer. As to this I say, that there is in the true belief of this commission a divine light, that doth witness and evidence in the spirit of true believers of it, that doth give perfect assurance, both of their election, and of their eternal salvation. This many can witness unto at this day in England, and some in those parts where they live beyond the seas.

Fifth question. Whether for resolution of any spiritual doubt, or removal of any eternal calamity, a man may address himself by prayer, to the divine majesty, or not?

Answer. To this I say, we lay no bonds upon any believers in that case, but leave it to their own freedoms. For this I see by experience, that some believers, whose faith is weak in the time of temporal calamities and troubles in eternal things, will make some application unto God, and it doth procure some satisfaction to their spirits, either to bear it more patiently, and willingly submit unto it, or else they find deliverance from it; yet God taketh no notice of their prayer, for the deliverance, it doth come from the seed within them; for God doth not work by outward and visible deliverance, as he did formerly, but more spiritual and invisible, because this is the commission of the Spirit,

So likewise some believers of this commission, their faith is so strong that they do not make any supplication unto God in the time of temporal calamity, and by faith they bear it, and do find as good deliverance as those that do pray.

So that whether you pray, or pray not, it is faith and knowledge that doth deliver in the day of trouble; so that you, or any believer of this commission of the Spirit, may do what they will in the matter, even as their spirits are moved unto, or their understandings are informed; for it will do no hurt, if it do them no good, if they know not how to satisfy themselves otherwise.

Sixth question. Whether this commission doth require the observing, or keeping any one day particularly, or particularly apart, for the service of God, as the two former commissions, or not?

Answer. To this I say, that this commission doth not observe any one particular day, for any worship, or service of God, as the former did; because the believers of this commission do worship God in spirit and truth. For no people under the sun doth worship God in spirit and truth, but the believers of this commission only: so that every day is a sabbath unto us. As to the rest of our minds concerning our eternal happiness, we can say we have rested from all our labour, as God did from his creation: so that we are not bound up in our minds, as all outward worshippers are, to meet every first day, and so bring themselves into trouble, for that which God doth not command. For though God commanded the apostles to observe the first day, and they laid the same upon their believers, that is nothing to Englishmen; for this is to mind that people are to observe every commission in its time and place. So that when Moses and the prophets commission was in being, the people ought to obey it; every commission in its time and place; so when Christ and his apostles commission was in being, the people in that time ought to obey it; so now the commission of the Spirit is in being, that ought to be obeyed. And look what worship is set up by these three commissions, in their time and place they ought to be obeyed, though they differ one from another; nay, they are observed and obeyed by the true believers of them, and not as all the world doth, to observe them traditionally; for Quakers and all other opinions do observe the sabbath, or first day, but traditionally.

Seventh question. Whether it may be any matter of conscience for a man to put off his hat, or to use the language of *thee* and *thou*, or to give titles of honour to the great men of the earth?

Answer. To this I say, that it is no matter of conscience for a man to put off his hat, but is only a civil custom used in the nation where we live; neither is it any tie laid upon the conscience of any man, neither by Christ himself, neither by any prophet or apostle; neither do we read any where in Scripture, that men were required to keep on their hats, though the blind Quakers do make it one of the chiefest articles of their faith; and as for the language of *thee* and *thou*, that may be used or not; for a man to tie himself to thee and thou to all persons, as kings and magistrates, this is but a traditional practice, imitating prophets of old, who were equal with kings, nay, whom princes have called them Lord, yet every silly man and woman, if they get to be Quakers, they will cry *thee* and *thou* to kings and magistrates of the earth; nay, they would count it a great sin if they should do otherwise.

This is a mere taking up of prophets and apostles words by tradition.

And as for giving titles of honour to the great men of the earth, to that I say, that great men of the earth, as kings, princes, and magistrates, they are called, in Scripture, Gods, though they die like men. And we find in Scripture, that prophets and apostles have given titles of honour unto kings and magistrates, as prophets have said to kings, *O king, live for ever*: As Daniel and Paul said, *Oh king, Agrippa!* and *noble Festus:* so that prophets and apostles did give titles of honour to magistrates. But if it be your lot to see that letter which I have sent to Thomas Taylor, in Stafford, that would inform you further in these things. If you do enquire for Thomas Barnet, of Utoxeter, perhaps he will shew it you; and if you did but see that book of mine, called The Quakers Neck Broken, you would see further in those things. I suppose William Newcombe, of Derby town, a bookseller, can help you to it.

Eighth question. Whether, after the belief in this commission of the Spirit, a man may fall back, or not; if so, whether there be a possibility of returning again, or not?

Answer. As to this I say, after a true belief in this commission of the Spirit, there is no possibility to fall away, (that is) if there be true faith in the heart; but if it be but a brain knowledge, or only in the head, he may fall back away, and never be renewed again. For this I must tell you, that all those that did seem to own the apostles doctrine of the gospel, and did afterwards decline from it, and turn to the law of Moses, they may be said to have faith in the head, and not in the heart. For none can be truly said to fall away, but those that fall away from the truth; and none can declare truth but he that is sent of God. Now the apostles being sent of God, all those that did seem to own their doctrine in their time, and did afterwards decline from it, and turn to the law of Moses, they may be said to fall away, that they had no true faith in the heart, but in the head only. For there can be no falling away, not properly, but they that fall away from truth, or from a true commission, when it is in being upon the earth. For men may fall away from all opinions of religion, or faith, upon the earth, and yet be safe enough; because all opinions in religion in the whole world are taken up by tradition from the letter of the Scriptures.

And so mens' faith become traditional also: so, that men may easily fall away from that traditional faith, and yet be never the worse. But if any shall fall from that faith he did seem to have in a true commissionated prophet, he shall never return again, but will certainly be damned to eternity. But if true faith doth arise out of the heart, he shall stand sure, and never fall; but shall have the testimony and assurance in himself of eternal salvation. For this I have observed by experience, since God made me a messenger to declare his will, I have observed three sorts of faith, or conditions in man. Some men I have seen to have faith and knowledge in the head, and pot in the heart: others again I have observed to have faith and, true knowledge in the heart, and not in the head. Others again I have observed to have true faith and true knowledge in the head and the heart. All these things I know by experience. Now there is but one of these three that is capable to fall away, namely, he that hath it in the head only; yet if a true prophet hath but charitable thoughts of him that hath it in the head only, he shall stand the longer. But if the prophet's good thoughts shall be taken from him, he will fall immediately, and his hopes within him will perish and die. But if men shall have true faith in the heart and head both, or in the heart only in this commission of the Spirit, they shall never fall away, but shall have the assurance of eternal life abiding in them. This many believers in this commission can witness so at this day.

Thus, as short as I can, I have given you an answer to your queries, which may somewhat more satisfy your mind as to your queries; but in the reading of the books, as to the true doctrine concerning the true God and the right devil, and the interpretation of Scripture, the books will give a great deal better satisfaction to the spirit if understood.

There is a young man of this faith that saw your letter, hath sent you a book, called, The Interpretation of the 11th of the Revelation, by your friend John Terry, with a letter also; his name is John Saddington: so that if satisfaction be not found in the commission of the Spirit, I say it will be found no where. For this I must tell you, that whoever owns free-will, as to the saving of his soul, after he hath heard of this commission of the Spirit, and of the doctrine of election and reprobation, declared by us, the witnesses of the Spirit, I say such will perish to eternity, let their righteousness be ever so great, or think of themselves what they will. For Moses did hold forth the doctrine of election and reprobation, and declared much against free-will, saying, *It is not in him that willeth, or in him that runneth, but of God, that sheweth mercy. And on whom he will have mercy, he will have mercy; and whom he will he hardeneth.*

Also it is the faith of us the witnesses of the Spirit, and of the believers of it, who can witness in their own spirits, that they are elected, and have certain and full assurance of their eternal salvation, and as certain that others are reprobated to endless misery.

But I shall say no more at present, but rest and remain,

Your friend in the true faith of Jesus, the only true God,

LODOWICKE MUGGLETON,

London, May 19, 1665.

A Copy of a Letter written by the Prophet Lodowicke Mugglelon, to one John Hyde, living in Jewen, a bookseller, bearing date October 27, 1665.

John Hyde,

I AM informed that you have very much exclaimed against me, as if I had dealt unjustly with you, as if I had done you a great deal of wrong, and not only so, but that I did gripe and exercise lordship over the consciences of others to keep myself in idleness. These are the best of your expressions; so that I shall not take much notice of them, though you have shewed the naughtiness of your heart, and a lie in it. But the thing I would discover unto you, and wherein your heart hath not been right is this: did not you proffer to bind me a quarter of a hundred of books single towards the printing, because you could not spare money, and that you would have one for yourself; indeed I was unwilling you should do it, and was loth to accept of it, and I said I would pay you for what you did bind for me, not expecting that you should be at the charge, no not so much as to buy one, or to work one out in binding; but you pressed upon me again and again to make up the quarter of a hundred. And you may remember I did ask you, in Mr. Medgate's shop, whether you did intend to have one of them altogether for the binding of a quarter of a hundred? and you said you would have one single. Mr. Medgate doth remember it. But if you would have had them altogether, you should have had them altogether, for that would very near have been worth the binding of them, for you did ask me but 5d. a piece to bind them, neither are they worth any more.

Likewise, did not you, when I was with you, with Mrs. Carter's book concerning the silver bosses, when I paid you 11s. for her book, and my wife's book, did you not then ask me to send so many books as would make up the quarter of a hundred, which was fifteen then wanting. So, through your pressing of me unto it, I did send by my wife, fifteen to make it up; for this I must tell you, if you had not pressed me to it, I would have bound no more than what I had present need of, but would have paid you for those ten that were done before, and there would have been an end of that business. For you might have had so much reason in you, that I would not go bind so many books to lie by me, for they will go off as well unbound as bound. So that the thing would have been no benefit to me to lay out so much money, and take it in by 6d. at a time, perhaps it may be a year or two before I receive the money in again.

Again, if you did not intend to perform your promise, why did you keep back that one book, according to your agreement, as if you meant to perform your promise; for if you did repent of your promise, you should have sent that book also, and a line or two, that you did repent of your promise, and I would have sent you money to the full, though they were bound contrary to my desire. But through the wicked hypocrisy of your heart, you take offence at me, and rage and rail against me, as if I were an unjust man, or had done such an unjust deed to you, by cutting off such a sum which you did expect. But this I would have you to know, that it was never my nature, when I was in my lowest estate in this world, to covet or encroach upon any, to get any thing from them., no not to the rich; and as to the poor, I was always tender of taking any thing from them, but would rather add unto them, even of that little that I had; though I had power, and now have power, to command what I think fit of those I know can or may perform it, yet I never did in my poverty, much less now in my plenty; for I considered their condition to be mine own, and that I would not have been dealt so by; so that the power I now have, did no ways alter my natural temper in this matter; neither have I got this plenty, whereby I stand in no need of any man, but all men do stand in more need of me, than I do; of them. I say I did not get this plenty out of the saints, but Providence hath given it me by my wife, else perhaps I might have been more troublesome to some of the richer sort of saints than now I am. But to let that pass: I will shew you wherein you have shewed the greatest piece of hypocrisy, that I have found in any man or woman, since I came to know truth: for you have acted just like Ananias and Saphira the Scripture speaketh of, who pretended to bring in their whole estates, and lay it at the apostle's feet, as if they were true believers of the apostle's doctrine, but the root of bitterness was in their hearts; they pretended one thing, but did another; that is, kept back part of what they pretended to give unto God. For whoever maketh a covenant with an apostle or prophet, he maketh covenant with God; and so Ananias became a liar unto the Holy Ghost, in that he did not perform what he pretended to do. And you may read what the effect of that sin did amount unto; for if he had not freely and voluntarily pretended such a thing, he might have kept his estate and his life both; for who required that thing at his hand? For he might have done with his own estate what he would, but when it was given unto God he could not; even so it is with you. Did I require any thing of you towards the printing of this book? Was it not your own proffer? Who required these things at your hands? But you pretending, as Ananias did, to be one that did believe, you would, as other saints did, offer up a sacrifice unto God, to help to promote the truth. And because I did accept of it, you revile and speak evil of me, as if I had done you wrong. Have you not done as Cain did, offered up a sacrifice unto God, that God will not accept of, but reject it altogether? For if the messenger of God doth reject it, it is as if God did reject it; for my soul doth abhor such a piece of hypocrisy, that shall pretend to give any thing for the honour and glory of God, and then repent of that deed, and not only so, but revile and speak evil of those they give it unto; for this I must tell you, that your sin is as bad as Ananias his sin was to Peter; for you have not only lied unto the Holy Ghost, but have spoken evil of it also; for I am as true a prophet as Peter was an apostle; so that Ananias did tell a lie unto the Holy Ghost no otherwise than what was in Peter. And have you not done the same unto me, though not in the same manner: for this I must tell you, it is a dangerous thing to dally with edge-tools; that is to say, it is a dangerous thing to make covenant with prophets, and not to perform your covenant, though you lose thereby. You must not think to deal with them as you did with other men. But seeing you have, through the hypocrisy and deceitfulness of your heart, acted like Ananias and Cain, as aforesaid, your sacrifice is rejected of me, and of God also; for I shall not accept of it, neither will God afford you any peace in it, but altogether on the contrary.

But this is not all: I understand that you, out of the pride, malice, and stubbornness of your heart, even with great wrath and gnashing your teeth, you expressed yourself thus, that if I did damn you, you would damn me, and that you had as great power to damn me as I had to damn you, if not greater, or to that purpose. Likewise you said, that I could not damn God's elect. I cannot damn God's elect; but if you had been one of God's elect, he would never have suffered you to have fallen into such a deep pit of eternal destruction; neither can any man be sure of his election, but by faith in the commission of God. But I will not stand to dispute that now, though I could give many reasons for it. Also you did threaten, that if I did damn you, then you would discover me what I am, as if you would persecute me, and those of this faith, but in what manner, and how, I know not But because you may execute your malice, I shall give you occasion enough to do it, for I had as lief you should do it as any other, if you can; for I shall serve you as Christ did Judas, he gave him a sop, on purpose that Judas might betray him; so likewise you shall have a sop given you, that if it is possible you may do as Judas did; so that your own fears and words may come upon you; for you have said many times, that you thought you should be damned by me, when as I thought not of any such thing, so that you said you had as good be damned at first as at last. This fear hath been in your heart ever since that business of Mrs. Harris, ever since your heart hath fallen; and according to the thoughts of your heart, it is now come upon you. Therefore, for this wicked piece of hypocrisy, about the books, and not only so, but for your unjust belying me, as if I had a desire to encroach upon you, and upon others, and your proud, malicious, insolent speeches against this commission of the Spirit, with many other wicked speeches, which would be too tedious to name, therefore, by virtue of my commission received from God, I do, for these wicked things aforesaid, pronounce John Hyde cursed and damned, both in soul and body, from the presence of God, elect men, and angels, to eternity, by

LODOWICKE MUGGLETON,

One of the two last Prophets and Witnesses to the High and Mighty God, the Man Christ Jesus in Glory.

You may now shake hands with Mr. Colebrooke, for your portions will be both alike, only I would advise you to take the money for binding the books, there is 7s.

6d. inclosed in your letter; you had as good receive it as not, for God hath rejected it, and I have rejected it. And further, if you will carry that one book more, which you have, to Mr. Medgate's, you shall have 3s. for it, and then you will have your full price for the quartern of books, at the rate of 5d. a-piece, which was your own demand, and so you may be rid of the doctrine as well as of the commission.

I would wish you to let that book go also, that you may have your money altogether; for it hath cost you dear enough in all reason, so that it is great pity you should miss of it.

October 27, 1665.

A Copy of a Letter written by the Prophet Lodowicke Muggleton, to Mr. Martyn, Minister of Orwell, in Cambridgeshire, dated from London, January 16, 1666.

I UNDERSTAND that you had a desire to see me, and to have some discourse with me, and that you were at a place in Orwell, to enquire for me. And not only so, but you brought also with you the high constable, and petty constable, and another man, to discourse with me. Do you think that any man that hath any wisdom, that can give any reason of his ways, Would think that your intent was good, to bring your armies with you, to discourse with a naked man; and not only an army of men, but great officers of the temporal sword, that they might not only bear witness of what words should pass between you and me, or catch me in what questions you should ask me; but, if they could have got nothing of me worthy of persecution, then, by virtue of the power of those two constables, you would have laid hold on me, as a deceiver of the people.

These things have been acted by such serpents as you, in former times, to prophets, apostles, and to Christ himself. How oft did the priest? and Levites, such as you are, tempt the Lord Jesus, by asking him questions, thinking to catch him in his words, that they might have therewithal to accuse him, before the temporal power!

It is not long since that I was served so by a priest or minister so called; and so caused the temporal magistrate to commit roe to prison. But what this minister got by it! It was no less than eternal damnation, which will assuredly be upon him, as it is upon murthering Cain, who killed his brother; and Judas, who betrayed his master; for how is it possible any persecuting spirit, who persecute men for conscience sake, not breaking any temporal law, should escape the damnation of hell? For this I must tell you, that persecution, merely for conscience sake, is the sin against the Holy Ghost; but more especially for men to persecute true prophets upon the account of deceivers, there is no pardon for this sin. But I have found by experience what the power of a prophet is, and I have; found by experience also? that none are so great enemies: to true prophets, as those called the ministers of the nation are. I find the prophets in the law were: persecuted more by those sort of men than any; and I have found those sort of men more active than any in persecution. So that the seed of the old serpent, the devil, it doth run in the line of those sort of men; it is as natural for those sort of men to persecute for conscience sake, and persecute prophets, and so sin against the Holy Ghost, as it is for fish to swim in the water; so that I do no ways admire the thing, but do see it must be so, and it can be no otherwise. But this I would have you to know, that if your intent had been real, then would you have come alone, and have discoursed with me privately, and not to bring great officers of the parish with you, to hear us discourse: so that your intentions were not good towards me, but by consequence very evil; and it was the ready way to have procured the sentence of eternal damnation. But in regard I do not hear that you did any ways revile and speak evil of me, or of the doctrine declared by me, by calling it blasphemy, or me a deceiver, or such like terms, whatsoever your intent was in bringing those men with you.

These things considered, I shall wave the sentence of damnation upon you at the present, for this your wicked intent towards me; only this yoke I shall put upon your neck, by virtue of my commission from God:

The thing is this, I understand that you, being a pretended minister of the gospel of Jesus Christ, (I suppose you will own yourself a true minister of the gospel of Jesus Christ; else what do you get up into a pulpit to preach to the people?) For yet you professing yourself a minister of Christ, I hear you present, or cause to be presented, divers of your parishioners for not coming to church. Is this the practice of a true minister of Christ? Surely no. Did you ever read in Scriptures, that any minister of Christ did so? Do you follow the example of the good shepherd? The Lord Christ speaketh of the good shepherd having an hundred sheep, and one of those sheep went astray, the good shepherd left the ninety and nine to seek that which was lost, or gone astray; and when he had found it, what did he do to it? He brought it home in his arms, and did nourish it and cherish it, and took more care of that which was lost, or gone astray, than he did of all the rest, that never went astray. This is the property of a good shepherd.

The moral is this: every true minister of Christ is a shepherd, and the people of his parish are his sheep, and the shepherd doth feed his sheep with such heavenly pasture; that is, with such saving doctrine, which giveth the sheep assurance of everlasting life; so that their souls are fatted with the joys of heaven, in the full assurance of everlasting life; and this heavenly pasture, it casteth out all fear of eternal death.

This ought to be your practice and your power, if you were a chosen minister of Christ; but how contrary to a true minister do you act: for if any of your sheep be gone astray to error, as you call it, and dissent from your worship, then, instead of bringing them home in your arms, and giving them bread to eat, and water to drink, to nourish their bodies, and good admonition, exhortation, and the true interpretation of the Scriptures, to feed their souls; instead of this, you present them, and labour to excommunicate them, and send forth the constables, church-wardens, and officers, to apprehend them, to bring them before the temporal magistrates, and so cast them into prison, or else get the wool off their backs, and leave them bare.

Is this the practice of a true minister of Christ? I suppose any conscientious man would be ashamed to own himself a minister of Christ, and yet do these things; but it is the custom of most national ministers to do so; therefore I do not marvel at it; because I know there is none of you chosen ministers of God; but being chosen by men, ye act as men, yea, as wicked men.

And seeing you are made a minister by men, and from men, and not from Christ, why are you not contented with that wages that men have appointed for you, and let mens consciences alone.

Therefore I shall say unto you as John Baptist said unto those soldiers that asked him, saying, And what shall we do? You know his answer was, They should be content with their wages, and do violence to no man. So I say unto you, be you contented with that wages the parish hath allowed you, and present and persecute no man for his conscience.

So, as I am a minister, messenger, and ambassador chosen of God, by virtue of my commission from him, I shall lay this burthen upon you.

That if you shall present, or cause the constables, church-wardens, or other officers, to present any man or woman under your ministry, for matters of conscience, or for not coming to church, let the people be of what opinion soever (always provided they pay you what is allotted for you, and the parish, and state-assessments;) but if you shall present, or cause to be presented, any, for the causes aforesaid, after the receipt of these lines;

Then, from the Lord Jesus Christ, the only wise God, I do pronounce you cursed and damned, both in soul and body, from the presence of God, elect men, and angels, to eternity.

LODOWICKE MUGGLETON.

A Copy of a Letter written by the Prophet Lodowicke Muggleton, to Mr. William Fershall, High Constable of Orwell, in Cambridgeshire, bearing date from London, January the 19th, 1666.

Sir,

I HAVE heard of you these four or five years, and I always heard a good report of you, for a moderate spirited man, and that your spirit is naturally inclined to peace and quietness; and that you are not naturally inclined to persecute any man for his conscience in point of worship: yet I hear, through the instigation and desire of the priest of your parish, that you, with the petty-constables, and the priest, did consent together, pretending to see me, and to have some discourse with me. And now what your intent was in it, I shall leave that to yourself; but that I know that your intents could not be good, towards me: for I know if you follow the advice of your minister, your intent cannot be good, but altogether evil; for it hath been the practice of the priests and Levites, in all ages, to persecute the truths and true prophets. So they did by the Lord Jesus himself; for it was always their practice to propound questions to entrap and ensnare the messengers of the Lord; and when they have words from a man, so to ground persecution upon it, then they turn it over to the temporal magistrate, and officers of the civil government, to put their wicked malice and hatred of truth, under the pretence of high blasphemy, or else horrible opinions, or great errors: I say, they turn it over to the temporal powers, and the temporal officers must put their wicked minister's intent in execution.

This I know by experience; for I have tasted of the priests cruelty before now. And this I suppose would have been the case now, had the priest and you met with me. But I am sorry that such men as you should be priest-ridden, to go a persecuting strangers at his desire and request, without a warrant: surely you did it out of ignorance, not knowing the power of an high constable, that he may choose whether he will stir in such cases without a warrant; or else you did sympathize with the minister, Mr Martyn, in his wicked design towards me. One of these two must be the motive to move you to go along with him. But I shall impute it to the want of the knowledge of your own power, rather than any desire of persecution in you. Therefore suffer me to give you a word of advice, and do not think scorn that such a one as I should give you advice; for I have given some judges of the land advice in point of persecution for conscience; how that judges of the land ought to mind the laws of the land, and to give righteous judgment according to law, and not to meddle with mens consciences in matters of worship; the conscience belongeth to God. What have judges to do with errors in judgment, there being no laws of the land broken, they ought not to meddle with any thing but what belongeth to the temporal law; so you being high constable, you ought to mind the place you are in; you are to keep the temporal peace where you live, and if any warrant come from any higher than yourself, if it be for treason, murder, felony, tumults, or such like, you are to search houses, or raise aid, and take prisoners such as are found guilty of such crimes, or suspected to be such persons, with many other such things of the like nature; yet all these things belong to the temporal laws: what is this to spiritual matters? What if a man be accounted a blasphemer, an heretick or deceiver, by an ignorant clergyman, or shall dissent from his parish church, through the tenderness of his conscience, will you exercise your temporal power to punish such men as never did you wrong, nor cannot break any of the laws, of the land? Yet because men are not of your opinion of religion, therefore they must be apprehended and persecuted to please the minister's malicious humour.

Therefore this charge I shall lay upon you by virtue of my commission from God, that if ever the minister of the parish, or any other, shall desire you to send after me, or any other person, upon a spiritual account; but if you shall voluntarily seek to satisfy the wicked wills of persecuting spirited men, being not forced unto it by a warrant, you ought not to stir at the request of any one whatsoever. For if you do persecute me upon this account, there being no temporal law broken, or any, other person for conscience sake: if you shall do these things aforesaid, after the, receipt of these lines, you will commit that unpardonable, sin against the Holy Ghost, and so be found a fighter against God, and; by consequence damned to eternity. For what have you to do with a man that is a free-born man of England, as yourself is, that cometh peaceably to see his friends?, Do we at London serve any of your country people so? Do we molest any of you, be you of what persuasion soever, provided you break not the king's peace?

I would have you to consider these things aforesaid before it be too late, and remember you were forewarned by one of the two last prophets and witnesses of the Spirit unto the High and Mighty God, the Man Christ Jesus in Glory.

Written per me,

LODOWICKE MUGGLETON.

London, January 19, 1666.

A Copy of a Letter written by the Prophet Lodowicke Muggleton, to Mr. James Brocke, bearing date from London, March 30, 1666, directed to Mile-End, near Stepney.

Friend James Brocke,

I RECEIVED a letter from you, wherein I perceive you have heard and seen divers papers concerning the Jews: and further you say, that I am charged, as though I were in an error concerning the Jews call, as doth appear as they say, (that is, I suppose enemies do say) from the 46th chapter of The Divine Looking-Glass: so that it seems that it doth lie upon you as a great weight and burthen, so that you see no way to get it off you.

Also you desire to be satisfied of me what the Lord hath revealed to me concerning those people of the Jews so much spoken of, that you might be satisfied yourself; and that you might stop the mouths of others, who are gainsayers, that do upbraid you with this, that it doth now plainly appear, as they say, that I have not truth on my side, in regard that I have written of no calling of the Jews into their own land, when the contrary (say they) is already manifest.

I was unwilling to give any answer to these things, because the thing is of no concernment whether the Jews be called into their own land, or not, what is that to the matter of salvation, whether they be or not? The truth is nevertheless on my side: neither need your spirit be ever the more troubled, in case you be thoroughly satisfied and grounded in the knowledge of the truth, that will thoroughly satisfy your spirit as to the matter of your salvation: so that no cavilling devil whatsoever need to trouble your mind, as to the foundation of true peace, though it lieth not in your power to answer every cavilling question that people shall ask from the letter of the Scriptures; neither will you be able to stop the mouths of gainsayers, though your knowledge in the Scriptures were greater than mine, or all mens knowledge in the world besides. You must not expect any such thing; and as for their saying that truth is not on my side, that is a small thing for me to bear: was there ever any prophet, apostle, or Christ himself, but the devil said they were liars, and in errors? Did not the Jews, who were devils, serve Christ himself so? Did he stop the mouths of those devils, notwithstanding his wisdom was so great that never man spake like this man, as it is said in Scripture? Yet he could not stop the mouths of those gainsayers, notwithstanding his great wisdom. And if he could not do it; how should I do it, much less you? It may be enough for you if you can satisfy yourself in those that are of absolute necessity unto salvation. As, first, the knowledge of the true God in his form and nature. Secondly, the right devil in his form and nature. Thirdly, the place and nature of heaven. Fourthly, the place and nature of hell. Fifthly, the persons and natures of angels. Sixthly, the mortality of the soul. The knowledge of these things are of absolute necessity unto salvation. These, with many other heavenly mysteries that are treated on in our writings, that whoever hath the true knowledge of these, things aforesaid shall not want peace of mind, though he cannot answer to every question the devil can ask from the letter of the Scriptures; but, however, I shall give you some answers to these things concerning the Jews, that you may be a little better satisfied in that point, if you can understand it; and that you may see there is no contradiction between the Divine Looking-Glass and the Scriptures.

First, As to Christ's people, called the Jews, which you have heard and seen so many letters of, who doth such mighty wonders, who are going to their own land; you are not sure it is true; nor nobody else; for I am informed,; it is nothing else but a point of state policy of the pope, and his council, to fill the minds of people with such things, that are at such a distance that none can disprove it; so that other things, that are of more concernment, for the state of the nations, might not be minded; for all people's minds in all Europe are striving after some deliverance or privilege but what it is they would have they do not know.

Secondly; if it were so indeed that those people were in such a great body as it is indeed reported of them; yet, this I say, there is never a one of them that doth, or will believe in that Christ, or Messiah, that died at Jerusalem, Which we believe in; for those Jews go to act over the law of Moses again, and their Messiah is yet to come; but ours is come and past.

Further, this you may observe, that these Jews in the Turks country are the children of those that put our Lord to death, whose father said, *Let his blood be upon us and our children*. So that these Jews will never be converted and believe in that Jesus which their fathers put to death; for his blood is upon them to this day, and will be to the end of the world; so that if they should get that land which Moses gave unto their fathers, yet they will never believe in that Christ or Messiah that we believe in, no. not traditionally, as most of Europe doth: so that I say, those Mosaical Jews will never be called to the faith of the gospel, neither do we in our writings meddle with the Jews going into their own land; if they do, that will be little benefit to me, or you, or any one else, as to our eternal happiness. But for their being called to the faith of the true Jesus, the only wise God, I am sure they never will be; nor those that upbraid me with truth not being on my side, neither is the contrary yet come to disprove me, nor ever will come.

Thirdly, I would willingly inform your judgment of the difference between those Jews the Scripture speaketh of, that shall be called to the faith of Jesus, and those Jews that shall not. This you are to mind, that there was many of the Jews nation that were moderate men, that had no hand in the death of Christ, neither did they give them their voice for the crucifying of Christ; so that the blood of Christ was not upon them and their children. Therefore mind what I say, in the destruction of Jerusalem, which was a matter of forty years after Christ's death, I say, then was all the innocent Jews taken by the Romans, with those Jews that were guilty of Christ's bloody and those innocent Jews, many of them being mixed in marriages with the Roman Gentiles, they have brought forth a generation of Jews of another nature, and of another profession. As thus, those Jews that kept to their own tribes in marriages, they professed only the law of Moses, they deny the gospel of Jesus, those shall never be called as aforesaid. Secondly, those Jews that mixed marriages with the Roman Gentiles, these Jews being of another nature, they are called to another profession of the gospel of Jesus: but I must tell you, it is but to an outward profession of the gospel; for few or none of those Jews do understand the faith of the gospel, though they profess it no more than the Gentiles do; for it is the power of the Gentiles that doth set up the gospel worship all over Europe.

Further, I shall distinguish who are Gentiles, and who are Jews, that do profess the gospel in a literal way: the Gentiles are all the priests and episcopal; these two sorts of people that profess Christ they are not Gentiles: the Presbyterians, Independents, Anabaptists, Ranter, and Quaker, are for the most part all Jews; and those all do profess the gospel of Jesus in the letter; but few of them in the spirit; so that saying is fulfilled, *Many are called, but few are chosen*; that is, many are called to the outward profession of Christ, but few that truly understand what this Christ is. Nay, I myself am one of those Jews of the tribe of Levi, according to the seed or spirit; and not only so, but God hath chosen me the last man to declare truth to those Jews and Gentiles, and many there is called to hear it, but few that truly believe it; yet some there is both of Jews and Gentiles that do truly understand and believe in the true Jesus, which is the true God, these things I do certainly know.

So that if you can understand these things here written, you will no more be troubled at the devil's words concerning the Jews: also, you will say, that truth is on my side, and will be on my side to the end of the world, when I am dead and gone; so I shall leave you to consider of these things, and if you can understand them you may be the better satisfied, because this is a universal interpretation, therefore more hard to understand.

So I rest your friend,

LODOWICKE MUGGLETON.

March 30, 1666.

A Copy of a Letter written by the Prophet Lodowicke Muggleton, to one Mr. Fletcher, of London, June 25, 1666.

Mr. Fletcher, who, as I understand, was formerly a Blacksmith by Trade, but now a Solicitor in the Law,

I UNDERSTAND that you are the man that hath managed Pittman's business against Mrs. Butler; and not only so, but you have got the better of it, your wisdom and subtilty being greater than ours in the tricks and queries of the law, which we were unacquainted with, though Mrs. Butler's case was as just a case as ever was, for Pittman did abuse and dishonour her good disposition very much, and he abused me much more, for I came in a fair way to Pittman, and told him Mrs. Butler had sent me a letter to receive the goods into my hands, and that I should pay Mr. Pittman half a years rent; and withal, she sent Pittman a discharge of her own handwriting, which discharge was given into his own hand; but he had not patience to read it himself, nor to hear any body else to read it, but did rage and rail at me upon a spiritual account, and called me blasphemer, with other base speeches, and did threaten to throw me at the fire back; whereupon I did pronounce Pittman damned, soul and body, to eternity, and he shall be sure to suffer those eternal torments according to my word, for he hath blasphemed against the Holy Ghost, a sin I am sure God will never forgive.

And I understand that you are so offended at me for passing the sentence of damnation upon Pittman, so that you have blasphemed against the Holy Spirit that sent me, and have raged and railed at me, and have called me blasphemer, a rogue, and have threatened me to persecute me, and to use your best endeavour that possibly may be to have me in jail in three weeks time, with many other venomous and envious railing speeches; which, since that your soul doth thirst after my blood, if you could take away my life, and not be hanged for it, I am confident you would do it if you could; yet I know no wrong I ever did you by word or deed, for I do not know you, neither do you know me; neither did you or I ever speak together as I know of, yet I am so railed at and abused by your evil tongue for nothing. Did you ever hear me speak evil of you for managing the suit in law against Mrs, Butler, though I was concerned in it, but I did rather commend you for it that did things so wisely, that you made a bad cause to be good in law, when as the innocent and true cause was overthrown through our innocency, and our ignorance together; yet in all this I never spake evil of you, not in the least, but could have wished I had known you before, that you might have been employed for Mrs. Butler's case, which was a just, righteous case; for certainly, if you did so well for a devil, and an unjust cause, certainly you would have done much better, when your wisdom had acted itself forth for an innocent person as Mrs. Butler, and her just, righteous cause, as before said; so that your best course would have been to have minded your suits in law, and have rejoiced that you overthrew the innocent in her right, which she must suffer patiently; yet this gives no content, except you could be revenged on me for damning Pittman.

What need, or zeal have been so great for Pittman's damnation? There was nothing said against you concerning that, you shall have minded the law of the land as aforesaid; for this I shall affirm to you, or before any judge, that God hath cursed and damned Pittman's soul and body to eternity, and he and his wife did Ananias and Saphira (his wife) like, consult together out of envy to me, to do Mrs. Butler that wrong to detain her goods against her order.

Therefore I say this, the Lord do so unto me, and more also, if the Lord doth not avenge himself upon Pittman and his wife, for their wicked, unjust dealings in this thing, and their blasphemy against God.

And now I shall speak a few words to you, Mr. Fletcher, who was before-time, as I understand, a blacksmith by trade, but now a solicitor in the law.

I do not repeat this out of any disparagement unto you. but because I know more men of that name Fletcher; so that I would not have the reflection of this; letter to reflect upon any but the right person, because I do not know your other name; so that the thing is this, that I shall say unto you, inasmuch as I perceive that you are of the seed of the serpent, a son of Belial, even a son of the devil, a reprobate, whom God hath appointed to be damned to eternity, therefore hath God raised you up, that he might shew his power upon you, in that he hath left you to sin against the Holy Ghost; and not only so, but you have vomited and breathed out cruel, threatening, envious speeches against me, who am innocent, who never had any discourse with you in my life; but I know your malice is, because I am the messenger of the most high God, and that you shall know to your eternal pain and shame, the wickedness you have committed, for which you must be damned. It is these, and such like; as, first, you called me a blaspheming rogue. Secondly, that I was a cheat and a deceiver, and it was pity I should live. Thirdly, and that you would persecute me what you could, and that, if it were possible you could by the law, you would have me in a jail, with many more cruel, envious speeches, which could not be spoken but by a reprobate devil, appointed to be damned, to one that scarce ever saw the man, and never asked me a question, neither spiritual nor temporal; yet this evil hath proceeded from you. And do you think in your conscience, if I were not a messenger of the Lord, but only an innocent man; I say, do you think that you can do these things, and yet escape the damnation of hell? Let any sober man judge between you and me.

Therefore Mr. Fletcher the solicitor, as I am the messenger of the most high God, for these your blasphemies against God, and your cruel murdering desires, and your wicked speeches against me, without a cause as aforesaid, I do pronounce this Mr. Fletcher cursed and damned, both in soul and body, from the presence of God, elect men and angels, to eternity.

This is the sentence of the Lord God upon thee, and because it shall surely come upon thee, neither shall you escape what I have said, for thy wickedness is great, and thy sin is gone up to heaven, and crieth for vengeance; therefore I say unto thee, God be judge between me and thee in this matter, and let God do so unto me, and more also than I have said to thee, if I shall do this without a commission from God; or if this thing doth not come to pass, which I have said unto and upon thy person, body and soul, then let it be upon me, that you and others may know that God hath honoured a man so far as to give sentence of eternal damnation upon the souls and bodies of reprobate devils, who speak evil things they know not.

LODOWICKE MUGGLETON,

I know you would gladly have something to accuse me of by the law of the land; but I would have you to know, that I cannot, break any of the laws temporal; so that I suppose the judges of the land will not meddle with things that do not belong to the law, that is, with things spiritual, for that belongeth to God, and to those whom he will chuse; for spiritual commissions are quite different from temporal commissions; and as judges of the land have commissions from the king, so God's messengers are judges, and have their commission from heaven; and the judges of the land, they judge according to the tenor of their commissions; so God's messengers, who are judges, they judge according to theirs, and they both have a rule to judge by; and you see, that when men have committed such things as the law saith, whosoever doth them shall die: you see likewise the judge giveth sentence for the man to die. Is it the judge that puts that man to death? Surely no; it is the man's: breach of the law that puts him to death; so that the judge is not to be blamed, but to be honoured, for giving sentence according to law: so likewise it is with God's messengers, for they are judges of spiritual things. Now, if a man shall sin against the Holy Ghost, or shew himself to be of the reprobate seed, if God's messengers shall give sentence of eternal damnation upon such a man, shall the man so condemned by God's messenger, fly in the man's face, and say it was the messenger of God that condemned him to eternal death? No, it was the mans sin that condemns him to eternity; the messenger doth but give sentence according to the demerit of the sin, just as the temporal judge doth in the case beforesaid.

So I say, as certain as you Fletcher and Pittman have seen many a one put to death, or hanged after the judge hath given sentence upon them, so certain do I and others see that you must to the damnation of hell. Now the sentence is passed upon you, deliver yourself if you can.

But because it is not executed upon you immediately, you may think there is nothing in it, but you will find it soon enough; for if such as you had lived in Moses time, you would have been cut off presently; for Moses did not stay long when the ground opened its mouth, and swallowed up those rebellious devils, such as you are; so those Elijah destroyed with fire from heaven, were such as you are; so Elisha, Isaiah, and other messengers of the Lord, and the apostles, as Peter, the sentence of these messengers of God, they were immediately executed; and had you lived in that time, you would surely have gone to the pot immediately with them; but your damnation doth neither slumber nor sleep.

Also, I understand you do intend to have the Lord Chief Justice's warrant for me, and that you have a great many of the damned crew to witness against me. Indeed they may truly witness they area company of damned devils, that have sinned against the Holy Ghost; and for my part, I shall witness before the justice, the thing is true, they are damned indeed; only I would desire you, when you go to the Lord Chief Justice for a warrant, that you will present this letter of your damnation to his honour, and see if his honour will give you any encouragement to prosecute me upon this account. I believe his honour will do, as other judges have done, he will say it doth not belong to the law.

How will such devils as you do then, for such matters as these do not belong to the law. It will be your best course to take Mr. Dagget along with you, for he and you have been brethren together in iniquity in this business of Mrs. Butler's and Pittman's, notwithstanding I did advise him to the contrary; but I perceive he hath ventured his eternal damnation upon Pittman; so according to what he hath done in relation to that letter, let it be unto him: but this I must say of Mr. Dagget, he is a far more moderate devil than thou art, for he acts more serpent like, but thou acts like a fiery dragon devil; but God will, by his mighty power of faith in me, see his Vengeance brought upon the dragon, and upon the serpent; so I shall stand still, and wait upon my God, and in a little time I shall see the downfal of most, or some of these my confederate enemies; so I shall see what you can do according to the laws of the land.

I have been more large than I did intend; but because these lines may be seen by more than the party himself, it was necessary people should understand the ground of things, so they may the better judge of these things.

LODOWICKE MUGGLETON,

The true Messenger of Jesus Christ.

June 25, 1666.

A Copy of a Letter written by the prophet Lodowicke Muggleton, to Mr. Harrison, called Minister of Blithfeild, in Staffordshire, dated from London, October 6, 1666.

Sir,

I UNDERSTAND you took a book from Joseph Whithworth, entitled, The Interpretation of the 11th of the Revelation; but I suppose it was by the justice's order that you had it to peruse, the justice conceiving that you were better able to judge of it than himself, you being a clergyman, or a pretended minister of the gospel; for pretended ministers of Christ, or false priests, having no commission from God for such a great work, they always become enemies to true prophets, apostles, and to Christ himself; none so great enemies and persecutors of truth as false priests, and false ministers. This the Scripture doth witness for truth.

Also I do understand that you did call the doctrine and interpretation of that book blasphemy and deceit, and a lie, with divers other wicked speeches against the doctrine contained therein; and not only so, but you did rail against me, the author of it, calling me a blasphemer, and a deceiver, and that you did believe that I was a Jesuit; and that you did believe I had received orders from the pope to divulge these things to deceive people withal, in regard my name was unknown unto most people, it being not a common name. These, and such like words, have proceeded out of your mouth, which doth discover unto me what your heart is: also I do see further into your heart, in that you did breathe forth threatnings of persecutions against me, in that you said I deserved fire and faggot, with other cruel punishments, as if you did not know what punishment was great enough for me. These, and such like words of yours, they shall be a witness against you in your own conscience, and God, angels, and men shall witness against you, that you have sinned against the Holy Ghost, as those Scribes and Pharisees did, which called the spirit and power by which Christ wrought those wonderful miracles, they called it a devil, so they sinned against the Holy Ghost. In the same manner have you sinned that unpardonable sin, which will never be forgiven you in this life, nor in the life to come, for you are the absolute seed of the serpent, a son of the devil. This I do certainly know, for none but that reprobate seed, whom God hath blinded their eyes, lest they should see the truth, when true light shineth before them, would have said as you have done; for this I must tell you, whosoever despiseth an embassador of Christ, despiseth him that sent him, and sinneth against the Holy Spirit that sent him, as you have done, in that you have blasphemed against as pure a truth as ever was spoken by prophet or apostle; for the same God that gave them authority to write the Old and New Testament, the same God gave me authority to write those things you have so much despised, and you shall find your blasphemy against those things punished with the same punishment as those that sinned against the Holy Ghost, when the prophets, apostles, and Christ were in being upon the earth.

This is not all, for you have shewed what a murdering devil you would be, if it did lie in your power; no less than burning at the stake, or some greater punishment, would satisfy your devilish spirit, could you accomplish it; just as the old serpent devil Cain, your grandfather; and bloody Bonner, your father; you know my meaning. But this I say, though you cannot accomplish your will, yet I know your desire is set on the fire of hell; therefore, according to your desire to me, it shall be done unto you; and look what measure you would have meted unto me, it must and shall be meted unto you again; for you have committed high blasphemy against the Holy Spirit that sent me, and in calling the doctrine contained in that book blasphemy, deceit, delusion, and a lie, with other wicked speeches against things you know not, which books such devils as you were not worthy to look into; and also for your serpentine nature, that would, if it were possible, persecute me to the death as aforesaid, a man that never did you any wrong, nor never saw you in my life to my knowledge; but by your own words you shall be justified, and by your own words you shall be condemned; therefore in obedience to my commission received from God, I do, for the aforesaid blasphemies against the Holy Spirit that sent me, and what measure you would have meted unto me if you could, the same shall be meted to you again, as burning and the like, I do pronounce Mr. Harrison, minister of Blithfield, in Staffordshire, cursed and damned both in soul and body, from the presence of God, elect men and angels, to eternity. Your body, which is now your heaven, shall be your hell, and your proud and envious spirit shall be your devil; the one shall be as fire, and the other as brimstone, burning together to all eternity.

This is the sentence of the Lord's messenger upon thee, and thou shalt remember that thou wert told so by a true prophet. Deliver yourself from it if you can.

LODOWICKE MUGGLETON.

To satisfy your evil mind that I have no orders from the pope, you may know that I was never above twenty miles by water in all my life, and that I am no Latin scholar at all, only I can read English, but not so perfect as many others can, yet God hath given me more knowledge in the Scriptures of the true sense of them in the English sense than any man in the world, so that I need not travel to the pope to learn knowledge from him. It was never the practice of prophets and apostles to seek after learned men for heavenly knowledge, for prophets and apostles were taught heavenly knowledge of God; so it is with me, my knowledge is of God, and not by education and learning from man. Also I am a freeborn Englishman, and a freeman of London by birth, and born there, and never was out of England in all my life: also I am known by person to thousands, and by name to hundreds, and to many that never saw me; so that you need not so much wonder at the strangeness of my name. Also I have been in three several prisons upon this account, and have had many persecuting enemies, and in every persecution against me there was a priest, or that you call a minister, with others that persecuted against me; but they got but little by it, but procured their further damnation; for what hath the law to do with mens damnation? The law cannot justify that which God condemns, for a sentence of damnation cometh not within the compass of the law. And so it was said by one of the judges of the land when I was tried; the judge said, the matter did not belong to the law, so I was quit: besides, I have had to do with a many of your priests, both episcopal and presbytery, and all other speakers; so that I have not been so obscure, but have been known to all sorts of people, though not to every particular man; so that you need not to question what I have said concerning you, for I shall justify that sentence upon you, and others of your coat, before any authority whatsoever, as I have done in former times.

I thought good to write these few lines, to satisfy your malicious spirit in that matter, concerning my going to the pope, (as you did suppose) and what I am, so that you may doubt no more of that matter; so that you may turn your persecuting spirit some other way, if you can tell how to state the malice of your heart according to law; you may do it, and see if that will ease you of your eternal damnation.

LODOWICKE MUGGLETON.

October 6, 1666.

The prophet Lodowicke Muggleton's Blessing to Mrs. Anne Lowe, now the wife of Alexander Delamaine, senior. Given to her July 5, 1667.

Dear Friend in the eternal Truth, Mrs. Anne Lowe,

ACCORDING to your request I shall write these lines as followeth: first, I looked upon you to be one of the blessed of the Lord, and seed of faith, before your aunt died; but I knew the seed was smothered and stifled in you through some temporal occasions, which could not be avoided, so that the seed of faith in you could not grow to perfection; no, not so much hardly to be seen; yet I saw, in that time of darkness, that there was a love in you unto the truth, though your knowledge and experience was very weak, yet I had a good opinion of you, that in time the seed of faith in you would spring forth, and appear in its own likeness; and, according to my thoughts of you, it is come to pass, which I know your own experience can judge of it; for now you can tell, in some measure, what difference there is between light and darkness, and between ignorance and knowledge.

Secondly, I do perceive, within a short time, even since your aunt died, that your faith hath grown very much, to receive a prophet in the name of a prophet, else would you not have requested such a thing at my hands; and because you would be sure you would not be satisfied with a word from my mouth, but would have it under my handwriting, though the word of a true prophet is as powerful to the party concerned, either in blessing or cursing, as writing is, only the party concerned cannot look upon words when they please; neither can they shew them to others, as they can writings, when I am dead and gone.

Therefore, to satisfy your request in this thing, I shall say this unto you, that I have so much discerning of what seed you are of, even of the seed of the woman, which is the seed of faith, that blessed seed, and not of the seed of the serpent, which is the seed of reason, that cursed seed; so that I am fully assured in myself, and do steadfastly believe, and my faith hath no doubt in it, neither in the blessed, nor in the cursed. Therefore, that you may be assured of your eternal happiness and salvation, without any doubt, I do, by virtue of my commission from God, and the faith I have in your eternal happiness, I do pronounce thee, Anne Lowe, one of the blessed of the Lord, both in soul and body, to all eternity; so that you need not fear, as Jacob did, when he received the blessing of his father Isaac, he feared a curse instead of a blessing, because he stole the blessing; yet, being blessed by the father that had power to bless, he was blessed, and it could not be taken off him again: so I say by you, being blessed by the last true prophet of the most high God, who hath power given him from heaven so to do, thou art blessed to eternity, and none can take it from you again.

Written by

LODOWICKE MUGGLETON,

One of the two last Prophets and Witnesses of the Spirit unto the High and Mighty God, the Man Christ Jesus in Glory.

July 5, 1667.

A Copy of a Letter written by the Prophet Lodowicke Muggleton, to Mrs. Ellen Sudbury, November 4, 1667.

Dear Friend in the eternal truth, Ellen Sudbury,

MY love remembered to you and your husband; I received your letter, and am glad to hear that you are both well; but as for those slanders and evil reproaches that are cast upon me by the damned crew, it is a small thing counted by me, for they did so by Christ, the only God, when he was upon earth, and would do so to him now if he did appear in mortality as I do, though now the seed of reason doth honour the words of the true prophets and apostles, who said by Christ, *never any man spake like this man*; but the seed of reason the devil did think then, never any man spake like him for error, pride, and blasphemy. What! make himself equal with God? The same case is with me, though I know never any prophet or apostle did or could speak, or declare those things as I have spoken or declared, and the seed of faith doth and will know it to be true what I have said and written; neither do I speak this out of any pride, but out of perfect knowledge, for true knowledge hath no pride in it: also I know the blessed of the Lord will witness unto it; and the more the devil layeth slanders and reproaches upon the truth, the seed of faith will be the more strengthened in their faith; for I am as a mark for every wicked man to shoot at, yet the archers cannot hit me so as to wound me, though many arrows have been shot at me, but my knowledge, revelation, and power remaineth in as full strength and power as ever. I know William Watson's brag of George Fox's book, and so are many more of the Quakers people; but that will yield them but little peace. Also I am desired very much by some that have been Quakers, but are come to own this, but are very weak, not able to give a reason of their faith in this, desireth me to write an answer to George Fox's book, which thing I have begun, and as soon as I can I shall perfect it.

I received the fifteen shillings, and I thank you for your kindness, and your kinswoman or friend for hers, and so doth Mrs. Bladwell, she is alive still, but very weak of body, but as confident of her eternal happiness as ever; also I have sent your kinswoman or friend a book all bound together, the price is ten shillings, they were always so. Our friends here are all pretty well, but in Cambridgeshire Charles Cleeve hath buried his wife, which is a great trouble to him for the present. This is all at present, but my wife's love remembered unto you. I rest your loving friend,

LODOWICKE MUGGLETON.

A Copy of a Letter written by the Prophet Lodowicke Muggleton, to Elizabeth Hooton, Quaker, January 26, 1668.

Elizabeth Hooton,

I SAW a letter of yours sent to James Brocke; it is supposed that you are the mother, or some relation to that Samuel Hooton of Nottingham, who was damned to eternity by me in the year 1662. It is no great marvel unto me that he proved such a desperate devil, seeing his mother was such an old she-serpent that brought him forth into this world. Also it is thought, that Dorothy Carter did give sentence of damnation upon you, as one of the seed of the serpent; but seeing it is not certainly known unto me, and in that you have written cursed, and many blasphemous speeches concerning me, for in that you have blasphemed and cursed me, whom the true God, the man Christ Jesus, hath sent; you have blasphemed against God that sent me, and have sinned against the Holy Ghost; and look what judgment is given upon your soul and body by me here in this life; God himself doth approve of it and not reverse it. If your letter had been only concerning James Brocke, I should have left it to him to struggle with you, though I know those curses you have pronounced against him, they will fall upon your own head, and not upon his; and what he said concerning George Fox, it was nothing but truth, and George Fox shall find it so in the end. But seeing the greatest part of your letter to him is against me, I shall give some answer unto it.

First. You charge me to be a sorcerer, and have opened (as you say) my mouth in blasphemy against the God of heaven and earth, and against the saints of the most high, meaning you Quakers.

Secondly. You charge me with a cursing spirit; and say, that woe and misery will be the portion of us both, meaning James Brocke and myself, and that it had been good we had never been born.

Thirdly. Be it known (say you unto us both) and to all our wicked crew, as you call them.

Fourthly. You say, woe unto thee, Muggleton, thou child of the devil, thou enemy of all righteousness.

Fifthly. You say, cursed shalt thou be in thy going out, and in thy coming in; and say, thou art a damned devil, as thou hast said unto others; so shall it be unto thee; and say, thou shalt roar in hell, and all such as be of thy spirit.

Sixthly. And say, for a sad day is coming upon thine head; and say, the same head that cut off thy brother Reeve, and shortened his days; and say, the same hand will cut off thee.

Answer. First, You do by me as those wicked Jews did by Christ, when he cast out Devils, and cured diseases by the power and spirit of God in him. They said he did it by Belzebub, the prince of Devils; so likewise do you Quakers say by me, because I do by the commission of the true God, and have cast out many devils out of many of you Quakers and others by a word speaking, and have subdued those witchcraft-fits within many of you Quakers, so that the strength of your witchcraft is much abated in you all, and you Quakers become many of you in your right minds, to your peace and comfort, and others of you Quakers are cloathed in your right minds, being not able to procure a witchcraft-fit as formerly, for it turns to a sensible rage, and malice and blasphemy against the true personal God, saying, I do these things by sorcery, as the Jews did by Christ, as aforesaid.

Secondly. You charge me with a cursing spirit, and say, that woe and misery will be the portion of us both.

To this I say, if I have cursed any of you Quakers without a just cause, or without a commission from the true God, let woe and misery come upon me indeed, according to your desire, and I shall bear it patiently, as I have testified in all my writings, that if those curses I have pronounced upon all you Quakers, and others, if it be not from authority from God, then let them be upon my head, as the desire of Quakers is; but I knowing God hath owned me these seventeen years, and hath made his power visibly appear in me upon the bodies and souls of many of you Quakers, and more especially in these six years time, and that God doth own that curse I have pronounced upon the Quakers people more than any other: Why? because the Quakers people are more Anti-christian than any other, though I confess the malice and temporal persecution hath been to me more from others than the Quakers; but the Quakers people being of a more Anti-christian spirit, and fighters against God, a personal God, than any others whatsoever, therefore the curse I have pronounced upon the Quakers people, it hath taken more visible effect upon them than any others; for the Quakers God and Christ is all within them, and from this God within them do they fight with my God which is without me, even the man Christ Jesus in that body that was nailed to a tree, as the Scripture saith, which is without me. For at what time did any man ever hear any that professeth the Scriptures, or the Christian religion, to say they would trample Christ Jesus, my God and me, under their feet as dung, and despise a God of five foot high, as you Quakers have done; for you Quakers know that I own no other God but the man Christ Jesus in glory, and he to be both God and man in one single person; yet you defy this God of mine, and say you would trample him and me under your feet as dirt, for which things hath the wrath of this God fallen upon you Quakers, and the curse pronounced by me, his messenger, hath taken place in some of the eminent Quakers; for the curse pronounced by me, God's messenger, is to part your Christ within you one from another; for you Quakers do not die, as you say, you do but go out of the body; but sure, when you do go out of the body, your Christ within you, sure your soul and he doth part one from another, and never shall see one the other more to eternity; and this hath been the effect of the curse, upon some of you Quakers, only to separate Christ's spirit from yours, that you may never see one the other more to eternity. And seeing these things have fallen out in these my days, and that God hath chosen me to stand as a wall of brass against all Anti-christian spirits, for every hypocritical spirit to shoot their arrows at me; but none can hurt me, nor make any entrance into me, because the whole armour of God is put upon me; my feet are shod with peace, my breast with the breast-plate of righteousness, and upon my head is set the helmet of salvation, and in my left hand is put a shield of faith, and in my right hand is put a two-edged sword, so that no fiery dart of the devil, man or woman, can enter me, or hurt me; and with this two-edged sword in my right hand have I fought with many men devils, and have overcome them, and yet received no wound myself. And now, last of all, there is a woman devil, namely, Elizabeth

Hooton; she hath shot forth her poisonous arrows at me in blasphemy, curses, and words, thinking herself stronger than her brethren, that if happily her poisonous arrows might pierce into me; seeing that so many of her Quakering brethren to fall before me, she was moved with great wrath against me, and zeal for her God and Christ within her, and madness, that some of her brethren, the Quakers, after the curse pronounced upon them for their blasphemy, they went out of the body, or laid down their bodies, as Thomas Leigh did. This moved her to pour out the poison that was in her heart, with her tongue set on the fire of hell against me, in curses and blasphemy, thinking her poisonous arrows and venomous tongue should have took hold or place in me, more than her brethrens curses did before; but as the men devils your brethren the Quakers, were made partakers of God's vengeance by the curse of his messenger, in that they blasphemed and despised the true God as aforesaid, in that they are damned to eternity, besides their going out of the body here as you think, so will the same curse follow you for your wicked, proud, presumptous speeches, in that you, being a woman, will undertake to pronounce woe and curses to one that hath a commission from God; yet you, from a light within you, and a Christ within you, a sandy foundation one, a puff of wind from a true prophet will lay it level to the earth: and would it not have been great pity, that such a she devil as you arc should have escaped the sentence of eternal damnation? Surely it would; and because you shall know for what you are damned, I shall rehearse some of your wicked speeches, curses, and blasphemy, which have proceeded out of your mouth.

First. You say, woe unto thee, Muggleton, thou child of the devil.

Secondly. You say, I have opened my mouth in blasphemy and cursing.

Thirdly. You say, I am cursed in my going out, and in my coming in.

Fourthly. You say, I shall roar in hell, and all such as be of my spirit.

Fifthly. You say, the same hand as cut off my brother Reeve, and shortened his days, the same will cut off me.

Sixthly. You have called me sorcerer, because I have cast the devil and witchcraft spirit out of some of you Quakers, and bound some quaking devils, unclean spirits, in chains of darkness and fetters of death, that shall never be let loose to eternity.

These things have been wrought and much more, by the commission of God in me, for which you call me sorcerer, as those devils did say by Christ when on earth. He cast out many devils and unclean spirits out of men and women, and they said he did it by Belzebub, the prince of devils. So say you Quakers by me; and you, Elizabeth Hooton, Quaker, have, in a high manner, like them, also sinned against the Holy Ghost that sent me, with great pride and high presumption, as may be read before.

Therefore, in obedience to my commission from the true God, the man Christ Jesus in glory, in heaven above the stars, I do pronounce Elizabeth Hooton, Quaker, for these horrid blasphemies and hard speeches against the truth, cursed and damned, both in soul and body, from the presence of God, elect men and angels, to eternity.

Your own body shall be your hell, and your proud raging spirit shall be your devil; the one shall be as fire, and the other as brimstone, burning together to all eternity. Your Christ within you cannot, nor God without you will not, deliver you from the sentence I have passed upon you.

Written by

LODOWICKE MUGGLETON.

One of the two last Prophets and Witnesses of the Spirit unto the High and Mighty God the Man Christ Jesus in Glory.

January 26, 1668.

The Copy of a Letter written by the, Prophet Lodowicke Muggleton, to Mrs, Parker, May 25, 1668.

Loving Friend, Mrs. Parker,

I HEAR by Mrs. Sudbury that you have been very ill, else you would have written to me yourself; I should have been glad to have received a few lines from yourself, if you can write, though it may be you may think you cannot express yourself as you would, yet let not that be any hinderance to you, for it is not the wisdom of placing words that I mind, but the sincerity of the heart; *for out of the abundance of the heart the mouth speaketh*, or writeth, whether it be in things that are good, or in things that are evil. I confess I do not know you by the sight of the eye, nor by writing; but I have heard a good report of you by others, as one that doth truly believe the truth, especially by Mrs. Sudbury. She giveth a good character of you, as one grounded in the true faith; as if your knowledge did arise very high, in believing all things declared by me, and that you have a good understanding in the rise of the two seeds, and how God became flesh, with other things; and that you have received much peace and satisfaction in your mind, since you believed in this commission of the Spirit. I do not in the least question the report that is given you by others, but am altogether inclined to believe it, especially from such persons as have experience in themselves, they can judge of the experience in others also; there are few persons that have a love for me, as a prophet of the Lord, but their hearts are right in the sight of God also. And as the foundation of your faith is built upon this commission of the Spirit, it will be as a sure rock that shall never fail you, though many storms of reason, the devil's temptations, may come violently upon you, yet it will not touch that inward peace of conscience in the assurance of everlasting life; for faith in the true God is that white stone in the heart, wherein is written a new name, which none can read but those that have it. This many can experience at this day. Also I doubt not but your faith will grow in you more and more, from strength to strength, so that the peace and satisfaction you have begun in you already may encrease to a greater measure of peace and satisfaction of soul to the things of eternity, to the full assurance of everlasting life, so that no, doubt may arise in, your heart.

I thought good to write these few lines unto yourself, to strengthen your faith, perceiving by Ellen Sudbury's letter it was your desire.

So at present I shall say no more, only my love to yourself.

I rest your Friend in the true faith,

LODOWICKE MUGGLETON.

The Postern, London,

May 25, 1668.

My wife, though unknown, remembers her love unto you.

The Copy of a Letter written by the Prophet Lodowicke Muggleton, to Mrs. Ellen Sudbury, May 25, 1668.

Dear Friend in the eternal Truth, Ellen Sudbury,

I RECEIVED your letter with the inclosed, and gave your husband's letter to Mr. Delamaine; also I am glad to hear that you and your husband are both well as to this present life, for I know your happiness in the life to come will be sure, in that my faith is in you, and your faith in me; and so by faith God is in us, and we in him.

This is that union men and women have with God, being partakers of the divine nature of God. Faith comes by hearing the word of God preached; and how shall he preach, except he be sent; that is, who can make known the true God, and declare the true righteousness of faith unto man, but he that is sent of God; and this righteousness of faith was in you, Ellen Sudbury, before you saw me, and my faith was in you before you saw my face, and before I saw your face, or heard your voice; but in your letters I saw that salvation was come to your house, in that you received a prophet in the name of a prophet, you could not miss of the blessing ©f eternal life; and you being the instrumental occasion of your husband's receiving the faith, whereby he hath peace and rest in his soul, as to his eternal happiness, as I find by his writings: so that it may be truly said, that salvation is come to your house, in that you received a prophet in the name of a prophet, you have received a prophet's reward, for every true prophet hath salvation attending on him. And as for our friend Mrs. Parker, I perceive she hath been very ill, and that she would beg a few lines from me. Now, what I write to her must be grounded upon your report, for I do not know that ever I saw the woman, or received any lines from her, yet I judge your discerning to be good, and the things true you report of her; therefore, upon your report, I shall write a few lines to her in particular; and as for my coming into the country this year, I think I shall not, neither to Cambridgeshire, nor no where else. I am desired much by Charles Cleve, and other friends there, to come this summer, and by friends in Kent also, but I have no intent to go from London; but for the devils malice I matter not what they can do unto me, for the devils must not go beyond the law, lest they bring themselves into a premunire; for had I known so much as I do know now, when I was taken at Chesterfield, I would have made the mayor, aldermen and constable weary of what they did. The devils malice could have done me but little hurt if I had been wise; but as the proverb is, *Wisdom is good when it is dear bought.*

Now I can certify you, that I have finished the answer to George Fox's book; it is ready for the press, therefore what you are pleased to give towards it send) as soon as you can with convenience, not wronging yourselves. I thought by our friend Tomkinson's letter to have seen him at London about Whitsuntide, but he did not come.

This is all, but my Love to yourself, and to: your husband, with my wife's love to you both.

I rest and remain your Friend in the true Faith,

LODOWICKE MUGGLETON,

London, May 25, 1668.

Direct your letter thus for me: for Lodowicke Muggleton, at the widow Brunt's house in the Postern, next door to the sign of the White Horse.

The Copy of a Letter written by the Prophet Lodowicke Muggleton, to Thomas Tompkinson, May 26, 1668.

Loving Friend in the eternal Truth, Thomas Tompkinson,

I RECEIVED in Mrs. Sudbury's letter, dated May 3, 1668, a letter of yours inclosed, dated April 20, 1668; in which letter of yours I am glad to hear you are well, and that your faith is so strong as I perceive it is; neither are you blamed by me for any slothfulness in you, for I am glad you are so well satisfied in yourself that you had no need to write to me. I could wish all saints were so satisfied in their minds in all things, to have no need to write unto me, neither for temporal nor spiritual satisfaction. I could be glad if every saint had it in themselves. Also I perceive in your letter that you had an intent to come to London about the tenth of May, but it seems some occasions did prevent you of that journey at present; and as for that book of George Fox's, I have written an answer unto it; I have now finished it; it will contain, as I suppose, a matter of twelve or fourteen sheets of print. There was great glorying in the Quakers people at the first in George Fox's book; but this answer will be as great a shame to them; therefore what you, or any others, are free to give towards the printing, let it be as soon as you can, for I do think to put it to the press about two or three weeks hence. You may, if you please, send it to Mrs. Carter's, or Mrs. Sudbury's, which you please, and they will convey it unto me. And as for that book Fox set forth against me, it maketh all wise men to see the weakness of the Quakers people more than they did before, for there is none rejoiceth in that book but those that are damned by me, or some ignorant shatter-brained people, that know not their right hand from their left in matters of religion; but such people as are serious, that do mind interpretation of Scriptures, they like it not, for he hath brought many places of Scriptures to prove me a false prophet and liar, but he giveth no interpretation; he leaveth the dead letter to speak for itself, and to condemn me; so that I am forced to interpret those Scriptures Fox hath left silent, which will appear in the reading of this answer to his book.

This is all at present, only to let you know that I am well; so with my love remembered unto yourself, and your wife,

I rest your Friend in the true Faith,

LODOWICKE MUGGLETON.

Postern, London,

May 26, 1668.

My wife, though unknown unto you, desireth her love remembered unto you and your wife.

You may direct your letter to me thus: for Lodowicke Muggleton, at the widow Brunt's in the Postern, London, next door to the sign of the White Horse, near Moor-lane.

A Copy of a Letter written by the Prophet Lodowicke Muggleton to Mrs. Dorothy Carter; being a relation of some Passages in a Discourse with George Whitehead, and Josias Cole, two Speakers of the Quakers in the Year 1668; as also some relation of that cursed Devil Thomas Loe, Speaker of the Quakers, and how the Ejects of God's Vengeance did seize upon him, immediately after the Return of an Answer to his cursed blasphemous Letter sent to me, and in less than three Weeks after was dead and buried.

1. THE first question or words Cole spake to me, as near as I can remember, were these: saith he, thou sayest God is in the form of a man, and thou sayest his hand is not much bigger than mine or thy hand; and thou seest what a little this hand will hold; yet, saith he, God is said to have measured the waters in the hollow of his hand, and behold the nations are as the drop of a bucket.

Why, said I, do you believe God to be so big to hold the waters in the hollow of his hand? That is spoken in relation to his great wisdom, power and dominion, and not relating to the bigness of his hand; for a king may conquer many kingdoms by the power of his sword, which his people have put into their hands by his command; and the king may say he hath won these kingdoms, and reduced them to obedience to his laws by the strength of his own hand; yet the king's hand is no bigger in bulk and bigness than another man's hand is: also I said, that I that am but a mortal man, have power over such a great God, whose hand is so big; for, said I, that God, whose hand is much bigger than thy hand or mine, I have power over to condemn: This was passed by, and no reply from them.

2. Whitehead said, he did hear one say that I had damned, that I should say I was as glad I had given judgement and sentence of damnation upon him, as if one had given me forty shillings.

This I did acknowledge to be true, for I have said so by several desperate devils, and I am justified in the sight of God, and in my own conscience, for so doing.

3. Whitehead said, that he did hear that I had cursed a man, and he changing his apparel, came afterwards, and did procure a blessing; and that this man, or some other, did smite or knock a pewter pot upon or over my head.

This I said was a lie, and false, for never did any man strike me over the head with a pot in all my life; and as for that report which Pope, that damned devil, in saying he was blest after he was curst, it is a false report, and a lie, that he hath reported several times amongst ranters and Quakers; for this Pope was a ranter when he was curst, which is about fifteen years ago, and is a worse ranter now than he was then, and that you Quakers know very well what a wicked piece he is, and the wicked lustful life he liveth now in; yet you Quakers will rather believe this damned devil, and wicked lustful person, than believe me, who have been kept innocent from the breach of any law, from my childhood to this day; but I know you Quakers, being of the same nature and seed of the serpent, as those Jews were in Christ's time, who desired of Pilate, that a thief and a murderer should be delivered from death, rather than Jesus, the Lamb of God that taketh away the sins of the world: so it is with you Quakers, you had rather believe this wicked lustful devil Pope, who hath from his youth, till now, had sin and wickedness reigning as lord and king in his mortal body: I say, you had rather believe him, even this notable sinner, than to believe me, who am the Prophet of the most high God, the man Christ Jesus in glory, and have power given of God, as Moses had, to set life and death before you; but I know you will say in the thoughts of your hearts, though not in words as those Jews did by Christ, away with Muggleton, let us have Pope, that wicked lustful man, that we might hear and inquire of him.

4. Whitehead espied a knot of ribbon upon the sleeve of my coat, and said, Why doest thou wear this vanity? Also I said to Whitehead, why doest thou wear silk buttons upon both thy coats? He said they were necessary; and I said no, he might wear hooks and eyes, or ilet-holes; so that was past by.

Again, I did say I did wear ribbons on purpose that I might not be taken or thought to be a Quaker, for I do hate the Quakers' principles; with that Whitehead said, that thou hatest all righteousness, and spake as if himself and Cole were writing against me, in answer to mine against George Fox, and some other things or words they had cateced from me in discourse to make me manifest: also one ugly flighting word did Whitehead speak against the personal God, which I do own, that he would trample him and me under his feet as dirt, with some other words of flighting and undervaluing my power; whereupon I did pronounce George Whitehead cursed and damned, in soul and body, to eternity: also I said his God within him is cursed, and that God he believed or trusted in without him was damned with him, and so ceased discourse with him.

5. When Cole had heard me speak thus unto Whitehead he was still, till I had ended with Whitehead, but I saw his eyes dazzle, and his spirit working within him, so immediately after he uttered these words, or such like: saith he, I have heard of several thou hast cursed, but, said he, I did not believe, had I not heard and seen, that a man could have spoken so presumptuously.

Then said I unto him, dare you say that I have spoken presumptuously? He said, he did believe it was presumption; then said I, on the contrary, I do believe thou art the seed of the serpent, and wilt be damned; and now see whose faith will be strongest, yours or mine; for my faith shall keep you down or under for ever. Under what? Said he. I said, under eternal damnation. Then said he, doest thou ground thy sentence upon my belief? I said yea I do, for you believe that I spake presumptuously, and I do believe you to be the seed of the serpent, and will be damned to eternity. Then said he, doest thou judge this to be a sentence upon me? Yea, said I, what should it be else? Then Cole rose up with a zeal for his God within him, and said, I told thee before that I would try thee and thy God, saying, they were setting forth a writing against me; and withal, Cole pronounced many curses upon me, with his eyes full of dazzled babies in them; and Whitehead, he came with great threatening of judgements upon me, they being both so full of curses together, that I can hardly tell what they said, their curses were so many and so various, so that I could not tell which curse of them both did most concern me to take notice of, only one passage I do remember Cole said, that I should sink in the pit of darkness, and such like words; he used the word darkness many times, but their words were both together, so that their words took no place in me, no not so much as to remember what they said; but I perceive Cole's curses were much like unto Thomas Loe's curses in his letter to me.

Many words more there was between us at that time, but these are the words and passages of most concernment at that time, and of a final judgement and sentence of, eternal damnation, that I gave that day upon Josias Cole and George Whitehead, speakers of the Quakers.

This I do discern and observe in these two men, first, that Josias Cole is of the Spirit of the Sadducees, and more fit to tempt, being more moderate in his words than the other was; for that devil that tempted Christ, spoken of Matthew, Chapter iv. was a Sadducee, yea a wise and prudent man, who se wisdom of reason is more qualified with moderation in discourse than the Pharisee is, so more fit to tempt than the Pharisee is; so I know that devil that tempted Christ was a man that was a Sadducee in his spirit, whatever he pretended to the rulers of the Jews, therefore more fit to propound questions to Christ than the Pharisees were; likewise I do know that Josias Cole sprang from that Sadducee that tempted Christ, and so was the more fit to tempt me, and I did like his spirit of moderation well, and was not offended at his temptations nor his questions until he called that presumption I said unto Whitehead. Also this I know, that George Whitehead, Quaker, is one of those Pharisees' spirits that carne to catch and entrap in his words, for it is the nature of the spirit of the Pharisee to watch and catch at words, whereby they may accuse or entrap them they talk with. This did the Pharisees to Christ, which made him call them serpents devils, yea, and that the devil was their father, because the Pharisee spirit is more secretly proud and mysterious than the Sadducee, which is the fittest devil to tempt; and Christ pronounced woes more earnestly upon the Pharisees than he did upon the Sadducees, or upon that devil that tempted him in the fourth of Matthew abovesaid; so it was with me, I was more offended at George Whitehead's pharisaical spirit, whose property was only to quibble and to catch at words, to turn the plain truth to another sense; for when a principle of truth is laid down infallibly, and plain Scripture words, that will not admit of innovation, then this Pharisee would neither affirm against it, nor deny it; but let it fall, and to another thing: Whitehead is of a Worse spirit than his forefathers the Pharisees in Christ's time, for they confessed they could not tell; but this Pharisee Whitehead, he would not say that he could not tell, but thought in his heart that he knew more than I did, therefore would neither affirm against those things I asserted or denied? but I know his eyes are blinded, his ears deaf, and his heart hardened, so that no true light of life might enter into him, lest he should have believed the declarations of the true God and the right devil, by the last true messenger of God, and have been converted and saved. Also this I say, that had Whitehead asked me, as Cole did several times, whether? I did discern him: to be the seed of the Serpent, but I would not tell while I saw further, but I would have told him I did, for I always hated the proud pharisaical spirit, who was as full of conceited knowledge of a Christ within him as his skin could hold, it was even ready to crack with that conceited light of a bodiless Christ within him; but a little time, and his Christ within him will be emptied out of him, as it is with Thomas Loe, and several others of the Quakers that are under the judgement and sentence of this commission of the Spirit; and where or whensoever this writing is read, it is recorded, that Josias Cole and George Whitehead, two speakers of the Quakers, were at this time, and in the discourse aforesaid, judged and condemned, both soul and body, from the presence of God, elect men and angels, to eternity.

By me,

LODOWICKE MUGGLETON,

One of the two last Witnesses and Prophets unto the High and Mighty God, the Man Christ Jesus, in Glory.

Thomas Loe, speaker of the Quakers, sent a blasphemous and cursed, envious, cursed letter unto me, dated the 16th of September, (which he calls the seventh month) 1668; and I sent him the sentence of eternal damnation by the bearer the same day in writing. Also the bearer is a Quaker that brought Loe's letter, and is damned also.

But people may see how soon this devil Loe was cut off this earth after that railing blasphemous letter, and gives no reason for what, but heaps up many curses, threatenings of judgements, and hellish expressions add high blasphemy against the Holy Ghost, or true God that sent me, so that I could do no Jess but give judgement and sentence of eternal damnation upon him; also the Quaker aforesaid was not willing to go without Loe's sentence, but Loe was cut off suddenly after. He was buried the 6th of October, 1668.

But I know the Quakers do not think the judgement of God, nor my sentence, was upon him, or over him, for his blasphemy, but they say he had been in a consumption fifteen years, and came lately out of Ireland. Very likely it maybe so; but sure if he had been sick when he wrote those lines to me, it shewed not weakness of nature in him, nor weakness of body; but it may be his spirit was so enflamed with the fire of hell in zeal for his God, or Christ within him, that he felt no weakness of body at that time; for his wrath was great and hot against me, as his letter doth shew; but you Quakers do believe that Loe's soul is not dead, but slipped out of his body, and gone you know not where, and into a power and spirit you know not what; but I say his soul is where you laid his body; they both came into this world together; they both despised the truth together; they both received judgment and condemnation together, and both died together, and were both soul and body buried together, and shall both rise again, every seed its own body; that seed of reason, which was his life, which he thought was the divine nature of God, but it was the nature or the devil or serpent, and that law written in his heart, he and you Quakers call the light of Christ, or Christ in you, which is nothing in you else but the law written in your hearts, your thoughts accusing and excusing; and when God shall raise him again, that seed of reason shall rise and bring a spiritual dark body with it, and that law, which was written in his and your hearts here in this life, shall quicken anew in that new, dark, spiritual body; and then shall he, and you despisers of a personal God, know, that your own souls, which you thought was the life of God, but it was the life of the devil, ye devils yourselves, and that law written in your hearts, which you called here in this life the light of Christ; but when this law doth quicken again, as I said before, it will prove the only and alone devil to torment you to eternity.

These things may seem strange sayings, and as a riddle unto you, and a thing impossible; but with God all things are possible which his own will moved him unto. And this I say, as it was possible for God to write the law in the angels natures, and by his secret determinations suffer one of those angels to become very man; and so the angels seed having the law written in it before God made Adam, and so by generation the law comes to be written in every man's heart, man finds it there accusing, but knows not how it came written there.

So it is as strange for you Quakers to believe that God will raise your souls, that were dead, again; and not only so, but the law shall quicken in you again; for as the law is strictly written in your hearts, but ignorantly written in the reprobate angel, so by Gods secret decree and power he will revive that law again in the reprobate seed of reason, as in Loe, and many of you speakers of the Quakers, and others of your brethren who are under the judgment and sentence of this commission of the Spirit, shall find my words to be true upon you and over you to eternity; neither shall you be delivered from it.

By,

LODOWICKE MUGGLETON.

A Copy of a Letter wrote by the Prophet Lodowicke Muggleton, to Mr. William Hall, in the Year 1668, concerning his Marriage.

I RECEIVED your letter, and I am troubled to hear of your trouble, and am perplexed in my mind to hear how you are perplexed, and that without a cause, about one that will love you whether you will or no; but, dear brother, I would not have you, through your weakness in judgment, and ignorance in experience, I would not have a good nature and an innocent mind enthralled and entangled, and bind itself with such cords that cannot be untied again, nor broken, but are as chains of iron; and seeing your mind is free, and you have no guilt upon your spirits in this matter, do not bring guilt upon your mind, through your weaknesses of judgment and want of experience, for I perceive you have broke no law to bring guilt upon your mind not in this matter; for if you keep yourself whole in these three things, the law of God, the law of conscience, and the law of the land, you need not be troubled in this business in the least of love; let it happen how it will, keep your conscience innocent in these three laws, and no guilt can be upon you in this matter; and for your better satisfaction, I shall open these three laws. The law of God is this: that if you shall covenant and promise, as in the presence of God, to take this maid to wife, none seeing or hearing but yourselves, then perform your vow as unto God. The law of the conscience is like unto it; if ye have in secret, between she and you, made any profession of Jove to her in that kind, to draw her affections unto you, or asked her whether she could love you in that kind, to draw her affections unto you, or asked her whether she could love you in that kind, or made her any promise or engagement to her in secret, which none heard or knew but yourselves; if not, your conscience is free from guilt or trouble in this business. And as for the law of the land; if you have promised before witnesses to have her to wife, yet if the maid be not there present to hear that promise, it signifies nothing, let witnesses witness what they will; except the maid be in the hearing of it, it signifies nothing. Now I am persuaded that you are innocent in all these laws, therefore why should you bring yourself into bondage to that you cannot love or fancy; if her love be so great to you, that she must do herself a mischief if she cannot have you to her husband, let the evil be upon her own head, she hath brought it upon herself, and would you cast yourself into hell, to marry one you cannot love, to raise her up into heaven? And whereas you pity her for the trouble and earnest affection to you for a husband; dear brother, be not more pitiful to relieve her troubled spirit, than to pity your own troubled spirit y such tragedies as these hath been acted upon the stage of this world before now; for if wives will force men to love them whether they will or no, it is not true love, neither are you bound to gratify that flame of desire; for it seemeth this act of hers, to savour more of boldness and impudence than of true love, to force love out of a man whether he will or no, or else she must die, or make away ourselves, this is but to put your tender nature into a fright, thinking to fright you to be her husband, lest she should do herself some hurt; but so as she can but obtain her desires, she cares not which way. Do not you believe that she doth this of herself, but as she is instructed by her mother, or some other friend, even as the damsel was that danced before Herod the King; the damsel knew not what to ask of the King, but went to her mother, and was instructed by her mother to ask the head of John Baptist; it was a woeful demand to John, and to Herod the King too, but for his oath-sake he must do it to his own ruin. Your case is something like it, for doubtless the maid is instructed to ask the body of you for her husband, and then the estate they know will follow; so the maid get you, they care not what trouble of mind you suffer afterwards, wherefore do not wound you? spirit where your gave no cause; if any will take offence, because you will not satisfy their desire, let the woe be to them that take the offence; for, first, they have made your passive nature the cause of offence, and except you will yield to their desires, they will take offence at you, and make you the cause of their trouble; but my advice is, that you will be Steadfast in your own mind, and resolve to keep the integrity of your mind, and the preservation of your own peace; let what will be the effect, your condition will be safe; and seeing you are in this streight at present about a wife, having so many proffers, I would resolve to have none at all, nor engage thyself at all to any at present. What if you stay a year or two longer, you are young enough, it will do as well, and your peace of mind will be preserved better; and who knoweth how Providence may order things in a little time, for a patient contented mind is more worth than riches, it maketh every condition a man is in to be comfortable.

LODOWICKE MUGGLETON.

A Copy of a Letter wrote by the Prophet Lodowicke Muggleton, to Mr. Edward Delamain, a Baptist Preacher, living in Marlborough, bearing date the 16th of June, 1668,

Edward Delamain,

I SAW a letter of yours, very large, sent to your brother Alexander Delamain, wherein I have found in it many passages so blasphemous against the Holy Spirit, which sheweth plainly unto me that you are of the seed of the serpent, and appointed to be damned to eternity.

And this I must tell you, when I spake with you I knew you were of the seed of the serpent, and appointed to be damned; yet I seeing you did not despise any thing I said, I let you alone, though I knew you well enough: your eyes were blinded, and your ears deaf, and your heart hardened; so that no light of heaven might shine into your heart: but if you would have spoken but one word to my face, as you did in your letter to your brother, you should have been damned then as your brother Noble who was the Baptist preacher; it would have saved you a great deal of pains writing those large letters to your brother, and your brother to you, for I said to him in my first letter he wrote to you, after you went away, that it would be good for him to send you the sentence of damnation then; but your brother having more mercy towards you (you being of so near relation to him) than God, or any off his messengers had; so did write to you again, though it was but to cast stones against the wind; for there is no. more possibility to convert you to the truth than; for him to reach up to the stars with his hand; for you are blinded and hardened as all reprobates are, who are conceited they know more by reading the letters of the Scriptures than any man's revelation, though it be the revelation of God, himself. I shall name some of those wicked passages in your letter.

As *first*, you look upon the letter of to Scriptures to be the lively oracles of God, to speak; unto you in these, days, and that you ought to give as great and real credit to them as if God had visibly; spoken.

Answer. The seed of the serpent is as well contented with the dead, letter of the Scriptures, better than they are with the spirit and life of the Scriptures; for, they that spake the Scripture, their words were spirit and life to those that believed them, and spirit and death to the reprobate seed; but the dead letter of the Scriptures is a lively oracle to the seed of the serpent, because they can give what sense, they please, saying; I conceive this is the meaning, the letter answereth not a word again: this pleases the seed of the serpent, because the letter lets them conceive what they will of it, and so it becomes a lively oracle to the reprobate's mind, because it cannot speak, now the men are dead, that spake it.

Secondly. You say the Scriptures were written in past times, and in present time, for the teaching and learning of those that should come in after time.

Answer. The Scriptures were written in past times for the teaching and learning of the seed of faith; but they were not written at all for the teaching and learning of the seed of the serpent, such as you are; neither doth the letter of the Scriptures teach or learn any man the way to heaven, by any spiritual knowledge, without a true interpreter, which I know there is none at this day, but us the witnesses of the Spirit only: but who so zealous for the dead letter of the Scriptures, as the seed of the serpent is?: Thirdly. You note the words of Peter, shewing, that he and others saw the glory of God's Majesty, and were eye witnesses of it, as in the second epistle of Peter, chap. 1. Peter, say you, was eye witness, and heard the voice of God himself, as much, if not more, than John Reeve, or any man can pretend to: yet, say you, he would not have the Christians pin their faith upon his revelation, or single voice of God.

Answer. How can you, being the reprobate seed, tell that God spake to Peter more than to John Reeve? And how can you tell that Peter and others saw the glory of God, and were witnesses more than John Reeve? John Reeve did see the glory of God, and God spake to John Reeve more than he did to Peter and Paul either. This John Reeve hath declared, and there is more ground to believe John Reeve than Peter; because John Reeve did justify the things a few years ago, and many now are living that heard him, and have the witness in themselves, that his voice was a true voice; but, as for that of Peter, there is none now living that heard him speak as they did John Reeve; yet the seed of the serpent honoureth the words of Peter, now he is dead many hundred years, and all that saw Peter and believed him are dead many generations past since; but the reprobate's faith is very strong in dead mens words; but when they were alive they were counted by the seed of the serpent deceivers and liars, as we are counted. And this I say, whoever did believe Peter's voice of God, and his commission to bind and loose mens sins, they did pin their faith upon his sleeve, that is, upon his commission and doctrine.

Fourthly. You say the Scriptures are more sure, and safer to be heeded and minded, than any revelation or vision of any man whatsoever.

Answer. Do you not shew your blindness and darkness in this thing? Did the apostles, when they came, with their revelations and visions, count the writings of Moses and the prophets to be more heeded and safer than theirs? Why did they then upbraid the Jews for putting their trust in Moses, and the worship of the law? For the Jews despised the Revelation of Christ and his apostles, calling it new doctrine, saying, they were drunken with new wine, because their revelation was new to the Jews, because they, declared a new doctrine and new worship, contrary to the old doctrine and old worship of Moses, and the prophets; even as the rulers said to the man that Christ opened his eyes that was born blind, when he asked them, saying; will ye be Christ's disciples? They said, no; they were Moses's disciples. Here the serpent gave more heed to the Scriptures of Moses, and the prophets, they being all dead, than they did to any revelation or vision of Christ and his apostles, when they were living. And those devils thought it more safe to put, their trust in dead mens' revelations, than in any man's revelation living whatsoever. So it is with you, being the Seed of the serpent, you look upon it to be more sure and safer for you to depend upon the dead letter of the Scriptures for life and salvation, than upon any revelation, or vision, or voice, this commission of the Spirit hath declared: but you shall find it more unsafe for your soul, in that you did put your trust in the letter of the Scriptures, and reject the revelation of the Spirit; for the letter of the Scriptures shall do you no good, neither shall you find any comfort by them; but they shall rather be your torment, because you did not hearken to man's revelation and interpretation of Scriptures, that is now living.

Fifthly: You say, you would have your brother to speak as Timothy did, boldly, from God's word, and not (say you) from supposed commissions, as you imagine.

Answer. Your brother doth speak boldly from God's word, as Timothy did, because he spake in the faith of a commission, and knows that this commission is the word of God, as much or more, than that word of God as Timothy spoke; because Timothy was chosen a bishop by men, and sent forth to preach the word of God by men, at the second hand: but John Reeve and myself were chosen by God himself, to be his two last prophets and witnesses, to preach the word of God; and as many as truly believe us shall certainly be saved, as those were that believed in Christ himself, when upon earth: also, we have power to ordain such as Timothy was, to speak the word of God boldly as he did, being ordained by the apostles, who were greater in power than Timothy was; so that your believing in Timothy's words now will do you no good; but those that did truly believe Timothy's words when that commission was in being, should have been saved by it, but now it will profit you nothing; for it is but a dead letter unto you now: do you not paint the sepulchre of Timothy now, as the Jews did the sepulchres of the prophets? They spake well of the prophets, when they were dead, and honoured them; so the Baptists speak well of Timothy, and honour his words now he is dead: but if you had heard him speak as you did me, you would have counted it more safe to have believed Moses than Timothy; for the seed of the serpent always counts it a more safe thing to put their trust in dead mens words, than in those men that are alive. And those words your brother sent you ought to have been believed by you as much as the words of Timothy, they would have done you far more good than the words of Timothy will.

Sixthly. You alledge Paul's words, *Galat. i. ver. 8.* where he saith, *Though we, or an angel from heaven, preach any other doctrine, or gospel unto thee, than that which we have preached unto you, let them be accursed.*

Answer. I can as truly say so as St. Paul doth, that if any angel from heaven should come and preach any other doctrine than that which we, John Reeve and myself, have preached, I will not say as Paul saith, *Let him be accursed*; but I say, we have power ourselves to curse angels or men to eternity, that shall dare to say we are liars, deceivers, or that the doctrine we preach is false: so that the power of this commission of the Spirit is greater in spiritual matters than that which Paul speaketh of; so that the Gospel of Paul, and others, preached at that time, will do you no good. It was life and salvation to those, that believed Paul at that time; but what is that to you Baptist preachers? Now, that which Paul preached will signify no benefit to you now, but rather do you more hurt; because you take upon you to preach as those vagabond Jews, the same Jesus that Paul preached, having no commission to preach from God so to do; for you should have harkened unto me, who make all unclean spirits subject unto me, as they were unto Paul: but the evil spirit in others, and the unclean spirit of reason in yourself, shall leap upon you, and rent, tear, and wound your soul to eternity, for preaching the words of Paul and of Christ, you being not sent of him.

Seventhly. You quote the words of John, 2 *Epist. ver.* 10. He saith, *If there come any unto you, and bring not this doctrine receive him not, nor bid him Godspeed.*

Answer. Do you, the preacher of the Baptists, bring that doctrine as John the apostle brought? If you do, it is either under your arm, or in your: pocket, in a Bible bound together that you bring; for you never knew that doctrine that John brought at that time,, when he was alive; there is none knoweth that doctrine that John brought and taught the people at that time, but us the witnesses of the Spirit, and them to whom we have revealed it; neither need the believers of this commission of the Spirit bid any of you, the seed of the serpent, Godspeed; for none of you know the doctrine of the true God, nor the right devil: but I know the Baptist-preachers will carry John's doctrine, the Bible, in your pockets, as aforesaid, and receive in it the notion of your brains, but I know you never did, nor ever will receive it in your hearts.

Eighthly. You say, verily brother, the great cause of errors, and delusions, and strong impostures, ariseth from slighting the Scriptures.

Answer. How can you, being the seed of the serpent come to error and delusion, and never was in truth? Do you think reading the Scriptures will give you to know what error and delusion is, whereas you were always in the darkness and blindness of your mind; and truth was appointed to shut your eyes, and harden your heart, and make your ears deaf, lest you should see, hear, and understand truth, and be converted and healed? This power hath God given unto me, to shut your eyes, make your ears heavy, and your heart fat, that your conceited knowledge of the letter of the Scriptures; so that you might not be converted and healed by this commission of the Spirit; so that your owning of the letter, and not adhering to the interpretation given by us, the Witnesses of the Spirit; for none knoweth the Scriptures truly but us, and this is the grand cause that you and others have fallen into such great errors, and strong delusions, because you slight the interpretation of the Scriptures, which I have given, and so have sinned against the Holy Ghost, This is the effect of your faith you have in the letter of the Scriptures; this will prove a great error and delusion indeed to you, and high imposture hath risen in you, in that you slighted your brother's advertisement in his letters to you, requiring you to lay down your preaching from the letter of the Scriptures, you having no commission from God so to do.

Ninthly. You say, your brother doth abuse the Scriptures, to call it a dead letter: take heed, say you, brother, you are not cheated of that reason God hath given you.

Answer. Why! Is it not a dead letter? Doth it speak any thing at all to you? If the Scriptures were not a dead letter, such serpents as you would not love it, but would hate it as those did when the Scriptures were alive; for when commissionated men spake the Scriptures, and declared their revelation, they were inspired with the Spirit, they were then alive, and their words were spirit and life, to those that believed; but you that are the pretended preachers of Scriptures now, are ministers of the dead letter; for there is no saving knowledge, nor spirit, nor life, in any of yours: nay, there is not one of you preachers that will be saved, for you do abuse the letter of the Scriptures, in that you make a trade of other mens words: and you will conceive what prophets, and apostles, and the words of Christ mean, and have no infallible spirit, nor gift of interpretation of Scriptures; for none can interpret Scripture but such as have the same spirit as spake them, which, I am sure, you have not, therefore the Scriptures will prove a dead letter to you indeed: and it is a great abuse unto God for you to take the Scriptures in any other sense, but as a dead letter; for it will prove a kiting letter unto you, even unto death eternal. And as for your brother being cheated of his reason; it is happy for him that ever he was born, that he was cheated of his reason in spiritual things; but you shall never be cheated of your reason, neither in things spiritual, nor in things temporal; for the reason you so highly esteem shall be the only devil that shall torment you, both here and hereafter.

Tenthly. Your brother saith, there is no other spiritual God or Father, but only within the blessed body of the Man Christ Jesus glorified.

This you deny, and say it is utterly false, and contrary to the whole Scripture, Also, you say, your brother's distinction of Christ's being Father, Son, and Spirit, is full of contradiction, and in, plain terms, say, it is a piece of nonsense, as you say you can make it appear by Holy Writ.

Answer. That there is no other spiritual God, Creator, or Father, but only in the blessed body of the Man Christ Jesus glorified. That is as true as truth itself, and I have abundantly proved that by Scriptures, in my other «writings, as in the Interpretation of the 11th Chapter of the Revelations, and the whole Revelations; but what should I say to blind men of interpretations of Scriptures? For there is light and life in the true interpretations of the Scripture to the seed of faith: but give the seed of reason, or the serpent, the dead letter without the interpretation, that he may conceive what meaning he pleases, and not be contradicted; for the fetter of the Scriptures is the prophets and the apostles dead bodies, as I have clearly opened in the: Eleventh of the Revelations: for your preachers do like unto the doctors of physic, they: get the bodies of men and women opened when they are dead; but when they are alive,: they dare not do it, to learn experience by their dead bodies, to cure diseases, as they think the better: so likewise it is with you that preach without a commission from God; you open the dead bodies, of the prophets and apostles, that is, their letter of the Scriptures, to see if you could find the cause of life and salvation there; by their dead bodies you learn experience and knowledge: to prattle and talk of life and salvation by the doctrines of Christ; but know nothing but what you pick out of the letter of the Scriptures, even as the doctors of physic do out. of the dead bodies they open; for when those men were alive that spake the Scriptures, you durst not take upon you to say, this is the meaning of Paul, and I conceive this is the sense of Peter's words; for when John said, speaking of Christ Jesus, that he was the first, and the last; that he was dead, and is alive; and behold he is alive for evermore, as you find in the Revelations. And likewise John saying, This is the true God, and eternal Life; durst you have denied these words of John if he had been now alive? And dare you say his words are utterly false, and contrary to the other apostles words? But you know there is neither one apostle, nor other, that can reply unto you again, that makes you so confident as you are; but I would have you to know that God hath chosen me in their steads, to give judgment upon you, and the letter of the Scriptures you put your trust in shall not deliver you from it; and that distinction your brother giveth of Father, Son, and Spirit, is true, and as good sense as men can speak: and what you deny in plain terms and words will be a seal of eternal damnation to your own soul.

Eleventhly. You call all the talk of the commission of the Spirit to be a mere whimsey of the brain, and you say, no less than mere delusion; and you say will prove so in the end, as true as God is in heaven.

Answer. Here you have shewed yourself of the reprobate seed; and that you have sinned against the Holy Ghost, as most of you Baptists do; a sin that God will not forgive in this world, nor in the world to come: and as sure as God is in heaven, you are appointed to be damned to eternity. This I know as sure as God is in heaven.

Twelfthly. You say your brother pleaseth himself with the face of a God, being in a form, and gives credit to no man that is rotten in his grave, and will not believe (say you) the living oracle, that says, he is a spirit And (say you) let your brother take God's form, but give you his power.

Answer. As for your brother's pleasing himself with the face of a God being in a form, to this I say, a man can have no true satisfaction in his mind, except he really believes God hath a face and form of his own, distinct from man and all other creatures. And for your brother's giving credit to a man that is rotten in his grave, your brother could not have had the assurance of eternal life in himself, but by giving credit to that man's words: but what think you? Are not the prophets and apostles rotten in their graves, many hundred years ago, and none living that ever saw them, or heard their voices. How comes it to pass you gave credit to their words, that were rotten so many hundred years ago? And you blame your brother for giving credit to a prophet of the Lord, who is yet in the sight and memory of many; for while I live, John Reeve liveth, and we are true as ever prophet and apostle were, and ought to be credited as they were.

And as for the believing the living oracles, that say God is a Spirit, the Scriptures you mean to be the living oracles. To this I say, the Scriptures do prove three places to one; that God has a form, and hath: a face, to one place where he is called a spirit. And the writings of us, the Witnesses of the Spirit, are more; living oracles than the letter of the Scriptures, and will give more peace and satisfaction to the souls of those that believe them, than the belief of the Scriptures will, now the prophets and apostles have been dead so many hundred years.

This many can experience, and witness in themselves, at this day; neither can any have the power of God but such as know the form and nature of God; which you, nor no man else can know, but such as believe the living oracles declared by us the witnesses of the Spirit.

Thirteenthly. You say, that Peter, nor Paul, or any other mortal whatsoever, hath, power to save, or damn to eternity: this is a work (say you) peculiar only to God, the Judge of all. Also, you marvel how many men dare to read otherwise than God speaks, or to put interpretation of their own brains.

Answer. That mortal men have power to pronounce the sentence of eternal damnation and salvation upon men and women, that is clear by the Scriptures: And it doth belong unto men, and not unto God himself; for God hath chosen men to be judges, to condemn men, and acquit men, according as they are found guilty or innocent by the law; but the king leaves it to the judges, and doth not meddle with it himself: so it is with the King, of Heaven, he gives power and commission to his prophets and apostles, and the witnesses of the Spirit, to judge and determine of people's eternal weal, or woe: and those keys of heaven and hell, that Christ gave unto Peter, was power to bless and curse to eternity; for whose sins be did remit; were forgiven to eternity, and whose sins he did remit, eternal salvation did come upon that man, so on the contrary, whose sins Peter did retain, that man's sins were never forgiven of God, being retained by Peter; so that eternal damnation is passed Upon that man whose sins are retained, and God will not revoke what his judge hath done; and this power God hath given unto us, the witnesses of the Spirit: but if you had read the book called the Quakers Neck Broken, you would have seen this point more largely proved; but I perceive you are ignorant of all things pertaining to salvation and damnation, but what the letter of the Scriptures dictates to your understanding and imagination: but we that are chosen judges of God are to read the Scriptures thus, and to give interpretation, according to the tenor of our commission; for the Scripture is given into mine hand, and no man knows the Scriptures truly but. myself; because God hath given me understanding of his mind in the Scriptures above all men in the world, and he hath made me judge of the Scriptures. Therefore what interpretation or sense soever you gather from the word of the Scriptures, I say it is but the imagination of your own brains.

Fourteenthly. You say nothing hinders mens salvation but their own wills: also, you say, there is no such thing as a doctrine of reprobation, whereby men are destined to destruction.

Answer. How comes it to pass then, that your freewill did not preserve yourself from being damned to eternity? It seems you had not power in your will to keep you from the sin against the Holy Ghost; if you had had power in your will, you would have believed your brother and me, when you saw your brother Noble damned by me: how comes it to pass your will did not submit, and be silent? You saw the trouble that Noble was in at the present; yet your will had not power to keep yourself from the same condemnation; but have you not read, that God hath blinded the eyes, and made the ears heavy, and the heart of man hard, lest they should see, hear, understand, and be converted? Why did not the will of those men convert themselves? The cause why, they were hardened of God: and why were they hardened of God? Because they were, of the reprobate seed, even the seed of the serpent; so it is with you, God hath blinded your eyes, because you are of the reprobate seed, the seed of the serpent, hated of God, as Esau was, and your brother Alexander beloved of God, as Jacob was. Here is the doctrine of election and reprobation manifest in you two; the one is taken, and the other left, by this commission of the Spirit. And do you not find in the Scriptures no such doctrine of election and reprobation? You may find and read it in the Romans very frequently spoken of; and had not you been of the reprobate seed, appointed to suffer those eternal torments, you would not have been so blind and hardened, but have believed, and have submitted to God's prerogative, power; but the reprobate seed thinks to be saved by his own will, whether God will or no; but you being destinated to destruction, hath caused you to write against it.

Fifteenthly. You say, one would think no man in his right wits should be so far deprived of his reason, as to admit of this for a ground to embrace the single, bare testimony of two men, whereof one hath been dead some years, and have but their bare words, that God. spake to them, and heard his voice; and such a commission strikes at the foundation and knowledge of the Scriptures, and the root of all religion and worship, at the very bottom of holiness and godliness, and also strikes at the very majesty of God himself: so you count your brother given over to strong delusions, to believe lies, because the Scriptures say, *In the latter days men shall be given over to believe lies, and the devices of their own brains.*

Answer. Had you been in your right wits, you would have made the single testimony of two men the only ground of salvation: but you being out of your wits, being blinded and hardened, you have embraced dead mens testimonies for the ground of your faith, men that have been dead many hundred years; so that your faith in those mens words will do you no good now: and it would have been as good for you if you had been deprived of your reason, as you think your brother is; for the reason in you is the devil, that shall torment to eternity, and good would it have been for you if you had been deprived of it: a little measure of faith to put your trust in the declaration of two single men, whereof one is now living, would have wrought the work of salvation in you, and have deprived you of reason, which reason now will torment you, because you are not deprived of it, but is wholly guided by it; and so your trust must be altogether in the dead letter of the Scriptures, and in dead, mens words, and you shall find nothing there for your soul but bare words; for there is no spirit and life in them, except you had hearkened and believed the single testimony of two men; those that do so, the interpretation of the Scriptures becomes life and spirit unto their souls: also, I confess the testimony of us two single men doth strike at the foundation of all hypocritical knowledge of the Scriptures, and at the root of all religion and worship, of all the formal worship of the Baptists and others, and at the very bottom of your hypocritical holiness and seeming godliness. This commission of the Spirit strikes at the very hypocritical majesty that you hypocrites seem to give unto God; for now is the axe laid to the root of that tree; it strikes to the root of all knowledge; wisdom, religion, worship, hypocritical holiness and godliness, that is practised in all the seven churches, as shewing, that the ministry of them all is false, none having a commission from God to preach? so that God hath by our hands, given the axe, and we have laid it to the root of the tree, and have cut down many of your preachers, and spoiled all your holiness and godliness, as dung and dross; neither shall your holiness, nor godliness, nor righteousness, avail you any thing, in that you are given over to a strong delusion, to put your trust in dead mens words, and hath despised the true interpretation of the Scriptures, which are alive; so that you followed the desires of your own brains to your endless misery.

Sixteenthly. You say to your brother, that God is everlasting and eternal God, and hath no beginning, nor will have no ending: but (say you) this their commission of the Spirit tells us of a God that no man knows in all the world but two men, and that no other can know the true God but those that believe in those two men; but, say you, what this new- broached light will come to, you will at present forbear judging, but leave it to the hands of the God of prophets and apostles.

Answer. As to that we own, that God is everlasting and eternal, and had no beginning, nor hath no enduing: and this is the same God this third and last commission tells you of, only there is no man in the world, at this day, that doth truly know this everlasting God, but us two, who are the chosen witnesses of this everlasting God, that knows him, and those to whom we reveal it; neither can any other man know the true God but those that believe in us two men.

Nay, farther, I say, as Christ did in another case, concerning himself: *Except* saith Christ, *you believe that I am he, you shall die in your sins:* so likewise I say, except you or any other do believe in our doctrine of the true God, and us two men, to be the last chosen witnesses and prophets of God, I say you shall all die in your sins, that is, in unbelief, and so damned to eternity; for this I must tell you, that whoever dies in unbelief, that hath heard the sound of a true prophet's words or writings, and believes them not, he dies in his sins of unbelief, and all sins else that he hath committed; so that he is cleansed from no sin at all, and what will follow upon that, that conscience that dies in his sins, let every man's conscience judge. But whosoever believeth in a true prophet's report and doctrine, his heart is purified by faith in himself, and doth not die in his sins, but is cleansed from the guilt and condemnation in his conscience of all sins, both original and actual, though the reason of man being the seed, counts the very act of faith that giveth peace to man's mind, they count the greatest sin of all: but great is the power of faith, and strong; but low is the power of reason, and weak; And as for this new-broached light, as you call it, I say it was new-broached by the God of heaven himself; and this light declared by us the witnesses of the Spirit, will come to centre itself in God, from whence it came, as the light of prophets and apostles did, who were sent of God, as those two men were whom you so much slight; and it would have been well for you if you had forborn judging, and left it to the hands of the God of prophets and apostles: but your reason hath undertook, by the dead letter of the Scriptures, to judge the greatest light that ever (God sent upon earth, and of a more higher nature than that of the prophets and apostles; but the light of heaven was ever slighted by the seed of the serpent, their hearts being darkened by the letter of the Scriptures, you have presumed to fight against: the fight of this commission of the Spirit, which God hath committed to two men, and you have judged it, and have not left judgment to God. These things aforesaid are the most considerable passages in your large letter to your brother Alexander, and the very quintessence of your knowledge in the letter, of the Scriptures, wherein you have taken up dead mens words, to fight with a man that is alive; you do as if a man should take the sheath of a sword in his hand, to fight with him that hath a glittering sword in his hand, with two edges, which cuts every way; for the letter of the Scriptures is but the sheath for the two-edged sword of the Spirit to be in: and God hath drawn forth this glittering sword with two edges, out of the letter of the Scriptures, and hath put it into two single men's mouths, and hath given us power to bless and curse to eternity: so that it doth not peculiarly belong to God but unto man; and had you believed in me, you should have believed God that sent me; but in that you have despised that two men should know more of God than all men in the world, you have despised God also, and have sinned against the Holy Ghost, and God hath made me your judge in his stead.

The blasphemies you have spoken are these:

1. That the letter of the Scriptures ought to be credited as if God did speak himself.

2. You prefer the words of Peter and Paul, being dead so many hundred years, to be of more consequence now than the voice of words God spake to John Reeve.

3. You call the commission of the Spirit a supposed commission and imagination.

4. You call the commission your brother owns and believes, error, and strong delusion, and high impostures, and pretended revelations and commissions.

5. You utterly deny the body, or person of Christ Jesus, to be Father, Son, and Holy Spirit: this you say is utterly false.

6. You say, the distinction your brother giveth of Christ being Father, Son, and Spirit, in plain terms, is a piece of nonsense.

7. You call the talk of this commission of the Spirit a whimsey of the brain, and no less than delusion. You call the doctrine of this commission of the Spirit a new-broached light.

These things being considered, I thought if some thing necessary to answer the things of most note in your letter to your brother Alexander; for in that you despise his advice and counsel, and doctrine and commission he owns, you have despised me and my doctrine. So I have collected the most wickedest speeches of yours out of your letter, wherein you may plainly see the cause of your condemnation is just upon you, if in that you think you have free-will to save yourself from eternal damnation; yet your free-will could not preserve you from the sin against the Holy Ghost, notwithstanding you saw Noble, the Baptist-preacher, damned before your face, for the same sins; yet he spake but few words to what you have done in your letter.

These things considered, in obedience to my commission from God, I do, for these your wicked speeches afore-written, pronounce Edward Delamain, Baptist-preacher, cursed and damned, both in soul and body, from the presence of God, elect men, and angels, to all eternity.

And it will be a marvelous thing if you do escape a very mean, low, even almost a vagabond condition in this life, besides your damnation hereafter; for this I must tell you, that sins of this nature seldom escape a double curse. But now you may go see if you can preach and pray this curse off you again; and if your will had any power in it, now you had best bestir yourself

Written by

LODOWICKE MUGGLETON,

One of the Lord's two last Witnesses and Prophets unto the High and Mighty God, the Man Christ Jesus in Glory.

A Copy of a Letter wrote by the Prophet Lodowicke Muggleton, to Mrs. Mary Parker, August 13, 1668.

Loving and kind friend, Mary Parker,

I RECEIVED your letter inclosed in Mrs. Sudbury's letter, and I find in your letter many excellent expressions, and words of faith and confidence in those truths declared by this commission of the Spirit: as in that great mystery, that God became flesh, and God did die to redeem the select seed? the seed of faith, from eternal death: and in that you have believed the report of us the witnesses of the Spirit, and have cast yourself wholly upon this commission of the Spirit, the arm of the Lord's saving health is revealed unto you in a measure already, in that you have found light and life in believing; and the salvation of the Lord shall be revealed unto you more and more, even from strength to strength, until a perfection of faith in you, so that no doubt shall arise in your heart as to your eternal happiness; but the light of faith in you, built upon this rock you have cast yourself upon, it will shew you how all the world doth lie in wickedness, ignorance, and darkness; nay, all religious, righteous, and good-natured people are in darkness, and ignorant altogether of this great thing, that God should become a child, and grow to a man, and eat and drink with man, and so suffer death by his own creatures, in that he poured out his soul unto death, in that he poured out the Godhead life, that was in the blood; therefore, the blood of Christ was no less than the blood of God; and whoever doth believe this, doth really and truly, by faith, drink the blood of God, and hath eternal life abiding in them; that is, the full assurance of eternal life abides here in them in this life, and so enters into eternal glory, when this natural life shall die; for there is no time to the dead.

I confess, I do not know that ever I did see you in my life; but your letter doth shew to me what your heart is, as I shall add this to your further confidence of faith and comfort of heart, that I do declare you are of the blessed of the Lord both in soul and body to eternity; in that I perceive you have received in your heart a prophet in the name of a prophet, you shall have a prophet's reward, which reward is no less than the blessing of eternal life.

So resteth your friend, though unknown by sight, but known by truth in the eternal truth,

LODOWICKE MUGGLETON.

Postern, August 13, 1668.

A Copy of a Letter written by the Prophet Lodowicke Muggleton, to Mr. Thomas Tompkinson, bearing date from London, September 21, 1665.

Loving and kind Friend, Thomas Tompkinson,

I UNDERSTAND by Elizabeth Bootham, that you have not received those books that came out of the press last, in answer to George Foxe; also I heard Mr. Delamaine's letter you sent to him, and you made no mention of the receipt of the books, which I did much marvel at; but I perceive by your letter to Elizabeth Bootham, that you have not received them yet; therefore I thought good to let you understand, that I did send five books to you; it is now almost six weeks since: also I sent a letter with them, and another enclosed from your maid, but it seems you have received none, which is a very base thing of the carrier, that could not have conveyed the letter to you before now; but I perceive it was partly your maid's fault, for she and my wife went together, and your maid delivered the books and the letter to the carrier that brought her up to London, which is Utoxeter carrier, and not by Ashbourne carrier, and this I suppose is the cause of the miscarriage; therefore I would desire you to call for the letter and five books of Laurence Foxe, Utoxeter carrier, which he received about five or six weeks ago. You will know by the date of the letter if you receive it. This Laurence Foxe inns at the Bell, in Smithfield, near the White Bear, London. Also I would desire you, if you have sold any of those books, to send the money for as many as you have sold as soon as conveniently you can.

This is all at present, only that we are all well, and do remember our loves to you and your wife, with all friends else there with you.

I rest and remain your friend in the true faith,

LODOWICKE MUGGLETON.

Postern, September 21, 1668.

Direct your letters to me thus: For Mr. Muggleton, at the widow Brunt's house, next door to the sign of the White Horse, in the Postern, near Moor-lane, London.

Elizabeth Bootham remembers her love and service to you and your wife; and she saith, she would not have you trouble yourself about sending any cheese, for she doth think she shall not stay here in London until All-holland-tide, therefore desireth to hear from you as soon as may be.

So resteth your servant,

ELIZABETH BOOTHAM.

A Copy of a Letter sent by the Prophet Lodowicke Muggleton, to Mr. Thomas Tompkinson, of Sladehouse, in Staffordshire, bearing date from London, December 14, 1668.

Loving Friend, Thomas Tompkinson,

THIS is to certify you, that I received your letter, dated December 7, 1668; also I received of William Osbourne the ten shillings you sent, and Elizabeth Bootham received her things also. There is little or no news here at London at present, for every sort of people here hath freedom of conscience to meet without any disturbance, only the Quakers people are much offended at me for setting forth this last book, called a Looking-Glass for Quakers; insomuch, that several of the chief speakers of the Quakers have come to talk to me about it, and have come under the sentence of damnation; and one Thomas Loe, a speaker of the Quakers, sent me a cursed, desperate, blasphemous letter, worse than ever I received of any from Quaker or other before; but upon the return of the sentence of damnation upon him, this said Thomas Loe fell sick the same night he received it, and never went out of his bed more till he was carried to be buried, which was in less than three weeks, which thing hath been great amazement to the Quakers, and hath moved them much against me; insomuch, that they have banded themselves against me, and have raked amongst all the damned devils they can hear of, to bear their testimony against me; and all false reports by this damned crew are taken for truth by the Quakers, that they might set forth a book against me. The chief speakers of the Quakers have consulted together, and, as I understand by several Quakers, have written nearly thirty sheets of paper against me, and intended to put it in print before now. I did expect to have seen it before now, but there hath fallen a cross upon them, for their printer press is broken in pieces, and the printer in prison for printing a book against the Presbyterians, and the man that wrote it hideth himself, yet a Quaker, and one of those that writeth against me; so that for the present there is a stop put to the Quaker's book against me, for no printer else must do it, it being not licenced.

I have written the chief passages in a dispute with some Quaker with me for memory sake, which, hereafter may come to light

So in haste, I rest, only my love, with my wife's love, remembered unto yourself and Wife, and all friends else there with you.

I remain your friend in the true faith,

LODOWICKE MUGGLETON

The Postern, London,

Dec. 14, 1668.

A Copy of a Letter written by the Prophet Lodowicke Muggleton, containing the Blessing of Eternal Life, sent unto Lydia Brooks, of Sheasby, in Leicestershire, (this was John Saddington's sister) bearing date from London, October 24, in the year 1668.

Friend Lydia Brooks,

I RECEIVED your letter of your brother John Saddington, wherein I understand how you came to hear of truth declared by this commission of the Spirit, and that the Lord hath opened your heart to believe the reports of our writings, and that I am a true prophet sent of God, It is confessed that I never saw you in my life; yet this testimony you give of your faith in your letter in the true God, and in this commission of the Spirit, giveth me assurance in myself that your heart is right in the sight of God, and that your faith is built upon a sure rock, that cannot fail; for whoever do only believe the doctrine declared by this commission of the Spirit, and believeth him whom God sent, they can do no less than receive God that sent him; and whoever receiveth a prophet in the name of a prophet, shall receive a prophet's reward, which reward is no less than eternal life; and that your faith may increase and grow, from strength to strength, as it is begun, I do declare you one of the blessed of the Lord to eternity, though I never saw your person; but by your words I saw your faith, and being justified by faith, you will have peace with God; for by words of unbelief are many people condemned, and by words of faith are many people justified; and as for your nearest relations, as husband and mother, being against you for not going to church, to that I say, be not you overcome to break the peace of your mind by the threats, or persuasions, or temptations of husband or mother, to defile your mind by false worship through slavish fear; but worship God in Spirit and truth as you have begun, as this commission hath declared, and you will become more than a conqueror in your spirit over husband and mother, and shall no more stagger in your mind through the persuasions or temptations of any whatsoever; and the wilderness where you now live will yield you such peace of mind, that will be as sweet as honey, or the honey-comb, though you have none with you to partake with your sufferings. This is all at present, only my love to yourself, though unknown.

I rest and remain your friend in the true faith,

LODOWICKE MUGGLETON.

Postern, October 24, 1668.

A Copy of a Letter written by the Prophet Lodowicke Muggleton, to Mr. Thomas Tompkinson, of Sladehouse, in Staffordshire, bearing Date from London, January 31, 1669.

Loving and kind Friend in the true Faith Thomas Tompkinson,

THIS is to certify you that I have sent seven books of the Interpretation of the Witch of Endor; I did intend the Answer to Isaac Pennington should have been printed also; but it did miscarry in the press.

I never was so crossed, in all the books as I have printed as in these two; for this of the Witch of Endor hath been for six months in the printer's hands; but with much difficulty, and trouble, and charge, I have got it safe out of the press: but because this printer was so base, and kept it so long, I put the other to another printer, thinking to have it done; before this, and so it would; but through the forgetfulness of the printer, not taking the copy in his pockets as he thought to do, he went out, and left the copy and proof of one sheet upon the press, with his servants, and the searchers came immediately up stairs and took it. and would have carried it to the council; but the printer made friends, for moneys else he would have been utterly undone; for it cost the printer seven pounds, and me five pounds, to pacify the matter, and not get it done neither. But I have preserved the copy, most part of it, and hereafter I do think to print it, but not at present, it will be no ways convenient. But I am glad it was not the Witch of Endor was taken; because 'tis of more value, and never written of before, by us, nor no other, and much desired, and objected by many: there is one for Thomas Turner, who gave 2s. 6d., one for Richard Grindy, who gave 1s. 6d., and one for John Grindy, who gave 1s. and one for Lawrence Waterman, who gave 1s., and there is three for yourself to dispose as you please, and pay for the carriage. These cannot be afforded under 1s. price, I sell none of them under, nor never will, while they last; I will not do as I did by the Mortality of the Soul, sell it for sixpence, and now I would give 2s. myself for one single. Here is Mr. Delamaine's letter inclosed. Thus in haste, I rest, only my love, with my wife's love, remembered to yourself and wife, and all friends in the faith,

LODOWICKE MUGGLETON.

Postern, London, January 31, 1669.

A Copy of a Letter sent by the Prophet Lodowicke Muggleton to Mr. Goodwyn, of Chesterfield, bearing date February 4, 1669.

Loving Friend in the true Faith, Mr. Goodwyn,

THIS is to certify you that I have sent you six books of the Interpretation of the Witch of Endor, desiring you to give Betty Smith one, and Betty Slater one, and two for your mother, and two for yourself.

Also I did intend the other should have been printed now; but things have fallen out very cross; for the other book was taken in the press, and the printer brought into a great deal of trouble; for it cost the printer seven pounds, and me five pounds, to pacify the matter; else the printer would have been utterly undone, and not get it done neither, and I could do no less to help bear him out, though it was altogether his careless forgetfulness that was the cause, and the business of the other printer, that kept this so long in hand, about six months: I have been more vexed about these than with all I did before; but yet I am somewhat comforted, that though I have staid long, yet, at last, I have got it out of the press, it being of more concernment than the other, and of a bigger volume, and a thing that was never written of before, by us, nor no other: and hereafter I do intend to print the other, if it be possible, when times are a little more open; for the copy is yet preserved.

This is all at present, only my love, with my wife's love remembered unto you, and your wife, and mother, and all friends else there with you, in haste,

I rest your friend in the true faith,

LODOWICKE MUGGLETON.

February 4, 1669.

Also I have sent of these books to William Newcome, desiring him to send two of the Mortality of the Soul for them: he said (when he was in London) that he had two of them, and that he would change With me for these. I would intreat you to be earnest with him, to look them up, and send them to me suddenly; because there is one or two friends in Kent, is extreme eager with me to get them for them; because I told them, I thought I should; and if he hath any more there, to let him send them, and he shall have what he will for them, either books or money; and this I would desire William Newcome, to sell none of these under twelve pence a-piece; for I will sell none under, as long as they last; for these cost twice the price printing of what the others did.

You may give William Newcome this piece.

A Copy of a Letter wrote by the Prophet Lodowicke Muggleton to John Lad.

Friend John Lad in the true Faith, &c.

I HAVE read over your letter, and I perceive your understanding is very much enlightened in the true saving light, and your faith strong in the doctrine of the commission of the Spirit. I have heard a good report of you before, as to your knowledge in truth in spiritual things, but by your expressions in your letter you have shewed a greater measure of faith in God, and knowledge in those things, those saving truths declared by us the witnesses of the Spirit, than was expected by me; but where the seed of faith is quickened by the words of truth, it will grow like a green olive-tree, as Christ said his words were spirit and life: also to every one that believes, the arm of the Lord's saving health is revealed to that soul, which is spirit and life to it, in that they are a savour of life unto life in them that are saved in that words of truth. It quickens that seed in man that was dead, and makes it alive, and so becomes spirit and life in man; so that the life a man doth live here is a life of faith, which is peace of mind, because this faith it shall live eternally with God, in whom he did believe. Here you have expressed a great measure of this faith, and it is that which I believe is in your heart is true faith, and will grow in you to a greater perfection, enabling, you to withstand all gainsayers whatsoever even in this life, besides the eternal happiness hereafter, when men shall receive the end of their faith, even the salvation of their souls. This is all at present, time being short.

I rest your friend in the true faith,

LODOWICKE MUGGLETON.

Postern, London, April 23, 1669.

A Letter from the Prophet Lodowicke Muggleton, June 14, 1669.

Dear Friend in the true Faith, Mrs. Parker,

I RECEIVED a letter from you heretofore before I had seen you, which made me sensible that your faith was true, and your heart was right in the sight of God; and I being the messenger of God, and an ambassador in God's stead, could do no less than give judgment and sentence of blessedness upon you; and I see and know that the word of a true prophet is not in vain, but standeth for ever; and I have seen the fruit of faith and love abound in you since I have seen you, and that part of those melancholy thoughts you were exercised with in your mind about temporal matters, are in a measure vanished away, and comfortable thoughts do run in the blood in the room thereof, which cheereth the heart in the assurance of eternal life, and happiness after death, knowing there is no worse thing than there is in this life. Oh, how comfortable is faith, without doubting, in the soul of man and woman! It removes mountains of darkness and great mists which lie before the understanding of man and woman; it giveth an hundred-fold of comfort in this life, and life everlasting hereafter; it makes a man or woman enjoy themselves in this life, and no bitterness of fear of damnation can come into the heart. These things I know you have seen, in a measure, and will experience them more and more. Oh, how beautiful are the feet of those that bring glad tidings of peace to the soul of man or woman! I have read of these things in Scripture in my ignorant zeal, but knew not what that peace was, neither did I know what that glad tidings was, until I was a chosen messenger of glad tidings myself; yea, I have been a messenger of glad tidings to you and many others, and I have been a messenger of sad tidings to many. These things I certainly know, yet am I noways lifted up with pride in this thing, nor cast down with any opposition of slanders and lies cast upon me by reprobate men and women: but I speak these things the more to strengthen your faith, being but of a short time standing, and having but little society with saints, and little of experience. I thought it necessary to speak kindly unto you, that your joy might be full; that you might have the penny of assurance of everlasting life, as those that have wrought in the vineyard of faith many years.

Thus, with my true love, and my wife's love remembered unto yourself,

I rest and remain your friend in the true faith, the eternal truth,

LODOWICKE MUGGLETON.

From the Postern, London, June 14, 1669.

We are all here at London in pretty good health.

A Letter from the Prophet Lodowicke Muggleton to Mrs. Ellen Sudbury, June 14, 1669.

Dear and well-beloved Friend in the eternal Truth, Ellen Sudbury,

I HAVE always remembered your faith and love to this commission of the Spirit from the beginning, wherein I received your first letter, wherein I found your faith and love was built upon a sure rock, even before you had seen me, or any of my writings, but Claxton's writings only; and I see how blest a thing it is to cast the soul upon a commission from God, not reasoning with flesh and blood, that is, to think to try the prophet's doctrine and declaration by the letter of the Scriptures, which cannot speak (as most people do) but you believing and did not see, in that you were more blessed than these that have both heard me speak, and seen me, and have believed as Thomas did also. You were one of the first, nay, I think the first in those parts, that did set to your seal, that the doctrine of this commission of the Spirit to be a real truth, and received a prophet in the name of a prophet, whereby you received a prophet's reward, the blessing of everlasting life, whereby you have grown in grace from strength of faith to strength, even to the full assurance of eternal life abiding in yourself; so that no doubt can arise in you to trouble you, as it doth in all others who build not upon this rock. Also you were for several years as one alone; for every Quaker, Bemonist, and others to be fried, that if it were possible by their cavilling spirits to have caused you to doubt or question your faith; but I have seen your faith hath grown stronger and stronger, and hath established your soul more firm, even like Mount Sion, which cannot be shaken, even while you stood alone; but in some space of time after to add unto your comfort in this life and the life to come; also God hath given your husband to be partaker of the like precious faith with you, and so will partake of the same glory with you hereafter, when time shall be no more; also there is given unto you for your further comfort in this life, another true believer fit for your society, one of your own sex, even your true neighbour, M. P.

Dear Friend,

This is to certify you that I came well home to London on Friday in the Whitsun-week, and all friends in London are pretty well, and were glad at my coming; but Mr. Whitehead went from Cambridge a matter of twelve days before. There is little news at London since I went, only the Quaker's testimony against me, upon whom I gave sentence of damnation, three hours before his death was written his testimony against me from his own mouth, which I received when I came home. It is of very little consequence, else I would have sent it you; but instead of that, I have sent you a book written by one that was a Quaker fourteen years, which will inform you more concerning the Quakers; and I would intreat you to convey the other book to Mrs. Carter, with the letter, as soon as possible may be.

Thus, with my dear love to yourself and husband, with my wife's love to you both, I take leave, and remain

Your Friend in the eternal truth,

LODOWICKE MUGGLETON.

The Postern, London, June 14, 1669.

A Copy of a Letter written by the Prophet Lodowicke Muggleton to Mr. Thomas Tompkinson, of Sladehouse, in Staffordshire, bearing date from London, June 19, 1669.

Loving Friend in the eternal Truth, Thomas Tompkinson,

I SAW a letter of yours to our friend Mr. Delamaine, and I received 9*s*. of him by your order; and I perceive by your letter it is exceeding great trouble to your spirit, that it was not your happiness to see me and those friends with me, being so near you. Mr. Whitehead, of Braintree, and Walter Bohenan, the Scotchman, were with me in all my journey, and we had good success and prosperous in all places and things we did intend, in that we saw all friends of the faith in Cambridgeshire, Leicestershire, Nottingham, and Chesterfield, and there was an intention and resolution to have seen you in us all, and all our care was when we were at Nottingham how to give you notice, that you might have met me either at Nottingham or Chesterfield; for Mr. Whitehead was to go, and did go, to Birmingham and Dudley in Staffordshire, joining to Worcestershire, to Mr. Finch, one that was formerly a Quaker, but now doth own this. Mr. Whitehead had some business with him in the way of his trade, being an ironmonger; so Walter Bohenan went with Mr. Whitehead to the place before-mentioned; it was above forty miles from Nottingham, but I stayed at Nottingham, being very weary with riding. We came to Nottingham to Mr. Sudbury's on Saturday; but Mr. Whitehead and Walter Bohenan went from thence the Monday morning very early; but I staid there till the Thursday following before I went to Chesterfield, and they were to meet me at Chesterfield, at Mrs. Carter's, on Thursday, as was intended, but they did not come there till Saturday; so I made a full account, and was almost confident they had found you out, which had caused them to stay so long; for they did intend, and it was concluded upon by us all, and by Mrs. Sudbury, that they should find you out. Being well horsed, as they were, if it were twelve or fourteen miles out of their way, they would have seen you, because Mr. Sudbury would have conveyed a letter unto you, to give you notice that I was there, but he could not; so I depended, and so did Mrs. Sudbury, that Mr. Whitehead and Mr. Walter Bohenan would have seen you, and the more, because they staid two days longer than was intended; but it fell out contrary to all our expectations, which made us all sensible of much trouble, that all things else in our journey had prospered well, and if we had seen you also, our joy would have been full; but missing this opportunity, our joy was somewhat diminished, to what it would have been had we seen you, even as much satisfaction as can be had in weary journies; but after a little rest there is joy in the morning. Mr. Whitehead would willingly have gone ten miles out of his way if he could have heard where Slade-house was; but none could tell them where; for they asked the country people for, or where Slade-house was, but none could tell them where, nor they did not know or remember any town near it, for they had forgot that I had told them it was about four or five miles from Ashbourne, by which means did this mishap fall out.

So, dear friend, I would not have you to think, or have any such thoughts, that it was for want of good will or love in any of us, or any slender thoughts in any of us more to you than to others; for we had and have the same affections of love and tenderness, and desire, to have seen you and your good wife, as to others; but none of us knowing the way, and by report a very bad way to your house from those parts, disheartened us to go any further.

Also I understand that Mr. Delamaine did give you to know that I was in those parts, else you would not have known so soon; but it was too late before he did know it himself; for he did as much marvel that I was in those parts of the country as you did, for there was no friends in the faith, nor sons nor daughters here at London, that did know that I would go any further than Cambridge, but my wife and one more, whose mother I was to go and See in Leicestershire, nor of Mr. Whitehead and Walter Bohenan's going with me, I kept all secret from friends here in London; but friends in Cambridgeshire knew of it; but I gave them notice to keep it secret from friends in London, till we came back again, which they did; so that none could give intelligence to friends in Leicestershire, Nottingham, or Chesterfield, so we came upon them before they were aware, unexpected, and so we thought to do by you, but did not attain our desires. For I knew if it had been known here at London, it would have been blazed about to them all before we came, and to you also, had it been known; for as soon as Mr. Delamaine did hear of it by a letter I sent to my wife, and one that Mr. Saddington's sister in Leicestershire sent to him, it was known that I was in those parts, then Mr. Delamaine, out of his exceeding great love to you, did send you word; but going by Ashbourne carrier, I perceive it came to your hand a day or two too late; for he could not have sent with safety to your house by the post; yet I perceive you had our friend Delamaine's letter before we went from Nottingham; for William Newcombe parted with us at Mrs. Carter's on Monday morning early, and he was to go that day to Bakwell, and we went to Nottingham, and staid there till Wednesday ten o'clock, and so departed thence the way we Came, till we came to Cambridge again; so Mr. Whitehead, as soon as he could, staid three days there, and went to his own home; but I staid a week longer; for I had promised them to stay with them at my return back.

Thus accidentally, I was the occasion that you did not see us; because it was secret and not known; but our desire and intent was to you as to others.

Thus I have given you a true account of the most considerable passages, and of our intents and desires, in this our journey.

So I shall say no more at present as to that; only to let you know that I am well, and so is my wife, and so are most of our friends in the faith here in London, pretty well.

Thus, with my love, with my wife's love to yourself, and your wife, and all friends else there with you,

I rest and remain your friend in the eternal truth,

LODOWICKE MUGGLETON,

The Postern, London, June 19, 1669.

I would desire when you send to me or Mr. Delamaine, if it be not too much trouble, whether that maid that fasted a whole year, as was reported, be alive yet, or no; because I heard at Chesterfield for certain that she was yet alive, and that it was a mere cheat to get money.

A Letter from the Prophet Lodowicke Muggleton, to Mrs. Ellen Sudbury, August 30, 1669.

Dearly beloved Friend in the true Faith, Ellen Sudbury,

I RECEIVED your letter, and was glad to hear of your welfare, and of the strength of faith in you: you are as one of the daughters of Sion, which rejoiceth. the heart of him that begot you to the true faith; for in the day wherein you first believed, before you had seen me, you were blessed of the Lord's messenger for your faith; for you have been like a green olive tree, that hath had the oil of joy, and gladness of heart, in the assurance of everlasting life, these many years, and I see the cruise of oil doth not staunch yet, but runneth more powerful than at the first, and so it will to the end; for the act of faith in you hath digged a deep well in the seed of faith in you, which will spring up in you, to satisfy your thirst here; so that no doubt or want of peace can come unto you, as concerning your eternal happiness, and it will spring up into eternal life. Also you may and do see, what an excellent language the heavenly language is; it differs from all the languages in the world; and you having learned the heavenly language of Canaan, you know the voice of it, wherever you hear it: in some it is more plain and easily understood than in others; yet, whoever doth speak it, though but in a stammering manner, yet the voice of faith understands the language of heavenly Canaan easily, which I know you can experience very easily; for you have understood and spoke that language this many years. Mr. Whitehead is well; he was at London the last week, and about Michaelmas he will be at London again. There is a great increase in the faith here at London, and in some countries. There have been with me of late, two or three German men, that were banished out of Germany, for not submitting to the worship set up by that power: there hath been grange things acted there about religion, as here in England; so these men came to see me, to see what difference there is between the revelation and declaration, declared by John Reeve and myself, and that revelation their countrymen have had; but the difference is as great as heaven and earth; for their revelation is like many that have been in England these forty years, as prophets and prophetesses, yet know not the true God, neither in form nor nature, nor the right devil, nor any true principle of doctrine nor commission, yet go forth as if the Lord sent them, yet know, not the Lord; the one of these is a doctor of physick, and the other was a minister in Germany; the minister could not speak English so well as the doctor; but the doctor bought all the bookstand hath written the commission-book into the. German language, and hath sent it among the Germans.; so what the issue will be, time will bring forth; for there is many would believe, did they but understand it in their own language.

You speak as if I should hear from Mrs. Goodwin, but I have heard nothing from them, since I was there with them, not as yet.

Thus, in haste, I shall only remember my dear love unto yourself and your husband, with my wife's love unto you both.

I rest and remain your friend in the true faith,

LODOWICKE MÜGGLETON.

From the Postern, London, August 30, 1669.

There is two little books, the one concerning witches, and the other an answer to Pennington the Quakers book, are ready for the press; therefore, what Mr. Sudbury is free to give towards the printing, is left to his own liberty. About five weeks hence it will be, I suppose, printed.

A Letter from the Prophet Lodowicke Muggleton, to Mrs. Mary Parker, August 30, 1669.

Dear and loving Friend in the true faith, Mary Parker,

THIS is to certify you that I received your letter, dated August the 8th day, 1669. It is a great while since, and I have returned you no answer, because I have been very much employed with writing and speaking with people, since I was with you; but I am not insensible of rejoicing in the growth of your faith and confidence in this commission of the Spirit, in that you have received a prophet in the name of a prophet, in the love of truth, and that the word of a true prophet shall stand for ever.

Now I know it will be unto you that believe, as the voice of God himself, as the law of the Medes and Persians, that cannot be altered; and now the light of heaven being set in your understanding, by your believing in the commission of the Spirit, in casting yourself upon the word of a man; I know you can tell the difference in yourself, whether your condition was better when you did not believe, or whether it is better and more satisfactory to your spirit now you do believe, than before: therefore, let no motions of reason in yourself, nor arguments of reason in others, make you to doubt; for this I say, there is such a thing as eternal glory hereafter, by believing, which will not be a minute of an hour, after death, before every believer shall enter into that personal glory, where they shall see their God, their King, and Redeemer, who hath redeemed us with his own blood, face to face. Also, there is such a thing as eternal damnation, which will not be a minute of an hour after death to the unbeliever, where they shall be capable of eternal torment, in utter darkness with the devil reason, for ever and ever.

I write not these things unto you, as if I did question or doubt the strength of your faith; but because I know your faith is built upon a rock, that cannot be shaken, and it might grow more strong, and peace might more abound in you, even while you live in this world, that you might rejoice, by believing an hundred-fold of satisfaction of spirit in this life; for in the life to come you shall have life everlasting. Thus being in haste, I shall take leave, only my dear love to yourself, with my wife's love remembered unto you.

I rest and remain your friend in the eternal truth,

LODOWICKE MUGGLETON.

From the Postern, London, August 30, 1669.

I have finished that writing concerning the Witch of Endor, and other witches, ready for the press: I have been desired by many to put it forth, with the Answer to Esquire Pennington, the Quaker. They are two little volumes, distinct of themselves; therefore what you are free to give, towards the printing of them, is left to your own liberty. It will, I suppose, be in print, about a month or five weeks hence.

Letter from the Prophet Lodowicke Muggleton, to Mr. Thomas Tompkinson, Sept. 6, 1669.

Loving Friend in the true Faith, Thomas Tompkinson,

THIS is to let you understand that I have written; a book concerning the Witch of Endor, spoken of in the book of Samuel, and of other witches and wizards, who deal with familiar spirits, shewing how n, familiar spirit is begotten, and how they may be said to speak out of the grounds and how Samuel may be said to speak unto king Saul, and how spirits may be said to speak without bodies, and how a man may be said to preach unto the spirits in prison, and how a man may be said to be in Paradise, yet not without a body, and how men may understand what that Satan is, whom the Scripture speaketh of, and what that Satan was, that tempted Job, and all other places of Scripture that seem as if spirits might speak, and appear unto people, without bodies: they are clearly proved and opened, and will much enlighten the understanding, to answer unto those things so commonly objected by most people. Also there is another book which I have written in answer to Esquire Pennington, a Quaker, his book, which he wrote against me, and many of our friends have a desire that I would put them two in print; they are but little volumes; the Witches, I suppose, will make five sheets, and I suppose the other will be less.

Therefore I thought good to acquaint you with it, and what you are free to give toward the printing, or any other friend there with you, it is left to your own liberty what; but I suppose there is hardly any there with you, but yourself, that can, or is free, to give any thing towards the printing. I suppose they will be printed about a month hence. This is all at present, being in haste, only to let you know that I am very well, and so is my wife, and so are all friends else here in London, pretty well.

So with my love, and my wife's love remembered unto yourself, and your wife, and all friends else in the faith there with you,

I rest and remain your friend in the eternal truth,

LODOWICKE MUGGLETON.

From the Postern, London.

September 1669.

When you send to me, direct your letter to me thus: "For Mr. Muggleton, at the widow Brunt's house, next door to the sign of the White Horse, in the postern, near Moor-lane, London.

A Letter of the Prophet Lodowicke Muggleton to Christopher Hill, September 9, 1669.

Loving Friend, Christopher Hill,

MY love remembered unto you and your wife. This is to certify you, that my wife hath been sick of the small-pox; they did appear the next morning you went away from us: she hath been very full, so that there was little hopes of life; but now we do conceive the worst is past for this bout; yet she is very troublesome still, being something light-headed, so that her nurse can have no rest, which is a marvellous thing, that she should hold out as she doth; for she hath not got an hour's sleep at once, not these twelve nights and days. My wife doth remember her love to yourself and wife, and to all the rest of her friends with you. And I would desire you to send me those two Commission-Books, and if you have any more of them, send them, and as many of the Mortality as you have, send; and if you have any of the Dialogue, and DevilBooks, and the Lost Sheep, send them up with the other, if you can, the next return of Haines the carrier.

I question not but this proclamation, which came out last, will both fright and incite you all to church now, to save twelve-pence a-week; for it will fare as well with those as never goes at all, as it will with those as go every now and then, except they can give a lawful excuse why they stay away: they must hear divine service, and receive the sacrament also like good national Christians. But those who are not stone-blind, may see what it is to make shipwreck of faith, and a good conscience; neither will that wisdom of reason, in bowing down to a false worship, gain that felicity of mind, nor wealth of this world, as was expected, but rather the contrary; for he that is willing to lose his life shall save it, and he that is willing to save his life, shall lose it: and those words of Christ, I find to be a standing truth, both in the spiritual, and in the natural, and happy and blessed are they which hold out to the end, that they may receive an hundred-fold of peace and quietness in this life, and in the life to come life everlasting. No more at present, but rest

Your friend in the true faith in the true God,

LODOWICKE MUGGLETON.

London, September 9, 1669.

A Copy of a Letter written by the Prophet Lodowicke Mugglinson, to Mr. Thomas Tompkinson, of Sladehouse, in Staffordshire, bearing date from London, October 4, 1669.

Dear and loving Friend in the true Faith, Thomas Tompkinson,

THIS is to certify you, that I received your letter, dated September 6, 1669, and I suppose I shall receive the money on Monday morning; for I was forced to write these lines unto you; before I could receive the money, because you might not miss of an answer this return; and I understand you have some thoughts to come to see us shortly, and that you might see friends in the way; therefore I shall give the names and places: I suppose you will come by Nottingham, and those friends you know there, only Mr. Sudbury and his wife, and Mr. Parker; and in Leicestershire, a matter of seven miles on this side Leicester, towards London, at a town called Arnesby, liveth one John Hall, and his mother, and two or three miles on one side, liveth Thomas Hall, the brother of John Hall, and have two brothers more in London that own the truth; and within half a mile of John Hall, liveth one who is sister to John Saddington, here of London, which owneth the truth; I saw her when I was there in my last journey: John Hall, or his mother, will send for her; so that they will inform you one of another: and as for those at Cambridge, it will be your best course to enquire for one William Dickinson, a butcher, in the Petty Cury, at Cambridge, and there is Thomas Parke, that will inform you of Charles Cleve, Mr. Hampson, and several others, there in Cambridge, and at Burton, two miles from Cambridge, Goodman Warboyes and his wife, and at Orwell, William Cakebread and his wife.

There is several others in those parts, which those friends aforesaid will inform you of. And if you should come into Essex, at Braintree there is one James Whitehead, an ironmonger, he that was with me when I was at Chesterfield.

This is all at present, being in haste, only my love, and my wife's love remembered to yourself and your wife.

I rest and remain your friend in the true faith,

LODOWICKE MUGGLETON.

From the Postern, London,

October 4, 1669.

I have received the 10s. since.

My love presented to all friends there with you.

A Copy of a Letter written by the Prophet Lodowicke Muggleton, to Mr. Thomas Tompkinson, dated from London, December 4, 1669.

Dear Friend in the eternal Truth, Thomas Tompkinson,

I RECEIVED your letter, dated November 29, 1669, and according to your request, I shall write a few lines unto you, this return, to certify that I am well, and so is my wife, and all friends elsewhere at London, and that my daughter White was well delivered of a son, which was a great comfort to her husband, and to us all, because they have none alive; but two weeks after it was born, it died, which is some grief to her and him; and as for Mr. Delamaine, he is well, and I shewed him your letter; and as for Mrs. Alsop, here in London, I do not know any such woman, neither do I know any that believes this commission in Lancaster; if there be any, it is more than I know. And as for that business concerning the Lord Mayor, he could do nothing to me, having no law on his side; for I said unto him if there were any matter of law against me, let him bind them (the accuser) over to prosecute, and I would put in bail to defend it; but he, having no law on his side, gave no heed to what I said, nor none of them proffered to be bound to prosecute; so the Lord-Mayor railed at me, and threatened me to do what he could, and as it is reported since, that he gave the Commission-Book to the Speaker of the House of Commons, being the Lord-Mayor's kinsman, to do what they could do; but I hear nothing of it since; for now he is out of his mayoralty, he is like another man. And as for the books you think long, as you may well enough, and so they do here in London; but the printer hath dealt so basely by me, he hath had them to do these four months, and hath done but one sheet and a-half; yet the two books will be about five or six sheets a-piece, so that I am forced to put one of them to another printer: but this man that hath dealt so basely by me, is one that I never employed before; for he that printed all the rest would not do them; so I was forced to get whom I could; but I hope I shall get them done by Christmas, or a little after; for all printers have been full of business this Term-time, with almanacks, and other things; but now they are over, I hope I shall get them done, and as soon as I can get them out of the press, you shall hear from me; and if it be so hard to get these two little volumes printed, what should I do to get those greater books printed? Therefore my advice to you and all other believers of these writings, is, to make much of these writings, and not to embezzle them away; for when these be gone that I have, they will not be had for any money; for I think they will never be printed any more, the charge will be so great, and the difficulty to get them done, will be the cause they will never be printed again.

This is all at present, only my love, with my wife's love to yourself, and to your wife, and all friends else there with you.

I rest and remain your friend in the eternal truth,

LODOWICKE MUGGLETON.

From the Postern, London, December 4, 1669.

A Copy of a Letter written by the Prophet Lodowicke Muggleton to Mr. Thomas Tompkinson, bearing date from London, March 20, 1670. Directed to Sladehouse, in Staffordshire.

Loving and kind Friend in the true Faith, Thomas Tompkinson,

I RECEIVED your letter, dated February 26, 1670, wherein I perceive your constant faith in this commission of the Spirit, which faith will uphold you in the day of trouble; and as for my being, I am where I was, in Wapping, and am pretty well in health, but confined from my own house still, because of that warrant which will last always, as long as the present power lasteth; yet my being in these parts hath been a means to establish many in this faith, who were Quakers and Baptists before; and, as it happened, one Mr. Atkinson, a Quaker, and Elizabeth Atkinson his wife, a zealous Quaker, who fell from the Quakers, and wrote against the Quakers, who came to me several times (perhaps you have had of her writings.) Her husband was loath she should come to me at the first, but she growing stronger and stronger in faith and argument by coming to me, she overcame her husband to see me, and hear me; which, when her husband did see and hear me, he was very much taken and affected in love towards me, and desired me to come to his house very oft, which I did by their inviting; so that the man was very much affected with my discourse, and had faith in this commission of the Spirit. But to be short; it happened, that after he had been acquainted with me but half a year, the man died; but he gave such testimony of his faith in this commission of the Spirit, with such wonderful expressions to his wife, and others that came unto him, exhorting them to stand steadfast in this faith, and let no doubt arise in them, for he did not think there could have been such peace upon this earth as he now did find, and that they should give glory to God that had sent a prophet upon earth now in these our days, who had declared to us the true God, and the rise of the two seeds, and all other things fit to be known; therefore let there be no doubt of these things, and said it would not be half a quarter of an hour before he should rise again, and be in glory, with many other wonderful expressions concerning the doctrine and faith of this commission of the Spirit, to the great amazement of those that heard him, and strengthening of the faithful, and convincement of the Quakers; for their mouths are stopped, and made silent by his testimony at his death.

This is one that had been a Quaker many a year. I thought good only to give you a little touch of these things for the strengthening of your faith; for it is more for one Quaker to die in this faith, and express himself so, than for one hundred of those that have professed it. But I shall say no more of that matter here.

And as for my advice and judgment concerning your factoring this next summer in butter and cheese to London; as to that, my advice is, that if you could deal with honest and able men, it would do well; but I have no skill neither in that trade, nor acquainted with any men of that trade, nor familiar acquaintance, only with Mr. Shelley; and I heard that he should say, that the carriage by land of those commodities did take up much of the cheesemonger's gain; but I had no discourse with him about it, therefore I shall not encourage you in it, nor altogether discourage you in it; neither am I at all acquainted with Mr. Ewer, or but little with Mr. Prince, especially in the matter of trade; therefore I can give but very little advice or encouragement in things I know not, neither will I dissuade you from it; but if you think your coming to London will not be too much hindrance c ш unto you, it would be best for you to come; for speaking with men face to face, will work more upon men than letters will, because a man may give many more reasons to objections by word of mouth than can be expressed by letters; therefore if you will venture the charge and trouble in coming to London only about this matter, whether you lose or win, I shall leave it to your own mind to resolve upon.

And this is all the advice I can give you at present in this matter, being unskilled in their way of trading, and unacquainted with the men; for I would gladly that you should do well, and should be very sorry you should be a loser; therefore be well advised in your own mind of what I have said before.

This is all at present, only my love and wife's love Remembered unto yourself, and unto your wife.

I rest your friend in the eternal truth,

LODOWICKE MUGGLETON.

London, March 20, 1670.

A Copy of a Letter written by the Prophet Lodowicke Muggleton to Mr. Thomas Tompkinson, of Slade-house, in Staffordshire, bearing date from London, April 25, 1670.

Loving and kind Friend in the true Faith Thomas Tompkinson,

THIS is to certify you and your loving wife, that we received your kind token, and do give you both hearty thanks for your kind love: and further, this is to let you know, that we are both well at present, and so are most of our friends here at London; and that since I came from Cambridgeshire, we received your kind token. There is one of our chief friends in Cambridgeshire dead, namely, the widow Adams, who lived at Orwell; but she was married above half a year to a friend of the faith, namely, Thomas Warboyes, a very honest-hearted man, and sufficient of the world's goods, who is in great trouble for the loss of her; but her daughter and son-in-law do live in Orwell still; but they being persecuted for not going to church, they do intend to remove from thence to Ware, about Michaelmas; so that this house at Orwell hath been a place of entertainment, like a stage-town, for many, twelve years to my knowledge; but now it will be broken up, and the saints will be scattered, but not out of England.

Also this act against meetings being so severe and cruel, it disheartens all sorts of professors of religion; but what the effect of it will be, time will bring forth; but however, it doth not reach us as yet; but yet we are sorry for the troubles of others; for it is their conscience to meet, else they can have no peace; but blessed be the God of truth, that hath given us peace, without outward worship, God's wisdom hath been mightily seen, in that he hath preserved this commission from all those laws, and powers of the nation, that have been made hitherto: and it is the most wise God, that hath sent a commission into this world, that giveth peace of mind in believing, without outward worship, so that truth runs clearly through the hearts of many; and the powers cannot tell how to stay it, nor make no laws against it.

This is all at present, only my love, with my wife's love, remembered unto yourself, and your wife, and all friends else there with you.

I rest and remain your friend in the true faith,

LODOWICKE MUGGLETON.

Postern, London, near Moor-Fields, April 25, 1670.

A Copy of a Letter written by the prophet Lodowicke Muggleton to Mr. Thomas Tompkinson, of Sladehouse, bearing date from London, December 7, 1670.

Loving Friend in the eternal Truth, Thomas Tompkinson,

I RECEIVED your letter, bearing date November 18, 1670, wherein I perceive you have not heard by any of our friends, nor by me, of the several troubles I have been in this whole year, but especially since Midsummer, so that I have not lodged at my own house these five months, nor dare not yet. I shall only give you a little hint of the cause, that you may understand, because I cannot enlarge upon particulars nor circumstances, but to give you a hint of the ground, and some passages of trouble that hath happened unto me this year about these books.

The first ground and cause of my troubles in this kind, I perceive now it was about this time twelvemonth, in this month December, there was a book of mine taken in the press as it was printing, and that did allude to the words in other books printed before, by which the master of the press did perceive there were other books printed without a licence; whereupon he sent twelve or fourteen men, some stationers, with the warden of the company, and some of the king's messengers, to search and seize upon unlicenced books; so there came twelve or fourteen men, and wrenched open the hatch before I was aware, and run into every room of the house; so they seized upon ten pounds worth of books, most of them unmade up; so they were intended to carry them all away, but they consulted among themselves, and said, Mr. Muggleton, we will be civil, we will take only some of these that are bound together, and leave the rest while further order; so they took what they would, and left the rest; but when they had perused them, they judging them to be blasphemy, they got a warrant from the council of state to take my person; so by chance I heard that there was a warrant out for me by my attorney at law, who saw it in the office; so I got out of my house immediately, and in a few days after came the messenger for me, but he missed of me; he came three times, but could not meet with me. A few days after came the Marshal of the Trained Bands, with a warrant from the militia, for my person to come before them; for not appearing upon the Trained Bands, they fined me five pounds; and I being not at home, but he thought I was, so he in fury threatened my wife and

Mrs. Brunt, and caused my wife to open the door, which she need not; but when he got into the chamber, he seized upon the best and heaviest chest, and caused two porters to carry it away to Guildhall, for five pounds, for not appearing upon the Trained Bands. The chest had in it books and linen to the worth of fifteen or sixteen pounds; so after he had done, he knew that he could not justify this act of his, by virtue of a military warrant, before the man of the house was apprehended; and he heard that I would sue him at the law for burglary and felony, to take away a man's goods before a man is convicted by the law: he hearing of this, pretended a great deal of love to my daughter White, as if he for her sake would do her father what good he could to get the chest again for a small matter, before the chest was broke up in the open court; and because I was not willing the court should see the books, «for there were, twelve pounds worth of books in it; but if they had been any other goods, I would have suffered it to have been broken open, and have seen whether they durst have sold them; but because of the books, I desired my daughter to comply with them, and get the chest off as cheap as she could; so with the help of this marshal she got the chest again, unbroken-up, for a matter of thirty-three shillings.

After this it came to pass, about Michaelmas last, there came eight or ten stationers, and other officers, and some of them the king's messengers, thinking to apprehend me for the old business at the first, and as it happened my wife was not at home neither, for if she had been at home, they would have broken in,. pretending to search for me, and there were many books at that time very easy to be taken; but she being not at home, they being very angry, went and searched the bookbinder's house for unlicenced books, so they found three of mine that were binding, and they took them away, and charged the bookbinder to bind no more; so there they fleeced thirty shillings more from me; so now I have removed my books out of my house, and shall prevent them from taking away any more; but now all their drift is to catch me, that they might get more money out of me, but I shall do my best endeavour to keep out of their hands, for I have not been at home to lodge these five months, nor shall not all this winter.

Thus in brief you may perceive some part of the troubles I have met with this year; and as for any spiritual matters, there is no other but what you have heard and seen; and if there were, it would be too tedious to write the revelations of faith; and as for parliament news, there is none here in London, neither hath the parliament determined any thing yet as I hear of, only to raise money for the king; but that way you speak of, is but talk; as to talk, there is no such thing, neither can there be any such thing as the state of things stands now.

This is all at present, being in haste, only my love, and my wife's love remembered unto yourself and, your wife.

I rest and remain your friend in the eternal truth,

LODOWICKE MUGGLETON.

London, December 7, 1670.

You may direct your letter to me as formerly, as your last, for my wife is always at home.

A Copy of a Letter written by the Prophet Lodowicke Muggleton to Mrs. Ellen Sudbury, of Nottingham, bearing date January 13, 1671.

Dear Friend in the eternal Truth, Ellen Sudbury,

I RECEIVED your letter, with the Quaker's letter inclosed, and I confess, it hath been a long time since I sent unto you; and I think I did receive two or three letters from you, and one or two from Mrs. Parker, and I gave you no answer, because I had no matter of concernment to write unto you; yet nevertheless my love was as great to you both as ever, though I did not write unto you; also I have hardly had time to write unto you since, for my time hath been much taken up all this summer with several Quakers that are fallen off from them, and are very firm in the belief of this commission of the Spirit, and are very well grounded in it, and their faith very firm, and none of the smallest persons neither; yet, as some have been exalted in their minds, and settled in the knowledge of heavenly things by me, so on the contrary, some, that were exalted in their knowledge by being in my favour, have rebelled against me, for which rebellion they have been cast down and out of my sight, because several innocent persons were drawn aside to join in their rebellion; but I have separated the sheep from the goats, that is, the obedient from the rebellious; and this act of rebellion hath been in agitation this whole year, but now it is brought to a period; and this hath taken up much time in writing and talking to other believers, to satisfy them in this rebellion; so that all are satisfied now, and more firmly fixed to me than before, only three or four of the grand rebels I have cast out, three cast out for ever, but one of the four repented quickly, and humbled himself, and I forgave him, but the others are hardened. And who do you think is one of the rebels? Even Walter Bohenan the Scotchman, his rebellion is great, for he hath joined with the other two without a cause, and he hath undertaken to plead their cause, and make their cause his own, and he hath written two base letters to other believers, to persuade them to rebellion against me, and to cleave unto the Scriptures; so that I see there is no place of repentance will be found for him; but perhaps you may hear more of this hereafter, for it would be too large to give you an account of the particulars and ground of this rebellion, therefore I shall not trouble you no further at present, only let you know we are all well at present; so with my love and my wife's love remembered unto yourself, and to our dear friend Mrs. Parker,

I rest and remain your friend in the eternal truth,

LODOWICKE MUGGLETON.

The Postern, London,

January 13, 1671.

And as for the Quaker's letter to the woman you sent, there is nothing in it to ground any answer unto it, neither by the woman, nor none else; they do as little children do, ask their parents such questions as cannot be answered by the parents, no more than the child that asks can tell; and do not they shew their ignorance and darkness to put queries to simple ignorant women to answer, which they cannot answer themselves, for they know not how to answer those queries they have put to the woman than a dog doth; if the mouth of the dog were opened to speak, he would say as much to those Quakers as they can; for if they knew how to interpret those Scriptures and queries, why did they not give the women to know them while they were of their faith; but now they be departed from them, now they come to learn knowledge of the women, and propound queries to them, as if those that depart from the Quakers people and principle are immediately endued with such knowledge as to answer any thing they do propound; and for the queries themselves, they have been answered over and over again in the Quakers Neck Broken, and in Fox's Looking-Glass, the women may read the answers to the Quakers there, and save themselves a labour. But there is one thing in the queries that I never heard before, that is, what complexion God is of; as for his stature and bigness is shewed in Fox's Looking-Glass, and for his complexion I could shew that also, but what good will that do Quakers to know; yet to satisfy you, I shall give you a little knowledge of it, what complexion he was of when he was upon earth, and what complexion he is of now; as thus, God became flesh, and dwelt amongst men, as in the first of John; likewise when he became flesh he was a Nazarite, as the Scripture saith. Now what complexion Nazarites were of, you may see in the Lamentions of Jeremiah, chap. iv. verse 7. The words are these: *The Nazarites were purer than snow, they were whiter than milk, they were more ruddy in their bodies than rubies, their polishing was of sapphire.* This was the complexion of Christ the only God when on earth; and what complexion he is now of in the kingdom of glory above the stars, may be seen Revelation, chap. i. verse 13 to 16. *And in the midst of the seven candlesticks John saw one like the son of man, cloathed with a garment down to the foot. 14. His head and hair were white as wool, as white as snow; and his eyes were like a flame of fire. 15. And his feet like unto fine brass, as if they burned in a furnace. 16. And his countenance was as the sun shining in his strength.*

Here is the full and true complexion of the person of God in glory in the kingdom of heaven above the stars; and this Son of Man in glory is the same Son of Man that was upon earth, even that very God, as I said before; so that you may see what complexion God was of when on earth in mortality before he suffered death, and what complexion God is of now in the kingdom of glory; he that can understand let him receive it. But what should the women trouble themselves to give answer to the Quakers queries? why do not the Quakers expound their riddles themselves, that people may love them for their doctrine and principle-sake, though not for their practice-sake? They shew themselves like ignorant foolish men, to ask wisdom of those that go out from them. And this I say unto the women, perhaps they went from them because of some evil practice among them more than for their doctrine; but I shall not accuse them for their practice, though by the reports of them that were of them, they were wicked enough; but as for their principle of doctrine concerning God, devil, hell, heaven, angels, and the mortality of the soul, they are altogether ignorant, and absolute antichristian, and great fighters against the truth of God; and yet they talk of truth more than any people whatsoever, but understand truth least of any.

I speak not this to persuade the women to believe me, neither do I do as the Quakers people do, to compel people to go to heaven whether they will or no, but leave it to the seed within them to work itself forth.

I have declared the mysteries of God, and of the right devil, and many other heavenly secrets, which have lain hid from the foundation of the world, never revealed to mankind till now; and whoever can hear and understand, will be made partakers of those heavenly truths.

There is now life and death set before the women, whether they shall cleave unto the Quakers, or unto this commission of the Spirit. Now they must venture their souls upon me, or upon them; if I be, true then they are false, if they be true then must I be false; for we cannot be both true, one of us must perish to eternity.

Now life and death is set before you, you must chuse or refuse which you will take; so that they must cleave to the one, and forsake the other, else they can have no peace at all.

But I shall say no more, but rest at present,

LODOWICKE MUGGLETON.

A Copy of a Letter wrote by the Prophet Lodowicke Muggleton to Mrs. Elizabeth Atkinson, bearing date London, February 12, 1671.

Dear Friend in the Faith, Elizabeth Atkinson,

OUT of tenderness and love to the welfare and peace of your mind here in this world, that you may be the more strongly established in the assurance of eternal happiness in the life to come, I thought good to write these few lines unto you by the way of counsel and advice, not compelling you, or laying any bonds upon you, but wishing you as well as my own children, and as my own soul; neither would I give you any counsel or advice, but what I would give unto you if you were my own natural child, as you are spiritual, being begotten by the faith of this declaration, which is as followeth: I do hear that you are somewhat intangled in your affections with that young man I saw once at your house, as if he and you are like to make a match together. Now if the case be so, indeed your condition is not good at present, neither will it be good hereafter in this world; for you will lose yourself exceedingly, and make shipwreck of your present peace, and of your personal estate; and your strong confidence of faith and knowledge of the true God, and faith in this commission of the Spirit, will be weakened in you, and you will become like unto Sampson when his hair was cut; he was strong before, but when his hair was cut he became weak, like another man; and the cause of his weakness was, in that he took a Philistine woman to wife; and what sad fruit and effect it wrought and brought forth! She was a snare unto him, and the cause that destroyed his strength: for Sampson was an Israelite, and it was unlawful for the Israelites to marry with the Philistines; therefore that evil came to pass upon Sampson. So likewise you are an Israelite of the tribe of Levi by birth, and I can say truly, since you believe as Christ did by Nathaniel, *Behold an Israelite indeed, in whom there is no guile*; and will you, that is an Israelite indeed, in whom there is no guile; and will you stain your wisdom, knowledge, and faith, and match yourself to an Egyptian, to a dark Egyptian episcopal man, who is as dark as pitch in spiritual and heavenly knowledge. Therefore I would have you to consider these three things: first, how unsuitable this match will be. First, he is no way suitable to your age. Secondly, he is no way suitable to your estate. Thirdly, his faith and religion is no way suitable unto yours. Your faith is now the faith of God's elect; and your religion is to worship God in spirit and truth, free from all idol worship, which is light and life. His faith is the faith of the Egyptians, and his religion as the darkness of Egyptians; and will you put light and darkness together. These things have been unlawful in the days of old, as it was by Sampson aforesaid; and if you match with this Egyptian, as he did with the Philistine woman, your strength will depart from you, as his did, and you will become weak like another woman; and that crown of wisdom, knowledge, and prudence, that hath been set upon your head, will be pulled off, and cast upon the ground, and you will be looked upon by the wise in heart as one of the foolish women. And because you are set free indeed by faith in this commission of the Spirit; for this faith doth make you free indeed, and will you enter into the spirit of bondage in Egypt again, by marrying with an Egyptian, whose worship is to worship a calf for his God? Consider how you will be intangled; your companions must be Egyptians, and you must dwell amongst the Egyptians, and your discourse must be the Egyptians language, and not the language of Canaan. For no people in the world can speak that language, though of this faith; and when all your familiar friends about you are Egyptians, how shall any of the Israelites of this faith have any society with you. And if you shall think by your wisdom and discreet carriage to convert him to your faith after you are married unto him, you will be deceived there of your expectations; and it will be a dangerous thing for a woman to venture that. Again, how will the Quakers trample over you, and say, Elizabeth Atkinson is gone back into Egypt again, and boast themselves against me, and say, this is Muggleton's doings; for it is like himself. But however, I can bear greater reproaches than these, as I have done in time past: therefore consider, and lay fond phantasy aside, and consider things of more weight. Let phantasy be but in one balance, and lay those three things aforesaid in the other balance, and see which will weigh heaviest in your mind, do you choose. And farther I say, seeing you cannot fancy Henry Hall, I would advise you to stay awhile longer, and not bind yourself to any, but keep yourself free from engagements and intanglements of this nature. Providence may order things so, that you may meet with one suitable in your years, suitable in estate, and suitable in religion: patience is a great virtue, and keeps the mind in peace, and doth things with deliberation and consideration; but phantasy runneth headlong to destruction; therefore I would wish you to be true; to your own soul, and do not dally with edge-tools, and intangle your own soul, and insnare the peace of your mind, and give way to no man, to intangle his mind, until you are resolved. For if you be true to your own self, you may resolve your own mind, and resolve him at two or three times speech with him; for long delays, and often companying with a man upon that account, is dangerous; and young men, that hath nothing but nature in them, hath many by-ends to raise their fortunes, whatever men may pretend to the contrary; and love above all things else. Yet if you were not a fortune, young men would not die for you, whatever they pretend; and that you may know right well to your trouble, if you make trial. For that man that pretends to let a woman give away her estate to her relations, and will take her with nothing, and yet hath no estate considerable of his own, he sheweth himself to be either a fool, or a knave, or both; neither can he mean honestly, whatever is pretended. For if this man had any considerable personal estate of his own, he need not fear having a wife with a considerable portion; but if a man's preferment dependeth upon kindred, he had need look after a wife with a considerable estate of her own; that he may pay back that relations hath laid out for him. But I hope your wisdom will preserve you from being catched as young birds are, with chaff instead of good corn; for the loss will be yours, and not mine, nor none else that hath a love for you. Thus I wishing you to mind your temporal quiet peace of mind, while you live in this world, that it may be added unto you as an hundred fold in this life, and I am sure it will not diminish the joy of the life to come, which is eternal. This I know by experience, and am sensible of the inconvenience you will sustain, if this match go forwards; but if these lines take place in you, so as to persuade you not to have that man for your husband, let me know it, by writing, or otherwise, and I shall give the best advice I can, to deliver you; but if these lines doth not take place in you, but you are resolved to have him to your husband, let me know it, and I shall not dissuade you from it, but leave it to yourself, to possess the comfort and the discomfort of such a match; therefore let it be considered in your mind, and so do. I thought good to write these words, because you may read by yourself, and consider of them; because things cannot be spoken so fully by words of mouth, nor without interruption.

So resteth your friend in the eternal truth,

LODOWICKE MUGGLETON.

February 12, 1671.

A Copy of a Letter sent by the Prophet Lodowicke Muggleton to Mrs. Dorothy Carter, of Chesterfield, March 23, 1671

Dear Friend in the eternal truth, Dorothy Carter,

THIS is to certify you, that I received your letter, dated March 16, 1671, and the enclosed I caused to be delivered as was directed; and I am very sorry for your great troubles now of late, in that you have lost your daughter, and your son; and now,

last of all, you are seemingly entering into a greater trouble than all the rest, and what advice to give you to deliver you out of it, I cannot tell; for I perceive you are so involved and entangled in your estate, and in your way of livelihood, by reason of your daughter's living with you, after she was married, that it will be hard to separate and divide, what is your own, and what is your son-in-law's own. These things are commonly the fruits that parents do reap, when children do live with them when they are married. I being sensible, and having had great experience of the inconveniencies of this, by several, it was always my advice to any friend, not to do any such thing, but would have had them to follow my example; therefore I gave my advice to your daughter, to have one that would have delivered her, and you also, out of all those temporal troubles, as it: is at this day, to that party that hath him. If she had been my own child, as she is yours, I could not have wished her better; but she did not hearken unto me, but followed her own fancy, and loved a man that I did not know at that time; so that I would not give her my advice in it, though desired by her; but she is gone to her rest from all her troubles in this world, and shall enter into those eternal joys, which natural eyes have not seen, nor the natural heart of man can understand.

And as for this maid Mr. Goodwyn hath a mind to marry, I never saw her in my life, only I have heard a good report of her, for a civil maid, and of a good meek nature; but as to religion, I never heard she was of any; but since she came acquainted with Mr. Goodwyn, she seemeth to have somewhat of truth in her; for I heard a letter of hers to Mr. Delamaine, and the letter was well composed, and did savour very much of truth; so that by that letter I cannot judge amiss of the maid, being of so short time standing, as to her spiritual estate: likewise you may remember your son Goodwyn, when he came first acquainted with your daughter, was as ignorant in the knowledge of truth, as this maid is, and I was unacquainted with him as I am with her; therefore when your daughter desired my judgment of him, I would give her none in that point; but since, you know, time hath proved that his heart is right, as to spiritual things, and as for his desiring to marry so hastily as you speak of, and forgetting your daughter so soon, you know that is a common thing with young men, and he is not the first, nor doth not marry the soonest of any.

And if you would not have him marry at all, because he hath two children alive by your daughter, that is something unreasonable to tie him up so close, neither was it wisdom in you to suffer any maid to come from London, to dwell with you as a servant, for bare wages, for I perceive it was he that hired her, and not you; and you might well think, that no maid that hath any breeding, would have gone from London, so far into the country, for a year's wages, if Mr. Goodwyn had not been a widower: these things maybe read in the hearts of men and maids, whatever is pretended; therefore I cannot blame either of them in this thing, if they marry or not marry; but the trouble of my mind is, that you cannot be set free, and at liberty, because things are so entangled between you and him: yet I perceive the trade and way of teaching scholars is in your hand, and not in his, and that his maid, if she be his wife, cannot manage the business without you, neither would I wish you to give up your employment unto her, as you would have done unto your own daughter; for these are both but children in law; for you have done much good in your generation, in your time, and you are not so old yet but that you may live to do a great deal more good before you die; you may live to see many younger than both them go before you: therefore I would advise you, to keep your own standing, and your liberty, and privileges, while you live; and whatsoever you know is right, do unto Mr. Goodwyn, only let him know what property he hath in your estate by reason of his wife, and what property you have yourself, keep; and as for his claiming promise to give your daughter all that you have, signifies nothing now she is dead; but if you had died before her, it is very like you might have left all your estate to her, and her children; but the case is altered now she is dead, and Mr. Goodwyn hath no ground to expect any such thing; except he were resolved to live single while you are dead, which I perceive he is not: and as for his reviving the bond of fifty pounds that signifies little, whether he will or no, as long as he and you live; the bond is made, I suppose, to you, and is in full force and virtue as long as you live, if you have the bond in your own possession. These differences, I suppose, may be composed between you; but here lieth the knot hard to be untied, how you two shall live together, and manage the employment together, as your own daughter and you did, seeing they are both children-in-law. Now where two are equal in power, or two mistresses, there will be some differences; but where one doth rule, and the other a servant, there is good government; neither would I wish you, in your old age, to become servant to any, except it be to your better advantage. And it is with you two, much like as it was with Abraham and Lot, one land could not bear them; so one house cannot hold two families, being both of one profession; and which way to separate you two is hard to judge, except you be both willing, as Abraham and Lot was, to let Lot take to the right hand, or to the left. Now you are in Abraham's state, and Mr. Goodwyn is in Lot's state, and it is to be feared, that if he goes from you, he will go into Sodom, as Lot did; that is, he cannot manage the way of schooling without you, and his own trade will not be sufficient for a livelihood; and how to persuade you to do to a daughter-in-law, as you did by your own, I cannot press you to it; for I could not do it, if I were in your condition; for you must expect, in time, young children by her, as you did by your own, neither can I persuade you to do as Sarah did by Hagar, to cast out the bond-woman, and her son, for he shall not be heir with her son; so the children of this woman cannot be heir of your affection and estate, as the children of your own daughter. Here I have opened the state of this matter, as far as I understand by your letter, so that you may see in part what my mind is, so far as I understand in this matter; but if there be any other secret contracts, covenants, or promises between Mr. Goodwyn and you, since your daughter died, or before, I am ignorant of it, and ignorant how you, being two families, lived as one, and how your gettings was, and how her gettings was, and yet kept union as one, I am altogether ignorant; but I suppose it cannot be so now; therefore I cannot give no absolute judgment, what you shall do in this case; but I shall leave it to yourself, to do whatsoever seemeth best for your own peace and quietness of mind, while you live in this world, as I did by your own daughter; but you have not that tie of nature to bind you now, as you had then.

This is all at present, only my love, with my wife's love, remembered unto yourself, and to Betty Marsden, and Betty Slater, and all friends else.

I rest and remain your friend in the eternal truth,

LODOWICKE MUGGLETON.

Postern, March 23, 1671.

A Copy of a Letter written by the Prophet Lodowicke Muggleton to Mrs. Ellen Sudbury, bearing date April 7, 1671, directed to Nottingham.

Dear Friend in the true faith of Jesus, Ellen Sudbury,

I RECEIVED your letter, dated March 28, with the enclosed to Mr. Hatter, which, he coming to my house at that time your letter came, I gave it to him, and which he was very glad to see; and he, reading of mine, was the more refreshed in his mind to hear of your love, faith, and steadfastness in this commission of the Spirit. Also I shewed it to my daughter and to others of the faith, which do much rejoice at your faith and satisfaction you have in the understanding of the truth, in that you are made partakers with us in the like precious faith, which doth consist in the right understanding of the true God, and the right devil, the rise of the two seeds, and the distinction of the three commissions, which no man in the world doth know at this day, but the believers of this commission of the Spirit only, because they have true spiritual foundation as a rock; but their foundation is upon the sand, even all the teachers of the world, and the Quakers' principle or foundation is the worst of all; though it seemeth to be the best of all in righteousness of life, yet the worst of all in point of doctrine, and that they will find in the end, that they may flourish for a time; for no Quaker, nor any other that hath heard of this commission of the Spirit, and of the doctrine declared by it, and doth not understand it, and believe it, that can be saved, let their holiness of life be ever so much; for God hath no regard unto the righteousness of life, except it doth proceed from faith in the true God, which no Quaker, nor any other man hath, but those that have faith in this commission of the Spirit; therefore it is that they do all fight against the true God, and against this commission of the Spirit: but I am refreshed at your experience and growth in grace and knowledge of the true God, in that you have eyes, and can see: as Christ said to his disciples, *Blessed are your eyes for they see; for many have eyes, but they see not.* Also I am glad to see that your understanding is enlightened to see the true interpretation of the Scriptures, which is given by this commission of the Spirit; and this book of the 11th of the Revelations is very little else but interpretations of many places of Scripture, besides the chapter itself, which will enlighten the understanding in the knowledge of the Scriptures, more than all that hath been written before; therefore I have sent you three of them, because if there should be any other besides yourself that should have any affection to them, that they may have one; but I shall leave that to your discretion, do what you will with them. I received a letter from Edward Frewterell, and your aunt Carter, with the money, bearing date March 19, 1671, but I have not sent them an answer as yet, nor no books; but I do intend to send this week, if the carrier be in town; but as for my coming down into the country, I do much rejoice at your and your aunt Carter's affections in desiring me to come, which I do intend to do, but I think it will be about James-tide; for I must go into Cambridgeshire about Midsummer, and after I have been there I do intend to see you: so being in haste,

I rest your friend in the true faith,

LODOWICKE MUGGLETON.

Mr. Hatter and my daughter remember their love to you, with several others of the faith.

A Copy of a Letter written by the Prophet Lodowicke Muggleton to Mr. Charles Cleve, Mr. Thomas Parke, Mr. Francis Hampson, all of Cambridge, bearing date April 24, 1671.

Loving Friends in the true Faith, Charles Cleve, Thomas Parke, and Mr. Hampson,

I UNDERSTOOD, by Mr. Hampson, that you three are in some trouble, and like to be in more for not going to church. Also I perceive, you are disputing and reasoning among yourselves, whether you may not go to hear common prayer once or twice to save yourselves from sufferings, seeing you do not deny your faith, neither do you suffer for your faith, only you would have my judgment in it.

First. As to this, my judgment is, that I cannot consent to any such thing; for you may as well go twenty times, or always, as once: for, if the image of Baal be set up, and you bow your knee before him once, you may as well do it always. Also you must mind this, that there must be some witness that you bowed your knee to Baal, else your suffering will be nevertheless. For to hear common prayer at your own church is part of worship to God, and it is the image set up in England for all people to bow to and worship; therefore consider what privilege this faith hath given you, and what sufferings it hath freed you from, in that it gave you peace of mind as to your eternal happiness; it hath freed you from formal bondage of worship; it hath delivered you from being tied up to meetings, as all others are: it hath preserved you from those sufferings, which have cost many one their lives: it hath given you liberty to pay tithes, and to defend yourselves by law, to keep yourselves from imprisonment and sufferings. You have only been tied up to do justly between man and man, to the utmost of your power, and to worship God in spirit and truth.

Only now you must consider, it is one thing to worship Baal by compulsion, for fear of sufferings; what do you else but to take the mark of the beast in your right-hand? And always, when you look upon the palm of your right-hand, there you will see the mark of the beast; for it will be printed in your minds, and the remembrance of it will remain to your lives end. And who would defile a pure conscience for fear of such a slight suffering as this? For it reacheth not to inflict any punishment upon the body; neither is there any resistance unto death, as hath been in other times for smaller matters than this. Also consider those three believers in Kent, who had the blessing of John Reeve; yet they, for fear of suffering and presumption together, because they had the blessing, they said, they could not be damned to eternity. So they bowed down themselves three times (that is, at church to Baal) and then gave over. But what hath been the effects of it? Since nothing but crosses, sickness, weakness, poverty and beggary hath, and is still, the fruits that action hath brought forth; besides, the author of hope is eaten over with rust in them. Also consider that loving and good man Dovey at his death; did any thing trouble him but his going to church? Poor man, he lost his peace by it, though I am persuaded the man will be happy, because he was true to the commission; but it would have been better for him to have had eternal life abiding in himself, and I should have been more joyful also. And if you shall reason in yourselves, that some that own this commission, and look to be saved by it, and yet can, and do go to church to save themselves, as Philip Williams and Goodman Singleton.

To this I answer and say, it is to be considered, that these men were never off from the church, because of one office or other in the parish where they lived, and therefore were under the more snares; and therefore, as Christ said, *the more hard for a rich man to enter into the kingdom of heaven*; indeed they have been men that have been rather for truth than against it, and so I have had a love for all such men, as the Lord himself had also. I know it is possible with God, though not with man, to make a rich man venture all his riches to worship God in spirit and truth, and to forsake all idolatrous worship, in hopes of everlasting life; but it is impossible with me, that am but a man, to do it. For let not men deceive themselves, it is not half the heart for God, and the other half for the world; for God will have the whole heart, or none. And he that seeketh to save his life by a false worship, or wrong means, shall lose it; and would you be contented with such a faith as theirs is, to give one half of the heart to God, and the other half to the world? I tell you, God will have all the heart, or none. And a man shall know in himself whether he hath given God his whole heart, by casting up what it will cost him. And if he is willing to give all that he hath for truth's sake, if it be required: for the whole heart carries all along with it; then shall he have his heart given him again, and all that he hath lost for his sake, shall be given him again in this life, and in the life to come, life everlasting. And except this be, a man cannot have the perfect assurance of eternal life abiding in him, but shall have sometimes hopes and sometimes fears. Also this you are to consider, that you have been kept innocent and pure, and have not committed spiritual fornication these many years, and would you now defile your conscience with idols? Oh! let your faith be steadfast, and have its perfect work in your souls, and hold out to the end, that you may receive the crown of life, which God will give you at that day, which will not be as an hour unto you after death before you are in possession of it.

I would advise you not to appear, for you will be condemned, and then your cause will be the worse; but keep out of the way at sessions-time, and if you be arrested afterwards, go to prison, and never put in bail for your appearance; if you do, your cause will be far worse. And as for Thomas Parke being a single man, he may keep out of the way all this summer; perhaps by next October things may alter. And as for Charles Cleve, if he find, when he is in prison, that there is no getting off without his utter undoing of his family, and destroying the peace of his own mind; let him cause all his goods and estates to be sold, and do what he will with it, and let his wife and children be all turned upon the parish, and let him live in prison himself: for, if he go to prison uncondemned, he shall have full power to sell his goods, and do what he will with them; but if he be condemned by a court, then he cannot, but they will seize upon his goods for such a parcel of money as they have judged him to pay, and take twice as much goods. And as for Mr. Hampson, he being better able in the world than you, let him keep out of the way in sessions-time, though he do lose trade for a little season, except he can employ one that he can entrust the while; and if he be arrested afterwards, let him put in no bail to the serjeant. If a bribe will not serve them, let him go to prison, and he will come off for a great deal less charges, being not condemned by a court, and save his conscience from any engagements; but if you are not able to endure a prison at all, then I cannot tell what to say to you, but must leave you to your own heart's disposing.

This is the best advice I can give you to save yourselves here, and keep the peace of your minds: for I cannot promise to free you from all troubles.

Your friend in the true faith,

LGDOWICKE MUGGLETON.

April 24, 1671.

A Copy of a Letter written by the Prophet Lodowicke Muggleton to Mr. Alexander Delamaine, senior, bearing date from Southampton, June 8, 1671.

Loving and kind friend in the eternal truth, Mr. Delamaine,

MY love remembered unto you, and to your wife. This is to certify you, that I delivered your letter unto our friends in the faith, and they were glad to hear it, and do much rejoice in reading your letters.

Mr. Fisher the elder hath been very ill, and is something crazy still; he is now at Southampton, but his son, the young man, and William Pedley, and myself, are in the country at the old man's house, very private, and they are very well, and do kindly remember their loves unto you, and to your wife. There is nothing here of any concernment to write of, but all is still and quiet.

Therefore I shall say no more at present, only desire you, that if my wife hath any occasion of business, or necessity to write to me, before the 21st of June, that you would be pleased to write it for her; but if there be no great necessity, do not put yourself to that trouble; for I do intend to be in London the 21st of this month. Pray give this letter to my wife, cut it asunder, and give it her.

So resteth your friend in the eternal truth,

LODOWICKE MUGGLETON;

Southampton, June 8, 1671.

A Copy of a Letter written by the Prophet Lodowicke Muggleton to Mr. George Gamble, a Merchant in Cork, in Ireland: the first to him after he came to set his seal to the true faith. Bearing date from London, March 6, 1672.

Loving Friend, George Gamble,

I RECEIVED your letter, bearing date February 14, 1672, and am glad to hear of your health, and the more, because I did hear, by a Quaker, that you were very sick, like to die: this was a little after Christmas. William Penn sent one of his books against me, and a letter with it, by one of the Quakers, to deliver it into my own hands: and when the man had delivered them into my hand, he asked me, when thou heardest from George Gamble, in Ireland? I said, I had not heard from you a great while, but once since you were here in London. He asked me by whom? I told him by Benjamin Capp; he said he knew him. Why, said I, do you ask? Said he, we did hear he is sick, like to die. I said, I heard nothing of it; so the man parted. And, as soon as the man was gone, it came into my mind, why he asked about you; it was, because the Quakers would have been glad in their hearts if you had been dead indeed; because they might have had occasion to ground a belief, that God's judgments did follow you so suddenly after you forsook the Quakers principles, and did cleave to Muggleton's doctrine, because several of the Quakers have died in a little time after they were damned by me: so they would willingly have some to die that fall from them; looking upon it as a curse upon them for falling away from their principles. But I see their hopes is prevented, and that you are in health, and not only so, but that the seed of faith in you is risen, even as the sun riseth, and hath shined in your heart, and hath given you to see that light of life eternal, in that you have faith to believe in the true God, and to love God; for no man can love God, but he that knows God; and no man can know God but by faith. And it is life eternal to know the true God and Jesus Christ, which is sent; that is, it is life eternal to know this Jesus Christ that is sent to be the true God, as we have unfolded in our writings, and that you do now believe in this commission, and that I am a true prophet, it is well for you that you was ever born; that your eyes of your understanding are opened, to let the light of life shine into your heart, in that you can be made capable to receive a prophet's reward; which reward is no less than the blessing of everlasting life. For prophets that are chosen, and sent of God, have eternal life always with them, that whosoever believeth their report, are made partakers of it. And it hath been a saying in old time, when prophets were more in request than now, how beautiful are the feet of them that bring glad tidings of peace and salvation. But now there is but one prophet in these last times, and shall never be no more true to the end of the world.

All professors of religion do say almost in their hearts, let this prophet depart from us, we desire not the knowledge of his ways, nor doctrine, because he is alive, to reprove us when we blaspheme against God, and against him; but give us those dead prophets and their doctrine, that cannot make answer for themselves; let us say what we will, they will let us alone, and say nothing to us. This is the nature of reason in most people, to love and honour prophets when they are dead, but to hate and despise prophets that are alive.

Likewise you say, that one Christopher Baton should say and affirm, that when I had given him the sentence, that he should never see, after the sentence, with his natural eye. This is as false a lie as ever was spoken; I never cursed the natural eye-sight of any person in all my life. But this I might say to him, as I have said to several, that I have given sentence upon, that after the sentence is given he should never see the face of God, nor the faces of elect men and angels, nor his own face, in the life to come, to eternity: so that he should see, in the life to come, no other God or judge, but that sentence I had given him, that should remain upon him to eternity; and he shall, in the resurrection, never stir from the place he is raised in utter darkness, where there is no light to answer the light of the eye. For there must be two lights, that in light we see light, else nothing can be seen; for one light can never see any thing of itself. As for example, though a man have light in the eye, yet, except there be day-light, fire, or candle-light, or some other light, to answer the light of the eye, the eye-light can see nothing, but is in darkness. Likewise, suppose a man be blind, and hath no light in his eyes, let the sun-light be ever so clear and bright, it makes not the blind eyes to see, and darkness is as good to him as light. This is that sentence I did pass upon him, and the blindness he should suffer in utter darkness to eternity, for his blasphemy against the Holy Ghost. And this he shall be sure to suffer according to my word, and it will not be a quarter of an hour after this life before he see the truth of that sentence upon him, let him flatter himself what he can. It hath been no new thing for hundreds of the seed of the serpent to belie, slander, and reproach me without a cause: for I never did any evil as to the breach of any law written in my heart in all my life. I never did any man wrong; yet all men, that are professors, speak evil of me, revile and persecute me, either in words or deeds, and for no other cause in the world, but because God hath chosen me, and hath given me wisdom and understanding of his mind in the Scriptures above all men, and authority to give sentence upon blasphemers. This is the cause I am so hated of the world, but wisdom is justified of her children.

As for William Penn's Book, the Quakers are very brag of it; yet there is no true wisdom in it at all, but some of the subtil serpent's wisdom there is in it, to make people more blind than they are by nature; and it will appear so to those who have the true light in them, when I have answered it; which perhaps may be towards the latter end of this summer. I would before, but I have promised to see some friends in Leicestershire, Nottingham, and other parts that way, which will take up the former part of this summer. I shall go in the middle of April, and, according to your desire, I have sent you a copy of Penn's letter to me, and a copy of Thomas Lee's letter to me, and a copy of a letter sent to me by a friend from Nottingham, that you may see and judge the better of it (in regard it was written by one that liveth there) than by my writing it by report, therefore I will give it you verbatim as it is sent to me.

I shall not enlarge further at this time, but take leave; only desiring you to remember my kind lave to Colonel Phaire, and his wife and family, and to all those there with you, that do love and believe the Lord Jesus, that was put to death without the gates of Jerusalem; who died, and rose again, and ascended up to heaven, to be the very true God and everlasting Father, Creator, and Redeemer of those that are saved by his own blood. Also my love, and my wife's love, presented unto yourself, and to Joseph Moss, I rest,

Your Friend in the eternal Truth of a personal God, God Man, the Lord Jesus Christ,

LODOWICKE MUGGLETON.

George Gamble,

This is to certify you, that I received the ten pounds you ordered for books, and I have sent you 17, at 18*s*. a-piece, which comes to 8*l*. 10*s*. 0*d*. and I gave to Mr. Godfrey, for 17 of the Mortality of the Soul, 26*s*.6*d*. and the postage of letters, and the box, and other trifling things, comes to 4*s*. 6*d*. This is the account of the 10*l*. I received upon your bill.

And seeing it is not convenient to direct your letters in my name, you may direct them to Mr. Alexander Delamain, at the Sign of the Three Tobacco Pipes, on Bread Street-hill, near Queen-Hithe, and it will come safe to me.

The Postern, London, March 6, 1672.

A Copy of a Letter sent by the Prophet Lodowicke Muggleton to Mr. Jeremiah Moss, Physician, living in Cork, in Ireland, being the first after his believing the Commission of Truth, bearing date from London, March 6, 1672.

Loving Friend in the true Faith, Jeremiah Moss,

I RECEIVED your letter, dated February 14, 1672, wherein I perceive that this record of the Spirit doth take place in the hearts of several in those parts; and doth give satisfaction to the minds of those that believe, and doth dissatisfy the reprobates, Indeed, words of truth are like a two-edged sword, that cut both ways; and he, that hath a commission from God, hath power as the Apostles had, as may be seen in the Acts: some were pricked or cut to the heart for their conversion and salvation, as in Acts ii. and 37th verse. Others again, by the words of truth, were cut to the heart for the convincing of them of the sin of unbelief; witnessing to their consciences, that they were reprobates, and would be damned to eternity, as in Acts vii. and 54th verse. So that true prophets, and true ministers of Christ, their words are spirit and life, to convert some, to open the eyes of their minds that were blind, and to let the light of life eternal shine into their hearts, in giving them the knowledge of the glory of God, in the face of Jesus Christ; that is, that Jesus Christ is the brightness of God's glory, because his face is the very true God's face; and this light of faith doth shine into the hearts of many, by the declaration or preaching of them whom God sends. And, on the contrary, this declaration is a savour of death unto death unto the seed of the serpent, in that words of truth do blind the eyes of them that think they see, and hardeneth their hearts, lest the word of truth should take place in them; and it maketh their ears heavy, or deaf, even as an adder; so that in hearing, they cannot hear nor understand; and in seeing, they may not perceive any truth in a prophet's words; and having hearts, but not understanding any heavenly or spiritual things, they despise and blaspheme against them, even the doctrine of the true God, lest they should be converted, and be healed with the assurance of everlasting life in themselves. Likewise you say, we think not the liberty convenient with you, which the believers with us take in passing sentence on those that blaspheme against the Holy Ghost. As to this, I never laid any bonds upon any believer, to give sentence upon any for blasphemy, except their faith be strong enough in themselves to believe, without doubting, that such a one is damned. For, if a man give sentence, and afterwards doubts, that sentence returns on a man's own head, and the party, so sentenced, is freed from the power of his curse. Neither shall I lay any bonds upon you, there to force you to give sentence upon despising, blaspheming spirits; if your own faith doth not move you to it, or is not strong enough in you to give sentence, then you may let it alone. But this I say, whoever doth hear men and women speak evil against this blessed truth, in despising and blaspheming against the Holy Ghost, and a man shall really believe that such a one hath sinned the unpardonable sin that shall never be forgiven in this world, nor in the world to come, and hold his peace, it sheweth a great weakness of faith in that person. For, if a man be saved by believing such a truth, and being glad in his heart, that he did not stir against the Holy Ghost himself, and doth hear others blaspheme against that truth he is saved by, and yet holdeth his peace, it sheweth much weakness of faith in that person. Besides, if all believers of this commission should be so weak in faith, then the devils might blaspheme against God without controul, and think they did well in it; so that none could receive the sentence for blasphemy but such as come to me: but where I give sentence upon one, there is ten that have the sentence given them for blaspheming by the believers of this commission of the Spirit, both here in London, and several parts in other countries, and their faith is made the stronger, by giving sentence every where upon despising spirits of truth; and when they neglect to give sentence, for some by-ends, for blasphemy against the Holy Ghost, their minds are troubled for neglect, and doth eclipse and weaken their own confidence; so that by this means the devils are met withal every where, because most of the believers here in England do give sentence upon the seed of the serpent, as they have occasion in discourse. And they are more justified in themselves than those that do not; and they are justified by me in so doing, rather than those that shall hear the devils rage, rail, and blaspheme, and say nothing to them.

Seeing it is not convenient to direct your letters in my name, you may direct your letters to me thus: for Mr. Alexander Delamain, at the sign of the Three Tobacco Pipes, on Bread Street-hill, near Queen-hithe, and it will come safe to me,

Thus, with my love, and my wife's love, remembered unto yourself, with my love to Colonel Phaire, his wife and family, and to all friends else there with you, I take leave, and rest,

Your friend in the true faith of Jesus,

LODOWICKE MUGGLETON.

The Postern, London, March 6, 1672.

A Copy of a Letter wrote by the Prophet Lodowicke Muggleton to Mrs. Preston, of Little Tower-hill, Mrs. Henn's Mother, and to her Father likewise, dated in London, May 14, 1672.

Mr. Preston, and Mrs. Preston your Wife,

I THOUGHT good to write these lines unto you both, but more especially unto your wife, because I have seen her once, and never but once, and she hath seen me once, and talked with toe, but as for the man I did not know that ever I did see him, or he me, but I make no question but Mrs. Preston hath heard of me by the writings, and by the reports of several other people, who are for the generality my enemies; but I have learned to go through evil report as well as good report: but the occasion of my writing unto you at this time is concerning your daughter Elizabeth Atkinson, and my speech is chiefly unto your wife, that if it were possible that the mother and the daughter might be reconciled together again, for I understand there hath been and is a great deal of trouble upon both your spirits about the match. Now I would have you to know, that this match was altogether contrary to my mind, as my letter to your daughter doth shew, if she hath shewed it you; it may come to pass that you may see it either of her or of me hereafter, and that will declare the truth of this matter more fully. First, I have been true-hearted unto your daughter ever since I came acquainted with her, and have wished her as well as my own children, and as my own soul: and if she had been my own child, as she is yours, I could not have given her better council than I have done: and what did I respect her so for, but because I saw she had a very good natural wisdom in her, and that she had the good seed of faith in her, but it was not then risen in her: but after awhile the seed of faith sprang up in her in heavenly wisdom, knowledge, and understanding, which was a crown of glory unto her head: but the crown is fallen off now by reason of this match, and the crown, of reproach set upon her head in the room thereof by many of her enemies, and a great dislike to several of her own faith, and I perceive an extraordinary grief to you her parents, insomuch as I hear you, her mother, hath renounced her, so as not to own her for your child: and further, that you have made a covenant and promise in your passion and anger, that you might never enter into the kingdom of heaven if you received her in favour, or own her to be your child. Again, to this purpose or words, I perceive you speak, and promised in your anger and passion. Now let me speak a few words between the mother and the daughter, and consider the trouble and torment of rash words and promises that are made out of anger and passion, they bring nothing but hell unto the mind, because they are groundless. Consider the rash oath and promise that Herod the King made, Mark iv and xxvi: but when he saw the woeful effects of that oath, he was exceedingly sorrowful; and for the sakes of them that were with him, he gave her John Baptist head. Now did not this wicked oath take away the life of the greatest prophet that was born of woman? And it brought hell-fire upon the conscience of Herod, and an extraordinary plague and punishment in this life, besides his eternal damnation; therefore, beware and take heed how you perform the rash vows and promises made in passion and anger; yet I confess vows and promises made unto the Lord, or to man, ought to be performed, else punishment will follow, but vows and promises made out of passion or anger ought to be broke, I confess it is an evil to make any vow at all out of passion and anger, but it is better to break that vow and covenant than to keep it, for it is better to err on the right hand than on the left; that is, if you break it you may find mercy and forgiveness, but if you perform it there is no hope of mercy nor forgiveness, no more than there was to Herod aforesaid. Also I would have you to consider, that your daughter's crime is not so heinous against you, her mother, as you take it to be, for she hath broken no law of God, nor law of the land, nor law of her parents; but what she hath done hath been against her own soul, it hath wounded her own spirit, and hath broken her own peace; she hath spoiled the treasures of rest and satisfaction in her own soul, and she must bear her own sorrow, and none to help bear her burthen, but rather add unto it, by excluding her unworthy of pity and compassion, even of her own parents, through anger and passion, without a cause; for she hath committed no evil to her parents in this thing, because she was a free woman, and hath had two husbands before, and hath not been under her parents tutoring, but hath been free of herself, to give her person to whom she will, and her estate; nor no others can hinder her, it is all in her own power: likewise she hath done nothing against God nor his laws in this matter, because there was no command laid upon her, neither by God, nor by his prophet, to the contrary; and for the law of the land, that doth justify her in it altogether; so that all the evil she hath done in this matter it is to herself, and to nobody else, as I said before; only this is her evil and trouble, that she did not hearken to the voice of Heaven, or to his prophet's advice on earth; and here lieth her trouble; but now the ting is done, and advice rejected, and cannot be undone again. What then is to be done unto her? I say, even to forgive her, and to make her burthen as light as may be; so that I have considered and weighed the whole matter and considered her condition, and have forgiven her neglect to answer my letter, and all things else that have impaired the peace of her mind as to life eternal; and she shall be settled as in peace of mind as to life eternal as ever, and that will make her life the more comfortable in the temporal; for I had compassion on her when I saw her troubled mind, because her faith was in me, and mine in her, so that she is forgiven of God, and forgiven of his true prophet also. I would you, her father and mother, to forgive your only daughter and to receive her into your favour again, and let her be as precious in your eyes as ever. Do as that good father did, as Christ speaks of in the parable, that had two sons; the one lost for a time, and when he was in want, he said in his heart, *I will return, and say unto my father I have sinned against heaven, and against thee, and am no more worthy to he called thy Son*, His father doth not dispute with his son, and ask him what hath thou done, in that thou wentest from me, or did any evil while he was gone; but he fell upon his neck and kissed him, and killed the fatted calf for him. This was always my practice to my own children, and I have had more experience in this kind than ever you had with your daughter; therefore let this thing be done: by you her mother, and let not your rash unadvised promise or vow, you made out of passion and anger, hinder you; for I understand she hath sent messengers as advocates to plead with you for forgiveness, and that your daughter hath humbled herself by them, to crave your favour and forgiveness, but you would not hearken to them, nor have no compassion upon the affliction of the soul of your daughter; likewise, that she hath sent to you a letter of her own hand writing, to crave your pardon and forgiveness, and to accept her into your favour; yet all will not prevail with you, but seemeth as if you could not for your oath sake. You are here just in Herod's condition; and if you should put it in practice as he did, you will be something like him hereafter, though not altogether so bad as his, because your oath will not produce so bad effects as his did; but you will have hell enough in your mind here, besides what will follow hereafter; therefore I would desire, and provoke you to hearken to my advice, and you shall do well, and be cleared of your oath. And though I be but a mortal man like yourselves, yet, being a chosen prophet of the Lord, it shall be as well with you, if you believe God, obey my voice, as if God himself had spoken to you; therefore I say unto you, break that oath and covenant that you made with hell and death, in the anger and passion of your mind, concerning this matter, and receive your daughter into favour again; and let her be taken into your affections again, even as one that was dead, and is alive again; and I will assure you your sin, in making such an oath as this shall be forgiven you of God, and forgiven by his prophet, and be forgiven in your own conscience, and you shall be clear from this oath, as if you had never spoken it; but if you will not hearken to my advice in this thing, but harden your heart against it, and say within yourself, that it is but mortal man's advice, and that you are loth to believe, except God himself, or some angel from heaven, did advise you; I tell you this, that neither God himself, nor angel from heaven, will never speak unto you, nor unto no man else upon the earth at this day, therefore do not expect any such thing; for if you will not believe me, you would not believe if one should come from heaven and speak unto you; therefore consider of it, and so do, if you do not hearken unto my words; however, your daughter shall have peace of mind, and you shall bear the trouble upon your own mind; but if you do hearken unto my words and advice, then both you and yours may be full; but in case, you do not hearken unto my words, your daughter shall have peace of mind, and be cleared of her guilt, and cause of your rash oath and promise, and you bear all the, trouble upon your own mind; for what hath parents to do with children that are free as themselves,. but to forgive them their offences; the law of God and the law of nature doth bind parents to have a care of their children, and to forgive them their offences, and not to cast them off and disown them in a passion; but children are not bound to have a care of parents; but if you do hearken unto my words and advice in this thing, and receive your daughter with the same love and affection as you did before this offence was given, you then shall be freed, and clear from any guilt of conscience, concerning your vow and promise in this matter, as if you had never made any at all; and then may your daughter and you both joy both be full.

So resteth your friend in what I say,

LODOWICKE MUGGLETON.

May 14, 1672.

A Copy of a better sent by the Prophet Lodowicke Muggleton to Mrs Elizabeth Marsden, of Chesterfield, May 20, 1672,

Dear Friend in the true Faith, Elizabeth Marsden,

I UNDERSTAND, by Mrs. Carter, you are very sickly and weakly, and that you have had very bad health ever since you were married, and much discontent of mind; and that you have a desire that I would pray for you, and that you might see my face once more before you go hence. I am very sorry to hear of your illness of body, and more especially that you should have discontent of mind; for it is a common thing to young woman, that are breeding, to be sickly and weakly, neither can it be avoided; and discontent of mind doth add further, to the weakness of nature; and peace and quietness of mind doth strengthen nature. For thoughts of peace and patience send forth strength into the blood, and strengthens nature, and makes it strong to encounter with sickness and weakness of nature, that discontent and grief hath produced in the body. So that discontent and content of mind doth produce both their several effects; so that the case is thus, as Christ said in another case, *To him that hath shall be given, and to him that hath not, shall be taken away, even that which he hath; viz.* To him that hath peace and content of mind, to him shall be given more peace and content of mind; because content and peace grows in him. And to him that hath not that, that hath no peace nor content of mind, but a little hope in; him to attain to peace, even that little hope: shall be taken from him, in that this discontent in the mind shall grow so strong, to swallow up all peace and content of mind into it, until it brings in death; and in this sense he hath not peace; even that little, or nothing, which he hath, shall be taken from him; that is, discontent shall take peace from him. I speak this that you may beware of discontent, and let not that enter into you concerning worldly things; for worldly sorrow causeth death: and I suppose it is worldly things that caused this discontent in you, and there is no removing it out of you, but by putting heavenly peace and content in the place. Let patience possess your soul: patience is a great virtue, and keeps the mind in peace; and remember the days of old, wherein I blessed you unto everlasting life. Likewise I have considered your faith and love to the Commission of the Spirit, in the day wherein you were but as a child for age; and my faith and love hath continued in you ever since, and shall uphold you. Also I blessed you to eternity when you were young, and that blessing shall remain with you to eternity.

Therefore let not your faith fail you in it, but look upon it as the blessing of Almighty God himself; for God hath given power to men to bless and curse to eternity. Therefore, let no doubt arise in your heart of your eternal happiness, and that will be a means to strengthen your nature, and to root out your discontent of mind, and settle your mind in patience and submission to the troubles of this World; and then your illness and weakness of nature will be either better borne, of your nature will be more strengthened to bear the troubles of this life. And this will he as a prayer unto God for you; for my commission is not to pray for temporal blessings: I never did pray for temporal blessings for myself; but the spiritual blessing of peace with God, and assurance of eternal life, hath always helped and strengthened me in the natural, and so it hath several others of this faith, and so it shall you; therefore let faith and patience have its perfect work in you, and you will do well. And as for your desire to see my face once more before you go hence; to this I say, I could have been very glad to have seen your face this summer, and did intend to have seen the faces of all our friends in those parts this summer; but here are new troubles fallen out here in London since Christmas, of wars and rumours of wars at sea, and pressing of men, that it is like to be a very bad summer with most people for want of trade, both by sea and land; so that I think not to go out of London this summer. Besides, my wife is to go into Kent, to see her relations, this summer; and I am loth to leave the house with nobody in it. But, however, be you of good comfort; it shall be well with you in the end, though you never see me more. Yet you may not be without hope of that; for providence may order things so, that I may see your face, and the faces of others, to my joy hereafter, and yours; for I am well at present, and I trust you may be preserved in health. So, with the blessing of the true God, the Lord Jesus Christ, the blessing of the true prophet rest upon you, and preserve you, both in this life, and in the life to come. I rest

Your friend in the true Faith,

LODOWICKE MUGGLETON

Postern, London, May 20, 1672.

P.S. My wife remembers her love unto you.

A Copy of a Letter written by the Prophet Lodowicke Muggleton to Mrs. Dorothy Carter, of Chesterfield, dated August 30, 1672, as followeth.

Dear Friend in the eternal Truth, Dorothy Carter,

I RECEIVED your letter, bearing date August 19th, 1672. And these are to certify you, that I am very well in health at present, and so is my wife, and most friends also here in London. I was indeed at Cambridge, at Whitsuntide, about a month, and after I came from thence my wife went into Kent to see her; relations; and. she returned again two weeks since, so that now we have done with-the country for this year. And as for your dream you spoke of, I perceive you give too much heed unto it, and do let your mind be too much exercised in the belief of it; I do confess in times past, that some dreams have been of great concernment, when it hath concerned the glory of God, as Joseph, in his dream, saw the sun, moon, and eleven stars bow down themselves unto him, that was his father and mother, and eleven brethren, should bow themselves unto him. Also that dream of Pharaoh King of Egypt, was of great concernment for the glory of God; likewise the dream of Nebuchadnezzar King of Babylon was of great concernment for the glory of God, when interpreted by Daniel; likewise Joseph, when he was espoused to the Virgin Mary, he was forewarned by an angel in a dream, not to put away his wife. Other places might be named, so that in the days of old; and in times past, some dreams have been of great concernment, and have been much minded; so that the interpreter of dreams hath been highly honoured of God, and honoured of kings, and of all men; not he that dreamed a dream, but he that could interpret dreams. Also let this be considered, that dreams have been always minded in such a time when there was no prophet upon the earth; as Joseph, when he dreamed a dream, it was before the law of Moses was given; and that dream of Pharaoh king of Egypt, interpreted by Joseph, it was before Moses, the first prophet that God chose: and that dream of the king of Babylon, which Daniel did interpret, it was when there was no prophet in Israel; for Daniel lived among the heathen, for it was the heathen that did generally mind, take notice, and follow dreams. Therefore, when they were frightful of dreams, they sought to their magicians and astrologers to interpret their dreams, and those were all the prophets the heathens had; and as for Joseph being forewarned in a dream by the angel, it was when there was no prophet nor apostle upon the earth. Therefore this is to be minded, that dreams ought not to take place in any man's heart, that is a believer in a commission, or in a true prophet: for those that followed the law of Moses, and hearkened to the prophets, never heeded dreams, nor minded them at all. So after Christ came, and the apostles commission was believed, they never minded dreams so as to trouble their thoughts about them: so likewise we that are under the commission of the Spirit, are not to mind them at all; for, if a dream does arise in a mail's sleep, let him tell it as a dream, but let him give no credit nor heed unto it, for dreams will arise through the occasion of troubles and griefs, and if they are not minded, they will pass away as if they had never been; for this I can say, I have had many such like dreams as yours is, but gave no heed unto them, for I know your mind hath been exercised of late with many troubles and grief of heart, in the death of your daughter and son, and other troubles which hath overwhelmed your spirit; and grief hath raised this dream out of your troubled soul. Therefore I say unto you, take no heed to your dream, but be of good comfort, that your days may be continued in this world, to do yet some more good before you go hence; knowing that you shall receive a portion in that everlasting kingdom above the stars, which is not made with hands, but eternal in the heavens, because you have believed his prophet's report.

As for my advice about Sarah Hatter, it is, that you would keep her till her time is out, and if you will not keep her longer, you must turn her home to her father, and her father must provide some other place for her, for he is not able to give her diet for a year, not for a week, as I can perceive; poor man, he cannot give himself diet, (not half enough) but goeth with many an hungry meal in a month, nay in a week, for ought I can perceive. Therefore, I would advise you to take no thought for her, what she shall do when you are gone; leave that to providence, your conscience bears you witness, and so doth his conscience bear witness, that you have been more like a mother than a mistress while you lived; and while you do live, let that satisfy as to that matter. I am glad to hear that Betty Marsden is pretty well, let her be of good comfort, and all will be well with her, both in this world, and in the world to come.

I do intend, if providence permit, to come to Nottingham, and perhaps to Chesterfield, the next spring; and then I intend to see you I hope all well, to my joy and comfort. Before I close this letter, I will give you a little hint of that which hath happened here in London, amongst the believers of this commission of the spirit, (it is above a year since it first begun, it may be you have heard nothing of it. There hath been a great rebellion against me, for some hard words that I have spoken in discourse, some have gathered them up together, and laid them as a charge against me, whereby they drew a party from me to cleave unto them, so that some were for me, and for those assertions that they drew up against me, and Some were against me, and against those assertions so that there was great strife amongst the believers, insomuch that I was forced to see who would be on my side; who, and that whoever did, those, with those rebels, let them be rich or poor, I would cast them off. There were four conspirators in this rebellion, the rebellion was hatched when I was absent from home, when the King's messengers sought after me, when they took away the books: the names of the rebels were these, William Medgate, scrivener; Mr. Whitehill, Thomas Burton the younger, and Walter Bohenan the Scotsman; these four were the grand rebels, for which rebellion I. damned two of them, and the other two I did excommunicate; three of these were believers, and the other seemed to believe also; but one of those that was excommunicated, namely Thomas Burton, repented of his rebellion, and asked forgiveness, so I received him into favour again; so that all those that were drawn away in the rebellion are returned to me again, only those three, William Medgate, he stands excommunicated still, and is hardened in his rebellion, so that I have little hope of his return. And for Mr. Whitehill the brewer, and Walter Bohenan, they two are cut off for ever: for Walter Bohenan hath acted the highest rebellion that ever was acted, since Korah, Dathan, and Abiram against Moses; for which cause I have given orders to all the believers in London and Cambridgeshire, and elsewhere, not to eat and drink with him, nor trade with him at all, as is more largely exprest the causes why, in the letter I wrote to him. Also I have answered those nine assertions which William Medgate hath drawn up against me, and the cause of his excommunication something large, which hath given great satisfaction to all the believers that have heard them, which hath established their minds more firm upon the commission of the Spirit than before.

I thought good to give you an account, and a hint, of what hath happened this years time; this rebellion hath caused me much writing since, because many of the believers would have one of the writings to themselves, to peruse at their own pleasures:

This is all I have to say at present, only my dear love to yourself and Betty Marsden, with my wife's love presented to you both, and to all friends else there with you.

I rest and remain your friend in the eternal truth,

LODOWICKE MUGGLETON.

From the Postern, London, August 30, 1672.

A Copy of a Letter written by the Prophet Lodowicke Muggleton, to one William King a Quaker, who came from New England, dated from London, October 3, 1672.

William King,

    I AM informed, that you have been a Quaker in New England, and that you have been moved, (as you say,) of the Lord, and sent with a message from him into Old England; to reprove and forewarn those people called Quakers, and others, of some miscarriages and bad accounts you know against them, and pretend to declare against them. But I understand the Quakers people will not hearken unto your message, nor own that the Lord hath sent you, but look upon you as a deceived person; and that your message is forged, and out of your own imagination, and madness of your own brains, making a disturbance in the Quakers meetings: what, is Satan divided against Satan, how then can his kingdom stand? Were not you of that faith as they are, how is it then that you find fault with them? Is not your God and their God the same? Is not your Devil and their Devil the same? Is not the light of Christ within them their only God and Saviour, and is not yours the same? There is no difference between them and you in point of doctrine, why then should you fall out, and find fault one with another? Cannot you let them alone in point of practice? If your practice be better than theirs, the comfort will be yours: so that you need not to have taken the pains to have come so far from New England, to Old England, to deliver such an ignorant foolish message, from the Lord and light within you.

    Also I am informed, that you have raged, railed, and reviled against me and the doctrine declared by me: I have heard of your wicked and blasphemous speeches against me, and the doctrine declared by me, several times; and I did patiently bear with you, but being informed lately of your exceeding great wrath and railing, and high blasphemy against that true doctrine declared by me. You said it was blasphemy to say that God died; doth not the Scripture say that Christ died, and poured out his soul unto death, and dare you say, that Christ was not God and man? The Church of England doth own that Christ was God and man, and that he died and rose again, and ascended up to heaven; this is that Alpha and Omega, who was dead, and is alive, and behold he liveth for evermore, as in the Revelation: this is he that poured out his soul unto death, as he was God and Man, and by this blood of Christ is my conscience sprinkled and cleansed from all sin, and by faith in this blood, am I justified, sanctified, and shall be glorified. Also you rage and rail at me, for saying that God hath elected some men to salvation, and reprobated some to damnation, before they were born: this you say is horrid blasphemy, and call me fool and ideot, and simple, silly ignorant man.

    To this I say, is not the Scripture full to prove, that God hath elected some from the foundation of the world to life and salvation, and some he hath reprobated and ordained of old, for eternal condemnation, even the seed of the serpent, of whom I know you are one, that was reprobated in your seed before you were born: for now the seed of the serpent doth reply against God, and say, why hast thou made me thus; as you have done, charging God with unrighteousness; for this I say, God hath a prerogative power, and is above all law, and may do with his creatures as the potter doth with dead clay; make one vessel to honour, and another to dishonour, for his own glory. And what if God willingly make you a vessel of wrath fitted for distruction, (that is, eternal torments) as I know you are, how will you help it? And if God willingly hath made me a vessel of mercy, fitted for eternal happiness, as I know I am, being of the seed of Adam, how should I prevent it? For God doth every thing for his own glory, and God will be as much honoured in your eternal damnation, as in my eternal happiness and salvation; for if I had not known such serpents as you are damned, I should never have known my own salvation, nor the salvation of others. For this I know, that God's glory would be eclipsed, if the seed of the serpent, (such as you are) should not be damned; for if all should be saved, then the glory of salvation would be lost because he that is saved is delivered from torment; and if all men were damned, then none could give glory unto God, nor praise him for his mercy. So that there is a necessity that the seed of the serpent (such as you are) should be damned, and that the seed of Adam should be saved, else God would have no glory by his redeemed ones, if not redeemed from hell and eternal torments.

These and many other things written by us, the witnesses of the Spirit, you have spoken against, which would be too tedious to rehearse; but you have shewed yourself plainly what seed you are of, and I having perfect knowledge what you are, and what you shall be hereafter, I shall proceed against you according to your wickedness: for you have raged, railed, and reviled at me without a cause, in that you have called me fool, simple, ignorant man, thinking yourself wise; you should have done as the apostle saith, suffer fools gladly, yet that foolishness of mine hath brought down the wisdom of many, and it shall bring down your wisdom, even to the lowest hell. Likewise you have railed against the true God declared by me, and have blasphemed against the true God that is in the form and person of a man: you have slighted such a God, you have denied that Christ was God become flesh, you have blasphemously said, that Christ's soul did not die, and the same that died did rise again, and ascend up into glory. Likewise, you have reproached the living God, denying his prerogative power to elect men to salvation that are the seed of Adam, and to reprobate some men, who are the seed of the serpent, to eternal damnation before they were born: you call the prerogative power of God unrighteousness, you say every man may be saved if he will. These, and several other wicked reproaches, and railing, and blasphemous speeches, have you uttered out of your mouth against me, and against God: for God hath chosen me to declare his mind, and not you; and in as much as you have reviled, reproached, and blasphemed against me, and the true doctrine declared by me, you have reviled, reproached, and blasphemed against God. You have done by me even as Rabshekah did to Hezekiah king of Judah, as in Isaiah xxxviii. 4. He sent to reproach the living God, so Hezekiah spread his blasphemous letter before the Lord, and prayed unto him to hear all the words of Senacherib, which he sent to reproach the living God; as in the 17th verse, so 23d verse, *Whom hast thou reproached and blasphemed, and against whom hast thou exalted thy voice? even against the holy one of Israel. 24th verse, By thy servant hast thou reproached the Lord. 29th verse, I know thy rage against me.* So likewise hath your imaginary God without a body, sent you, William King, out of New England into Old England, to reproach the living God, the Lord Jesus Christ. And I have spread your blasphemous words before the Lord, and do believe he will hear all the words wherewith you have reproached the living God; for whom have you reproached and blasphemed, and against whom have you exalted your voice? even against the very true God Christ Jesus, who is in the form of a man: this is that God whom I serve, and by whose power I do act; by him the worlds were made, and without him was nothing made that was made. And this is the Lord you have reproached and blasphemed, for I know your rage is against him; if he were in my place, you would say to him as you do to me: and seeing God hath chosen me his last true prophet and witness of the Spirit, and hath set me in his place here on earth, to give judgment upon all proud blasphemous despising spirits, who blaspheme against the living God, as you have done in a high nature; therefore, in obedience to my commission from God, for the aforesaid raging and railing against me, and reproaches and blasphemies against God, I do pronounce William King cursed and damned, soul and body, from the presence of God, elect men and angels, to eternity. Deliver yourself from this curse if you can: that God which sent you hither cannot; nor the true God will not deliver you from that judgment and sentence I have passed upon you, and you shall know to your endless pain and shame, that God hath chosen mortal man, like yourself, whom you have reviled; and hath given him power to curse you to eternity, and none shall deliver you from it: for your soul shall die two deaths, the first death is natural, the second death is eternal; and when God shall raise you again in the resurrection, which will not be a quarter of an hour to the dead, so that you shall pass through the first death into the second death, where the worm of conscience shall never die nor the fire of hell shall never go out, in utter darkness, where is weeping and gnashing of teeth for evermore. And you shall remember you were told so by the last true prophet, and witness of the Spirit.

Written by me,

LODOWICKE MUGGLETON.

October 3, 1672.

A Copy of a Letter written by the Prophet Lodowicke Muggleton to Mr. Thomas Tompkinson, bearing date from London, October 16, 1672.

Loving and kind Friend in the true Faith, Thomas Tompkinson,

THIS is to certify you, that I received your kind token of love, the cheese; and we give you many thanks for it. Also I have now sent you the answer of the assertions, and the true copy of these nine assertions that William Medgate wrote to me, with his own hand; also I have sent you the letter that I sent to Walter Bohenan, the Scotsman, in answer to his rebellious letters. I have placed Medgate's nine assertions in the beginning, and Walter Bohenan's letter at the latter end, desiring you, that if Walter should happen to come to see you, that you would not let him see the answer to the assertions, for the rebels are mad, because they cannot see them. I could not send them to you sooner, because several believers have desired them before I could write them. So having no more at present, being in haste, I shall take leave, only my love, and my wife's love, remembered unto yourself, and to your wife, and all friends else in the faith there with you.

I rest your friend in the true faith,

LODOWICKE MUGGLETON.

The Postern, London, Oct. 16, 1672.

A Copy of a Letter written by the Prophet Lodowicke Muggleton to Mr. Thomas Tompkinson, of Sladehouse, in Staffordshire, bearing date from London, January 19, 1673.

Loving Friend, Thomas Tompkinson,

I SAW your letter to Mr. Delamaine, wherein you desire some of my advice; I do not know well the ground of this matter to give advice in, but so far as I understand by your letter. I shall give what advice I can. I perceive there is three particulars that causeth your landlord to take an occasion against you: *First*, Because you did not pay the tax he was to pay, and bear the loss yourself. As to this you did wisely, in that you did not keep to the letter of the law, that is, to the act of parliament, and have paid no tax for your landlord at all, but have strained his cattle for it; likewise I perceive you have stopt some of your landlord's rent in lieu of the tax you have laid out for him, which cannot be justified by law; but what tax you paid for your land that was for your landlord to pay, the law will bear you out; but to stop rent for other disbursements you laid out for your landlord, will not stand good in law, therefore it is dangerous for collectors to pay taxes for other men, except it be as far as his own tax for his landlord; but perhaps the court will take it into consideration, seeing the tax was for the king, and they will perceive the dishonesty of your landlord, for it will be a great disparagement to a person of honour to have such a wicked deceit discovered and made appear in open court, and perhaps the court may relieve you, seeing the tax was for the king.

Secondly. You speak as if your cattle had committed some trespass upon your lord's grounds; as to that, I suppose may be referred to men that know what damage your landlord hath sustained, and what they judge you shall give to satisfy him for the trespass done, do you pay it, and let no money be spent in law in that business. I suppose these two things may be blown over with a little charge, and that the landlord and the priest knows well enough; but that which they think to do most mischief in is about spiritual matters, for not going to church, and baptizing your child, and such like, and that will advantage them nothing at all but to do you a mischief, neither can that disinherit you of your right in the temporal, nor prevent him from paying you that which he oweth you, therefore I shall inform you in some measure the strength of the spiritual court. First, they have power to proceed so far as to excommunication, and when they have done so, you may go to the proctor of the court, and take it off for money as Mrs. Carter did; she stood excommunicate several years, and took it off at last for twenty shillings; and Mr. Sudbury was the like when he was alive, and his was sued to a *Capienda* writ, yet he got it off for fifty shillings; but the spiritual court itself doth commonly proceed no further than a bare excommunication, except some envious person will be at the charge to sue out a *Capienda* writ, and that they sue out here at London; all *Capienda* writs are fetched out of the High Court of Chancery, the writ doth cost thirty shillings itself, besides other charges; and when they have got it, they must have the hands of several bishops of two or three courts, and he that layeth out this money never hath one penny of it again if it be executed, so that except a man were made up of nothing but malice, he would never put himself to that trouble, charge, and vexation of spirit, to have nothing else for his pains and charge; and when a *Capienda* writ is executed upon the person of a man, it cannot take away of his cattle nor goods, nor hinder a mail of his right in any suit of law, except it be for paying of tithes and other church duties; but for the things aforesaid, for not going to church, nor baptizing children, that writ doth not touch the estate of a man, nor take away his right in law, only this, if a man have this writ sued out upon him, if he overthrow the adversary, the judge and jury will give him the debt and charges, for the court cannot give away a man's just cause and right because he is excommunicated, but this a *Capienda* writ will hinder the man, that he cannot have an execution upon his adversary's person nor goods until the excommunication be taken off. There was an example of this awhile ago, there was a widow-woman, a friend of ours in Kent, and there was a neighbour of her's that was at law with her about a field that joined to her's, and she was an excommunicated person a great while; the suit was brought to trial, her adversary put himself to the charge of a *Capienda* writ against her, thinking that she should not have had the benefit of the law by reason of that writ, but the judge and jury gave her the verdict against him both debt and charges, only she could not have an execution granted her upon his person nor goods until she had taken the excommunication off, which she did, and it cost her four pounds to take it off, and then her adversary paid what the court ordered, for a *Capienda* writ is only for the person of a man; and if it be served upon a man by officers, there is no bail to be taken, he must pay the debt, and the charges, promise to conform, or else go to prison; but no goods can be touched except a man be sued to an outlawry, which must be some extraordinary occasion.

Thus I have given you a hint of the effects of a *Capienda* writ. Now I shall write a, few words to satisfy you, that my answer to William Penn's book is got safe out of the press, but with great charge and difficulty; the volume is pretty large, nineteen sheets and an half, and there is variety of matter in it that is new, never written before, very pleasant to read; the books are half a crown a-piece, I will not let one go under to friend nor stranger, therefore if you please to make those friends acquainted with it that will go to the price of ft, let them send money, and I will send as many of them as the money doth amount to at half a crown a-piece. You wrote to me a great while ago for a book bound altogether for our friend Thomas Hall, I sent you an answer of that letter concerning that book, but I have heard no answer of it never since.

This is all at present, only my love, with my wife's love, remembered unto yourself and wife, and all friends else in the faith there with you.

I rest your friend in the eternal truth,

LODOWICKE MUGGLETON.

The Postern, London, January 9, 1673.

A Copy of a Letter wrote by the Prophet Lodowicke Muggleton to William Penn, Quaker, bearing date from London, January 23, 1673.

William Penn, Quaker, that blaspheming reprobate Devil,

I THOUGHT good to send thee an answer of thy wicked anti christian pamphlet, where thee mayest be convinced, though not converted, but the more hardened in thy blasphemy against the true God in the form of a man; and that sentence and judgment that I passed upon you, in the discourse between us, may be more surely established upon your heart, even so strongly, that your God, that is an infinite formless spirit without a body, cannot revoke it, nor take it off you to eternity; and you shall find these heavenly secrets, which you call foolish dreams and impostures, to be too strong for your anti-christian spirit of reason the devil in you, which you call God; neither can I wish for your soul's sake, that you may think in time, and have a deep repentance, and come to find forgiveness with the true God, because I know he did reprobate you in the seed of the serpent; and that you are predestinated in the seed to blaspheme against the true God, as made man in his own image and likeness, that you might justly be damned to eternity; so that, if it were possible that you should be convinced now, I have given sentence upon you for your blasphemy, I then must of necessity be damned if you believe; but I know in whom I have believed, in that God that hath given me power to give sentence upon such anti-christian devils, that deny the body and person of God; and I am justified of God, and justified in my own conscience; neither will it stand with God's glory to save us both; and if those revelations of Reeve and Muggleton's hath declared be filthy, devilish, and sottish imaginations, as you call them, then certainly our end will be endless pain indeed; but if we be true, as I know we are, then you have given just sentence upon yourself, that your end will be endless pain from the never-dying worm in your conscience in the resurrection, when eternity doth begin to rise, and time doth end.

LODOWICKE MUGGLETON.

Postern, London, Jan. 23, 1673.

A Copy of a Letter sent by the Prophet Lodowicke Muggleton to Mr. George Gamble, in Ireland, Feb. 14, 1673.

Loving Friend in the true Faith, George Gamble,

I SAW your letter bearing date the 30th of January, 1673, wherein I perceive the seed of faith is much risen in you, since the time I saw you; in that you do believe in a personal God, and in his messengers whom he hath sent, to declare the true God in this last age, what he is in his form and nature: and that you do believe this God will raise the dead at the last day, the true believer to everlasting glory, and the unbeliever to endless misery. For without this faith, it is impossible for any man or woman upon earth to have true peace in the soul, as to life eternal; because this is that peace which the world cannot give, because it riseth from the seed of faith in man, which is the seed of God in man; but the peace of this world, it ariseth from the seed of reason in man, which is the seed of the serpent, the lost angel in man. Therefore the peace which this world gives is full of doubtings, and accompanied with fears that a worse thing will follow after death; but the act of faith hath no doubt in it, but doth say to this mountain of fears, that presents itself to the mind, *Be removed, and cast into the bottom of the sea.* The seed of faith in man, that is less than a grain of mustard seed, doth this and more: Out of this doth the day-star arise, that enlighteneth every man that believeth, so that he cannot walk in darkness as the seed of reason doth; but seeth the strait and narrow way, that leadeth to life eternal: but the seed of reason walking in darkness, his way is large and broad, that leadeth to destruction. This seed of faith in man, is that single eye in man, *Therefore, if a mans eye be single, his whole body is full of light*. Neither doth this single eye of faith offend a man, but most men in the world, having the eye of faith and the eye of reason in them, (that is, the seed of reason and the seed of faith disputing in man's soul,) which doth offend man's mind, which Christ calls the right and left eyes, or two eyes. And because the seed of reason is the elder brother, (being the serpent's seed) it is called the right eye; therefore, Christ saith, *Matth. 5, 29. And if thy right eye offend thee, pluck it out, and cast it from thee; for it is profitable for thee, that one of thy members should perish, and not that thy whole body should be cast into hell.* The meaning is, that if the right eye of reason in man do offend him, by reasonings and disputings in a man's soul, against God and his prerogative power, offend a man, as I have had great experience of, when I was a Puritan; so that my right eye of reason did offend me so much, that I was forced to pull it out and cast it from me; and submit to the prerogative power of God to do what he would with me; else I saw that both my eye of reason and my eye of faith, also body and soul, must have perished in the resurrection, in hell-fire, to eternity. For Christ did not mean that a man should pull out his bodily eye, that doth offend him with a cold rheum and other distempers, and cast from him; neither would the pulling out of both his bodily eyes save him from being cast into hell in the resurrection, if such a thing should be done by any man; neither can a man pull out his own eye that offends him, it must be another man must do it. But this right eye Christ spake of, that offends a man's mind, he must pull it out himself, and cast it from him, and he shall see the way to heaven better with one eye, than he did before with two eyes. So that it is better for a man to go to heaven, with one single eye of faith in the true God, than to go to hell, with two eyes of reason and unbelief, and faith with doubting. Therefore the right eye of reason in the things of heaven, must be pulled out in man, and cast from him, as Christ said to those Jews, Why reason you in yourselves, saying, *We have Abraham for our father; for God is able, of these stony-hearted Gentiles, to raise children unto Abraham*. Because they should believe the truth declared by his apostles, they should pull out the right eye of reason, and should see by the single eye of faith; in that they should believe the apostles doctrine, the strait and narrow way to heaven, better with one eye than they could with two eyes. Therefore the right eye of reason in the things of God, that doth offend a man's mind, ought to be pulled out, and cast from him; else he will be in danger of being cast into hell-fire, in the resurrection, which will not appear to the dead soul a quarter of an hour, from its death to its rising again.

I only give you a hint of this, because I see you have faith in the resurrection, that you might be more strongly confirmed in it, and established in the spiritual meaning of the Scriptures, which were spoken by holy men of God, the prophets and apostles, and by Christ himself; and interpreted in this last age, by us, the witnesses of the Spirit.

This is all at present, only my love, with my wife's love, remembered to yourself, and your good wife, being of the seed of faith as you say, which I am very apt to believe, and not without some ground though I never saw her. My love to Doctor Moss, and Colonel Phayer, George Rodgers, and the rest in the true faith of God's elect, in that one personal God, Christ Jesus, that was manifest in the flesh, that is, God become flesh, and dwelt amongst men here on earth.

So I rest your friend in the eternal truth,

LODOWICKE MUGGLETON.

The Postern, London, Feb. 14, 1673.

Friend George Gamble, I received the four pounds of Mr. Delamaine, and have sent you twenty-nine of those books in answer to William Penn; they come to 3*l.* 12*s.* 6*d.* And I have sent you five of John Saddington's books, which come to 5*s.* And as for the box and line, and carriage to Bristol, Mr. Delamaine will give you an account, for I have left that to him; likewise, I am sorry that the Divine Looking-Glass and Mortality of the Soul was taken away, for I could have helped you to some of the other single, but cannot help you to one of them single; and especially the Divine Looking-Glass, because that is of great consequence, and will never be printed more while I live. But for the Mortality of the Soul, this answer to William Penn doth treat upon that point, sufficient to satisfy any man that hath faith, that his soul doth die. Only that book is desired the more, because it was of John Reeve's writing; but seeing it cannot be had, people must be content with what they have. Therefore I would wish you and all others to make much of them you have; for when those few I have be gone, you will not get one of the whole volumes for love nor money. I have had experience of that already, by that book which I sold for sixpence; I could have had five shillings of several, and some friends had it, and could have spared it; yet would not part with it. I have gotten now a bookbinder, that doth bind the whole volume together, so that all the Divine Looking-Glasses are bound to the set, so that if any will have that, they must have all or none.

So resteth your friend,

LODOWICKE MUGGLETON.

The Postern, London, February 14, 1673.

A Copy of a Letter written by the Prophet Lodowicke Muggleton to Mr. Thomas Tompkinson, bearing date from London, February 16, 1675.

Loving Friend in the true Faith, Thomas Tompkinson,

I RECEIVED your letter you sent to our friend Delamaine, dated from Waydley, January 3, 16'73, wherein I perceive your great enemy hath brought himself under the law, which is the same measure that he would have meted unto you if he could, but his unrighteous intents unto you is come upon his own head; likewise you desire that I would send you three books to the answer of William Penn;

also I went to Mr. Shelley, and shewed him your letter; and he looked in his book, and said it was not so much as three shillings and eleven pence; but rather than I should send but three books to you, he gave me half a crown, that I might send four books; and so I have sent you four of those books by Ashbourne carrier; so there remains seven shillings and six-pence due to me.

This is all at present, only my love, with my wife's love, remembered unto yourself, and to your wife, and all friends in the true faith there with you.

I rest your friend in the true faith,

LODOWICKE MUGGLETON.

The Postern, London, Feb. 16, 1675.

A Copy of a Letter written by the Prophet Lodowicke Muggleton to Mr. Alexander Delamaine, senior, May 16, 1673.

Loving Friend in the true Faith, Mr. Delamaine,

I HAVE thought it convenient, seeing that I am in trouble about these books, lest they should be taken away by the enemy, who would destroy them and me also if they should catch me; therefore I do intend to write to all the believers of this commission, that are able and willing, to buy one of these books bound altogether; the price is eleven shillings, and some friends will have two of them to help me away with them, for I do intend to sell no more of the three great volumes not single; that is to say, The Divine Looking-Glass, The Eleventh of the Revelation, and The Whole Revelation, but what are bound altogether; so that the believers may do me a great pleasure to take some of them off my hand, and do themselves no great harm; for the time may come, ere long, that they may have more for them than they give me; but, however, as the old proverb is, they will eat no bread, it will be only so much money lie dead: so that if you be free to take one, and send eleven shillings by my wife, and she shall bring one to you.

So resteth your friend in the true faith,

LODOWICKE MUGGLETON.

Postern, May 16, 1673.

A Copy of a Letter wrote by the Prophet Lodowicke Muggleton to John Harriot, bearing date from London, July 16, 1673.

John Harriot,

YOU may remember that I did send to my cousin Elizabeth White, two books, the one was concerning The Mortality of the Soul, and the other: was The Interpretation of the 11th of the Revelations; it was many years ago, I suppose nine or ten years ago, since I sent them to my cousin White, but I could never hear that they were received by her, or no other; but now of late I am informed, that you her son-in-law, that married her daughter, did receive them, and not only so, but you have burned them. I do remember that you, and Samuel Butler the tanner, had some discourse with me and Mr. Hudson at that time; you did then a little shew yourself what seed you were of at that time, even the seed of the serpent; yet for cruelty's sake, because you married my cousin's daughter, I did take little notice of your words at that time; likewise you were desirous that I should send your mother-in-law those books, because she could not read, that you might read them to her; but it seems that you were so offended at them, that you burned them: you should have burned that which was your own, you never paid a penny for them, neither were they sent to you, but to my cousin, and if you had not liked them, you should have given them to others, or have sent them to me again, then should you have escaped that unpardonable sin against the Holy Ghost, which God will not forgive in this world, nor in the world to come: for you have done despite unto the Spirit of Grace, in that you burned those writings that were penned by the Revelation of the Holy Spirit of God in us. I know you would have burned me as you did them, if you could with as much ease as you did them; also I know you would have done as much by Christ himself, if he were upon the earth, as you do by me; and in burning those books, you have committed high blasphemy against the Holy Ghost, a sin that will never be forgiven, neither in this world, nor in the world to come; and it would have been good for you if you had never been born: but you have shewed yourself of the reprobate seed of the serpent, appointed for eternal damnation; therefore, in obedience to my commission received from God, for this your wicked, envious, malicious burning those books without any cause, I do pronounce you cursed and damned, in soul and body, from the presence of God, elect men and angels, to all eternity. And you shall remember in your death, and in the Resurrection, that you were told so by one of the two last Prophets and Witnesses of the Spirit; neither will God deliver you from this curse which I have pronounced upon you, but it shall be as sure upon you, as if God himself had spoken it; for God always gave his Prophets and Apostles power to bless and curse to eternity, that is, to forgive sins, and retain sins; and this sin and blasphemy against the Holy Ghost, in burning those books, that you have committed, is that unpardonable sin, which Christ saith will never be forgiven in this world, nor in the world to come: besides, sins of this nature doth seldom escape a double curse, even crosses and poverty in this life, besides your damnation hereafter. Your sin hath lain hid a long time, but now is brought to sight. Furthermore, I understand, that Samuel Butler, and Mr. Smith the minister, were confederates with you in advising and counselling you to burn them; for I perceive you three are all of the Presbytery religion, and you three are in union, and do rule the whole town in matters of religion, if not in temporal affairs» because you three can prattle upon the letter of the Scriptures than any others in the town, yet more blind and ignorant in the knowledge of the true God, and all heavenly and spiritual knowledge, than the ignorant men of the town that is in his right senses; but because you think, and say within yourselves, you see, therefore your sin of blasphemy and blindness of mind doth and shall remain upon you; and as to Samuel Butler, I shall say this, that if he were confederates with you to burn them, or any other way, or had any hand in it whatsoever, I do pronounce Samuel Butler cursed and damned, soul and body, from the presence of God, elect men and angels, to eternity; but if he be innocent, and not guilty in no kind whatsoever, then this curse shall take no place in him, nor be of no effect; but if guilty, then it shall remain upon him to eternity, as aforesaid. Likewise if Mr. Smith, your minister, hath been confederates with you in burning those books, in giving his advice or counsel, or persuading you, or had any hand whatsoever in your burning those books, then I do pronounce Mr. Smith, your minister, cursed and damned, both in soul and body, from the presence of God, elect men and angels, to eternity; but if he be innocent and guiltless of this crime, then this curse shall be of no effect upon him; but if he be guilty of the burning of those books in any kind whatsoever, then shall this curse remain upon him to eternity. Furthermore, if any other persons, either men or women, that had any hand, or gave their consent willingly to the burning of those books, whoever they be, they are cursed and damned, both in soul and body, from the presence of God, elect men and angels, to eternity.

Written by

LODOWICKE MÜGGLETON.

July 16, 1673.

A Copy of a Letter sent by the Prophet Lodowicke Muggleton, to Cork, in Ireland, being the sentence of damnation upon twenty-six Quakers there.

Cork, in Ireland, the 11th of July, 1675.

AT the quarterly meetings of Quakers, they have drawn up a declaration, or testimony, in the behalf of all the Quakers, against John Reeve and Lodowicke Muggleton; whereunto six and twenty Quakers have set their hands, as a testimony against Reeve and Muggleton.

The true Copy of this Testimony, as it came to my hands, is as followeth, viz.

The God of eternal glory, who, by the arm of his living power, hath in these latter days of the world, gathered a remnant to himself, and brought them into fellowship and acquaintance with him; in whom he hath poured out of his Holy Spirit, according to his promise, as the prophets and the holy men of God in ages and generations past, whereby they are enabled, with an infallible discerning, (as in his holy covenant and council they abide) to try the spirits that come into the world, whether they be of God or not.

And whereas there is a spirit, that hath come forth into the world, and lain lurking in secret places for a season, and now begins to enlarge itself, by the erroneous doctrines of John Reeve and Lodowicke Muggleton, setting forth themselves to be the two last witnesses of the Commission of the Spirit; the former of which is dead, and the latter, named Lodowicke Muggleton, surviving, hath presumptuously arrogated to himself the power of blessing and cursing, and that, irrevocable to all eternity. Also that he, the said Lodowicke Muggleton, is the only interpreter of Scripture in the world, and the only and alone judge what shall become of men and women after death; neither shall they whom he damns, see any other God or judge but himself. And that he knows more of spiritual things, than ever prophet or apostle did since the beginning of the world; and some of whose principles, exactly taken out of some of their own books, hereafter follow: viz.

John Reeve sets forth in his book, called Transcendent Spiritual Treatise, that, Feb. 3, 4, 5, 1651, God, whom he saith is above the stars, spake to him by voice of words, saying, I have given thee understanding of my mind in the Scriptures above all the men in the world; and also said, I have given thee Lodowicke Muggleton to be thy mouth. And page the 5th, the said Reeve, page 32. Elias was exalted upon the throne of glory for a moment, to represent the person of God the Father, and he was made the protector of my God, when God became a child. And it was Elias that filled the Lord Jesus with those great revelations of his former glory, that he possessed in the heavens, when he was the eternal Father. And it was Elias that spake those words from heaven, saying, *This is my beloved Son.* And the said Reeve affirms, that if a man had no sin in their bodies, they might live and die, and naturally rise again by their own power, and in their own time, as the Lord of life did.

Page 33, John Reeve and Lodowicke Muggleton, in their book called, A Divine Looking-Glass, on that Scripture, saying, *The Lord said unto my Lord, sit thou on my right hand;* and that is to say, then the everlasting Father spake to himself. Page 46', Lodowicke Muggleton, in his book called, The Neck of the Quakers broken, saith, you can never know Christ, nor the Father, nor the Holy Ghost, by the words of Scripture, nor the light of Christ within you, without an interpreter, there being none in the world at this day but myself, as in page 25. Page 45, saith, I am sure I do know more in spiritual things than ever prophet or apostle did since the beginning of the world. And, page 47, he saith, I am the only and alone judge what shall become of men and women after death; neither shall those that are damned by me see any other God or judge but me. Page 15, he saith, and what person soever we determine judgment upon, it is so, and there is no revoking of it. Page 53, he saith, though Christ be the truth and the life, yet I am the only declarer what this truth and life is: and though Christ be the door, yet I have the key given me to open the door to life eternal.

And forasmuch as a false rumour hath been spread abroad, that we, or some of us, whose names are hereunto subscribed, have received the doctrines and principles of the aforesaid Reeve and Muggleton; whereby some honest-hearted may seem to stumble and startle: we therefore, the people of the Lord, called Quakers, at a general meeting in Cork, for the province of Munster, have very seriously, in the council of God, weighed and considered the principles and doctrines of the aforesaid Reeve and Muggleton, and the Spirit from whence they flow, and do, in the name and authority of the Holy Spirit of Truth, deny that spirit, as the spirit of error, and give our testimony against the same, warning and admonishing all people in the fear and dread of the Lord God of Heaven and Earth, to turn from it, and avoid it. The 19th day of the fourth month, 1673.

Let this be read in the publick meeting in the City of Cork, and the same to be recorded in a book to stand as a testimony against this blaspheming spirit, for ages and generations to come.

The Names of those that subscribed to this Paper, are as followeth, viz

WILLIAM MORRIS,
WILLIAM EDMONDSON,
ROBERT SANDHAM,
WILLIAM EDWARDS,
JOHN FENNELL,
THOMAS WIGHT,
JOHN FOSSAGE,
FRANCIS ROGERS,
JOHN BURNEGATE,
GEORGE PATTESON,
JOHN GETTAS,
JAMES DOWLYN,
THOMAS ALLEY,

WILLIAM EUD,
PHILLIP DYMOND,
CHR. PENNRICKE,
DAN. SAVERY,
WAR. PHLLLIPS,
THOMAS WHEDDEN,
JASPER TREYOS,
WILLIAM HAWKINS,
JOHN HAMMOND,
GEORGE NEGNOE,
TIMOTHY THOHOYMOUTH,
RICHARD BERRY,
ARTHUR JOHNSON.

The Answer of Lodowicke Muggleton, to this Paper as followeth

I SHALL separate the Quakers words in their paper from those words of Reeve and Muggleton, which they have picked out of our books, being all in print already, it will be needless to repeat them over again.

Therefore I shall only give answer to those words of the Quakers, which these twenty-six persons above written, have subscribed their names in the behalf of all the rest at their general meeting at Cork.

The words of concernment in their paper I have divided into six heads, which are all their own words; but as for the rest of their paper, being Reeve's and Muggleton's words, as they have picked out of their books already, and will remain upon record to the world's end, and to eternity, both upon the souls and bodies of them which truly believe in this commission of the Spirit, who are blessed, and upon the souls and bodies of all those that have actually despised and blasphemed against the doctrine and commission of the Spirit, declared by Reeve and Muggleton, who are cursed by them.

Therefore I shall direct my words only to the twenty-six persons above written, that have subscribed their names to this paper, and not to the whole assembly that professeth to be Quakers, though you say you subscribe your names in the behalf of all the Quakers. But I shall deal more justly in my judgment than you Quakers do in your judgment; for Penn, and other Quakers have not only given judgment against me, but upon all those that believe me. But I shall do by you as I have always done, set my face against none but those that are found in actual transgression of blasphemy against the Holy Ghost; for whoever despiseth us, the Witnesses of the Spirit, despiseth God that sent us. And if you had lived in the days when Christ was upon earth, you would have said as much to him as you do to me.

1. First. The Quakers say, the God of eternal glory, who, by the arm of his living power, hath, in this latter age of the world, gathered a remnant to himself, and brought them into fellowship and acquaintance with him; in whom he hath poured out of his Holy Spirit, according to his promise, as the prophets and the holy men of God in ages and generations past, whereby they are enabled, with an infallible discerning, (as in his holy covenant and counsel they abide) to try the spirits that come forth into the World, whether they are of God or not.

Muggleton's reply. That the God of eternal glory is not the Quaker's God? Why? Because he hath a spiritual body, form and shape, like man, therefore said to make man in his own image and likeness; therefore it is that angels, and all other creatures in heaven, do give glory, praise, and honour to the person of God their creator. For this I say, there is no honour, praise, and glory can be received by the creator, except he hath a body distinct of his own; neither can any creature, that hath life in the body, ascribe honour and glory, but to a personal God, that hath a body of his own. But the bewitched Quakers, through their ignorance and blindness of mind, do praise and magnify an infinite spirit without a body, that cannot be seen, nor comprehended by angels, nor man, nor no other creature. So that the Quakers are the absolute one alone people, that are led and guided by the spirit of Anti-Christ in this last age, who deny both Father and Son to have a body; for they have imagined the Spirit of God and the

Spirit of Christ to be all one Spirit, as is most true; they are but one Spirit: but they have imagined likewise, that this one spirit hath never a body of its own; therefore the Quakers people are absolutely of the Anti-Christian spirit, that denieth the Godhead Spirit to have a body of its own. For this I say, a spirit hath no existence no where without a body, but is a meer nothing at all. And this imaginary God, a Spirit without a body, is the Quakers God of eternal glory, which they worship, even a nothing at all, but a God of their own imagination: so that their fellowship and acquaintance is only with such a God as they have imagined; a spirit without a body is the Quakers God of eternal glory; and this God, an infinite nothing, hath poured out of his unholy spirit of imagination of reason upon the people called Quakers, such a spirit, which hath enabled them to defy the living God, that hath a body of his own in heaven, above the stars. And this imaginary God, a spirit without a body, hath given the Quakers discerning and counsel to fight against the true God, that hath a body, and to blaspheme against him and those he sends: so that the spirit of reason, the devil, in the Quakers, think they can try the spirits, whether they be of God, or not, yet stone-blind, and know not the true God.

2. The Quakers say, and there is a spirit that hath come forth into, and lain lurking in secret places for a season, and now begins to enlarge itself, by the erroneous doctrines of John Reeve and Lodowicke Muggleton, as they call them.

Answer. That this spirit, that hath come forth, which you say hath lain lurking in secret places for a season, it was the Spirit of Christ, the only wise God, that hath a body now in heaven, which you Quakers so despise, that did authorise John Reeve and Lodowicke Muggleton, to declare against that Anti- Christian spirit that reigneth in the world in all professions of religion; in that every man, by nature, is ignorant of the form and nature of the true God, and that God made man in his own image, in respect of his bodily shape and likeness, as well as his soul. But all men, by nature, being blind in spiritual things, as we ourselves were, have imagined and framed to themselves a God that is not, only a spirit without a body. And this dark apprehension of God hath taken such deep root in all mens hearts by nature, it being an established doctrine in the world above these thousand years, even from one generation to another. And the cause why this utter darkness hath remained upon all men, as well upon the elect as upon the reprobate, is, because God hath not sent one man, by commission, to declare the true God this many hundred years, until now, in this last age of the world, he hath sent Reeve and Muggleton. And that hath been the cause the whole world hath been over-spread with this conceit, that God is an infinite, formless Spirit, that hath no body, form, or likeness of his own. But Reeve and Muggleton were Sent forth by the authority of this God, that hath a body of his own, to try the spirits of all professors of the Scriptures in the world; which we have tried, and we do perfectly know the height and depth of every man's faith in the world in spiritual things concerning his God. And by this spiritual knowledge of God, his form and nature, we know the forms and natures of all things else, in heaven above, and in the earth beneath; and in the trial of all mens religion, we have tried by what spirit the Quakers are come forth in, and we find, by the knowledge of the Scriptures, and by the faith of the prophets and apostles, that the Quakers people are carried forth, by the spirit of Anti-Christ, with an imaginary God, a spirit without a body. And that there are no professors of religion in the world so absolute Anti-Christ as the Quakers people are. To be plain, the Spirit, which they call God, or Christ, or the light of Christ within them, is nothing else but the imaginations of reason, the devil in them, they finding the law written in their hearts, their thoughts accusing and excusing, they do imagine this law to be God; and this law hath never a body distinct from man. Therefore the dark imagination in the Quakers hearts doth think, that this law, written in every man's heart, must needs be God. This is the Quakers God, that hath never a body of his own, but man's body to dwell in: but this God of yours within you will prove your only devil to torment you to eternity.

And whereas you say, this spirit, meaning Reeve and Muggleton, hath been lurking in secret places for a season.

To this I say, it hath been almost as openly declared as the Quakers spirit hath, and almost as long it hath appeared in this last age of the world, for matter of time, as the Quakers Anti-Christian spirit hath appeared. It is almost twenty-two years since this commission of the Spirit hath appeared; and the spirit of Anti-Christ in the Quakers hath appeared but few years more. And when Reeve and Muggleton did appear at the first, this declaration and doctrine was far more publick than the appearance of the Quakers; why? Because we wrote our faith, doctrine, and commission, and printed it to the world, whereby the people took more publick notice of us than of the Quakers; for at that time, there were but few Quakers of note; neither did they print any thing of their faith and doctrine, what they would have the people to believe; and I suppose, that, if the first book the Quakers wrote to vindicate the principles of the Quakers doctrine could be produced. it would not bear so long a time as Reeve's and Muggleton's Commission-Book doth. But however, the Quakers at that time had witchcraft-fits, which did rather fright the beholders of them than inform their judgments. But since that, Muggleton hath cast out that devil out of many of them, by the sentence of damnation upon the chief of them: so that it hath eased the whole body of the Quakers of those witchcraft-fits, that were formerly very rise in the Quakers people; so that now there is hardly a witchcraft-fit can be procured amongst them. So that this spirit, that Reeve and Muggleton were guided by, hath not lain lurking in secret places. For I do believe, that we have written and printed, if it were possible to gather them all together, in publick, more than most of the Quakers in England have written; however, our books trouble the world more than any Quakers books do whatsoever. Likewise we were publick enough twenty years ago with you Quakers, when we gave sentence of damnation upon four of your chief leaders, if not the first broachers of the Quakers Anti-Christian doctrine, viz. George Fox, the elder and younger, both, Francis Howgell, and Edward Burroughes; these four, as I remember, were the first Quakers that were damned for denying that God hath a body of his own, distinct from man, and all other creatures. So that you Quakers have the least cause of any people whatsoever to say, that this spirit hath lain lurking in secret places; for this spirit hath had more power over those people called Quakers, than any other people whatsoever. So that you Quakers, of all people in the world, have the least cause to say, this spirit hath lain lurking in secret places. Indeed, we have not followed the practice of you Quakers, to compass sea and land to gain proselites, as many of you have, and you have made them twofold the children of the devil than they were before, in that they are more hardened, and more uncapable to understand the mystery of the true God becoming flesh, and the devil becoming flesh.

And whereas you say, now it begins to enlarge itself by the erroneous doctrines of John Reeve and Lodowicke Muggleton, as you call them.

To this I say, the Anti-Christian spirit in the Quakers hath enlarged itself very much within these fifteen years, which hath been the cause that the Spirit of the true Christ in us hath enlarged itself, in opposition to the Spirit of Anti-Christ in the Quaker, and more especially since John Reeve's death; for in his time, there were but few Quakers in comparison to what are now, and little notice taken of them in his time; but since they have encreased and multiplied exceedingly; but since Muggleton began to oppose them, by writing against their bodiless God within them, it hath put a great stop to them; and not only so, but this doctrine of Reeve and Muggleton hath delivered many innocent souls out of the snares of the Quakers, which leadeth men to eternal perdition, which denieth the body of the Lord of life to be without them. Besides, the spirit did not lurk in any secret place, when I wrote to Edward Bourne, Samuel Hooton, William Smith, Thomas Taylor, and several others, which is near twelve years ago, wherein they were damned to eternity for despising that doctrine you call erroneous; and ever since that letter to Samuel Hooton and William Smith, I have not been suffered to lurk in secret places. For you Quakers have caused me to be the publickest man in the world; witness that

Richard Farnesworth, Thomas Taylor, George Fox, Isaac Pennington, as may be seen in The Neck of the Quakers Broken, and in Fox's Looking-Glass, and the Answer to Pennington; besides letters to other Quakers, more than I can remember; besides the Interpretation of the 11th of the Revelations, and the whole Revelations, and The Interpretation of the Witch of Endor.

These things do manifest, that I have not lain still in secret, but do manifest me to be the most publick man in the world in spiritual things; because I am not only hated of you Quakers, but am hated of all the speakers and ministers of all the seven Churches of Europe, besides thousands of their hearers; so that it is an impossible thing, that I should have lain in any secret place. And this hatred have we procured of all people in the world, for no other cause at all, but for declaring this doctrine, which you call erroneous, and the authority of our commission, given by voice of words from the Lord Jesus Christ, the only wise God, who hath a glorious body, in the form like a man of his own; as we have written in The Transcendent Spiritual Treatise, when God gave this commission, in the year 1651.

3. These Quakers say, forasmuch as a false rumour hath been spread, that we, or some of us, whose names are here under subscribed, have received the doctrine and principles of the aforesaid Reeve and Muggleton, whereby some honest hearted may seem to stumble and startle.

Answer. If such a rumour hath been spread, and it was false, the more will be your misery. And you that have subscribed your names as a testimony that you have not received the doctrines of Reeve and Muggleton, but have utterly denied it, in subscribing your names as a testimony against it: I say, it would have been good, if none of you had been born; for in denying those doctrines, you have denied us; and in denying us, you have denied the true God that sent us;, which hath given me just occasion to give sentence of judgment upon all you that have subscribed your names.

And whereas, you think by this means that you have removed the stumbling stone out of your way, that the honest-hearted might not stumble and startle, and that you might establish your Anti-Christian principle the more sure; but you will be prevented; for God hath laid this doctrine and commission, which you deny, as a stumbling stone in Sion. So that many of you Quakers, and others, shall stumble at this stone, and fall, and never rise again; but there are some of those people that shall be preserved from stumbling at this doctrine of the Witnesses of the Spirit. For whoever is left to fall upon this stone, as you have done, shall be broken into pieces as to the peace of their minds here in this life; and on whomsoever this stone, or sentence of damnation, shall fall upon, it shall grind to powder in those eternal torments, which the wicked despisers and fighters against a personal God and his messengers, whom he hath sent, in utter darkness; so that there shall not one motion of peace arise in them to eternity. And farther, I say, I never did, nor never shall persuade any man or woman to believe this doctrine, or commission; for I have done my duty to God, in that I have declared the whole council of God beyond all that have gone before me, or that shall come after me; and whoever doth understand and believe, it will be for their eternal good; and if there should none believe this doctrine, yet should not I question the truth of it; for I have peace in myself, in that I have declared the mind of the Lord freely, as it hath been revealed unto me; neither did I ever encourage or persuade any person to believe. I set life and death before them, as Moses did, to chuse or refuse; if they did truly believe the doctrine of the true God, and the commission of the Spirit, they should live, and have eternal life abiding in them; this many can witness: but if they did refuse, deny, despise and blaspheme, as you have done, against the commission of the Spirit, then they chose eternal death rather than eternal life; this many hundreds can witness in their consciences if they would. For it was never my custom or practice this twenty years, to persuade any man against his conscience, nor to believe me, after they have had several discourses with me. I gave them liberty to go to any opinion whatsoever, and if they could find any man speak like this man, or give them better satisfaction to their questions than I have, let them go, and come no more at me. It was never my custom nor practice to compel people to enter into the kingdom of heaven, whether they would or no, as you Quakers do. I was always inclined to let the kingdom of heaven to suffer violence, that the violent desires of men and women, after salvation, might take the kingdom of heaven by force, and not be compelled to enter in. For you Quakers keep a great bustle to keep your disciples to you, for fear of losing them; I never did endeavour to get your disciples from you, yet there are many of them that are come to the life of this doctrine of Reeve and Muggleton, which you call erroneous. And if they could not have found rest in this doctrine and commission, they had liberty to return to you again. And can you Quakers tell the reason why so many of your disciples, that were absolute of you, should come to me, and never return to you again; and it is a more admirable thing, that there should not be one of Muggleton's disciples, or true believers of him, to fall from him to the Quakers, not this fifteen years; I know not one; neither do they stumble or startle any more, if they truly believe Reeve and Muggleton's doctrine.

4. Say they, we therefore, the people of the Lord, called Quakers, at a general meeting at Cork, for the province of Munster, have very seriously, and in the council of God, weighed and considered the principles and doctrines of the aforesaid Reeve and Muggleton, and the spirit from whence they flow.

Answer. That these people, called Quakers, at a general meeting at Cork, were not the people of the true God, but the children of that serpent devil that beguiled Eve. And your serious council in God, as you say, it was in the council of your imaginations of reason, the devil within you, which is the Quakers God they take council in, and in your imaginations of your hearts, which is your God, you have weighed and considered the principles and doctrine of Reeve and Muggleton, as you say, and the spirit from whence they flow.

5. They say, and do, in the name and authority of the holy spirit of truth, deny that Spirit as the spirit of error, and give our testimony against the same; warning and admonishing all people, in the fear and dread of the Lord God of heaven and earth, both to turn from it, and avoid it.

Answer. Here the Quakers do prate of the name and authority of the holy spirit of truth, yet know not the body of that God, from whence the holy

Spirit of truth proceeded; for this I say, that a spirit without a body can give no council at all; neither can any council proceed but from a spirit that hath a body of his own If mens spirits had not bodies, how could they give council to one another? Neither can that God, that hath never a body, be the true God, or give any council at all. Yet the Quakers people doth take council of a spirit that hath no body, which they call God; which God is nothing else but the law written 4n their hearts. So that this conclusion must needs follow, that you Quakers take council, in your own hearts, with a spirit without a body; the light of Christ within you: this you call God's Holy Spirit of truth, in which you take council. Now the light of Christ within you is not the true God; it is nothing else but God's law written in the heart, which doth accuse the conscience when you do any thing contrary to it. And when you do commune with this, righteous law, written in your hearts, you do imagine that you take council in God, a spirit without a body. Here lieth your great mistake, in that you take God's righteous law, written in your hearts, for God himself. A man may as well lake the law of a king for the king himself: only here is the difference; a king's law is visible, and himself is visible to the natural eyes; but God's law is invisible, written in the hearts of men, and God himself is that invisible God, yet a person distinct from this invisible law, written in man's heart. Now shall I say, that this law, written in my heart, is God; because I cannot see it with my natural sight, nor know how it came to be written, there, it being invisible. So that the Quakers do worship the law, written in their hearts, for God; and the light of this law, is that light of Christ they so much talk of within them: and this law is their God and Saviour, and they have no other God to save them, but the light of this law within them. This I know is the Quakers holy spirit of truth they so much talk of, which is no other spirit, but the law, written in their hearts, in the life and soul of them; and when their souls doth die, this law, written in their hearts, doth die also; and so, by consequence, their imaginary God, a spirit without a body, is dead also; and so they lie all three in the earth together, viz. the soul, the law. the imagination that God was a spirit without a body, all dead in the earth, until the day that my God, that hath a body of his own, shall raise them again in the resurrection, then shall the soul and the law, written in their hearts, which was their God, a spirit without a body, and their imagination, that created in itself such a God, a spirit without a body, they shall all rise again together. And this law, written in their hearts, they called God, a spirit without a body while they were in this life, shall be the only devil that shall torment them to eternity in the resurrection. And this law, aforesaid, the light of it, is the Quakers holy spirit of truth, which doth deny that spirit that doth declare God to be in form and shape like man, as the spirit of error, and they do give testimony against the same; and not only so, but they do admonish all other people, as well as their own, in the fear and dread of their imaginary Lord God of heaven and earth, both to turn from it, and avoid it. But this I say, whosoever doth adhere to the Quakers admonishment, or to their God, he doth adhere to A God of his own imagination, which hath neither body, form, shape, nor substance; which cannot deliver you in the day of trouble.

6. And, *lastly*, the 19th day of the fourth month, 1673, let this be read at the publick meeting in the city of Cork, and the same to be recorded in a book, to stand as a testimony against this blasphemous spirit for ages and generations to come.

Answer. Here the reader may see what care and pains the Quakers doth take to uphold their kingdom of Anti-Christ; and to bind themselves together, at their general meetings, to fight against the Spirit of the true Christ, and his doctrine, declared by Reeve and Muggleton, but more especially against me. These ten years, and better, have I only engaged against the whole host of Quakers, they being many, and I but one man; yet being chosen of God to oppose that Anti-Christian spirit that would have spread itself over the face of the earth: but God hath letted them, by sending two men to make war against them; and I, even I, have fought many battles with them, and have, by faith in the true God, that hath a body of his own, broken the jaw-bone of the Quakers strength to pieces, and have shattered them in confusion.

There hath come forth against me many of their mighty men of valour; they have shot their poisonous arrows at me, but could not hurt me. Oh! how many of your Anti-Christian companions, captains, and mighty men of war of Anti-Christ's army, have come out against me, more than I can well name: they came with their weapons of war as Goliah, as it were like giants with their weavers beams; yet I being but one in the world, by the help of my God, that hath a body in heaven, above the stars, being cloathed with the whole armour of God, the breastplate of righteousness, the shield of faith, the helmet of salvation, and the two-edged sword of the Spirit, I have fought with many men of valour, and have overcome them, as David did Goliah, and have scattered their followers, even as the host of the Philistines were scattered. These things are written more at large in another place, which will be upon record, and in publick, after my death: so that you Quakers, if you were sensible, might say, Oh! what is become of our valiant leaders, our captains, and mighty men of war, that listed, as under the spirit of Anti-Christ? Oh! how are they fallen by the sword of the Spirit put into Muggleton's mouth? Alas! alas! our mighty men are fallen into eternal damnation, when, as we thought, that their spirits did but go out of their bodies; but, alas! it is otherwise: they are gone to eternal darkness, where they shall never see bright day more. But, here of late, since William Penn hath survived the place of a teacher, a leader, and captain of the Quakers host, he hath been more zealous for the spirit of Anti-Christ, than the former that went before him; and he hath defied the living God, that hath a body of his own, more glorious than any that went before him. And for this he is damned, body and soul, to eternity; and it will not be long before he shall possess the reward of his blasphemy, which is this: his soul, which he saith cannot die, it shall die two deaths; it shall pass through this first death, which is natural and appointed unto all men once to die, and enter into the second death, which is Vernal, in utter darkness, where he shall never die, nor never live in comfort, even a living death, and lying life: this is the second death, which God hath Prepared for the seed of the serpent, such as Penn, and others, that despise such a God as hath a body, form, and shape like man; and he shall remember, that he was told so by me.

Furthermore, I suppose William Penn's book against me hath been some cause that hath stirred you, in Ireland, up to band yourselves thus, at your general meeting, to declare against the doctrine of Reeve and Muggleton. So that the Quakers come now of late in troops; they do not come two or three at a time, as formerly; but, as it were, in bands: for it is not long since I had a testimony against this doctrine and commission of the Spirit, at a quarterly meeting of women Quakers, no less than twenty-eight, their names subscribed; and at a quarterly meeting of men Quakers, about thirty, that subscribed their names, as a testimony against the doctrine of Reeve and Muggleton. William Smith wrote the testimony of them both, and a little while after he died. And now here cometh a band of men out of Ireland, twenty-six, who have given testimony against Reeve and Muggleton's doctrine, calling them erroneous, and do deny them as the spirit of error and blasphemy.

These words are the sin against the Holy Ghost; and inasmuch as God hath chosen me, on earth, to be the judge of blasphemy against the Holy Ghost, so that I have considered your testimony, and the names of all you that have subscribed to that paper; your names are written at the beginning of this paper. And you having all jointly set your names, as one man, to this testimony above written.

Therefore, in obedience to my commission from the true God, I do pronounce all those twenty-six persons, whose names are aforewritten, cursed and damned, in their souls and bodies, from the presence of God, elect men and angels, to eternity.

Written by me,

LODOWICKE MUGGLETON,

One of the two last Prophets and Witnesses of the Spirit unto the High and Mighty God, the Man Christ Jesus in Glory.

I wish you to read this answer at your general meeting, that the whole congregation may hear it; and, if you please, to record it for ages and generations to come.

Let these two sheets of paper be delivered to the hands of some of the Quakers, at their general meeting, in Cork, in Ireland, to be read, if possible, to the congregation.

The Postern, near London Wall,

in London, Aug. 11, 1673.

A Copy of a Letter sent by the Prophet Lodowicke Muggleton to Mr. Joseph Moss, a Physician, in Cork, in Ireland, August 11, 1673.

Dear Friend in the eternal Truth, Joseph Moss,

THIS is to certify you that I received your letter, with the Quaker's testimony. I am glad to hear you are well in health, and of George Gamble's health; but as for satisfaction of that life eternal I suppose you do not want, for true faith, without doubting, doth remove mountains of objections in the mind to be cast into the sea, where they shall sink, and never rise again to stand before the understanding. And inasmuch as God hath been pleased, in this last age of the world, to chuse two men to be a light unto the world, and to declare the Lord's saving-health unto as many as shall receive it, that hath enlightened many that sate in darkness and in the shadow of death, that have been instruments or candlesticks to hold the light of life before people, whereby those that have oil in their lamps may enter into the gate of heaven, (that is, faith in their hearts) may enter into heaven while the door is open, and may sup with the God of Heaven.

This commission of the Spirit is the door of heaven in this last age, and he that believeth in the doctrine of the true God and his commission, doth enter in at the door of heaven: and though these times may be the worst of times as to temporal affairs, yet it is the best time to the seed of faith to exercise itself, that hath been above this thousand years; for who knew the form and nature of God till now, and the form and nature of the right devil; the knowledge of the one causeth the soul to mount up to heaven, and the knowledge of the other maketh the soul descend into the lowest hell, and ascend out of it again. These things are wonderful hard to understand by them that have no faith, but to those that have faith in the true God, and in the commission of the Spirit, it is very easy; which I do not question you nor George Gamble, though I thus speak.

Friend Moss,

I hope the books that were sent to George Gamble did not receive much damage, though they passed through great casualties. Likewise I heard that George Gamble was in some trouble about quartering of soldiers, but I hope it is not so bad as it was reported. I am a writing an answer to William Penn's book, and as soon as I can I shall get them printed; but I know not how any can be conveyed safe to you in that country.

This is all at present, only my love and my wife's love remembered unto yourself and George Gamble, and my love to Colonel Phaire and his wife, and all friends else in the faith there with you.

I rest your friend in the eternal truth,

LODOWICKE MUGGLETON.

Postern, August 11, 1673.

Friend.

I would desire you to deliver this paper enclosed to what Quakers you think will faithfully read it in the Meeting; I have sent it unsealed for you to read, and, if you think it worth your pains, to take a copy of it before you deliver it to them; because if they should deal deceitfully with that, and hide it from others, you have a copy of the same may the better convince gainsayers.

A Copy of a Letter written by the Prophet Lodowicke Muggleton to Mr. Thomas Tompkinson, of Sladehouse, bearing date from London, August 11, 1673.

Loving and kind Friend in the true faith, Thomas Tompkinson,

I RECEIVED your letter, bearing date June 27, 1673, but I could not well give you an answer of it since, because I have been much employed in writing, both in the answer to Penn's book, and otherwise; so that I cannot perfect the answer not as yet, because of several occasions doth happen which doth hinder me; and as for that business concerning the oaths, and receiving the Sacrament, it doth not belong to you, and if it should come to be forced upon you, it is not lawful for you to take it; for whoever doth take it now, will as soon take an oath to the contrary, when occasion is, for this business will not hold long at the lock it is now: but I suppose our friend Mr. Delamain hath given you some satisfaction in this business before now; and as for our friend Hall, that doth desire me to send a book bound altogether, I thought it convenient to let you know before I send it that I had none bound, until about two weeks since I have met with a book-binder that hath bound me some, and there is all the books bound together, except The Mortality of the Soul, and there is none of them to be had, nor hath not been a long time; neither is there any clasps to them that are bound now, it being dangerous to put clasps on, but they are well covered with good strong covers; besides, there is never a Divine Looking-Glass single to be had but what is bound in the whole set, if you would give twice the price, therefore I would wish you to make much of them you have, for they will be very hard to come by ere long; so that if our friend Hall will have one of them as they are, without The Mortality or clasps, I will send him one; the price of it is eleven shillings, as it always was; so if he do like of it, let me know by what carrier I shall send it, and I will send it to you.

So being in haste I shall take leave at present, only my love and my wife's love remembered unto yourself, and to your wife, and Thomas Hall, and all friends in the faith there with you.

I rest and remain your friend in the eternal truth,

LODOWICKE MUGGLETON.

The Postern, London, August 11, 1673.

A Copy of a Letter written by the Prophet Lodowicke Muggleton to Mrs. Dorothy Carter, bearing date January 16, 1674.

Dear Friend in the true faith, Dorothy Carter,

THIS is to certify you, that I received your letter dated January 8, 1674, and am glad to hear that yourself, and all the rest of friends you make mention of are in health: and as for Mr. Goodwyn taking no notice, nor speaking any thing concerning his faith in this commission, do not you be troubled at it, neither do you speak to him about it at all, except he speak to you first; for if his heart be falling from that affection and love he had once to it, in the days of your daughter's life, let him go, for every one must stand by his own faith; but his faith, which will not hold out to the end, will miss of the end of his faith, which is the salvation of his soul; and if he did procure a blessing from me, through your daughters prompting him on to ask it of me, yet if he stick not to it with all his heart, and with all his soul, to his life's end, he will lose the benefit of it as others have done; but seeing he doth not rebel against it, nor speak for it, let him alone; if he be contented, I am contented; if he make no mention of it, I advise you to do the same, and there is no question but he, will find trouble enough in the world, even as the sparks fly upwards, which is the portion of every man and woman in the world, more or less; but happy are those that have peace in the faith of this commission of the Spirit.

Also you say William Newcombe is intended to go to Virginia, and take two of his children along with him. I wonder what is in mens minds to run amongst the heathens, that are without God in the world; besides, the climate doth not agree with the English nature to live there contentedly; but some men, when the world frowns upon them, having not patience to submit, they run into a present destruction: just as if a man should seek the living among the dead, so doth all that goeth out of England for want of livelihood, thinking to find it there. I have known several hath done so thinking to find life, but they have found death instead of life. My nature is so contrary to go out of the land of Canaan, of England, amongst the heathen, that I had rather live in prison here all days of my life. But where men cannot bear the Cross patiently, they seek deliverance by running into a present destruction; which frees men from all troubles, but not with peace of mind As for those books he saith he hath of mine, which he thinks come to fifty shillings, I cannot think he hath so many; I know not what counsel to give you concerning them, neither would I hinder you from doing the man good, for I know money is scarce with most people now-a-days; but I shall lay no bonds upon you in this thing, but leave it to the freedom of your own hearts; but if you do buy those books of William Newcombe, I would not have you send them to Virginia amongst the heathen, it will signify nothing at all; I have lost several books that way, so that I will never send book morel by sea; I would wish you to keep them yourselves, and if you cannot tell how to bestow them, if you please send them to me, and I will put them off as I can. This is all I can say as to this, but leave it to your own liberty; and as for Capt. Wildey, Mr. Cawley, Mr. Delamain, Mr. Saddington, they are all well, but Mrs. Whalley is dead and buried; she got an extreme cold in her head and teeth about Michaelmas last past, and she would needs be let blood; so the doctor let her blood, till her life was almost gone, but with much ado she was preserved alive in a great deal of misery a quarter of a year; she was buried upon New-Years day, when I was at Braintree, in Essex, at Mr. Whitehead's house; but I saw her before I went, and she was very well satisfied in her mind as to her eternal happiness; she had not the least doubt in her; if she had not been let blood she might have lived many years; and as for Mrs. Griffith she is out of town, and will not be in London this two weeks, as I hear by my daughter White, neither have I seen Mrs. Griffith since she brought me your letter, which desired me to lay out six shillings for Sarah Hatter, which I let Mrs. Griffith have; and as for Sarah I have not seen her since I came to town, but I hear she goeth out to work a-days, and comes home to my daughter's at night; I heard: nothing, but that she is pretty well, and that she cannot write to you as she would, she being so bad a scribe; and when she is at leisure then her father is not, and when he is at leisure then she is not. When Mrs. Griffith cometh to town she shall have your letter, hoping she will satisfy you further.

This is all at present, only my love, with my wife's, remembered unto you, and, Betty Marsden, Betty Webster, Anne Mallate, and all friends else.

Your Friend,

LODOWICKE MUGGLETON.

Postern, London, Jan. 16, 1674.

A Copy of a Letter written by the Prophet Lodowicke Muggleton, to Mrs. Frances Man, containing her blessing, dated January 23, 1674.

Loving Friend in the true Faith, Frances Man,

I UNDERSTAND that you are not in health, so that you cannot conveniently go abroad, neither is there freedom for me nor my wife to come and see you: therefore I thought good to write these few lines unto you, to comfort and bear up your spirit in your trouble, as followeth:

I have had experience of late days of your faith in the true God, and in this commision of the spirit, though I know it was long before your heart did close with it; but when you received me in the name of a prophet, you did set to your seal, in your own soul, that I was true, and sent of God; so that when you received me, you received, him. that sent me, even the true God; so that after you believed, you were sealed with the holy spirit of promise, which is the blessing and assurance of everlasting life, then did the day-star arise in your heart; that is, the act of faith is the star that did arise in your heart, to enlighten your understanding in the things of eternity, in those deep hidden mysteries of God becoming flesh, and the devil becoming flesh. Upon these two foundations standeth eternal life, and eternal death, and the act of faith in man is that which giveth the assurance of everlasting life, which assurance of it doth abide in yourself, which hath appeared in you, in that you have not been ashamed of your faith before men, but have justified your faith in this commission of the spirit against all gainsayers; so that you, being justified by faith in your own soul, I know you have peace with God, and so the assurance of your eternal happiness on the other side of death: so that I can truly say by you, as Christ did, when on earth, to his disciples that believed on him, *Blessed are your eyes, for they see, and your ears that hear, and your heart that understands the things that belong unto your peace*; which is the peace of God that passeth all understanding, which none upon earth have but those that truly believe in this commission of the Spirit; and because you have stretched forth the hand of faith, and have taken and eat of the tree of life, you shall live for ever; for by faith you have eaten of the flesh of God, in that you have believed that God became flesh; and you have drank of his blood, in that you have believed that God died, and shed his most precious blood to redeem the seed of Adam; so that faith in his blood it hath purified your heart from that thick darkness of unbelief, which lieth upon all people in the world but those of this faith. That is that water of life that doth quench the thirsty soul, so that you shall never hunger and thirst more after the forgiveness of sin, nor after the assurance of everlasting life; and these words of mine shall be as the leaves that fall from the tree of life, which is for the healing of the nations, so shall they be for the healing of your troubled soul with the seed of the serpent in this life. This faith is the faith of God's elect, that removeth that mountain of darkness and ignorance that lieth before the understandings of all mankind by nature; this faith is that which doth ascend up to heaven, and pierceth through the sky, and beholdeth our God, our king, and our redeemer, upon the throne of his glory: which faith is an evidence to the soul, that we shall see him face to face, who was dead, but is alive; and behold he is alive for evermore.

These things considered, let faith and patience bear up your soul in this troublesome world, and after a little season you shall enter into the possession of those eternal joys, and endless pleasures.

This with my love presented unto you, I rest and remain your friend in the eternal Truth,

LODOWICKE MUGGLETON.

January 23, 1674.

A Copy of a Letter written by the Prophet Lodowicke Muggleton to Elizabeth Dickinson, Jun, being her Blessing, bearing date March 6, 1674.

Elizabeth Dickinson the Younger,

I UNDERSTAND, by Goodwife Love, that you are not well, but rather drawing near the grave, and that you would gladly have seen me before you die; yet being comforted in yourself that you shall see me hereafter in heaven, I was desired to write a few lines unto you, to add to your comfort before you go hence, and shall be seen no more. I have considered your tender age, and weak distempered body, ever since you were born; yet with tender looking to, your weak distempered nature hath been preserved and upheld to this day, yet the root of your disease doth still remain, and cannot be cast out but by death, it being born with you; but in the resurrection this vile distempered body of yours, which is now mortal, shall rise an immortal, spiritual body, capable of eternal joy and glory, where no diseases, pain or sorrow can come, where body and soul shall live in joy and pleasure for evermore. And though I know there can be no fears of death to arise in your heart, because of the tenderness of your age, you being uncapable of actual sin, the sting of death is taken away from you, for the sting of death is sin, and the strength of sin is the law; but that being not capable of the breach of any law, so no sting of death can lay hold of you I knowing this, would add a word of comfort to strengthen your spirit here, and to your happiness hereafter in the kindom of eternal glory, where is joy and pleasure at the right-hand of our God and King, and our Redeemer, for evermore. And that you may be the more satisfied and comforted in the assurance of everlasting happiness in the life to come/I do declare you, Elizabeth the younger, one of the blessed of the Lord, both in soul and body, to all eternity. And if you do live till Whitsuntide, I do intend to see you if possible.

So resteth your friend,

LODOWICKE MUGGLETON.

The Postern, March 6, 1674.

Postscript of a Letter to Mrs. Futerell.

SOVEREIGN means to give you peace in this life, and in the life to come; and you seem to be very well satisfied in it ever since; but now about the death of this child, I perceive your faith faileth you, in that you have let such a conceit (that your child was bewitched) to enter into your heart, to cause this melancholy humour in you, that maketh shipwreck of your natural peace here, and will eclipse your spiritual peace hereafter, if it be not reasoned out in your own soul, for my faith is stedfast in what I said unto you, therefore let your faith be stedfast in me without doubting, and you shall never perish in the peace of your mind, neither in this life, nor in the life to come, but shall have everlasting life; and let not melancholy thoughts of your child's being bewitched, or evil surmise, enter into your mind, but let your faith on God, and in this commission of the Spirit, and patience in temporal troubles, possess your soul, then will you receive an hundred fold of peace and satisfaction in the life to come, and life everlasting.

This is the true way to have peace in this life, and in the life to come; and what can I do more for you than I have done to settle your mind in peace? Yet if you have conceived any prejudice in your heart against any believers, though it be causeless, yet I shall part you asunder, so that you and your husband shall have no society with them, nor they with you, do more than any stranger; so that you may be satisfied, and your peace may be perserved, all shall be well.

This is as much as can be said in this matter, and all I can say at present, hoping you will take my advice in what I have said in this paper, that my words may take place in you to your peace of mind here, and eternal happiness hereafter, as it hath done in several others.

This with my true love remembered to yourself, I rest your friend in the eternal Truth,

LODOWICKE MUGGLETON.

Postern, London, June 11, 1674.

A Copy of a Letter wrote by the Prophet Lodowicke Muggleton to Mrs. Hampson of Cambridge.

Dear Friend Mrs. Hampson,

I UNDERSTAND you have some trouble upon your mind about the death of your child, as if it was bewitched; I thought your faith, in what I had declared concerning witches, had been stronger than so to think that witches should have power over infants, which are not capable of fear, for fear and belief is the inlet to all witchcraft, fear entered first into the mind, and belief enters into the blood, and so men, women, and children comes to be bewitched; but I suppose your child was not capable of any of these two; likewise frights to children may cause fits, like to witchcraft fits, yet not bewitched in the least; besides, children in the conception, when they are conceived in the womb, may partake of that melancholy blood in the nature of the parents, or of any other distemper or disease in the parents, as I by experience do know by my own children, two sons by my second wife, as sweet children as eye could look on, yet partakers of their mother's nature, who was a comely woman to see to, yet of a melancholy dropsical nature and humour, if things did not go well in this world, as no man can assure his wife all things shall prosper always, because troubles are as sparks of fire that fly upwards, and fall down to its centre again, especially where children are. The first-born son was stricken with a convulsive fit, when it was a year old, as it sat upon my knee, when it was merry, and it lived till it was three years old; afterwards the second son I had by her did grow up and prosper till he was three years old, after that the evil did break out, and it encreased to the running evil from place to place, and he lived thus till he was nine years old, though I used means to help him, but all in vain; and when the child died I was glad, knowing all the children I had by her did partake of her melancholy and dropsical nature, and not any witchcraft powers in the least; and I know your nature is given much to melancholy and discontent of mind, produced out of your own surmisings, which are as false as God is true, so that you have created to yourself fears where no fear is, and sorrow where you might have had joy, and grief where you might have had comfort; and though you are not sensible of the hurt it doth your person, it being grown strong, yet your mind being troubled, it corrupts your nature, in that it enters into your blood; and the grief your husband hath to see you in this condition, that nothing will comfort you, it hurteth his nature also, which never was very healthful since I knew him; so that what evil is produced in your body by fears and melancholy, you must expect your children must partake at one time or another, and you have no remedy but patience; therefore I shall say this unto you, I remember when you were first married your melancholy mind wanted rest, not only in this life, but you wanted peace and assurance of happiness in the life to come, and for that purpose you desired a blessing of me, which upon your request I gave you, and you seemed to be satisfied in it ever since; and my faith is stedfast in what I said unto, therefore let yours be stedfast in me, without doubting, and you shall never perish, but have everlasting life; and let not these melancholy thoughts of witchcraft, or evil surmises, enter into your mind, but let your faith in God, and in the commission of the Spirit, and patience in temporal troubles, refresh your soul, then will you receive an hundred fold of peace and satisfaction in this life, and in the life to come life everlasting. This is the true way to have peace in this life, and in the life to come; and what can I do more for you than I have done, to set your mind in peace?

Yet if you have conceived any prejudice in your heart against any of the believers, though it be causeless, yet I shall part you asunder, so that you nor your husband shall have no society with them, nor they with you; so your peace can be preserved, all shall be well. This is as much as can be said in this matter, and all I shall say at present, hoping you will take my advice in what I have said in this paper, that my words may take place in you to your peace of mind here, and eternal happiness hereafter, as it hath done in several others.

This with my true love remembered to yourself and husband, I rest your friend in the eternal Truth,

LODOWICKE MUGGLETON.

Postern, London, June 11, 1674.

A Copy of a Letter written by the Prophet Lodowicke Muggleton to Isabella Malum, Quaker, dated from London, October 1, 1674, directed to her at Nottingham.

Isabella Malum,

I RECEIVED a letter, dated Nottingham, the 12th of the fifth month, 1674. I know it is not of your hand-writing, but it is the testimony of your own heart, as you have declared; wherein you have shewed what seed and nature you are of, even the seed of the serpent, in that you have been left to the reasonings of your own heart, as King Saul was to reject the prophet of the Lord, in sinning against the commandment of the prophet Samuel, and go to a witch; so that the good Spirit of the Lord departed from him, and an evil spirit of the Lord was sent unto him; so it is with you: you have rejected and despised me, the prophet of the Lord, and have given your testimony against the good Spirit of the Lord, and did strive with your evil spirit of reason, the devil in you; which good spirit would have led you through that narrow gate which leads to life eternal, which few do find, or enter therein. But I perceive the evil spirit of reason in you hath prevailed, and hath the victory over you, and hath led you captive, insomuch that it hath caused you to despise and reject the good Spirit of the Lord, in his messenger, which brings glad tidings of salvation to all that truly believe in him.

1. This Spirit of truth you call a seducing spirit of Lodowicke Muggleton; which you say leads to death and destruction; so that the good Spirit of the Lord that did strive with you, and had almost persuaded you to join with it, as you have expressed in your testimony, is now departed from you; and the evil spirit of reason in you is now to be your guide; and the good Spirit shall strive no more with you; for you shall be given up to a reprobate mind, as Saul was; and the hope of such hypocrites as you shall perish.

2. You say, it is now upon your heart to declare something how you came to lose your condition, and to backslide from the Quakers, and from that light within, which you call the light of Christ, which did reprove you of sin, and convince your conscience of the vanities, and customs, and fashions of this world.

As to this, I say, if you had been at rest, and peace of mind, in the Quakers principles and practice, you would never have backslidden from them. For the cause why people run from one thing to another is, because they are not at rest where they are. For this I say, if religious people could find peace, and rest of mind, in the doctrine and practice of the seven churches, there would never a man or woman believe me; for there is none believes me, but those that are lost; for I am in the same condition as Christ was when upon earth; he came but *unto the lost sheep of the house of Israel*, not to those that were settled in a form of religion, as the Scribes and Pharisees were, and as all the seven churches are now: so that if you had found rest in the Quakers way, why did you not keep there? Why did you backslide from them? Certainly, if the Quakers way had been the truth, (as you say now,) it would have given you rest then. And are you so bewitched, to think that you shall find more peace in that truth you backslided from now, than you did when you were in your innocency? Will the Quakers love backsliders better than they did before? I am sure, the true God, nor his messengers, doth not love backsliders, nor hypocrites, nor rebels, as they do integrity and uprightness of heart. But the Quakers people being ignorant of the true God, perhaps their God, an infinite Spirit without a body, or that God in them, will be more merciful than the true God: perhaps their God, an infinite Spirit, will love you better for your backsliding from them; and the more because you had like to have been catched in Muggleton's snare, as you say. But I can do as Peter did by his, pick out of his snare or net the good fish, and cast the bad away. I can spare such as you are very well. And whereas you say you backslided from that light within you, which you call Christ, which did reprove you, and convince your conscience of sin, and of the vanity of this world; this light of Christ was nothing else but the law written in your heart, which did accuse you when your mind was vain; and when your mind did not run after vanity, the law written in your heart did excuse your conscience.

Indeed this law was written in every man's heart by Christ, the only God; therefore may be called the light of Christ, *that enlighteneth every man that cometh into the world*: but Christ's person is distinct from this law written in man's heart; and this light of the law is distinct from Christ; and whoever maketh the law written in his heart, that accuseth and excuseth, to be the very Christ, as the Quakers do, that Christ within them shall prove the greatest devil to all eternity.

3. You say, you desired to see Lodowicke Muggleton's books: you say you heard some places here and there read, and you were asked the question, whether ever you heard friends declare such things? And you said, nay. Likewise you do confess, you were bid to take heed of judging or speaking against him. Here was the desire of reason, the devil in you, to see those books: and you say you heard them read. Did those that shewed you those books, force them upon you, without your desire, and contrary to your mind? They were lent unto you; for I am sure you bought none. What provoked you to desire to see them for your own hurt? Likewise you had a charge given you, not to speak against them; but you contrarily have spoken evil of them in a high nature, insomuch that you have spoken against your own soul; for had you not been of that reprobate seed, you would have had a care of speaking evil of those books that were so lovingly lent you: they cost you nothing: had you been of the elect seed, though you could not have believed them, or not liked them, you would have been kept from speaking evil of them.

4. You say you had got some of his books, and reading of them, your heart became dark, having lost your guide, which caused you not to believe in him, as the only prophet and messenger of the most High God. Here the spirit of reason was struck dark in you, by reading those books, because the doctrine contained in those books did so far surmount the doctrine or principles of the Quakers, as the sun in its brightness doth the twinkling star; so that the light of the law in you, which was but as the light of a star in you, which is nothing else but the light of nature, which guideth men to do things honest and just between man and man. And this light of nature is that light of Christ in you, and that truth you so much talk of; for this I know, that there is never a Quaker in the world that hath any other light of Christ in him, but the light of nature, not as he is in the state of a Quaker; and this was the cause you were stark dark in the reading those books, because the light in you was put out, and caused you to walk in darkness; having lost the light of nature, you lost your guide; which, if you could have stood still awhile in patience, you should have seen the salvation of the true God, and have been brought out of that darkness into his marvellous light, which is heavenly, far exceeding the light of the law in you; which would have caused you indeed to believe him to be the true prophet and messenger of the most high God; but you being the seed of the serpent, heaven was not appointed for you, but hell only.

5. You say, I sent a letter to a follower of mine at Nottingham, that if the two women that were fallen from the Quakers, would turn to them again, let them return; but if they do, they will perish for ever. Likewise I said in that letter, if I be in the truth, all that believe in my commission shall be saved; but if I be not in the truth, all shall be damned that believe in me. These, or to this effect, you say, was part of my letter. Further you say, the hearing of this letter struck you to the heart, and much trouble seized upon you, that you should venture your salvation upon the words of a mortal man.

Also you say, Oh! how you cried to the Lord, that you might once more be worthy to be a door-keeper amongst the congregation of the faithful, before you *go hence, and shall be seen no more.*

As to this, I did send a letter to a follower of mine at Nottingham, that if the two women that were fallen from the Quakers would return again to them, let them return; for I did understand, that the Quakers did solicit them much, with exhortations, and persuasions, and by letters to them, to return to them again. The letters I have yet to shew; and I find in those letters, that those two women were in a great streight in their minds, to give the Quakers an absolute answer, whether they would return to them, or keep to Muggleton. I heard those two women were in a great quandary, whether to keep to me, or return to them; and especially Isabella Malum was inclinable to fall back to the Quakers. Whereupon I wrote that letter to my friend, that if they would return back to the Quakers again, let them go; but if they did, they would perish for ever; and so you will; for whoever setteth the hand to the plough of faith, in this commission, and looketh back, will perish to eternity.

And further I say, that if I be a true prophet, as I know I am, all those that truly believe me, and hold out to the end, shall surely be saved; but if I be a false prophet, as you say I am, then all those that believe me shall be damned, and I myself shall be damned, for being deceived myself, and deceiving others.

This must be ventured by all men and women, else no salvation can be attained unto in this life.

Therefore it concerns all you ministers and speakers, to be sure you are not false ministers of Christ yourselves, to deceive others; for I can assure you, if you are, you will be damned to eternity yourselves and all those that are deceived by you will perish also.

Likewise you say, the hearing of this struck you to the heart, and much trouble seized upon you, in that you should venture your salvation upon the

As to this I say, it had been well for you, had you ventured your salvation upon the words of a mortal man. Was not all the Scripture given forth by mortal men? Was not Moses a mortal man, who set life and death before the people; and those that put their trust in his words did live; but those that did not venture their lives upon his words were put to death, as may be read abundantly in the Scriptures. Were not Peter, and the rest of the apostles, mortal men? yet the keys of heaven, and of hell, were given unto them; and whose sins were forgiven by them on earth, were forgiven by God in heaven; and whose sins were not forgiven by them here on earth, were not

Now ought not those that heard them, and believed them, to venture their salvation upon the words of these mortal men, that preached life and salvation by Jesus Christ unto them; yea, all that were saved by faith in their doctrine, ventured their salvations upon the words of those mortal men; and whoever did not venture their salvation upon those mortal mens words that heard them, were damned to eternity: so likewise, if you had ventured your salvation upon the words of me, the Lord's true prophet, which am but a mortal man, you should assuredly have been saved, as many others can witness: but in regard you could not venture your salvation upon the words of a mortal man, you will assuredly be damned to eternity; for this was God's way ever since he chose Moses, to give authority to mortal men to bless and curse to eternity; and that men and women should believe them, and venture their salvation upon their bare words.

Also you say, Oh! how you cried unto the Lord, that you might be once more worthy to be a doorkeeper.

Here you speak like an ignorant, silly, foolish woman, that desires to be a doorkeeper amongst the congregation of the faithful.

To discover your ignorance, let me tell you, that there is no door-keepers of the congregation of the faithful but men, and they must be such as prophets and apostles, who have the keys of heaven and hell. Such men as these do open the doors of mens hearts here on earth, and letteth the spirit or soul of man out of that prison of darkness, which every man and woman's souls are in by nature. Such mortal men as these have the keys of the door of heaven, to open the door of man's heart, that he may see the light of heaven, and the glory of God in heaven, with the glory of saints and angels, in form like men, by the preaching of Christ, as Peter did: he opened the door of Lydia's heart, and shewed her the glory and benefit she should receive, even life and salvation to eternity, by the death, resurrection, and ascension of that man Christ Jesus, which the apostles preached.

Such men as these are door-keepers of the house of God here on earth; which house is the congregation of faithful believers. Therefore it is that David, who was a king and a prophet, desired to be but a door-keeper in the house of the Lord, and God granted his desire, and gave him the key of heaven, that is, to prophecy of the coming of God in the flesh, who was Christ, who was the door, the way, the truth, and the life; and no man could enter into life eternal, but by this door, and none could open this door but those that have the key; and none hath the key but commissionated men, as Moses, the prophets, the apostles, John Reeve and Lodowicke Muggleton.

These mortal men were made door-keepers in the house of God here on earth; but they shall sit upon thrones of glory in heaven.

But I never read of any woman that God made door-keeper of his house here on earth; so that your choice shall not be granted you, but the contrary; for you shall have the door of hell opened unto you, where you shall go among the congregation of the faithless and unbelieving reprobates, where is utter darkness for evermore.

6. You say you had a book written by Lodowicke Muggleton in your house, called, A Looking-Glass for George Fox. You say a most wicked book; and you often wished it out of your house; it being an aggravation of your trouble, when you thought of it.

It seems this book became a wicked book to you, and an aggravation and trouble when you thought of it. The cause why it was an aggravation to your mind was, because you were the seed of the serpent, as aforesaid; for those books are an aggravation to the mind of none but reprobates; for the book cost you nothing. If you had bought it, you would have esteemed better of it, and it would have been no trouble to your mind; and if you could not have believed, you would have been kept from speaking evil of it. But I perceive for the most part, those that have these books lent them for nothing, are the greatest despisers, and do stumble most at them, as you have done. But I know the cause why they have been such an aggravation and trouble to your mind is, because you thought if you should believe Muggleton's writings, there will not be so many loaves and fishes in believing this, as there will be among the Quakers people; for he promises no loaves nor fishes at all; and there is so few that believe him in those parts; so that you cannot expect but very few loaves and fishes here. But the Quakers people are many, and there is more loaves of bread and fishes to eat; therefore said you in your heart, I will return to the Quakers again; for you are of the same mind as those hypocrites were that followed Christ for the loaves; for I am confident that if I had promised more loaves and fishes than you found among the Quakers, you would never have returned to them again. But, much good may you do the Quakers, now they have got you back again; they have laboured hard for you. For this I say, it never was my practice to hire people to believe my doctrine; for if I could but promise all those that believe me loaves and fishes, then should I have more disciples than the Quakers have; therefore it is. that so few poor Quakers believe me, hardly any; (but a many rich Quakers believe me), because I cannot feed so many of your hypocrites with five loaves and two fishes as Christ did when on earth; for there was very few of those five thousand, but poor; and that they were hypocrites is clear by Christ's words, *John* vi. 26. *Jesus said, verily, verily, I say unto you, ye seek me not because ye saw the miracles, but because ye did eat of the loaves, and were filled.* So likewise you would have followed me, not for my doctrine-sake, but for the loaves-sake; if I could have fed you with loaves to the fill; for I know your desire of heart is only to *labour for the meat which perisheth*, and not for the *meat which endureth unto everlasting life*; which all those that do truly believe my commission and doctrine do eat of, and are satisfied, in the assurance of everlasting life, which God shall give them in the resurrection at the last day, which will not be a quarter of an hour after their death; for there is no time to the dead; time belongeth only to life.

7. You say, now it is in your heart further to declare, that you do for ever judge and condemn that spirit of darkness that did lead you from the light (as you say) to join with Lodowicke Muggleton. You say you do also believe that Lodowicke Muggleton is a false prophet, and seducer, and a blasphemer of the living and true God, who is an infinite and unchangeable Spirit, and lives and walks in his people, meaning the Quakers.

Here you have brought death and destruction upon your own head. You have sought after eternal death as for hid treasure, in that you, being an ignorant sottish woman, should undertake to judge a prophet, whose revelation and knowledge of God's mind in the Scriptures is beyond the knowledge and revelation of all the men in the world at this day, as my writings do declare. You, who have not the common knowledge and learning of women, and that without a cause, did never persuade you to believe me, or my doctrine. I never gave you any enticing words to encourage you to believe me, Were not the books lent you freely? they cost you nothing: was there not the wine, milk, and honey of heaven given you, without price, without money; yet your full stomach loathed the honey-comb of heaven. Were not you left to your liberty to eat or not to eat, to chuse or to refuse; but you must take down into your stomach that which could not be digested, which caused you to vomit up such blasphemy against that holy Spirit that sent me, and against me that God sent.

First. You have called the holy Spirit that sent me, a seducing spirit, which leads to death and destruction.

Secondly. You call that book that was lent you, a wicked book.

Thirdly. You do judge and condemn that spirit that wrote that book, which had almost persuaded you to be a true Christian, to be the spirit of darkness.

Fourthly. You say you do believe that Lodowicke Muggleton is a false prophet, and that he is a seducer and a blasphemer.

In these words you have blasphemed against the holy Spirit that sent me. And seeing such sins as these are unpardonable, both in this world and in the world to come; therefore what measure you have met, shall be met to you again, in that you give judgment first; therefore what judgment you have judged you shall be judged with.

Therefore, in obedience to my commission from God, for this your blasphemy against the Holy Ghost aforesaid, I do pronounce Isabella Malum aforesaid, cursed and damned, both soul and body, from the presence of God, elect men, and angels, to eternity.

Your body shall be your hell, and that spirit of reason in you, which you call the light of Christ, shall be your devil; shall be as fire to torment you to eternity. And while you are in this world, you will hardly escape the exemplary judgment of God in this life, besides your damnation hereafter; neither can that infinite spirit without a body (which you call God, which lives and walks in you, as you imagine) deliver you from the curse a mortal man hath passed upon you.

Written by

LODOWICKE MUGGLETON.

London, October 1, 1674.

I did not write this so large only for your sake, but for the sake of others that shall come to see it, or hear it read, because it shall be recorded for the age to come.

A Copy of a Letter wrote by the Prophet Lodowicke Muggleton to John Gratton, of Derbyshire, bearing date October 8, 1674.

John Gratton,

I UNDERSTAND you sent a letter to Thomas Page; I perceive you are the man that lives in Derbyshire, and was acquainted with some of my friends there; which thereby you came to see some of my writings, for I think you never bought any but what you borrowed: also I remember you writ a letter to me then, to answer some questions you propounded; and you pretended to our friend at that time, as if you did believe many things in the book; to which I sent you an answer, that you deserved the curse rather than an answer to those questions: this is many years since; I have not heard any thing of you since till now; and not only so, but you are turned Quaker, and a speaker of the Quakers, so that now you are a two-fold child of the devil more than you were; before you were a child of the devil, when you writ to me, and you turning Quaker made you a two-fold child more than what you seemed to own my writings; for being a speaker of the Quakers, it is impossible for you to repent, or to be saved; for God hath given you up to a reprobate mind, in that you did not like to retain your true God, who hath both form and nature; I say you did not like to retain him in your knowledge, therefore he hath given you up to a reprobate mind, to be a Quaker, to believe that there is no God, but what is in you; and that the light that is within you, that convinceth you of sin, is the very God, and very Christ; so that your God hath never a body, nor your Christ hath never a body neither; this is the absolute spirit of Antichrist in this last age; so that I perceive by your letter, that you have not only slunk away from that doctrine which you did once seem to like, but have spoken evil of that, and me also, and your letter is a sufficient witness against you to me, that you are the seed of the serpent, a reprobate, who is given over to a strong delusion to believe a lie, that there is no God but what is within you; who denies God to become flesh, and that all the fulness of the Godhead dwelt in him bodily, as saith the Scriptures: this is denied by you anti-christian Quakers; foe which thing sake hath the wrath of the true God fallen upon many of your leading Quakers. And now you have taken upon you to be a teacher, or leader of the anti-christian army of Quakers, so that you may expect the same wrath that your brethren have undergone before you; for this your wickedness beforesaid, I do pronounce John Gratton cursed and damned, both soul and body, from the presence of God, elect men and angels, to eternity. Your light of Christ within you, nor that God within you, shall not deliver you from that curse a mortal man hath passed upon you; and you shall know, to your endless pain and shame, that Muggleton's words will reach your life, which you say is in God; so that your God and your life shall perish together; and my God, which you say will be found no God, shall keep you and your imaginary God, a spirit without a body, in utter darkness to eternity.

Written by

LODOWICKE MUGGLETON.

From the Postern-gate, October 8, 1674.

A Copy of a Letter written by the prophet Lodowicke Muggleton to Mr. Thomas Tompkinson, of Sladehouse, in Staffordshire, dated from London, July 1, 1675.

Loving Friend in the true Faith, Thomas Tompkinson,

THIS is to certify you, that I received your letter, dated June 17, 1675; as also to let you know, that I received the cheese that, our friend Anthony Half, and his wife, sent me; and I give them many thanks for their kindness.

Also this is to let you know, that Mr. Delamaine saith to me, that he hath received the coat, and those things you speak of in your letter. I suppose he hath given you notice of it by writing, before this will come to your hands.

And for the difference with the parliament, it is true there was a great difference between the House of Commons and the House of Lords, about privileges, insomuch that the House of Commons did send several great lawyers to the Tower; insomuch that the king was constrained to prorogue the parliament to the third of October next. The contention between the House of Lords and Commons was so great, that it is thought by many, that they will hardly ever agree again; but the next morning, these lawyers the Commons had committed to the Tower, were delivered by a *Habeas Corpus* out of the prison, contrary to the vote of the House of Commons: so that there is no act of parliament this sitting at all; neither is there any thing done touching persecution of conscience at all, but things stand as they were: so that many justices that were hot upon persecution, are cooled. And as for London, and all about London, the meeters are quiet, and not one justice doth stir. And as for your being churchwarden this year, I would advise you by all means to put it off this year. Who knows what the next year will produce?

Thus in short I have given you a hint of things, as they, are at present; and being in haste, I must take leave, only my love presented unto yourself and wife, and to all the rest of our friends in the true faith there with you. I rest

Your friend in the eternal truth,

LODOWICKE MUGGLETON.

Postern, London, July 1, 1675.

A Copy of a Letter wrote by the Prophet Lodowicke Muggleton to Mr. Henry Henn, bearing date from London, August 20, 1675.

Mr. Henn,

I RECEIVED a letter from you by the hand of a boy; the substance of your letter was, a complaint against yourself of your wicked actions, and great sin against God, and against your wife; and of your great sorrow, and unfeigned repentance for it; I do confess I have not been altogether ignorant of your wicked proceedings against your wife, yet because you have writ to me in your necessity of your own accord, and hath confessed your sins, and laid open yourself in your confession, and it is to be minded by me, and I remember that saying in Scripture, *that whosoever confesseth his sins, and forsakes it, shall find mercy.* You have made a good confession of your sin and wickedness towards your wife, and her friends, and if you do but forsake them, as you have promised in your letter to me, there is no question but you will find mercy in the thing you require of me; and as to your liberty only; this I must tell you, how you came to have so grievous a fall: it was because you were ignorant of the words in Scripture, which saith, *Man shall forsake his father and mother and cleave to his wife*; but you have done quite contrary; you have forsaken your wife, and cleaved to your relations, which were not so dear unto you as father and mother; and what fruit have you found or reaped by it? Have you not destroyed your wife's estate, in what you could, and your own interest in it? You have utterly destroyed it, by forsaking your wife and cleaving to your relations; this is the first entrance into sin and wickedness; and so brought destruction upon your wife and yourself in the estate; you being not content here, but added sin to sin, far worse than the first; in that you made yourself the member of harlots that was unclean, which act of yours did not only defile your soul, as a breach of God's commandment, but defiled your body; and the effects of this sin is the very cause of that separation between your wife and you; she would with ease pass by all that wrong you did in wronging her in her estate; but this nature itself doth abhor, that is not given over to a reprobate mind. After this, you proceeded on to a sin of cruelty, to abuse your wife, by laying violent hands upon her; putting her in such frights, as if death had possessed her, which caused her friends to fear you do intend to murder her; which is the cause they do intend to put you in prison, to prevent her from being murdered, and you from being hanged; for it is to be feared, by your rugged carriages to her, that you have made a covenant with death and hell, and that you can be but hanged if you kill her, or do her some other mischief; then hell must follow after death; this is the very cause that her friends do seek to prevent you from doing this wicked deed; and not merely for your wickedness done unto her estate, in forfeiting your bond; she and her friends could and would have passed that by; and not have troubled your person for it, but have sat down in silence in the loss of it; considering that your person being in prison, would do her nor them no good; but this violent practice of yours towards your wife, both in words and actions, doth give all her friends and acquaintance suspicion that you do intend to murder your wife, or do her some other mischief, if you meet with opportunities; therefore it is that they will endeavour to secure your person, to prevent you; but seeing you have made your request to me, and have desired me to use my utmost endeavour to your wife, her father and mother, and brother Atkinson, to let you have your liberty, to try you this once more, and that you will never disturb nor abuse your wife more, either in words or actions, unbecoming an honest man, let you endure all the punishment that is possible to be inflicted upon you: you have spoken with your pen as good words as can be spoken, and if your heart be right to perform what you have said, it is pity but that you should find mercy in the thing; for this I say, it is a dangerous thing to dissemble with God and man; for whoever dissembles with his own heart, dissembles with God; for God hath placed his law in man's heart, as his watchman, to tell God of all his doings, either good or evil; but I am apt to believe that you do not dissemble with me; but I will perform what I have promised concerning your wife, that you will never abuse her more, in words nor actions, and I will do my best endeavour that you shall have your liberty. The case is this; I know your wife and father, out of tenderness to you, though you have done them this great wrong, is willing to pass it by and let you alone, but the power of the law lieth in Mr. Atkinson's hands, and he can prosecute the law, whether your wife or father will or no; and if you had not writ these lines unto me, you would assuredly have been prosecuted; so that my business is only to persuade Mr. Atkinson to let you have your liberty, and I think you need not doubt but I shall prevail with him, that you shall have your liberty; do you keep your promise, and he shall keep his; this shall be sufficient to satisfy you that you shall not be arrested by him for any of your former faults. Written by me, your friend in this matter,

LODOWICKE MUGGLETON.

August 20, 1675.

Since I wrote this letter I spake with Mr. Atkinson, and I have prevailed with him to call back that warrant from that serjeant that was to arrest you, so that now you are relieved from him, and those that are related to him, for the present. Witness my hand,

LODOWICKE MUGGLETON.

A Copy of a Letter written by the Prophet Lodowicke, Muggleton to Mrs. Susanna Moss, of Dublin, in Ireland, bearing date September 5, 1675.

Friend in the true Faith, Susanna Moss,

I RECEIVED your letter, dated August 23, 1675. I confess you are a stranger unto me, but not unto the doctrine of the true God declared by me: for I have heard of you several times, of your faith in the commission of the Spirit, and that your husband died in the faith of it also.

Likewise I perceive by your letter, that you have procured by your faith the hatred of your relations, and others; but this I know, that the peace of your mind is more worth, than the whole world; especially that peace, which the world cannot give, even the *Peace of God which passeth all understanding.*

And this peace of God, it doth arise from the seed of God, which is God's own nature, in that it doth believe in his prophet's report; so that the arm of the Lord is revealed to that soul, according to that saying in Isaiah; *who hath believed our report, and to whom the arm of the Lord is revealed.*

And what is the arm of the Lord, but his saving health; that is, the assurance of everlasting life, abiding in the soul of man, which cannot be attained unto any other way, but by believing the prophet's report.

God hath honoured all his chosen prophets with heavenly wisdom, knowledge and power, above all other men; therefore it is said in Scripture, *How beautiful are the feet of them that bring glad tidings of salvation*; and of that saying, *Whoever received a prophet in the name of a prophet, shall have a prophet's reward.* And what is a prophet's reward, but a blessing of everlasting life: for he that receiveth him that is sent of God, receiveth God that sent him.

Now consider, that all religious men in these our days, do confess and say, they do believe the prophets of old that are dead, and the apostles that are dead, and that they wrote and spake as they were inspired by the Spirit of God; but doth utterly deny that God shall send any prophet in these our clays; saying, that prophesy and revelation is now ceased, yet they will undertake to preach the word of God, as it is written, without any revelation from God.

So that you may observe that the seed of the serpent, the seed of reason in man, doth always believe dead prophets, but would never have believed them when they were alive. So on the contrary, the seed of faith, the seed of God, doth always believe live prophets, rather than those that are dead; because the living prophet gives them to understand the meaning of those dead prophets' writings, and would have believed them dead prophets had they been alive: according to that saying of Christ to the Jews, *Had you believed Moses, you would have believed me.*

So can I truly say, that if people did truly believe the prophets and apostles, as they say they do, they would believe me; for God hath chosen me one of the two last prophets and witnesses of the Spirit, as truly as he chose Moses, Aaron, and the prophets and apostles in their time: and there is as much ground for professors of the Scripture to believe me, and more, than to believe those that are dead, i Why? Because God hath give me understanding of his mind in the Scriptures, above all the men in the world; nay, if I did not know more of God's mind than those that wrote the Scriptures, I would not speak or dispute with men about spiritual matters; neither do I speak this out of a conceited pride of heart (as most wise men in reason do), but out of true knowledge; for true knowledge is never proud.

But the Lord of Heaven, who hath redeemed my soul with his most precious blood, and hath given me my part in the first resurrection, in that the seed of faith in the true God, which is the day-star, is risen in me, and hath freed me from the fear of the second death. And he hath set me as it were upon a hill, for the seed of reason to shoot their poisonous arrows at me; but the shield of faith, and the breastplate of righteousness hath preserved me.

Also he hath set me as a light upon a hill, to give light upon the earth in these last days; so that in light men may see light; so that you, the seed of faith, who hath the day-star risen in your hearts, hath light, and in light you shall see light.

This light hath shined into darkness in this last age; but the darkness doth not comprehend it, but doth hate the light, and me also; because some people do believe in the light of heaven; that is, in the hidden mysteries in the Scriptures declared by me.

As, *First*, What God was in his form and nature from eternity; and how he became flesh, and dwelt amongst men here upon earth.

Secondly, What the right devil was in form and nature before his fall; and how he became flesh, and dwells among men here on earth.

Thirdly, The place and nature of hell, and the devil's torment.

Fourthly, The place and nature of heaven, with the joys the saints shall have.

Fifthly, The persons and natures of the holy angels.

Sixthly, The mortality of the soul.

These, and many other heavenly mysteries, have been declared by us, the two witnesses of the Spirit; so that the light hath shined through darkness in this last age, and hath made the rough ways plain, and the crooked paths strait to some.

And I can truly say, I know I am of God, and the whole world lieth in wickedness, and darkness, and blindness, not knowing any one of these heavenly mysteries aforesaid.

So that I can truly say to you, as Christ did to his disciples, *Blessed are your eyes that see the things that belong to your peace,* and your ears that hear, and hearts that understand the secret mysteries of God, revealed by his two last prophets now in this last age.

This is that hath made the world to hate me; for when I was a zealous professor, a puritan, yet ignorant and blind, the world did love me, and religious men did love; but now they hate me, because I do not walk in darkness with them; for when I was blind and ignorant of the true God, and the right devil, as they were, we did agree well enough; but this commission and knowledge of God in the Scriptures, above all men in the world, causeth all men to hate me; so that they hate you that believe, for my sake; so that they do not only hate you, but they hate me, and they hate God that sent me; for if they could avenge themselves of me, they would love you *i* but because they cannot, therefore they hate you. But consider, every true prophet cometh to bring a sword upon the earth, to set the nearest relations one against another: but blessed are those that are not offended with such a prophet.

It was Christ's own words and practice when on earth; for when the world expected he should have brought peace upon the earth, he brought a sword, and instead of making peace between relations, he caused a greater difference between the most nearest relations than ever; even against husband and wife, father and son, mother and daughter; the husband and wife being in bed together, the one was taken by his doctrine, and the other was left in ignorance and darkness. The father and son being in bed together, the one is taken, and his eyes opened to see the glory of God, even life and salvation to his soul!; and the other is left in ignorance and blindness of mind, and hardness of heart, to perish in his ignorance and unbelief to eternity. The mother and daughter being in bed together, one was taken as aforesaid, and the other was left.

These things I have had great experience of these twenty-three years and more, since I received my commission: and I have seen those words of Christ fulfilled in these my days.

Also I have seen two grinding in the mill of the affairs of this world together; and by this doctrine, declared by John Reeve and myself, the one hath been taken out of ignorance, and the other hath been left.

These things I have had perfect knowledge of, being the last prophet that God will ever send to stand in the place of God here on earth, to act the same things as he did when he was upon earth and as he was hated of all men, for his doctrine-sake, and saying he was the Son of God, so I am hated of all men for my doctrine-sake, that hath laid the axe to the root of the tree of all opinions and religions in the world.

And that I am the last true prophet that God will ever send to the end of the world, which hath caused the world to hate me; for I have no dealing with the world; I neither buy, nor sell, nor trade with them; I owe the world nothing; I never wronged any in the world the value of sixpence in my life, to my knowledge; yet all the world hates me, both righteous and unrighteous, only because I am of God, and they are not of God. If I could love the ways of the world, and speak well of them, and their religion, they would love me; and then I should be a liar like unto them. For if I should say, that I do not, know more of God's mind, in the Scriptures, than all the men in the world at this day, I should be a liar like them.

This is that strait and narrow gate that leads unto life eternal, but few do go therein.

Consider the parable Christ spake, *There was a man had an hundred sheep, and one of them went astray*; and there was an hundred righteous persons, and one of them went out from his righteousness, and was lost in himself, as the sheep that went astray.

Now the shepherd went out, and found that one sheep that went astray, and brought it home, and rejoiced over this more than the ninety-nine that went not astray. So there was joy in heaven of the holy angels, more over that one sinner that repented, than over the ninety-nine just persons that needed no repentance.

The interpretation and meaning is this, that the ninety and nine just persons were all damned; and that one person that repented, was saved; and so of the sheep.

For if the ninety-nine just persons, that needed no repentance, were saved; and that one repented, saved also; then the whole hundred were saved; so that none were damned. This is the judgment and opinion of all professors of the scriptures.

But the seed of faith knoweth to the contrary; that the meaning of Christ was, that all the ninety and nine just persons were damned. Why? because they needed no repentance: therefore the angels did not rejoice over them at all.

[From this place it is torn out.]

This is the Copy of the Answer of the Prophet Lodowicke Muggleton's, unto a Letter which our brother Lad had sent him.

John Lad,

I RECEIVED your letter, dated August 1, 1676, wherein you have expressed your faith and confidence in the doctrine declared by us the witnesses of the Spirit, and persons of us, who were sent of God, to bring glad tidings of peace and salvation to as many as shall receive our report, and to whom the arm of the Lord's saving health is revealed, to lead those that were in captivity, in ignorance and darkness, captives into that glorious light of life eternal, and to open the prison-doors of mens hearts, and to let their souls that were prisoners go free. This many can experience in these our days; and what can be said more than what Christ said to his disciples, and those that believed in him, *Blessed are your eyes that see, and your ears that hear, and your hearts that understand the things that belongs to your peace* Thus it is with every true prophet that is sent of God; and what things can a man understand that belongs to his peace, more than to know the true God in his form and nature, and the right devil in his form and nature, and angels their persons and nature, and to have the prison-doors of mens hearts opened, and to let the King of glory enter in? These are things that belong to a man's eternal peace, which none can have or receive, but those that do receive a prophet in the name of a prophet, receiveth God that sent him; for whoever believeth in a prophet for his doctrine sake, shall see the treasures of heaven, both new and old. That is what the prophets of old did lay up in heaven, believing that God would become a little child, and grow up to a man, and suffer death, and rise again, that he might give them in the resurrection life eternal, and a crown of glory to wear for evermore. This is that treasure the prophets of old did lay up in heaven, therefore called old treasures, and the treasures the apostles laid up in heaven were counted new by Christ in that time, in that he compared the kingdom of heaven to u good scribe, that brought forth of the good treasures of his heart things new and old; likewise we the ministers of the Spirit have brought forth out of the good treasures of our heart things new and old, we have declared unto you the deep things of old, the very foundation of God's council of old, which he revealed to Moses, the righteous fathers and prophets of old, and so of the apostles. And now is the new wisdom of God and treasure of heaven brought forth to the view of the world, by us two prophets and witnesses of the Spirit, in a more abundant measure than all that went before us, as may be seen by our writings; and there will never be no more new treasures of heaven brought forth into the world, any more than what is declared by us while time is no more. And seeing God hath chosen me to be one of his two last prophets and messengers unto this bloody and unbelieving world, and that caused and preserved me to be the longest liver, and hath lengthened out my days and years; and he hath made me a scorn to fools, that nothing understand; yea, he hath set me as a mark for every wicked man to shoot at me, yet faith in my God hath preserved me from being wounded by the cunning archers. He hath made me as a wall of brass against all men, both righteous and unrighteous. They have all strove to bear me down, both with spiritual weapons and carnal weapons, but he hath delivered me from them all. I did not think, when I was chosen a messenger of God, that I should have been so hated of all men for declaring of truth, but rather thought all men should love me; but when I went into the sanctuary of the Lord, I found it quite contrary; for when I had considered the trouble Moses and the prophets went through, both with the wicked and the righteous, even with those that served in the tabernacle of God, how did they rebel, which caused Moses to wish himself blotted out of the book of life, rather than to undergo the burthen of the Lord; but more especially the prophet Jeremiah, the burthen of the Lord was so heavy upon him, that he cursed the day of his birth, and desired God to send whom he would send, so he would let him alone; but God would have him and none else to deliver his message, else he would consume him before the people: so it was with John Reeve and myself, God would send none else but us two, which was sore against both our desires; but being forced by a curse from the Lord, and I being the last liver, the burthen of the Lord hath lain heavy upon me this many years but what am I! And what was Moses! Or what was Jeremiah, and the rest! that we should resist the voice of God to stand in the gap in God's stead for every legal righteous man to shoot at us, and every wild beast to rend and tear, blaspheme, reproach, revile, despise, even bloody-minded men, whose soul do thirst after my life as for sweet wine! my blood would be more sweeter to them than honey, or the honey-comb! But knowing it was so with God himself when on earth, and that they would do so by him as they do by me, where he in my place, the consideration of these things doth bear up my spirit, and causeth me to strengthen myself, my God, my King, and my Redeemer. I have had great experience of David's condition, how he prayed to be delivered from his enemies, as Psalm lix; and so have I in like manner, *Deliver me from mine enemies, O my God; defend me from them that rise against me; deliver me from the workers of iniquity, and save me from bloody men, for lo! they lie in wait for my soul*, not for any sin I have committed, or any wrong I have done to any man, but merely because I have declared the true God unto them, and because I say God sent me, therefore have they waited for my soul to kill it; and were it not for the outward law of the land, they could not be prevented; for they have altogether stifled. that righteous law God hath written in their hearts, and hath made it useless unto them, so that my life could not be preserved, were it not for the outward law of the land; so that I have just cause to say, Lord, be not merciful to any wicked transgressors that hateth me for truth's sake, let not the Lord be merciful to Such wicked men; but God hath and will let me see my desire upon mine enemies, and bring them down to destruction, O Lord my God, for they have hated me without a cause, and hateth thee that sent me. Also I have had experience of the prophet Jeremiah's condition, Jer. ii. ver. 19. I know not that they had devised devises against me, saying, *Let us destroy the tree, with the fruit thereof*; that is, let us destroy this Muggleton and his doctrine, which is the fruit of the tree, and let us cut him off from the land of the living, that his name may be no more remembered. I have had great experience that wicked men have had several devises against me, saying in their hearts, let us destroy the tree, with the fruit thereof; and let us cut this Muggleton off from the land of the living, that his name may be no more remembered. Every true prophet is the tree, and his doctrine is the fruit thereof. The reprobate, the seed of the serpent, cannot endure that any man should eat of the tree of life, and live for ever; the serpent would have all to eat of the tree of knowledge of good and evil as himself doth, therefore he devises how to destroy the tree, that is, the prophet, and the fruit thereof, that none of the seed of faith might receive his doctrine, that is eat of the tree of life, and live for ever; therefore it is that the seed of the serpent hath devised devises against me, to destroy me and my writings, which is the fruit, that I might be cut off from the land of the living, that my name may be no more remembered; that is, if wicked men could but destroy me, and burn my writings, then my name would be cut off from the land of the living, and be no more remembered, as they think, because then none could believe me. Thus I have been compassed about with wicked ungodly men, and sometimes with subtil serpents, who hath had many devises against me, to destroy me and my writings; but the God of my salvation hath delivered me out of their hands hitherto, that my life is yet preserved; and the Lord God of truth, that judgeth righteously, that triest the reins and the heart, let me see thy vengeance on them that are thy enemies as well as mine; for unto thee have I revealed my cause, and shall wait on thee for the execution of thy wrath upon those wicked, ignorant, blind-dark devils, that hath not so much as the light of thy law written in their hearts. Thus I have given you but a little account of my long experience of the burthen of the Lord upon me; I have complained as little of it as ever any prophet did, but of these late years I have been compassed about with wicked men more than heretofore, yet I have given less cause of late than before; but as the saints hath increased, so hath mine enemies increased more and more. I have writ these lines unto you because you did beg them of me, because it is seven years since you received a letter from me, so that I could not well deny your request; so I have presented these lines unto you for your further consolation, with my love to you also.

I take leave, and rest your friend in the true faith of the true God,

LODOWICKE MUGGLETON.

Postern, near Moor-Lane,

London, August 26, 1676.

A Copy of a Letter written by the Prophet Lodowicke Muggleton to Mr. James Whitehead, of Braintree, bearing date from London, December 31, 1679.

Loving Friend in the true Faith, James Whitehead,

I RECEIVED your letter, dated December 26, 1679, by the hand of your neighbour. And I had an hour or two's discourse; but the man said little, and objected less against what I said; only that he was troubled that he had lived to this age, and should be so ignorant of the Scriptures, and of matters of salvation; yet he stuck at continual prayer unto God. I gave him advice to let prayer alone, and to act righteousness between man and man, and let God do what he would with him after death.

This did I do when I was in your condition; for, said I, there is no question but you have prayed unto God this many years, to give you peace of mind and assurance of salvation. For that is the desire of all men, that the soul might enter into rest in this life; then doth a man cease from his labour of prayer and worship, which he worketh in the fiery furnace of his mind, to make up his full tale of prayers and holy duties, thinking God will reward him with peace of mind, and life, and salvation, seeing he hath wrought eleven hours in the day in God's vineyard of the righteousness of the law; yet we see that man that wrought but one hour in God's vineyard of faith, he received his penny of everlasting life presently, which was the assurance of life everlasting in himself, even in this life; so that his work is done, and is entered into his rest, as God entered into his rest from the work of creation.

Likewise the penny those had that wrought eleven hours of the day, it was credit, reputation, and honour, amongst men of the world, being righteous godly men, by the people of the world. This is that penny that most religious people do receive for their prayers and holy duties. This I know to be true; and it is a good penny to have honour and credit with men in this world; but this penny doth not satisfy the mind of those that work eleven hours in the day, as that penny doth that worketh but one hour in the righteousness of faith; which was the cause those men did grumble; and it is the cause now that righteous men do grumble, that a few men that believe Muggleton should be sure of their salvation in this life; and we that have wrought all our lives long in the righteousness of God's law, cannot have that penny of satisfaction of mind.

Indeed this would cause any righteous man to grumble, as I myself did when I was in their condition; so that the penny of this world is that penny God doth give to all legal righteous men: and the penny of assurance and satisfaction of mind, is that penny God doth give to those that truly believe in his messengers, though it be in the last hour of their lives.

Many things were spoken, and the man said little, only complained of his ignorance. The man is moderate enough, and able to hear and bear what was spoken; nor doth not deny, nor receive any thing for absolute truth, to receive it for his own satisfaction, as I can perceive.

It is something a hard thing, when a man is old, to enter into his mother's womb to be born again, as Nicodemus said; but as Christ said, It is possible with God, and it is possible with faith, though it be impossible with reason to understand; for I have known elder than he have been born again by this commission of the Spirit.

I would not have you let him hear this letter; but if he come to you perhaps he may speak something to you, whereby you may perceive whether he did like or dislike any thing he heard or saw.

Thus, with my love, and my wife's love, remembered unto yourself, and to your wife, and Mr. Nicholls, and the rest.

Also Mrs. Man doth remember her kind respects unto yourself. I take leave, and rest,

Your friend in the eternal Truth,

LODOWICKE MUGGLETON.

London, December 31, 1679.

I am willing that John Lad, and you, and all of you, if it be convenient, to have a meeting with this Finch, as he requireth, to see what he can say for himself; and if he give occasion of a sentence, you may pass it upon him: if he denieth and forsaketh the blessing, and sold the books in contempt and dislike, or doth any ways say he was deceived by believing them or me, then you may justly give sentence upon him, never to have any discourse more with him in matters of religion; and if you think it convenient, you may read this letter of mine which follows, unto him, or as many as he will allow to hear it; but let your discourse be first with him, then will you have the better ground to give sentence, and read my letter. And as for that Finch you spake of, I do remember you and he were once at my house, and the man was much troubled in mind, and did buy some books; but that did not satisfy him without the blessing; for, said he, I would have all things that might give me satisfaction and peace of mind, I told him I could give him no sentence of blessedness, except he did believe in me that I had such power; which after a while discourse he said he did believe: upon which I gave him the blessing, in which he did continue (as I did hear) several years, and he himself did rejoice in it, and did boast of it

As that woman that came in the coach with me, when I came to your house, as you may remember it, none being in the coach but she and I, she asked, if I went any further than Braintree; I said, no. She asked, to whom there? I said, to your house, naming your name. Then she asked, if I did not know one Finch? I said, I did. Then she mistrusted that I was the man that had given this Finch the blessing; for the woman had great troubles of this world upon her that time, besides the fear of a worse trouble after death; for, said she, would I could meet with that man that blessed Finch, to bless me; for Finch, said she, was in a sad condition in his mind, and low in the world heretofore; but, said she, he is now cheerful, and saith, he is sure he shall be happy hereafter, and did thrive in this world. He was asked, how he came by this peace? He said, by the blessing of that prophet Mr. Whitehead believed in.

This and much more did the woman speak concerning Finch, as we rode in the coach; but I took no notice that I was the man; but was glad to hear that Finch had found such peace of mind.

But it seems by your letter, that now he is turned back again to the Quakers, and hath sold his books to John Lad, and doth request a meeting with him, thinking himself so strong now he is at the brink of the pit of destruction eternal, as the push of a little finger will shove him into the pit of eternal destruction; for he doth practice the same thing as those did in the apostle Paul's time, as in Hebrews vi. who did fall back from that faith they had in his doctrine. Observe what judgment the apostle gives upon those, *For it is impossible for those who were once enlightened, and, have tasted of the heavenly gift, and were made partakers of the Holy Ghost, and have tasted the good word of God, and the power of the world to come; if such fall away, it is impossible for them to be renewed by repentance.* That is, it is impossible that they should have true repentance again, that would restore them to the same peace again that they had before; but in the room thereof they will assuredly be damned to eternity.

This is the case of this man; for he was enlightened by believing in me, and received the Holy Ghost, in that he received the blessing; and he tasted of the good word of God in reading those books, and of the powers of the life to come, in that he rejoiced in the peace he received in that faith for a season, as aforerelated; but now it seems he is fallen from that faith he had in this commission of the Spirit, and sold the books, not for want, but for contempt, as not worthy to be looked into by him: he hath despised the blessing which he once rejoiced in, as Esau did his birth-right, and hath sold all his interest to heaven, for to trust to the motions of reason, the light within him, the Quakers mess of pottage, for salvation; for there is no salvation in their principles; if there had, why did he not keep to them before? Doth he think to find rest there now? Surely no.

Therefore, if this man be guilty of this great fall, as I suppose he is, it *had been good for him that he had never been born*; but he cannot help it; for it is a dangerous thing to be an hypocrite to God, and to his own soul; for a true prophet represents the peace of God here on earth.

This man is like one of those branches Christ speaketh of, John xv. 6. *If a man abide not in me, he is cast forth as a branch, and is withered, and men gather them, and cast them into the fire.* This Christ spake unto his disciples, he being the true vine, and the believers of him were the branches; he knowing that some that pretended to believe in him that had no true faith, therefore brought forth no fruit, nor did not continue in that faith to the end: so it is with every true commissionated prophet; he is the vine that God hath placed in his vineyard in this earth, and the believers of this prophet are the branches, and by faith they are ingrafted into this vine; and those branches that bring forth fruit of faith, and love to God, and abide in the vine, it bringeth forth new fruit of peace and joy to the end. But those withered and dried branches, which do not abide in the vine, are to be cut off, and cast into the fire of hell; or, as the fig-tree that had leaves upon it, seeming to be a good tree, but when Christ came to eat of the fruit, he found none; therefore he cursed it to wither and die, never to bring forth fruit more to eternity. I have had great experience of such like branches as these since the time of my commission.

Written by me,

LODOWICKE MUGGLETON.

London, December 31, 1679.

A Copy of a Letter written by the Prophet Lodowicke Muggleton to Mr. George Gamble, in Cork in Ireland, bearing date the 12th of January, 1678.

Loving and kind Friend in the true Faith, George Gamble,

I HEARD a letter of yours read, dated the 19th of December 1678[1], to our friend Mr. Delamain, of the great troubles you are in, concerning the affairs and dealings of this world. I was sorry, and grieved in heart to hear it; but, considering in myself, that it is a common thing, especially in these troublesome days of late years, for men that are incumbered with great affairs and business in this world, to fail, and bring trouble upon themselves. It is grown a common thing, in these late years, as if it were a thing in course in this world. All men have trouble to get a little food and cloathing, let it be ever so small; it cannot be had without care and trouble. But where incumbrance is, and great profit, it creates great losses, and so great trouble. Those things doth befall both to saint and devil sometimes; so that the peace which this world gives is taken away almost from all men, both saint and devil.

---

[1] This date appears to conflict with the letters date but both the 1755 and the 1820 texts are identical on this point.

As to the troubles of this world, both of the losses and crosses, you must wade through it as patiently as you can: do that moral righteousness between man and man, in these matters of the world, as you would have others do unto you; and you shall have that peace of mind as moral righteousness will afford: but as for that peace which the world cannot give, which is that *peace of God which passeth all understanding*, which I perceive you have tasted of, in that you have believed this third and last record of the Spirit. I have had several testimonies, in your letters, of your faith in the true God, and in me his true messenger; and this faith of yours will bear your up into everlasting life; for this doctrine of the true God, and the right devil, the knowledge of these two, their forms and their natures, the one giveth the soul the assurance of eternal life, and the other frees the soul from the fear of any devil, or eternal death, which many can witness at this day. It is life eternal to know God as he is, which no man in this world at this day doth, but those who have believed our report. God hath hid these things from the world, and hath revealed them only to his chosen messengers; for the world is so blind that it counts it a needless thing to know God in his form and nature: but, blessed be the God of heaven, that hath blinded their eyes, and hath opened our eyes, to see by faith, that God hath both form and nature, in that he created man in his own image and likeness; for all the comfort of prophets, apostles, and saints, lieth in the knowledge of God's form and nature: his form is brighter than the sun, swifter than thought, yet a glorious spiritual body, in form of a man from eternity; and that this glorious, spiritual, heavenly body, in fulness of time, transmitted itself in the virgin's womb, and became a pure natural body, the Child Jesus, *God manifest in that flesh*; or more fully, *God became flesh, and dwelt among men*: so that eternity became time, and time became eternity again; and immortality became pure mortality in that body of Christ Jesus. And as immortality became pure mortality, so pure mortality became immortality again. Therefore it is said in John's Revelation concerning Christ, that his face shone as the sun in its strength, and his head, and his hair was white as wool. And in another place he is called, *The Ancient of Days*: and he calls himself, *The first and the last, the beginning and the end; he that was dead, and is alive, and behold he is alive forevermore*.

This is that spiritual body that was from eternity, that became time; that immortality that became pure mortality, is now become eternity and immortality, that was brighter than the sun, swifter than thought. That eternity that became time, that immortality that became pure mortality is now become eternity and immortality again; therefore called *The Ancient of Days*, because he was; that eternal God that created the two worlds. This is that great mystery of, *God became flesh, and dwelt among men*; which mystery the holy angels desired to pry into; which the tongue of man is notable to express but in a small measure; this is that mystery of God that was to be finished in the days of the voice of the seventh angel, when it doth sound; which is fulfilled in these our days, and will sound till time be no more: this is that foundation which God hath laid for his elect to believe, to change his own glorious immortal body, first into pure mortality, that we his servants, the prophets and apostles, and you the true believers, may understand the better the power of God, how he will *change our vile bodies and make them like unto his glorious body*; and that *this mortality shall put on immortality*: and that you that believe may understand, that the Godhead life, when he became flesh, did but change his garment, laid dawn his spiritual body in the womb of the virgin, and cloathed his Godhead life with flesh and bone, as a new garment, or new body, which he will wear to all eternity.

These things are hard to be understood by the reason of men, but by faith only: this is that God I have declared unto you the seed of faith, and unto this wicked generation for which I have suffered persecution and imprisonment in several gaols; but the God of my salvation hath preserved my life to this day. This faith and knowledge, I perceive, is the comfort of your soul in this your great afflictions and troubles you are in at present. And what can I say more, but to strengthen your faith more and more in the true God, that he counted you worthy to believe his prophets report in these last days. Oh! it is a blessed thing, to know by faith in this commission of the Spirit, that you shall see God face to face, because you have believed God hath a face. This is the faith of God's elect, and by this faith we know God hath elected us from the beginning of this world. This faith gives us to know the certain knowledge of our eternal happiness. This faith gives us to know God as he is in himself, both his form and nature; and that these vile bodies of ours shall be raised spiritual bodies, and be made like unto his spiritual and glorious body, and shall sing praises unto our God, our King, and our Redeemer, in that kingdom of eternal glory. By faith I know these things will be as if I saw it with my natural eyes; for true faith is as certain an evidence to the soul of man, of things not seen with the natural eye, as the clearest sight of the natural eye can witness to any natural truth whatsoever here upon earth. This will come to pass at the end of the world, which the soul of man will not be sensible that he hath been dead a quarter of an hour, when he is raised again; for there is no time to the dead; so that the righteous doth but pass through this natural death into eternal life and glory; and the seed of the serpent doth but pass through this natural death, into eternal death and misery.

I have been more large than I thought, but I know it will not be burthensome for you to read, because things of this nature cannot be expressed in a few words; so I shall take leave at present, only my love, with my wife's love, remembered unto yourself and good wife, though unknown to me; and all the rest of friends whom you know in those parts. I rest your friend in the true faith of the one personal God, the man Christ Jesus in glory,

LODOWICKE MUGGLETON.

London, January 12, 1678.

In particular, pray remember my love to Mr. Rogers, whom I once saw, and had discourse with him at our Friend Delamain's house.

A Copy of a Letter written by the Prophet Lodowicke Muggleton to Major John Dennison, of Dublin, in Ireland, bearing date February 24, 1678.

Loving Friend in the true Faith, Mr. John Dennison,

I HAVE received several letters from you, wherein you have expressed yourself to have faith and confidence in this commission of the Spirit; but I have quite forgot that ever I sent you any answer in particular; but having this opportunity to send by your son, I shall write these few lines unto you, as followeth:

I perceive that you have found out that strait and narrow way that leads to life eternal, which very few do find, which is in believing this last record upon earth; which narrow and strait way to life eternal hath not been shewn to any man this thirteen hundred years and more, till within these twenty-seven years God chose John Reeve and myself, who have declared Jesus Christ to be the very God and very man, who is the way, the truth, and the life. This is that strait and narrow way that leads to life eternal, which so few do find in these our days; yet more do find this narrow way, at this time, than have a thousand years before.

I doubt not but you have put on the armour of God as I have done, for whoever goeth this narrow way to heaven shall meet with enemies great store, both spiritual and natural. And if a man be not well armed with the armour of God, the spiritual enemies in his own heart will overcome him; for if a man conquer his own heart, he may conquer the whole world. The armour of God is the shield of faith; a breast-plate of righteousness, instead of a breast-plate of iron; a helmet of salvation upon a man's head, instead of a silver head-piece; the sword of the spirit in a man's mouth, instead of, a sword of steel with a silver belt tied to his side. This helmet of salvation, it casteth out the fear of eternal damnation. This breast-plate of righteousness, it keepeth off the fiery darts of the devil's accusations in the conscience. The shield of faith, it keeps off all doubts and questions that would arise in man's heart, concerning his eternal happiness. The sword of the Spirit is the words of faith, which cuts unbelief in sunder, both in himself and others. This is that armour that doth overcome death, hell, and the devil in man, even as Christ did without man. Oh! blessed and happy are all those that do fight the good fight of faith, there is laid up for them a crown of life, which God the righteous Judge shall give at that day, even that crown of life which he purchased with his own blood. Oh! how few do understand those things that belong to their peace. I perceive you have read our writings, and some of those letters I wrote of late, concerning my sufferings for God's cause. It was the cause of Moses, the prophets, Christ's, and the apostles' sufferings. And, last of all, it hath been the cause of my sufferings. We read the prophets and apostles of old, how they complained of the *burthen of the Lord was heavy upon them*; insomuch that Moses desired to be blotted out of the book of life, rather than be troubled any further with a rebellious people. Jeremiah the prophet was so weary of his messages of the Lord to a gainsaying people, that he cursed the day of his birth, and wished he had never been born. Paul also wished himself *accursed from Christ for his kindred and relations in the flesh*, he being sensible of the miserable condition they were in to be *damned to eternity through unbelief.* People think it is a brave thing to be a prophet, but we find it by experience to the contrary. Our honour and glory is put upon us after we are dead by the world; but while we are alive, hated and despised beyond all other men, only for speaking the truth, which the Lord hath forced us to speak; for if the world be told any judgment shall befal them, or that God will execute any vengeance upon them, either spiritual or temporal, they will hate us, and dispitefully use us: for we cannot speak peace to the people of the world, but to some few that are chosen out of the world. But to give you to understand why such great prophets and messengers of God should curse the day of their birth, and be blotted out of the book of life, and accursed from Christ, after God hath given them so full assurance of eternal salvation.

Answer. That Moses did not desire to be blotted out of the book of life, as to eternal salvation, and so to suffer eternal damnation, for that he knew could not be; but his desire was, that God would errase his name out of his book as a commissioner, or that God would take away his commission from him, and give it to another man, so that he might be freed from that trouble. And as for the prophet Jeremiah cursing the day of his birth with such a heavy curse, it was because he knew that if he had never been born, or died in his childhood, he should never have known trouble or sorrow; for he was so sensible of the multitude of his enemies that sought his life, and his sufferings for being a true prophet of the Lord, that he was unsensible of any glory, salvation, or happiness in the life to come; so that the persecutions and troubles of this present world, weighed in the balance of his mind more heavy than an eternal kingdom of glory hereafter: so that he wished he had never been born, then should have lain still, and have been quiet, and not have been sensible neither of joy nor sorrow. I myself have had experience of this a little, before I was chosen of God, or knew what revelation was. It came to pass that my thoughts were troubled about salvation and damnation; and the dispute within me grew very great; and the motions of faith, though I knew it not, were so strong in me, against the motions of reason in me, which then I knew not neither; but the motions of faith being so well grounded upon the Scriptures, did prove to my reason, that there was a necessity, that some men and women should be saved, and the greatest part should be damned; so that I saw there was a certain damnation and salvation, and both eternal; but which way to gain the one, and escape the other, I could not tell, or what course to take; loth I was to be damned to eternity; and how to gain the assurance of eternal salvation, I knew not, because it lay in God's prerogative power to make me a vessel of wrath, or a vessel of mercy, which he pleased. I saw my righteousness, nor prayer, nor any good deeds I could do, would not save me, if he had made me a vessel of wrath; so that my hope was cut off, and almost utter despair in the room; so that I wished in my heart that I had never been born; or that I had died in my mother's womb; for I did not desire so much to be saved, so that I could but escape being damned: I knew no evil I had done why I should be damned; but God's prerogative will not be limited by any law whatsoever but his own will; if he will have mercy, or if he will not have mercy, how should I, his poor creature, gainsay it. This lay heavy upon my soul, so that I was forced to summon it to God's prerogative power, and immediately after I found rest to my soul; and not many hours after, the Heavens were opened and the windows thereof, and it poured down showers of revelations, and knowledge in the Scriptures above all the men in this world, at this day; and it hath and doth remain with me to this day; which is now almost twenty-eight years. This is but a hint of those things I have had experience of, after I had revelation to interpret Scripture, and satisfaction in my own soul, and assurance of my salvation. I was well contented, for no man can certainly know he shall not be damned, unless he first be sure he shall be saved.

This I know to be true, and when I had all this laid up in my heart, as a treasure in heaven, where no doubt could arise, nor in the least think that God would choose me to be a prophet. I always loved the prophets of old, but was very unwilling to be one myself; so that I have wished since (as Jeremiah did) that God would have chosen some other man, and have let me alone; but God chose whom he will, and who shall gainsay it: and blessed be the God of Heaven that hath redeemed my soul with his own blood, and hath freed me, and many others, from the fear of eternal death, which is the second death; who hath preserved my life from the mouth of the lion, and from the paw of the bear; from the great men of this earth, and from the poor of this wicked generation, these many years, and hath carried me through many dangers, persecutions, and imprisonments, for his name's sake, and for the good of others that do truly believe in this third and last record of the Spirit. I know I shall be missed, when I am gone, by the saints, but the devils will rejoice, because there will never arise another true prophet after me, like unto me, while this world endureth. I have been longer than I thought, but I hope it. will be no great burthen for you to read. But shall take leave at present, only my love, with my wife's love, remembered unto yourself, not forgetting Colonel Phaire, Mr. Gamble, Mr. Rogers, and Captain Gale, with the rest of that little flock in those parts, I rest

Your friend in the eternal truth,

LODOWICKE MUGGLETON.

London, Feb. 25, in the Year 1678.

A Copy of a Letter written by the Prophet Lodowicke Muggleton to Michael Pett, in Kent, bearing date the 25th of February, 1678.

Loving friend, Michael Pett,

I RECEIVED a letter of yours by the hand of Mr. Shelley, wherein your desire is, that I would satisfy a question or two of your wife's, she being, as it seems to me, unsatisfied in her, mind, concerning her salvation; and she would willingly attain the assurance of her eternal happiness by prayer. For, say you, your wife questions if we are not to pray with motions in the mind for assistance, for want of satisfaction.

In this question you are sore afflicted with fears and doubts.

The second question is, if the revelation which Mr. Claxton writes of, proceeded from God, or if it proceeded from faith.

Likewise you say, if God do not give his in-shining light with all. For instance, you say, see Matthew, the 7th chapter and the 7th verse.

This is the whole substance of the matter. Now, I know not whether this affliction of fears and doubts doth arise from yourself, or from your wife, her soul being afflicted not only for want of her eternal salvation, but the present fear of her eternal damnation, or endless misery. This is that which maketh the hearts of all men and women, to fear, doubt, and fail. I understand your wife was to see me, with your father Harris, when I was in prison; but I have quite forgot the favour of the woman; neither do I remember her at all; neither do I know whether she did ever believe any thing of the doctrine or power of this commission of the Spirit or no; yet if she hath not been a despiser, blasphemer, or opposer of the doctrine or declaration of this commission of the Spirit, in calling it blasphemy, delusion, and lies, or any thing of that nature, which cometh under the sin against the Holy Ghost; I shall give her any satisfaction, and it shall be effectual to comfort her troubled soul, if she can but believe.

And as for your first question, whether you are not bound to pray with motions in the mind for assistance, seeing you want satisfaction of mind. And for example, you think you have Christ's words for it, in the 7th chapter of Matthew, and the 7th verse, where he saith to his disciples, *Ask, and it shall be given you; seek, and you shall find; knock, and it shall be opened unto you.*

This you are to mind, that they were Christ's disciples, that did believe in him; therefore he gave them this exhortation, to pray in faith, knock in faith, and so in faith they should find in their own souls the assurance of everlasting life; so that heaven-gate should be opened unto them, and they shall enter into their eternal rest, even while in this world; as you may see the like words of Christ, Matthew the 21st, and 22d verse, speaking to his own disciples, who did believe in him, saith, *All things whatsoever ye shall ask in prayer, believing, ye shall receive*; so that there is nothing to be had of heavenly peace, joy, or glory, or the assurance of everlasting life, by prayer, except it be the prayer of faith; that is, to believe in the true God, and to believe that messenger he doth send. Likewise in Mark, the 11th chapter, and 24th verse, *Therefore I say unto you, what things soever ye desire when ye pray, believe that ye receive them, and ye shall have them*; so that there is no heavenly gift whatsoever to be had, but by the prayer of faith, which is to believe, as I said before. So James the first, and 5th and 6th verses, saith, If any of you, meaning believers of his commission, lack wisdom, let him ask it of God; that is, heavenly wisdom, which maketh men and women wise unto salvation; but let him ask it in faith, nothing wavering, nor doubting; for if the soul doubt, he shall receive nothing of the Lord. This is that prayer of faith which did heal the sick in the apostles time; and this is that prayer of faith that healeth the wounded soul of every man and woman in these our days, who have set to their seals, in believing the doctrine and declaration declared by us the witnesses of the Spirit, and that we two are the two last witnesses and prophets that God will ever send, to the end of this world: this is that faith that many men and women have, by it, removed mountains, and high hills, of ignorance and darkness, which lay before their understandings, by the power of faith in this commission of the Spirit, into the bottom of the sea, that is, into utter oblivion; so that peace of mind enters into the soul, and bringeth the assurance of eternal life into the soul; so that eternal life doth abide in them, and are entered into their rest, having no need to pray any more; for where the assurance of eternal life is granted, what need that soul pray for the same thing again, which he hath in possession. This prayer may be called the prayer of faith, which is the motions of the mind in secret; and so we pray in secret, and our faith, peace, and joy, and heavenly knowledge, being increased in secret, in the mind or soul, it comes to be rewarded openly in the kingdom of glory: but as for publick prayer to be heard of men, that is the practice of all hypocrites; they do imitate the words of Christ, which he said to his own disciples and believers; therefore it is they pray, but are never heard; they ask for peace, and assurance of God's mercy, but never receive any: they knock at heaven-gate a thousand times, but the gate is never opened unto them, because they are like the foolish virgins, *that have no oil in their lamps*; so they have many prayers to heaven, but no faith in their hearts; so that in the day of death the door of heaven is shut against them; then are they forced to go the broad way into utter darkness: but the prayer of faith, if it be but once in his life-time, it is of that power with God, that he will open the gate of heaven, and let him in, even as the door of his heart was opened to receive his prophet's report, and let the King of glory, that is, the knowledge of the true God, his form, and nature, enter into his soul here in this life.

This prayer need not be said day after day. Let any man or woman pray this prayer of faith but once in their life-time, and the gates of heaven-shall be opened unto them, and they shall enter into the Paradise of peace here on earth, and into the assurance of eternal glory hereafter.

This experience hath shewed me, and many others, both men and women can witness the truth of it; so that you may well perceive, that if you have no faith in your prayer, and do not believe God will answer you in peace, you had better let it alone, and submit to God's prerogative power, let him do what he will with you after death. This was my way, and many more that have followed me have found rest to their souls; for so long as you practise that which was others duty to do, you will never find peace of mind here in this life, no more than all professors of religion do, notwithstanding the multitude of prayers they make; yet not a man of them hath true peace and assurance of their salvation in themselves. Why? Because they act over the apostle's commission again, which was given to those people that believed them. Therefore I shall say this unto the woman, that if she can but believe me, and follow my advice, and let prayers alone, though I know she cannot hinder the motions, if she could she would, her soul would be quiet; but if she can but let God alone, and submit to his prerogative power, in matters of salvation and damnation; for there is no striving with the Creator, neither will he be intreated to alter his will or purpose. If she can but take this yoke upon her, it is but easy and light, but seems very heavy to reason. My soul for hers she shall be saved; and in a small time the day-star of light in her understanding will arise, and bring peace and rest to her soul.

And as for Claxton's revelation, it proceeded from the seed of faith in himself, from that faith he had in John Reeve and myself, and not from God without him; neither did God choose him as he did John Reeve and myself, by voice of words. But however, the things he wrote concerning God and devil were true; but you need not concern yourself any ways with him as long as I am alive.

I have written the more large, on purpose to satisfy your troubled soul, if possible. So take leave, and rest,

Your friend in what I may,

LODOWICKE MUGGLETON.

London, Feb. 26, 1678.

A Copy of a Letter written by the Prophet Lodowicke Muggleton to Mr. Thomas Nosworthy, in Antigua, bearing date the 3d of March, 1678.

Loving friend in the true faith, Thomas Nosworthy,

THIS is to certify you, I received your letter, dated Antigua, July 12, 1678, by the hands of our friend John Saddington. I am glad to hear of your health; also to let you know, that we received your kind token you sent to my wife, the barrel of pickled limes, and a box of sugar; for which my Wife and myself do return you many thanks; but as for those commodities which you sent, and whether any friends will venture any thing in way of traffick for those commodities that country or island doth afford, I leave it to Mr. Saddington to give you an account of it; for I have not commerce with any men of the world. Also I am glad to hear, that your faith is so strong in the true God, and in this commission of the Spirit: and as for the thing you request of me, to satisfy your conscience as to matter of fighting, in case you are forced to it, I confess the power of liberty in this case lieth only in me. But I have considered, that we have no express command from the Lord to lay that bond upon every believer, let his case be ever so desperate or dangerous, in a strange land, where no hiding-place is, nor none to suffer with himself to utter ruin, the enemies being not of the same profession, neither in the temporal affairs; nor of the same profession in religion; neither is it in those strange islands, amongst the heathen, as it is here in England, Ireland, and Scotland, who profess all one faith, though very few have true faith. Besides, here is many hiding-places here, and safer to be in prison than to go to war, so it be for that cause only: but in those islands people must do as they do, else utter ruin will befall. Therefore, as the old proverb saith, "If you will live at Rome, you must do as Rome doth."

Upon this consideration I do give you leave to submit to the laws and customs of that island, which are for the defence and preservation of the temporal life, and the estates of the people, against the heathen, and any other enemies that seek to invade that island, and you shall be justified in your conscience, as if you had never borne arms at all. Let these lines satisfy you in this matter.

I was intended to send an answer to you long before now, but could never hear that any ship went to Antigua before now.

Mr. Saddington saw Captain Broad, and he said, that he setteth out for Antigua the 10th day of March next.

This is all at present, hoping these lines will come safe to your hands, and find you in good health, as I and my wife are at present, only my love, with my wife's love remembered to yourself, with my love to her that was Mrs. Heathcocke, and tell her that Mrs. Griffith is yet alive.

I rest your friend in the true faith,

LODOWICKE MUGGLETON.

London, March 1678.

The Prophet Lodowicke Muggleton's Blessing to Alexander Delamaine, junior, bearing date November 18, 1678.

Loving Friend in the true Faith, Alexander Delamaine, the younger,

I HAVE considered the tenderness of your age, and the innocency of your nature, and more especially the love and growth of your faith in this commission of the Spirit, in so short a time, even in the sixth hour of the day; and seeing you have desired a line or two of my own hand-writing, I do know what your request is for; and I, having this opportunity, cannot but grant your desire. Therefore, in obedience to my commission, I do pronounce you blessed in soul and body to eternity. Only I shall say unto you, as Christ did when on earth, to some that he had done some notable miracle upon; he bade them go their way, and tell no man, what good they had received from his words; but they blazed it abroad so much the more. So likewise I say unto you, let no man see this writing but your father and mother, if you can possible, lest you provoke others to do the same, as several of our friends have done the same heretofore, for want of my giving them a caution to the contrary.

Written by me,

LODOWICKE MUGGLETON.

A Copy of Mrs. Elizabeth Roe's Blessing:, written by the Prophet Mr. Lodowicke Muggleton, bearing date December 5, 1678.

Loving Friend in the true Faith, Elizabeth Roe,

YOU have made choice of two persons, whom I love well, to intercede for you, namely, Ann Delamaine, formerly Ann Hall, and my wife, to prevail with me to give you a blessing in writing; which thing I have refused to do unto several, and to yourself, because I gave it to you by word of mouth.

But your desires are so extreme, as the woman's was to the unjust judge, though he neither feared God nor honoured man, yet, because of her extreme suit unto him, for his own greatness-sake, he would do her justice upon her enemies; or as Jacob, that would not let God go till he blessed him. Here God seemed to put Jacob off without it; but through his great strength of faith he prevailed with God to bless him. Besides, we see by the Scriptures, that God, for to try a man or woman's faith, doth condescend to be counted by the reason of man, to be an unjust judge: and the woman's faith, that was so strong to be troublesome and wearisome to him, as justices are with a brawling woman's tongue; for that parable was spoken, and related to heavenly things.

I write not these lines to you, as thinking you unworthy of a blessing; only I do not usually give it in writing, and by word of mouth both; but considering your desires are so important and urgent, and your advocates aforesaid so well beloved of the Lord, and of me, I do declare you, Elizabeth Roe, one of the blessed of the Lord, both in soul and body, to eternity. And this blessing shall bear you up in the resurrection into eternal life, where you shall see our God, our King, and our Redeemer, face to face, to eternity.

LODOWICKE MUGGLETON.

December 5, 1678.

A Copy of a Letter written by the Prophet Lodowicke Muggleton to his Kinsman, Mr. Roger Muggleton, of Wilbarston, in Northamptonshire, bearing date December 14, 1678.

Dear and loving Cousin, Roger Muggleton,

I RECEIVED your letter, dated November 26, 1678, and am glad to hear of your recovery of the mishap that befel you, to put your ankle out of joint. Indeed I had great hopes to have seen you at Cambridge. I went about the fair at Sturbridge to find you out, and so did several others of our friends, persons of quality, from London, and out of the country, knowing that I would be there, not only for my sake, but hoping to see you, because you are a Muggleton, and my near kinsman; they love you, not only for my sake, but for your own sake, because the name of Muggleton is precious in the eyes of all the saints, but despised and hated of the world, and of reprobated men and women. God hath honoured the name of Muggleton above all the men in the world at this day, in that he hath preserved my life these many years, to be his last chosen prophet and witness of the Spirit, that God will ever send to the end of the world; and the next age and generation, after I am dead, shall call me blessed, though their fathers said, when I was alive, Muggleton was a blasphemer, a false prophet, a liar, and deceiver, a man not fit to live; but their children shall call me blessed, and say, had we lived in our fathers days, we would not have reviled nor persecuted this Muggleton, as our fathers did that hath declared such heavenly mysteries beyond the prophet sand apostles that went before him, or any that shall come after him, to the end of the world.

Dear Cousin,

I am glad the God of Heaven hath preserved you, of our father's house, to keep up the name and house from whence I sprang. Our fore-fathers were all plain men, yet downright honest men; men of no great repute in the world, nor of base report, as ever I could hear. And it was always God's practice, in all ages, to chuse men of low degree, and raise them up to the greatest honour and dignity. As for example, what was the first king in Israel, Saul, but a keeper of his father's asses? And David a keeper of sheep, yet made a king? What were the prophets of old, many of them, but herdsmen? and the apostles, but fishermen? Very mean employments; yet God hath honoured them with great honour, that hath made poor men kings, prophets, and apostles. And why should it seem strange to the world, that God should chuse two taylors, namely, John Reeve and Lodowicke Muggleton, to be his two last true prophets, and witnesses of the Spirit, in this last age of the world? A taylor is more honourable with kings, and princes, and noblemen of this world, than herdsmen and fishermen: but no prophet or apostle hath honour in this world, while he is alive; for the honour the world puts upon a prophet is after he is dead; and so it will be by John Reeve and myself.

I write these lines to strengthen and comfort you, in that the God of Heaven hath chosen one of your father's house, and hath revealed unto him life and salvation, as you will find in those writings you have; and I wish you may peruse them as much as you can; they will enlighten your understanding in things of eternity.

I have great encouragement to believe you are one of the blessed seed of faith, and my cousin Anne, though you have been kept in darkness, and unacquainted with me, till within these few years; so that I perceive you do not love me only because I am your kinsman, but because the light of faith which is the day-star, is risen in your heart, though but dimly, yet in truth, which will bear you up into everlasting lifer which none of my relations ever did receive before, but my two daughters, this twenty-seven years almost, since I was chosen of God.

I shall not trouble you further at this time, only to let you know that my daughter Whitfield is well, and my son White is well, and myself is very well in health at present; only I am so racked and taxed, upon that small visible estate in houses, and tenants so bad to pay rent in these troublesome times, the, oppression is so great that I am forced to leave my house, and let it stand empty.

Therefore, dear cousin, if you do come to London at the spring, which I hope you will, for I would be glad to see you, or send any letter in the mean time to me, direct your letter, or your person, to Mr. Alexander Delamain, upon Bread-street-hill, a tobacconist, at the sign of the Three Tobacco-pipes, and it will come sale to my hands.

This, with my love, and my wife's love, presented unto you and your wife, and to my cousin Anne; I take leave, and rest

Your loving Cousin,

LODOWICKE MUGGLETON.

December 14, 1678.

A Copy of a Letter written by the Prophet Lodowicke Muggleton to Mr. Thomas Tompkinson, bearing date July 29, 1679; directed to Slade-house, in Staffordshire.

Loving Friend in the true Faith, Thomas Tompkinson,

I RECEIVED your letter, dated July 15, 1679, wherein I am glad to hear of your health, and more glad to hear of the joy and comfort you do receive in your soul, by your faith in this commission of the Spirit: for indeed there is no true peace of mind to be found in any man or woman's soul here upon earth, but in the doctrine, declaration, and commission of the Spirit, which God gave unto John Reeve and myself. And as it hath pleased God to preserve me to be the longest liver, I have not been idle in the work of the Lord, since the burthen of the Lord was laid upon me, which is above twenty years since John Reeve died.

I have wondered in myself of late, how I have been enabled to go through those many troubles and persecutions from devils, and to write so much as I have, both in books and letters. It is almost unspeakable, were they calculated all that I have written: besides the many and various disputes, in answering the questions, both in saints and devils, both in prison and out of prison. But the God of my salvation never let that well that was digged in my soul, before I had a commission from him, to stand dry; but the well of living water did continually spring up in my soul, with new revelations, in opening the scriptures; and to answer to every person's question and objection that could arise out of the heart of man. All questions in spiritual matters were easy to me; the revelation of faith in me never studied what answer to give; for as Christ saith, *He that believeth in me, out of his belly shall flow rivers of living water*. Now, true faith in the soul doth dig a well in a man's belly: Why? Because the heart of man doth lie in the upper part of a man's belly; so that out of the heart of man, which lieth in the belly, doth flow rivers of living water, or rivers of water of death: for there is a well of water in every man, and this well is always springing up: if the well that faith hath digged, then springs up revelations, heavenly wisdom, peace of conscience, joy in the Holy Ghost, the assurance of everlasting life, and never to study for to live a good life, or to gain more faith and knowledge. For out of this well doth spring living water, that satisfies the soul: it taketh away the desire of more knowledge, or more faith, than it hath; for the well-spring Of life is always rising in the heart, with motions of peace, the growth of faith, with new and fresh knowledge and experience in those things it hath believed; so that it is a man's own faith that makes him whole. Only God gave faith in the original, in the seed, but God's messengers digged this well in every true believer, in that faith comes by hearing the word of God preached, *and how can he preach except he be sent*? So that he that preacheth the truth diggeth a well in his heart that believeth his report. For believing is faith; and this faith comes by hearing the word of God preached, And this faith which came by hearing the word of God preached, is that seed that was sown in good ground, or that faith which digged a well in man's heart, which in it is that water of life Christ speaketh of, which whoever hath this well of water in him shall never thirst more after heavenly peace, or assurance of eternal life.

These things many can experience at this day, besides myself.

Also the seed of reason, that the reprobate angel gave in the original, hath a well of water in them also; and this well is digged in the souls of men and women, by false preachers, that went before they were sent; and out of this well doth arise water of death, instead of water of life. From this well of water in men and womens' souls, or hearts, doth arise unbelief, a troubled mind, a wounded conscience, the fear of eternal damnation, despair of hope of God's mercy. This is that river, or well of water, that floweth out of the belly of the seed of reason in reprobate men and women. Prom these two wells of water in men doth spring water of life eternal, and water of death eternal; and from no other wells whatsoever. But blessed and happy are you, and all those that have and do drink of that living water that floweth out of his own belly, by believing, or having faith of, this commission of the Spirit, in this last age. And miserable, and cursed, will those be that hath, and doth, drink the water of death, that floweth out of his own belly, by unbelief, and persecuting of the commission of the Spirit in this last age.

These lines may give you some light into things that have not been treated upon heretofore. And that I can truly say, as the apostle Paul to those that believed in him, that I have declared unto you the whole council of God, as it hath been revealed unto me. I have kept nothing secret, but have revealed it upon the house-top of men's understanding.

I shall not trouble you further; but take leave, and rest,

Your Friend in the true Faith,

LODOWICKE MUGGLETON.

July 29, 1679.

A Copy of a Letter written by the Prophet Lodowicke Muggleton to Mr. Thomas Tompkinson, bearing date from London, July 24, 1680.

Loving Friend, Thomas Tompkinson,

I PERCEIVE your brother and sister is in some trouble, and desire my advice in it. I cannot tell how to give advice in that which I do not know the ground and cause. You say there is coming out a distress upon them, or rather a sequestration of the third-part of their estate of land, being proceeded against as persons offending, and taken in with some papists, and thereupon an order came from the sheriff to repair to him such a day, and to pay him eight pounds, as a debt due to the king for his lands, upon default of which two of the sheriff's men came and distrained; but he loosed his goods, and. paid the money.

This is the whole substance of the matter. Now, whether your brother Burton hath been sued as a papist, or been confederate with papists, and sued as an offender, I know not; or whether he hath been sued as a nonconformist, or for not going to church. If they take away the third-part of his land, for not going to church, and that is the only fault he hath committed, he being a Protestant, he may have relief by the law hereafter, but not at present; for it is the grand-jury that giveth away all the privileges of the people, especially if they be Dissenters: the jury doth so in other counties, as well as yours; and they do strive what they can to do so to all those called fanatics, if they could; only this city of London is a curb which causeth several counties to forbear; but if he be a Papist, or not paying of tythes, it will be a vain thing for any person to stand against it, because of Queen Elizabeth's laws; and several proclamations have been put out lately against them; therefore to no purpose for papists to stand it out. And if your fault be nothing else but for not going to church, it is dangerous for any sheriff to take away the third-part of a man's land: but how shall any man help it in these times, being given by a jury? My advice should be to you, as it was to a friend of mine in Kent lately, who was sued at several quarter-sessions, for not going to church; and the man was freed, and declared by the judge of the court not to be guilty of any penalty; yet, after the judge was gone from his seat, the grand-jury brought him in guilty, and ordered that his land should be measured, and the third-part for the king.

Now, I advised him to let them measure his land, and see who dares buy it. Nobody dares buy land, or give any money for it upon such an account; he must be exceeding wicked that would do such a thing.

But how this matter is ended I cannot tell; My advice to you is the same, if your land be your own, and not farmed; if farmed, they cannot meddle with it; and if it be your own, let them sequester, and sell the third-part of it, if they can; for they must not meddle with none of the crop nor stock upon the land; they are to have nothing but the bare land: and who will buy it of the king, or for the king? Perhaps some will beg it of the king, and sell it for a small matter to the person himself.

But I perceive by your letter, that the sheriff's men have distrained his goods instead of his land; and that your brother hath paid eight pounds in money; so that the sheriff's men, and the sheriff himself, is satisfied. In that you have paid to the sheriff the eight pounds, you have satisfied the king's debt, and satisfied for your fault, whatsoever it was: so that your goods and your land are both redeemed, and your fault forgiven for the present, till the next fault is committed; then perhaps half your land may become indebted to the king, and so on, till the king hath it all. If it proves so, let him have it; for you cannot help yourself; so that you need not to have sent to me for any advice in this matter, seeing you have paid the sheriff the eight pounds already: the eight pounds is the sheriff's; he receiveth all the king's debts that is due, of that nature; so that the sheriff hath got the third-part of your land; so he hath left you worth twenty-four more in land. He might, if he would have any mercy for you, have taken half the money; but the other second-part of your land will serve the next sheriff. This sheriff hath got his share. You must bear it patiently; and being for conscience-sake you suffer the loss of your land, your peace will be greater, if you keep your confidence to the end. Your mind will be made free to part with all your land for conscience sake. You will receive an hundred-fold of peace and content in this life; and you will heap coals of fire upon the heads of your enemies; for the sentence upon you was only out of envy and malice.

This is all at present, but rest

Your friend, LODOWICKE MUGGLETON.

London, June 24, 1680.

POSTSCRIPT.

After the writing of this, I understand, that your brother Burton and sister did suffer upon the account of being Papists, because they durst not confess they owned Muggleton; because the name of Muggleton at that time was very odious in this nation, and the Papists at that time was very much favoured by the nation in general, and by the powers of the nation were assisted; but Muggleton was altogether despised, and trod under foot; so that you chose rather in the time of persecution, to shelter yourself under the Papists, to save your estate, than to own the name of Muggleton.

Was it the faith you had in Muggleton's doctrine, that caused you to refrain from going to the church of England to worship? Or was it the Papist principle that caused you to refrain, or their liberty? You seemed to own me before the believers of this commission; but before your enemies you durst not confess me before them; so that you disabled yourselves to give a reason of the faith and hope that was in you, to any enemy that should ask you. You have fulfilled the words of Christ, that saith, *He that denieth me before men*, that is, before enemies; for no man denies Christ before the believers of Christ; therefore, whoever denies Christ before his enemies must be denied of him before God. The case is the same now; whoever denieth the commission of the Spirit before men, even their enemies, denieth God's messengers, therefore ought to be denied by him; but whoever confesseth Christ, or his messengers, before men, they will confess him before the God of Heaven: and whoever doth lose house or land for truths sake, shall receive as much peace and content of mind in this life, as will weigh in the balance equal with house and land, besides life everlasting in the world to come. But I perceive you have lost the third part of your land for a lie, for being a Papist, which I do think you never did own in your heart; but your silence in not denying it, nor confessing your faith to the contrary, you have received judgment and sentence in not going to church, as an absolute Papist, and not as a Muggletonian. Now many of the judges of the land, and many of the clergy, and bishops of the land, and all the courts of England, both of London and elsewhere, and gaol-keepers, and all sorts of people, do know that Muggleton himself is no Papist; witness those many hundred books they took from me, and the universities are furnished with: and my standing upon the pillory hath witnessed to the whole nation that Muggleton is no Papist; and most of the believers of England and Ireland are known by the name of Muggleton, to be no Papists; neither was ever any person that hath suffered for not going to church; as I have known several that were Muggletonians; and the judges did know that they were Muggleton's people; but none suffered as a Papist: but now you have given an example.

LODOWICKE MUGGLETON.

Lodowicke Muggleton's Letter to Robert Peirce, concerning the Holy Ghost.

Loving Friend, Robert Peirce,

I RECEIVED a letter from you, dated July 9, 1680, wherein I perceived you received a letter from me, and that you being not at home, but your brother was, and through the ignorance or the covetousness of your brother, the letter was carried back again, for want of one penny more than usually the post hath; it was very weakly done, for posts will not abate any thing of what the letter is marked, so that the letter is absolutely lost, except you go to the post-house in Taunton, and ask for a letter so long ago, directed to Robert Peirce, at St. James's, in Taunton; it was a large letter, but it was not from me, it was from a friend of mine, his name is Alexander Delamaine, from the Three Tobacco-pipes, on Bread-street Hill, tobacconist; he wrote that letter to you.

The other thing of concernment in your letter is, you desire me to shew you the meaning of two places in Scripture, which I perceive you would desire to know, in what sense you may believe and satisfy your mind, whether the Holy Ghost did descend upon Christ, when he was baptized of John, in a bodily shape really? or whether it is to be understood in some other sense? To which I answer and say,

That the Holy Ghost that descended in a bodily shape on Christ like a dove, it was really so; for when all the people were baptized of John, Christ being the last that was baptized of John at that time; and after Jesus was baptized he prayed, *and the Heavens were opened, and the Holy Ghost descended in a bodily shape, like a dove, and it lighted upon him.*

Now to give you to understand that none saw this Holy Ghost descend upon Christ in a bodily shape like a dove, but Christ himself and John the Baptist; neither did any person see the Heavens open, nor heard the voice from Heaven, which said, Thou art my beloved son, in thee I am well pleased. I say no person did see the Heavens open, nor hear the voice, but Christ, and John the Baptist.

Now it may be rejected, whether that voice was from that bodily shape like a dove, that was upon Christ, or from some other person in Heaven.

To which I answer, the voice from Heaven was not from that which appeared in a bodily shape like a dove, the voice was from Elias, that was in Heaven, and it was he which said, *Thou art my well-beloved son, in thee I am well pleased*, Luke iii. ver. 22. This was the same Elias that spake here, that spake the same words in Matthew xvii. ver. 3. *And behold there appeared unto them Moses and Elias talking with Christ.* And in the 5th verse, *While he was yet speaking, a bright cloud overshadowed them,* (that is) *Peter, James, and John; and behold a voice out of the cloud, which said*, This is my beloved son, in whom I am well pleased, hear ye him. Here it is clear, that Elias acted his part in Heaven as God the Father of Christ, while Christ that was God became flesh, or God manifest in the flesh: while he went that long and sore journey here upon earth, it was of great necessity that he should put a faithful governor in Heaven to represent the person of the Father, and he invested him with all power in

Heaven above while he passed through death, and quickened into life again, and ascended up into the same glory which he had before the world was.

Here you that have faith may see the bright cloud that brought Moses and Elias from Heaven, and that the presence of them talking with Christ caused his face to shine as the sun, and his raiment was as white as the light; and this bright cloud carried Moses and Elias to Heaven again, which cloud, as it ascended up to Heaven, it overshadowed Peter, James and John, and Christ himself; and out of this cloud as it did ascend Elias spake through the cloud; so that James, Peter and John, and Christ himself, heard the voice out of the cloud, which said, *This is my beloved son, in whom I am well pleased, hear ye him.* This voice confirmed Peter, James and John in their faith, that Christ was indeed the Son of God; but Christ charged them to tell no man the vision until he was risen from the dead; neither did they tell it to any man, until afterwards they told it to Matthew, Mark, Luke, and others, for none of the Evangelists nor Epistles were written until after Christ was risen and ascended: so that none saw this bright cloud, nor heard Moses and Elias voice but these three, Peter, James and John, and Christ himself; and no man saw the Holy Ghost descend in a bodily shape like a dove unto Christ, but John the Baptist, and Christ himself; yet Matthew and Luke, that never saw any such thing, they must write and publish it by revelation, which is as it were at the second hand, yet ought to be believed, as if God himself had spoken to every man in particular.

And why the Holy Ghost did appear in a bodily shape like a dove? It was only to signify the innocency of his person, and innocency of his practice, and innocent actions, that there should be *no guile found in his mouth*; and to confirm John in his message, *whose shoe-latchets he was not worthy to unloose.* And this is to be minded, that Elias being immortalized of God, before God became flesh several hundred years; but when time appointed was come for God to fulfil the promise made to Adam, and was expected by Enoch, Abraham, Isaac, and Jacob, and the prophets, that the seed of the woman should break the serpent's head; which should be done no other way, but in that God became flesh; so that Christ is very God became flesh, as the Scripture saith.

Now upon this wonderful mystery, before God did become flesh, he did ordain, appoint and invest Elias with power and glory, and majesty, to sit in the throne of God as God, on the same throne of glory as he himself was in before he became flesh; so that Elias did govern the Heavens above, and watch over Christ's person as God the Father, all that time that God was become flesh, until he ascended into the same glory which he had before the world was.

And when the Holy Ghost doth descend upon a person or persons, as it did upon Christ in a bodily shape like a dove, it was to endue him with an extraordinary power above all other men, that have the gift of the Holy Ghost in a bodily shape like a dove.

It did impower, or give power to Christ after he was baptized of John, to increase in wisdom, knowledge, patience and meekness, above all, and did impower him to work miracles, to open the eyes of the blind, the lame to walk, and dumb to speak, and the dead to be raised, which no man else could do: this power was given to Christ when he was baptized of the Holy Ghost, that descended upon him in a bodily shape like a dove; and Elias being in the glory of the Father, sent his appearance like a dove upon Christ, he being then in the condition of a creature, though without sin: for this is to be minded, that Christ never did any miracle till after the descending of the Holy Ghost upon him, then it was he received his commission from Heaven, to teach and preach, and work miracles, signs and wonders; so that where the Holy Ghost doth appear in any visible form, one or more, it is because some great and mighty work is to be done by that person or persons to whom this visible appearance of the Holy Ghost is presented, as you may see, *Acts* ii. *ver.* 3. When the apostles were met together, and were to receive their commission to preach from Heaven, as Christ had told them before he was ascended, that he would endue them with power from on high; and now he is ascended into the glory of the Father again, he sendeth the Holy Ghost in the visible shape of *cloven tongues, like unto fire*; and this Holy Ghost sat upon each of the twelve apostles, as in the third verse, *And there appeared unto them cloven tongues like unto fire, and it sat upon each of them*: and the fourth verse, *And they were filled with the Holy Ghost, and began to speak with other tongues, as the spirit gave them utterance.*

Here you may see, that when Christ was ascended into the glory of the Father again, the same glory which he had left with Elias while he became flesh and in the condition of a creature. I say, when he ascended into that glory again, he sent the Holy Ghost to sit upon each of them *like cloven tongues of fire*.

Now mind, no person saw the visible shape of these *cloven tongues like of fire*, but the twelve apostles, who were commissionated, but they declared it to others.

Here we see these cloven tongues of fire was the Holy Ghost, which Christ sent from Heaven to impower them to preach the gospel to all nations, and to speak with other tongues, which they never were taught nor learned in, and to work miracles; and so, many signs and wonders were wrought by them: to be plain, these cloven tongues, as of fire, was the Holy Ghost, which gave the twelve apostles their commission to do these things aforesaid.

Now observe, when Elias was in the glory of the Father, he sent the Holy Ghost in the visible shape of a dove, and it descended upon Christ really in that form beforesaid, but the Holy Ghost that Christ sent down from Heaven, when he was in the glory of the Father, it descended and sat upon the apostles, in the visible shape and form, was cloven tongues like unto fire; yet both these shapes are called the Holy Ghost, which did impower both Christ to act those miracles, and the work of redemption for the elect seed, and did enable him to suffer the pains of death, and to quicken out of death, and to rise again, and to ascend into Heaven: and the apostles were enabled by the Holy Ghost, which sat upon them like cloven tongues as it were of fire, to preach life and salvation to the world by this Jesus, who suffered death, and rose again, and ascended up into Heaven, whereof they were witnesses; and these cloven tongues as of fire was a visible shape to the apostles.

Now to satisfy you further, this Holy Ghost that descended upon Christ, in the shape of a dove, nor that Holy Ghost that descended upon the apostles in the shape of *cloven tongues like fire*. I say, this Holy Ghost was not God, but proceeded from God; and Elias being in the throne and place of God, he had power to send the Holy Ghost in the shape of a dove.

And when Christ was in his throne again, he had power to send the Holy Ghost on the twelve apostles, like cloven tongues as of fire; for the person of God never was in the form of a dove, nor in the form of cloven tongues like fire, but his person was in the form of a man from all eternity; therefore it is that *he made man in his own likeness*. Therefore I say, let not any man imagine that this Holy Ghost was God, and so ground three persons in the Trinity, as the blind reason in man doth; for God's person was always in the form and shape aforesaid.

Some may say, what then is that which is called the Holy Ghost?

To which I answer, that this Holy Ghost spoken of in the Scripture, is the Spirit of God, and doth proceed from God; so that every true believer may be said to receive the Holy Ghost, or to have the Spirit of God in him, because he believeth the report of those that have either the spirit of prophesy or revelation, or that hath the Holy Ghost by way of vision, as Christ had, and the apostles had in a more extraordinary manner; for he that hath the spirit of prophesy, revelation, or inspiration, hath a great measure of the Holy Ghost in him, but not so large a measure as those that receive the Holy Ghost by visible appearances. Now all this doth come by receiving the Holy Ghost, which is called the Spirit of God.

And when this wisdom and knowledge ariseth in man's heart secretly, as beforesaid, it is not for such outward visible public work as it did to Christ and the apostles.

Likewise Stephen was a man full of the Holy Ghost, but he was filled with the Holy Ghost by secret inspiration and revelation; and so it is said that David by the Holy Ghost did prophesy concerning Christ, but this was secret likewise, Acts viii. ver. 15. *Peter and John prayed, and the people received the Holy Ghost*, for as yet the Holy Ghost was not fallen upon none of them; and the 17th Verse, *Then laid they their hands on them, and they received the Holy Ghost*; and in the 19th Verse, *one Simon proffered Peter and John money, saying, Give me also this power, that on whomsoever I lay my hands, they may receive the Holy Ghost*. Here you may see, that Peter and John, that were in the state of mortality, had power to give the Holy Ghost on whom they laid their hands.

If mortal men, that received their commission and power from Christ, the only God, when he had passed through death, and ascended into the same glory, could give the Holy Ghost to whom they laid their hands on, why should it seem strange to any man, that Elias, who was immortalized and glorified, who sat in the throne of the Father, even of God, while Christ the God went that far journey in the flesh; it may well be called far, for it was from heaven to this vile earth; was he not able to give the Holy Ghost in a bodily shape upon Christ like a dove, being then in the state of immortality, and he in the state of immortality and glory? And by the power of this Holy Ghost, did Christ do all his miracles when on earth.

LODOWICKE MUGGLETON.

August 2, 1680.

A Copy of a Letter written by the Prophet Lodowicke Muggleton to Mr. Edward Burton, in Derbyshire, bearing date the 12th of January, 1681.

Loving Friend Edward Burton,

I RECEIVED your letter dated the 3rd of January, by our account here at London, 1681, but by your account 1682; and as for your other letter from your brother-in-law Tompkinson, I received, and the cheese: the token of your love I received also, and do know that your brother-in-law, and your son, have spent a great deal of money to get your release by the laws of the land, but to no purpose.

I cannot see but that all your labour, charge and expence is all lost; neither do I know any thing of the proceedings in those cases; but do understand that he that was employed to manage your cause, hath deceived you of your money, and the courts also. Therefore if you can get any of your money again of him that hath deceived you, it will do well; but to the thing you desired of me, is whether you may or not go to the church once or twice, seeing they require no more; but as for the receiving of the sacrament, you say you will not do; but you hearing I gave Mr. Powell leave to go to the church, you made bold to send to me, whether you may go to the church or no, to free you from the malice of your enemies, whereof you say you have suffered the loss of 100*l*. all ready.

Answer. That since I have seen the bad effects of giving leave to Mr. Powell to go to church but once, I am resolved never to give leave any more to any person whatsoever; for after he went once to churchy that the priest had got fast hold of his right-hand, he would not let him go, till he had fast hold of his other hand also: that is, till he had made him go to church often, and to receive the sacrament and to baptize his child, which hath been a great dishonor to me and all the believers of this commission of the Spirit, and an everlasting shame to himself amongst all that know him, both to saints and devils; neither is he yet delivered out of his troubles, notwithstanding he has wounded his own soul, and lost his credit in this world, (which I fear will never be repaired again,) and wasted his estate to keep himself out of prison; so that I see he had better have gone to prison at the first, and never have put in bail, but stood the trial of the court; then would he have seen an end of all his troubles in a short time, and would have had the love and pity of all saints, and of many devils; but by submitting unto them, hath lost them all; for this I must tell you, that the ecclesiastical authority doth now ride upon the temporal power, even the laws of the land. So that if a man be sued in the spiritual court, or upon a spiritual account, even that knack of not going to church, the temporal law, which is the birth-right of every Englishman, cannot free, and deliver any man from punishment. This I have had experience of in my sufferings; and had I known as much at the first as I did afterwards, I would have saved a great deal of charge and expence in putting in of bail, and court charges, so often as I did, but would have lain in jail at first, and have spent that money in prison; then would my sufferings have been ended quickly.

Therefore he that would keep his conscience clear as to God, must be sure to suffer persecution for his conscience sake, or lose the peace of his conscience, which is of more value than all the riches of this world.

Now what I have suffered upon a spiritual account, it was merely for the commission of God, put upon me, and the cause of Mr. Powell's sufferings was for extravagant words, which he ought not to have spoken; and I understand that the cause of your sufferings, is not because you were a believer of Muggleton, but rather a sider of papists; which has been the grounds of all your sufferings, and how to deliver you out of this I cannot tell. But seeing you cannot sell nor let your land, nor put your son into it without paying such a sum of money in goods and chattels and conformity to the church of England, against the peace of your own conscience, my advice is, that you should rather go to prison as others do; as Quakers, Baptists, and others do, and spend your estate in the jail, and leave your estate to the management of them you can confide in; for the law of England cannot imprison a man's body, and take away his goods and land too; for suffer you must. I see, either make shipwreck of the peace of your conscience, or shipwreck of your estate: but I would rather advise you to keep your faith and a good conscience towards God; and in a little time you may see a deliverance; for I have seen several persons that have been in the jail upon the like account; yet in six months time of imprisonment have been delivered.

This is but cold comfort that I can give you; it is like a cup of cold water in the name of the disciple. But it will be the reward of a disciple's peace of conscience, as cold water to cool the tongue of conscience from reasoning, to and fro in the mind. But I perceive by your letter, that they will not accept now of your person going to prison; neither will they put you in prison, but had rather have your goods or land; and because you did not appear at the first process or first summons in your own person, and make your defence what religion you were of, then would the court have fined you so much money as 20*l*. for the first fault, or have sent you to prison for six months, without bail or mainprize. But in regard you made no personal appearance from Sessions to Sessions, they knowing you to be a man of estate, they had rather have your estate than have your person in prison; and your employing a false-hearted man to manage your defence according to law, hath cost you more money than would have satisfied your adversaries, and hath done you no good, but a great deal of hurt, in that it hath enraged your enemies, so that nothing will satisfy their rage but your utter ruin, either of your peace of conscience, or else of your whole estate; first of your goods, and afterwards of your land; so that your condition is desperate, and I am afraid you must be forced to make a desperate cure, which will be thus: before any other process can come forth, to drive all your cattle off your own land, and sell them by degrees; and as for your household goods, corn, hay, and whatsoever is moveable, take it off the land, and carry it away; and take your wife and children, and live in some place, and hire ground in some other place, and leave the bare land for the king to take away; for the king cannot sell it, neither dare any man buy it; and in a little time your land may be restored to you again, or to your son, upon reasonable terms. I know an example much like this in Kent: there was a landed man, and his land, some of it was let to other tenants of his, but the man himself had no goods nor chattels but what he could remove; so that they could not get any goods considerable; so they went to seize his land, the third part for the king; but no man would buy any such land of the king, because his title was not good to a free-born man's land, and this was for not going to church, but they agreed with the man for 20*l*. only; it cost him 10*l*. more charges, bailiffs, and others; so the man enjoyed his land ever since.

For my part, I cannot see how you can possibly be delivered from utter destruction, and keep the peace of your mind, but this way, you may leave your son, and whom you will, upon the land, to look after it, and some necessaries for them that is not of considerable value, and let the officers and them do as well as they can. This is my advice in this matter, but leave it to your own consideration to do as you please.

So, with my love, with my wife's love, remembered to you, and to your wife, I take leave, and rest your friend,

LODOWICKE MUGGLETON.

January the 12th, 1681.

The Copy of the Prophet Lodowicke Muggleton's Blessing, sent to Mrs. Sarah West, of a place called Uver, in Cambridgeshire, dated February 22, 1681.

Loving Friend, Mrs. Sarah West,

I RECEIVED your letter, enclosed in our friend William Dickinson's letter, in which you do acknowledge me to be the only true prophet of the high, immortal, glorious God, Christ Jesus, and that you have believed this many years in this last commission, and that you had an intent to have come to London to see me, but weakness of body did hinder you, and for no other cause, as I perceive, but for a blessing of everlasting life, before you depart out of this natural life here in this world; and I understand, by our friend Dickinson's letter, that you were sorry, or blamed yourself several times since, that you did not ask it when I was there with you. Indeed, you had then a good opportunity, which will hardly ever be again in this life; for salvation was then come to your house, not only in myself, but several other friends, who had the assurance of salvation abiding in them.

I speak not this to daunt you for your neglect, but do say unto you, as Christ said unto Martha, who was troubled with many incumbrances about victuals to entertain Christ and his disciples; for indeed, your husband and yourself did entertain us with several feasts as princes, which will not be forgotten as long as any of us do live. And this I have perceived in you ever since I came acquainted with you, that you: have not had that great experience to talk or discourse of your faith as several others have, but your love to it hath been expressed constantly to this faith ever since I first saw you; and in this letter you have expressed your faith more than ever, in that you do believe that I am a true prophet of the Lord, and have power given me of God to give a blessing to those that truly believe in this commission of the Spirit.

These things considered, I do pronounce and declare you, Sarah West, one of the blessed of the Lord, both in soul and body, to all eternity; and this blessing shall bear you up in death, and free you from the fear of that second death, which is eternal; and in the resurrection you shall remember you were told so by the last true prophet that God will ever send to this unbelieving world, to your everlasting joy and comfort, though you never see me more in this world.

Therefore trouble not yourself with bad times, for in this world there will be troubles, let what come that will come, but let your peace be in God, and in the assurance of your eternal happiness.

I rest your friend in the true faith,

LODOWICKE MUGGLETON.

A Copy of a Letter written by the Prophet Lodowicke Muggleton, bearing date August 22, 1681, to Charles Yeeles, Thomas Millerd, and John White, in or near Cork in Ireland.

Charles Yeeles, Thomas Miller John White,

I RECEIVED a letter as from you three, by the hand of Rebecca Stratton, dated July 22, 1681.

I perceive by your letter that you have viewed some of our writings, and that it hath pleased God, in the reading thereof, you have found great satisfaction, and by faith do believe our commission to be true, and by the same ye are come to believe in the true God, and to know the right devil, with an increase of daily satisfaction in yourselves, though much to the discontent of the children of this generation. I perceive some of you have been Quakers, and that it is but lately that you have seen any excellency in those writings of ours; and it is God's great mercy indeed, that your eyes are opened to believe the true God, and to know the right devil. The knowledge of these two, their forms and their natures, giveth great satisfaction to the mind of man, and without the knowledge of the true God and the right devil, there can be no satisfaction nor assurance of eternal life abiding in any man while upon this earth; for God hath blinded the eyes of all men by nature upon the earth for these many generations, that he might give light unto two men in this last generation, to enlighten the understanding of many in those deep hidden mysteries, how God became flesh, and dwelt among men here on this earth, and how the devil became flesh, and doth dwell among men here on earth now, and of that great mystery of the two seeds, namely, the seed of the woman, and the seed of the serpent; and from whence these two seeds came; the original how they came to be seed, and of their production; what those two seeds did produce, even eternal salvation to many, and eternal damnation to millions of men and women; with many more sacred things that did belong unto God only, as the form and nature of angels, which were known to God only that created them, which he hath revealed to Reeve and Muggleton only; and we are as a pipe of wood in the earth, that hath conveyed that water of life into many earthen vessels, whose souls shall drink of the water of life, and doth never thirst more. It hath been in the souls of many that have believed our report, as that oil the prophet Elisha filled that woman's vessels with, even enough to keep her and her son as long as she lived in this world.

Thus I have given you a little hint of those heavenly mysteries which have been revealed unto me, which you will find more abundant in those books Mrs. Stratton doth bring, if she come safe to Ireland, as I hope she will; and I do wish you may understand what you read, for I cannot give you understanding, it must arise out of your own seed, and understand with your own hearts the things that belong to your eternal peace; and you must expect the discontent and ill-will of many; for God hath made me, as he did the prophet Jeremiah, to stand as a waif of brass against Israel and Judah, which was only to two kingdoms; but God hath made me a wall of brass not only to three kingdoms, England, Scotland, and Ireland, but unto all Europe that professeth the Christian religion. I am hated of all nations for nothing else but for the commission of God put upon me, and the most zealous and righteous people of all hate me most of all; yet the God of my salvation hath preserved my life almost these thirty years, in several persecutions and imprisonments, and my life is still within me, without any distemper of body, only age groweth on, which must be submitted unto.

I take leave at present, only my love remembered unto you all three, and unto Jeremiah Stratton, George Gamble, and his wife, George Rogers, and Elizabeth Flaggetter, and all the rest of our friends in the true faith in those parts.

I rest your friend in the true faith in the Lord Jesus Christ, the only wise God, blessed and praised be his name,

LODOWICKE MUGGLETON.

London, August 22, 1681.

The books which Rebecca Stratton paid twenty shillings for are these, and the price:

	£.	s.	d.
1. The Divine Looking-Glass, at	0	5	0
2. The Interpretation of the 11th Revelation, at	0	5	0
3. The whole Revelation, at	0	2	6
4. Fox's Looking-Glass, at	0	2	6
5. The Witch of Endor, at	0	2	6
6. The Answer to William Penn, at	0	2	6

The whole Revelations and Penn's Were always at that price, because I have some of them two left still; but all the other are hard to be had single for any money, but what are bound altogether, and they be very dear.

A Copy of a Letter written by the Prophet Lodowicke Muggleton to Mr. James Whitehead, of Braintree, in Essex, bearing date from London, August 30, 1681.

Loving and kind friend in the true faith, James Whitehead,

THIS is to certify you, that I received your letter, bearing date March 23, 1680; wherein you commanded your daughter to dine with me on Saturday last, but upon some occasions it was put off until Monday, which was more convenient, and at a more convenient house, where my wife and I, and other friends, did dine with your two daughters, I suppose to the content of both your daughters, and of us also.

And as for those two things you desire of me, to give you an account concerning your eldest daughter, her lineage and faith, I shall give you my judgment, as far as I can discern, by what I have heard and seen by her myself, and by her letters to Mr. Delamaine, and discourse our friend Delamaine and his wife hath had with her, and experience they have had of her; as thus;

Your daughter Priscilla is of the lineage of Rebecca and Rachel, that is, of the race of the Assyrians; for Laban the Assyrian was Rebecca's brother, and Rachel's father.

Now to give you the reason why I judge the Assyrians is the best of natures amongst the Gentiles, for these causes:

Firsts Because they are generally honest of their bodies, both men and women.

Secondly. They are in their natures generally just persons in their dealings, especially if they be the seed of faith, or have but the least measure of faith in them.

Thirdly. They are generally wise in their natures, and given to covetousness with moderation; which is indeed but to preserve for another day, that they might not be servants to Canaanites, nor subject to proud Moabites, nor stout-hearted Ammonites, nor scoffing Ishmaelites, nor prophane Esau's; so that they may be subject to none but Jews only. This is counted covetousness by all these sort of people.

These things aforesaid, I do discern are in your daughter's nature, which came by the mother's side, of Rebecca and Rachel, as aforesaid.

And as for her faith in the true God, and in this commission of the Spirit, she hath expressed before Mr. Delamaine and his wife, and me and my wife, besides what she expressed in her letters formerly as much, and more than could be expected, having so little occasion to draw it forth as she hath had; for it cannot be expected that, her faith should appear visibly strong as those that had their faith, tried in the fiery contests of the world, even as gold is tried, even as you know some have here in London; yet her faith is true, and grounded upon a rock; and time may cause her faith to be tried, as others have been, in the fire of opposition, and come forth to the visible view of this world, as others of her sex, as gold purified seven times in the fire.

Thus I have given you a small account of those two things you desired, and I know you will perceive by these lines more than can be expressed in Writing.

Therefore I shall say no more at present in this thing, but present my love and my wife's love unto yourself, and to your good wife, and to Mr. Nicolls,

And rest your friend in the eternal truth,

LODOWICKE MUGGLETON.

A Copy of a Letter wrote by the Prophet Lodowicke Muggleton to William Wood, of Braintree, in Essex, dated September 26, 1681.

Loving Friend in the true Faith, William Wood,

I RECEIVED a letter from you, dated August 15, 1681, wherein you desire to have a line or two from me; and since that, John Lad was very earnest with me on your behalf, to write a few lines unto you; saying, it would much rejoice your heart.

I was unwilling to Write where there was no need; because at that time, I had a great many long letters to write, both into Ireland, and here in England, which were something burthensome unto me, yet did not intend never to write unto you; but now having a little more leisure and opportunity, I shall gratify your desire, and write these lines as followeth.

I perceive by your letter, that your faith is strong in the true God, even the Lord Jesus Christ; which faith and knowledge in the true God and man, should be but one single person, even the Lord Jesus Christ, which our writings have declared is life eternal to know.

Also, I perceive by your letter, that your faith is strong in this commission of the Spirit, and that, by your faith in us, the witnesses of the Spirit, you do in believing know those divine secrets, and heavenly revelations, which are hid from all the world besides, and revealed to none, but those few that believe our report: to them few is the arm of the Lord's saving health revealed.

Again, I do discern by your letter, that your faith is strong in those words I spake unto you when you were at London; and that they were as a seal in your forehead, sealed up unto the great day of God Almighty, unto eternal happiness in the kingdom of glory, in that world above the globe, where the person of God himself, and angels in the persons of men, do inherit; ascending and descending to one another with messages, and praises, and thanks, glory and honour, unto God the Creator eternally. And we that are his chosen prophets, and you his saints, ever since the creation of this world, shall sing the song of Moses, and the song of the lamb of Moses, and the song of the lamb unto our God, and our Redeemer, hallelujah, salvation, and glory, and honour, and power, be to the Lord our God, as he is our Redeemer. And the holy angels shall ascribe all honour, glory, and praise unto the same God, as he was their Creator, but not as their Redeemer, because God redeemed none but the seed of Adam fallen into mortality, and into death. So that by the death of God, and his quickening into life again, he hath redeemed us, not only from this natural death, but from eternal death. And as he quickened himself out of death, and made his pure natural body in the quickening, a spiritual body, to live eternally, and by the power of this quickening Spirit will he raise our souls; and our bodies that were natural, shall rise in the quickening spiritual bodies, capable of ascending in the clouds of heaven, to meet the Lord in the air.

This is the power of our God, as he is our Redeemer.

This is a great mystery, hard to be understood but by the spirit of faith, which is the evidence of things, which the spirit of reason cannot see. For this I say, that the spirit or seed of faith in me hath been carried up into the third heaven, where God, and the holy angels were resident; where I saw things unutterable. And when the spirit of faith descended upon earth, it brought the abundance of Revelation with it, as hath been declared by word and pen in a great measure, as many can experience and witness it this day. And many that are fallen asleep in the experience and faith of these great mysteries, which have been declared by the abundance of revelation that hath proceeded from the spirit of faith, which did first arise in me in the beginning of the year 1651, which is thirty years ago.

I would not have you think, because I speak thus, that I would lay any burthen upon you, or any other believer of this commission of the Spirit, as to expect that every one should have such a measure of faith as I speak of; but that you may by these lines grow and increase in the knowledge of these heavenly mysteries, according to the measure of faith in you.

Thus I have written these lines to answer your desire, and more than I did intend, because I know you will let other friends there with you, see it or hear it. So I shall take leave, and rest, and remain with my love, and my wife's love unto yourself,

Your friend in the true faith in Jesus Christ, the only wise God, blessed for ever,

LODOWICKE MUGGLETON.

My love is remembered to Mr. Whitehead, and his wife, and Father Nicolls, John Lad, Goodman Thorndike, with all the rest of our friends unnamed, as those named.

A Copy of a Letter written by the Prophet Lodowicke Muggleton to Mrs. Mary Scott, of Bristol, bearing date October 12, 1681.

Dear Friend in the true Faith, Mary Scott,

I RECEIVED a letter as from you, written to Mr. Jenkins, dated the 8th instant, 1681, concerning your son John being troubled in mind concerning his future state and condition; and that he cannot by no means be satisfied about it; therefore you desire me to send down my answer concerning it, to satisfy your son thereabout; wherein you desire me, and all our friends, to put up our petitions to the Lord for him.

As to this, your request is a thing something contrary to the practice of this commission of the Spirit, for me to send an answer, or to take off the trouble of a man's mind, which I have had no experience of his practice of life, nor of his faith in the true God, nor in me, the messenger of God, neither do I know what is the cause of his trouble of mind, whether it be for some sin he hath committed, even some actual sin, for actual sin hath the sting of eternal death in it; for the sting of death is sin, and the strength of sin is the law, as the apostle saith; or whether this trouble of mind doth arise from his own ignorance in the knowledge of the true God, and the right devil, fearing God's prerogative power in election and reprobation; and that he may be a cast-away by God's prerogative will and pleasure; and who shall gain say it?

These two things are the cause of all men's trouble of mind in this world, both saint and devil: but actual sin is most generally the cause of despair, which doth wound the spirit of men, which is more than he can bear.

So that I cannot give any judgment upon him, neither good nor evil; not absolute good, because he hath not believed our doctrine nor commission; nor evil, because he hath not despised any thing declared by me. Yet this I will say for his comfort, that if sin be the cause of his trouble of mind, let him confess it to you his mother, as in the presence of God, and forsake it, and act it no more, and he shall find mercy and peace in his soul. And if the trouble of his mind doth arise from the other thing aforesaid, or any other cause but sin, then I would desire him to submit to God's prerogative power, to do what he will with him after death; do righteous and just things between man and man, and do not trouble himself what shall become of him after death; and I do assure him he shall have peace of mind for the present, and may come hereafter to the knowledge of the truth, which will give him the assurance of everlasting life in himself, as you his mother, and many others, have at this day.

These lines will prove a good prayer unto him, if he do but believe and do it.

This is as much as I can say, in answer to your letter, and as to your son; and I wish my words may take place in him, then will salvation encrease in his soul.

So I shall take leave and remain your assured friend in the eternal Truth,

LODOWICKE MUGGLETON,

London, October 12, 1681.

A Copy of a Letter wrote by the Prophet Lodowicke Muggleton to Mrs. Dorothy Carter, of Chesterfield, in Derbyshire, bearing date from London, February 1, 1682.

Dear Friend in the true faith, Dorothy Carter,

I HAVE seen two letters, which our dear friend Elizabeth Marsden (whom I always loved well ever since she was a child, in comparison of age) sent to our friend Mrs. Griffith, which two letters are in your behalf, as if they had been writ by yourself; the one is dated January 16, 1682, and the other is dated January 24, 1682; and I perceive by these two letters that you are sick of body, and have great trouble of mind upon you, and that your burthen is very great, and lieth heavy upon you, and that you are afraid you have displeased me, because I have not writ to you all this while. As to that, I shall deal truly with you, that I never was offended at you, nor with you, for what you writ concerning John White, but did what you required me to do in your letter to Mrs. Griffith; neither did that letter require any answer from me, which was the cause I did not write unto you all this while; but these two letters coming to my hand so lately, causeth me to write these lines unto you as followeth, as thus: I perceive this great trouble and grief of heart, and burthen that lieth upon you, it is but temporal, about your grand-children; if your trouble had been upon a spiritual account, I could have eased you of your burthen immediately; but; people would willingly have prophets to give them peace of mind, and assurance of their eternal salvation in the life to come, but would have the prophets to free them from all troubles in temporal things also; but this I would have you to take notice of, that prophets, apostles, and Christ himself, that gave those that believed in him the assurance of everlasting life abiding in themselves, it was to strengthen them, that they might be the more able to encounter and bear the troubles of this world; I say as Christ said to those that believed in him, *In me you shall have peace, but in the world you shall have trouble*; so that if a man have true peace in God, he shall rather have the more trouble in the world, much less be delivered from all trouble in this world: this I have found by experience, therefore do you mind your faith, which you once received in this commission of the Spirit, and the blessing I once declared upon you, and that will strengthen you, and enable you to bear those temporal troubles the better, knowing that you shall be free from them in death, and that there is no worse thing after, which is more than all the world can say beside, but those whose faith is truly grounded upon this commission of the Spirit.

And now, dear friend, I perceive there is contained in these letters the ground of your great temporal troubles, and they are about your own grand-children, and those two persons concerned with them. I would not have you offended, nor let your spirit be troubled, nor overcharged with grief, and especially where things cannot be helped, nor called back again; but let your joy be in God. Besides, I look upon it very expedient, that you might know the utmost of your troubles, and not to hide it from you; because you will be delivered out of all your troubles, which I am sure a wounded spirit would receive ease, if it did but know that this natural death would end those eternal torments, which it shall endure hereafter. As for those two troubles, which is, and hath been, I shall endeavour to satisfy you in the one, and advise you in the other.

First. You seem to be more troubled at the lesser trouble than the greater.

As for John White's neglect of binding your grandson, I did as you desired me; I spake with his wife, and left word with her, that I would have her husband to bind John Carter at the hall, and that he should order it so at the hall, that his time should go on from the time he was bound by the scrivener, so that the boy should lose no time, to satisfy his grandmother: she told me her husband did intend to do so, and promised me that her husband should bind him at the hall suddenly; and in a little time shortly after, John White, the same day he bound him at the hall, came to my house, and the boy with him, and said he had done as I had ordered him, and said that John Carter was to send his grandmother word, to satisfy her that it was done; so I thought all was well, and that you were satisfied, and did wonder that he should be such a great trouble to you now; nor wherein he is unjust, seeing he hath bound him at the hall according to law, and that he will make him a freeman of London from the time he was first bound, I cannot see any ground of trouble you need be at in this matter, except he hath been cruel to the boy since, which I have heard nothing of.

The second thing is, I know you have had great cause of trouble with your grand-children by Mr. Goodwyn, but you know that I would not, nor ever had any concern in Mr. Goodwyn's affairs, not from the first, when he married your daughter; for I saw he was not of a prosperous nature, only I was loath to discourage your daughter, or you either. I never did meddle in the marriage of his wife, neither was I ever his counsellor in any of his concerns whatsoever; neither would I concern myself now to speak of him, but only for your sake, that you might be armed with patience to undergo the trouble that do follow by reason of him

First, in that you are forced to keep his two children which he had by your daughter; and as for other concerns you have with him I know not, but I suppose it is certainly true that Mr. Goodwyn is dead, and that his wife would willingly cast that child there in the country upon you to keep for your own; but what advice to give you I cannot tell: the child is no more relation to you, than it is to any stranger; so that if you cannot send it home to the mother, nor put it upon the parish where it was born, you must keep it yourself. One of these three must be done.

So I shall leave it to yourself to consider it, and take leave, only my love, with my wife's love, remembered unto yourself and Elizabeth Marsden,

Remain your Friend in the eternal truth,

LODOWICKE MUGGLETON.

London, February 1, 1682.

A Copy of a Letter written by the Prophet Lodowicke Muggleton to Mrs. Elizabeth Flaggerter, of Cork in Ireland, bearing date from London, June 22, 1682.

Loving and kind Friend in the true Faith, Elizabeth Flaggerter,

I RECEIVED your letter sent by your son, dated Cork, May 3, 1682, wherein I perceive you are very much comforted, and have great assurance of all your four children being happy.

As to that I shall not discomfort you, nor in any wise weaken your assurance you have in your childrens happiness, either in this life or in the life to come; but am glad you are so well persuaded in your mind of them, you having the experience of their natures, and of their actions, by the light of faith in you, besides the light of nature, as they are your own children, and I not knowing any of them, only I have seen this son two or three times; but I never asked him any question about heavenly things, neither did he enquire after any. It was never my practice to compel or thrust men into the kingdom of Heaven, whether they will or no; neither do I use to open the gate of heaven, but to those that do know themselves; for where true actual faith is in the heart risen, it will knock at the gate of Heaven, and it shall be opened unto them. As Christ said to his disciples, which had faith in themselves, *Seek, and ye shall find; knock, and it shall be opened to you.* And of that laying, *To him that hath shall be given; and to him that hath not shall be taken away even that which he hath.*

These sayings are quite contrary to the reason of man; for, saith reason, must none knock at the gate of Heaven, but he that received faith from Heaven first? What need, saith reason, that he should knock at Heaven-gate that hath received the joys of Heaven by faith in his heart already? There is more need that Heaven-gate should be opened to him that wants faith in his heart when he knocks, because he wanteth that heavenly peace of mind which the other had before the gate of Heaven was opened unto him. And is it not fit, saith reason, that he which hath not peace of mind, should have some heavenly peace given him, rather than he that hath peace already shall have more given to him. And is it not more fit, that he which is in want should seek, that he might find; and knock, that it might be opened unto him, than the other that hath enough, and yet must have more given. And that which is worst of all is, that he which hath nothing, yet this nothing must be taken from him also. This seemeth, saith reason in man, to be injustice and partiality, and not equal dealings in God. These words might be opened, but it would be too large. But I perceive by your letter, that the gate of Heaven which hath been opened unto you, when you knocked, and the cause why, in that you had faith in your heart to believe in this commission of the Spirit, when you heard the sound of it in your ears, by our writings and speakings; for which you do thank God, that experimentally you can speak this, that by his last messengers you have attained to that knowledge here, and assurance of being an inheritor of incomparable joy and glory hereafter.

Herein the door of your heart was opened by these messengers declarations, as the heart of Lydia was opened at the preaching of Peter: for this I say, that every true messenger that is sent of God doth keep the gate of Heaven, because none but such persons as God sends, have the keys of Heaven given unto them: and there is but two keys, nor but two gates, the one belongeth to Heaven, and the other to hell. And God delivereth these two keys into the hands of those he sends; so that God's messengers are not only door-keepers of heaven, but door-keepers of hell also. I have known several persons in my time, that have desired but to be but a door-keeper in heaven; but I never knew any person that desired to be a doorkeeper of hell. But we his messengers are forced to be door-keepers both of Heaven and of hell; because God hath given these two keys into our hands; and these two keys that do open these two gates, is the knowledge of the two seeds of faith and reason. The key of faith opens Heaven-gate, and enters into that kingdom, and seeth indeed what God is, in his form and nature: and this key of reason openeth the gate of hell, and entereth into that kingdom, and seeth Lucifer, the prince of devils (even that reprobate angel that deceived Eve, which became the first man-devil, which begat millions of devils like himself;) his form being the form of a man, and his nature being pure reason, fallen from its purity.

This is not a usual language. But seeing, as I said before, that you have knocked at Heaven-gate, and it hath been opened unto you, by us, God's messengers, therefore to you that have understood the mysteries of God becoming flesh, by which you have peace here in this life, and assurance of eternal life hereafter, in yourself Therefore to you it shall be given to understand these three great mysteries of God's dealing with men, as followeth:

First. That God doth choose and ordain some particular man, and doth furnish him with revelation, to declare unto the people what the true God is, in the time of his commission. The first man God chose, after the fall of Adam, was Enoch; and God did furnish him with revelation to write books, wherein he did declare to the succeeding fathers of old, that were of the seed of faith, or seed of Adam his father; and this revelation of his walking with God, and what God was: he left this revelation to Noah, and Noah left it to Shem, and Shem left it to his sons, until it came to

Abraham, Isaac, and Jacob. So that Enoch's revelation and declaration to the fathers of old, and all that did believe the books of Enoch, they were as a parliament, to enact it as a statute-law to their children, from generation to generation, for ever. And so it was with Moses and the prophets, and with Christ and the apostles.

The second secret is, that great difference that there is between reason's Heaven, which they do imagine, and the seed of faith's Heaven, which they are fully assured of; for the seed of reason's Heaven is without substance; there is no persons with bodies in reason's Heaven; there is none but spirits without bodies; there is neither God nor man to be seen, so no joy nor glory at all. But the seed of faith's Heaven hath a real substance to stand upon; and the person and body of God to be seen, and the persons and bodies of the holy angels, and of men, and all other creatures, to be seen in joy and glory, in that Heaven that God hath prepared for the seed of faith: so that there is a vast difference between the seed of reason's Heaven, and the seed of faith's Heaven.

The third secret; that though the prophets and apostles have declared in several of their writings, of that great and wonderful mystery of *God manifest in the flesh*; yet, in all their writings, from Enoch's to Moses's writings, nor the prophets writings, nor the apostles writings, nor Christ himself when upon earth, did ever declare or make known, not plainly, nor clearly, that great mystery of the devil become flesh, and doth dwell among men; and that there is no devil to suffer eternal torments, but men and women, to the end of the world, and to eternity. I say, no writings of prophets or apostles have made known this great mystery, which concerns all mankind, but John Reeve and Lodowicke Muggleton, whom God chose in the year of the world 1651, as our writings do declare.

These things I have written for your sake, and the sake of others of this faith there with you. Take leave; only my love remembered, with my wife's love, unto yourself, George Gamble and his wife, and to all the rest of this faith there with you. I rest and remain,

Your friend in the eternal truth,

LODOWICKE MUGGLETON.

London, June 22, 1682.

A Copy of a Letter wrote by the Prophet Lodowicke Muggleton to Mr. William Sedley, a Weaver and Dyer, a Believer of the Commission of the Spirit, living in Southampton, bearing date from London, the 12th day of January, 1683.

Loving Friend in the true Faith, William Sedley,

I RECEIVED your letter, dated January 4, 1683, wherein you complain of your great troubles you have gone through in these late years; what in oppression, I suppose you mean oppression for conscience sake. And your greatest troubles, I perceive, hath been in the natural concerns of this world; in respect of your first wife being dead, and leaving a charge of children behind her; and I perceive you have married another wife, and hath some charge by her also, which, you say, are in number five; thus poverty must needs come upon you like an armed man. These troubles are common to all married men and people, both poor and rich, but especially to the poor that do live by trade; for if trade doth fail, poverty doth increase and grow exceedingly; for trade is a very uncertain thing, especially in a time of persecution; for trade and commerce hath taken the wings of the morning, and fly away in these our days; so that poverty cometh in upon the poor as a flood upon the dry land; this thousands can witness in this, nation, as well as you, for want of trade. And poverty is the great common enemy in the nation at this day and time; and in regard this poverty and want of trade is so common, and so natural in this world, therefore it is that no eye pitieth the poor, let him be saint or devil, righteous, or unrighteous. Also I perceive by your letter, that all the rest of your faith in those parts are backslided, and hath forsaken their own peace, and hath conformed for fear of the loss of some of their worldly goods, or fear of imprisonment, even against their own conscience; some only upon threats, others having lost some of their goods, for fear of losing more, or all, have submitted and conformed; so that now you are left alone: these are days of trial, but few are able to stand the trial, to keep faith and a good conscience; and especially in most counties in England several hath conformed:. so that in saving earthly riches, they have lost heavenly riches.; for they will never recover that peace and assurance of eternal life, which they once had abiding in themselves, hot while they-live in this world; for you may read in the Scriptures; that he that doth fight the good fight of faith, and holdeth out to the end of this life, shall receive the crown of eternal life and glory; but he that looketh back, as Lot's wife did, to fetch something that was in her house, which she thought might do her a pleasure when she was got out of the flames of fire and brimstone, so it is with those that go back from the principles of truth, which led them to Zoar, a refuge of safety; of peace and content of mind to free them from the fear of the fire and flames of hell in the conscience, which we see the Sodomites of this world are in; which makes them blaspheme against the God of Heaven, and persecute stedfast and faithful men; it is a dangerous thing for men that have tasted the good word of God in spirit and truth of heart for many years, according to the commission of the Spirit, which is now in these last days in being; and now, because of a little persecution, to fall from it, and worship that, which all the ignorant and unbelieving people, and those that doth not know God, doth worship. How doth such persons think to recover their peace with God again! Neither doth God regard such worshippers, neither doth God's messenger regard such worshippers, that can suffer nothing for their faith, and they will reap the fruits of their own doings, which is the loss of their peace of their own minds, while they live in this world, and the fear of eternal death hereafter, to save themselves in this world for a little time: for this commission hath laid but an easy yoke, and a burden which is very light upon the necks of the believers of it. Christ said to those in his time, *That his yoke was easy, and his burthen light*; yet those that would take his yoke upon them, must forsake father and mother, wife and children; if persecution should occasion it; nay life itself must go rather than cast off his yoke, else no crown of eternal happiness, life, and glory is to be had; this seems to the eye of reason to be a heavy yoke, yet Christ calls it easy; and the eye of faith doth count it easy. Still you say, that they have made a distress upon you already, and that you are left to wrestle with them, meaning your persecutors, which say you, according to reason, I am worst able: as to this I say, you are best able to wrestle with them, for these reasons: 1. Because you have suffered for your faith already. 2. Because you are a poor man, and hath a great charge of children, and hath little or no estate to lose; for poverty and a great charge of children, is a fortress, or a tower of defence, against your persecutors; for what town, or city, will persecute a poor man, to cast him out of the town, or put him in prison, that hath committed no crime against the law of God, nor the laws of the land, and that hath nothing; to lose, to bring upon the town a great charge? For you may, by the laws of England, throw all your children upon the town, and so shift for yourself elsewhere; and the town must, by the laws of England, provide for your children, and bestow them as they please; if they do persecute you, and throw you into the streets, then do you throw your charge upon the town, and shift for yourself. So that being poor, will make you the more able to encounter with your persecutors, and preserve the peace of your mind, and your faith, that fail not to the end of this natural life, that you may enjoy that eternal happiness hereafter: for riches of this world is a great snare; and many men, rather than lose this earthly riches, and honour among men, they let go their hold of eternal life in the world to come; because that is at a distance, and this is in present being. I hope these lines may satisfy you, and bear up your spirits in the day of trouble, and deliverance will come in its due time.

So resteth your friend in the true faith,

LODOWICKE MUGGLETON.

London, January 12, 1683.

A Copy of a Letter wrote by the Prophet Lodowicke Muggleton to Mr. Capp, upon his death-bed, dated from London, the 15th of March, 1683.

Loving Friend, Mr. Capp,

I PERCEIVE by my son John White's letter, and by that since of your own writing, that you are very sick and weak, even near the point of death; and that you have a desire that I would come to see you, which I cannot do at this season, because you live at such a distance so remote from me; neither can I travel at this time of year so far a-foot, as formerly I could; neither can I come by water, because there is an antipathy in my nature against it; and a coach would be too chargeable; for these reasons I cannot come to see you: I am sorry you are so near your death, as I apprehend you are, but I always looked upon you not to be a long-lived man, but that your life would be but short in this world; but should be glad that you might find the assurance of eternal life abiding in yourself, for the world to come, before your death; I have known you several years; I never knew any harm by you in my life, but that you were a very honest moral man, which I dearly love in all men that hath it; moral wisdom is commendable, both in the sight of God and good men; but spiritual and heavenly wisdom is that which speaketh peace to the mind of man in the hour of death, and giveth assurance of entering into death, and through death into eternal life: likewise you have had a taste of that truth which hath been declared by this commission of the Spirit, you know what I mean; you have in part owned it, secretly in your heart, but not publicly before men, nor before me, but I hope that secret faith of yours will bear you up in the hour of death: in the assurance of your salvation, and in regard you never did publish your faith to me in this commission of the Spirit, I cannot give that sentence of blessedness upon you, as I could had your faith been publick; neither will I give any judgment against you in the least to discomfort you, or to weaken your hope within you; but would rather strengthen your hope, and leave you to wrestle with death, that you might have an easy passage through death; then will you cease from all the troubles of this life, and, I hope, from the troubles of the life to come. Thus with my love and my wife's love remembered unto you,

I rest your friend, in what I may,

LODOWICKE MUGGLETON.

March 15, 1683.

My son read this letter and wept, and six days after died.

A Copy of a Letter wrote by the Prophet Lodowicke Muggleton unto Mrs. Rebecca Hall, of Arnesby, bearing date from London, May 1, 1683.

Loving and kind Friend in the true Faith, Rebecca Hall,

THIS is to certify you, that I received two pair of gloves from you, one pair for myself, and another for my wife, by which I understand that your husband is dead, which we are all very sorry to hear; for Mr. Delamaine and his wife, and myself and wife, had a great love for him; but we feared when he was sick before, that he was not long-lived, therefore his sister Delamaine and myself had a great desire to see him once more before he died, and were glad to hear of his recovery; so that we did not neglect that opportunity, but did come to see him as suddenly as we could, which was, and is great satisfaction to our minds, that we did see him once more before his death.

I know it cannot but be a great grief to you to lose such a loving and good-natured husband, as I suppose he was, yet your sorrows are not the worst of sorrows, but the best of sorrows, in these two things.

First, though he hath left you three children, I suppose he hath left an estate answerable to bring them up, besides your own estate you brought unto him, which will make your sorrows the easier and lighter.

The second thing is this, which is greater than the other is, by your matching into the family of the Halls, you have come to the knowledge of the truth, whereby you shall come to have the assurance of your own salvation, and the assurance of eternal life abiding in yourself, which is of more worth than the whole world; and this I say, if you had matched into any other family in the country, you would never have come to the knowledge of what you do know, and shall know, as to your eternal happiness in the life to come, though you might have been saved, being elected, if you had matched into another family, but you would never have had the assurance of it in this life; why, because you would never have seen the commission of the Spirit, nor the commissioners, nor the believers of it, as now you have: it is we only that doth make our calling and election sure in ourselves, so that our faith being built upon a rock, even the knowledge of the form and nature of the true God, which shall never fail, which all the people in the world, both religious and irreligious, of only these few, that doth believe in this commission of the Spirit; and for your own part, I did perceive by your writing, and your love to us when we were there with you, that you are one of those grains of wheat which the God of Heaven did sow in the field of this world, even the seed of faith, though but weak, yet it was sown in good ground, even in the heart, not in stony ground, which is in the head only to talk of, nor by the wayside, for the foolish phantasies of the mind, called the fowls of Heaven, to devour the good doctrine you received by those writings or books of your husband's, and those letters you received of Mr. Delamaine, and your sister-in-law, his wife; but I judge, and my judgment is true, that you received the truth in the love of it, and do advise you to prize those books of your husband's as much as you can, and I make no question but your understanding will be more and more enlightened in the knowledge of the truth, and grow in experience, and strong in faith, and in the assurance of your eternal happiness in the kingdom of eternal glory, where you shall be with us, your God, your King, and Redeemer, face to face. These lines I have written unto you, that your faith in the true God, and in the commission of the Spirit, might be strengthened and encreased to your further assurance and comfort while you live in this world. No more at present, but my love and my wife's love remembered unto you.

I take leave, and remain your friend in the eternal truth,

LODOWICKE MUGGLETON.

London, May 1, 1683.

My wife and I do give you thanks for your kind token you sent by the hand of Mr. Delamaine.

A Copy of a Letter wrote by the Prophet Lodowicke Muggleton to Mrs. Elizabeth Flaggerter, of Cork, in Ireland, bearing date from London, June 25, 1683.

Loving Friend in the true Faith, Elizabeth Flaggerter,

THIS is to certify you, that I received your letter by the hand of your son, dated May 24, 1683, wherein you complain of your own heart, that though it doth will to do that which is right in the sight of God, yet you cannot do it; and in that your heart doth will that which is good, and doth not do it, that which is acting; but to will ill in the mind is no action; therefore it is said, *Do this and live*; and it is said, *Thou shalt not commit adultery; and thou shalt not eat of the tree of knowledge of good and evil*; so that the not doing of evil is an affirmative action, for he that doth refrain from evil actions, it is counted a good action in the sight of God, and of righteous men. Likewise it is said, *Thou shalt love the Lord thy God with all thine heart, and with all thy soul, and with all thy strength.* This is a good action, *Do this, and thou shalt live eternally*; but if a man shall blaspheme, persecute, and defy the Lord his God with all his heart, and with all his soul, and with all his strength, as many doth at this day, this is an evil action; and he that doth this shall die a death eternal; for it is not good nor evil in the mind of man that doth make a man happy or miserable, but it is the doing of good or evil actions that doth make a man happy or miserable, therefore I say to all of the faith, that it is good to will well, and better to do well. If these two go together, there will be peace with God, and peace of conscience in themselves, which I perceive you have by your faith in the true God, even in Christ Jesus our Lord, as you say he speaks peace to your soul, and carries you through all your troubles and difficulties of this world; and I am glad to hear you have that assurance in yourself, and of his peace and love, that doth bear up your Spirit in these days of trouble in this world, which I perceive you have had of late in the temporal, but our troubles here in England are altogether in the spiritual. These troubles in the: spiritual are at this day all over England, and more especially in this City of London, so that no friend can help one another. This persecution for conscience-sake is against all professors of religion, and Dissenters of all kinds whatsoever, that will not conform; but blessed are those that do stand in the day of trial, that can keep the peace of their own mind; for peace of conscience is of more value to me than the whole world; and so it is in every man that is sensible; for if a man loseth his peace by conforming against his conscience to save himself, he loseth his peace, which is his life and strength; in seeking to save a man's life, he shall surely lose his life; for peace of conscience is the life of every man and woman in this world; and if you are but sensible of the truth of these lines, as I have been about thirty years since, what it is to want peace of conscience, and afterwards receive that peace of conscience which the world cannot give, even the peace of God that passeth all understanding. This peace is that which will enlighten your understanding, and quicken your weakness of Spirit, and give you boldness in your passage, not only in the kingdom of grace here, but to the throne of glory hereafter, where you shall see the face of God in his bright burning glory to eternity. This peace will take off your complaint of your spirit, being willing, but your flesh is weak and dull; neither would you any more complain of imperfections, for if the eye be single, the whole body is full of light; so if the conscience be at perfect peace with God, the whole man is at peace, no imperfections to trouble the mind. As to things appertaining to God, salvation, life eternal, or any matter or things of that nature, are utterly expelled. These lines I have written unto you, that your spirit may be strengthened in peace, for in peace life is set before you, and in unbelief and doubting is death set before you; the God of heaven hath, by his chosen prophets and apostles, and us the witnesses of the Spirit, every one in their time, hath set life and death before all people, by writing and speaking; but how few doth chuse life rather than death, and how few hath believed our report in this age! Thus I take leave, only my love and my wife's love remembered unto yourself, Mr. Gamble, and his wife, and the rest of our true friends in the true faith there with you.

Remain your friend in the eternal truth,

LODOWICKE MUGGLETON.

London, June 25, 1683.

Copy of a Letter wrote by the Prophet Lodowicke Muggleton to Alexander Delamaine, senior, dated in London, June 25, 1683.

Loving and kind Friend, Mr. Delamaine,

I WAS at Mrs. Hooper's this week, and she did complain to me of the sad condition of Our friend Ann Oakebread, now her husband is dead, and hath a great charge of children; I told her that the town, ought to maintain her children, but I know she will be loath to expose her children to the parish. Mrs. Hooper said, she would never do that, whatever she suffered. I gave her no encouragement at that time that our friends would do any thing in that matter, because of the troubles that are now generally upon our friends in all parts of England, and in this city of London also, so that one friend cannot help another; but since I have considered, that she and her husband both hath suffered many things for their faith, almost continually, above these twenty years, and hath kept their consciences free from any defilement in the worship of the nation; likewise her house hath been a house of entertainment for all friends of this faith in all parts of England and Scotland also; and she did entertain the prophet Reeve when she was a maid, and was his handmaid, to guide him to other friends houses, before I ever saw her; and since I have seen her, she hath not been wanting to express her kindness, in entertaining both me and my friends from time to time, as occasion hath had need, to the utmost of her power. These things I have considered, and am moved in my mind to write these lines unto you, knowing that as to yourself, you are always willing to contribute to such a good deed as this is; but my desire is to put it upon you to speak to others of this faith, to those that are rich in this world, in her behalf, because I am not willing to be seen in this business. I suppose it not convenient to speak to any of our faith; but those that doth dine with us on the 19th day of July, those are the most able of this faith, for it is not convenient to ask of the poorer sort of this faith; for if they give but one shilling a-piece, they will make a great noise; and besides that, they will look for the like to be done unto them upon the least trouble that falleth upon them; therefore I think if we could get a matter of ten pounds amongst us this once, it would do the woman a great pleasure; and as for my part, I will give ten shillings towards it, for the great love I bear towards her. I do think it will not be your best course to speak to any of these friends that are to meet the 19th of July about this business, because that day will be chargeable; but let that day be over first, and two weeks after will be time enough. My love to you and your wife,

LODOWICKE MUGGLETON.

June 26, 1683.

A Copy of a Letter written by the Prophet Lodowicke Muggleton to Mrs. Mary Scott, of Bristol, bearing date from London, July 19, 1683.

Loving and kind friend in the true Faith, Mary Scott,

THESE lines are to eerily you, that I have received the books again safe, and that I have received your letters from our friend Mrs. Jenkins, the last of yours, dated May 22, 1683; likewise I received from Mrs. Jenkins's hand both your tokens; the token of your love was five shillings, and this last was ten shillings. Your love and kindness hath far exceeded my expectation, for indeed I did not expect one penny: but I see that your love for truth's sake, I may say is almost boundless, in that you do those things out of your own free heart, without the least hint of any advisement from me; but I perceive the truth hath made you free indeed, that your faith hath built upon a rock, even upon the Rock of Ages, even upon the eternal God, that was in the form of man from eternity, and in time humbled himself so low as to become a man-child and grew up to be a perfect man, making himself capable to suffer the pains of death by his own creatures. This Jesus Christ is that child the prophet Isaiah saith to us, *A child is born, to us a child is given; this is that shall be called the mighty God, the everlasting Father, the Prince of peace*; and now is fulfilled that saying in this commission of the Spirit, for no people in the world at this day doth truly believe that that child Jesus is the mighty God now, nor the everlasting Father, but those few that do believe the doctrine of this commission only. This is that greatest mystery of God, God manifest in the flesh, or God become flesh, and dwelt among men. This is that great mystery which the angels desired to pry into, but God letted them, and revealed it to unlearned men, that we might declare it to unlearned people, as at this day, for unlearned people are the most capable to understand the mysteries of the kingdom of heaven;, and so they come to have assurance of eternal life abiding in themselves. Thus the, poor and unlearned people being filled with good. things, but the rich and learned was sent empty away. These things are fulfilled in these our days; and as for those books you have sent again, I did believe they would be too dear, which made me loth to send them at all; but because I could not furnish you with those four or five books single, as you desired, caused me to send you the whole volume; and I am very well pleased you sent it again, because there is never another left so perfect as that is, to be had for that money; and as for those five books single, which your son Markes in his letter writeth for; that is to say, The Divine Look-Glass. *Secondly*, The Interpretation of the 11th of the Revelation. *Thirdly*, The Interpretation, of the Whole Revelation. *Fourthly*, The Mortality of the Soul. *Fifthly*, The Transcendent Spiritual Treatise.

These five books single, if they could have been had, would have been five shillings a-piece, both great and small, which would have cost twenty-five shillings, for there is none to be had single of the Transcendent Spiritual Treatise, nor of the Mortality of the Soul, nor the Divine Looking-Glass, nor of the Interpretation of the 11th of the Revelation, There is none of these four books to be had single for any money, but what are bound altogether, and they are very scarce to be had also; therefore I would advise you, and all others of the faith, to make much of those books you have; for if you let: them go, you will never meet with the like again for; any money while you live. Notwithstanding that, shame and reproach I have suffered from writing those books, there are several persons of honour; that would willingly pry into those books, as the holy angels did into the mystery of Gods becoming, flesh; but as God would, not reveal this secret mystery unto the holy angels, because, though their natures were pure reason, that they might never understand that great mystery, how their fellow-angel, after he was cast down from heaven, became flesh, and so became a man-devil. This mystery did God hide from the holy angels, and is hid from, them to this day, that; they might never know that there is a possibility in the holy angels, whose nature is pure reason, to fall into, the same condition as their fellow the reprobate angel did; but God hath revealed, those two secret mysteries unto his our seed of faith, the prophets, apostles, and us the witnesses: of the Spirit only; and we have declared, and made unknown unto you that believe a prophet's report, to your present peace of mind, and to your full assurance in this life of your eternal happiness in the life to come, which no people in the world hath, or can have, but those only which do truly believe in this commission of the Spirit; therefore it is I am willing to hide these writings of ours from the great men of this world, and learned men, that they might not pry into them while I am alive; for great and rich men, and learned men, are generally of the seed of reason, which came of the reprobate angel, which he and his seed are kept in chains of darkness in their own bodies, till the judgment of the great day, when God shall raise all the seed of faith to eternal happiness, which they did believe in this life, and he will raise the seed of reason in chains of darkness, ever since the reprobate angel became flesh, when he deceived Eve; so am I willing that the seed of reason, that the great and learned men of this world, who are the children of that reprobated angel, should be kept in chains of darkness, from reading any of our books and writings, till the judgment of the great day, when God shall raise all of them to their eternal pain and shame: for this I do know, that there is two seeds, and that these two seeds, the original of them, came from two distinct persons, who were celestial, spiritual, and heavenly persons; the one was all faith, and the other was all pure reason fallen. Now these two persons transmuting their spiritual seed into mortal seed, so that now there is but two seeds of men and women in the world, as the scripture saith; namely, the seed of the woman, the seed of faith, which is the seed of God, and the seed of the serpent, the seed of reason, the seed of the devil; and of these two seeds hath millions of men and women came, both righteous and unrighteous; and here lieth our peace of mind, even that peace of God that passeth all understanding; and in that we know by faith without doubting, that we are of the seed of faith, and shall be raised at the last day to eternal happiness, where we shall see God face to face, in whom we have believed: likewise we do perfectly know that the seed of the serpent, that live to men and womens estate, shall certainly be damned to eternity; and when they are raised again at the last day, they shall never see the face of God, nor the faces of one another, but shall be in utter darkness to eternity. Thus I have written these lines unto you, not only to strengthen your faith, but to comfort your spirit in these evil days wherein we live: so with my love, and my wife's love presented unto yourself, and to your son John Markes, and the rest of friends there with you, take leave, and remain your friend in the true eternal God, the man Christ Jesus in glory,

LODOWICKE MUGGLETON.

London, July 19, 1683.

A Copy of a Letter wrote by the Prophet Lodowicke Muggleton to Mrs. Eleanor Sudbury, in Nottingham, bearing date from London, August 6, 1683.

Dear friend in the true faith, Ellen Sudbury,

THIS is to certify you, that I received your letter, by the hand of Mr. Delamain, and I am sorry to hear of your trouble you are like to fall into; but I considering this kind of persecution at this time, for conscience sake, it is not only upon you/but generally upon all dissenting persons every where. The decree is gone forth among all Dissenters, in all parts of England, and the golden image of common prayer (called divine service, and the Sacrament of the Lords Supper,) is set up, in every town and city in England: and whoever doth hear the sound of the cornel; (which is the citation or summons,) and doth hear the sound of the dulcimer, (which is the informer,) and doth not come; to church, and hear divine service, and receive the sacrament, must be east into prison; which is a far more easy punishment, than to be cast into the lion's den, or to suffer any other corporal punishment upon the body, as I have do lie. I look upon this to be as easy a punishment, as ever any power of a nation did inflict upon a people, where liberty of conscience is not granted: and truly, friend, what advice to give you in this case I know not, for I cannot advise myself, how to deliver myself out of any of these troubles; no other than to submit, and let the flood of this persecution run over us: and if we be swallowed up of it, it will be well with us, because it is for our faith and a good conscience; which is of more value than the whole world. Only this advice I would give you, in this particular; not to give or enter into bond for your good behaviour, for it is of dangerous concernment, though the things proposed unto you seem ever so fair, innocent, and just, which you may justly keep; but if one informer afterwards do put you in for the least misdemeanour in the world, the justices of the county must be judges then, whether you have forfeited your bond, and not behaved yourself according to the tenor of your bond, let your innocence be never so great, you must pay what fine the justices will lay upon you, or lie in prison for it: Therefore, my advice is, to deliver up your body into prison at the first, rather than be bound for your good behaviour; for who knoweth what the justice will call good behaviour? Keep the peace of your mind whatever you do, suffer merely for your conscience sake; be not guilty of the breach of any law of the land, nor of the law of God in point of worship; and time may produce deliverance, either by death or otherwise. Faith towards God, and in the true God, and patience in tribulation, will make persecution for conscience sake very easy, and bear your spirit up in all your troubles: and for your further encouragement, I shall give you the same advice as the apostle Paul did to the believers of his doctrine of Christ, in his time; he adviseth them to put on the whole armour of God, for God hath armour to put upon his saints here upon earth, as earthly kings have armour to put upon their captains, and mighty men of war, only God's armour is spiritual, and the world's armour is temporal, suitable to this earthly kingdom: and God's armour is spiritual, suitable to that heavenly kingdom above the stars, where his residence is. Now this armour of God, I do know that you and many more hath put on in part, above these twenty years, and now of late more fully. The armour of God put upon you, is, *First*, There was put upon your head, after you believed in the true God, and our report, there was put upon your head the helmet of salvation, in that the memory is placed in the head; so that you shall never forget it to eternity. In the second place, there was a breast-plate of righteousness of faith put upon your breast, when your heart set to your seal, that Jesus Christ is God and man, in one single person. *Thirdly*, You being true-hearted to that principle of truth you received, at the first sound of this declaration, there was a girdle of truth girded about your waist, to strengthen you in your principle you once received. *Fourthly*, In that your stedfast believing the doctrine of this commission of the Spirit, your feet are shod with the doctrine of heavenly peace. *Fifthly*, When you first heard of this heavenly doctrine, about twenty years since, you received then the shield of faith; which made you able to oppose strongly those Bemonists and Quakers, which would, and did, shoot their fiery darts of slander and reproaches upon me and mine; thinking to have made you revolt and decline from me, and from the truth you once received. *Sixthly*, That when you received the truth first, there was put the two-edged sword of the Spirit into your mouth, that made you able to contend for the faith, and to convince several, and to convert some, and to give judgment upon others, to eternity. So that the two-edged sword of the Spirit hath been put into your mouth, and it hath proceeded out of your mouth, some to their eternal blessedness, and some to their endless misery. This armour of God is still upon you, and upon all the believers of this commission of the Spirit: and this armour must preserve you still, and strengthen you to bear, and to suffer what trial soever befalls you in this life, until the day of your death. Then shall you and I, and all saints, put off this armour of God, and lay it down in the dust for a moment, and in the resurrection our God will make us of the host of heaven, which shall follow our God, our King, and our Redeemer, upon white horses, clothed in white linen, white and pure; this is God's armour we shall be clothed with in heaven, in the kingdom of glory. This is better armour we shall be clothed with in the kingdom of glory, than that armour of God was, which we had upon us in the kingdom of grace; which being exposed to all manner of sufferings, even to death itself. But blessed be the God of truth, that clothed us with this armour first, else we should never have been clothed with that glorious armour of heaven, which we shall never put off again to eternity. This is all the advice I can give you in this matter: I have been more large than I thought, being not very well in health these three weeks, nor am not yet; I grow old and crazy, and writing is now somewhat burthensome to old age, which formerly was very easy unto me, as these many writings of mine in the world, and what is not yet seen, will witness when I am gone, after my death: yet I was willing to add some comfort unto you, to strengthen your spirits in these days of trouble; that you may bear your cross the more easy, and take leave; only my love and my wife's, remembered unto yourself, and to your two daughters, and to our dear friend Mary Parker.

I remain your friend in the eternal true God, the man Christ Jesus in glory.

LODOWICKE MUGGLETON.

London, August 6, 1683.

A Copy of a Letter written by the Prophet Lodowicke Muggleton to Mrs. Ann Jackson, living in York, bearing date from London, August 29, 1683.

Loving Friend in the true Faith, Ann Jackson,

THIS is to certify you, that I have received, from the hands of Mrs. Hatter, your letter, dated the 3d. of August, 1683; also I received of her, at the same time, your kind token of your love, which you sent by her, thirty shillings, and one shilling to drink, in remembrance of you; which we did, for I was glad to see her, in that I have not seen her these several years, never since her husband's death, and before.

And as for your part, I do not remember that ever I saw you in my life; I do remember I did write to you many years since, which I did promise to your maid servant; which at that time, as I remember, did deliver me a ten shilling piece of gold, as from you, as a token of your love at that time. I suppose that letter, which you have received so long since, doth give you an account of the receipt of it; so many years ago since I wrote to you, and not hearing no answer from you of the receipt of that letter these many years, I have quite forgot what was contained in it; but I am very glad you did receive it at last, and am very well pleased that it was, and is, so welcome unto your mind, as you have expressed both in word and deed, in that your love hath far exceeded my expectation, or hearing from you any more. But I say by this your letter, that the good seed of faith was sown in your heart many years ago, by those books and letters; and your soul was that good ground, and I was the sower which God sent forth to sow in these latter days. Reeve and Muggleton hath sowed the doctrine of truth, which is the good seed in this world; and some hath fell by the wayside, which the fowls and phantasies of men and women hath picked up; we have cast some of this good seed among thorns, and the cares of this world hath choaked it up, as soon as ever it began to appear, and so came to nothing. Likewise we have cast this good seed, very much of it, into stony ground, and it came up very quickly into a blade, very green and pleasant; but when the sun of persecution did arise, it scorched the green blade, and made it wither and die. And some of this good seed we have cast into good ground; as you and many others can witness at this day, both in England and Ireland, and other places; insomuch, that they have brought forth good fruit, even the fruit of faith, some thirty, some sixty, some an hundred fold, of peace of mind, the assurance of everlasting life in themselves, while in this life, in that they did believe the true doctrine declared by us, the witnesses of the Spirit, they brought forth the knowledge of the true God, in his form and nature, which causeth them to see God; for no man can love God, but he that doth know God in his form and nature; therefore said, this is life eternal to know the true God, which no man or woman in the world, at this day, doth know the true God in his form and nature, but those men and women only, that doth believe the doctrine and declarations written in these books, set forth by the witnesses of the Spirit; so that we can truly say, we do know the true God in his form and nature, because we have the assurance of eternal life abiding in ourselves. Likewise all true believers of this third and last commission of the Spirit, hath the knowledge of the form and nature of the right devil; so that all fear of seeing the devil is taken away; for the right devil is man, or Mendinaeas; because the right devil is incarnate, the devil became flesh; so that no man of this faith need to fear, or be frighted, at the sight of the devil; except a man-devil comes with a warrant to carry him to jail for debt, or some other misdemeanor. But the whole world lieth in ignorance and darkness in the knowledge of the right devil, as they do in the knowledge of the true God. The religious, and the expounders of the scriptures, are as dark in these too main points, of absolute necessity for every man to know, concerning the true God and right devil, even as the heathen, that never had the scriptures to read; therefore all professors of the christian religion hath created in themselves a devil which God never created, a Spirit without a body, that is invisible, to fright themselves withal. These two great mysteries, and many more heavenly secrets, are declared and plainly opened in those books you say you have of mine, and of Lawrence Claxton; and I would advise you to preserve those books you have, for it is hard to get some of them you have for any money: and if you do seriously read them, I make no question but your understanding will be opened to comprehend those deeper and secret mysteries contained in those books, which will increase your faith and knowledge in those heavenly truths, to the great satisfaction of your own soul, and to the joy of me, the minister of glad tidings of life and salvation to you and others, even as many as the Lord our God shall call to the belief of the doctrine of this commission of the Spirit, and to the glory of our God, the man Christ Jesus in glory. I perceive that you were one of God's elect; that you were not overcome by the temptations of the devil. For those Quakers, and other professors, which persuaded you to fling those books in the fire and burn them, for they were all nought; I say they were all devils, the seed of the serpent, and will be damned to eternity; but in that you preserved them out of love and care to keep them, out of love to them, you have shewed yourself to be one of God's elect vessels, of the seed of the woman, of the seed of God; one that is appointed to life and salvation, which you shall have the witness in yourself, in the believing and understanding these heavenly mysteries contained in those writings of the prophets and apostles; which is a clear proof to me, that if you had lived in the days of the prophets, or in the days of the apostles, you would have believed them; and would have been saved by your own faith in them, as you will now be saved by your own faith in us, the two last prophets that God will ever send to the end of the world. For I can truly say, as Christ did to the Jews, who said they believed Moses, that God spake to him; but as for this man, that calls himself Christ, we know not whence he is; Christ said to them, *If you had believed Moses, you would have believed me, for Moses wrote of me*; so I say that whosoever would have believed the prophets and apostles, in their time, will believe us now in this last age of the world; for the prophets and apostles wrote of us, as I could prove by the scriptures, but it would be too large. And as for the Quakers reporting that I was dead, I cannot much blame them for it; because there was a printed pamphlet cried about the streets, that I was dead, and that I died in the Marshalsea, naming the day when, about four years since: the man that cried the book, in the same yard where I dwell, the boys knowing I was well, called the man lying rogue, and brought him to my door; and when the man saw me, he asked my pardon, and said he would stop selling of those books that day, and so he did; but many of them was spread up and down London, and sent into many countries, as truth; but the God of heaven hath preserved me to this day with my life and health. Thus I have touched upon all the material things in your letter; whereby you may know that I am yet alive. So that I shall take leave at present; only my love, and my wife's love, presented unto you, though unknown by face to us both, I remain,

Your friend in the eternal truth,

LODOWICKE MUGGLETON.

London, August 25th, 1683.

If you send any letters to me, direct your letters thus: These for Mr. Alexander Delamain, at the sign of the three Tobacco Pipes, upon Bread Street Hill, London, and it will come safe to my hands. I would willingly hear whether you receive this letter.

The Copy of Mrs. Anne Tompkinson's Blessing, given her by the Prophet Lodowicke Muggleton, dated in London, July 10, 1684.

Loving Friend in the true faith, Anne Tompkinson,

I UNDERSTAND by my wife, that your desire and request is, that I would give you the blessing in writing before you go into the country; it is not a usual thing in me to give a blessing in writing when the! person is near at hand, and may have it by word of mouth; but when persons are at a distance and could not have it by word of mouth, I have given it in writing to many, as is upon record at this day, as I know you are sensible of since you came to London; and I know your desire is to be bound in the bundle of life with God's elect, and that your name might be recorded in the book of life with the blessed of the Lord, both here in this world, and in the world to come. And to grant your request, I shall say this unto you, I have considered the tenderness of your age, even a child, and that the seed of faith did begin to arise in you about twelve years of age, but could not shew itself, for want of more years of age to strengthen your understanding; and that you are but a child as yet, though your understanding and experience hath been much increased in the knowledge of truth since you came to London, and that you have been called to the knowledge of the true God, and to have faith in this commission of the Spirit in the sixth hour of the day of your life, before you had done either good or evil; for there is but three hours in which every man and woman is called to life and salvation, either by God's service stirring up the seed of faith in the hearts of his elect, to keep themselves from actual sins, which never heard of a true prophet or messenger, or minister of God, or else they be called by a true prophet, messenger, or minister, which God sends to believe the doctrine declared by him, and that he hath power to bless them that truly believe him, as I know you do, and to curse those that despise him; and in any of these three hours of the days of a man's life is every one of the elect of God called to life and salvation; this is to say, in youth is the sixth hour, as it is with you and several others, which I know; the ninth hour of the day is the middle age, the eleventh hour of the day is old age. These things I have had great experience of; so likewise I have considered your innocency, your tender age, your great experience, and your strong faith in this commission of the Spirit; and to grant your request, I do pronounce you, Anne Tompkinson, one of the blessed of the Lord, both in soul and body, to eternity, where, in the resurrection, you shall see the face of my God; and your God in the kingdom of eternal glory.

Your friend in the eternal truth,

LODOWICKE MUGGLETON,

July 10, 1684.

A Copy of a Letter wrote by the Prophet Lodowicke Muggleton to Mrs. Ellen Sudbury, of Nottingham, bearing date from London, July 19, 1684.

Dear Friend in the eternal Truth, Ellen Sudbury,

THIS is to certify you, that I received your letter dated July 8, 1684, by the hand of Mr. Delamain, with the two cheeses, and that which was written in your note to Mr. Delamain; I confess it was a great, while: since I wrote to you; the reason was, I had nothing, of consequence to ground my letter upon to write unto you. I am glad to hear of your liberty of conscience still, but I perceive by your letter they do proceed against you still, as they do to others. This persecution for conscience, is not only to you in particular, but unto all persons whatsoever in cities and countries, that are dissenters; so that all persons that are concerned in it, are put to their shifts what course to take to deliver themselves from it. All people would willingly keep the peace of their minds, and their estates also; but it is a hard thing in these days to keep both; therefore it is that people run some way, and some another; some run beyond the sea, others follow the words of Christ, which gave liberty to his disciples, if they were persecuted in one city to fly into another; this is practised very much in these days, which is the main cause of so bad trading; others, considering that their persecution doth not reach to life, only a man must make shipwreck of his conscience, and conform, to save his estate, and to keep out of prison; and so lose the peace of his mind, which is of more value than all the world's riches; which peace of mind, if it be once lost, will be hard to get again, as long as they Jive in this world; so that there is but these two ways for you, and those of this faith, to preserve the peace of their mind, and their estates; that is, to remove from that place where they are persecuted, or to deliver themselves up to prison; this will preserve the peace of their minds, and their estates both, if they can submit to either of those two; but if none of this faith can submit to either of these two, they must suffer. The loss of both these things I have had experience of in these late years, in several persons, of this faith, because they could not bear the cross, but hath spoiled the peace of their minds here, and lost their assurance of eternal life hereafter; so that nothing but a bare hope is left in them, only to save the riches of this world; and others, for a morsel of bread, to preserve this natural life. And as for Thomas Wyld you speak of, he was twice with me about six weeks ago, with one of his daughters, and he hath placed her with a friend of ours, one John Thomson, a taylor, in Bedlam, his wife keeps shop, and sells hoods and scarfs, and many other things in Old Bedlam. If I had known at that time that he did owe you so much money, I would have persuaded him what I could to pay you; but I have not seen him since I received your letter. I sent my wife to his daughter, to know if he were in London, or not, that I would speak to him; she said that he was gone into the country, a matter of forty miles from London, but when he came to London again she would send him to me; but I will enquire of her mistress, when he comes to town to give me notice of it; and when I have spoke with him, I will certify you of it: this is all that can be said of this matter at present. Also I would desire you to let our dear friend Mrs. Carter know that Mrs. Griffith is dead; she died the 16th day of July, about six of the clock in the morning: I having the opportunity to write to you, I thought it convenient, that you might certify Mrs. Carter of it as soon as you can.

This is all at present, only my love, with my wife's love and thanks unto you for all your kindnesses, I take leave, and

Remain your Friend in the eternal Truth,

LODOWICKE MUGGLETON.

London, July 19, 1684.

Pray present my love to Mr. Parker, and your daughters.

A Copy of a Letter wrote by the prophet Lodowicke Muggleton to Mr. James Whitehead, of Braintree in Essex, bearing date from London, August 12, 1684.

Loving Friend in the true Faith, James Whitehead,

I HAVE read over your letter you sent to our friend Delamaine, dated July 30, 1684, wherein you make mention of me to be the judge of this great difference between Henry Hawkes and you, as if I should do justice between you two, which if it did belong to me to give judgment upon two persons that doth both believe in the same God, and in the same messenger of God, my judgment would be very heavy and terrible to that person which hath, through covetousness and passion of this Spirit, broke forth into such outrage, railing, reviling, reproaching, scandalous judging and condemning a man of his own faith, which hath been longer and stronger in the true faith than himself, and a more righteous man in nature than himself; but in: regard this: difference between Hawkes and you hath been produced and occasioned through your temporal dealings together so that it doth not concern me to divide the inheritance between two brethren of the true faith; but if the difference had been in matters of religion, or in spiritual debates or matters of faith, I would willingly have given my judgment between you; therefore I shall leave it to yourselves to agree or not agree, it lieth in your power to forgive him, upon his acknowledging his sin against you, because he hath sinned only against you; and if he doth not confess his sin against you, but is hardened, as old Medgate was against me upon a spiritual account, who said he would perish first before he would confess his sin against me; so it lieth in your power to deal with Hawkes, to cast him out of your society, and have no dealings or commerce with him, neither to eat or drink with him, and you will see that all the rest of friends in your town in a little time will follow your example, which will be punishment enough to Henry Hawkes; for I understand by your letter, that you did employ Henry Hawkes to buy a part of a house for you, but it seems he had a mind to get something by it, not that he would do you that kindness for nothing, therefore he bought it for himself, thinking you would willingly have given him five pounds for his buying of it, seeing you had a desire to have it bought for you; but you seeing he had, through covetousness, bought it for himself, not for you, he thinking to have got five pounds by it; but when he saw that you were not Willing to meddle with it, nor buy it at all, this occasioned his passion to break forth into such base and wicked, reproachful expressions, to one that was a better man than himself, both Spiritual and temporal: which if he had spoke such words to a man of this world, they would have made his body and his purse to have paid for it, and would not have left him worth a groat; for of all the men and women I have known, neither saint or devil, these thirty years, did ever act or speak such words to one which he had dealings with, or more especially to one of his own faith, or one of his own principle in religion; he hath derogated beyond all morality of nature, much: more of grace therefore I shall relate his bad unhuman words and expressions against a brother of his own faith, as asserted against him by several witnesses, as followeth: First, That Henry Hawke came with one of the constables to your door, and Doctor Milford, and your cousin Ladd, that is now dead, meaning John Ladd, and many other neighbours, which you can produce to witness Henry Hawkes called you liar and fool, saying, that you could not carry any errand over the way, in a most abusive manner did taunt and rail, and went from your door to the; Black Lion, were brother Thomas Ladd was met with his partners, where he did, to the great grief of brother Thomas Ladd, lash out behind your back with the most basest language, saying you was as great a liar as one he named of your neighbours who lies under that odium, and that you was a silly fellow, not fit to carry an errand five rod, and further he said, you had been distracted this half year. As to this I say, if Hawkes had not been distracted himself with envy and. madness, he would never have uttered such mad expressions to a sober man, that was more in his senses then ever Hawkes was in his life; for it doth not belong to that tribe and nature that Whitehead is of, to be distracted in his, brain; but distraction of brain belong, to the Gentiles, such as he is, Amorites and Moabites, and Canaainites; and the race of the Gentiles, but not to the Jews, who are zealous of the law of God written in their hearts; but the Gentiles, such as Hawkes is, through their experience of business in this world, and their passionate humours many of them came to distraction, and to be distracted in the brain, which causeth them in the heat of their minds to utter such expressions out of their mouths, which are unsavoury and unseemly, which causeth repentance, else nothing but hell followeth. As to all these base reproaches, and undervaluing words, and despising speeches aforesaid; I perceive by your letter that Henry Hawkes did acknowledge his fault unto you, and that you did acknowledge in your letter, that you have forgiven him this tresspass against you before. But now, last of all, in this month of July, 1684, Henry Hawkes hath committed a greater fault against you than the former; for, say you, Mr. Clarke, who owns the other part of the house, that is to say, that part of the house that you was about buying of Henry Hawkes, you having agreed with him. Likewise, you say, for no other cause as you know, than for refusing to allow the one half of the five shillings and two-pence charge which you said was needlessly bestowed, and that Mr. Clarke, your partner, and yourself, told the workmen that you would not allow Henry Hawkes it; but he before your partner, Clarke, and Richard Amis, did call you a damned knave, and damned rogue, and that you were a likely man to buy a house, when as you owed him money, and could not pay it. These are abominable words, which no man could or should have borne, had he not professed the same faith as you do; however, except he doth repent and acknowledge his fault to you, that you might forgive him, in that he hath sinned only against you in a high nature, you may do as I said before, cast him out of all concerns with you, even as the Jews did the Samaritans, have: no dealings with him. If the house be yours and Clarke's which Hawkes lives in, and that he doth pay one half the rent to you, and the other half to Clarke; if he be a tenant to you both, as I perceive he give a letter of attorney to any other man whom you can trust, to receive your part of the rent quarterly, or half year, as the tenor of your lease runs; but if he hath no lease, but a tenant at will, you may advise with Mr. Clarke, and turn him out of the house according to law, and let it to another to put him out of the house; then you may do as aforesaid, and free yourself from having any dealings with him. This is all the justice I can give you in this particular at present, but take leave,

And remain your friend in the eternal truth, both natural and spiritual,

LODOWICKE MUGGLETON.

London, August 10, 1684.

A Copy of a Letter wrote by the Prophet Lodowicke Muggleton to Mrs. Elizabeth Wheately, of Andover, bearing date from London, dated September 24, 1684.

Dear Friend in the true Faith, Elizabeth Wheately,

THIS is to certify you, that I have read your letter you sent to our friend Mr. Delamain, dated the 3d of September, 1684; wherein we have received the kind token of your love also; I am glad to hear of your good health, and more especially of the strong faith you have in the personal true God, the man Christ Jesus in glory: I know your faith in him is built upon a rock, a sure rock; which all the fiery darts of reason, (the devil in man) shall not prevail against you; you being fully assured in yourself, that there is no devil to affright you, but men and women devils. And your faith is built upon a glorious spiritual personal God, in the form of a man, whose nature is all faith, which faith is all power; and you being of the seed of faith, it is the great support of the peace of your mind here in this world, and doth give you the assurance in yourself, of that eternal life and glory in the world to come. So likewise, your faith in the true God doth give you the knowledge of the right devil, his form and nature; which knowledge doth keep you from all fears of the devil when you see him, knowing in yourself, that there is no devil to be damned but men and women: for as men and women are the seed of Adam, which is the seed of God, are appointed to be saved, because the seed of faith is risen into an act of faith, to believe God's messengers; and so come to have assurance of eternal life abiding in themselves, yet they are but men and women that are to be saved: and the cause why men and women are saved, is, because they are of the seed of Adam, which is the seed of God, and for no other cause. So likewise, there is no other devil to be damned to eternity, but men and women. Why? Because men and women are the seed of the serpent, and the serpent's nature, being reason fallen: and no creature else hath the seed of reason in it, but men and women; therefore it is, that when the seed of reason doth arise in man and woman, into an act of rebellion; and so the breach of the moral law, which God hath written in the hearts of men and women I then doth the fear of eternal damnation arise in the heart of the seed of the serpent, which are no other but men and women so that as Adam and his seed are all appointed of God to be saved, both of men and women; so likewise, the serpent and his seed are appointed of God to be damned to eternity, which are men and women: for there is but two seeds, that is, the seed of faith, and the seed of reason; and herein lieth your eternal happiness, and all others, in that you have believed a true prophet's report; whereby you come to know yourself to be of the seed of faith, of the seed of Adam, of the seed of God. This is that peace of mind, and comfort of heart, which the world cannot give; neither can any religious man in the world whatsoever, attain to this peace of mind and comfort of heart in these days; but those few that do believe in this commission of the Spirit. I have added these few lines, for the increase and strengthening of your faith, that your joy may be full, and so take my leave at present; only my love, with my wife's love and respects, presented unto you.

I remain your friend in the eternal truth,

LODOWICKE MUGGLETON.

London, September 24, 1684.

I perceive you have earnest desire to Mr. Delamain, to procure you these two books of Claxton's writing; namely, The Dialogue betwixt Faith and Reason, and that book, called, Look about you, for that Devil you fear, is within you. Friend, it is a great wonder that we could help you to both, or to either of them; but as it happened, Mr. Delamain looking over all his books, he found one Dialogue that was perfect, and no more, and I myself had the other devil book that was perfect, and no more. The price of the one Dialogue is 2s. and 6d. and the other 1s. and 6d. our friend Delamain will take care to send them.

A Copy of a Letter wrote by the Prophet Lodowicke Muggleton to Mrs. Rebecca Hall, of Arnesly, in Leicestershire, bearing date from London, October 18, 1684.

Dear friend in the true faith, Rebecca Hall,

THIS is to let you know, that I saw a letter of yours to our friend Mr. Delamaine, dated September 21, 1684. In which letter I understand you are like for to come into a great deal of trouble, about your not going to church, and not receiving the Sacrament: these two things are of late the snare to catch every tender conscience; and this snare is spread over all the land at this day, so that no tender conscience can escape being taken in this snare, but by suffering or conforming; so that his conscience must be wounded to save himself from suffering. This sacrament is as a net spread all over the land, to catch not only the fowls of the air, but also the fowls that fly in the midst of heaven, are catched in this net. To open the difference betwixt the fowls of the air, and the fowls that fly in the midst of heaven, (mark!) the fowls of the air be these, viz. the dissenting Presbytery, Independents, Baptists, and Quakers. These be the fowls of the air, that dissent from the church, and yet doth the same things among themselves, and do believe the same doctrine as the church doth: their God is all one, and their devil is all one; their heaven and hell are all one, and their souls are all immortal, and do slip out of their bodies, and never dies, but goes to heaven or hell. This is the spirit of reason in all men; and the seed of reason is risen more higher in all religious dissenters than in the common, ignorant, dark church people; that is, the righteous law of God is risen, and written in their hearts, more than in other people; which causeth them to be more righteous, that is, more legal righteous, to perform and keep the moral law written in their hearts, than those that are born churchmen, and never knew any other righteousness than to go to church, and to hear a church-boy say grace, and read prayer to a whole congregation. These Dissenters, aforesaid, are the fowls of the air, because the imaginations of reason goeth out of them, seeking and thinking by reading the Scriptures, and by, their righteous life, to obtain eternal life: yet being ignorant of the true God, in his form and nature, and the right devil, in his form and nature; upon these two foundations dependeth the secret decree and council of God concerning life eternal, and death eternal, to all mankind. And these fowls of the air being ignorant of these two foundations aforesaid, that is to say, the true God, his form and nature, and the right devil, his form and nature, they cannot enter into rest: neither can they have eternal life abiding in themselves; for their God is an infinite spirit, without any body or form at all; he fills heaven and earth with his vast spirit, the air and all places; he cannot be confined to no particular place; neither in heaven above, nor this earth, nor the air, cannot contain him. Likewise they have imagined a wrong devil; a spirit without a body, which is in hell-fire, and in chains of darkness; yet this chain is so long, that he comes out of hell upon this earth, and into the air, and at noon-day, to tempt men and women to murder, and adultery, and all manner of wickedness.

Thus the seed of reason in all Dissenters feedeth upon these serial notions; therefore called the fowls of the air. But the fowls that fly in the midst of heaven, are the saints that are Dissenters. And why do they dissent from the church? Because they know the true God in his form and nature; and therefore they serve God, because they know God; for it is life eternal to know the true God. Likewise we know the right devil, in his form and nature; therefore we do not fear any other devil but the men devils that seeketh to devour us, in our lives and estates; for I am sure no other devil can do us any harm, but men and women devils. And we, the fowls that fly in the midst of heaven, do receive the true sacrament every week; because we do, by faith, eat the flesh of God, and drink the blood of God, and feed upon the true God in our hearts, by faith with thanksgiving.

I have administered this sacrament to many, and you, and several others of the fowls that fly in the midst of heaven, have received the true sacrament of the Lord's Supper, in that they have eat the flesh of Christ, which is God become flesh; and they have drank the blood of Christ, which is the blood of God; for God could not become flesh without blood, for no living flesh can be without blood, for blood is the life of the flesh; therefore it was as Christ said when he was upon earth, *Except ye eat my flesh, and drink my blood, ye have no life in you*: that is, you have no assurance of eternal life abiding in you. Now you that have believed our. report, who are the witnesses of the Spirit, as you say, let us comfort ourselves in the Scriptures of truth, and in the prophets writings, that bears witness to the truth of them. These words of yours proceeds from the strength of your faith, which faith of yours will make you perfectly whole, as to the peace of your mind here in this life, and to eternal life in the world to come, because you have believed our report; and have believed our report, and hath believed our doctrine, concerning the true God, in his form and nature, and how he became flesh, as our writings hath declared; so that by your faith in them, you do eat the flesh of God, and drink his blood; so that your mind doth feed upon the flesh of God, and drink his blood continually. This is the true spiritual sacrament of the Lord's Supper, which we, the fowls that fly in: the midst of heaven, do eat of while we live in this world': this flesh of God is meat indeed, and his blood is drink indeed. This meat and drink doth satisfy the soul, so that it doth thirst no more, nor hunger no more after salvation, nor eternal life; because we know the seal and assurance of eternal life, abiding in ourselves; so that you, and all true believers of the commission of the Spirit, do, by faith spiritually eat the flesh, of Christ, which is the flesh of God, and drink the blood of Christ, which is the blood of God; so that you have received the true sacrament of the. Lord's Supper and that you have supped with the true God here in mortality, upon this earth; and all those that hath supped with the great God here, when he was upon earth, in that state of mortality, they shall be invited together with all the fowls that fly in the midst of heaven, to come unto the supper of the great God, now he is: glorified; that is, to sup with him in shame in mortality, and suffered persecution for his name sake in mortality. So likewise, in the resurrection, their shall be immortalized, and gathered together, to sup with the great God of heaven in glory; and, as the apostles did, by their preaching, invite the fowls of heaven in their time to sup, that is, to believe in the name of the Lord Jesus Christ, they did sup with God, so likewise Reeve and Muggleton, the two last prophets and witnesses of the Spirit, Gold hath chosen us two in this last age, to meet God's elect, the fowls of heaven, and you being one, and you have believed our declaration concerning the true God, how he became flesh, and dwelt amongst men, and hath supped with them here in mortality, you shall be invited to sup with the great God of heaven in glory; and that when you, and all the fowls of heaven, shall have to up with the great God in this last age to eat, will be the flesh of persecuting kings, and the flesh of persecuting judges, and justices of the peace; and the flesh of persecuting captains of trained bands, and the flesh of mighty men of war; and the flesh of pampered horses, and them that sat on them and the flesh of all persecuting men for conscience sake, both small and great; as churchwardens, constables, informers, and all inferior officers. This supper with the great God will be when he hath gathered his elect, the fowls of heaven, from the four winds, at the day of judgment, in the resurrection, when the sheep, which is called by John's Revelation, The *fowls that fly in the midst of heaven*, shall stand on God's right hand, and he shall say, *Come ye blessed*, because when I was upon earth in shame you believed in me, and believed my servants, the prophets and, apostles, and my two last prophets reports; therefore inherit the everlasting kingdom, which I have prepared for you before the foundation of this worldly kingdom was laid; so likewise the seed of the. serpent; as persecuting kings, fudges, captains, mighty men, both small and great; which are called in Scripture reprobates, goats; in the resurrection they shall stand on God's left hand; he shall say, *Go ye cursed into hell-fire, which was prepared for the devil and his angels*; because, when he was upon earth, you persecuted me, and put me to death, thinking in yourselves that I should never rise again. Also, you persecuted the prophets, and did kill them that did foretel of my coming; and ye persecuted my servants and messengers I sent unto you in all ages; therefore go ye cursed, both great and small, into everlasting torments, *where there is weeping and gnashing of teeth* for evermore. Then shall all the prophets, apostles, and we the witnesses of the Spirit, and you the fowls of heaven, shall sup with the great God of heaven, that redeemed us with his own blood: so that God himself with us shall eat the flesh of these persecuting reprobates beforesaid. That is, God himself, the prophets, and apostles, and we the witnesses of the Spirit, and you the fowls of heaven, shall rejoice in the everlasting damnation of these your enemies, the whole race of that serpent-devil Cain; the first man devil in flesh. For this will be the last supper that God will ever make with his saints, because there will be no wickedness acted between the seed of God, and the seed of the serpent, for ever, to eternity; and this is that we shall eat to eternity, which will be our joy. Thus, with my true love, and my wife's true love, remembered unto yourself I take leave, and remain

Your friend in the eternal truth,

LODOWICKE MUGGLETON.

London, October 18, 1684.

Dear friend,

I PERCEIVE, by your letter, you have proposed several ways to yourself, what course you should take, how to deliver yourself out of this persecution for conscience sake, and yet keep your conscience free, that the peace of your mind may not be lost; for I perceive that the churchwardens and the constables have taken their oaths at the Sessions, which the justices keeps to persecute their neighbours for conscience sake; so that the churchwardens and the constables are the informers against you, and hath put your name into court, I perceive for one month, which will cost you twenty pounds, by the law which was made in Queen Elizabeth's days against the Papists; but now in these days; it is put in execution against all dissenting Protestants. There is three ways to punish all kinds of Dissenters, both rich and poor: *First*, They proceed upon rich by Queen Elizabeth's law, aforesaid, upon the twenty pound act, to take their goods, and not their persons to prison. *Secondly,* They proceed against the poor Dissenters by way of excommunication, that they might keep their persons in prison, and not their goods; so that many of the rich do conform to save their goods; and many of the poor do conform to save their persons out of prison thereby. The law whereby they do persecute Dissenters As for meetings; the speaker twenty pounds, the housekeeper twenty pounds; and if any hearers be rich, he must pay five shillings a man, for a hundred persons, which they will levy upon his goods. This law was made by the Parliament since the King was restored; now you being rich is well known to the informers aforesaid, therefore your persecution is grounded upon Queen Elizabeth's law aforesaid.

Now you have thought upon several ways to deliver yourself from all; but I cannot say that any of these ways you have proposed to yourself will do you any good; but the remedy will be worse than the disease. *First,* You say you told the churchwardens you thought to go to your mother, and then, if she were questioned about it, they may say you were gone from home. This will do you no good, except you could carry your lands, your chattels, your corn, and all that you have in the house, and all upon the ground, along with you to your mother; for it is your goods that they come for, or your money, and not for your person. *Secondly,* You say, if they bring you into trouble, you say you shall be fain to move to some other, place. To this I say, unless you could remove your land, and all your other foods, to some other place, it will do you no good.

Thirdly, You say you think you shall be willing to go to prison, To this I say, they will not let you go to prison, neither will they put you into prison; and if you go to prison before you take your land and goods with you, else that will do you no good at all. *Fourthly,* You say you think you shall be forced to make over your chattels and goods to some of your friends, for the use of your children. This you may do according to law; but your land must be made over also; but this I must tell you, if you should make over your estate to any friend whatsoever, your condition will be seven times worse than to stand to the persecution of the nation, let their persecution extend ever so far. Therefore let me advise you, that is now a freed woman, a widow, that hath full power as any lord in the land, over your husband's estate, for the good of your children; and though there be overseers, yet the power lieth wholly in you, as it did in the man; so you are the lady of all, and hath the possession of all, as your husband had; and for yon to make over your estate to another man, you will become a mere servant, and your children mere servants to another man; therefore I will give you my advice and judgment in this matter: I have always given my advice and judgment for the widow and the fatherless, for their good, and those that did follow it did prosper; and those that would not, if they did miscarry, I could not help it. Therefore my advice to you, and judgment is, that you should not make over your estate to any man, nor to remove to any other place; but keep at Arnesby for the good of your children. Neither let your mother be grieved, but let your enemies proceed as far against you as they will; and when they come with their warrant to seize your goods for the twenty pounds, do you pay them the twenty pounds down quietly, and let them not be put to that trouble to seize your goods; and it will convince and melt the hearts of the most implacable enemies you have, in that you know you are an innocent, harmless woman, that suffers this only to keep the peace of your conscience; so that perhaps they may never trouble you more: if they should trouble you again, I am confident it will be a great while first. Thus I have given you the best and safest advice I can in this matter.

Your friend,

LODOWICKE MUGGLETON.

London, October 18, 1684.

A Copy of a Letter wrote by the Prophet Lodowicke Muggleton to Mrs. Ann Jackson, of York, bearing date from London, October 18, 1684.

Kind and loving Friend in the true Faith, Ann Jackson,

I SAW a letter of yours to Mrs. Hatter, dated August 27, 1683; in which letter of yours to Mrs. Hatter, you do order her to pay forty shillings to my wife; and you give it her to buy a piece of plate, as a token of your love. I confess your love is very great for truth's sake, for I know of no other inducement to move you thereunto; for I nor my wife never saw your face in our lives, I think, nor you us, neither had I ever any concerns in temporal matters with you; so that your faith in those books and writings of ours, the witnesses of the Spirit/ it hath opened your eyes to see, and your ears to hear, and your heart to understand the things that belong to your peace of mind here in this life, and in the world to come life everlasting; in that by your faith you do understand the form and nature of the true God: so that you do know God; for none can love God, but those that know God in his form and nature; which none in the world doth, but those that have faith in this commission of the Spirit. Likewise by your faith you do understand the form and nature of the right devil; which knowledge of the right devil, it casteth out all fears of seeing any invisible devil whatsoever, that hath no body. These are two great mysteries the Scripture speaketh of and upon these two, the mystery of God become flesh, and the mystery of the devil become fleshy proceedeth all other spiritual and heavenly knowledge, and secret decree and council of God, concerning the weal and woe of all mankind in the world, which is hid from the world, in that their eyes are blinded, and are kept in chains of darkness in their own minds until the last day, even to the end of the world; so that none can be partakers of these heavenly and spiritual enjoyments, and assurance in this life, but those few that have believed our report, and doth understand those two great mysteries aforesaid; therefore I may truly say unto you, as Christ did, when on earth, *Blessed are your eyes that see at such a distance, and your ears that hear, find your heart that understands these things, that you have read at such a great distance; whom I never saw, nor discoursed with.*

This is to certify you, that Mrs. Hatter was in the country with her children, at that time, when you sent that letter, dated August 27, 1683, only her son James was in London, and it was almost August again before she came to London; and upon the 13th day of August, 1684, my wife received the forty shillings of Mr. Hatter, and she bought a piece of plate, which is as you directed, and will keep it for your sake; and doth give you many thanks for your great kindness. I could not write to you before now, till the thing was accomplished, that I might certify you of the receipt of it; neither have I had time of late to write, through one occasion or other. Thus, with my love, my wife's love remembered unto you, I take leave, and remain your friend in the true faith, in the personal God, the man Christ Jesus in glory,

LODOWICKE MUGGLETON.

Pray James Doe deliver this letter to Mrs. Ann Jackson, directed for his loving sister Jane Doe, in the Betheren, in York, but for Mrs. Ann Jackson, of the same city.

A Copy of a Letter wrote by the Prophet Lodowicke Muggleton to Mrs. Rebecca Hall, of Arnesby, in Leicestershire, bearing date from London, January 20, 1684-5.

Dear Friend in the eternal truth, Rebecca Hall,

I SAW a letter of yours, sent lately to our friend Mr. Delamaine, wherein you sent him a token of your love, and another to me; in which letter of yours I find that your faith doth grow very strong in the doctrine of the true God being in the form of man, and in us the witnesses of the Spirit, which doth comfort your soul, and bear up your spirit, in the troubles you do and shall meet with, in this troublesome world; which I am glad to hear of your strong faith in that personal God the Man Christ Jesus, now in glory, as our writings have declared. And blessed are you that have believed our report; to such as you, and no other, is the arm of the Lord's saving health revealed unto.

Also I find by your letter, that your troubles are like to increase more and more. You say that your brother Barker told you, when he was at your house, that you was indicted for one month; and that at Michaelmas assizes; and that he wrote you word, that if you did not come to church before the next sessions, he thought that you might be indicted for three months, and in the court too. Now what he meant by the court too, I cannot tell; neither doth he nor you relate who it was that put you into the sessions court first, at Michaelmas, for one month; whether it was the churchwardens of your town, or the constable of your town, which you say presented you: which of these it was you have not declared, nor, I perceive, do well know; and why your brother Barker should write for you to come to church before the next sessions, else he thinks you will be indicted for three months. As to this advice of your brother Barker, you cannot do; for if you should appear at church, the minister must be made acquainted with it, and he will examine you, and you must stay and hear common-prayer read, called divine service; and then he will tell you of a sacrament that you must receive, and that he will give you a certificate to carry to the justices at the sessions, and so you may save your goods, and lose the peace of your mind, which is of more value than the whole world.

Likewise you say, you were presented by the constable of your town, and not by the churchwardens: and you speak as if you are loth it should come to an excommunication. Likewise you desire to know, whether you had best take a lawyer's advice, or whether they can excommunicate you if you go from Arnesby. I cannot understand how they should proceed against you in the spiritual court, to excommunicate you; and sue you, or indict you, upon the twenty pounds act also. For excommunication is always out of the spiritual court, and that extends no further than to put your person in prison, and to keep you there until you do conform, and to pay the charges of the court besides. Before they excommunicate you, they are to cite you before the chief doctor of that court, and to instruct you, and to give you time to conform; and after that time is expired that was given you, if you do not conform, they must publish your excommunication in your own church, by your own minister of your town. Do you know who it is that doth prosecute you in this spiritual court? Or do you know who hath presented you into this spiritual court? or whether they have proceeded, and how far, in relation to an excommunication? If you know these things, it will be your best course to employ a proctor that belongs to that court; he can do you the best good to get you off, for money, of any man.

Likewise I perceive by your letter, that they prosecute you in both courts, both in the spiritual court, and in the temporal court, where the justices of the peace are to be judges; and both for one thing, for not coming to church to hear common prayer, called divine service; and receiving the sacrament, which is a very cruel deed to the widow, and the fatherless children; that is to say, the clergymen, they are to have your soul and body into a prison, whereby to make you confess, that you might utterly destroy the peace of your mind, and that your faith might fail in you; so that they might have full power over you, both in soul and body.

And as for the temporal court, the justices of the peace, they are to prosecute you upon the twenty pounds act, made in Queen Elizabeth's days, and they came by this act for your goods, and not for your body and soul. The justices have left your body and soul to those pretended spiritual men, as the priests of the nation. I confess these things are very hard to be done unto the widow and fatherless children; to suffer thus merely for conscience sake, having broke no temporal nor moral law of the land; for the conscience belongs to God only to judge of, and not to man. You are edged in on both sids; so that it is hard to give you any advice to do you good: but this I say, you had better fall into the hands of the justices of the peace, rather than into the hands of the pretended spiritual men; because the justices will be content with your goods, or money; but the other will not be content without your soul and body doth conform unto their worship; which you cannot do without destroying the peace of your own soul, which is the peace of God, *which passeth all understanding*; a peace which the world cannot give.

Now I perceive by your letter, that you had rather fall into the hands of the justices, to take away your goods, than into the hands of the clergy, that will keep soul and body in prison, except you will fall down and worship that great image of common prayer, called divine service, and receive the sacrament to eat a bit of bread, and to drink a spoonful or two of wine, and so destroy, and make shipwreck of, the peace of your mind, and of that comfort and assurance of everlasting life, which you have received already, by eating by faith in your heart the flesh of Christ, which is the flesh of God; and in that you have drank the blood of Christ, which is the blood of God. This is the true sacrament of the Lord's Supper; for the flesh of God is meat indeed, and this blood of God is drink indeed; and as oft as you do eat of this bread of God, and drink of this blood of God, you cannot choose but remember that comfort, joy, and assurance of eternal life, abiding in your own soul, abiding in you whilst in this world; besides those unspeakable pleasures in the kingdom of glory, where you shall see your God, whose flesh you did eat of here in this life. I say, you shall see the same God, in the same flesh glorified, which you did eat of here in this life, in his bright burning glory, face to face, in his eternal kingdom of glory; which whosoever doth eat that bit of bread, and drink that spoonful or two of wine, in a sacramental way, as an ordinance of God, against his conscience, to keep himself from suffering, he doth eat and drink his own damnation, not discerning the Lord's body; he doing that which is so directly against his own conscience. It is a dangerous thing to worship a God, which he knows is not the true God.

Dear friend, I would willingly give you the best and safest advice, so far as I understand, in this business of yours, that you might keep the peace of your mind that your own conscience may not condemn you; that you may always look with boldness to the throne of grace. For the conscience of every man is of God's side, and pleadeth for him; and that you might come off the great troubles you are like now to go through, as easy, and with as little loss, as you can;—which is this; if you be indicted and presented into no court, but the court of justices of the peace, which prosecute you only upon the twenty pounds act, then I look upon it your best course to go yourself in person to one or more of the moderate justices of the peace, and plead with him, that you are a widow, and hath so many small children to bring up; and that you never broke any of the King's temporal laws; neither did you ever go to any private meeting, contrary to the act of parliament; you always went while your husband lived, to the church of England, and since your husband died you have stayed at home, and do read the Bible, which is the scriptures, and am very well satisfied in my mind, and hath peace of conscience towards God, and peace with all men; I do wrong to no man; I meddle with no man about religion; every man ought to worship God as his conscience doth dictate to him; and if any person should do any thing contrary to his conscience., his own conscience will condemn him; which if I should do, that which I am indicted for, before your worships, my own conscience would condemn me greatly, which I dare not do, though I suffer much for it: I know it lieth in your power to do me good or hurt; therefore I shall leave it to your consciences to do what you will by me; I must suffer it as patiently as I can.

Again you say you are loth it should proceed to an excommunication: I cannot blame you for it, because the spiritual court had rather have your soul and body in prison, that they purge out, through your sufferings, the sincerity of your heart, and that strong faith which you now believe, to fail, and question whether you may not be saved, though you do hear their doctrine, as they call it, and eat their bit of bread, instead of Christ's body of flesh, which you did eat of before; and that you may drink a spoonful or two of their wine in a golden cup, the priest hath in his hand, instead of that blood of Christ which you have drank many times of before, which hath proved water of life unto your soul; and that it will be *as a well of water springing up in your soul unto eternal life*: so that you need not come unto this well which is digged, and set up by the powers of the nation, to draw any water, because their well is dry; and you have no pitcher, that is, no affection in your soul to draw of that water out of the world's well, because, after the drinking of that water of the world's well, you will be more thirsty after the peace of mind, and the assurance of salvation in yourself, than if you had never taken it at all; therefore it is a dangerous thing for any man or woman, that hath tasted of the good word of God, that is, that hath tasted of Christ's flesh; for he is that word of God which was in the beginning; and hath tasted of the powers of the life to come, which is eternal; for it is he that hath purchased by the body of his own flesh, and by his own soul, that was in the blood of his flesh, being poured out unto death, and rising again, hath all power, both in heaven and in earth, to give everlasting life to all those that truly believe in him; which faith in him is to eat his flesh, and drink his blood; so that if those that have tasted of these things aforesaid, do fall away to the worship of the nation for fear of suffering, contrary and against their conscience, it is impossible, as the apostle saith, to be renewed by repentance.

I would desire you to satisfy yourself in these things following:

First. Whether you be presented or prosecuted in the spiritual court, and Sessions court, indeed, or but in one?

Secondly. Whether the church-wardens of your town did indict you to the sessions or no?

Thirdly. Whether the constables of your town did present you into the spiritual court, or at the sessions court only, or into both courts, aye or no?

Fourthly. Whether the minister of your town hath any hand in this business, against you, aye or no?

I could wish you to speak with the church-wardens of your town, and with the constable of your town, and with the minister of your town, and they will inform you how they do proceed against you, that you may know how to make your defence the better.

This is all I can say at present in this matter; only my love, and my wife's love, remembered unto you, and remain

Your friend in the eternal truth,

LODOWICKE MUGGLETON.

London, Jan. 20th, 1684-5.

A Copy of a Letter wrote by the Prophet Lodowicke Muggleton to Mrs. Mary Gamble, of Cork in Ireland, bearing date from London, March 6, 1684-5.

Loving Friend in the true Faith, Mary Gamble,

THIS is to let you know, that I received your husband's letter and your's, dated Feb. 3, 1684: and because I never saw your face in my life, to my knowledge, nor received a sign from your hand-writing before now but I have heard of you by the hearing of the ear, but mine eyes, never saw you, nor you me; therefore it is that I shall direct or write these few linens chiefly unto you, as a true believer of this commission of the Spirit, and of the doctrine declared by; us the two last prophets and witnesses of the Spirit, that God will ever send, while this world endureth. I perceive by these few lines of yours, that you have a true affection unto the truth, and to me the messenger of glad tidings of life and salvation, in that you have a full assurance of your eternal happiness in the world to come, as you have expressed, and as hath been reported of you by others; so that I can truly say by you as Christ did while on earth, that you *Mary hath chosen the better part, which shall never be taken from you*, in that you have believed our report at such a distance: your faith is so much the rarer, in that you never saw me, nor heard my voice in the streets: for I say by experience them words of Christ to be true, that *a prophet is not without honour, save of them of his own house*, or of his own neighbours: for this I know by experience, this thirty-three years that I have been in this commission, there hath not one neighbour, or acquaintance, or kindred here in London, as I knew of, that hath believed my report, save my own children: but I perceive you have read our own writings, which your father, and mother-in-law, and your husband, brought into that land. These three I have seen, and discoursed with in the days of their ignorance; and since they all believed, I have written letters to them, to strengthen their faith in the knowledge of the true God, his form and nature; and in the knowledge of the right devil, his form and nature: these two are the foundations both of hell and heaven, which I perceive you have heard, and read, and hath built your faith upon that rock, which no fiery darts of reason, the devil, shall enter to wound your soul, as to question your salvation, or to fear your eternal damnation; only I would strengthen your faith a little further, in what you have read in our writings, concerning these two foundations aforesaid, of hell and heaven, or of God and devil.

Mind, this God and devil were those two trees spoken of by Moses, which stood in the midst of the garden; namely, the tree of life, and the tree of knowledge of good and evil. From these two trees came hell and heaven; that is, eternal life and eternal death. These two trees were two spiritual bodies in the forms of men, as I have declared in my other writings; and they both descended from Heaven, and they differed in their natures; the spirit and tree of life was God the father, and Creator of both worlds, and his nature was all faith, by which he created all creatures that hath the breath of life; therefore he is called the tree of life. Likewise the tree of knowledge of good and evil was, in his creation, an angel of light, and his nature or spirit was pure reason; but he falling from his created estate, his glory was changed into an angel of darkness, a serpent, a tree of knowledge of good and evil.

Now from these two trees did proceed hell and heaven: likewise these two trees, because these two trees had two several god-like wisdoms in them; that is to say, the tree of life had the wisdom of faith, which is all power in him; therefore God created Adam in his own image and likeness; not only in his inward soul or spirit, but in his outward bodily form also; only his body was earthly, and God's bodily form was spiritual and heavenly: and this spirit or seed of Adam ought to have eaten of the tree of life, by the motions in his mind continually; besides the fruits of the wooden trees that was good for earthly bodies to eat, and have lived for ever in that state of innocency. Likewise the tree of knowledge of good and evil, it was a spiritual and heavenly body, cast down from Heaven, which lost his ascending power by his disobedience to his Creator, when he was a companion with the holy angels. This tree of knowledge of good and evil was in the form of his bodily shape of Adam also, though a spiritual body, and his spirit or nature was alt reason fallen; and why Moses calls him a tree of knowledge of good and evil, is, because the Creator hath written the law of obedience unto their creator in the seed of reason; therefore it is written, *Thou shalt worship the Lord thy God, and him only thou shalt serve.* Now, as all men and women in this world, by generation, doth come to be partakers of these two seeds, which came from these two trees, namely, the tree of life, and the tree of the knowledge of good and evil; now that man or woman soever, in their conception, doth partake most of the seed of faith, it is from the tree of life; and so it will stretch forth the hand of faith, and take and eat of the tree of life, and live for ever. And what man or woman soever, that doth partake of the seed or spirit of reason, which is from the tree of knowledge of good and evil in their conception, the spirit of reason in them will put forth its hand, and take and eat of the tree of knowledge of good and evil, and die to all eternity.

Now how these two trees came to be in flesh, and to dwell among men on this earth; that is to say, how he should become very God and very man; and how the angel should become very devil and very man: these are the two great mysteries that hath produced an eternal happiness to the seed of Adam, the seed of God; and an endless misery to the seed of the serpent, the seed of the devil; but these things are more large in print. It is the glory of God's prerogative power to make one vessel for mercy, and another vessel for misery; else how could we, that do believe in the true God, and hath assurance of his everlasting mercy, praise and magnify our God, our King, and our Redeemer, for his infinite wisdom, and secret prerogative decree, to make us vessels of mercy, if he should not, by his prerogative power, wisdom, and secret decree, make vessels of wrath fitted for eternal destruction; or, as I may say, fitted for eternal damnation, to the seed of the serpent, the seed of Cain. So that God's prerogative power, he being above all law, hath made a necessity of two seeds, and a necessity of an eternal salvation unto the seed of Adam, and a necessity of an eternal damnation to the seed of the serpent: and who shall withstand a prerogative power, that is absolute above all law; that made himself capable to die, and to quicken out of death into eternal life again? By this means be hath purchased an eternal life and glory to the seed of Adam, his own seed; and an eternal death to the seed of the serpent; else there would have been no eternal life to the one, nor eternal death to the other. And by this means hath the God of Heaven prepared a kingdom of Heaven above the stars, with thrones of glory for Moses and the prophets, and for the faithful elders of Israel, and for the fathers of old, and for the twelve apostles, and for us the witnesses of the Spirit, and for all true believers in every commission called saints, shall, in the resurrection, enter into that kingdom of glory, where we shall see our God, our King, and our Redeemer, in whom we believe in this life, face to face. Also by this means of God's dying, and rising again, or quickening out of death into eternal life again, which no life could do but the godhead-life which was eternal; by this means he hath purchased a kingdom of hell for the seed of the serpent; and this kingdom of hell must be upon this earth here below, where the seed of the serpent hath acted all their wickedness; and this kingdom of hell will be in eternal darkness, or eternal death: that is, a living death, and a dying life; that is, always dying, yet never dead to all eternity. These are wonderful things, which God hath appointed and decreed; and I know them to be true, and will come to pass in their time; and I do not doubt but that your faith in this commission of the Spirit will make you suitable to understand these great and wonderful mysteries of God's secret decrees concerning mankind, in that he hath been pleased to honour his poor creatures, the prophets, apostles, and witnesses of the Spirit, in revealing those wonderful things unto us, that we might make them known unto his elect saints, as I perceive, and do know you are one; which hath caused me to write so large unto you, being as it were a stranger, and at such a far distance, and would be glad to see you with these natural eyes, if with your conveniency, here in London, before I go hence, and shall be seen no more; for I am old, and cannot live long by the course of nature; but shall take leave at present, only my love, with my wife's love, remembered unto yourself, and to your husband, rest and remain,

Your friend in the eternal truth,

LODOWICKE MUGGLETON.

London, March 9, 1684.

And as for our friends here in London, there is put a stop for the present to that persecution that was before, only the meeters are a little prosecuted still; but let us stand still, and see the salvation of God, and we shall see this summer what the effect of these things will amount unto, whether for liberty, or for bondage.

A Copy of a Letter written by the Prophet Lodowicke Muggleton, to Mrs. Priscilla Whitehead, containing her Blessing, bearing date from London, September 24, 1685.

Dear friend in the eternal Truth, Priscilla Whitehead,

I RECEIVED your letter dated September 11, 1684, wherein your request and petition, as you say, unto me, is, that I would be pleased to give you the blessing of eternal life with my own hand writing. You do by me as Hezekiah the King, did unto the prophet Isaiah, when the prophet told the king, that the Lord had added to his life fifteen years more, which pleased the king very well, that his life should be preserved fifteen years longer; but this did not well content him, but the prophet must shew him a sign, else he could not be contented; then the prophet must propose what sign he would have, whether of these two, whether the sun should go ten degrees faster in the dial of Ahaz than was its usual course, or ten degrees backwards; the king was sure to ask the hardest sign; therefore the prophet said, thou hast asked a great thing, yet, notwithstanding, it shall be granted thee; so likewise I do partly remember, that I did once already declare you one of the blessed of the Lord to eternity by word of mouth, and you were well pleased and satisfied with it; but since that, I perceive you have read at Mr. Delamaine's in that you call the book of life, where several of the saints are recorded to have the blessing of eternal life and salvation pronounced upon them by me; so that now you are not contented with the blessing of everlasting life and salvation by word of mouth, but doth sue and petition, as it were, for a sign; I may say for a sign, and that an hard one two, because it is not usual for me to give the saints a blessing by word of mouth, and writing too; but, however, your petition shall be granted you. I do perceive, that though you have the assurance of eternal life and salvation abiding in yourself by your faith in the first blessing, in that you are recorded in the book of life in heaven. When that book is opened at the resurrection, you are written one of God's elect; but I perceive your desire is to have your name written in the book of life here on earth, that is, to have your name recorded amongst the blessed of the Lord, that the age to come that shall believe, shall call you blessed. You have given in your letter sufficient testimony of your faith to be true and strong in the true God, and in this commission of the Spirit; therefore, to grant your request, I do pronounce Priscilla Whitehead one of the blessed of the Lord, both in soul and body, to eternity.

Written by

LODOWICKE MUGGLETON.

One of the two last Prophets and Witnesses of the Spirit that God will ever send to the end of the World; with my love, and my wife's love remembered unto you.

London, September, 24, 1685.

A Copy of a blessing wrote by the Prophet Muggleton, to Mrs. Mary Whitehead, of Braintree, bearing date

Dear Friend in the true faith, Mary Whitehead,

THIS is to certify you, that I received your letter, dated May 18, 1686, written with your own hand, and with your own heart hath indited it, wherein you have expressed the sincerity of your heart, which I do believe: a child, as may call you so young, or as a tender plant that is watered with the dew of heaven, which makes; you grow in faith, and in the knowledge of the true God, as you say, doth cause you to increase: every day more and more. I am glad to hear that there is that well of the water of life digged in your heart, that will spring up in you unto eternal life, so that you may not go to draw any water out of the world's well, that is, the world's doctrine and worship, to satisfy your soul as to things of eternity. Besides, this I can say, as Christ did when on earth, in another case, concerning children, *That of such is the kingdom of heaven;* so I do say by you that do believe, even in your nonage as it were a child, so I say that of you and such as you are, is the kingdom of heaven prepared for. Likewise you say you long to be with me, and that you could live with me night and day; as to that, I perceive your love is great toward me, and other friends here in London, but I perceive it is not expedient at present; but wait a-while, and who knows but that good providence of God may bring things to pass in time, that may satisfy your desire in the natural; but this I can assure you, in things spiritual and eternal; that you shall live with rue, where there is no night at all, but all day; that is, an eternal day, or a day that shall never end, then shall you live with me, and with all true believers of this commission of the Spirit, in that boundless kingdom of glory, which no mortal eye can see, only the eye of faith doth see it at a distance here in mortality; but when our God shall change these our vile bodies, and make them like unto his own glorious body, then shall we see as we are seen of God, that is, when our bodies are spiritualized and immortalized, then shall we see spiritual bodies, as spiritual bodies doth see us, so that my faith here in mortality is the only evidence of those things we shall see in the state of immortality and glory, which will be fulfilled, when our God shall raise the dead; and we that die in this faith, doth die in the Lord with all the elect, God will raise first before he doth raise any one reprobate. This may seem to the reason of man at a great distance, and impossible to be done; but to a strong faith, without doubting, it is possible and easy for God to do; for the act of faith, without doubting, always taketh God's part, knowing that their is no time to the dead; therefore when you and I am raised again, we shall live eternally together; and, as you being but a child in age, yet a woman grown in faith and experience, as you have expressed, that your knowledge in the true God doth increase in you every day more and more, so that your faith is always working, so that your mind is of that world to come. These things I have considered, and of your great love to me as the prophet of God, it doth proceed from a true heart, being but a child for age, and an Israelite, in whom here is no guile; therefore, that the grace of God, which you have received already, may increase in you more and more, to the full and perfect assurance of everlasting life abiding in you, I do pronounce you, Mary Whitehead, one of the blessed of the Lord, both in soul and in body, to eternity.

Written by your friend in the eternal truth,

LODOWICKE MUGGLETON,

One of the two last Prophets and Witnesses of the Spirit unto the, High and Mighty God, the Man Christ Jesus in Glory.

London, June 1, 1686.

A Copy of another Letter wrote by the Prophet Lodowicke Muggleton to Mrs. Anne Delamaine, Widow of Mr. Alexander Delamaine, Senior, bearing Date from London, February 3, 1687.

Dear Friend in the eternal Truth, Anne Delamaine,

THIS is to certify you, that I received your letter, and your kind token, by the hand of our friend Thomas Ladd. I am very glad to hear from your own hand-writing, but should be far more glad to see your face, and enjoy your good company at your own house again, and so would many friends more here at London; but seeing it cannot be as yet, we may bear it more easy with patience, seeing you do bear it so patiently yourself, that is more concerned in it than we are. Faith and patience are two great virtues, which doth enable a man or woman to go through great troubles; faith makes a man to remove mountains of troubles, that is many great troubles, and patience, on the other side, doth enable a man to bear mountains of troubles, that is, many great troubles, and not sink under them, as many of this world doth. Faith in the true God doth enable and cause a man to love God so that faith, love, and patience are the three virtues that doth adorn a man or woman's life, and makes it peace. These three virtues I know you have had ever since I first came acquainted with you, which caused me to say I loved you more than other common believers of this commission of the Spirit, you following my advice in all things more than any womankind of this faith, nay, more than my own daughter's, which caused my daughter Sarah, which you knew very well, to express these words to a company of women at a woman's labour, that you, when your name was Anne Hall, were the beloved disciple of her father of all the women in London. The words were true enough, though I never did express it to any person myself. Indeed this cold weather is very unfit for you to take any journey, or to go into the cold air at this present. You give us some good hopes that your cough is breaking away, and that your nature is sound and strong still, and that, about the latter end of March, you do not question but you shall come to London; which doth increase our hopes to wait with patience. So with my love, and my wife's love, remembered unto yourself in particular,

I take leave, and remain your friend in the eternal truth,

LODOWICKE MUGGLETON.

London, February 3, 1687.

Postscript. My love with my wife's love remembered to Mr, Whitehead, and his wife, and to Priscilla and Mary Whitehead, and give her thanks for her kind token she sent me by Thomas Ladd. Our love to all friends there with you.

A Copy of a Blessing wrote by the Prophet Lodowicke Muggleton to Mr. John Mellford, of Braintree, bearing date from London, April 12, 1687.

Loving and kind Friend in the true Faith, John Mellford,

I DO understand you do truly believe the doctrine of the true God, the Man Christ Jesus, and how God became flesh, and dwelt amongst men upon this earth. This is the greatest mystery of all unto this world; and the second mystery is like unto it, how the devil became flesh, and dwelt amongst men, here upon earth. Upon these two standeth hell and heaven; and in the true knowledge of them both doth arise peace of mind, joy of heart, and the assurance of everlasting life; and on the contrary, the ignorance of both, not knowing these two great mysteries, doth arise the fear of hell and the fear of a devil, that hath no being at all in their sins, and of their eternal torments; which devil is that worm of man's conscience, that doth kindle a fire in the mind of man, which will never be quenched, because the worm of man's conscience doth never die in the body of man to eternity: upon these two dependeth all those wonderful secrets of God's council, which he hath revealed to the fathers of old, as Enoch, Moses, the prophets, the apostles, and to us the witnesses of the Spirit, as is declared in all our writings, which I do perceive you do truly believe them; else why did you ask a blessing of me by words of mouth; but that will not serve your turn now, but you would have it in writing. But I knowing you are capable to understand more than you have yet read in our writings, I shall inform you yet a little farther of these great secrets of God's dealing with men. *First*, He doth chuse and ordain some particular man, and doth furnish him with revelation to declare unto the people what the true God is; he did to Enoch, and he declared it unto the fathers of old; and all that did believe the books of Enoch, they were as a parliament to enact it as a statute law to their children, from generation to generation for ever; and so it was with Moses and the prophets, and Christ and the apostles. *Secondly*, That great and vast difference that there is between the seed of reason's heaven, which they do imagine, and the seed of faith's heaven, which they are fully assured of. Things, that though the prophets and apostles hath declared in several of their writings of those great and wonderful mysteries of God becoming flesh, and God manifest in flesh; yet in all their writings, from Enoch to Moses' writings, nor the prophets writings, nor the apostles writings, nor Christ himself, when he was upon earth, did ever declare or make known not plainly, nor clearly, that great mystery of the devil becoming flesh, and dwelling amongst men to the end of this world, and to eternity: I say, no writings of prophets or apostles hath made known this great mystery of the devil becoming flesh, but John Reeve and Lodowicke Muggleton, whom God chose in the year of the world 1651, as our writings doth declare. And now, dear friend, I do not question but you do understand these things I have written to you before, and by your faith you have set to your seal, in believing that God hath chosen me the last prophet and witness of the Spirit, that God will ever send while this world doth endure. This for your farther satisfaction and assurance of your eternal happiness in the world to come, when our God shall come in the clouds of Heaven to raise the dead, then shall we, that die in the faith of the true God, rise first to meet our God in the air; and because my faith hath no doubt in it, I do pronounce you, John Mellford, one of the blessed of the Lord to eternity, both in soul and body, and that you and I, and all true believers of this commission of the Spirit, that doth hold out to the end of their life, shall arise spiritual bodies, like unto the glorious body of our God, in whom we did believe in, and that we shall be capable to enter into the clouds of Heaven; for they shall come down, and receive us, and carry us up to that place, where we shall be glorified, as our God, the Lord Christ Jesus, was after his resurrection. This, with my dear love, and my wife's, unto yourself, and to all our friends there with you, I take leave, and remain your friend in the true faith of that one personal God, which did die, and hath redeemed us from that second death, which the reprobates, the seed of the serpent, must suffer, where the worm of conscience shall never die, nor the fire of conscience shall never be quenched to eternity.

LODOWICKE MUGGLETON

April 12, 1687,

A Copy of a Blessing wrote by the Prophet Lodowicke Muggleton to Thomas Ladd, of Braintree, bearing date from London, July 15, 1687.

Loving and kind Friend in the true Faith, Thomas Ladd,

I PERCEIVE your desire is very earnest that I should give you a blessing in writing, you being not content with the blessing by word of mouth, because you have seen or heard of the blessing I gave to those two virgins in writing, which you know very well, and of Mr. Mellford's blessing, in which he did, as it were, wrestle with me, as Jacob did with God, that would not let him God go, except he would bless him: so I would willingly have put him off with the first blessing, by word of mouth; but he would not be satisfied with that: I did plead against it; so that he prevailed with me to give it him in writing. Likewise you know, when I was there with you, you pleaded with me to give it you in writing; but I gave you no encouragement that I would do it; neither did I absolutely deny it, but was silent, and was glad I did escape so. But since I came to London, I understand that you have chosen Mrs. Delamaine and Priscilla Whitehead to intercede for you in this matter; so that they have prevailed with me to give you the blessing in writing. Therefore, that I might satisfy your strong desire, I shall say as followeth: I have had several testimonies of your faith, both in your discourse, your words and actions, of your strong faith in the true God, and in me, his true prophet; and this faith of yours will bear you into everlasting life; for this doctrine of the true God, and the right devil, the knowledge of those two, their forms and their natures, doth free the soul from the fear of eternal death; for men would never be so afraid of this first natural death, if there were not a second death, and hell, which is eternal, that doth follow upon the first death, and hell doth follow the second death; these three doth go, or join, hand in hand together, which causeth the soul of every man, which hath not the assurance of eternal life abiding in himself, to fear, which none hath in these our days, but those that doth truly believe this doctrine and commission of the Spirit, as you and many more can witness the truth of it; I say, is the cause that most men in the time of sickness are so afraid of this first death, because the second death and hell doth follow at the heels of the first death; for it is life eternal to know God as he is in himself, he having both form and nature; his nature being all faith, which is all power, which no man at this day doth know, but those that hath believed our report. God hath hid these things from the world, and hath revealed them only to his chosen messengers; for the world is so blind, that many think it a needless thing to know God in his form and nature, but think a good life and good actions a great deal better, as the Quakers do; but blessed be the God of Heaven, that hath blinded the eyes of the wise and prudent men of this world, that cannot understand that God, the Creator, can admit of any form or nature at all, and yet they do acknowledge that he created all forms and natures, both of man and beast, and all other creatures, yet had no form nor nature of his own. How blessed and happy are we, whom God hath opened our eyes to see by the eye of faith in our souls, that God, Creator of all forms and natures, had both a glorious form, and a powerful nature of his own from eternity; and from the knowledge of God's form and nature, we come to know the right devil's form and nature; and this is to be minded, that the two seeds are the two natures, or the two keys of faith, that doth open the strait and narrow gate that leadeth into Heaven, and into the presence of God; and the other key, of reason in man, doth open that great and wide gate that leadeth into hell, and into the presence of the right devil (one which has been so long imagined by the seed of reason, to be a spirit without a body) which hath been so long feared; but God hath given these two keys into the hands of none but unto his commissionated prophets and apostles, and unto us, the two last true prophets that God will ever send while this world doth endure. Mine, with the eye of faith, I have opened the straight and narrow gate that leadeth you, and many more into Heaven, where you shall enter into the presence of the true God, in whom you did believe, where you shall see his person in the form of a man, and that he hath a face as you have, even that same face which our God had when he was upon this earthy being glorified; you and I, and all true believers, shall be spiritualized and glorified: then shall we see our God, our King, and our Redeemer, face to face. This will not seem a quarter of an hour's time after our death; there being no time to the dead. Likewise I having the key of reason in my hands, I have opened that great and wide gate that leadeth into hell, whereby you may see many go therein at, and shall come into the presence of the right devil, Cain which they did imagine in this life was a spirit without a body, which they called a devil and his angels, they supposing that the devil and his angels were all spirits without a body, which they called the devil and his angels, that were reserved in chains of darkness until the judgment of the great day; but when they came into hell, they found that the devil and his angels had all bodies, and saw that they were grossly mistaken in this life; but now it was too late to repent. This doctrine we have declared, hath opened your eyes, to see the blindness of the seed of reason, that; lieth upon almost all the wise and learned men in this world at this day; which is the cause of that great fear of hell and of eternal damnation, when this first natural death doth appear. Likewise I have given to you, by print, and by discourse, many wonderful deep secrets of God's dealing with man, and how God always makes use of man to declare his secret councils, ordered by himself; but man hath declared unto man: Moses and the prophets were men; Christ and the apostles were men; so that God himself became a man, that he might be numbered among those holy men that were inspired to write or speak the Holy Scriptures, which is called the Old and New Testament; and now, last of all, God hath chosen John Reeve and Lodowicke Muggleton, to be the only interpreters of those secret mysteries, hidden in the Scriptures, according to those words God spake to John Reeve, which said, *I home given thee understanding of my mind in the Scriptures, above all the men in the world*; which words of God hath proved true, both by our writings and speakings, as I know you can very well experience the truth of it, in that you have believed the prophet's report; for without faith in the prophet there is nothing can be done. So that by faith we know the worlds were framed by the word of God; and it was God's own faith that moved him to speak those words that framed the world; in that he said, Let such a thing be so, and it was so. So likewise it is by faith that you came to understand those hidden mysteries, and deep secrets, which God hath revealed unto us, his messengers, which we have declared unto you; so that, by your faith in God's messengers, it is given to you to overcome the motions of reason in yourself, and to overcome the enemy without you; so that it is given to you to eat of the tree of life, which is in the midst of the Paradise of God; and it is given you to eat of the hidden manna, and to have that white stone in your heart, and in thee a new name written by the finger of your own faith, which no man knoweth, saving he that receiveth it. This is the true sacrament which I have administered to you, and to many in my time, in that they eat of the tree of fife, which is the flesh of Christ, the same that stood in the midst of the Paradise of God; Christ being the same God, and tree of life, as stood in the midst of Paradise in the days of Adam; and in eating of the hidden manna, is when the mind of man doth, by faith, feed upon those heavenly mysteries, and deep secrets of God's council and decree, which God hath revealed unto his servants the prophets, apostles, and us, the witnesses of the Spirit, as we have declared in all our writings, as the mystery of God's form and nature, and how God became flesh; and the right devil, of his form and nature, and how he became flesh, which is a great mystery, with many other deep secrets, which are hid from all the world besides: therefore by the spirit of revelation this hidden manna to your great satisfaction, so that you need not hunger no more after the assurance of your salvation; and this white stone, which is given unto you, is your faith, that hath purified your heart, in that you have eat of the tree of life, and have eat of the hidden manna: So that, by faith in the blood of God, your heart is cleansed and made white as snow, therefore called a white stone, because your heart is enlightened in the knowledge of the true God, and in all those wonderful deep mysteries and secret councils of God, which is hid in the Scriptures, which we have declared unto you; and the hearts of all unbelievers may be called black, stony hearts; because their hearts are overspread with blindness, and thick darkness, therefore may be called black stony hearts: so that they can neither see with their eyes, nor hear with their ears, nor understand with their hearts, that they may be saved. And as for a new name written, which none knoweth saving he that receiveth it, this name is to be called the Son of God; that is, he that hath the assurance of eternal life in himself, hath the white stone in his heart, and hath an assurance abiding in himself that he is an elect vessel, and that he is a Son of God, which is the new name written in his heart, which no man else in the world can know, but he that hath received it, as you have done. These things I have written unto you for your greater satisfaction, knowing that you do truly understand these great and deep mysteries, spoken aforesaid in this letter; and for the further satisfaction of your mind, and strengthening of your faith, I do declare you, Thomas Ladd, one of the blessed of the Lord, both in soul and body, to eternity.

Written by me,

LODOWICKE MUGGLETON,

One of the two last Prophets and Witnesses of the Spirit unto the High and Mighty God the Man Christ Jesus in Glory.

London, the 15th of July, 1687,

A Copy of a Blessing wrote by the Prophet Lodowicke Muggleton to Mr. James Whitehead, of Braintree, bearing date from London, August 27, 1687.

Dear and loving Friend in the true Faith, James Whitehead,

I RECEIVED your letter by the hand of our friend Ann Delamaine, dated August the 24th, in the year 1687, wherein I perceive you do follow the example of others that are far more younger in the true faith than yourself is; for I think you may be esteemed the father of all the believers of this commission of the Spirit that is in your town. And indeed I have written more letters to you than to all the people in that town; and I have justified your faith and your person to be one of the saved of the Lord in all my writings unto you, besides the blessing of eternal life in the world to come, by word of mouth; yet all this will not satisfy you, without I give you a blessing of eternal happiness with my own hand-writing; which request of yours I cannot well deny, knowing you so long to be a true believer, and a chosen vessel in the seed which God hath elected, even the seed of Adam, which is the seed of God; and as you say you was like that lost sheep, that wandered from the ninety and nine sheep that were never lost, and so never were found by God's shepherd; for all God's sheep were lost in Adam's fall, and are found again by the second Adam, the Lord from Heaven; therefore it was Christ said he came to seek and to save that which wets lost, and he came to none but to the lost sheep of the house of Israel; and this I can say, though God hath chosen me to be the last true shepherd unto this bloody unbelieving worlds these five-and-thirty years, there is not one man nor woman that hath believed our report, but those that were lost. So that it is happy for you, and all the rest, that they were of those lost sheep, which were lost in the fall of the first Adam, those only are found by the second Adam, the Lord Jesus Christ, the only true God. But all those that did fall in the fallen angels fall, were never found any more, neither by God himself, nor by his prophets, nor by his apostles, nor by us, the two last witnesses of the Spirit: they are left in utter darkness in their fallen state, that think they see, but are stark blind; and *have ears, but hear not*; and have hearts, but understand not any heavenly mysteries at all, yet conceited in themselves that their wisdom of reason is wiser than the wisdom of faith, which is Gods own nature; and those be those ninety and nine just persons that never were lost, nor needed no repentance; therefore God hath left them to perish in their own conceits to eternity. So that it is happy for you that you are one of those lost sheep; for I was a lost sheep myself for several years, and whither to go I could not tell; but in the year 51, I was found of God himself twice in that year, and yet I knew not God, neither in his form nor his nature; but in the month of April, in the same year, there fell upon me a great trouble of mind about my salvation, and in the multitude of the thoughts of my heart, there arose the spirit of revelation in me, which opened the Scriptures unto me, and that spirit of revelation did grow and increase in me exceedingly: so that no question was too hard for me to answer; and I was well pleased, and was well satisfied, and did not mind what became of all the people in the world besides; and was resolved to live a private life, and not to discourse with any man more about religion. So this continued with me, till the month of February, in the same year, God spake to John Reeve, by voice of words, to the hearing of the ear; then God chose John Reeve to be his last messenger, and gave me to be his mouth, as he did Aaron to be Moses' mouth; so that I have been chosen of God twice in one year, as aforesaid; which forced me to be the publicest man in the world; and in God sparing my life so long upon this earth, I came to understand the Scriptures, and to understand the tribes of Israel, and to distinguish between the Heathen and the Jews; and how God had placed the priesthood upon the tribe of Levi, in that Abraham did pay tithes unto Melchisedech, which was the true God and Creator in those days; and Abraham paid tithes unto him in the person of Levi before Levi was born. So that Abraham did act the person of Levi, signifying that the priesthood should be confirmed upon that tribe; therefore God did chuse Aaron to be Moses' mouth, Aaron being the first high priest that God ever chose, or did ordain, which did continue many generations; and now, in this last age of the world, God hath chosen one of that tribe of Levi to be the Lord's high priest in this latter age, according to those words God spake unto John Reeve, in that he said, *I have given thee* Lodowicke Muggleton *to be thy mouth*; and this is to be minded, that the Lord's high priest had always power to bless and curse: but our commission is altogether spiritual, therefore the blessings and the curses are all spiritual: also it reaches to eternal life, and to eternal death. These things I know you will understand, because you are of the tribe of Levi, as I am; and I have the greatest respect for you, being of that tribe, hath caused me thus to write; and knowing that your judgment will be informed some more than it was before; therefore I shall not trouble you, nor myself neither, to enlarge any farther, only I do declare and pronounce you, James Whitehead, one of the blessed of the Lord, both in soul and body, to all eternity.

So resteth your friend in the true faith,

LODOWICKE MUGGLETON.

August 27, in the year 1687.

A Copy of a Letter wrote by the Prophet Lodowicke Muggleton to Mary Gamble, dated August 29, 1687.

Loving and kind friend in the true faith, Mary Gamble,

THIS is to certify you, that I received your letter, dated the 9th of July, 1687, which Mr. Rogers caused to be left at my house, for I was in the country when Mr. Rogers was at my house; so that I never saw, him, nor he me, which I was sorry that it was my lot to miss of him; but the chiefest matter of concernment in your letter, I perceive, is concerning, a sister of yours, that is now afflicted, as you say, with very wicked, vile,: blasphemous, evil thoughts, and cannot get rid of them by any means. You say she hath had what spiritual comforts you thought needful; but you say evil tomes, and turns it all aside., You say she hath taken physick several times, and been let blood, yet it is all one. You say she desires in her spirit, and by prayer, that it might please the Lord to remove that evil from her; for it hath made her despair of ever finding mercy. You say, though you tell her that Mary Magdalen had seven devils cast out of her, and many more of the elect, yet she thinks her condition worst. You say, she would willingly use all the remedies that can be thought on, and hath a desire to see me; you say truly you are free, if the rest of her friends would consent. You say you fear it will produce madness, if it run too long. You say, to all outward appearance, she seemeth to be well enough. You say, O! that it might please God, by his prophet, or some other way, to rid this poor soul of her torments. This is the whole substance concerning your sister.

To which I shall give you this answer as followeth: in the first place I do not know your sister's name, neither do I know the cause of this trouble of her mind, or that melancholy spirit that is produced in her, whether it be from some sins which she hath committed, but loth to confess it to her sister, or any other, for fear of shame, if it should be known: for secret sins hath generally a secret punishment in the mind: pr whether trouble of her mind doth arise for want of assurance of her salvation in the world, to come; from one of the two that melancholy spirit doth generally arise, which doth cause a despairing in the mind; and it was very ill done to give a woman that hath a melancholy troubled spirit, to give her physic, or let her blood. It was the only means to procure an absolute despair, and to procure madness of. That is the cause the keepers of Bedlam doth practise to every person that is distempered in the brain; by physic and letting of blood, they make the spirit of the person so weak, that they can never get strength in the brain more to the day of their death. But if you had given her nothing but kitchen physic, that is, all kinds of broths, or spoon-meats, your sister's spirits would have been strengthened, and have been made strong, to reason out those melancholy thoughts: yet, notwithstanding, if your sisters trouble of mind doth arise from either of those two causes aforesaid, or any other cause whatsoever, let her confess it to you, her sister; and if she can but believe that I am a true prophet of the Lord, and hath power to bless some to eternity, and to curse some to eternity, as yourself and several others hath believed, and are blessed both in soul and body to eternity; and you have assurance of eternal life abiding in yourself, by the blessing and faith you have in me that God hath sent; for without faith in God's messengers it is impossible to please God: therefore I shall say this unto your sister, though unknown unto me, that if she doth declare the true ground and cause how this melancholy did first arise in her thoughts to you, her sister, Mary Gamble, and to nobody else, it shall be as well as if she had declared it unto me myself. And let the cause be what it will, I will assure her, if she can but believe my words in this letter, that her sins are forgiven her, and that her faith in me shall give the assurance of everlasting life that shall abide in herself. Thus, with my love remembered to your sister unknown, and unto you, Mary Gamble, and to your husband in particular,

So resteth your friend in the true faith of the true personal God, the Lord Jesus Christ, upon his throne of glory,

LODOWICKE MUGGLETON.

And if your sister can read print-hand, let her read our books, and if she doth but understand what she reads, it will be great satisfaction to her mind, and cast out all evil thoughts, and will settle her mind in peace.

August 29, 1687.

A Copy of a Blessing wrote by the Prophet Lodowicke Muggleton to Mrs. Mary Whitehead, the Wife of Mr. James Whitehead, of Braintree, bearing date from London, November 17, 1687.

Dear friend in the true faith, Mary Whitehead, the Wife of James Whitehead,

I UNDERSTAND by your husband that you are not satisfied with the blessing which I gave unto you by word of mouth, except I give it you in writing, as I have to several others of this faith. I had thoughts never to have given the blessing in writing to any person more, which had received it by word of mouth before; for that blessing by word of mouth will be as sure and true as the other, in case they that have it by word of mouth, doth hold out in their faith to the end of their lives, and not rebel against it, as some which you know have done; but indeed I never did knew any person, neither man nor woman, that did revolt or rebel, which had the blessing by me in writing, not this five and thirty years; but because you made your husband your advocate unto me in this thing, I having no writing nor request from your own hand, nor your own mouth, as I have had from all others, I may say, as one did in the Scriptures, thou hast asked a great thing, yet, notwithstanding, your request shall be granted in this thing. I always had a respect for you in the days of your ignorance, because you did not speak against this commission of the Spirit, though you could not truly believe it; but since you have truly believed the doctrine declared by this commission of the Spirit, wherein you have received in your understanding the knowledge of the true God, in his form and nature, and the right devil, in his form and nature, with many more heavenly mysteries and secrets of God's dealings with mankind; and in that you have believed my report, and have owned me to be the last true prophet that God will ever send to this bloody unbelieving world, while this world doth endure, and that I have power to give you a blessing of everlasting life, both by word of mouth, and by writing, by this I do know, that you do set to your seal that I have that power from the true God, as I have declared in all my writing; therefore your request in this thing shall be granted you. This is all I shall say unto you, my dear friend Mary Whitehead, the wife of James Whitehead, I do declare you one of the blessed of the Lard, both in soul and body, to eternity.

Written by

LODOWICKE MUGGLETON,

One of the two last Prophets and Witnesses of the Spirit unto the High and Mighty God the Man Christ Jesus in Glory.

London, November 17, 1668,

A Copy of a Letter written by the Prophet Lodowicke Muggleton to Mrs. Sarah Delamaine, Daughter to Mr. Alexander Delamaine, Senior, Wife of Robert Delamaine, bearing date December 14, 1691.

Dear and loving friend in the eternal Truth, Sarah Delamaine,

YOUR desire it was to me to give you the blessing of everlasting life in writing, notwithstanding I have given you the blessing by word of mouth many years ago, which I was unwilling to do; but you being so urgent upon me to do it, made me promise to give you the blessing in writing; so that I have considered that you have read in that book which your own father did send for, those letters that were sent to me for the blessing of everlasting life to eternity in many parts of England and Ireland, and many other parts of this world, which many of them never saw me in all their lives, yet were satisfied in their minds, and had the assurance of eternal life abiding in themselves while in this natural life, by believing in this commission of the Spirit, which is the last commission that God will ever send unto this bloody, unbelieving world, while this world doth last; and that book which your husband hath, it was your fathers care and charge, and your mother-in-law's too, to get it recorded for the ages to come after my death, and it will be found at the last day as a book of life to all those whose names are recorded therein, to be the blessed of the Lord, because they shall have their part in the first Resurrection, so that the second death shall have no power over them; for God will raise the saints and the elect of God first, before he doth raise one reprobate or devil. And this I do know, that your own father and own mother, and your mother-in-law, and your own brother, Alexander Delamaine, and your own husband, Robert Delamaine, will all be saved, being all blessed of the Lord to eternity, in that they truly believed in this third and last commission of the Spirit which God will ever send, when they were alive, while this world doth last or end.

And you, Sarah Delamaine, the only daughter of your father Alexander Delamaine that is alive, doth truly believe in this commission of the Spirit, and that God hath given me power to pronounce you blessed to eternity, as I have done to many others; and your desire is, that I would give you the blessing in writing, that you might be numbered amongst the blessed of the Lord; therefore, to satisfy your desire, and in obedience to my commission, I pronounce you, Sarah Delamaine, blessed, both in soul and body, to all eternity.

Written by me,

LODOWICKE MUGGLETON,

One of the two last Witnesses and Prophets of the Spirit unto the High and Mighty God, the Man Christ Jesus in Glory.

London, December 14, 1691.

FINIS.

Printed by W. SMITH, King Street, Long Acre.

A

STREAM

FROM THE

TREE OF LIFE:

OR, THE

THIRD RECORD

VINIDICATED.

BEING THE

COPIES OF SEVERAL LETTERS AND EPISTLES

Wrote by the two last Witnesses of Jesus Christ.

WHEREIN

TRUTH RIDES TRIUMPHANT AND IMAGINATION IS CONFOUNDED.

These were not included in the Volume of SPIRITUAL EPISTLES because of the great expence.

Printed from the original Manuscript in the year of our Lord
M.DCC.LVIII.

To all those that fear not the sudden appearing Of JESUS CHRIST.

BRETHREN,

IT is a great pleasure to the only true Church of Christ, to see so great a progress, in not only re-printing but also putting in print what never was before, things of the highest eternal consequences to the seed of faith, at a vast expence. It is surprising how it is so far accomplished, considering what a handful we are, and how few of that handful have substance sufficient to support so great an undertaking. Notwithstanding all this, love hath carried on the work, insomuch, that within these seven years, we have printed, besides this, The Interpretation of the Eleventh Chapter of the Revelations, The Divine Appendix, The Soul's Mortality, The Answer to William Penn, the volume of Spiritual Epistles, [never printed before], The Transcendent Spiritual Treatise, The Looking-Glass for George Fox, and The Neck of the Quakers Broken.

So there is nothing now scarce, except The Acts, and The Divine Looking Glass. And if we are preserved in the same love and harmony we are in at present, their printing will soon be effected also. For no other way can we serve God, than by making The Third Record on Earth public to his friend, the captive seed of faith. For a candle is not lighted to be put under a bushel; and what is done to his seed, he accounts it as done to himself.

So wishing love may increase in the Church, as without that no heavenly virtue can inhabit the soul, I subscribe myself an unmoveable believer of these glorious truths, which will remain unshaken to eternity.

JOHN PEAT.

THE CONTENTS.

	PAGE
A Copy of a Letter to W. Medgate, proving that God takes no immediate notice	326
To Walter Bohenan, on the same subject	332
To James Whitehead, answering six queries	338
To Colonel Phaire, concerning eating the flesh of devils; as also explaining the mustard grain, Luke xiii. 19.	344
To Edward Fewterell, concerning witchcraft	348
A discourse between John Reeve and Richard Leader, wherein philosophy is confounded	354
To Thomas Tomkinson, relating, in part, the Prophet's sufferings for declaring truth	361
An Epistle to a Quaker, showing the blindness of those people	362
An Epistle of the Prophet Muggleton's, proving his power to give sentences; also explaining how the devil entered into the herd of swine	367
To Christopher Hill, containing his own, Thomas Martin, William Young, and Elizabeth Wyles's blessings	373
To Alice Webb, containing the Six Principles, and her blessing	374
To a Friend, concerning true and false preachers	376
An Epistle concerning Spirits	378
To Isaac Pennington, Esq. concerning God's visible appearing in flesh	382
The death of Moses unfolded	386
An Epistle, proving Christ had inherent power to die and live again, without assistance from any in heaven or on earth	387
To Ann Adams, showing the peace of a pure life	391

Here followeth the Copies of several LETTERS and EPISTLES, taken from the original Manuscript, for the further Consolation of the Elect.

The Prophet Muggleton's EPISTLE to the Believers of the Commission, touching the Rebellion occasioned by the nine Assertions.

AND now I shall speak a few Words unto him, and the rest of Believers, as followeth:

And because one of the Conspirators in Rebellion hath repented of his Rebellion, and asked Forgiveness before it was too late, and I forgave him his Trespass against me, and against God; (namely, Thomas Burton.) He did well to agree with his Adversary while he was in the Way, for the Prophet is an Adversary to all Rebels against God.

And this I would have you to know, though it be now too late, that Obedience is better than Sacrifice; that is, Obedience to the Prophet is better than all the legal Righteousness you have performed between Man and Man all your Days; yet this ought to be done, but not to leave the other undone. And this you may know, that Rebellion is as the Sin of Witchcraft, for Rebellion against the Prophet is Rebellion against God; for when King Saul rebelled against the Prophet Samuel's Words, he rebelled against God, for it was the Prophet Samuel that gave the King a Command, and it was he that reproved the King for his Disobedience and Rebellion, for God never spake to him, nor never gave Judgment upon him, it was the Prophet only. Now ought not King Saul to have minded the Prophet only? But Saul minded God only, as you have done, and rejected the Prophet Samuel; and because he minded God only, in that he thought to please God better by offering up the best of the Cattle in Sacrifice to God, he thought it was better to mind God than the Prophet's Words: But how did God reject him for disobeying the Prophet? And his Sacrifice was rejected also. Now had not Saul better have minded the Prophet only? then would it have been well with him; but he minded God only, and disobeyed the Prophet, and rebelled against his Command. What a woful Effect did fall upon him! and so it will upon all Rebels against Prophets. Thus it is with Men that think themselves wiser and more righteous than their Fathers; for whosoever disobeys a true Prophet, disobeys God, and it is accounted so of God; therefore it is good for Men to mind the Prophet only, and pin their Faith upon the Prophet's Sleeve, else there can be no Peace nor Safety, because no Man can come unto God to reason or dispute with him but by his Prophet only. This hath been the Way God hath walked in all Ages; and now I being the last Prophet of all, God hath put me in his Place here upon Earth, and hath raised me up as he did that good Man Joseph, Genesis the last, the 19th Verse, who said unto his Brethren, Fear not, I am in the Place of God; and Verse 21, Now therefore fear you not, I will nourish you; and he comforted them, and spake kindly unto them.

So God hath raised me up to be his last Prophet, and hath set me in the Place of God, to nourish his People, who have believed his Prophet's Report, with spiritual and heavenly Knowledge: For true Prophets, true Apostles, true Ministers, have made Saints in all Ages; so that, without these, no Saints at all; they may be elect Vessels, but not Saints; for no Man or Woman can properly be laid to be a Saint, except they come actually to believe in a true Prophet, true Apostle, or true Minister of Christ.

And further I say, that whoever doth not act well, by that Law written in his Heart, and doth not stand in Awe of that, and fear to offend that Law of Conscience, as if God himself did stand by, and take notice of all his Actions; therefore he doth well, because God's Eye is over him, else not. I say, all his well-doing is but Eye-service, and respected of God no more than the cutting off a Dog's Neck. And that Man is in the Depth of Darkness, who will do nothing that is good, except God doth take notice of him, to reward him for every good Deed he doth; but if he doth Evil, then he desireth God to take no notice of it, but blot it out of his Remembrance, as if God were beholden to Man to do well, when there is a Blessing in the Deed doing, and a Curse in evil-doing. But this I say, if there were no God to reward the Good, nor to punish the Evil, yet could not I do any otherwise than I do; for I do well, not because I expect any Reward from God, or refrain from Evil, because God will punish me, or that he doth mind me in it; but I do well to please that Law written in my Heart, so that I might not be accused by that Law in my Conscience, as God hath placed for his Watchman, to tell me when I do well: So am I justified by Faith in God, in my own Conscience, and being not condemned by the Law written in my Heart, I have Boldness to the Throne of Grace. Neither do I refrain from Evil for fear of God's Person seeing me, and he seeing me will punish me; but I refrain from Evil, because the Law written in my Heart seeth all my Doings, and that Watchman God hath set there to watch me, will tell God of all my Doings; so that God need not trouble himself to watch over every Man's Actions himself, for he hath placed his Law a Watchman in every Man and Woman, to give notice of all their Doings, whether good or evil.

Thus, in the Original, God taketh notice by his Law, written in every Man's Heart, both of Saint and Devil; and no otherwise doth God mind to take notice of his Saints in particular at all. Not that I do own this Law written in Man's Heart to be the very God, as the Quakers do; but God is a distinct Person of himself, and distinct from this Law written in Man's Heart. And in this Sense, God may be said to take no notice of his Saints, nor doth not mind them at all.

True Believers are my Brethren and Sisters, and the Prophet hath spoken kindly unto them, and hath nourished their Souls with Bread of Life, as Moses, he hath fed them with heavenly Manna; also the Prophet hath been like John Baptist, a burning shining Light in this last Age, as John Baptist was in his Time; a shining Light that hath discovered the Darkness in all the World, for it is Light that discovereth Darkness; and hath not the Prophet enlightned the Understandings of many, that in Light they see Light? Hath not the Prophet fed them with Bread of Life? He hath given them the Flesh of God to eat, he hath given them Water of Life to drink, even the Blood of God to drink, to satisfy their thirsty Souls; also, he hath brought them to the Knowledge of the true God, his Form and Nature; he hath brought them to feed upon the Flesh of God, and to drink his Blood by Faith, whereby their Souls have never hungred nor thirsted more after the Forgiveness of Sins or Satisfaction of Mind as to Things of Eternity; for who hath fed the People with the Knowledge of God, the Knowledge of the right Devil, the Knowledge of Scripture, and all other heavenly Secrets which are hid from all the People in the World, besides? Hath not the Prophet taken the People by the Hand, and pulled them out from the Spirit of Bondage, which kept them under Fear, and hath pulled them out from under the Task-masters of Superstition in Egypt? The Prophet hath led them through the Wilderness of their Minds, and hath brought them into the Paradise of Peace, and hath shewed them where the Tree of Life flood in the Midst of the heavenly Canaan above the Stars, and many of them have stretched forth the Hand of Faith, and have taken of the Tree of Life, and eat and live for ever, and so are set down at Rest there. And doth not all the People in the World else perish for Want of Knowledge, but those few who are led and guided by the Prophet? He hath blessed many of them, and hath led them into the Way of Peace, a strait and narrow Way, that few can find; and when they have wanted Comfort of Mind, he hath comforted them; and when they have been weak in Knowledge, he hath strengthned them; and when any of their Brethren have been too strong one for another, he would not suffer the Strong to trample upon the Weak and Feeble, but would lift him up, and uphold him with his own Knowledge, so that no People under the Sun live better for the Generality than those People who are obedient unto the Prophet, or under him. Hath the Prophet been a Burthen, or oppressive to any of the Faith, let them speak, and he will restore them two-fold; or hath he favoured the Rich, or oppressed the Poor; nay, hath he not forced the Rich to help the Poor? Nay, the Yoke laid upon the Neck of these People by the Prophet is easier and better, both spiritual and temporal, than the Yoke of any other People whatsoever.

And now I shall speak unto you in particular, and ask the Reason why you rebelled against me. What Cause did I give you to rebel? Were you offended at my Words? And because I did bear with many Weaknesses of some of your Brethren in the Faith, and had Compassion on them, and would not suffer them to be so much oppressed in Spirit for the Guilt of their own Sins, and judged and condemned by their own Brethren in the same Faith, because they were of corrupt Natures, so doth God himself bear with corrupt Natures; the Prophet must bear with corrupt Natures, as well as with pure uncorrupt Natures, though you cannot, for Prophets are not sure that all uncorrupt Natures will believe them; so that if a Prophet hath not Power to uphold some corrupt Natures that believe him, to what Purpose then should God send him? And will you find Fault with the Prophet for being merciful to corrupt-natured Men, whore Nature is more corrupt than your's? Yet the Prophet hath upheld you these many Years. You may remember when you came acquainted with me first, that there was some Difference between Claxton and you. Claxton was high in Knowledge at that Time, and yourself weak and low in Knowledge at that Time, and his Knowledge and Faith was over you, and above you, and did keep you under him, though his wicked Life had been worse than your's, yet your legal Righteousness between Man and Man could not have delivered you from his Power, had not the Prophet kept him down; and when you made your Complaint to me I strengthned you against him, and upon your Request I blessed you, and you became in my Favour and when any spoke against your wrathful Nature, Words and Actions, I pleaded for you, and upheld you against them; also I led you in a Way which you knew not, and in a Path which was not known to any but myself, even the Way and Path of Peace; I brought you into the Assembly of Saints, for there is no true Saints on Earth at this Day but those that are under the Prophet; I brought you with the rest of the Saints from under Mount Sinai, that is, from being under that fiery Law written in your Hearts; I led you by your Hands through the Wilderness of your Minds; I led you unto Mount Sion, the City of the living God; I shewed you the holy Hill of Sion; the Habitation of the holy God is Mount Sion, the City of the Living, and the holy Hill of Sion signify the holy God himself, from whence Prophets, Apostles and Saints receive their most holy Faith, Revelation and Prophecies in the Original; also I brought you to the Spirits of just Men made perfect, as Noah, a Preacher of Righteousness by Faith, he built an Ark, and Lot by Faith received two Angels, therefore called righteous Lot; Abraham by Faith would have offered up his Son, therefore called the Father of the Faithful; Isaac and Jacob, Moses, the Prophets, David, the Apostles, these were all just Men, made perfect by Faith, yet several of these just Men, whose Spirits were made perfect by Faith, they committed Evil and Sin after the Blessing was given of God; as, Noah he was drunken with Wine, and discovered his Nakedness; Lot was drunken with Wine, and committed Incest with his two Daughters; Abraham told a Lie, because of his Wife; Jacob lied to his Father, when he stole the Blessing; David, a Man according to God's own Heart, was guilty of Murder and Adultery; Peter, the Rock upon whom Christ built his Church, plaid the Hypocrite, and dissembled, when he circumcised Timothy; Paul dissembled, and plaid the Hypocrite, when he pretended a Vow, and shaved the four Men's Heads. These, and several other just Men, whose Spirits were made perfect by Faith, committed Evil, after the Blessing was given them of God; but their Faith never failed, and should not he uphold them that blessed them? But this Prophet is blamed for upholding smaller Sinners than some of those that believe. Now if these Men's Spirits were made perfect by Faith, and so said to be the Spirits of just Men made perfect, so are all true Believers of this Commission of the Spirit, whose Faith holds out to the End, are counted of God the Spirits of just Men made perfect by Faith, and so may be laid to come unto the Spirits of just Men made perfect. Also I led you into the Paradise of Peace, where the Thief went that Day he believed in Christ: I brought you, with the Rest of Believers, to the Tree of Life, which stood in the Midst of Paradise; you said you saw it, and you liked it well; and if you had stretched forth the Hand of Faith as others did, and have taken and eat of the Tree of Life, and have lived for ever, then had you not rebelled. I shewed you the Tree of Knowledge of Good and Evil, you saw it, and understood what you saw; I shewed you the New Jerusalem, that came down from Heaven, and that is said to be four square, the Length and Breadth are equal. The New Jerusalem that came down from Heaven, it was when God became Flesh in the Virgin's Womb, and its being four-square, the Length and Breadth equal; it was when Christ was nailed to the Cross, his Arms being spread abroad were equal with his Head and Feet, and so may be said to be four-square, and so is every perfect Man: And so the New Jerusalem that came down from Heaven, the Person of Christ, may be said to be four-square, the Length and Breadth equal. Likewise I brought you to an innumerable Company of Angels, I shewed you their Forms and Natures. These Things I did for you, in the spiritual, and many more; and the Prophet hath not been the least beneficial to you, in the temporal; I have not been your Hindrance, but your Furtherance, in what lay in my Power; I never was beholden to you in any temporal Matters, and did not satisfy you for what you did. And when several Believers did complain of your rude Speeches, your wrathful Words, your merciless Judgment, I have pleaded for you against them, and have upheld your corrupt Nature, else you would have been forsaken of several Believers before now; but those I have done most for, and have been the least beholden unto, have lift up their Heel against me, so that you have been offended against me, and rebelled against me without a Cause, which hath caused you to be cast out of my Sight, and out of God's Sight, as Cain was, and out of the Society of the Saints. And now, may all your own evil Words and desperate Wishes which you have uttered, come upon your own Head.

First, You say, if Claxton were saved, you would be damned; how do you limit God's Mercy to your Wrath?

Secondly, You say, that if God did not take notice of you, then would you had been a Toad, a Dog, or a Serpent, or any Thing but a Man.

These, are desperate, Words, and it will be a Wonder if you have not Cause indeed, to wish yourself a Toad, Dog, or Serpent, rather than a Man.

Thirdly, You call the Prophet, Devil; Peter might as well have called Christ Devil, for calling him Sathan; for Peter's Offence was out of Love and Pity to Christ, but your Offence to me, was out of Pride and Rebellion; for I was your Master and Judge, as Christ was Peter's.

Fourthly, You slighted the Blessing from the Prophet, and in a rude and uncivil Language, said, you cared not a Fart for it.

Fifthly, When Burton bid you burn the Assertions, and humble yourself to the Prophet, as he did, you said you would perish first.

Sixthly, You despised the Government of the Commission of the Spirit, saying, it is poorly and weakly managed.

These are desperate Words against God, and against the Prophet, and high Rebellion; I do not think it could be paralelled, not by all the Prophets and Apostles, since the World began. And if this Rebellion be forgiven, then let it be said, that this last Prophet and Witness of the Spirit had Power to do more than any Prophet or Apostle ever did in the Time of their Commissions.

Written by

LODOWICK MUGGLETON,

One of the two last Prophets and Witnesses of the Spirit unto the High and Mighty God, the Man Christ Jesus in Glory. Amen. In the Year 1671.

A LETTER written by the Messenger of God, Lodowick Muggleton, to Walter Bohenan, of Condemnation for Apostacy, January 23, 1671.

Walter Bohenan,

THIS is to let you know, that I have seen three of your rebellious Letters, for which Cause I was not willing that any Rebel should see the Answer to those Assertions laid down by William Medgate, that grand Rebel. Your Letters are full of Nonsense, and not good English; and you have laid down the Assertions false Lies, and not true. Those nine wrote by Medgate were well laid down, and I own them all to be true as they are laid down; and I have given an Answer to them all, but no Rebel shall see them if I can help it.

But it seems that you have undertaken, not only to answer the Assertions, but to give Judgment upon them; and not only so, but you vapour and threaten me, that you will force me to give Answer to them, as if so be you were commissioned to judge me. I shall not speak of many of your wicked, nonsensical, rebellious Words; it would be too tedious, only these few:

First, You say you do believe that I, and all the Devils in the World, cannot hurt you; for my Power, you say, you are not afraid of it, no more than of a Child of one Day old.

Secondly, You say, That if I do give Sentence upon you before I have answered the Assertions, you say you will force me to it, if you and I do live in England; and that you will bring me on the Stage. This is Judas like.

Thirdly, You say, You have more Ground to be offended with me than I have to be offended with you: For, say you, I do affirm that you are fallen from the Truth, and have gone about to overthrow John Reeve, and have contradicted myself: This is Devil like, to judge his Lord and Master.

Fourthly, You, say you, will make me believe a Lie, and more than one, but many Lies, contrary to all the Prophets and John Reeve's Writings. Here is the Mark of a Reprobate, to charge his Teacher with Lies from dead Men's Writings; these are but a few of the Fruits of your Rebellion, but there is enough to condemn one Rebel to Eternity, if there were no more; but this I shall say unto you, that you have shewed yourself a right Scotchman, a dissembling false-hearted Man, of the Scottish Nature. And it would be a rare Thing to meet with a true-hearted Scotch-Man or Woman, that is upright in Heart, either to God or Man: For I have been in this Commission almost twenty Years, and I never knew but two, one a Scotch-man, and a Scotch-Woman, that made a Profession of this Faith, and they proved both false-hearted, both to God and Man for the Woman did fall from John Reeve in his Time, for which he branded her with a Title of false-hearted Scot, and you, the Man, is fallen from that Faith, you once had in me, to Rebellion, for which I shall brand you with the Mark of Reprobation, for you have shewed yourself a Reprobate, a falsehearted Man a Cast-away. Did you not say, that you did believe that I had Power to give a Blessing unto you of eternal Happiness, else you would not have asked it of me.

And upon your Request, saying you did believe that I had such Power, I gave you a Blessing, and you continued in my Favour, and in the Favour of many Believers for a While; but now you have despised the Blessing as Esau did his Birthright; for the Blessing of a Prophet is a good Birthright, if it be not despised; but you have despised and disowned it, and forsaken the Blessing of a living Prophet, and do cleave unto dead Men's Words, and to the Doctrine of those that are dead. John Reeve is dead, and those that wrote the Scriptures are dead, but he that God hath preserved alive, to be the Judge of John Reeve's Writings, and Judge of the Writings of the Prophets and Apostles, which you never knew, neither did you ever receive any Light or Knowledge from them, but what you received from me; yet have you lift up yourself in Rebellion against me, and have despised the Blessing, therefore you shall have the Curse of a Prophet in the room of it, and see, if that will stick more close unto you; for this I say, you shall never cast that off, as you have done the Blessing, but it shall remain upon your Spirit to Eternity; for your Condition is much like unto King Saul's: The good Spirit of the Lord departed from him, and an evil Spirit was sent from the Lord to him; that is, while he kept in Obedience to the Prophet Samuel, the good Spirit of Peace from the Lord in his Seed gave him Peace of Conscience; but his Rebellion and Disobedience to the Prophet Samuel, caused that Peace of Conscience to depart from him; and the evil Spirit in the Seed of Reason, of Rebellion, and Disobedience, was sent unto him, and that became a Worm in his Conscience, that never dies, and a Fire in his Conscience, that will never be quenched.

This will be your Condition for your Rebellion and Disobedience unto me; for while you were kept in Obedience unto me, the Prophet of the Lord, the good Spirit of the Lord in your Seed, that believed in his Prophet, it preserved you in Peace of Conscience, in that I gave you the Blessing; but now, through your Disobedience to the Prophet of the Lord, and Rebellion against God, for it is all one, if God himself were in my Place, you would say as much to him as you do to me; but the good Spirit of the Lord is departed from you, and an evil Spirit, from the Lord, is sent unto you, even the Fruit of your Disobedience and Rebellion, which is the Curse of God, you being rejected of God and of his Prophet, and cast out from the Society of the Faithful for ever; so that the Worm of Rebellion will never die in your Conscience, nor the Fire of Hell will never be quenched in you; so that you shall know this Torment is for nothing but your Disobedience and Rebellion against the Prophet.

And as for your vapouring that I, nor all the Devils in the World, cannot hurt you, and that my Power is no more feared by you than a Child of a Day old, these Words you have learned of Medgate, that Dragon Devil, who hath roared out his Rebellion like a mad Bull; and you have learned of him to call the Prophet of the Lord Devil, who was his Lord and Matter, and yours also. But for all your Vapour, you shall find that my Power shall reach you wherever you go; if you ascend up to Heaven in your Imagination, my Faith and Authority shall pull you down from thence; and if you go down into Hell, I shall find you out there, and your Act of Rebellion shall be executed, and my Judgment shall be executed upon you there. And if you go to the uttermost Parts of the Earth, you shall not flie from that Curse that shall follow you; so that you shall know that the most High hath chosen me, and rejected you. And as for your threatning me that you will force me to answer the Assertions, if you and I live in England, and that you will bring me upon the Stage, do you not shew yourself a Cain and Judas Devil; you would both betray your Lord and Master, as Judas did his, and kill, as Cain did his Brother, because he was accepted, and Cain rejected. So, because God hath accepted of me, and hath let me in his Place, and hath rejected you, therefore you would betray me, to bring me upon the Stage. Your evil Spirit is willing, I perceive, but your Power is weak. And will you dare to talk of bringing a Man upon the Stage, that is freeborn, and free by Service, by you, that are a Foreigner, a Stranger, and Alien, one that is by Act of Parliament counted a Vagabond, a Runagate, a Fugitive in a Nation which is not your own, who is not free-born, nor free by Redemption; yet you will dare to bring me upon the Stage, because I condemn you for your Rebellion. And this I say, if I were treacherous in Heart, as you are, I would quickly cause you to be removed from Ware, if not out of England but I shall let that pass; and I would fain know how you can force me to let you see the Answer to the Assertions, or to bring me upon the Stage; you may do what you can now, I provoke you to it, but here you may see the Pride and Presumption against your own Soul, in that you have lifted yourself up against your Lord and Master.

And whereas you say and affirm that I am fallen from the Truth, is not this the Word of a Rebel, that learned and was taught the Way of Truth, and what Truth is; neither had you any Light or Truth at all, but what you received from me, your Lord and Master; and yet the Spirit of Rebellion in you is grown so wise to judge your Master that taught you, to be fallen from Truth, so that you know how to teach your Master better than he can teach you. But how can I expect any better from the Spirit of Rebellion? Also you say, I would make you believe Lies: Who made you a Judge, what is a Lie, and what is Truth? You say, I go about to overthrow John Reeve, and that I would make you believe many Lies, contrary to all the Prophets and John Reeve's Writings:

To this I say, What have you to do with John Reeve's Writings, now he is dead? Neither have you to do with the Prophets nor Apostles Writings; they are all given into my Hands, that is alive, and you ought all to be taught of me that am alive, or else you cannot be taught of God. And whereas you say, I contradict John Reeve:

To this I say, I have Power so to do, and I had Power so to do when he was alive, and did contradict him in some Things, when he was alive; and John Reeve wrote some Things that was Error to me, and Error in itself, which I did oppose him in to his Face, and he could not deny it. And yet notwithstanding John Reeve was infallible, and did write by an unerring Spirit. This will seem a Riddle, except it be unfolded thus: As to the doctrinal Part contained in our Writings, the six Principles were written by an unerring and infallible Spirit in John Reeve, and the Interpretation of Scripture written by him was infallible; but John Reeve's Experience and Apprehension of God's taking immediate Notice of every Man was Error; and that God did supply every Man and Woman immediately from his own Person, this was Error in John Reeve's Judgment and Experience, as I did prove to his Face; but the Things being written before, and they were of no Consequence as to eternal Happiness, they were let pass. Besides none can judge of a Prophet's Writing or Judgment, but he that is equal in Power and Judgment with him. Being chosen of God, I had Power to contradict him in his Judgment; and though it was Error, it would have been Rebellion in any Believer to do as I did. And now, I being the last Liver, it is Rebellion in you to call any Thing Lies or Error that I do justify to be true; for none is to call me to an Account, or to refill my Judgment in spiritual Things or Matters, but God only. And I am sure he hath and will justify me in what I have done, and in what I do of this Nature. Besides, where Men are chosen equal in Power, they may contradict one the other in some Things, and yet both infallible Men in Doctrine, but not in Judgment and Practice.

As for Example, Peter was an infallible Man, and did write by an infallible and unerring Spirit, as to the Doctrine of Christ, yet he erred in his Judgment and Practice, and circumcised Timothy, contrary to his Commission from Christ; and it was a great Error in Peter, and Paul being an Apostle, and in equal Power, withstood him to his Face, and reproved him of Error and Dissimulation. Now should any Believer of Peter's Doctrine have said to Peter, thou art a Liar, and no true Apostle, nor hath not an infallible Spirit, but art in Error, if this should have been spoken by any private Believer, as it was by Paul, who was equal in Power, I would not have been in that Believer's Condition for all the World.

Again: Did not Paul write by an infallible Spirit? As to the Doctrine of Christ, Peter and he did agree in that; but Paul committed an Error in his Judgment and Practice, when he pretended a Vow; this was a great Error in him, it had like to have cost him his Life. And should any dare to say that he wrote his Epistles by an erring lying Spirit? So likewise Paul and James do absolutely contradict one another: Paul saith, Rom. iii. 28. You see then by Works a Man is justified, and not by Faith only. Here is a quite Contradiction to Paul. And should any Believer, in their Time, dare to say, that either of these did write Error and Lies, and that they were not infallible Men, in their Doctrine of Christ, because they differed in Judgment, in Point of Faith and Works; this was much like John Reeve's believing God did take notice of every particular Man, and my Judgment that God did not.

Now shall any dare to say, that either of us are Liars, because we differ in Judgment in some Things? Besides, this is a common Thing in the Scripture, for Prophets and Apostles to differ in Judgment and Practice, but not in Doctrine; as the four Evangelists, they contradict one another very oft, and the Words of Christ himself contradict one the other, in many Places, which would be too tedious to name now. Now because Christ's Words do contradict one the other, shall any dare to say he spake Lies, and taught Error, and that which he spake was contrary to all Truth, or that he was not a true Christ? None but Devils did say so, when he was upon the Earth. And should any, in the Apostles, Matthew, Mark, Luke, and John's Time, dare to say that any of them wrote Lies and Errors, because they contradicted one another, in point of Judgment and Experience? None but Devils did find Fault and cavil with them, when they were alive. And so it is now, with John Reeve and me; none but Devils would have made a Fraction and Disturbance amongst the Believers, about John Reeve's writing of Error; for this I must tell you, that no Man upon Earth is to judge what is infallible, and what is not, but the Prophet only that is alive; and if Men will not take Things upon his Words and Judgment, whoever refuseth is upon his bare Word, will perish to Eternity; therefore the Spirit of Rebellion hath deceived you, and made you forsake the Prophet that is alive, and to cleave unto John Reeve, that is dead, and to trust to the Scriptures, that were never spoken to you, nor given unto you; but those People they were spoken unto, did receive Benefit by them, if they did believe in Time, when that Faith was in Being. But John Reeve's Writings, nor the Scripture, will do you no good, now you have rebelled against the Prophet that is alive; neither will that Faith in them deliver you at all from those eternal Torments, neither will those dead Prophets deliver you from your Rebellion, nor help you to the Knowledge of Truth, now they are all dead; but this live Prophet shall torment you, and those dead ones shall not deliver you from my Power.

And as you have walked in the Steps of Korab, Dathan and Abiram, those notable Rebels, who rebelled against Moses and Aaron: And what was the Fruits of their Rebellion? Did not Moses, the Prophet of the Lord, cause the Ground to open and swallow them up alive. And this you shall know, though I cannot cause the Earth to open its Mouth as Moses did, yet this I can do, by my Commission of the

Spirit, I can open Hell's Mouth, and that shall swallow you up alive, and keep you there eternally, where your Worm of Conscience shall never die, and the Fire of Hell shall never go out, that you may know to your endless Pain and Shame, that you rebelled and forsook the Blessing of a true Prophet alive upon Earth at this Day. And for all your Pride, Presumption, and Vapouring, lifting yourself up against the Lord's anointed chosen Prophet. And it will be a Wonder, if God's Vengeance doth not make you exemplary in this World, to be a Fugitive and Vagabond upon the Face of the Earth before you die, betides your Damnation hereafter; for Sins of this Nature are punished with a greater Punishment than any other Sin whatsoever, but Murder; and it would have been good for you and Medgate, if you had never been born. Therefore, in Obedience to my Commission, for this your Wickedness, in falling from the Faith you once had in the Prophet, now alive, to Rebellion against him and against God, and for many base, proud presumptuous Speeches in your Letters, I do pronounce you cursed and damned, in Soul and Body, from the Presence of God, Elect Men and Angels, to Eternity. And now do you see whether God will take Notice of you, to deliver you, or whether he will own you or me; or whether your Faith be stronger than mine; or whether you have declared Truth or I; neither shall any of this Faith eat or drink with you, or trade any more with you, if I can help it; for you are cast out of God's Sight for ever, and cast out of the Prophet's Sight, and cast out of the Assembly, or the Society of the Believers, for ever; and now you may seek new Acquaintance in the World, and see if you can find a better Sort of People than those you find Fault with. And you need not fear as Cain did, that every one that meets you will kill you; but your own evil deceitful Heart to your Principles, and rejected Spirit, may meet your Conscience, and kill the Peace of it.

Written by

January 23, 1671.

LODOWICK MUGGLETON.

A COPY of a LETTER written by the Prophet Lodowick Muggleton, to Mr. James Whitehead of Braintree in Essex, bearing Date June 13 1682.

Loving Friend in the true Faith, James Whitehead,

I Received a Letter as from you, but I suppose not of your Handwriting nor inditing; but I perceive you do own it as your's by the Direction of it, and your Name being at the latter End of your Letter, being your own Hand-writing, wherein your Desire and Request is, That I would answer those six Queries you have laid down, as followeth.

Query 1. Whether there be such an Estate attainable in this Life, that a Man may be certainly assured of eternal Life on the other Side of Death?

Answer. To this I say, That the Scripture is full to prove, that the Fathers of Old, as Moses and the Prophets do declare, and there was such an Estate attainable of the full Assurance of their eternal Happiness in the Kingdom of Glory after Death, even while they were in this mortal Life; else how could Abraham, Isaac, and Jacob have blessed their Children? Shall an Man imagine, that their Blessing did extend no further than the Things of this Life? Or shall any Man think, that those they blessed had not the Assurance of eternal Life in themselves?

As for Example, Christ said when on Earth, Whoever believeth, in me shall not perish, but have everlasting Life abiding in him. So that, if Christ, when on Earth, was assured of his own eternal Life and Glory after his Resurrection, when he had passed through this first Death, I say the very same Assurance was attained unto in this Life in every true Believer in that Commission, who continue stedfast to the End.

For this you must understand, that those Men God hath chosen, and hath given Power to bless and curse, must needs have Assurance of eternal Life in themselves, else they could not give a Blessing of eternal Life to those that believe them: So that Person that doth truly believe hath the same Assurance of eternal Life abiding in himself, as he hath that gave the Blessing, else what Peace and Satisfaction can any Person have in this Life; and if this Peace and Assurance be not attainable in this Life or in this World, it will never be attained to in the Life to come; but I know that you and many others have attained the Blessing and the Assurance of everlasting Life in yourselves now in this present World, which will endure to Eternity.

Query 2. If attainable, whether a Man having once attained it, can finally fall away, and be reduced to a State of Damnation?

Answer. That if a Man hath attained the Assurance of eternal Salvation, and that it doth abide in himself, he cannot finally fall away, nor be reduced to a State of Damnation; but if a Man do attain to the Assurance of eternal Salvation in his Head and in his Tongue only, such a one may finally fall away, and be reduced to a State of Damnation. Why? because this Assurance of eternal Life did not abide in him, that is, it did not sink down into his Heart, it remained in his Head and Tongue only, so that it taketh no Root in the Heart; so that the Assurance of eternal Life in such Men it springeth up; and maketh a fair Shew quickly; but a little Opposition causeth it to wither, and finally to fall away, and be reduced to a State of Damnation.

This I have had Experience of, by some Persons you know, for he that hath attained the Assurance of eternal Life after Death, abiding in his Heart, then it is in himself; for it is Paid, Thou shalt love the Lord thy God with all thy Heart, with all thy Soul, with all thy Strength; so that, whoever hath attained the Assurance of eternal Life here in this World in his Heart, shall hold out to the End of this natural Life, and shall not fall away, nor be reduced to a State of Damnation.

Query 3. Whether our Justification and Peace of Mind ariseth not purely from the Act of Faith from the true God?

Answer. That the Justification and Peace of our Mind, it doth arise first from the Act of Faith in the Messenger of God; for a Man must first believe he is a Man of God, or sent from God, else why should any Man enquire of him after heavenly Things: Therefore it was the Prophet said; Who hath believed our Report, or to whom is the Arm of the Lord revealed? So that if People do not believe the Prophet's Report, that bringeth glad Tidings of Life and Salvation in the first Place, he cannot have any Act of Faith in the true God, because it is the Prophet that doth declare the true God; which is the Prophet's Doctrine; so that our Act of Faith doth first arise in believing the true Prophet, and that leads us to the Act of Faith in the true God, for there must be a receiving which is believing, which is an Act of Faith in him that God sent in the first Place, and then you shall receive God that sent him.

And so Justification and Peace of Mind ariseth purely from the Act of Faith in the true Prophet, who hath declared unto you the true God, which is the Rock to build your Faith upon, that will say unto you in that Day Come, ye Blessed, because you believed my poor despised Messenger, when on Earth, enter into the Joys of Heaven, which is Life eternal, which my Messenger I sent declared unto you; and in as much as you believed him which I sent, you believed in me.

Thus do true Believers come to have Justification and Peace of Mind in this Life, by the pure Act of Faith that ariseth in their Hearts while here on Earth.

Query 4. Of what Use is the Moral-Law to us who have received the Commission of the Spirit in the Love of it, and have yielded Obedience thereunto, and have chose rather to suffer under the Odium that evil Men have laid upon it than to enjoy the good Report the Men of this World give to false Worshippers.

Answer. That the observing and yielding Obedience to the Moral-Law is of great Use to all those who have received, and that have Faith in this Commission of the Spirit, and that have yielded Obedience unto it in the Love of it. Why? Because the Moral-Law is the second Commandment; for as Christ Paid, when on Earth, There is but two Commandments; that is, one Commandment on God's Part, and the other on Man's Part.

The Commandment that is for God, is evangelical, spiritual, and heavenly; that is, Thou shalt love the Lord thy God with all thy Heart, with all thy Soul, and with all thy Strength. This Commandment no Man, in the World, can keep, or perform, but those that do truly believe in this Commission of the Spirit: Why? Because no Religion in the World, at this Day, Both know the true God in his Form and Nature, but those that believe in this Commission of the Spirit. Therefore no Man can love God with all his Heart, nor with all his Soul, nor with all his Strength, because he doth not know God. For how can a Man love him with all his Heart, which he doth not know; but by Reading the Scriptures or the History of a God, a Man may know God in his Head by the Imagination of Reason, and in his Tongue to talk of a God, and so love that which he doth not know with all his Head, and all his Tongue, and all his Imagination.

This is the State and Condition the whole World lieth in, as well Professors of the Scriptures, as others; For none can love God with all his Heart, but such as know God by Faith in this Commission of the Spirit: This is a strait and narrow Gate, which few do enter in at.

And the second Commandment is like unto it, Thou shalt love thy Neighbour as thyself; because the Moral-Law is written in every Man's Heart, which Law doth speak in every Man's Mind: Do as thou wouldst another should doe to thee. For this I know, that there is never a Man in the World, but would have every Man to do justly and honestly by him; but he will not do so by others. For this Moral-Law, written in every Man's Heart, is on Man's Part to keep and perform; that is, whatsoever he would have another do unto him, let him do so to another; for if all Men did walk by this Moral-Law, written in every Man's Heart, then there would be no Wickedness acted upon this Earth; for observe, there is no Man that hath his Senses or in his Wits, and his Reason in him, that would willingly have another Man to commit Adultery with his Wife, whom he loves, or to commit Fornication with his Daughters. The Nature of Man doth loath and abhor this in another Man, yet himself will commit Adultery with another Man's Wife, and commit Fornication with other Men's Daughters.

This is not to do as he would be done unto; and so of the Rest of the Particulars in the Moral-Law, written in every Man's Heart; and he that breaketh one of these six Commandments is guilty of the Breach of all the Moral-Law written in his Heart, which is contained in the second Commandment, which is on Man's Part, to do as he would be done unto; which is this Moral-Law, written in Man's Heart, which if this Moral-Law were kept, performed, and done by all Men, there would be no Disobedience to Parents, no Adultery nor Fornication committed, no Murder, no Stealing, no Covetting his Neighbour's Wife, his Ox or his Ass, or any Thing that is his; so that the Moral-Law is of great Life to the Believers of this Commission of the Spirit, and to all religious Men, as well as wicked, in all Ages. And especially since Moses published this Law written; for where the Righteous doth break this Moral-Law, the Worm of Conscience will gnaw in the Righteous now in these Days, as it hath done in the Days of old. As David, for his Murder and Adultery, who brake the Moral-Law written in his Heart, in a high Degree; he was loath that another should have done so by him as he did to Uriah and his Wife, in that he gave Judgment himself; That another Man should die that did do as he had done, not thinking in the least, that he was the Man. It was a very bad Example of a Righteous Man, and to all Kings that should come after him; for the Breach of this Moral-Law caused him to make a great Outcry to the God of Heaven, and to his Prophet to take off this Burthen of his Soul, I have had the like Experience of some that shall be nameless, since I have been in this Commission. So that the Moral-Law is of great Use both to Saint and Devil. And I could wish that all the Believers of this Commission of the Spirit might be observed from the Breach of the Moral-Law in Act, as I have been from my Childhood: For this I say, Millions of People are damned to Eternity for nothing else, but for the Breach of the Moral-Law, written in their Hearts, and Millions of Men and Women, who are legally righteous, and many of them never break the Moral-Law in Act, yet being of the Reprobate Seed, have despised the Truth, and others being shut up in Unbelief of the Truth, will perish to Eternity.

Query 5. What is that which gives Trouble and Distraction, in the Hour of Death, to some Believers in this Commission, when as we know and believe, that being justified by Faith, we have Peace with God, and Peace with Death? What then, I say, is it that seems to separate us from that Peace and Joy we had in the Time of Health, to the great Dishonour of Truth?

Answer. It is Sin, after they have believed the Truth; say, it is the Breach of the moral Law, written in his Heart, in some Kind or other, after he received the Truth, which gives the Trouble and Distraction in the Hour of Death, to some Believers of this Commission, as I have had Experience of, in my Time, of several; and of some I have taken off the Trouble of the Mind, and restored them to their former Peace and Assurance they had in their Health (as the Prophet Nathan did to David and others) that have fought to me, in the Trouble of their Minds, to ease them of their Burthen, but I would not, but left them to the moral Law written in their Hearts, and their Sin, after they received the Truth, to grapple together; so that which got the Mastery, the Soul muff be subject unto. Their Persons on both Sides shall be nameless.

Likewise, I do know that every true Believer in this Commission is justified by Faith; they have Peace with God, but have no Peace with Death, but fight with it. Neither is Death at Peace with any Man that hath Life in him; for Death and Life is always at War, one with another; and Death is never at Peace with Life, until Death hath conquered and overcome Life; then is Death and Life at Peace one with the other; for Death is the King of Terrors; so that the God of Heaven, when he was on Earth, was made capable of the Fear of Death, which caused him to cry out, if it be possible, this Cup of Death might pass away from him; but he, knowing that he could not be Death's Death, no other Way but by suffering of Death, to have the Conquest of the Godhead Life for a Moment; so that Death and the Godhead Life was at Peace, one with the other, for a Moment; but this Godhead Life, being the quickening Spirit, it quickened out of Death again, into a new and eternal Life; and this new eternal Life is Death's Death, and hath conquered Death, Hell, and the Devil; that is, by his quickening out of Death into an endless Life, he hath procured an eternal Death, that is, a living Death, and a dying Life; so that Death shall always live in Hell, and Hell shall always live with Death, and the Devils, which are Men and Women in the Resurrection, shall live with Death and Hell, in utter Darkness, to Eternity.

This did Christ purchase, by his suffering of Death, and his quickening again into Life eternal; else there would have been no Death eternal to the Seed of the Serpent, nor no Life eternal to the Seed of the Woman, which is the Seed of God.

These Things are deep and secret Mysteries, the Tongue of Men and Angels cannot express.

This is more largely treated of in my two Books of the Revelations, and what that is that seems to separate us from that Peace and Joy we had in the Time of Health, to the great Dishonour of Truth.

To this I say, it is the Guilt of some Sin which is secret and hid in a Man's Heart, which in his Health he would willingly hide from his Brethren of the same Faith, left he should lose his good Reputation and Credit among his Friends, and of the World, that had a good Opinion of him, thinking in his Health that in Time he shall order his Matters so as to satisfy his own Conscience, and that none shall know that he ever did any Evil at all to any Man. This was David's Case, he thought he hid his Sin of Adultery, by causing her Husband to be killed; but Death appearing presently after the Act of Sin, Sin appeareth also; for Death and Sin always goeth Hand in Hand together, to accuse the Conscience, and Hell followeth at the Heels. As for Example, when Adam had sinned, his Sin, his Sin did not accuse him, but thought himself well enough, till the Voice of the Lord called, Adam, Where art thou? immediately after his Sin was committed, and said, Hast thou eaten of the Tree of Knowledge of Good and Evil, which I forbad thee to eat of?

So likewise when Cain had killed his Brother Abel, he thought all would be well with him; but when God called unto Cain, and said, Thy Brother's Blood crieth from the Ground unto me for Vengeance, then Sin and Death joined together in Cain's Conscience, which caused him to say, his Punishment was greater than he could bear.

And so it was with David, he thought himself well when Uriah was slain, till the Prophet Nathan in his Parable had convinced him of his two Sins in Act of Adultery and Murder, then Sin and Death went Hand in Hand together against his Conscience, which made him cry out, he had sinned against the Lord.

And this is that, as I laid before, that doth seem to separate a true Believer in this Commission of the Spirit from that Peace and Joy they had in the Time of Health, which is to the great Dishonour of Truth, which no Prophet, nor God himself when on Earth, could prevent, the Fear of Death being not at Peace with Death in Health.

Query 6. Whether a Person dying so, may be accounted true in the Faith, and may notwithstanding obtain a Crown of Righteousness from the God of our Hope at the last Day?

Answer. That a Person so dying in Trouble and Distraction in the Hour of Death, if his Trouble and Distraction of Mind doth arise through some actual Sin, after the receiving of the Truth, then, except he can procure a Forgiveness from him that is the Head of that Doctrine which he received the Truth from; I say, such a Person that hath dishonoured the Truth, and hath committed Sin in Act, after he received the Knowledge of the Truth, he may not be accounted true in the Faith, neither can he obtain a Crown of Righteousness from the God of our Hope at the last Day, except he can procure Forgiveness of that Person as aforesaid.

Thus I have answered your six Queries, according to your Request; and having no other Matter, at this Time, to write unto you, I shall take Leave, and remain, in that eternal Truth, which none knoweth, but those that truly believe in this Commission of the Spirit,

Your Friend,

London, June 13, 1682.

LODOWICK MUCGLETON.

A COPY Of a LETTER written by the Prophet Lodowick Muggleton, to Colonel Phaire, and the rest of the Believers of the Commission of the Spirit. Dated in London, February 16, 1680.

Loving Friend in the true Faith, Robert Phaire,

I Having the Opportunity to send unto you by our Friend Mary Stone, the Daughter of Mrs. Penson, who came on purpose, as the faith, to see me and Saddington; therefore it was necessary that I should write a few Lines unto you, upon her Request, to signify unto you that she hath been with me; which Lines unto you are as followeth:

I have had great Experience of your stedfast Faith in the true God, and in this Commission of the Spirit, ever since you first heard of it, even above twenty Years; you have been, as it were, the Corner-stone, that was laid in that Kingdom of Ireland, which many have stumbled at, and have dashed their Foot against a Stone; and others again have built their House upon this Stone, as upon a Rock, so that no Winds nor Storms of Persecutions, Reproaches, Slanders, and Lies, could make it fall, or shake this Doctrine of the true God, in his Form and Nature, and of the right Devil, in his Form and Nature, which Reeve and Muggleton have declared in our Writings, which I perceive you and others are very well satisfied in, do truly understand and believe; for there can be no true Faith in the Heart, except the Understanding be enlightened first. And these two Forms and Natures are two Pillars; the one Pillar bears up Heaven, and the other bears up Hell.

Now, God's Form is spiritual, heavenly, and glorious, yet in the Form of Man, and his Nature is all pure Faith, which is all Power: Therefore all true Believers do partake of the Divine Nature of God, even the Seed of Faith, which is but as a Grain of Mustard Seed , a very small Seed; yet is able to remove that Mountain of Ignorance, Darkness, and Unbelief, that lyeth before the Understanding of every Man by Nature; so that by Faith we come to know the Worlds were framed by the Word of God; that is, by the Power of Faith in God. And by Faith in these our mortal Bodies, we come to know God in his Form and Nature; and by Faith we see God here in Mortality, as in a Glass, as the Apostles faith; and when this Faith is immortalized in the Resurrection, then shall our vile Bodies be made like unto his glorious Body, then shall Immortality appear, and shall see the immortal God in the Form of Man , Face to Face; even as we are seen of him, according to our Faith here in this Life, shall it be unto us.

Furthermore, by Faith we do feed upon the Flesh of God, and drink his Blood, as Christ said, when on Earth; Except you eat my Flesh, and drink my Blood, you have no Life in you; for his Flesh is Meat indeed, and his Blood Drink indeed.

And this I say, None upon Earth, at this Day, doth eat his Flesh, and drink his Blood, but those that do truly believe the Doctrine of this Commission of the Spirit: Why? Because no Man hath Faith to believe that God became Flesh, and dwelt amongst Men here upon Earth, who doth not believe that the Flesh of Christ was the Flesh of God, and the Blood of Christ to be the Blood of God; and who hath not Faith to believe, That the Godhead Life died when Christ was offered up unto Death through the eternal Spirit; no, not any but those that believe our Report.

Therefore it is that all religious Men perish for Want of Faith in the true God, they cannot eat the Flesh of God, that is Meat indeed, to satisfy their hungry Souls; neither can they drink the Blood of God, which is Drink indeed, to quench the thirsty Soul of Man. But blessed are your Eyes that see, and Ears that hear, and have Hearts that understand the Things that belong to your Peace; for God hath given you his own Flesh to eat, and his own Blood to drink, which hath assured you that you shall drink of those new Joys, and new Pleasures, and new Glories in the Kingdom of Eternal Glory.

This is that Wine that Christ, our God, our King, and Redeemer, will drink a-new with his Apostles, and us the Witnesses of the Spirit, and you the Believers, in the Kingdom of eternal Glory.

And this I say, all those, or all us, that have eat of the Flesh of God, and drank his Blood by Faith here in the State of Mortality, we shall be gathered together in the Resurrection (as the Fowls) to fly in the Midst of Heaven, being immortalized, shall come to the Supper of the great God, that we may eat of the fame Flesh as he eateth of, which is the Flesh of persecuting Kings, and the Flesh of Captains, and the Flesh of mighty Men, even of Judges, and the Flesh of Horses, and of them that sit on them, and the Flesh of all Free-men and Bond-men, and of Small and Great; that is, all wicked reprobate Men, both small and great, that have persecuted and hated the Lord's Prophets, Apostles, and Messengers, which he sent in this World.

Oh! how blessed are we that shall sup with the great God of Heaven, in the Destruction of our Enemies; for as God was hated when he was on Earth, so are we for his Sake; and as God is pleased to make his Supper with the Destruction of the Souls and Bodies of the Seed of the Serpent, to Eternity, and he hath invited us, the Fowls of Heaven, to sup with the great God, why should not we rejoice in this Supper which the great God hath made, even in the Destruction of this wicked World; for this Earth is a Habitation of Devils, while the World doth endure. And for my Part, I could willingly sup with the great God of Heaven, that hath redeemed my Soul, in the Destruction of this World, that I might eat the Flesh of mighty Men; Mayors, Judges, Juries, small and great Devils, that have hated me without a Cause. Oh! how happy are we that shall sup with the great God, that is, in the Assurance we have, that God hath ordained wicked persecuting Kings, and high Captains, and Judges, and mighty Men, and all other inferior Devils, both small and great, more than the Sand of the Sea-shore, which cannot be numbered, to be damned to Eternity, to suffer those eternal Torments.

These I know shall be cast alive into a Lake of Fire, burning with Brimstone, to all Eternity; and we, the Fowls of Heaven, shall eat or feed upon the Miseries of these mighty Men, as in a Supper with the great God, praising and magnifying him that redeemed us with his own Blood, from being Devils incarnate, or Devils in Flesh. And in this we shall eat the Flesh of Kings, and the Flesh of high Captains, and the Flesh of mighty Men-Devils, and the Flesh of small and great Devils. And this Supper, I know, we shall have with the great God in the Resurrection, when we shall ascend in the Clouds of Heaven, and meet the Lord in the Air, and leave the Devils, the Serpent, and his Seed, here upon this Earth, where they shall be tormented Day and Night for ever, and evermore, even to Eternity. This is the true Interpretation of John's Words, in the xixth Chapter of his Revelation, concerning the Supper of the great God, and the Fowls of Heaven; for God hath sowed in this World the Seed of Faith, which is counted the small Seed, even as one Grain of Mustard Seed, which indeed, as Christ saith, Matt. xiii, and 32, is the least of all Seeds; but, when it is grown, it is the greatest among Herbs. And it is a Tree, so that the Birds of Heaven came and built in the Branches thereof: So in Mark the ivth, and 31st, the Kingdom of God is compared to a Grain of Mustard Seed, which, when it is sown in the Earth, is the leaf of all Seeds; but after it is sown, it groweth up, and is greatest of all Herbs, and beareth great Branches, so that the Fowls of Heaven may build under the Shadow of it. So in Luke xiii, and 19, then said he, What is the Kingdom of God like? It is like a Grain of Mustard Seed, which a Man took and sowed in his Garden, and it grew and waxed a great Tree, and the Fowls of Heaven made Nests in the Branches thereof.

This small Grain is the Grain of Faith that was in God from Eternity, by which he created the Heaven and the Earth, and all Creatures else, in both Worlds, by this little Grain of Faith, no bigger than a Mustard Seed, hath he done all his Wonders. By this Grain of Faith did he sow himself in this Earth or Garden, which was in this World, which was in the Virgin's Womb, and brought forth himself a Man-Child, in pure Mortality. And this Grain of Faith, that was sown in the Field of this World, it grew up to be a Tree, that is, a Man, whose Branches spread themselves forth so thick, that the Fowls of Heaven do make their Nets in the Branches thereof.

This Tree of Faith, which is compared to a small Grain of Mustard Seed, was Christ, the only God, become Flesh; when he was in the Glory of the Father, he was that Man that sowed that Grain of Faith in the Field of this World, or in the Garden of Eden, when he breathed into Adam and Eve the Breath of Life, and they became living Souls: Then was this little Grain of Faith no bigger than a Grain of Mustard

Seed, sowed in the Field of the elect World: So that, all that are Partakers of this little Grain of Faith, they build their Nests in the Branches of this Tree, by having Peace, Salvation, and Life eternal abiding in them.

These are the Fowls of Heaven, that build their Salvation upon Christ's Death, Resurrection, and Ascension, which none in this World doth at this Day, but those that truly believe this Doctrine declared by Reeve and Muggleton. We are the Fowls of Heaven in this last Age, that have received a Measure of this Grain of Faith, which doth cause us to make our Nests, and rest quietly in the Branches of God's free electing Love, in his Redemption and Salvation.

Thus I have given you the true Interpretation of the Excellency of this little Grain of Faith, as small as a Grain of Mustard Seed, which you, that have but a Measure of it, can experience the Truth of it. Therefore I shall say no more at present, but remember my Love to yourself and good Wife, your Sons, and Daughters, that are Partakers of this precious Faith, and to all the Rest of our Friends in the true Faith, in that Kingdom, I take Leave, and remain,

Your Friend in the eternal Truth,

Feb. 16, 1680.

LODOWICK MUGGLETON.

A COPY of a LETTER written by the Prophet Lodowick Muggleton, to Mr. Edward Fewterell of Chesterfield, bearing Date from London, March 29, 1660.

Friend,

I Received your Letter, wherein I perceive you are a Man that hath been led through several Opinions, yet not suffered to join with any, but have been made to wait upon Jesus Christ, the only God, for Satisfaction; and now it hath been his great Love, which he hath loved you, to let you have a Sight of those infinite Truths written by the Hands of his two Witnesses, and Lawrence Claxton, which Writings of ours, I perceive, perceive, by your Letter, have given you more Satisfaction than any that ever you read before.

Only this I perceive, that you did, and do, still much approve of Jacob Bemon's Works, and for this Cause; because you were, as I perceive by his Writings, exhorted to resign your Will unto God's Will, and to come unto that happy State, neither to will or desire any Thing, but to abide in the Will of God, which is Jesus Christ, into which Estate the Lord did twice bring you in some Measure.

Also you say, that it is a hard Thing to cast out that Devil that is in us, nor can it be done, as we say, or think, but by that Resignation and Faith in the true God.

Likewise you say, that you were a great Disputant against all Forms and formal Worship, till the Lord silenced you, and did let you see it was but a vain Thing to wrangle and jangle with the Devil more.

But I shall pass by Part of your Letter, and I shall answer you to those Things that are of most Concernment.

You say, that there was that Portion of Scripture brought into your Remembrance, of his Promise, I will send the Spirit of Truth, which shall guide you into all Truth; and there have you had your Rest reposed.

In the last Place, I find that you would have some Answer to some Doubts, concerning that Devil that doth appear to Witches, and suck of their Bodies and what that is that doth appear to Conjurers, and the Authors of lying Wonders of John Robins, though you do believe there is no Devil but Man. You do believe also, that the Soul of Man is mortal, and must needs die, and so cannot appear, though you thought otherwise in your Reason.

You say, Whether is there a Spirit in Man, that surviveth, and is allured by them, or do they stir upon awaking the Power of the first fallen Angel through their devilish Faith; or is these Things from their vain Imaginations? If so, how? If not, what it is, is your Desire to know of me.

To which I shall give you some Answer, both to the first Part of your Letter, and also to the latter Part of it.

First, You say, That you have been made to wait upon Jesus Christ, the only God, for Satisfaction thereof.

I would have you to consider, how could you wait and be satisfied in the Belief of such a God, which you never knew? For the Letter of the Scriptures did never declare to you, that Jesus Christ was the only God; neither did God commissionate no Prophet nor Apostle for to declare it, though their Declarations was as necessary to be believed, in their Time and Place, as this Commission of the Spirit; which Commission of the Spirit hath deeper Mysteries held forth in it than the other two Commissions had: For God never did give to any Prophets or Apostles the Knowledge of his own Form or Nature, before he became Flesh; if they did know it, they did not reveal it; but he hath given it to his two last spiritual Witnesses and Prophets, John Reeve and Lodowick Muggleton, who were those chosen Witnesses of God, which should have more Understanding of the Mind of God, in the Scriptures, than all the Men in the World.

Which Knowledge of God's Mind in the Scriptures doth consist of these six Heads:

First, Of the Form and Nature of God, before he became Flesh.

Secondly, Of the Form and Nature of the Devil, before he became Flesh.

Thirdly, Of the Place and Nature of Heaven.

Fourthly, Of the Place and Nature of Hell.

Fifthly, Of the Nature and Persons of Angels.

Sixthly, Of the Mortality of the Soul.

Upon the Knowledge of these six Principles depends the eternal Happiness of many. And the Knowledge of the two Seeds is those two Keys that doth open those two, namely, the strait and narrow Gate, that leadeth unto Life, and the broad and wide Gate, that leadeth to Destruction. And those two Keys are given unto us two aforesaid, which hath the Commission of the Spirit given unto us.

So that there is no coming unto the Knowledge of the true God, nor the right Devil; but where the Declaration of this spiritual Commission doth open the Doors or Gates of Men's Hearts, and lets them see what Seed they are of. And so Men come to know the true God and the right Devil. And then a Man may truly say, that he can resign his Will to God's Will, as you say Jacob Bemon in his Writings doth declare.

Yet this I would have you to know, that Jacob Bemon had no personal God at all, not to resign his Will unto; but his God was an infinite, incomprehensible formless Spirit, as all the World hath; neither had his Devil a Person, nor Form; neither had his Angels he speaketh so much of any Body, or Form at all; but they were all Spirits without Bodies, which in Conclusion was no more but so many Letters, that is, three Letters, G. O. D. And so of the Devil and Angels.

And yet this Man would resign his Will unto God's Will, and yet his God had no Form nor Nature at all. Therefore there could be no Will in his God, whereby any Man should resign his Will into God's Will; whereas there can be no Will in God, except he hath both Form and Nature.

And this is that Will of God, which you call Jesus Christ, into which Estate the Lord did twice bring you; which Estate of yours in that Faith of Jacob Bemon's could not be a true Estate, because there was not the Knowledge of the true God. And where there is not the Knowledge of the true God, there cannot be the Knowledge of the right Devil.

Without the Knowledge of these two, there can be no true lasting Peace in Man.

And as for your being a great Disputant amongst all formal Worship, I do not question the Thing, because I know that the Wisdom of Reason, which is the Devil, doth love to be uppermost in Disputes.

But, how can you say, That the Lord did silence you, and made you to see the Vanity of all Disputes, whereas you did not know any other God, but what is generally believed on in the World; that is, an infinite, incomprehensible Spirit; not minding whether God had any Nature or Form at all?

Therefore it could not be the true Lord that did silence you, but it was something that did arise out of your own Seed, which did shew you the Vanity of all Disputes.

In the next Place you say, That there was brought into your Remembrance that Portion of Scripture concerning his Promise, that he would send his Spirit of Truth, which should guide you into all Truth, and there have you had your Rest reposed.

Answer. That this Place of Scripture did not belong unto you, nor to any Man in the World, at this Day; for that Promise was given only unto his Disciples, which Disciples of his, to whom those Words were spoken, were afterwards made Apostles of Christ; so that the Promise which Christ did Promise to his Disciples, before his Death, was that of the Blood, which was given unto his Apostles, which was called the Spirit of Truth; because it should lead them into all Truth; because they should witness unto the Truth, that is, unto his Death, and Resurrection, and Ascension.

Therefore take Notice of this, That that Promise was fulfilled upon his Apostles after he was ascended up to Heaven, as you may read in the second of the Acts, and not to every Man, that doth read the

Promises, which God did make to his commissionated Apostles, it doth not belong to every Man that doth read them; but every Man is to mind that Commission which he is under.

Therefore, for you to repose your Truth upon such Promises as were given to other Men in their Commission, that Peace will not endure to the End, but will vanish like Smoak in the Fire.

In the next Place, I shall give you some Answer to those Doubts which you spake of, concerning that Devil which doth appear to Witches and Conjurers, and how those lying Wonders were acted by John Robins.

Answer. There is a twofold Witchcraft, the one is natural, the other is spiritual

Now this natural Witchcraft is acted by such as are called Witches and Conjurers. Now as for those ignorant Women, which are Witches, their Witchcraft lies in their wicked Nature, by giving themselves up to believe that there is no God at all, but Nature only, and so by that strong Faith that they have in Nature, they have Power over those whose Understandings are of a lower Capacity than themselves; and so People being ignorant and fearful of them, doth many Times disturb and search their Blood with the Extremity of Fear, which they have of one that is suspected for a Witch, and so by their own Fear and Imagination they come to be bewitched. As a Man being overcharged with extreme Grief, or being prevented by one that he loves, he goes distracted, or runneth mad, which is no other but his being bewitched. And so it is with all those that are ignorant and overcharged with Fear; and as for those Children and Cattle that are bewitched, it is by some other Sorcery, which they do use, with Herbs and Plants, and some other Things of Nature, they having some small Knowledge of that Sympathy and Influence the Stars have over those Bodies and Herbs; and so mixeth their Faith and Experience together, pretending to do all Manner of Good, but intendeth nothing but Evil; so that there is no such Thing as People do vainly imagine, as for Spirits to suck Witches; but all the Devils that is, is their own dark Reason, and that Spirit that doth bewitch any Creature, it doth arise out of their own Imagination. And as for Conjurers and Magicians, their Reason is more enlightened than the others is, because they do go altogether by the Figure, which is an Art by which the Reason of Man hath produced Characters and Figures for the several Stars and Planets; and so they came to imagine the Influences of those Stars and Planets upon the Bodies of Men; and many Times they do affright, yet it is still but Witchcraft, for it is nothing else but the Imagination of Reason, that doth prye into the Secrets of Nature. And the first Witchcraft that ever was, it was produced by learning of Numbers and Figures, I say it was first from the Egyptians Arts, and from thence came Conjuration, and the Knowledge of the Influence of the Stars and Planets, and the Knowledge of Physick, which are no other in the

Original but Witches; only this their Witchcraft is more tolerated by the Powers of the Nations; but I am confident that there is more People in the World bewitched with them, than there is with the other Sort of Witches; that is, they are deceived both in Body and in Mind, and Estate; for when a Man is deceived in his Expectations and Faith which he had in that Art, he may very well be said to be bewitched. But as for the railing of Spirits, without Bodies, there is no Witch, no Conjurer, or Magician, nor the greatest Artist in the World, can do; neither can any Spirit assume any Body but its own.

So much for natural Witches.

And as for those lying Signs and Wonders which John Robins did act, it was by a mere spiritual Witchcraft; his was not by the Knowledge of the Stars, though he had some Skill in that too; but the Power of his Witchcraft did lie in the affirming and taking upon him the Title of the great God, as you may read in our Books; and so that his Reason being more excercised in the Scriptures, upon spiritual Matters, because the whole Body of the Scriptures doth consist of spiritual and heavenly Matter; and he having more Knowledge in the Mystery of the Scriptures, at that Time, than all Men in the World, therefore he had many that did fall down and worship him, because his Knowledge in the Scriptures did surpass other Men, and so produced Voices in himself, and could present lying Signs and Wonders unto all those that were deceived by him, or that were afraid of him. Yet he did not deal with Spirits that had not Bodies, but all that Wisdom and Witchcraft that he did shew, it came or arose out of his own Spirit of Reason, which was inclosed in his own Body. And there is the Influence of the same Spirit of Witchcraft doth now remain upon those People called Quakers, notwithstanding their seeming Holiness; for they have many Times such fleshly Fits falling upon them, which doth seem as if they had the Falling-Sickness, and be as Men dumb, and will not speak a Word for three or four Hours together, and upon a sudden, they will break forth into a strong Language, as if the Spirit did immediately move them to speak. This, I say, it is nothing else but an Influence of John Robins's spiritual Witchcraft, which is produced out of their own Spirit within them, and not from any Spirit which hath no Body, without them. And all this is because they have no Knowledge of the true God, or the right Devil.

Therefore it is that the greatest Part of the World doth lie under Witchcraft, either a natural Witchcraft or a spiritual Witchcraft; there is a very few, that is delivered from being under one or both of them. There is none delivered but those that are come to have Faith in this spiritual Commission, which is now extant in the World; for Faith in it doth lead Men to the Knowledge of the true God and the right Devil, with all those deep Mysteries, which doth depend on them, the Knowledge of which doth free a Man from all Witchcrafts whatsoever.

Therefore, I would advise you to read the Book of ours, called The Divine Looking-Glass; for that you may see there, that there can be no Spirits without a Body; neither can any Witch or Conjurer raise any

Spirit without a Body: But these Conjurers may do, through the Ignorance and Darkness of Man's Reason, and that Fear and Belief that is in the Ignorant, they may, by their ignorant Power, raise a Shadow of Things, as if they were real Bodies, or Spirits, in the Shape of Bodies, as the Egyptians did before Pharaoh, King of Egypt; they did seem to raise Frogs and Grasshoppers in the Sight of Pharaoh, King of Egypt but I say they were not real Frogs and Grasshoppers, but Shadows of such Things, which as soon as ever their Witchcraft Power Art was over, their Frogs and Grasshoppers were gone also, else would the King and his People been as much troubled at those Frogs, which the Magicians did bring up on their Land, as they were with those which Moses brought up, which went into their Houses. And now, if Moses had not raised Bodies, as well as Spirits; or if he had raised Spirits without Bodies, they would have been as little troubled at those Things which Moses did, as they were at those Shadows, or seeming Things, which the Magicians of Egypt did. There is some more of the Letter; but I have not Time to writ it. Vale, so resteth your Friend,

London, March; 29, 1660.

LODOWICK MUGGLETON.

A DISCOURSE between John Reeve and Richard Leader, Merchant; recited by Lodowick Muggleton, one of the two last Witnesses and Prophets of the most high God, the Man Christ Jesus in Glory.

THIS Richard Leader, not withstanding he was well satisfied in spiritual Things, as to his eternal Happiness, yet there was some Things as to temporal Matters, which we had declared, that he could not as yet consent unto, because it was contrary to the Rule and Art of Astrology and Philosophy; for I asked him what it was; he said, you declare the Sun is not much bigger than it seemeth to be, and our Art saith it is threescore Times bigger than the Earth: Also, said he, you say the Moon doth not borrow any Light of, nor from the Sun: Likewise you say, that the Heavens is not much above six Miles high from the Earth; and we by our Art do say, the Heavens are Thousands of Miles high from the Earth; these Things, saith he, seemeth something strange.

Then I answered, and said unto him, You are a Man, that have travelled through many Parts of the World, and you have been in that Place, called the equinoctial Line, where the Sun is nearest to the Earth of any other Place, where the Heat is so great, that no Creature can scarce live, the Sun is so hot; did the Sun seem any bigger to your Sight, when it was near to the Earth, than at other Times, when you were at a Distance? You saw the full Proportion of it, did you not? He answered, and said, he did. Then said I, did the Sun seem any bigger to your Eye-sight, where it was near to the Earth, than at other Times? He answered, no not any bigger, as he could discern. Why then, said I, will you believe your lying Figure, before you will believe your own Eye-sight? You must either say, the Sight of your Eye is false, or the traditional Figure you depend upon is false; now hath not God appointed the Sight of the Eye to be Judge of that it sees? But Men hath chose rather to believe their lying Imagination, which they never saw, nor never can see, nor knows not what it is; therefore it hath erected a Figure, that Man might be led into Darkness, imagine Things that are not; and make People believe, that the natural Sight, that God hath given Men in their Creation, to be Judge of what it sees, to be a false Sight, and a false Judge; and your dark Imagination and Figure to be a true Light, and a true Judge of the Bigness of the Sun. For consider,

That the Imagination of Reason in Man, doth always judge God to be bigger than he is, or lesser than he is; likewise Imagination being blind, it judgeth God's Power to be greater than it is, or lesser than it is; and so it doth in the Works of Creation: As for Example; the Imagination of Man judgeth, that God made this vast Earth and Waters of Nothing; which is more than God could do, for he never made any Thing of Substance of Nothing, for of Nothing comes Nothing; for what Thing or Creature, that God made of Nothing, God will turn it to Nothing again. Then would it be well for all wicked Men, if the Earth was made of Nothing, and Men made of the Dust of the Earth; then, when this Earth is turned to Nothing, its Original also; but this Earth was an eternal dark Chaos, and shall return at the last Day into Darkness again, and wicked reprobate Man shall live upon this Earth in eternal Torments, in utter Darkness, for ever and ever.

So that neither the Earth, nor wicked Man, the Seed of the Serpent, shall neither of them both be turned to Nothing, but shall be in utter Darkness to Eternity. Again, the Imagination judgeth the Sun, Moon, and Stars, to be of vast greater Bigness, though they seem to be small Bodies to us; so that the Imagination of Man, being blind, judgeth every Thing bigger than it is, or lets than it is; though God hath made the Sun, Moon, and Stars, little Bodies, to give Light unto the Earth and Waters, and in their Light, the Creatures here on Earth do see Light; and God hath made these Lights, Bodies in Heaven, to answer to that Light that is in little Bodies here on Earth. And shall a Man say, the Light of his Eyes is no true Light, but the Imagination, that seeth not at all, is called true Light; thus it is with Astrology, and Philosophy, that judgeth God to be bigger than he is, or lesser than he is, and his Power to be greater than it is, to create this vast Earth and Waters of Nothing; and the Sun, Moon, and Stars, of such a vast Bigness, all out of Nothing: So that the lying Imagination hath created to itself a bigger God than the true God, and this God hath a greater Power, and hath created Things of a more bigger Magnitude, than the true God ever did, and could do, as to make this Earth of Nothing, and the Sun, Moon, and Stars, of such a vast Bigness, far bigger than ever the true God made them. But to tell the Imagination of Man of the true God, that created Man in his own Image, he became Flesh, and became a little Child, and grew to a Man, and suffered Death by his own Creatures. O! no, faith the Reason in Man, God could not die, it is impossible for God to die; here God's Power is looked upon, by the Imagination of Men's Hearts, to be less than it is.

Objection 1. Said he, The Sun may seem to be but a little Body, because of the great Distance from us: As for Example, let a Man upon the Top of Paul's, and at a Distance he will shew as little as a Crow. To this he answered and said, Indeed a dark Body at a Distance doth shew less than it is. But, said I, let a light Body, as a Torch, or Candle, be but a Mile above the Earth, if it were possible, and it shall shew bigger a hundred Miles Distance from it. As for Example:

When a Beacon is let on Fire, it seemeth a greater Blaze forty Miles Distance, than it doth near at Hand, for it is but a little Thing of itself; yet nevertheless, it is the Nature of all light Bodies, to shew rather bigger at a Distance, than they are of themselves; and it is the Nature of all dark Bodies, to seem less at a Distance, than they are in themselves. When he heard this, he was convinced; and did acknowledge, that it must needs be so in Nature, that light Bodies did show bigger at a Distance, and dark Bodies less; so that the Sun being a bright Fire, light Body, and running so swift in its Course, it could not be much bigger than it seemeth to be, notwithstanding he had long imagined the contrary.

Objection 2. Saith he, We by our Art doth judge, that the Moon doth borrow her Light of the Sun, because; saith he, In far as the Sun is right against the Moon, so far the Moon is light, and when the Moon is at the Full, the Face of the Sun is right over it; so that sometimes the Moon seems to have a dark Body, only a little Piece of it forked, why is it then, said he? Because the Sun is right against no more of the Moon, and so much of it as the Sun is against it, it receiveth Light from the Sun, and the rest of the Body of the Moon seemeth dark: To this I answered and said,

If this should be so, then that Saying of Scripture, Gen, i, v. 16, must be laid aside, where it is said, God made two great Lights, the greater Light to rule the Day, and the lesser Light to rule the Night. Certainly the Moon hath Light in itself to rule the Night, else those Words cannot be true; for if God made the Moon a dark Body, and that it hath no Light in itself, but what it receiveth from the Sun, then God made but one great Light, and one dark Body, and not two great Lights; for if the Moon hath not Light in herself, but doth borrow of the Sun, then the Moon had no Light in her Creation: A Man may as well say, That a Man is a living Man, that hath no Life in him; for if a Man hath not Life in himself, he cannot move no farther, than a Man that hath Life doth carry him; so likewise if the Moon were a dark Body, and had no Light in itself, how could it move to rule the Night? The Sun, that hath always Light in itself, must carry the Body of the dark Moon, and move it about the Firmament of Heaven, to rule the Night, which would be a great Trouble to the Sun to do two Bodies Works; for God hath set every Thing in order, and every particular Thing shall do it's own Work; the Sun shall rule the Day, and the Moon shall rule the Night, and the Stars shall give their Light; so that every Thing that God hath made, shall do their own Works, according to the Law God hath placed in their Natures. If the Moon must rule the Night according to God's Command, certainly he gave the Moon a Light in itself to rule with, else it could not rule; for borrowed Lights never ruleth well. A Man that is Stone-blind, may as well say to another Man that can see, I would borrow your Eye-sight, that I may see the Light of the Sun, as you do: This cannot be done, for in Light we see Light; for there must be two Lights, else a Man cannot tell that there is any Light at all.

For that Man that was born blind, could not tell that there was any Sun or Light at all in the Day-time, but as he heard others say; but when Christ opened his Eyes, then he law Light, because he saw Light in himself; and when he received his Light, was not this Light of his Eyes in himself? Was it any borrowed Light, or Light for Christ? I trow not, for God hath made every Creature, that hath Light in itself, to see another Light that is out of itself; so that in Light we see Light; there must be two Lights, else Things cannot be distinguished; for dark Bodies, that hath not Life and Light in itself, cannot borrow Life and Light of any other; neither can the Moon borrow any Light of the Sun at all, for it hath an inherent Light in itself in it's Creation, as the Sun hath in it's Creation; so that the Words of Moses are true, that God made two great Lights, the Sun to rule the Day, and the Moon to rule the Night; only the Moon hath a lesser, but both hath a Light in themselves, and doth not borrow one Light of the other; else how could the Moon fight with the Sun in the Eclipse sometimes; if the Moon were a dark Body, and had no Light in itself, could it oppose the Sun as it doth, that the Moon even darkens the Sun in the Fight? Can a dark Body fight with the Light of the Sun? You may as well say, that a dark Body may fight with a living Man: But these Fictions of Men's Imaginations, hath deceived the whole World, and keepeth the People in Darkness, and putteth out their own Light of their Eyes, and calleth Darkness Light, and Light Darkness, even in Things that are visibly seen.

Objection 3. Then said he, How comes it to pass, that there is so many new Moons, and sometimes we see but a Piece of the new Moon, and do discern the rest of the Body to be dark, and so the Moon doth intrace the dark Bodies filled up with Light; so that in a Matter of fifteen Days, the Moons full and all Light, and in a little Time, it is quite gone, and seen no more in our Horizon. To this I answered, and said,

Were you ever up in the Firmament of Heaven? Do you know by your Imagination how God hath framed it, and how many Chambers he hath made in it? And how many Planets, Stars, and Lights, he hath put in every Chamber, in the Firmament of Heaven? You Astrologers yourselves say there is twelve Houses and four Housons, are you sure there is no more Houses in the Firmament of Heaven, but twelve? And do you know how many Lights there is in every House, and when these Lights do remove out of one House into another? Or do you know whether one Star doth take its Light from another Star? Or hath every Star Light in itself? Or doth the Light of the Stars and Planets remain in their own Bodies, and neither increase nor decrease their Light, since they were made and fit in the Firmament of Heaven? Is there any of those Stars or Lights in the Firmament of Heaven missing, that were made at first? Or hath any of them lost their Light God put in them at first, when God created the Heavens and the Earth?

If you can tell this, then you can say something, as the Moon borroweth Light of the Sun; but to give you a little further satisfaction; God hath placed the Sun, Moon, and Stars in the Firmament of Heaven, and every one of these, Houses of their own, that is, the Place where they first began to give Light, and to shine upon the Earth, that is, the House of the Sun, Moon, and Stars; now God that made them, knoweth the House and the Place of the Firmament of Heaven, where they first began to give Light; because he had measured out the Firmament of Heaven, because he made it; but Man doth not know, nor cannot know by his Imagination, Art, and Figure; also God hath given these Lights Power to go out of their own House, into any of the Chambers of Heaven, even as a Man doth out of his own Dwelling House, into more remote Parts, yet the Man retaineth his own Wisdom and Knowledge, when he is remote from his own Dwelling House, as at Home; so it is with the Sun, Moon, and Stars, though they go out of their own House, yet they retain the same Light in themselves, wherever they go. And if God hath made the Sun so swift and bright, to run through all the Houses of the Firmament of Heaven, in twenty-four Hours, yet that is the Sun's own House, where it went first from, and it is the Work God hath appointed the Sun to do every Day and Night; and when the Sun is absent, in its Place, the Moon supplieth her Light, and the Moon not being so swift as the Sun, it cometh not so soon into our Horizon as the Sun doth; betides, it passeth throughout the same Region as the Sun doth, but in a Region of a lower Degree in the Firmament of Heaven, than the Sun doth; and the Cause why the Moon sheweth the Light, but a little Piece of her, when the is but a Quarter old, so by Degrees she increaseth, till she is at the Full, so that the Full Face and Light of her, may be seen by the Light of the Eye. The Cause why we see her by a little and a little, is, the cometh out of one Chamber or House of Heaven into another, and as the Houses and the Firmament of Heaven be at such a Distance one from another, so we see her Light the more, and we see her sometimes half light and half dark; now the Piece that seemeth dark, it is because she is not come out of that House or Region; but when she is come to that Horizon, where the was at the Full, then she is all Light and no Darkness at all; not but that she was all light in herself before at all Times, but she was in some Chamber of Heaven, which shadowed her so, that we could not see her whole Light of her whole Face. As for Example: Suppose a Man stand in a Bottom, and there be two high Hills before him, at a Distance one from the other, the Man standing in the Bottom, discerneth a Man upon the Top of the farther Hill, so seeing him come down the Hill a pretty Way, but a little lower he loseth the Sight of the Man, until such Time as the Man cometh up that Hill nigh to him, and when he cometh to the Top of this Hill before me, I do discern first his Head, then after his Face, then after his Body, so that I see it is a perfect Man which I law at first, but this Hill before me hindred the Sight of him till he came to the Top of it: So it is with the Moon, a Man cannot discern the full Face of her, till she hath passed in her Journey thro' all those Houses of the Heavens, which lieth lower in that Region where she is, so that the Hill and Mountain of the Earth doth hinder the Sight of her, until she cometh to the Top of the Hill of our Horizon, then can we see her whole Face; for the Earth is as a Ball, standing upon and in the Air; that is, the Power of God's Word hath made the Air a Foundation for the Earth to stand upon; therefore it is, that the Earth standeth upon Nothing as a Man can see; and this is the Foundation God hath laid this vast Earth upon: And who could lay the Foundation of this Earth upon such a Foundation as the Air? None but God only, whose Power is infinite and unspeakable. Likewise the Earth about with the Element, then the Earth must needs interpose and shadow the Light of the Moon, so that she cannot be seen in her perfect Light, until she stands upon the Top of the Ball; but those that are on every Side and underneath the Ball cannot see her. for she is always at the Full in herself, tho' a Man cannot see her so perfectly, but when she is at the Full; yet the Moon is the same Light in herself always, as when she is at the Full, tho' those on the Sides and underneath cannot see her; neither is there any Newness in her, but she is the same Today, Yesterday, and same for ever, as long as the World lasteth; ever the great Light, which God created and appointed to rule the Night in one Place or other of this World continually: This is Truth, and Moses's Words are Truth, whatever Man by their Imaginations do say to the contrary.

Objection 4. Well, said he, how will you make it appear, that the Heavens are not above six Miles high from the Earth?

I answered and said, that I will make it appear by Scripture and Reason. That will do well, (said he.) Then said I, see that Scripture, Gen. xi. 4. And they said, Go to, let us build us a City, and a tower, whose Top may reach unto Heaven: And in the 5th Verse, And the Lord came down to see the City and the tower which the Children of Men builded: And the 6th Verse, And the Lord said, behold the People is One, and they have all one Language, and this they begin to do, and now nothing will be restrained from them, which they have imagined to do. Here, said I, it is plain, that there was a Possibility for the Sons of Men to build a tower up to Heaven; now if Heaven had been Thousands of Miles high, as the lying Art of Astrology saith, there could have been no Possibility to build up to Heaven, and that these Men's Reason know well enough, neither could they have laid a Foundation to build Thousands of Miles high; now the Imagination of Reason in these Men were more right, which went by no Figure, nor Rule of Art, but by the Sight of the Eye, and their Reason and Sense; and they did imagine by the Sight of the Eye, that it could not be above three Miles to the Clouds, which the Philosophers grant by their Art, the Clouds to be but three Miles high from the Earth; so they imagined that the Firmament could not be above three Miles higher; and we do imagine, said they, in themselves, that they might lay a Foundation to build six Miles, and thought they, when we come up to the Clouds in Building, we shall see then how far it is to the Firmament, and so build up unto it. Now, the Lord himself said, it was possible for them to do what they had imagined, for (saith he,) Nothing will restrain them for what they have imagined to do. So that God knew there was a Possibility to build up to Heaven, else he would never come down from Heaven himself, to prevent them, in confounding their Language, if the Heavens had been Thousands of Miles high: Besides, said I, do you think, when Christ ascended up to Heaven, after he was risen from the Dead, that he ascended with that Body thousands of Miles high, from where he ascended up to Heaven? It is said Acts i 9. While the Men beheld, a Cloud received him out of their Sight. That is, they saw him ascend up as far as the Clouds, which is half Way to the Firmament of Heaven; for the Clouds opened for him to pass through, and closed together again, out of their Sight; for they could not see no farther than the Clouds: Likewise, when the Prophet Elijah went up to Heaven in a fiery Chariot with Horses of Fire, Do you believe that he had thousands of Miles to Heaven? He said, No: Besides, there is a Possibility to build up to Heaven now, as there was then, only it is forbidden of God: But this I say, if it were lawful, and that a Man was fore to live 7 or 800 Years upon this Earth, as they did then, then a Man might as easily build up to Heaven now, as then; were it lawful, as I said before.

So that God hath not made the Heavens so high, as the lying Imagination of Reason hath; for Reason imagineth the Heavens to be higher than they are; and Reason imagines Hell to be lower than it is; so that Heaven is so high, that Reason can never ascend up to it, and Hell so deep, that Reason can find no Bottom; therefore called, A Bottomless Pit, when indeed Hell is but six Miles Distance from Heaven to this Earth, where Men acted all their Wickedness, shall be that Place of Hell for all the Damned, and the Place where the Devil and his Angels, which are wicked Men and Women, shall be tormented to Eternity.

But the Seed of Faith knoweth the Heighth of the Heavens, and but a few Miles high, and can easily ascend up to it; and Faith knoweth the Bottom of Hell, and knoweth it is upon this Earth, and no deeper than this Earth, and that the Bottomless Pit, so much feared by Man, it is in a Man, and not without a Man: Therefore, said I unto him, your Figure, Rule and Art, must be laid down; but Arithmetick and Numbers is necessary only for Things on this Earth, to measure Land, and other Accounts between Man and Man here on Earth; your Arithmetick and Figures is not to measure the Heighth of the Heavens, nor the Depths of Hell, that belongeth only to the Seed of Faith, being God's own Nature.

Faith measureth the Height of Heaven, and the Deepness of Hell: Therefore, in these Things, you are to lay aside your Figure Art, and depend wholly upon Belief of what we have said in there Things, because your Reason, Skill and Art, let it be never so great, cannot disprove a stedfast Faith.

When he heard this Discourse, with much more than is here written, he was very well satisfied in there Things, and many others, and he grew very mighty in Wisdom and Knowledge, both in natural Wisdom and heavenly; so that every great Man of his Acquaintance did submit to his Wisdom, and loved him for his Knowledge; so he continued in it all his Life: But about a Year or two after John Reeve died, he died at Barbados.

A LETTER from the Prophet Muggleton.

Loving and kind Friend in the true Faith, Thomas Tomkinson,

MR. Delamaine would have written sooner, but being in great Trouble, had not Leisure to write; for the Shepherd being smitten, the Sheep were all scattered. Upon the 17th Day of January last past, Judgment was given upon me, to stand upon the Pillory in three several Places of the City of London, and the Books they took away from me were divided into three Parts, and were to be burnt before my Face, those three Days I stood on the Pillory.

So they offered up the Books as three Burnt-offerings, to the unknown God; and they offered me up as a Sacrifice, to be slain by the rude Multitude; and it was a wonderful Providence I was not slain outright.

I was exposed to the uttermost Rigour of the Law, more than any ever did, that suffered in that Time however, they have shed the Blood of the last Prophet, although not to Death. Oh! what shall be done to this bloody City, for shedding innocent Blood! The God of Heaven will say unto this bloody City, You shall be punished with Poverty, Beggary, and Imprisonment.

But those that have had a Hand in the Persecution and Blood of my Servant the Prophet, shall be cast into that bottomless Pit, in utter Darkness, where shall be wailing and gnashing of Teeth for evermore, where they shall never see bright Day, to Eternity.

This, I am sure, will be the Effect upon those that have had a Hand in these Sufferings of mine. I cannot enlarge in particular of these great Sufferings of mine, that hath hapened to me of late, it would be too large a Volume, to relate the Particulars of it; but you may understand by a little what a great deal means. So being in Haste, I shall take Leave, and rest, only my Love to yourself, and my Wife's Love to yourself and your Wife, and all Friends else there with you,

I rest your Friend in the true Faith,

From the Press-yard, Newgate,
    April 23, 1677.

LODOWICK MUGGLETON.

An EPISTLE To a QUAKER

Dear and loving Friend,

I Shall not salute thee about perishing Natures, or empty Observations, for the exalting of an Idol; but the Desire of my Soul is, that we may be found real in the Things of the Spirit, that we may be impowered to perform our Christian Duties to each other, in the Things of Flesh; which is that which girts the Spirit, or strengthens the Soul with lasting Peace.

Is it not a real Comprehension of him that made us, by Virtue of his heavenly Light or Love abiding in us? If this be true, as I am certain it is, how is it possible then, that we should be one in Spirit, or in the Flesh either, until the true God be made manifest to us, or in us? Indeed Time was when I was strongly deceived with an Imagination of the eternal Salvation of all Mankind, though they lived and died under Power of all Manner of Unrighteousness whatsoever. And this Error arose in me through a lying Doctrine, founding in my Ears, of a pretended universal Love to the whole Creation, from those People called Ranters, which gilded Love I found at length to be nothing else but carnal Lust, in the Bottom of it; why, because it had no spiritual Foundation to build his Faith and Hope upon, but within itself only.

Peradventure, thou at this present mayst imagine, that thy Society, called Quakers, are endued with more excellent Light than all others whatsoever; but if I should condescend to such an Imagination, I must belye the Light of all Things, which, through his eternal free Love, hath lately shined into my dark Soul; but it hath not so shined into it as to persuade me to mind no other God or Christ, present Light, or future Glory, but what is within me only, as formerly I did, when I was deluded to idolize my own lying Imagination with Titles of divine Glory, by worshipping of it with the holy Name of eternal Jehovah, or Jesus, and calling of it the high and lofty One, or holy One of Israel, the only begotten Son of God, the everlasting Father, the Daughter of Sion, the Glory of all Perfections, with many other such like heavenly Expressions, which indeed belongs only to a glorious personal God, eternally living without me, and not to any spiritual God or Christ, Light or Glory, that is, or may be within me, in the least.

For whilst I groped after Light and Life, only within myself, behold I met with nothing but thick Darkness, and a secret Fear of an everlasting Vengeance; but since I came really to understand that all the spiritual Godhead is wholly abiding, remaining, or dwelling in the glorified Body of the Man Christ Jesus, and that by the Light or Virtue of his Spirit only, he lives by his redeemed Ones, I have enjoyed much sweet Peace, and pure Hopes of spiritual Glories, in that Life to come, which are eternal.

Moreover, though the Variety of spiritual, or temporal Joy and Glory, be of none Effect to the Creature, without an inward Manifestation of it, yet, when I feel a Want of new and heavenly Consolations, to satisfy my hungry Soul, thro' the manifold Temptations of the Flesh, behold I seek not for it from any spiritual Light or Life that is within me, or within Men or Angels, because, by woful Experience, I certainly know it is not there to be found; but the Light in me ascends up on high without me, even into the glorious Body of the everlasting God-Man Christ Jesus, the Lord both of Quick and Dead, whose spiritual Godhead wholly died with its Manhood, and lived again alone by his own Power, and from thence, from whence alone all spiritual Excellencies proceed, received I divine Satisfaction in this Life, according to my present Necessity, with a full Assurance of a transcendent bodily Glory in that Life to come, at the Resurrection of all the Souls and Bodies of Mankind that are dead, asleep in the Dust of the Earth, when Time shall be no more.

I say again, as aforesaid, that all the true Peace, Joy, or Glory, which the Creature doth or shall enjoy in this Lifer or the Life that is to come, proceeds not from any spiritual God or Christ, Light, or Life, or Glory, that is within the Spirits of Men or Angels, in the least; but it flows only from an infinite Fountain of spiritual Glories, which are wholly dwelling in the Man Christ Jesus, that is without them, the personal Majesty, in the Sight of many true Witnesses, visible ascended far above all imaginary bodiless Gods, Heavens, Angels, or Men.

Furthermore, notwithstanding all this, if thou shouldst still imagine, that both our Lights may or will produce eternal Life in us at the last, though we should be at Variance about the Knowledge of the true God and his divine Worship, to our Lives End, I am not of thy Mind. Why? because as there is but only one true God, so likewise I certainly know there is but only one true Light or Worship, appertaining to his glorious Person, which Worship of his is now only spiritual and invisible, suitable to an invisible Glory.

Now thou mayst suppose thou art guided by an inward pure Light, yet certainly know, that instead of spiritual teaching, grounded upon a firm Foundation, thou art in Bondage to outward Forms and empty Declarations, proceeding from Man's carnal Spirit, who, through fleshly Guilt and Loftiness of Spirit, with a pretended pure Language and Practice above all other, Pope-like, are violently hurried about, to proselyte the whole World to themselves, which cunningly they endeavour to bring to pass by the Sword of the Tongue, for Want of a Sword of Steel in their Hand, deluding their own Souls, and many of their Hearers, vainly to imagine, that all Men and Women have so much true Light in them, which will make them eternally happy, if they will.

But the Light in me witnesses the contrary; for by it I am really informed, that there are select Numbers of Mankind, who, in the free

Love of the Creator, were set apart for the Enjoyment of the Light of Life eternal, even before the Foundation of the World was laid.

So likewise, on the contrary, I am fully satisfied against all Gainsayers, that there is a Generality of Men and Women, who, in the Foreknowledge or Purpose of the living God, were ordained to an Estate of Unbelief in his glorious Person, and the spiritual Mysteries of his heavenly Kingdom, that they might everlastingly perish, even for Want of the Light of Life eternally shining in them: So that it is clear to a spiritual Eye, that it is not in him that willeth, nor in him that runneth, but in God alone that sheweth Mercy unto eternal Salvation, or withholds his divine Light or Love to himself, unto everlasting Condemnation, as aforesaid.

And who shall be able, in the great Day of Accompt, to look on his Face, and to say unto him, Why haft thou made one all glorious, and another altogether miserable? Woe be unto them that contend with their Maker, by speaking Evil of him and his secret Councils, which they know not, which he hath not revealed to the dark Multitude, nor never will, no, nor to any Speaker that hath handled a Sword of Steel to slay Mankind, or hath defiled his Marriage Bed, under what Pretence whatsoever.

Again, I say unto thee, that the Light in me disowns those Men to be spiritual Commissioners, or Witnesses unto the true God, that say they are guided by an infallible Spirit, through which they speak against all deceivable Preaching or Writings to the People, and yet do the very same Thing.

Moreover, the Light in me bears Witness against all Kind of publick or private Meetings in the World, in a ministerial Way of Worship, as not by a Commission from the Holy One of Israel, Why? Because of the great Ignorance I find in them of the one spiritual God, and personal Glory, prepared for his Elect, and bodily Misery ordained for the Reprobate, at the last Day; therefore, as before, I certainly know, that such Men have no Authority from the living God, to prophecy, preach, or speak of heavenly Things to the People, but only from their own lying Imaginations.

Furthermore, I say again, the Light in me bears Witness against those Men that own no other spiritual God or Christ, but what is within the Creature, or within this Creation only, to be for the present in the deepest Darkness of all Mankind, concerning heavenly Things, or that worship the literal Word Light, instead of Jesus Christ, the eternal Word, who alone is both God and Man in one single Person, glorified as aforesaid, whole ever-blessed Body is a fiery glorious Substance, distinct from all Things and Places, that he alone is worthy, may have the Pre eminency over all, and in all, who above all is worthy, having purchased it from himself, by Virtue of the pouring forth of his Godhead-Life, Blood unto Death, and quickening that divine Life again, in the very same Body that died, into transcendent ravishing Glories, even out of silent Death, or Darkness itself.

Now I am compell'd from undeceivable Experience, to let thee know, that thou haft never heard such a Language of seeming glorious Enjoyment, from any imaginary God or Christ abiding within the Creature only, as I have done; therefore it is not the Words of Men or Angels that can now convince me in the least, that they are in the Truth, unless they are able plainly to declare who or what that God or Christ is, both in his Nature, Form, and Essence, from whence they suppose they enjoy such spiritual Consolation above all others, that are not endued with the same Light.

For as Men's painted Words will not fill the Belly, nor cloath the Back, without Food and Raiment; so likewise an imaginary God of goodly Words, only living within the Creatures, will not satisfy my hungry Soul, without the real Knowledge of a glorious Substance to feed upon.

But peradventure, thou mayst reply and say unto me, that every rational Man and Woman, hath so much true Light in them, that will lead them to the real Knowledge of the true spiritual God, whereby they may attain everlasting Happiness if they will, by hearkening unto it with a diligent and obedient mind; Many are called, but few are chosen, for all Men have not Faith: Wherefore to this I answer, if this thy supposing of all Men possessing spiritual Light in them, were as true as it is false, indeed then there would be no need of any other spiritual God to instruct Mankind but what is within them only.

Again, if every rational Soul were possest with never so little of Salvation Light in it, how is it possible that it should live and die in Wrath with God or Man, as commonly it doth? What, is Man principally guided in spiritual Things, is it the Light of his own Spirit or another Spirit? Now if you acknowledge it to be the Light of Gods Spirit that bears Rule in the Creatures, what is it then that purifies the whole Man from all Filthiness of Flesh and Spirit, and leads it into Righteousness? is it the Light or Will of his own Spirit, or of the Spirit of God, as aforefaid? Now if it be the Light of another Man's Spirit, that opens Man's dark Understanding, enabling them, in some Measure, to comprehend the glorious and wonderful Things of Eternity, and not the Light of their own Spirit, as I am certain it is; it is not then in the Power of any Man's Will, at his Pleasure to obey or disobey the Light that is in him, as many Men vainly imagine. But it is the Power of God's Will only by his most blessed Spirit, to perswade Man's Spirit to be willing to yeild Obedience to the Light that he hath freely given him, or sometimes it is his Pleasure to leave him to his own Strength, through which he rebels against the Light that is in him, to the wounding of his own Soul, That he may learn to know, that the Power by the Virtue of which he is perswaded from Eternal Ruin, is not in himself but in the living God that made him, who freely gives the Light of Life eternal, to whom it pleaseth him, but neither can nor will give his Glory to Men or Angels, or to the Light that is in them; why, because the Tree of eternal Life and Glory is not within them, but the Fruit of that heavenly Tree only, as, abundantly aforesaid.

Wherefore, whither Spiritual Obedience, Praise or Glory belongs to the Fruit or the Tree, judge ye.

Now thou mayest know there is a twofold Light in Mankind, a natural and a spiritual, the natural Light comprehends natural Things or Notions only, but the spiritual Light comprehends heavenly Things that are past, present, and to come, and is not ignorant of natural Things neither; for the natural Light enthralls the Soul with fleshly Whimsies, literal Observations, censorious Madness, and what not.

But the spiritual Light lets the Soul at perfect Liberty, from inward Wrath and outward Rage, carnal Whimsies, or invented Formalities, leading the Soul into all spiritual Loveliness and Peace, to the utmost of its Power, with all Mankind even all its Days, not that it can have any heavenly Communion, with any but those which enjoy its own Light. What Communion hath Light with Darkness, or Life with Death; Now in that personal God and his Light declared in this Epistle, I am thy loving Brother in the Flesh and in the Spirit for ever. I do fully expert thy Answer to this Writing, and shall with Patience wait for it, that the true and saving, Light may distinguish between the Spirits that set Pen to Paper.

JOHN REEVE, One of the Lord's two last Witnesses unto the Foundations of all Truth, and Pen-Man to this Epistle.

An EPISTLE written by the Prophet LODOWICK MUGGLETON.

THE Occasion of this Writing, is in Answer to some Objections made against me. The first is, that there is no Power given of God unto Man, to give Sentence of Damnation upon Man for his Wickedness and Blasphemies against God and a true Prophet. In Answer to which, I say, it is recorded in the Old Testament, That he that despised Moses's Law died without Mercy; these are the Words of a mortal Man, and where there is no Mercy, there remains nothing but Condemnation or Damnation, which is all one, Again, is it not said, Jacob have I loved, and Esau have I hated, before they had done Good or Evil; but this is to be observed, God had appointed them to live to be Men, and two Nations to come out of their Loins; so when they were come to be Men, the one had the Seal of God's everlasting Love in his Soul from his righteous Actions: The other had the Seal of God's everlasting Vengance from his wicked Actions. Is this any other than Blessing and Cursing, or Salvation and Damnation? And there are the Words of a Man, that had Power from God to set Life and Death before all Men; and this I say, Happy is that Man that hath the Seal of God's everlasting Love in his Soul; and miserable is he, that is sealed up, through the Evil of his own Heart unto eternal Condemnation, which all Men are that have committed the unpardonable Sin, by despising the Teachings of God's Holy Spirit, and blaspheming against it. By this you may see there is a prerogative Power in God, above all Law, to place his electing Love where and in whom he pleases; and to fix his rejecting Power where and on whom he will, without any Motive to it, for the Advancement of his own Glory: For this I say, God will have as much Glory by reprobate minded Men, as he hath by the Elect: For as the one setteth forth his Love and his Mercy, so the other setteth forth his Justice, Power, and Wrath, without which the Glory of God would be quite lost: For Mercy cannot be called Mercy, if there be no Justice to punish Wickedness; take away the one, and you destroy both. He that pleads against this Doctrine and Power opposes an infinite Being; and who art thou that contendest against it? For Infiniteness is above all Law. The Apostle Paul hath spoken positively and fully to this Point, which I refer to your Consideration. This Doctrine is owned, I suppose, by the Church of England, but is very coldly maintained; for I don't remember I have heard it preached to any Purpose in my Time. And now I shall return to my first Proposition, and prove, in the second Record, that Power was given unto Man to give Sentence of Damnation upon all such as refuse to believe, or rather despise the Doctrine of the Apostles. For it is Paid: He that believes and is baptized shall be saved, and he that believes not shall be damned.

Is not this a positive Sentence of Blessing and Cursing, or Salvation and Damnation? And these were Men who pronounced it; and this Power was given to the Apostles when the Keys of Heaven and Hell were given to Peter. These Keys were the Gospel of Jesus, by which they opened the Hearts of all such as had Faith in their Doctrine to Salvation; and to shut the Gates of Heaven upon all such as despised and persecuted it unto Condemnation. This was opening the Gates of Hell in the Hearts of all despising, blaspheming spirited Men that villifye God's Prophets, Apostles and Saints, when Salvation is offer'd to them, by calling them Blasphemers, Liars, Herticks, and their Doctrine false Delusion, persecuting the Name of Christ afresh, and yet expect to be saved by the same Name which they persecute, this is a Sin not to be repented of, and will never be forgiven. This I speak of Men that had their Commission from Heaven given of God by Voice of Words, as Paul, and Moses, and several of the Prophets had; and he that speaks Evil or persecutes a false Prophet, will do the same by a true Prophet, for he knoweth not who is false and who is true, and all Persecution is of the Devil, and will be punished with eternal Death; as well he that persecutes a false Christian, as he that persecutes a true Christian.

Note, The same Power that was given to God's chosen Messengers in the two past Records, the same Power was given to his two last Witnesses in this third and last Record that God will bare to this World, and which will last to the End of the World; and that Ministry that hath not Power to bless Men for their Faith and Obedience to God, and to curse Men that are disobedient to the Teachings of his Holy Spirit in his chosen Messengers is not of God.

The next Objection I shall answer is, these Sayings in the Scriptures where the Devil was cast out of the Man that had an unclean Spirit, and suffered to enter into the Herd of Swine: But first I shall endeavour to discover the right Devil from the imagined Devil, which Man hath created to affright himself with all, how fain would Man have a Devil distinct from himself: But there is no such Thing, the right Devil is the Seed or Spirit of Reason in Man, from whence the Imagination flows which was first seated in Cain, and runs in the Line of his Seed to the End of the World, therefore Cain is branded with the Title of a Devil, and Judas was a Devil, and those Jews that pleaded they had Abraham to their, Father. Christ tells them, they were of their Father the Devil, which was a Murderer and a Liar from the Begining and his Work they would do, and so they did, for they crucified him, and put him to Death. These were all Men Devils, and I can find no other Devils mentioned in Scripture. Esau was a Devil, and would have murdered his Brother Jacob, had not his Mother by the Revelation of Faith sent him out of the Way. Now observe, it is said, all Evil is of the Devil, not only actual Evil, but all, such Evils as are Incident to the Nature of sinful Man, for by Sin came Death; and Diseases being the Forerunner of Death, these are the evil Spirits or Devils that Christ cast forth of Men, that were afflicted with them, and the Man out of whom the unclean Spirit was cast, was a lunatick Person, and was distracted in his Senses, as may be seen by his Breaking of Chains, so that by his rageing Madness, his Strength was doubled to him; and Christ commanded this unclean Spirit to come out of him, whereby his Senses were restored, and he became in his right Mind as before this unclean Spirit, Devil or Disease took Place in him, and went away praising or giving Glory to God for his Mercy toward him, so likewise Christ call out the Fever. Now I would not have Men think that Christ cast out a Spirit, an Existence in itself distinct from the Body of Man; for there is no such Thing as Spirits without Bodies, for Spirit and Body is one inseparable Being, and cannot be parted from its own Body; and as to the calling out this unclean Spirit, Christ by his commanding Power, caused this Spirit or Disease to cease and have no longer Power in him; for he became whole and in his right Mind: And as to the Devil or Disease entering into the Herd of Swine, I affirm the Devil did not enter into Hogs, for there were no Hogs. in that Country, but Hogs the People, and they abhor Swine's Flesh, for the Swine the Devil entered into, were Men of a brutish, swinish Nature, a stubborn, ungovernable, unruly People, that would neither be obedient to the Law of God nor Man, but always resisting the Power of Christ, when he was upon this Earth, as you may see, where they accused Christ of calling out Devils by Beelzebub, the Prince of Devils; and these unclean Spirits that entered into them, arose out of their own Souls or Spirits; for Soul and Spirit is all one. And it is said, they run down a steep Hill into a Sea or Lake, and were drowned: Now this Sea or Lake was not a Sea or Lake of natural Waters, neither was that Hill a Hill of Earth; but it was the Worship of the Law of Moses was that Hill they are said to run down; for these Gadareans were a zealous People in the Worship of the Law; and those high and lofty Imaginations they had of that Worship, was that steep Hill; for that Worship was esteemed as a Mountain, overtopping all other Worships; and this was that high Mountain the Devil tempted Christ upon, where he shewed him all the Glories of the World; and these Waters were spiritual Waters, wherein they were choaked or drowned: For the Testimony that Christ did bear, in declaring the Gospel of Peace, and the Miracles he wrought, and with the lunatic Man's declaring him to be the Son of God, it took away or destroyed their Peace they had in the Worship of the Law; so that no true Hope of Salvation remained in them: Thus they may be said to be drowned in the Fears of eternal Death; these were those spiritual Waters they were drowned in.

Again, I never read, that Christ destroyed any Man in his temporal State, while he was upon this Earth: He came not to destroy, but to save Sinners. I wonder that Men should be so dark in their Imaginations, to think that the Devil entered into Hogs. Were not all Things made for the Use of Man, and to support him with Food whilst he is in a State of Mortality, and so to end and be no more? The

Beasts cannot sin, nor be tempted of the Devil, nor suffer eternal Torments: It is the Devil and his Angels, or his angelical Seed of wicked reprobate Men, that will be cast into Hell-Fire at the End of Time. And now observe; this lunatic Man is said often to frequent, or have his Dwelling amongst the Tombs: These Tombs signify a Burying-Place or Church Yard, near unto which might be an Assembly of People to be instructed in the Worship of the Law of Moses; and for their Unbelief, and despising Christ's Power and Miracles, they are called a Herd of Swine; for they were many in Number; and those Herdsmen were their Teachers, which went to the City and told what was done, which brought a Fear upon them; so they came humbly to Christ, and besought him to depart their Coasts. Again, it is said, Cast not your Pearl before Swine: It is not meant, cast not natural Pearl before Swine; but those Pearls they were forbid to cast before Swine, were those Salvation-Secrets that tend to Mens everlasting Happiness; these are those Pearls such swinish Men are not worthy of. Thus, if your Eyes are opened, you may see something into the spiritual Meaning of those Scripture Sayings.

   And now I shall discover the Devil Man hath created out of his lying Imagination of his own evil Heart. This Devil is a Spirit without a Body, and hath no Form of his own, but borrows some other Form to represent himself in; for he can assume what Shape he pleases; he can whip into a Man, and tempt him to all Manner of Evil, which once committed, he can whip out of him again, and leave the Man to suffer for his Sins; he is invisible, and yet visible; he is in Hell-Fire, and yet out of the Fire; he is chained, and can go no farther than God suffers him; and yet at Liberty, and can tempt Millions of Persons at the same Time: He is a Monster of a Devil; for he hath Horns and never a Head to place them upon; he hath Wings, and never a Body to fix them to: I have seen him represented with Claws to tear and torment People with, but still hath no Body of his own. This is the Devil Man hath made to affright himself withal.

   The next Thing I insist upon is to distinguish a true Minister from a false, which I have in a Measure explained before, as thus; a true Minister is one that God hath chosen and fitted for his Purpose, by inspiring him with the Revelation of his Holy Spirit, and then giveth him a Commission to go forth in this World, to propose Terms of Salvation or Condemnation to his People. Thus he is made Christ's Ambassador, and is impowered to set Life and Death before all Men, and this Power is blessing all such as believe, and are obedient to his Doctrine or Declaration to them, and a Curse upon all such as refuse to believe or rather despise it: For God doth not come now into this World himself to treat with his People, But giveth Power to a mortal Man to be a Prophet, an Apostle, Minister, or Ambassador of God, the King of Heaven; as the Kings of this Earth do to their Ministers. And these commissionated of God, stand in God's Stead, and represent the Person of God the King of Heaven, as an earthly King's Minister doth represent his Person and Power, and such Men are true Ministers of

Jesus Christ, and happy are those Men that are made obedient to them, and miserable are all such as despise their Declaration.

A false Minister is such a one as may be distinguished by the Contraries of the foregoing Discourse, that hath no Commission from Jesus Christ by Voice of Words, spoken from Heaven to the hearing of the outward Ears, but counterfiteth a Commission from the Letter of the Scriptures, but have none of the Spirit that declared them, nor no Authority from God. Some of them justify themselves by the Authority of the national Power, and if this will serve their Turn at the last Day, it is well with them. Others think the Letter, which was other Mens Words, that had their Commission from Heaven, to be as good a Commission as that of the national Power; And if this will bare them out, it is well with them also; others think themselves as good Ministers as those before mentioned from the Light within them, these are the People called Quakers; but this Light I know to be only the Law written in their Hearts, which no Man can keep, therefore serves only for Condemnation. So that when all those Ministers comes to plead in their Hearts and say, Lord we have preached in thy Name, prayed in thy Name, cast out Devils, and done wonderous Things; their Answer will be, Go ye Workers of Iniquity, I know you not, I sent you not. Thus you may see God will not own them, because he did not send them; there are some of the Ministers have got away of whining and toning in their preaching, as if their Words had not the same Meaning, without toning as with it. Again, they shall repeat one Word or short Sentence, three, four, or six Times together. Thus they go on, till they have filled their Noddles, topful, and when they have tired themselves and their Congregations, then they depart, and in half an Hour or an Hour's Time, their Sculls are as empty as before they came together, and if they talk together as they go Home, they shall admire their Teacher, he is a precious Man, a great Gift in Prayer, a sound Preacher. These are such as by their canting Language climb into the Hearer's Affections, empty their Pockets, and fill their Heads and Hearts with Nonsense. It was my Chance to hear a Clergyman say, if he had a Horse or any other Goods to expose to Sale, and if this Horse was all over Faults he was not obliged to discover any Fault at all, except it was demanded of him to discover them, to which I agree; by the Laws of the Land, he may conceal them; but by the Law of Moses, which is the Law of God, by which the Law of the Land is made, I can find no Justification for Man to deceive his Neighbour by Concealment; but because Men can find no positive Words to forbid this Deceit, therefore Men justify themselves in it; yet the Law is good, and doth not allow any Man to be deceived by his Neighbour, and he that lives by over-witting or any wordly Deceit, will be found to deceive himself; if Man was not corrupt in his Nature by Sin or Evil, which is of the Devil, he would abhor such Deceit in himself, and not encourage it in others. There is a new Law given, which is to do as ye would be done unto; and I believe no Man is willing to be deceived or wronged in any Kind; and if this Man had instructed Men in the Christian Law, I should have approved of it much better. This Law of Christ faith, love your Enemies, do good to them that hate you, and evilly intreat you; and such Men that seek to pervert the Law of Christ, or Christian Law, are rather to be esteemed Ministers of Deceit, than true Christian Ministers: Men are apt enough to take this Liberty to deceive their Brethren, although it disturb their Consciences; therefore they need not be encouraged in it.

He that peruses this Writing, and considers it in his own Mind, may see that God doth give Power unto Man, to judge, and give sentence upon Men, of Salvation or Condemnation, according to their Obedience or Disobedience to God and a true Prophet. Likewise he may see, that the Evil that arises out of a Man's Soul, is the Devil, and no Spirit without hath Power to tempt him to any Evil. Again, he may see, that he that takes upon him to be a Minister of Jesus Christ, and hath not a Commission from Heaven, as Paul had from God's own Mouth, I say, he commits spiritual High Treason against God, and will be punished with everlasting Death for so doing, if he continues in it.

LODOWICK MUGGLETON:

AN EPISTLE of JOHN REEVE to his loving Friend Christopher Hill.

Brother Hill, in the Eternal Truth,

MY Love to you and the Rest of our Friends. This is a spiritual Love Letter that I am moved to write unto you, wherefore by Virtue of my Commission I pronounce thee Tho. Martin, William Young, and Eliz. Wyles, the Blessed of the, Lord to Eternity; the Remembrance of this the Lord's Blessing, will do you no harm when I am in my Grave; in the mean Season, our good God cause you to love one another more than your temporal Enjoyments, and that will become a Heaven upon Earth in your innocent Souls; Faith fetcheth spiritual Comfort, the Fountain to each particular Soul; but Love fulfilleth all Righteousness both to God and Mans Oh! the transcendent Excellency of the Love of Christ in his new born People, it is not to express'd by the Tongues of Men or Angels.

JOHN REEVE.

A copy of a LETTER wrote by the Prophet JOHN REEVE to Mrs. Alice Webb, containing her Blessing, and the Six Principles, on August 15, 1656.

Loving Friend,

DESIRING your Eternal Happiness in that Place of Glory above the Stars, I am moved from the Spirit of the Lord to write these Lines unto your serious Consideration.

This I know as sure as God knows himself, that Jesus Christ from his Throne of Glory spake to me by Voice of Words three Mornings together, which Speaking of his hath opened my dark Understanding to declare such spiritual. Light to the Chosen of God, as never was so clearly manifested before, especially in, these six Foundations.

First, What the Person of the true God is, and his Divine Nature.

Secondly, What the Persons of the holy Angels are, and their Nature.

Thirdly, What the Persons of the Devils are and their Natures, and what the Person of the Devil was before he became a Devil, and begot Millions of dark Angels or Devils, it being all one.

Fourthly, In what condition the Man Adam was created, in and by what Means he lost his first Estate and the Effects of it.

Fifthly, What Heaven and Glory is, and the eternal Residence of it.

Sixthly. What Hell and eternal Death is, and the Place where it shall be to Eternity.

This I know certainly, That before the Lord sent me to declare his Pleasure unto his People, no Man upon this Earth did clearly understand any one of these six fundamental Truths, which to Understand is Life eternal, and to be ignorant of them is Death eternal. Now the Lord hath sent his two Messengers to declare them, I mean, to all those that may be informed in these spiritual Things, and do reject us (that are the Lord's Messengers of these Things of Salvation) through the Love of carnal Things, they must all perish to Eternity.

Again we know from the Lord by that infallible Spirit that he hath given us, of divers Persons that shall be eternally blessed with us: and all that we pronounce Cursed to Eternity are eternally Cursed, as sure as Jesus Christ the Lord of Life is Blessed, because it is his Curse and not ours.

Again, if the Lord Jesus do not bear Witness unto our Testimony, and make it evident that he hath sent us in a few months, than you may conclude, that there never was any true Prophets nor Christ, nor Apostles, nor Scripture spoken from the Mouth of God to Men. But there is nothing but the Wisdom of Men and Nature their God. But we know, that those that are joined with us, are Partakers of the Truths, and shall be blessed for evermore, and shall in the mean Time patiently wait the fulfilling of our Prophecy, and shall have Power over their Thoughts, Words, and Deeds, purifying their Hearts by Faith in the Person of God even as he is pure, trampling all the Riches and Honour of this World, under the Feet of their Souls as Dung, because they have tasted of that Glory to come, that no Tongue of Men or Angels can express, and this makes them not only love one another in carnal Things, but for the Truth's sake they are ready if (need require) to forsake all Relations, and Life itself for one another , and is that Power of that one only Faith and Truth, declared from the Spirit of God, the Man Jesus by us, which none enjoys but those of this Faith.

Much more might I write, but speaking Face to Face; (if it may be) is far more profitable: Farewell.

JOHN REEVE, the true Prophet, of the only true Personal God, the Lord Jesus Christ upon the Throne of immortal Glory in the highest Heavens.

An EPISTLE of JOHN REEVE to a Friend, written in May, 1657.

Shewing,

THAT Elect Angels are distinct from him who visibly beheld him Face to Face; and what that reprobate Serpent-Angel was in his Creation, which by the secret Council and unsearchable Wisdom of God, fell from his created Glory like Lightning from the invisible Heaven above, to this visible Earth beneath; and through his super-seeming God like Counsel, he overcame innocent Eve; and the yielding unto him, he wholly entred into her Womb, and naturally changed himself into her Seed, and so became the first-born Son of the Devil, and afterwards a cursed Cain, and the Father of all those Cananitish Reprobate Angels, spoken of in the visible Records of the Scriptures; Not as Cain, who was of that wicked one, and slew his Brother; the 1st of John, the 3d Chapter, 4and 18th Verse. And the Tares are the Children of the wicked one, Math. 13th Chapter, and the 18th Verse. Also in what Condition Adam was created in, and how he came to fall from his created Estate, and what that Sin was that Eve and he were guilty of, and how Sin came first in their pure created Natures.

Again, what that heavenly Glory is and where it is, that God's Elect Wheat, which are the Seed of Adam, and not of Cain shall possess when time shall be no more, and what that shameful Eternal Death is, and where it is reserved for the Seed of Cain, and not of Adam, who are either a Spirit given up to persecution of Men's Consciences, or else they are left in Darkness to condemn the Things of Eternity, because they cannot comprehend them for want of a true distinguishing Spirit, which is a Gift of the Holy Ghost, unto him which is immediately sent by the Lord of Glory, that he may be distinguished by the new born of God, from all those counterfeit or deceived Preachers or Speakers in the World, who are apt and ready to judge Men in Darkness, if they soberly ask them needful Questions concerning things of Eternity; the understanding of those glorious Excellencies, which is the Saints inheritance, being utterly hid from them, because they went before they were sent.

Friend and Brother in the Eternal Truth,

By this infallible Demonstration, you may know a Man that hath not a Commission from the true God, to preach and speak unto the People.

If a searching Speaker or Writer, deliver any thing unto those People that joyn with him, then for fear of his Weakness or Ignorance being discovered, he will counsel the Hearers to stick close to the Ordinances in the Word of God, or to hearken to them, or to that in their Consciences, and to beware of false Christ's and false Prophets, and such like borrowing Scriptures Languages, to prevent the People of ever hearing the Glorious and dreadful Things of Eternity from the ever-living God, revealed both by Voice of Words without, and Inspiration within, unto his two last despised true Messengers.

Thus it is clear, they have not the true Spirit of Paul in them, who gave the true Saints Liberty to try all Things or Opinions of Men, (for that was his Meaning) but to hold fast to that which was good.

Again, that Speaker or Preacher to People, whether publick or private, that declares against all Appearances that are contrary to his Way, discovers himself to a discerning Spirit not to be of the Lord, unless he can demonstrate a Spiritual Commission received by Voice from Heaven, from the Mouth of the Lord Jesus Christ, so that no Man can disprove him, though few from a true Understanding received him.

Again, he that preaches or teaches only of a God or Christ in Men's Consciences, doth he not question the Scripture Records concerning the Resurrection and Ascension of the glorious Body of the Lord Jesus Christ, who through Faith in his invaluable Bloodshedding, the Consciences of the Elect being sprinkled, are purified from the Power of all Unrightousness of Flesh and Spirit, and so doth he not question the Resurrection of Mankind after Death.

Again, if after Death there be no bodily Resurrection for the Spirit to possess an immortal God like Glory, or to suffer an eternal Devil-like Shame, according to their Deeds done in their Bodies; is it not one of the vainest Babblings under Heaven, for Men to talk of a God or Christ, or of Righteousness, or Purity, or Mercy, or pure Love without Envy, or of any Spiritual Excellency whatsoever, unless it be for Gain or Glory amongst Men.

The eternal Spirit and alone everlasting Father, which essentially reigneth in the glorified body of our Lord Jesus Christ his eternal Son, and spiritually, and motionally, or virtually liveth or reigneth in elect Men and Angels, bear Record between me and you for Everlasting, or World without end, whether this Witnessing be not sent unto you, and all the Elect that shall view it principally for the re-establishing of your tender Spirit, upon that spiritual Rock of all Ages, the Lord Jesus God and Man, in one distinct Person Glorified and everlastingly Honoured, with all Variety of Spiritual new Songs and Praises, from his Redeemed or Elect Men or Angels, when all Time or Times is swallowed up into Eternity or Eternities.

JOHN REEVE.

Another EPISTLE of JOHN REEVE's

SIR,

YOUR Replication to mine doth but still harp upon the same Matter as your former, and yet you suppose you have given such Arguments as may quite silence my former Assertions, were that there are no Spirits without Bodies, but such as mere Shadows and that God is not a bodiless Spirit, but hath and ever had Form, Substance, and Shape, and that is no other but the Form of a Man.

This is Contradicted by you, and so you affirm these Particulars following.

1st, You take at those my Words which said, that if a Spirit have no Body or Shape, then it is no more then a meer Shadow: This you deny, by saying, that a Shadow is only privative, but a Spirit, say you, is possitive.

2dly, You further say, that there is such immaterial Substances, which have a separate Existence from such gross Bodies which we have about us; witness say you the Soul of Man, which is immaterial, and lives after the Body is dead, which is, say you, confirmed by Paul, 2 Tim. i. 10. which saith, that the Gospel brings Life and Immortality to Light.

3dly, This Doctrine, say you, was known by the Light of Nature to the Heathen Philosophers, and hath since been confirmed by Scripture of the New Testament to us, and so conclude it no ways repugnant to right Reason.

4thly, You charge me with quoting the Scripture falsly, when I said, that Christ reply'd to the young Man, saying, That no Man was good but one, which was God; therefore say you it is false that the Scripture saith, that God is a Man.

To each of these take this particular Answer, 1. If your Spirit have neither Shape nor Substance, it is but a Shadow and no more than what the Egyptians Sorcerers produced before Pharaoh, what Moses brought up were real Substances, but their's no other but Shadows, but therefore a Spirit without Substance is not positive; for that which is privative can have no Being without a positive, because that which is positive hath a Being or Substance: Now he that will not admit God to have a distinct Being of himself, his God that he worships is nothing but a Shadow.

2dly, Where you speak of Spirits being immaterial Substances if they be immaterial, how are they Substances, and what Existence can they have, and how can a Soul be immortal in a mortal Body; it is said, the Soul that Sins, it shall die; yet you, it is immortal and cannot die, and would prove it in Tim. i. 10. when as that Place shews plainly, that it was Christ's Death and Resurrection which brought Life and Immortality to Light; so that if there be not a Resurrection, then can there be no immortal Life.

Therefore it is, that the Scriptures doth affirm, that there can be no Salvation without a Resurrection, so that if the Dead should not rise, then were all Faith vain, and God the God of the Dead (seeing Death is not abolish'd) and not of the Living; so that there is no Spirit that can subsist or have any Existence without a Body, either Spiritual or Natural.

Again, doth not the Gospel bring Life and Immortality to Light, and is this Life and Immortality brought to Light without a Body, but it will have a Spiritual Body suitable to that mortal Spirit made immortal. And doth not the Scripture affirm, that it shall have a Body like unto God's own glorious Body, and yet you say, God hath no Body, and a Soul hath no Body.

Do you not read also, that Christ had a Body, and that it was after the express image of his Father's Person: Would you trace substantial Truth into an Allegory, and say Righteousness, Knowledge, and Holiness is the Image of God, and yet must have no Body to act forth itself in. When God said, be ye holy, as I am holy, must we turn our Souls out of our Bodies, to make them like your bodiless God.

When we are said to worship God in Spirit and Truth, is this spiritual Worship performed without a Body, although there is a Mental, Privy, and Praise without a vocal Expression, yet it muff arise from a Heart, and that Heart mutt be placed in a Body.

There is no Light without a Sun, no Stream without a Fountain, and no Spirit without a Body.

3dly, As to your third Particular, this I must tell you, that no Light of Nature can discover Spiritual and Evangelical Truths, and it is very gross for any Man to subject the Spiritual Truths of the Gospel, to the heathenish Principles of Philosophers, making the New Testament no other but for the, Confirmation of the Principles of Nature, which Nature you call right Reason, which say, you never repugns the Gospel, nor the Gospel it.

By this your Discourse I find, that you own that Christ came, but to confirm the heathenish Principles of Nature, as, that God, and Spirits, and Angels, were all without Bodies, being immaterial Beings, and you know not what.

Now give me leave to be plain with you, and to tell you, that I could never read that the Gospel of Christ was ever sent to enlighten Nature, Nature or Reason hath no Interest in it at all. In the moral Law it hath, and therefore it is written, the Law came by Moses; and what to do, but only to enlighten Reason unto whom the Law was given: But as to the Gospel, it came by Jesus Christ, and particularly belonged to another Seed; namely, to the lost Sheep of the House of Israel; so that you can no more distinguish between the Law and the Gospel than between the two Natures of Faith and Reason it is all a Mystery to you. Do you know what right Reason is, if you do, you must ascend up into the Kingdom of Heaven, and view it in the holy Angels; for you will not find neither pure, nor right, nor uncorrupted Reason any where in this Orb below the Stars; For it is evident that Reason's Notion can never be capable to comprehend Spiritual Truths, as from the Power of its own Nature, it only serves to comprehend natural and temporal Things, it being but natural itself; but Gospel Truths are comprehended by another. Light, according as it is written by David saying, in thy Light shall we see Light, &c.

So that from what is said, we need not fear (as the World have) of the Heathens rising up in Judgment against us, for maintaining Gospel Truths against their Darkness of Reason.

4thly, As to your fourth Point, where you charge me of fathering upon the Scripture those things that are not, and you make a Wonderment of it, that I should say, that God was a Man, and to quote Christ's Words for it, telling the young Man, that there was no Man good but one, which was God, this you tell me was false, for you say, the Text saith that none is good but one, which is God. Here your ignorance appears very great, and may be wonder'd at considering your great Learning and continual Study; but it appears, it is but in those heathenish Philosophers; for observe for better instruction, did not that young Man call Christ Master, and own him to be a Man and no more: Now to this you may find that Christ's Answer did tacitly imply, that if he was but a Man, he was not perfectly good, and that no Man could be perfectly good.

And furthermore for a more full Answer in the Old Translation, attending to mark it, is render'd thus Word for Word that there is no Man good but one, which is God.

This is plain Scripture, and yet you are ignorant of it; I perceive you are not very conservant in Scripture, your Philosophy turns you out of all Scripture knowledge. But to proceed farther, cannot you find by Scripture that God was ever called a Man, did not you ever read that Scripture that faith, God was a Man of War.

Much more might be said of this and several positive Proofs from Scripture might be produced to confirm it withal, but because it is not the general received Opinion, therefore it must be quarrelled with; for the Honour of this World must be both fought after and submitted to.

And whereas you farther say, that the Apostles of Christ did ever teach after they had received their Commission, that Spirits were immaterial and could subsist without Bodies, now answer to this:

It is most certainly evident, that the Apostles never taught, that any Spirit could subsist without a Body, but the contrary altogether; for their Doctrine was, that as the Soul and Body lives together, so it dies together, and at the Last Day rises together, and is ever without Separation.

When the Apostles said, That many Spirits were generate into the World, which denied that Christ was come in the Flesh, did he mean Spirits without Bodies: And when Paul said, that the Spirit speaketh expresly, that some shall depart from the Faith Now what Spirit was that, but Paul's own Spirit of Faith, in his own mortal Body; for without a Tongue it could not be expressed.

And where the Apostles tells of the Doctrine of Devils were those Devils bodiless, and teached damnable Doctrine?

So that the Apostles never taught that there was any Spirits without Bodies, but always Spirit and Body went together, and so makes Longitude and Latitude profoundly, as your Philosophical Notions teacheth, although you cannot apply it to any sublime or spiritual Thing, you knowing nothing of it but all is nothing and of no Substance; and so in that your Darkness I leave you, seeing you are no Friend to the Lights and rest yours in all civil Respects,

JOHN REEVE the only true Witness unto the very true God, amongst many pretended Spiritual Messengers in this confused Age.

An Epistle wrote by the Prophet JOHN REEVE to ISAAC PENNINGTON, Esq; dated 1658. concerning an Answer to a Book of his, with several Mysteries and Divine and Spiritual Revelations declared by the Prophet, concerning God's visible appearing in the Flesh

IN your Self-return, you seem to mourn over the sunk Spirit of both Creations, so termed by you. Also you write as though many from a satanical Spirit write most accurately, both of the Works of Creation and Mystery of Redemption by an immediate Gift of God from our Lord Jesus Christ. To this I answer, a little Season will produce Mourning enough in you, when you shall see your angelical Motions like Lightning, cast down with Confusion of Fear, from their former Perfection of imaginary Glory, rational Dreams and Visions, Revelations, Inspirations, Experiences, or Voices proceeding from an incomprehensible Spirit.

Again; I have both read and heard a Voice to say, that the Secrets of the Lord are his choice Treasures, reserved only for Redeemed ones; but I never read or heard from any spiritual wise Man before now, that any satanical Spirit was able to intellect deceived Persons, exactly to write of the hidden Mysteries of the Everlasting God. Again, you pretend unto no such Revelations as I proceed upon, but say you, there is another Way more certain than Reason or Revelation, which whether as I presume you were led into, the Lord will one Day make manifest, from the true Light of Life Eternal. To this I answer, your Light as terming of the true Inspirations of the Lord Jesus Christ, written by me to you, is because as yet his Holy Spirit viels them from your Eyes; but as for your new Sound of teaching them from your God, more certain than Reason or Revelation, from the Divine Voice spoken in the Ear, through the glorious Mouth of my Lord. I declare that in all Ages the Elect loft Sheep of Israel, did never read or heard of any more than two original Ways either natural or spiritual in Mankind, whether you call them Creature or Creator, Light or Darkness, Truth or Error, Revelation and Reason, Inspiration and Imagination, Truth and Unbelief, Flesh and Spirit, and such like.

'Tis confessed, that visible Appearances of God or any else unto Mortals is teaching of all, but he that expects that kind of Teaching any more until Men are immortalized, lieth under at present as great an imaginary Deceit, as ever yet appeared in this Land. It is also granted that the most holy God speaketh to his Chosen Messengers by Voice of Words, even to the hearing of the Ear unto which Truth for Ends belt known unto himself, by his gracious Power only, can bear Record in this present Generation, unto the Grief only of all angelical

Wise, envious, proud, inglorious, hypocritical Reprobates that hear of it.

Moreover if your more sure Way of teaching from God were Vision itself, yet it is impossible for you to enjoy any true and lasting Peace, unless it swallows up all your former Writings produced from your own Spirit, without an immediate Commission from God, and in the Room thereof, perswade your Soul to pour in your Oil, into the natural Wounds of oppressed Persons, under what Opinions or Appearances whatsoever.

Again, you say, O Lord God, pity the Captivity of Man, yea, pity the Captivity of thy own poor Seed, hear the Prayers of that Spirit that interceedeth with thee for every Thing, not according to any fleshly Imaginations, but according to Truth and Righteousness of thine own Ballance. From the God of Truth, to this I answer, concerning that spiritual Captivity of the Elect, in Reference of a right Understanding of the Creator, you need not trouble yourself about that, unless you think through much importuning the unchangeable God, may be perswaded to loose their Bonds before the decreed Time thereof; but if you think that Glory of God's eternal Love towards them, will provoke to their spiritual Darkness through the invisible Appearances of his own pure Light, then you may know, until his own glorious Season, that all the Desires of Men or Angels are of no Effect, no nor of the Son himself, if you imagine a Father besides. 'Tis confessed, when the Time draweth near of some great Deliverance of the Chosen of God, usually the Lord provokes his People to cry unto him with Sighs and Groans, which cannot be uttered but from the innocent Spirit of his spiritual redeemed Ones, as his Due, he may receive all. Honour, Praise and Glory for their Deliverance out of their natural Darknesses, unto his marvellous Light.

Again, I declare from the true Light of the true aft that the Spirit which interceedeth with the Creator for all Mankind, upon the Account of his eternal Happiness, was never principled upon a spiritual Foundation of Truth, whatever subtile Expressions of God's righteous Ballance procedeth from him. Moreover, is it not the new heavenly Glances of Christ Jesus in Man's dark Soul, which upon an immortal Account, becomes all Light, Life, or ravishing Glory in him; and of the contrary, is it not the absenting Voice or Virtue of the uncreated Spirit of the Lord Christ Jesus, that occasions Men's Spirits to be full of satanical aspiring Wisdom about the Creator; and whence think you cometh this to pass, or possible could be of the Spirit, if the Creator were, and Angels were essentially living in one another there.

Again if your literal Request unto the Lord God, as in Reference unto the miserable Captivity of poor Mankind, lying under the miserable Yoak of unmerciful rich Tyrants, especially over his own innocent Seed or chosen People, then this will most necessarily follow; nay, you cannot deny it, if there be any Light in you, that all your conceived Spiritual Speakings, or Writings, or Prayers, in the great

Day of the Lord Jesus Christ, will became but fiery burning Death in you of utter Darkness, according to the true Saying If that Light in you be Darkness, how great is that Darkness? Unless as before said, answerable to your Profession of Love unto God, and Pity unto Man, you ate a bountiful Reliever of his oppressed Ones, according to his Bountifulness towards you, then mind the Virtues of Christ Jesus thus shining in you, will occasion from the refreshed Bowels of his own Seed new spiritual Acknowledgments, and a loving Return in the Lord for you, Why? because it is rare to find a merciful rich Man.

Friend, I certainly know that if you are one of God's Elect, you cannot be offended with me for writing the Truth, though at present, I be contrary to you in Spirit. Again, you write that you would beg unto the Lord for me, both with Tears and Blood, and you would speak somewhat concerning me, but you are afraid to open the Spirit before the Season thereof. Friend, As to that if ever the Lord of Life and Glory manifest himself to your Soul, then you will see clearly the Vanity of those Words.

Moreover, if I should tell you, that in the pure Eyes of the Lord Christ Jesus, that one handful of your Silver Tears, are of more Value than a Horse Load of your Tears and Blood, you might account it a very strange Paying from me; truly I unfeignedly believe it will be found a principal Truth, when our Lord Jesus Christ shall say in the day of Judgment,Come ye blessed of my Father; inherit the Kingdom prepared for you, for when I was hungry, you fed me; Go ye Cursed into everlasting Fire, when I was hungry ye fed me not: So that without Controversy, there is nothing in Man comparable to Love, Mercy and Forgiveness, even to his greatest Enemies.

Again, it is a marvellous Thing, if you or any other Man, should have a Spiritual Gift to distinguish between divine and diabolical Appearances, and yet defer the Examination thereof to another Season, or did the most wise God ever commission any Man or Angel to make a Discovery of any spiritual Counterfeits, and yet that Messenger remaineth dark in his own Understanding, concerning the Creator that sent him. I remember such a like Scripture Saying as this, him "whom you ignorantly worship, declare I unto you. Moreover, if the most wise Creator, either visible or invisible by himself or Angel, hath appeared in your Spirit, whereby unto your thinking, I was clearly discovered as a deceived Person among the rest, is it not a strange Thing that you should have Power over that Light above Men or Angels before you, for the Producing of it at another Season, the Creator himself will visible make it manifest, even so come Lord Jesus Christ, for thy glorious Name-sake, come quickly, and in the visible Sight of Men and, Angels bear Record whether thy Holy Spirit sent me (as I have declared almost these three Years) or no. Again, when the Lord made Choise of such a simple poor Man as I was, as many can witness in the City of London, that have known me about these twenty Years, that I might instrumentally discover the two principal Heads of mischievous Darkness in the Land; as namely John Robins past, and

John Tawney almost spent, truly I had no Power in me to put by his Message until another Time; why because (whether you can believe it or no) his Voice was so glorious in me, that it shone as the Sun, and it was of Motion swifter than Thought, and so pleasant to be declared by Tongue; yet for all that Godlike Glory piercing in me, and through me there arose a Desire in me to be eased of that Burden of the Lord committed to my Charge, because of that sharp Sentence that I was to declare against any Man that should despise it; then the Lord spake again unto my Soul, Words of burning Death, of sensible unutterable Darkness, answerable to that Jonas-like Rebellion in me, against so great convincing Glory; and truly I was compelled immediately to cry unto him for Deliverance from the Wounds or Anguish of my Soul, that I might presently obey his Word that shined in me with such Light, and Majesty, and Glory in whatsoever it should command me.

Wherefore, Friend happy are you if preserved from slighting an Appearance, that is contrary unto your Light, though it strike at the Foundation on which is built all your Spiritual Enjoyments; for alas, you know in the End, all false Lights will be made manifest unto those that possess the true Light of Eternal Life in them; blessed therefore are those, that in Obedience unto the Creator from a purified Spirit are compassionate to all Men, but especially to those innocent Appearances, in the Name of the Lord, though they all differ in their Declaration for them. If there be but one true Messenger from the Lord amongst the rest, they shall as formerly, receive an Angel of God unawares, and with him be Partakers of the glorious Secrets of the everliving God, to their eternal Consolation: for this I know, from the Spirit of Truth, that those that are left under a Spirit of rejecting and despising of false Appearances, coming forth in the Name of the Lord, they not clearly knowing them to be so, they will as readily despise a true Messenge of the Lord to their eternal Hurt; wherefore are all those, that neither Honour nor Life itself is dear unto them, but upon an Account of Spiritual Wisdom amongst wise Man, when the Glorious Things of Eternity, though in base Appearance presented unto them, from that Spiritual Rock of all Ages, which is our Lord Jesus Christ, God and Man, is one district Body or Person glorified, for whatsoever Men dream from their imaginary Gods, of two or three Persons, or a vast incomprehensible Spirit, essentially living in all Things and Places; from an immediate Voice from the highest Heavens, I positively affirm against Men or Angels, that there neither is, nor ever was any other God or Creator, but that God-man Christ Jesus, which was nailed to the Cross, the which Glorious God will one Day visibly appear with his mighty Angels, to the everlasting Terror of those that reject his Person, as to love a Thing for an infinite God to dwell in or to be; yea this very true God in Opposition to all other Gods, Men or Angels, is already come with his invisible pure piercing Light, to make an everlasting Distinction between the imaginary notional Misteries of Men in rational Darkness, and the spiritual

Misteries of his everlasting Kingdom, by true Inspirations from an holy and unerring Spirit. Even so come Lord Jesus Christ, visibly also according to thine own Word, come quickly. Amen.

Yours with all the Elect, in that only wise very true God, which in the Sight of Men and Angels visibly appeared in Flesh, and in that very Body of Flesh and Bone, is ascended far above all Gods, Heavens, Angels, or Men, and there to remain until the Resurrection of all elect Things, or the Judgment-Day, whose uncreated Spirit of fiery Love, is all Variety of immortal Crowns of new ravishing Glories, prepared for all those that long for his visible appearing, to make an everlasting Separation, between the merciful Elea, and unmerciful Reprobate.

JOHN REEVE, the only true Witness unto the very true God, amongst many pretended Spiritual Messengers in this confused Age.

And Moses was never buried.

The Testimony of the Prophet Muggleton, concerning the Death of Moses, the first Commissioner from God to the Children of Israel, he saith, That Moses went into the Mount, and there died, and God raised him again in a Moment of Time, and translated him into Heaven, but Enoch and Elias were both translated, and did not taste of Death, and God not thinking fit to bury Moses by the Hands of the Children of Israel under the Earth, because till he had laid down his God-head Life himself, he could raise none from the Grave.

As concerning who gave John the Baptist: his Commission, whether Elias, or Christ, the Prophet Muggleton's Testimony is that Elias gave it to him from Heaven, therefore saith the Scripture, he came in the Spirit and Power of Elias.

Is There any Evil in the City, and I the Lord hath not done it; the Interpretation is thus, when a sinful Land committeth all Manner of Sins and Wickedness, which in the committing to them is pleasant, but when God cometh and bringeth the Evil of Punishment, as Plagues, or Fire, or Sword, then he bringeth the Evil upon them.

An EPISTLE of the Prophet REEVE. Written in the Year, 1656.

BLESSED are all those that shall read, or hear this Epistle with a meek Soul, and are kept from judging Things that seem strange at first Appearance, but by sober searching of the Scriptures, compare spiritual Things with spiritual, as those noble born did in the Apostles Time, being made patient to wait the Lord's Leisure, who reveals his Secrets to such only who with a pure Conscience hearken to his Spirit; He that believeth maketh not Haste.

In the 6th Chapter of St. John 36th Verse, are these Words, The Words that I speak unto you are Spirit and Life; and in the 10th, 17th, and 18th Verses, it is thus written, I lay down my Life that I may take it again: No Man taketh it from me, but I lay it down of myself I have Power to lay it down, and Power to take it again. Therefore, that you may increase in your most holy Faith unto your eternal Glory, which are appointed to believe in that distinct glorified Body of the Lord Jesus Christ, the only God and everlasting Father, from the Holy Spirit, I shall shew you wherein that Power did consist of Christ dying and living again.

This his Power was secretly hid in the Truth of his Word speaking. Why? Because the Nature of Christ's Soul within his blessed Body was only one Voice of spiritual Faith and Truth. Therefore, you may understand, whatever he spoke in that Word speaking, was all Power to effect the Thing spoken of. The Words that I speak unto you are Spirit and Life, that is, as if Christ should have said, "My Words tend not to Joy in carnal Things that perish, but in the rejoicing in spiritual Things which are eternal; or, as if the Lord should have said, "My Word is all spiritual Light and Love, Meekness, Patience, with all Variety of immortal glorious Joys beyond the Comprehension of the Spirit of Men and Angels."

Again, Christ's Words are said to be Spirit and Life, because all Spirits in the Creation were made by his Word speaking only: Furthermore, because his Word only, is the original Cause of all Light, Life and Glory in Heaven and Earth, and in Men and Angels; I have Power, said Christ, to lay down my Life, and Power to take it again. I declare from the Holy Spirit, none in Heaven and Earth could ever truly speak those Words, but that Man Christ only.

Again, it is as if Christ should have said, "I only have all Power within my Soul, by a Word speaking, to die and live again".

Moreover, Christ Jesus being Lord of Life and Death, did believe without any Motion of doubting in him, that whatsoever he spoke should come to pass, and that gave a Being to the Thing spoken of, and that made him to say in the 24th of St. Matthew, ver. 25. Heaven and Earth shall pass away, but my Word shall not pass away.

So that Christ being the only God of all Truth, you may underhand that it was his Faith in that living Truth, or Virtue of his Word speaking, which gave him Power to lay down that divine Soul, or spiritual Godhead Life in the Hell of the Grave, and to quicken his spiritual Life again from Death, to reign in immortal Glory to Eternity, in that very Body of Flesh wherein he suffered Death. For I declare, from the Holy Spirit, from that everliving Virtue continually flowing from the former Suffering of God on this Earth, in the Body of Christ, the Tongue of Men nor Angels can never express the Variety of new glorious Joys, the eternal Spirit of God the Father hath in that glorious Garment of Flesh he hath clothed himself withal.

Again that divine Faith of Christ in that living Truth and Virtue of his Word speaking gave him Power over Life and Death, that by his precious Blood shedding, he might purchase from himself the Lordship of the Dead and Quick.

Again, If God had not been able to have made his Soul to die in his Body, and by the living Virtue of that almighty Word of Truth, spoken through his holy Mouth, to quicken a new and glorious Life again, O then would it be impossible for him at the last Day, by the Power of his Word to quicken and make alive, all the Souls and Bodies of Mankind that are dead asleep, and buried in the Grave.

You may understand, that living Virtue of his divine Word of Truth, spoken before he died, was that God, which raised the everliving God from Death to Life again.

Therefore, because the Lord your God liveth, ye which are to live eternally with him with astonishing Wonder and Admiration behold your God, that was absolutely dead and alive at one and the same Time.

Therefore Christ spoke those Words to his Apostles of the Power of Faith, Matt. xxi. 21. and Jesus answered and laid unto them, Verily I said unto you, if ye have Faith, and doubt not, ye shall not only do what I have done to the Fig-tree, but also if you say to this Mountain, take thyself away, and cast thyself into the Sea, it shall be done; and in Matt. xix. and 26. But with God all Things are possible, and in Gen. xiv. Is any Thing hard to the Lord.

Woe, Woe, Woe therefore, to all that are left under the Power of carnal Reason, that they may ever war against that incomprehensible Power of spiritual Faith and Truth essentially reigning in the glorious Body of the only wise God, your alone Redeemer, which long for his Appearance, which by the almighty Power of his Word speaking of that Substance of Earth and Water, created both Worlds, and all living Forms that in them are, into that Order they appear now to be, whether for a Time; or for Eternity, which also twice changed the Condition of his glorious Form by the almighty Power of the Spirit of Faith and Truth speaking thro' his heavenly Mouth.

Moreover, his divine Godhead died in the Flesh and quickned in the Spirit, not only to redeem his elect loft Sheep of the House of Israel, from the bitter Cup of eternal Death, but also to prove his infinite Power and Wisdom of Truth speaking, and for the disproving of all lying Reprobates, which always either in Heart or in Tongue, speak against that glorious Power of their Creator.

You know, that it is a common Thing for them to say, that it is Blasphemy for any Man to say, that God could possibly die, with many such like cursed Speeches against incomprehensible Power. And why do atheistical Hypocrites say, that God could not die? Because of their lying Imagination they cannot comprehend by what Means God should possibly live again if he were dead.

Thus they measure that incomprehensible Power of divine Faith or heavenly Truth, by the narrow Compass of their blind Reason, and bottomless Pit of lying Imagination, which understand nothing of that spiritual Power of true Faith.

And because they are not able to comprehend the spiritual Ways of the Lord Jesus Christ, they hate both him and his Elect, and call him a Liar to his Face, both in his Person and in his Word, and in his Prophet, and in his People.

Moreover, because they see no Power in themselves, neither to live nor to die, presumptuously they take upon them to judge the God of all Power over Life and Death, by their no Power at all.

Again, if that God that said, I have Power to lay down my Life, and Power to take it again, did not die, and was buried both Soul and Body in the Grave, and after the decreed Time of three Days and three Nights, by a quickening Spirit revive a new and glorious Life again in Despite of Death's Power, then (angelical Reprobate) the following Scriptures were Words of Truth, spoken from the Spiritual Mouth of the everlasting God, that sent me to declare this Secret, who did die, but cannot possibly lie; for lying is of a mortal Man, like unto thyself. In the Words of Isa. lv and the last Verse, Because he poured out his Soul unto Death. In Psal. 16. ver. 11. For thou wilt not leave my Soul in Hell, neither wilt thou suffer thine holy One to see Corruption. In Acts ii. 27, 31. Because thou wilt not leave my Soul in the Grave, neither wilt thou suffer thine holy One to see Corruption; he knowing that he before spoke of the Resurrection, of Christ, that his Soul should not be left in the Grave, neither should his Flesh see Corruption. Rom. xiv. 9, For Christ therefore died and rose again, and revived, that he might be Lord both of the Dead and and Quick. In Rev. i. 17, 18. Saying unto me, Fear not, I am the first and last I am he that liveth, and was dead, and behold I am alive for evermore, Amen; and have the Keys of Hell and Death. And Rev. ii. 8. These Things saith the first, and the last, which was dead and is alive.

If this Truth be not sufficiently cleared by the Letter of the Scriptures concerning Christ's Soul and Body being both dead and buried in the Grave, and living again by his own Power, I would it were. This I am certain of, that they that deny this Truth, are not only naturally blind, but wilfully also do shut their Eyes, and flop their

Ears, and call the Scriptures Lies, because of the Cross of Christ, without which there is no Crown of Glory.

Again, if the everlasting God for a Moment could not have, died, and left himself void of all Light, or Life, spiritual or natural (as the Condition of all Mankind is, which are dead asleep in the Dust of the Earth) then he could not possibly have experimentally known the State of the Dead, whether elect or reprobate. Moreover, neither could he possibly, in his Creatureship Condition, be capable of entering into the immortal Glory of his Creatorship again, but by his entering into Death, that he might live again, and upon his glorious Head, instead of a Crown of Thorns, wear a double Crown of eternal Glory.

Again, that he might also shew unto his elect Men and Angels, his almighty Power and unsearchable Wisdom, by quickening an immortal, transcendent, glorious Life, out of Death itself.

Thus the Lord of Life and Death, by suffering all Conditions in his innocent Soul and Body, did purchase, at a dear Rate, from himself, a prerogative Power of being Lord and King over all Conditions whatsoever; and from hence he experimentally knows what immortal Crowns and Glory are most suitable for all suffering Conditions his blessed ones undergo; and, by Virtue of his unspeakable Sufferings at the Hands of Jewish, Canaanitish Devils, he knoweth what Measure of eternal Death in utter Darkness is most meet for the Souls and Bodies of all the Sons and Daughters, proceeding from the Bowels of cursed, bloody Cain, that reprobate, angelical, old wise Serpent-Devil, and Father of all the Damned; who through the Decree of God, was call out of Heaven into this World, that he might bring forth his generation of proud, envious, scoffing, persecuting wise Serpent-Devils; not only to war against the Lord of Life and the Truth of Holy Scriptures, but also against his Holy Spirit of divine Faith or Truth, in all the elect lost Sons and Daughters proceeding from the Loins of *Adam:* So that their eternal perishing by the secret Decree of God, being hid from them by his Wisdom, they might justly be damned in themselves from the everlasting Remembrance not only of all their Actions of vainglorious Hypocrisy, but unmerciful Cruelties.

This will be that gnawing Worm of Conscience which never dieth, and that fiery Curse of the Law, of the Wrath of God in Mens Souls, that never goeth out.

And much concerning that everlasting Word of Truth that was spoken by the glorious Mouth of the everlasting God, that Man Christ Jesus, upon the Throne of all immortal Crowns of Glory and Majesty, far above all Heavens, Angels, and Men.

Yours, who love the Lord Jesus, more than this perishing World.

JOHN REEVE.

A Copy of a Letter written by the Prophet LODOWICK MUGGLETON, to ANN ADAMS of Orwell, in Cambridgeshire, bearing Date from London, March the 27th, 1663.

My Dear and Loving Friend, Ann Adams, the Wife of William Cakebread, my Love remembered unto you.

THESE are to certifie you, that I came well Home, therefore I thought it convenient to write these Lines unto you, as followeth: First in that thou wast honoured of God to be an Handmaid or Guide unto a Prophet, unto John Reeve, when thou wast but in thy Infancy concerning the Knowledge of Things of Eternity, but the Seed of Faith which was in you, though it was but small, yet it hath taken deep Root downward in the Heart, and hath brought forth Fruits of Faith and Love upwards; for thou hast and shall find it no vain Thing to receive a Prophet in the Name of a Prophet, and the reward is no less than Peace of Mind here, and eternal Life hereafter in the Kingdom of Glory, let the World esteem of it how they will.

There is one thing which I shall always have a Love to thee for, in that thou wast kept innocent in the Days of thy Ignorance, for that was a Thing which I always did love in myself in the Days of my Youth and Ignorance, and it Both yield me a great deal of Peace, the Remembrance of it now; because the World cannot say justly, that there is any Evil found in me, neither is there any Blot upon my Mind, for I can say truly as the Prophet did in another Cause (where he saith) whose Ox have I stolen, or whose Ass have I taken away; so I can say whose Wife have I committed Folly with, whose Daughter have I deflowered, which is a great deal of Peace to me, and it may be some Satisfaction to all you that are innocent; and for others of the Seed of Faith, which have been guilty in the Days of their Ignorance; for this I would have thee, and all the Seed of Faith to mind, that almost all those that have gone forth upon the Account of Prophets, and Prophetesses, and Speakers of every Sea, they have been for the generality of them guilty of Lust, many of the Baptists and Quakers have been guilty. Therefore impossible they should be Messengers or Ministers of Christ's whatsoever they pretend, yet we the Witnesses of the Spirit can bear with those that have been guilty; but it was always my natural Temper to be more affectionate to that which hath been kept undefiled from their Childhood, and as that Seed of Faith lay secretly hid in thy Nature.

The Declaration of the commission of the Spirit hath brought it forth to publick View; and as Nature hath beautified, thy outward Form or Person, so likewise hath that Grace of Faith beautified thy Heart and Mind, in that your Understanding is enlightened to discern betwixt Faith and Reason, God and Devil, with many more heavenly.

Secrets which is hid from the Eyes of the World; and as thou art Partaker of the like precious Faith with us the Witnesses of the Spirit, so likewise thy shall be Partaker with us of the like spiritual and heavenly Glory; and the stronger thy Faith is in this Commission of the Spirit, the more bright will you thine in that Kingdom of eternal Joys, where Pleasure will run as a Stream or as a River out of your own Person, and not only so, but you shall see your God Face to Face, of whose Seed and Nature we are, and this will produce those Pleasures that are at his right Hand for evermore.

I thought good to write these few Lines unto thee; not but that I am well perswaded before of thy eternal Happiness, but only that you mayst know that the Blessing of the true Prophet is as if God had blest thee himself; and thy so receiving of it will grow to a perfect Peace here, and to eternal Happiness hereafter.

No more at present but my Love to your Husband, and to your Mother, and Goody Candy, as being in the same Faith with you, and your Husband's Brother Symonds.

I cannot enlarge, because I have so many Letters to write and other Business to do, because of my long Absence; therefore I shall take leave, and subscribe myself your dear and Loving Friend in the true Faith.

LODOWICK MUGGLETON:

My Daughter Sarah, and her Husband with other friends in the Faith, remember their Loves to you, your Husband, and Mother, with all the rest in the Faith with you.

London, March 27, 1663.

FINIS

SUPPLEMENT

TO

THE BOOK OF LETTERS,

WRITTEN BY

JOHN REEVE AND LODOWICKE MUGGLETON,

THE TWO

Last Prophets of the only true God

OUR

LORD JESUS CHRIST.

BELOVED BRETHREN,

WITH the authority of the Church we have made diligent search through the Manuscript Records of the Church, and have found the following Letters, not in print in the "Book of Letters." The following Letters may be considered the conclusion of all the Writings of the Prophets REEVE and MUGGLETON, both of spiritual matter and temporal advice, as far as the Church is in possession of.

JOSEPH & ISAAC FROST.

LONDON:

PRINTED BY R. BROWN, 26, ST. JOHN STREET, CLERKENWELL.

1831.

SUPPLEMENT

TO

THE BOOK OF LETTERS,

&c. &c.

An Epistle of *JOHN REEVE* to *CHRIS. HILL.*

> *Dear Friend in the eternal Truth, my love to you and the rest of our spiritual friends remembered.*

Brother Hill,

IT seems very strange to me, that you with the rest of former friends, make no enquiry after me whether I am dead or alive. What, have the unnecessary things and cares of this world swallowed up your former love to the truth? Though I am moved in this manner to write unto you, I trust you have not so learned Christ.

Friend, the reason of my not sending unto you this long season is this, because my wife and I were both very sick and weak, of which sickness the 29th of March last my wife died.

Immediately after I had buried my wife, the Lord our God called me to visit some of his people living near the City of Cambridge, as he once called me to visit you; yea, it was in the very same manner, for one of the chief speakers of the Ranters being convinced by this truth, who formerly had deceived them, took a parcel of my books and presented them to them, upon which they greatly desired me as you formerly did; I hope there is about half a score of them that have received the truth in sincerity of heart; they are husbandmen and tradesmen that labour for their bread as you do; they rejoice in those that really possess this truth though by face unknown.

Christopher Hill,

You seem to forget your engagement to your father-in-law, you know the time is expired concerning your payment of the money which was lent to you, and not to him; wherefore as you love the truth, I desire you to send me the fifteen shillings remaining behind speedily, that I may restore it to the right owner.

Now concerning my own condition, it is thus; on May Day last, I was senseless two or three times, insomuch, that if a faithful friend had not been by me to relieve me with a little cordial, I had immediately died. I still continue very sick and weak, so that of necessity I must either mend or end in a little space. As for relief now I have most need of it, it hath been very small of late; I wish it may not be a burthen to the conscience of some when I am gone; the widow's mite will be a witness against all carnal excuses in those that own this truth. It may be you may think I have no need of your charity now, because the merchant for a little season allowed me five shillings a week; but if you think so you are much mistaken, for I have had none from him a pretty while, neither do I know whether I shall have any more from him at all, for when he took ship for Barbadoes, he had not wherewithall to leave for his wife and children, through the unjust dealings of unreasonable men. Brother Hill you may remember you sent me word, that if the London Christians would contribute weekly or monthly to my necessity, you would do the like, you will do well to keep your covenant.

And so I commit you to the most High, and remain yours in all righteousness,

JOHN REEVE.

My dwelling is in Bishopsgate Street, near Hog Lane End, with three sisters that keep a sempstris shop.

Direct your letters, to our brother MUGGLETON, to be conveyed to me, and the fifteen shillings to him for me, you know where he dwells; it is in Trinity Lane, over against a Brown Baker's

London, June 11th, 1656.

Another Epistle of JOHN REEVE'S to the same person.

For his loving friend CHRISTOPHER HILL, Heel Maker, in Stone Street, in Maidstone, in Kent. These

Brother Hill,

I HAVE received your letter and your kind token, for which I acknowledge your kindness to truth.

As for my neglect in writing to you, my great troubles of sickness and mortality hath hindered it, I hope whilst I am able to write for time to come you shall not charge me with any such neglect; in the mean season I do not desire your charity unless you can spare it. Remember my kind love to your mother Wyles, to Thomas Martin, and Goodman Young, and I rejoice in the Lord for you that the truth abides in you. As for the fifteen shillings I am glad of your care for the truth's sake, because it was lent to me upon that account.

No more at present, but desiring my God abundantly to establish you in all spiritual excellencies, unto whose infinite grace I commend you all, and remain yours in all righteousness,

JOHN REEVE

London, June 30th, 1656.

The Prophet Lodowicke Muggleton's blessing to his Son-in-Law, Mr. John White, bearing date in London, 18th Nov. 1665.

Son John White,

YOUR wife shewed me your letter unto her, in which letter I understand your desire of the blessing, if I may count you worthy of it.

As to that I say, God hath counted you worthy of it, else you would never have had such interest in the faith of this Commission of the Spirit as you have in your wife and the rest of the true believers of it. But I thought you would have been well enough satisfied without the declaration of it, for my thoughts were the same towards you before as to your eternal happiness. Yet, to satisfy your request, and for your further confirmation of your faith, in the assurance of your eternal life and happiness, I do declare and pronounce you to be one of the blessed of the Lord both in soul and body to eternity.

P. S. As for things of temporal affairs, I suppose your wife will certify you in her letter, but I thought it necessary to satisfy your desire with these few lines, though I be in haste, and could hardly spare time at present, so that I had thoughts to have let it alone till another time, but I thought you might be troubled a little at it, if it had been delayed.

Written by

LODOWICKE MUGGLETON,

One of the two last Witnesses of the Spirit.

London, 18th of November, 1665.

Copy of a Letter written by the Prophet Lodowicke Muggleton to Mr. Sudbury, January 31st, 1669.

Loving and kind friend in the true faith, Mr. Sudbury,

This is to let you understand that with much trouble and charge, I have got the interpretation of the Witch of Endor safe out of the press; but as for the other to Isaac Pennington, Quaker, I have had bad success, for it was taken in the press and the printer like to be undone; but money did buy it off. It cost the printer seven pounds, and me five pounds to pacify the matter, and not got it done neither; but most of the copies are preserved, and hereafter when times are something better, I will get it printed if it be possible; for the winter is the worst time to print in of all the year: but I am glad this of the Witch of Endor hath escaped, it being of more value than the other, because it was never written upon before by us nor no other; for I have been much crossed in the printing of it and very fearful it would have miscarried as the other did, because he kept it so long; these six months he hath had it in hand, but with much ado I have it safe home at last, so I have sent you four of them, desiring you to give Mrs. Parker one, and the rest you may dispose of as you please yourself.

I did hear by a letter from Mr. Tompkinson to Mr. Delamain, that you were very ill, which I am very sorry for, but where nature is overcome by natural diseases, death will get the victory, and swallow up life into death; but I am persuaded that your faith is so strong in the true God, and in this Commission of the Spirit, that you are sure you shall find everlasting life hereafter, according to your faith, and according to my word; and though the word of a prophet now in these days cannot cast out natural distempers and natural diseases that are seated and settled in the blood, yet the word of a prophet can cast out all fear of eternal death.

Therefore that your confidence may be strong in yourself, in the assurance of your eternal salvation, I do confirm that; word of blessing to eternity which I once did give unto you.

So being-in great haste, I shall only present my love to yourself and to your dear and loving wife, and to our dear friend, Mr. Parker.

I rest and remain your friend in the true faith,

LODOWICKE MUGGLETON.

Postern, London, 31st Jan, 1669.

P.S. My wife desires her love remembered to yourself, your wife, and Mrs. Parker.

A Copy of a Letter written by the Prophet Lodowicke Muggleton to Mrs., Dorothy Carter, bearing date, the 23rd of April, 1670.

Dear friend in the, eternal truth, Dorothy Carter,

This is to certify, you, that I received your letter, dated 27th February, 1669, with one from William Newcome, and one to Mrs. Griffith, and one to Mr. Hatter which letters I did deliver as you did appoint; but whether you have received any answer from them since I know not, also, you may think it something long that I did not send you some answer of the things you desired, but I seeing the matter contained in your letter did not concern me, and that there was such impossibilities in Mr Hatter to perform what you expressed in your letter, as what he promised in his other letter, that I did forbear writing unto you; and in a little time after I went into Cambridgeshire, and being now returned, I thought it necessary to write a few lines unto you for satisfaction in the thing you desired, concerning Mr Hatter's daughter.

My opinion and knowledge is, that Mr Hatter is as uncapable to provide for his daughter at present, as ever he was since I knew him; for he is as a man of sorrows, always in straits and wants, and the more comfortless to all of the faith, because there is like to be no end in this life; and his sorrows are the greater because he brought them upon himself, that the saints cannot deliver him, not with small matters; for there hath been done for him by me and other believers more than to all the saints besides, yet not delivered at all; yet we cannot but look upon him with an eye of pity, in respect his heart is right towards God, and strong in the faith of this Commission of the Spirit, and many other natural endowments which few men have the like, which doth cause both saint and devil to respect him, and to have tenderness towards him; but his troubles are so many, and tied with cares---with many fast knots, so that neither saint nor devil can loose them, as I said before. His wife is now gone into Yorkshire, it may be if she prospers any better than heretofore, there may be something done for that child you keep; but my hope in this matter I fear will be much like the hope of the hypocrite that perisheth. Therefore as to my judgment concerning the maid and you, I am very loath to give any, yet because I would not have you altogether unsatisfied, I shall tell you my thoughts.—That seeing the God of truth hath moved you and your daughter, for truth's sake, to take the girl when she was fit for nothing, and have brought her up so long and so many years for nothing, neither do I think you will ever have any thing for this time past; therefore, I suppose, you must add this good work to your faith, and let it follow you in the resurrection in a degree of glory above your fellows; when the saints shall differ in glory as one star differeth in brightness from the other, which will not be a quarter of an hour's time after death before you will receive the reward. I know not whether Mr. Hatter hath sent you any answer concerning it, but seeing you have done all this for her when she was fit for nothing, I think now you have made her fit to do something towards her living, it will be best in my judgment to keep her still a while longer, and see if her father may be in a better capacity than at present to take her off your hands.

I speak this not to force you to keep her against your will, but only to let you know how the case is with her father, neither doth her father know that I write unto you, nor desired me, but of my own will I thought it convenient to let the naked truth be laid open before you, and leave it to your own consideration.

And as for Mr. Fewterill requiting you evil for good, that is a thing something common with poor people and yet for my part I never heard him speak a word of ill of you since he came to London, nor before; therefore, if he hath done you wrong by thought, word, or deed, it is unknown to me, neither do I love to enquire after people's evil or weaknesses; neither do I question but he and she have both carried themselves unworthily unto you for all your kindness towards them, but I am unacquainted with it, and by your patient bearing, knowing your own innocency, you will help coals of fire upon their heads that do you wrong.

I shall be glad to see you here at London this summer if your strength will bear the journey. All the news here in London is now about this new act for the preventing of meetings, it puts a damp to all trade exceedingly, it is so strict and cruel, that all people are almost against it, but what effect it may produce, time will bring forth.

It was the great wisdom of God, that this Commission of the Spirit should not be tied to outward worship, so that no act the powers have made yet, doth reach us, but truth is preserved in secret, and no envy can have any law to hinder it or suppress it.

This is all at present, only my love and my wife's love remembered to yourself, Mr. Goodwyn and his wife, Thomas Marsden and his wife, Betty Slater, William Newcombe, and all the rest of our friends in the faith there with you.

I rest and remain, your Friend in the true faith,

LODOWICKE MUGGLETON.

From the Postern, London, April 23d, 1670.

Copy of a Letter wrote by the Prophet Lodowicke Muggleton, directed these, for his loving Friend, Colonel Robert Phaire, in Ireland. Give this with care.

Dear Friend in the true faith, Robert Faire,

Sir,

I HAVING this opportunity to send by Elizabeth Faggetter, I thought good to write these lines unto you, to certify you, that I received your letter by Mr. Greatreakes, dated Dublin, this 27th day of May 1675, wherein I perceive your great faith and love to the true God, and to this Commission of the Spirit, not only in this letter, but in your former letters, in March 1669. I have heard a good report of you both by Saint and Devil; also, I have had experience ever since you received the doctrine of this Commission of the Spirit, you turned well that declared us to be true witnesses of the Spirit, ambassadors sent of God, in that you have obeyed the truth in believing God hath sent us; you know what great power is in a commission that is given by the powers of a nation or earthly kings, you have had experience of that yourself; and are not those happy that obey the commission of earthly kings as far as kings can reward them with honour in this life, and those that disobey his commission are they not punished, the case is the same with John Reeve and myself, God hath chosen us two in this last age to be his two last Prophets and Witnesses of the Spirit, and hath a commission from God to give sentence of blessing and cursing to eternity; to seal the foreheads of true believers unto everlasting life, and to seal the reprobate and unbeliever in their foreheads, unto eternal torment, which is abundantly declared in our writings; and ought not this commission of God from heaven to be obeyed, yea it is obeyed by some few, but the enemies of it are more than can be numbered. I write not this to you as questioning your faith, but rather to make your faith the more strong, for I know your heart did close with it ever since you first saw the writings; and when you received me in the name of a prophet, you received him that sent me, even the true God, whereby you were sealed with the Holy Spirit of promise, even the spirit of faith, which giveth assurance of everlasting life, which doth abide in yourself, which hath appeared in you have not been ashamed of your faith before men, but hath justified your faith in this commission of the Spirit against all gainsayers, so that you being justified by faith in your own soul, I know you have peace with God as to your eternal happiness on the other side of death; likewise I can truly say by you as Christ did when on earth to his disciples that believed on him, blessed are your eyes that see, and ears that hear, and hearts that understand the things that belongs unto your peace; not that peace which the world gives, but that peace which faith in the true God gives, which shall endure for ever, both in this life and in the life to come, even to eternity; and because you have stretched forth the hand of faith, and have taken and eat of the tree of life, you shall live for ever; that is, by faith you have eat of the flesh of God, and drinked the blood of God, which is that water of life that doth quench the thirsty soul, so that you shall never hunger nor thirst more after the forgiveness of sin, nor after the assurance of everlasting life; and this doctrine and words of mine shall be as the leaves that fall from the tree of life, which is for the healing of the nations. This faith is the faith of God's elect, that removeth that mountain of ignorance and darkness that lieth before the understanding of all mankind by nature, and all that hath the light of faith in the true God. This faith is that which doth ascend up to heaven, and pierceth through the sky, and beholdeth our God, our King, and our Redeemer upon the throne of his glory, which is an evidence to the soul that we shall see him face to face in the resurrection, which will not be a quarter of an hour's time to the dead soul before it shall quicken again into an everlasting life and glory; likewise this faith of the elect doth descend into hell, and seeth the form and nature of the right devil, and seeth the place, manner, and nature of the devil's torment; it doth, as David said concerning God, if he should ascend up to heaven God is there, and if he should descend into hell, he is there by his power to keep them in utter darkness; so I say, let the reprobate and unbeliever's imagination go down into hell, the faith of this commission will find him out there also; and though the seed of the, serpent doth rage, rail, and revile against me without a cause, and cast out their malice as floods out of their mouths; they being, as David said in his time, my enemies are more than can be numbered, yet by the power of faith I know I Shall prevail over them all. I write these lines only to certify you I received your letter, and for the further strengthening of your faith, having at present this faithful friend to deliver it to you, else I should not have wrote to you at this time, so at present shall only remember my true love unto yourself, and to your dear wife, which I once or twice saw in London, whose faith I understand is grown very strong since that time, which causeth my love the more in her, she having that faith in her, that works by love, for none can love God but those that have faith in the true God, then will they love him that is sent of God, and rest your friend in the eternal truth,

LODOWICKE MUGGLETON.

My love remembered unto your son-in-law George Gamble, and your dear daughter his wife, and to Doctor Moss, and to all the rest of our friends in the true faith there with you.

The Postern, London, Aug. 9th, 1675.

SIR;

I HAVE discoursed with Mr. Greatreakes three times, and he told me what the token was you mention in your letter, and who it was that gave it, and that he would pay it, but it is not yet paid, for he is now gone into Devonshire, perhaps he may send it to Mr. Delamain's before he goeth out of England, if he does you shall hear of the receiving of it, for I did not think to have wrote to you at all till I had received it, but because of Elizabeth Faggeter being here.

You speak of a token in your letter, dated the 20th of March 1669, and now in this letter, dated 27th of May 1675, if this be the same token and same party that sent it, Captain Gaile, I give him many thanks for his love and kindness, in that his heart was free, though I never received it.

So rested your Friend,

LODOWICKE MUGGLETON.

The Postern, London, Aug. 9th, 1675.

Copied from the original Copy of the Prophet Muggleton's own writing.

A Copy of a Letter written by the Prophet Lodowicke Muggleton, to Mrs. Dorothy Carter, bearing date February 22d, 1676.[1]

Dear Friend in the true faith, Dorothy Carter,

I SAW your letter to Mrs. Griffith, dated February 13th, 1676, in which your desire is, if it were possible, to have a few lines from my own hand. To satisfy your desire I shall give you a small account of my sufferings, and how my wife and I do fare at present.

My sentence was, to stand upon the pillory three days, and the books they took from me were about four hundred, and they were to be divided into three parts, and burnt by the common hangman before my, face every day. I stood upon the pillory. The sentence was executed upon me with the greatest severity, beyond any felon or cheat that ever stood upon the pillory before. I was drawn in a cart like a thief to the gallows, without cap or hat, and stood upon the pillory bare-headed; I was exposed to all the shame and reproach that

---

[1] I think that this date must be in error, as the events described took place in January 1677, which is therefore probably the correct year for this letter.

possibly could be invented; I was led as a lamb or as an ox to the slaughter, there was no mitigation at all of the rigor of the sentence, but rather more punishment added to it. The books were offered up in three burnt offerings unto the unknown God; and I myself was offered upon the pillory, to the rude multitude to be slain or stoned to death, and it was the wonderful providence of God that I escaped with my life, or being maimed in my limbs, which would have been worse than to be killed outright. Now is my testimony finished, in that the last true Prophet that God will ever send, suffered for the truth as all his servants the Prophets did that went before me. The world shall never have Prophet of the Lord more to persecute while the world doth last, for the mystery of God is finished, both by declaration and suffering, as was declared by his Servants the Prophets and Apostles of old. Wait but a while with patience and we may see, how God will pour out his wrath and vengeance upon this wicked world, and especially upon the City of London, who has shed the blood of the last true Prophet that God will ever send, though not unto death; my innocent blood will be a testimony against them, and will cry to heaven for vengeance, for they thirsted after it as for sweet wine, and now they have drank it both great and small, their thirst is not yet quenched because I am yet alive; God doth seldom let sins of this nature go unpunished in this life, besides the punishment in the life to come, but gives them their own blood to drink by destruction, for they are worthy that touched God's anointed Prophet, and doth them harm.

The effects of these things will come to pass and be made manifest! I cannot give you an account yet about the fine, it is £500. I am yet in Newgate, but removed into the Press-yard, a little better place than I had before. I have a handsome chamber for ten shillings a week by myself, where my wife and friends may come freely to me. I am indifferently recovered of my wound, but the cold and cough doth cleave to me still, but not so extreme as before, I hope I shall outgo it and be well again. My wife is not very well, her grief and troubles have been so many and so great of late, that it is a wonder she holds up so well as she doth.

As for the copy of the indictment it is very large, and cannot be had, my Attorney hath it, but the whole indictment, every word of it was taken out Of the Book called the Neck of the Quakers broken, and in no book else at all; and as for the paper pinned to my breast, it cannot be had, it was so daubed with dirt; but the words were these Lodowicke Muggleton standeth upon the pillory for publishing and printing a heretical, seditious and blasphemous books; these were all the words of it in great letters.

Thus I have given you an account of the substance of things that have happened unto me; particulars would make a volume. I was willing to satisfy your desire with my own hand-writing, with my love and my wife's love remembered to yourself and to Betty Marsden, your maid Ann, and all Friends else there with you, I take leave and remain your Friend in the eternal truth.

LODOWICKE MUGGLETON,

From the Press Yard, Newgate, London, February 22d, 1676.

A Copy of a Letter written by the Prophet Lodowicke Muggleton to Mr. Thomas Tompkinson of Slade House, in Staffordshire bearing date from London, 14th of November, 1676.

Loving Friend, Thomas Tompkinson,

I SHALL give you a little account of those things that were then upon me when you were in London last, which caused me to absent my own house, neither have I been at home never since, nor know not when I shall, for the king's messengers have been to seek after me several times, but have missed of me; and if I can keep out of their hands, (as will do my endeavour,) I shall deal well enough with all my enemies, which are many, yet I see the law, and money will bridle them all; so the bit of the bridle be of silver to put in their mouths, it will keep their necks strait to the law, and turn their heads aside every way. I have been a whole year in law with two persons that do trespass upon the widow Brunt; and after her death it fell into my hands, so I commenced two suits of law against them, but they had several put offs, which caused a great charge the more to me and some to themselves, but I following it as fast as the law would permit; they perceiving the law went against them, they devised to put me into the Spiritual Court, thinking to get me excommunicated, that I might not have the benefit of the law in these two causes; but I defended myself in the spiritual court, so that would do them no good.

They seeing that would not do, they devised another device, to inform the Warden of the Company of Stationers, that I had printed blasphemous books, being unlicensed, which caused six men that belonged to them to break open four doors, and took away fifty pounds worth of books, under the pretence of being unlicensed. After these men had broke open my doors and took away my books, they finding that I would sue them at the law for what they had done, they got a warrant from the council table for my person, but I have kept out of their hands hitherto, and have overthrown them men in law, and cast them and recovered my title to the ground that was the Widow Brunt's:— likewise I have arrested two or three of those men that broke the door, and do proceed in law against them, and do intend to put in our declaration in court this week, so we shall go right to bring it to a trial next term. Also I have proceeded in the spiritual court so far as to get out their libel to see what they charge me with, and do intend to carry it out of the spiritual court into the court of king's bench, then I shall be the plaintiff in both suits, for they hang together, and now I have done with the other two causes, I shall the better follow these two.

I have acquainted several of our friends here in London, and advised with them, that if they of our faith that are of ability, will assist me in these two causes to wage law with them, and they are very free and willing to contribute towards the charge of law; we being many, the burthen will not be very great upon any particular person, it is left to every one's freedom whether they will give any thing or no. It concerns all of this faith, and I will stand in the gap to manage the law by my attorney, and if I do overthrow them in both courts as I hope I shall, it will be upon record, so that none will meddle with me more about those books for ever. I have advised with the council that they have done that which the law will not justify them in what they have done, for it is contrary to law and to several acts of parliament; however it goeth, on my side or not, it will be good for the age to come, not to suffer any envious devil to do as they have done; if I lose my books they shall not have them for nought, and make others afraid to do the like.

Therefore if you please to propound this to as many of this faith as you know, whose minds are free to contribute what they please towards this business, I shall be very willing to accept of it. Thus I have given you as short an account as I can of those matters and troubles I have passed through one whole year, and how long my troubles will last yet I know not.

So I shall say no more at present, only my love and my wife's remembered unto yourself and wife; I take leave and rest your friend in the true faith,

LODOWICKE MUGGLETON.

11th Nov. 1676.

A Copy of a Letter written by the Prophet Lodowicke Muggleton, to Mr. Thomas Tompkinson; bearing date April 23d, 1677.

Loving Friend in the true faith, Thomas Tompkinson,

THIS is to certify you, that I received of Mr. Delamain ten shillings at one time, and thirteen shillings and sixpence at a another time, which you and the rest of friends did send to him for me according as their particular names were set down; but I gave Mr. Delamain orders to give you an account that he had received the money both times, and had given it to me according to your order, but not that he should mention every person's name nor every particular shilling that every person gave. It was both troublesome and needless, and very inconvenient if the world should have seen it; therefore a receipt in general was enough, for if we received all that was sent, we must needs understand the names of them that sent it and all particulars.

I hope you nor the rest of friends do not doubt of Mr. Delamain's faithfulness to deliver to me whatsoever is sent to me by any friend of ours in any parts of the world, both by sea and land; whatsoever hath been directed to him to be given to me, either letters or any thing else, he hath faithfully delivered unto me, and I have desired him to give a receipt for me in general, when I have not been capable to write myself, and it hath satisfied all friends else; so that it was partly my fault more than his, that he did not write any larger at that time, for I and he and all our friends else here in London were in great trouble, and had not leisure to write at that time, for the shepherd being smitten, the sheep were all scattered.

Upon the 17th of January last past, judgment was given upon me to stand upon the pillory in three places of the City of London; and the books they took away from me were divided into three parts, and were so burnt before my face the three days I stood on the pillory; so they offered up the books as three burnt offerings unto the unknown God, and they offered me up as a sacrifice to be slain by the rude multitude; and it was a wonderful providence I was not slain outright; I was exposed to the utmost rigour of the law, more than any man that suffered in that kind. However they have shed the blood of the last Prophet, though not unto death; oh! what shall be done unto this bloody city for shedding of innocent blood! the God of heaven shall say unto this bloody city, "You shall be punished with poverty and beggary; but those who have had a hand in the persecution and blood of my servant the Prophet, shall be cast into the bottomless pit in utter darkness, where is weeping and gnashing of teeth for evermore, where they shall never see bright day to eternity." This I am sure will be the effect upon those that have had a hand in this suffering of mine.

I cannot enlarge in particulars of those great sufferings hath happened to me of late, it would be too, large a volume to relate the particulars of it; but you understand by a little what a great deal meaneth.

So being in haste, I shall take leave and rest, only my love to, yourself, and my wife's love to yourself and wife, and all friends else. there with you.

I rest your loving friend in the true faith

LODOWICKE MUGGLETON.

From the Pres Yard, Newgate,
April 23rd, 1677,

A Copy of a Letter written by the Prophet Lodowicke Muggleton to Mr. George Gamble of Cork in Ireland, bearing date, August 20th, 1677.

Loving friend in the true faith,

THESE lines are to inform you of the truth concerning my sufferings; I shall only touch upon the chief heads of the whole matter, for particulars and circumstances would make a volume, which shall be left upon record, with many other acts and sufferings done by John Reeve and myself, which will be published after my death.

But as to this present suffering of mine, upon the 17th day of January, 1677, I was tried and condemned.

And in the trial I would note to you this, the judges were divided in themselves, the judges did not give consent to that sentence; therefore not to repeat circumstances nor particulars, I shall note this passage unto you that one of the judges said.

"Gentlemen of the Jury,

"I cannot see by the laws of England how you can bring this man in guilty," with many words to that purpose, "therefore," said he to the jury," look to it."

Then stood up another judge, chief of England, and said, "that if it were not law we will make it law," and many other words to that purpose, to provoke the jury to bring me in guilty, else they would be partakers with me in that horrible blasphemy; so the jury did hearken to him, and brought me in guilty.

Upon which the sentence was given in thus, THAT the court had no love to my person, and were sorry that the laws of England were so unprovided to punish such crimes of this nature. Therefore saith he, we shall give you but an easy punishment, that is, you shall stand upon the pillory three days in three of the most eminent places in the

City of London, two hours at a time, from 11 o'clock in the forenoon till one of the clock in the afternoon, and a writing shall be tied upon your breast, to show the cause why you suffer, and that my books should be divided into three parts, and burnt by the common hangman before my face every day I stood upon the pillory, and that I should be fined five hundred pounds, and after the fine was satisfied, I should put in bail for my good behaviour during my life, and that none should be bail but such as were not of my principles.

This is the very substance and almost verbatim, the words and truth of this sentence.

This sentence have I suffered in every tittle in the greatest rigour that could possibly be inflicted upon man; they made me ride in a cart as a thief, or a murderer, bare-headed, without hat or cap, which never was done in England before: I stood bare-headed, which no cheat nor bawd ever did; I was set as a mark for every one to throw a stone at me, my books were offered up in three burnt offerings, at three sacrifices unto the unknown God before my face, and I myself was offered up as a sacrifice to the rude multitude, I was bruised and battered with dirt, mud, rotten eggs and stones; and my innocent blood was shed, though not unto death; it was the wonderful providence of God I was not slain outright. That my life was preserved being exposed to the rude multitude, even to unreasonable men, such as Paul in the like case desired to be delivered from; so that the blood of the last true Prophet that God will ever send hath been shed by this bloody city of London; which innocent blood doth cry to heaven for vengeance on them that have had a hand in it, because it was shed for God's cause only therefore the sin is the greater; I was willing to have been stoned to death by the rude multitude, and would have gone off the pillory to be stoned to death, but the officers would not let me come down.

When this was over and my wounds washed, and the blood stanched, I was put into the cold cellar again the same day at night; I went three pair of stairs to my lodging, and the next day I would willingly have kept my bed all day, being not well of my wounds, but the keeper said, if I would not come down into the cellar in the afternoon, they would put me into the common side, so I was forced to come down into the cellar, which had more need to have kept my bed; but there is no mercy in prison for in hell there is no mercy but justice only; neither is there any mercy in prison keepers at all without profit; and I was very well satisfied that God's hell which he hath prepared for all persecuting devils will be worse, neither will there be any mercy at all there, but justice only, and in the assurance of this I rest satisfied. And when I was in the celler, William Penn and William Mead came to talk with me, which I was unwilling at that time to talk with any man in prison, yet Penn asked me "if I had peace in this, my suffering?" I said I had, and that now I had finished my testimony and sealed it with my blood; and that I should never suffer more for it while I live, which I know I shall not.

Those are the words that he grounded that report, "that I had denied my commission." Further, he and several Quakers, upon a report that the Quakers were the authors of this my suffering, because the indictment against me was taken wholly out of that book, called 'the Necks of the Quakers broken,' there was not the least syllable in the indictment taken out of any other books but out of that only. But I answered Penn and the rest, that I did not think that the Quakers had any hand in this my suffering, but do clear the Quakers from having any hand in this matter, though I knew may of them were glad in their hearts that it was done by others.

Now I have given you a small account of my sufferings, let me give you a small account of my deliverance: while I was in the press-yard a prisoner, the sheriffs sent several times by the goal keeper to see what I would do about the fine, but they were at no certainty what fine they required; at last the clerk of Newgate said, they would take a fifth part which was one hundred pounds, I was loath to give so much, and let it alone for a quarter of a year longer for some reasons I had, and after that time I appointed was over, I sent a letter to the Sheriffs to treat with them about the fine, but they were very high, and would not abate one shilling of an hundred pounds, and the cause why, I understand, they were proffered by some of the goalers and others, an hundred pounds to keep me a prisoner for ever, or else to have a larger sum of money for my ransom, I perceive had not the sheriffs honour laid at the stake, I had been bought and sold as Joseph was in Egypt, a prisoner during life or till such ransom was paid, it would have been a great disparagement to the sheriffs if they had sold me, such as never was done in England before. But they having an eye to credit and somewhat to conscience, they would not do such wickedness; but however it caused them to abate nothing of an hundred pounds, neither would they give any time, but to lay down the money presently; so we borrowed an hundred pounds the next day and gave it to them upon the 19th day of July, 1677, and the same day at night I was released out of prison.

I was prized at a goodly price, far higher than the Lord of life was prized when he was on earth, he was valued but at thirty pieces of silver, but they valued me at one hundred pieces of silver; the thirty pieces of silver was thirty pounds they valued Christ at, else it would not have bought the potter's field, and the hundred pieces of silver they valued me the last true Prophet, and Witness of the Spirit, it was an hundred pounds; and the cause why they valued me at such an high price above my Lord and master, it was because they knew I had some inheritance and interest in this world, but the Lord of life had not a place to lay his head, therefore was he valued at such a low price; and because they knew I had some interest in the world, and many followers of me, therefore they valued me at such a high price of a hundred pounds of silver; and as the thirty pieces of silver was the price of innocent blood, therefore not fit, to be put into the treasury to be expended upon any holy use, or to relieve the poor, but to buy a potter's field to bury the stinking carcasses of strangers, thieves, and murderers, so that the thirty pieces of silver was bestowed upon the basest way suitable to the purchasers, being the price of innocent blood; so likewise the hundred pieces of silver I am valued at, it is the price of innocent blood also, a very goodly price; and this money will not be put into the treasury to repair churches, or relieve the poor, but will be spent basely in lusts and drunkenness, and voluptuousness to the purchasers of it, being the price of innocent blood.

Thus have I given you an account of the whole matter as short as I can, both of my sufferings and delivery out of all these troubles, and that I am indifferent well in health; being restored to my own house again I thought good to write these lines unto you, to satisfy you in those parts touching all those things that have happened unto me of late here in London. If you please you may shew this letter to those of this faith, if you think fit, but shew it to none of the contrary party, let the blind lead the blind, that they may both fall into the ditch together.

So not to trouble you any further, but do remember my love, and my wife's love unto yourself, and to your good wife, unknown to me by the natural sight of the eye; but the time shall come, she shall see me face to face, when I in a better condition than now I am even upon a throne of glory, though now I have been upon a throne of shame and reproach, even a pillory. My dear love remembered to Colonel Phaire and his good wife, to Major Dennison and Captain Gale, to whom I am much engaged for his kind token long ago, and to all, the rest of the friends in the faith there with you. I take leave and rest,

Your friend in the eternal truth,

LODOWICKE MUGGLETON.

The Copy of a Letter written by the Prophet Lodowicke Muggleton, to Mr. Thomas Nosworthy, in Antigua, dated from London November 4th, 1679.

Loving Friend in the true faith, Thomas Nosworthy,

THIS is to certify you that I received your letter about the beginning of Oct. 1679, with your brother's letter from Virginia, and that you received my letter with the rest, that we received your kind tokens. I am glad you receive satisfaction of mind though it be but in temporal affairs, is more than all the riches of this world, what is it without peace of mind; but that peace that floweth from the assurance of eternal salvation in the life to come, all the kingdoms of this world is not to be compared unto it, but when this temporal peace and eternal peace doth meet together in one soul, which I do not question, but they do in you, so that nothing under the sun can be compared with it.

I have read over your brother's letter, he writeth very well as to moral wisdom, and as to temporal affairs, but stone blind as to spiritual and heavenly wisdom, even like unto those David speaketh of, who said to those prophets that came in the name of the Lord, "we desire not the knowledge of thy law, therefore depart from us. So doth your brother by those books you sent him, for he doth count the truth of God and the wisdom of heaven a stumbling block indeed unto them.

And you may see what reward you have for your good will, you are counted a poor weak man by it, and fallen into a greater error than you were in when you were a Quaker, and in effect they desire not the knowledge of God's law nor of your books, but do wish you had never sent them; neither would they have yourself to believe them, but to depart from them as they have done, for they desire not the knowledge of them neither.

Therefore do you do as Christ did, he went to his own, but his own received him not, neither did he do any miracle because of their unbelief; so you sent books to your relations, but they received them not in love, neither could they convert any of them, because of their unbelief. It is a vain thing to write or send any heavenly matters among the heathen, for they will count you the greater deluded and in the greater error; therefore let no heavenly wisdom come there no more. I am glad you are recovered to your health again, and except the truth were locked up in a chest and never opened, it will meet with oppositions as I perceive you do.

I have been more sick of a fever and ague this spring than ever I was in my life, but now I am in health again, and as for your sending three thousand pounds weight in sugar, and consigning it to our friend Mr. Saddington, this is to let you know that he is dead a matter of six weeks, almost before your letter came to my hands: likewise, I asked Mr. Clarke if he would undertake that which Mr. Saddington should have done, but he saith, he will not concern himself in such matters at all, so that there is no friend at all, that I know of, that is of any ability that will meddle in it, nor have any concerns in ship affairs, and if those that are poor should undertake it, perhaps they will sell the sugar, and spend the money, so you may lose all. And as for my part, I never could, endure to concern myself with any ship or sea affairs if it were ever so much for my profit. Therefore I thought good to acquaint you and give you notice, that you may appoint some other man that you can confide in, that you know hath been used and knoweth the custom and manner of sea affair, and of the custom-house; we are all very ignorant of these matters, therefore unwilling to meddle in it. And as for your sending me a further token of your love, I know it is out of pure love, but my desire is, that you would not send any thing to me at all, and I shall take it as kindly at your hands, and have as great a love for you, as if you had sent it, because I have enough in this world and have no need, neither would I have you to think that I do refuse your kindness out of any scorn, but out of true love, knowing that I have less need than yourself, neither do I love trouble myself to trouble others.

This with my love and my wife's love presented unto you, and to those two friends you speak of in your letter; I take leave and remain your friend,

LODOWICKE MUGGLETON.

London, 4th Nov, 1679.

A Copy of a Letter written by the Prophet Lodowicke Muggleton to Mr. James Whitehead of Braintree in Essex, bearing date from London, October 18th, 1680. Beginning as following.

Dear friend James Whitehead,

I received your letter dated October 12th, wherein I perceive that the country justices have agreed and drawn up an order for the compelling of all persons to come to their parish church, according to the act made in the first year of the reign of Queen Elizabeth.

I cannot conceive how the justices of peace in any county have authority and power to put that act in execution in these days, except an act of parliament to authorise them, which no parliament ever did since his Majesty was restored; for that act was at that time made only against the papists, far all protestant episcopal and puritans did go to church generally; there was no Dissenters then as there is now, there was then when this act was made but two denominations, that is to say, papist and protestant; so that act the intent of it was only against the papist, and not against the protestant in the least, and none refused to worship in the protestant churches but the Papists; but it is said that this act is in force to dissenters now in regard it stands unrepealed.

In answer to that, As that act is not repealed by parliament, neither hath it been confirmed and put in execution by any act of parliament since the king was restored, so that no justices ought to put it in execution; for this is to be minded, that this act hath been laid aside in England, Scotland, and Ireland, and three or four governments and parliaments have laid that act aside, as in king James's time, and king Charles the first, and the government of that, called the commonwealth, and since king Charles the second was restored, all these governments laid aside that act of Queen Elizabeth, and made laws of their own for the quiet of the nation, not meddling with that act of Queen Elizabeth, that was made against the papists only. But to satisfy you further, the execution of that act hath been endeavoured by several justices in England and practiced by them, for when I was prisoner in Derby goal there was twelve men of the baptist people in prison, for not paying twelve-pence a Sunday for not going to church and the justices of that county did commit them to prison for nothing else; because the king had set forth a proclamation suitable to that act, that every person that did not come to church every Sunday, should pay twelve-pence; but it was alledged before judge Tyrrell that the Baptists some of them should say, that the king's proclamation was no law; the ,judge said nothing to that, neither to justify the king's proclamation nor deny it, but acquitted them without paying any thing for not going to church, only the fees of the prison. After this trial that practice was laid aside by the justices in those parts ever since; several of our friends did pay twelve-pence a week for a while, it did not last long, After, this the justices in Cambridgeshire were very hot upon this act of Queen Elizabeth, and made several of our friends and other dissenters to pay twelve pence a week for not coming to church; our friends did pay it for a while, but the justices not being contented with twelve-pence a week, they proceeded further to another act of Queen Elizabeth, made against the papists, "that if any person were cited into the quarter sessions for not going to church three weeks together, he should pay but 3s. but if he were cited in for not going to church a whole month, then it was 20s. this did our friend Dickenson suffer, and other dissenters, but this did not last long but fell to the ground.

I suppose that the justices of the peace for your county do think and hope that the parliament when it sits, will make an act to establish their order they have drawn up. This is but a bad time for justices to combine together to force the consciences of three parts of the nation; but it is hoped the parliament hath matters of more consequence and weight for the good of the nation, than to humour the malice of a few justices.—And wait patiently a while, and you will see this fall as other things and this nature have done.

Thus I have given you a little light concerning the law, and how justices have acted contrary to law, and many have suffered by unjust men that have made their own wills a law, being backed by authority; and how could the innocent help themselves, but bore down their necks and take the yoke that wicked men have laid upon them. And as for my advice in this thing is this, that if this order to compel all persons that can not bow down to their worship, if it come to be general and take place in the nation that those of our faith that are able to give twelve-pence a Sunday, rather than let

[The remainder of this letter by some accident torn out.]

A Copy of a Letter written by the Prophets Lodowicke Muggleton to Mr. John Whalley, bearing date, May the 11th, 1681.

Mr. John Whalley,

I received your letter, dated February 12th, 1680, in answer to mine; and I give you thanks that you gave me your answer which causeth me to write this once more unto you, concerning this business.

First, you say that I was misinformed in that you stopped Nurse Holland's legacy for her abusing you; but you say the truth of the matter was, you stopped her legacy, because you found that you lost from your fathers death to that time of what was committed to her charge more than eight pounds; this, you say, caused you to forbear the payment of her legacy.

Answer. Why did you not then sue her for this at the law? but you sued her at the law for her abusive words to you. And Mrs. Middleton, and she and you together, did ruin the poor woman at the law, and made her spend all her wages she had of the captain and Mrs. Middleton, and you got nothing by it; you two punished her enough for her abusive words, which I blamed her very much for; and though the cause was Mrs. Middleton's yet you did appear in it, so that by the effort there was no great mistake that the legacy was stopped for her abusing you, in that you did not sue her at the law for what you charge her, with, but now the case is altered, the legacy is mine, as sure as if it had been given in the will; neither do you know what I and my friends have done, and must do in relieving her in that miserable, poor, and sick condition this long time; so that she could do no less than make that legacy over to me.

Secondly, you say that your father left his estate so much in debt, in mortgages, bonds, bills and book debts, that it was very little worth more than the legacies have charged it withall, especially if I consider how miserably out of repair he left the house

As for that, I understand, that the greatest part of that money Mr. Cally was engaged for upon them houses, his own house he lived in did pay; for I am informed, you had two hundred pounds fine and ten pounds a year for that house ever since, and that now you have eighty pounds a year coming in for their rents, besides ten pounds a year ground rent to the College, besides your father's goods, plate and jewels, and whatsoever is your son's is in your possession. Which fine and rent this three years and a half, I suppose may defray all mortgages, bills, debts, and legacies, which I conceive cannot be much less than £100, which, I suppose you are to pay out of the estate; but what is this to me, if it were twice as much more I have nothing to do with it, the law hath given you the rule of it, and power to dispose of it, as a man in trust for your own

Thirdly, you say, that till the mortgages, bonds, bills and honest debts be paid you cannot lawfully pay her legacy; and if the law do allow it, you say, her legacy shall be the last that shall be paid when the estate is cleared, and you get money over or out of it, which is as much as to say, you will never pay that legacy at all; for who shall know of you when the estate is clear, and when you have money over and above out of the estate, sure no counsel told you that to be law or justice.

Fourthly, you say, if you have paid off debts or legacies, it was to preserve the estate and your father's reputation.

What you have done of that nature it was to preserve your own interest, and your own child's inheritance; you being executor in trust, else the child and you both might have been disinherited; for there was estate enough left to discharge all things in your father's will to my knowledge; therefore you need not plead your father's reputation, for this I must tell you, I have been an executor myself to houses that have been mortgaged, and legacies given, and debts to pay, and money owing to me besides, yet I have been faithful in my executorship, to pay the mortgages and honest debts that were due, and all the legacies according to the will of the deceased, before I paid my own debt or had received it out of the rents; for this I must tell you, that legacies are to be paid whether we received it out of the rent or no: besides it is a very unjust thing and guilt upon the conscience of man not to fulfil the will of the dead; I have known a woful effect upon one that I knew for not fulfilling the will of the dead.

Fifthly, I make no question but you have paid your own legacy of £50 to yourself, and that you have paid your father's kinswomen's legacy of £30, and that you have paid Mr. Butler's legacy of £50, debt and legacy, and all other legacies mentioned in the will. Certainly the estate would have paid this £10 legacy as well as the rest if you had pleased, and you may pay it now to me if you please; and you have reason so to do because it is my right and the law requires it.

Sixthly, you say, if I am resolved to sue you in her behalf, you say, for my sake, you will put me to as little charge as you can, and answer me in any court; likewise you say, that an executor in trust pays no costs.

As to this, I am unwilling on my own behalf to sue you in any court at all, if you will pay it me, or any other I shall appoint quietly, for she hath nothing to do in this matter now: also, I know an executor in trust pays no costs, yet this must tell you, that you must pay the legacy, and if you put me to spend ten pounds to get ten pounds, it is not the first ten pounds I have spent in law to get that which is my right; besides, though you pay no costs you must loose your own costs as I do mine.

Seventhly, you say, that you disbursed moneys for me when I was in troubles.

To this I say, you were the man that put me upon that way; I being innocent and ignorant of that proceedings, was led as a lamb before my potent enemies, and was not to open my mouth, for my dependance was wholly upon you, and those you employed in that business; and when I came before the court you durst not appear yourself nor those you did employ, neither counsel nor attorney, nor no other durst appear to speak a word for me in my behalf. The Judges called for one Rous, answer was made, he was sick a bed.— The Judges called for two men more, answer was made to the court, That they were gone into Southwark about earnest business; so that I was made a scoff and derision to the whole court; and Jeffreys pleaded to the Judges, that this was but one of Muggleton's cheats, and that I did not owe Mrs. Hall any thing, for she was called in; and one King that you employed which managed the business was called for, but there was none to answer, nor to receive me, so that I was returned back again to Newgate with great disgrace, and with great charges; and I seeing I was so basely abused by them you did employ, and had spent such a deal of money in vain, I was resolved to take a chamber in the Press-yard, which I did, and not to remove to the Kings Bench if you would have given me ten pounds to remove thither

Yet after I was settled in the Press-yard, you put me upon the same thing again, and said, that a mark more would get me turned over, and that you would appear yourself; and I like an ignorant fool, did hearken unto you, and put myself to thirty shillings charges more, besides what Mrs. Hall spent, and all her trouble she had, and you did not appear yourself, nor none else durst appear before the sheriffs of London, but that poor old man in all this business.

But I understood by those that knew, that the King's Bench officers dare not appear in court in my business; so that your putting me upon this way, cost me first and last, at least ten pounds. Besides, this last bout made the sheriffs and jailers so mad with me, because I did not stand to their courtesy, they would not bate one shilling of an hundred pounds fine, which would before have taken forty or fifty pounds at the most, and would have saved me four months imprisonment.

Thus have I suffered greatly for hearkening to your advice in this matter. Likewise you know Mr. Brocke gave you two guineas which is mine which you have towards your disbursements in my troubles; if you laid out, more, it must be your own loss, for mine hath been great; and to prevent a law-suit or quarrel, as we always, have been friends hitherto, I shall propose this unto, you, that if you will pay me this ten pound legacy quietly, I will return you forty shillings of it back again and give you a full discharge of the whole, and you shall see the deed and will annexed together as sure as law can make it. I do beg your answer once more, whether you will or not; if you like, appoint your time when.

Direct your answer as you did your other letter.

LODOWICKE MUGGLETON.

May 11th, 1681.

A Copy of a Letter written by the Prophet Lodowicke Muggleton to Mrs. Dorothy Carter, of Chesterfield, Sept. 21, 1681.

Dear friend Mrs. Carter,

I SAW a letter of yours to my son White, concerning your grandson being an apprentice with him, and your great desire is to have my advice and judgment in it.

Truly friend I would willingly have waved the thing, for these reasons following.

First, if I should help the boy to never so good a Master, and of a good trade, yet if it be not in the boy's nature to be obedient unto his master and apt in nature to learn the art of his trade, the parents of the boy are apt to blame the master of the child for his neglect in not learning the apprentice his trade and art in his trade according to his covenant and promise, which default may be in the apprentice, because his nature could not receive it himself; and if his master should be cruel and beat the boy, thinking by that means to force the boy to learn his trade, and yield obedience whether he will or no, the master will then be cried out upon as a cruel tyrannical master, which was the cause the boy never came to learn his trade to any purpose.

Secondly, the experience I have seen by one dear friend Ellen Sudbury by her son; I was not only myself, but prevailed with other friends to help her son John Sudbury to a place, to be apprentice both to a good master and a good trade; truly I do think he was one of the best and patientest masters in London, and a very good trade which did not require strength but, fitted his fancy very well, for his idle nature never loved much labour; yet he being naturally proud and disobedient to his master, insomuch that I have had much ado to keep him in his place so long as he hath, and have persuaded his mother several times to part with money to please his fancy, else he would go away from his master; yet his master is blamed for letting him have so much liberty, which if his master had been strict he would never have stayed half so long as he hath; and were it for a great necessity that lieth upon him, he would never stay that little time he hath to serve; for now he must serve out his time, or else fall into the hands of destruction, or else be a burthen to his mother, which I am sorry for his mothers sake.

And now, dear friend, I know you have a tender love and a great care for your grandson, but you must not think that a master can have the same tender affection to apprentice as a grandmother hath, neither do you expect that he is put to apprentice as one to nurse or to beard, but you put him out to be a servant, an apprentice to learn a trade to get his living another day; and when he cometh out of his time, he will the better know how to take an apprentice himself, and then he will know what it is to be an apprentice, and the difference of be in brought up with his parents, and learning a trade.

And as for my son White, I gave you my judgment before, and do give you the same still, that I do not know of any better master, nor of any better trade in London than he is. And as for his trade, he is not only a bare brazier, but a curious artist, which is only in request in these times, which will not be so heavy nor require so much strength as a plain brazier doth, besides he worketh much at home himself now, which is very good, for an apprentice will the sooner learn his trade; and as for your grandchild's mistress, she is as good a woman as lives, as far as I can discern; and for liberty of conscience, he shall have with him more free than any people, whatsoever, in the world will grant him.

Also, I perceived by your letter, that you are resolved to give no more than fifteen pounds with him, because of three grand-children to provide for by you.— I know, you speak truth and that your care hath been great, and is great still, as I said to my son White. And upon this consideration, he said these words: that in regard of this and former kindnesses that he hath received at your hands, he would take him with that fifteen pounds and well-clothed, and that he would have you send him up as soon as you can, for I say it is better to send him now, because he may be seasoned with London air this winter, than stay till the spring when hot weather comes on apace.

Thus my son White is agreed to take your grandson, and if you and your grandson are agreed with him you may send him to him as aforesaid.

Thus according to your desire, I have given you my judgment and advice in this matter, and take leave and rest and remain,

Your friend in the true faith,

LODOWICKE MUGGLETON,

London, Sept. 21st, 1681.

A Copy of a Letter written by the Prophet Lodowicke Muggleton to Mr. William Pedley, a Weaver and Dyer, a believer of the Commission of the Spirit, living in Southampton, bearing date from London, the 12th day of January, 1683.

Loving friend in the true faith, William Pedley,

I RECEIVED your letter, dated January 4th, 1683, wherein you complain of your great troubles you have gone through in these late years, what in oppression, I suppose you mean oppression for conscience sake; and your greatest troubles I perceive, hath been in the natural concerns of this world, in respect of your first wife being dead, and leaving a charge of children behind her; and I perceive you have married another wife, and hath some charge by her also, which you say are in number five, thus poverty must needs come upon you like an armed man; these troubles are common to all married men, and people both poor and rich, but especially to the poor that do live by trade, for if trade doth fail, poverty doth increase and grow exceedingly, for trade is a very uncertain thing, especially in a time of persecution; for trade and Commerce hath taking the wings of the morning and fly away in these our days; so that poverty cometh in upon the poor as a flood upon the dry land; this thousands can witness in this nation as well as you, for want of trade; and poverty is the great common enemy in the nation at this day and time; and in regard, this poverty and want of trade is so common and so natural in this world, therefore it is that no eye pitieth the poor, let him be saint or devil, righteous or unrighteous. Also I perceive by your letter, that all the rest of your faith in those parts are backslided, and hath forsaken their own peace, and hath conformed for fear of the loss of some of their wordly goods, or fear of imprisonment, even against their own conscience, some only upon threats, others having lost some of their goods, for fear of losing more or all, and have submitted and conformed, so that now you are left alone, those are days of trial, but few are able to stand the trial, to keep faith and a good conscience; and especially in most counties in England several hath conformed; so that in saving earthly riches, they have lost heavenly riches, for they will never recover that peace and assurance of eternal life which they once had abiding in themselves, not while they live in this world; for you may read in the Scriptures, that he that doth fight the good fight of faith, and holdeth out to the end of his life, shall receive the crown of eternal life and glory; but he that looketh back as Lot's wife did, to fetch something that was in her house, which she thought might do her a pleasure when she was got out of the times of fire and brimstone; so it is with those that go back from the principles of truth, which led them to Zoar, a refuge of safety, of peace and content of mind to free them from the fear of the fire and flames of hell in the conscience, which we see the Sodomites of this world are in; which has them blaspheme against the God of heaven, and persecute steadfast and faithful men. It is a dangerous thing for men that have tasted the good word of God, and the powers of the life to come, that hath worshipped God in spirit and truth of heart for many years, according to the Commission of the Spirit, which is now in these last days in being, and now men because of a little persecution, to fall from it and worship that which all the ignorant and unbelieving people, and those that doth not know God doth warship. How doth such persons think to recover their peace with God again? neither doth God regard such worshippers, neither doth God's messengers regard such worshippers, that suffer nothing for their faith, and they will reap the fruits of their own doings, which is the loss of their peace of their own minds while they live in this world, and the fear of eternal death hereafter, to save themselves in this world, for a little time; for the Commission hath laid but an easy yoke and a burthen which is very light upon the neck of the believers of it. Christ said to those in his time, that his yoke was easy and his burthen light; yet those that would take his yoke upon them, must forsake father and mother, wife and children, if persecution should occasion it; nay, life itself must go rather than cast off his yoke, else no crown of eternal happiness, life and glory is to be had; this seems to the eye of reason to be a heavy yoke, yet Christ calls it easy, and the eye of faith doth count it easy. Still also you say that they have made a distress upon you already, and that you are left to wrestle with them, (meaning your persecutors,) which say you, according to reason, I am worse able. As to this I say, you are best able to wrestle with them for these reasons.

First, because you have suffered for your faith already.

Second, because you are a poor man and hath a great charge of children, and hath little or no estate to lose, for poverty and a great charge of children is a fortress, or as a tower of defence against your persecutors; for what town or city will persecute a poor man to cast him out of the town, or put him in prison, that hath committed no crime against the law of God, nor the laws of the land, and that hath nothing to lose, to bring upon the town a great charge; for you may by the laws of England throw all your children upon the town, and so shift for yourself elsewhere; and the town must by the laws of England provide for your children, and bestow them as they please. If they do persecute you and throw you into the streets, then do you throw your charge upon the town and shift for yourself; so that being poor will make you the more able to encounter with your persecutors, and preserve the peace of your mind, and your faith that fail not to the end of this natural life, that you may enjoy that eternal happiness hereafter; for riches of this world is a great snare, and many men rather than lose this earthly riches and honors among men, they let go their hold of eternal life in the world to come; because that is at a distance, and this is in present being. I hope these lines may satisfy you, and bear up your spirit in the day of trouble, and deliverance will come in its time.

So resteth your Friend in the true faith,

LODOWICKE MUGGLETON.

London, Jan. 12th, 1683.

A Copy of a Letter written by the Prophet Lodowicke Muggleton, to Mrs. Elizabeth Flaggetter, of Cork, in Ireland, bearing date from London, August 5th, 1684.

Loving Friend in the true faith, Elizabeth Flaggetter,

THIS is to certify you, that I received your letter, dated July 3d, 1684, wherein I perceive your son hath been hindred of his purpose, which is a thing very common in these days, and that your time would not hardly permit you to write those few lines; I know where people are concerned in the affairs of this world, must be carried and spurred on both in body and mind; the business of this world is that which causeth all people in the world to forget God, some striving for riches and honour, so that there is no room left in the heart, not to have any hope in a God, or any other heaven, nor the fear of any hell but what is in this world; and the poorer sort of people their hearts are so full of the cares of this world, how to get bread to feed their families and themselves, and to cloath their nakedness as Adam and Eve did; so that no fear of hell, or of a worse condition than poverty can enter into their hearts, but look upon the rich and honourable people to be in heaven, and do wish he could attain to the same condition or hell after death, than poverty in this world, or any better heaven after death than riches and honour in this life or world, no more than Dives the rich man did till he came into hell in his conscience. And happy are you and all those that are chosen out of this world by this Commission of the Spirit, which hath shewed you a better heaven than the riches and honour of this world, in that you are made rich in faith in the true God, in his form and nature, which no people in the world besides doth know, but those that doth believe our report, to them the arm of the Lord is revealed at this day, and to no other. Likewise we have shewed you a worse hell than the poverty of this world, and by your faith in this Commission of the Spirit, you will escape falling into that hell which is eternal; though you be poor in spirit, this kind of poverty is blessed of the Lord; Christ did not say, blessed are the poor of this world, but "Blessed are the poor in spirit for they shall see God." I perceive you are all there in peace and in quietness of mind, which all the riches of this world will not give; I am glad to hear of your steadfast faith in the true God. I have not written these lines to discomfort you, nor with the believers there with you, but for the comfort and strengthening of you all to hold out to the end, because you will not have a prophet always with you; I being old cannot by the course of nature live many years longer, but those writings I have left behind me will endure to the world's end.

This is all at present, only my love with my wife's love remembered unto you, and to George Gamble and his wife, and all the rest of our friends in the true faith with you. I take leave and remain,

Your friend in the eternal truth,

LODOWICKE MUGGLETON.

London, August 5th, 1684.

A Copy of a Letter written by the Prophet Lodowicke Muggleton to the Widow Mrs. Elizabeth Marsden, of Chesterfield, bearing date from London, April 18th, 1685.

Dear friend in the true faith, Elizabeth Marsden.

I HAVING an opportunity at this time to inform you, that there is a design in agitation that will be for your good, and your children's good also, as long as your natural life in this world, if you please to accept of it. I thought it convenient and necessary to give you timely notice of it, that you may not be surprised, but may have time to consider of it. The business is this, there is a friend of ours that is a widower, that is of this faith, that is a shopkeeper and of a genteel trade, namely, a salesman and a tailor both, that selleth all new apparel, and he hearing that you are a shopkeeper though of another trade and of this faith, and of a good natural temper, doth conceive you would make a good wife to live here at London, if you shall think good;— the man's name is John Croxen, he liveth at the corner house at Houndsditch, it is the best house for trade in all the street, being a corner house; his trade doth bring in at least two or three hundred pounds a year; and as for his person I suppose you will not dislike—and for his age it is very suitable unto yours, he is about four or five and forty years old is the most, and I suppose you are seven or eight and thirty years old, which is very suitable, and this was one of this faith we own, and we know him to be of as good a natured man to a wife as any I know in the world; I know you may live in as much splendour and credit as any merchant's wife in London doth, if you have him to your husband you shall have a maid servant, and men servants to be at your command; for my wife's brother's son is apprentice with him, and hath served now at Midsummer, five years of his time, which if I had not known him to be a good natured man, and a good trade, he should never have him put apprentice to him. All the rich believers here in London doth very well approve of his having of you to wife, and of your having of him to your husband, and would be glad to have you live at London, that you may be numbered among the rich in this world, as well as being numbered with the rich in faith, rich in the world to come, as I know you will; besides I cannot conceive how you can raise yourself, or prefer yourself or your two children, if you should match with any man there in the country, though it were with a man of a hundred a year, yet your person will be made a mere drudge, and your children mere slaves, neither is there any of this faith there in that country as I know of, that is worth any thing considerable; and for you to match with one that is contrary, it will cause shipwreck to be made of the peace of your mind, which is of more value than the whole world.

Now I shall tell you how the state of this man's condition is, that if you cannot bear with it you shall have your liberty to chose or refuse, and save him a journey; this John Croxen hath had two wives, and hath at this time five children all alive, two by the first wife before I knew him, and those two are both out of the way; the daughter geteth her living, being a good needle-woman, or at service, or might be married, but her father doth not like the man that she would have, because he hath no trade, for a trade is the surest thing to get bread in this England, if a man be a good husband; the other is a boy that is apprentice to a silk weaver, which hath served great part of his time, so that he will be no trouble nor charge to his father nor his wife; and by this last wife he hath three daughters, the eldest is I think a matter of twelve or thirteen years old, and she is put apprentice to a friend of ours for five years, to be a shop-keeper; so that there is but two young daughters that is at home with him, the one of them is about eight years old, and the other I think about four years old, these two must be at home, yet no great trouble to his wife, because the maid can make them ready and send them to school; for if you should be his wife you would do more good ten times, in looking to the shop and selling of garments, and to know the prices, and learn the trade, that in case he should die before you, you may drive the trade yourself; thus I have given you an account of the whole matter. Now he and William Chaire a batchelor, doth intend after Whitsintide to make a journey into those parts to see you and other friends in Staffordshire; Mr. Croxen cometh only to you, upon that account as to make you his wife, if you like the man when you see him; and William Chaire he cometh on purpose to Elizabeth Burton, to make her his wife if she will accept of him, he had a great love for her when she was here in London.

But now, dear friend, the case is thus, that you must send me word whether you are resolved to keep yourself a widow always, or whether you are minded to keep yourself a widow always, or whether you are resolved to live there where you are always, or whether you are minded to change your condition you are now in, or whether you will suffer him to come to see you; and if you do not like him when you have seen him, you shall have liberty in your mind to refuse him; for I would not persuade you to any thing against your own mind, nor advise you to any thing that were not for your good; therefore I would desire you to send your answer unto me as soon as you can conveniently, and as short as you can to those particulars, in the latter part of this letter; likewise, I desire you not to let any of our friends in those parts to see this letter, neither would I have you to mention it to any one, till after you have given me your answer; and if you do incline in your mind to hearken to the conditions contained in this letter, then keep it to yourself, and let none know of it, until Mr. Croxen and William Chaire doth come to see you and the rest of our friends, which will be after Whitsintide So with my love and my wife's love remembered unto yourself, I take leave and remain,

Your friend in the true faith,

LODOWICKE MUGGLETON.

London, the 18th day
of April, 1685.

Direct your letter unto me, thus, for Mr. Delamain, upon Bread Street Hill, at the sign of the "Three Tobacco Pipes," in London.

A Copy of a Letter, written by the Prophet Lodowicke Muggleton to Elizabeth Phaire, bearing date the 29th of June, 1686.

Dear friend in the true faith, Elizabeth Phaire, the Wife of Robert Phaire, who hath been dead some time since.

THIS is to certify you that I received your letter, dated May 25th, 1686, by the hand of our friend Mrs. Stratton; and I am glad to hear of your good health, but more especially of your strong faith in the true God and in me his messenger, and in that the God of heaven hath preserved my life here upon this earth these many years, and hath delivered my soul out of many prisons and persecutions, and hath restored me to my own habitatation again, without any limbs broken, or bruises, or maimed, and am as perfect in nature from all diseases and distempers as ever, only I am grown old and cannot live many years longer, by the course of nature. I have looked upon you as one of God's elect in the day when I first saw you, when your husband first brought me to your father's house, when you were, as it were, creeping out of your ignorance and blindness of nature, which is near twenty-four years since, so that, I doubt not, but that you shall hold out in your faith to the end of your life, here in this world, because your faith is built upon a strong rock, even upon the true God the man Christ Jesus in glory, as we the commissioners of the Spirit have declared, so that you shall with us in the resurrection arise first, and shall ascend in the clouds of heaven into that glory, where we shall see our God in whom we have believed, when in this life, face to face, and receive that mansion of glory according to the measure of faith we had in this life. This is all at present, only my love, with my wife's love presented unto you. I take leave, and remain,

Your friend in the eternal truth,

LODOWICKE MUGGLETON.

London, June 29th, 1686.

A Copy of a Letter written by the Prophet Lodowicke Muggleton to Mary Gamble, dated June 29th, 1686.

Dear and loving friend in the true faith, Mary Gamble,

THIS is to certify you, that I received your letter, dated the 27th of May, 1686, by the hand of Mrs. Stratton, wherein you make a good excuse why you did not return me an answer to my letter which you so joyfully received, and will as carefully keep for those that are growing up after you. I am very well satisfied in the causes you make mention of, and as for your inclination still to see me here at London, I should be glad it might be so, if it might not be too much to your prejudice, you being so far remote, and at such a distance from me, it would be no trouble to me, but joyous to me to see you before I go hence and be seen no more; but if it should be so, that you could not see me here in this life in the state of mortality, you shall be sure to see me in the state of immortality, when this vile body shall be made like unto our God's glorious body, then shall I be worth the seeing, and thrice happy will you and all those be that hath truly believed our report, in this life, in that you shall be made capable to see me and our God face to face, in that kingdom of eternal glory; these things will come to pass in their time, which will be finished in the resurrection; which will not seem a quarter of an hour's time between the death of your soul and the resurrection of it to eternal life and glory; for there is no time to the dead, all time is to this mortal life; and in this regard our state doth far differ from the state of the whole world, because it lieth in ignorance and darkness of their minds, of the knowledge of the true God and the right devil, which is the cause of all men and women's fear of death, they having no faith in the true God, nor knowledge what the right devil is; this is that, that causeth the fear of death and hell; for death and hell join hand in hand together against the soul of man, which hath not the shield of faith in him of the true God, and in this Commission of the Spirit, to keep off the fiery darts of the devil, off his heart in his life and at his death. And as for your desire of my advice, whether it would be more peaceable for you to live in England than there; as to that, I do know that it would be more safe and peaceable living in England than where you are; could you leave your concerns there where you now are without any extraordinary great loss and ruin of your estate, it would be far more safe and security of your lives here in England, than there will be where you are; now for this I am well persuaded, that England, is the safest place for peaceable and quiet people to live in, that is in the whole world; besides, notwithstanding, it is bad enough in conscience, and wicked enough, yet the most righteous place in the world at this day; neither will there, nor can be such a thing acted here in England, as you fear will be acted there where you be now; therefore, as I said before, if you can without too much undoing yourself in your estates, it will be safer for your lives to live in England—you must venture something—your lives are better than lands, and your bodies are better than raiment.

This is all the advice I can give you in this matter; so I shall take leave, only present my love and respects with my wife's love unto yourself and to your husband. I rest and remain,

Your friend in the eternal truth,

LODOWICKE MUGGLETON.

London, June 29th, 1686.

A Copy of a Letter written by the Prophet Lodowicke Muggleton to Elizabeth Farmer, bearing date from London, June 29th, 1686.

Loving and kind friend, Elizabeth Farmer, tho' to me unknown

THIS is to certify you, that I received your kind token by the hands of Mrs. Stratton. I perceive by her, that you are one of this faith, and that you are Mary Gamble's sister, and daughter to Colonel Robert Phaire. I knew your father very well, and your mother-in-law, and your sister Gamble by letter, but I never saw her person in my life: but I perceive, you are one that doth own and believe the same doctrine and commission of the Spirit as your father and mother-in-law, and, your sister doth, else why should you send a token of your love to me, which is evident you have a love to the same truth as those aforesaid named; yet because I received no line from you concerning your faith. I shall take leave at present, only my love, and my wife's love and respects remembered unto you, shall take leave, rest and remain your friend in the true faith of a personal God, the man Christ in glory.

Your friend in the eternal truth,

LODOWICKE MUGGLETON.

London, June 29th, 1686.

A Copy of a Letter written by the Prophet Lodowicke Muggleton to Mary Wakeham, dated June 29th, 1686.

Dear friend, though unknown, Mary Wakeham,

THIS is to certify you that I received your letter with your kind token of your love, by the hand of our friend Mrs. Stratton; and as you say, I never did hear of your name before, but I perceive you have heard of my name to your unspeakable joy and comfort. I perceive, by your few lines, that your understanding is greatly enlightened, in that you have faith in the true God, our blessed Redeemer, and Lord Jesus Christ, and that you have received us his messengers in the love of our doctrine, which we received commission from God to declare also you have received me in your heart as a messenger sent of God, though you never saw me nor I you, but the sound of this doctrine and Commission of the Spirit hath gone through many parts of the world, and here and there one hath ears to hear the sound, and eyes to see the truth of it; so that in your receiving of me as a messenger sent of God, you shall and do receive him that sent me, and it will be your eternal happiness and your good lot that you did receive me as a messenger of God to direct you in the way of truth; indeed the number is but few, even like the gleaning of the field of this world; the world carryeth cart loads of sheaves into their barn, that is into their heaven, because they have a multitude of messengers and teachers to drive people to heaven whether they will or no; but God's Messengers are sent but one at a time; if he should send two at a time the world cannot bear one, much less two; so that God's messengers are glad to gather a sheaf or two in one land, and three or four in another land in comparison, so that God's barn or heaven is very empty; there is room enough for you and such as you are being one of that scattered flock, you being numbered amongst God's elect in that you have believed his prophet's report.

So resteth your friend in the true faith,

LODOWICKE MUGGLETON.

My love and my wife's love remembered unto you though unknown.

London, June 29th, 1686.

A Copy of a Letter, written by the Prophet Lodowicke Muggleton to Mrs. Ann Delamain, the widow of Mr. Alexander Delamain, senior, bearing date from London, December 26th, 1687. Beginning as followeth.

Dear friend in the truth, Ann Delamain,

THIS is to give you an account of our proceedings, and what we have done this last long term, in my wife's kinsman, Thomas Martin, concerning his being heir at law to that house and lands which his mother bought for her and her heirs for ever, in the days of her widowhood; I knowing that nothing would be done with his father-in-law by fair means, but by law, therefore I sent him first to see if he could get the deeds how his mother bought this house and lands; so his father-in-law let Thomas Martin, his son-in-law have the key of the chest, where was nine pair of sheets and other linen, and all the writings with it; so Thomas Martin, being a good scholar both in writing and reading English, he took out of the chest those writings which concerned his house and lands, and locked the chest again, and gave his father-in-law the key again; for no man could give the young man any advice until we had seen the deeds; and after we had the writings he advised with an attorney at law, and his advice was at first, to have a writ of ejectment upon the tenant out of possession, except the tenant would own him to be his landlord, and he would give the tenant a bond under his hand to bear him harmless; which thing was done by this means, his father-in-law was turned out of possession of the house and lands; the next advice was given, to get a letter of administration upon the chest of linen and other things, and upon fourteen pounds rent, and upon two bonds of eight pounds which was unpaid to his father-in-law, which is twenty and two pounds; the third advice was, for him to have a writ to arest his father-in-law for all the rent which he hath received for this house and land this eight years, which is now in suit of law, and the next term they do proceed. I shall say no more at present, but do hope I shall see you ere long at your own house, where I shall give you a full account of this matter; therefore I shall only remember my dear love with my wife's love to yourself in particular, and to Mr. Whitehead and his wife, and Priscilla and Mary his two daughters, and all the rest of our friends in the faith with you. I take leave and rest,

Your friend in the eternal truth,

LODOWICKE MUGGLETON.

Dec. 26th, 1687.

A Copy of a Letter written by the Prophet Lodowicke Muggleton, to his loving friend Mary Wakeham, dated from London, August 15th, 1688.

Loving and kind Friend in the true faith, Mary Wakeham,

THIS is to certify you that I received your letter, dated the 29th of May, in the year 1688, by the hand of our friend, Mrs. Stratton; wherein I perceive you have a desire to come to London to see me. I should be very glad to see you, if it were possible; but I may say unto you in the temporal, as Abraham said unto Dives in the spiritual; he being in hell, and Abraham in heaven, that there was such a great gulph between them, that Abraham could not come to him in hell; neither could Dives come out of hell and ascend up to heaven to come to Abraham; so likewise there is a great temporal gulph between you and I, as to the hundred miles by land, that might easily be done, but that gulph by sea will be very hard for you to come and see me; and I have such an antipathy in my nature, that if I might have ten thousand pounds; I would not come through that sea gulph to see you, though I have travelled several thousands of miles in England in my time by land, so that if you can come through this sea gulph to see me, I shall be very glad to see you, but as you say if you cannot see me in this state of mortality, you will be sure to see me in the state of immortality, in a better condition than now, when you and all others, that are true believers shall see me and John Reeve set upon thrones of glory, and there you shall see the twelve apostles and all the prophets, with Moses and Elias that represented the person of God the Father, while Christ the only true God went that journey in the flesh; all these and many more shall you see to sit upon thrones of glory, distinct one from another; nay, further I say, that we the two Witnesses of the Spirit being upon thrones of glory, shall say to those the believers of this Commission of the Spirit, Come, we will lead you up into the kingdom where our God sits in his glorious throne, with all his holy angels round about him; there you shall see him face to face, because you did believe in him when he was in shame, when he was upon earth; this is that unspeakable glory and pleasures which my faith tells me, which we and all true believers shall see and enjoy those pleasures at his right hand for evermore. This is all at present, only my love, and my wife's love remembered unto yourself I take leave, rest and remain your friend in the eternal truth.

LODOWICKE MUGGLETON.

London, August 15th, 1688,

FINIS.

www.ingramcontent.com/pod-product-compliance
Lightning Source LLC
Chambersburg PA
CBHW071435300426
44114CB00013B/1451